NOTABLE PLAYWRIGHTS

MAGILL'S CHOICE

NOTABLE PLAYWRIGHTS

Volume 3

George Ryga – Paul Zindel
751 – 1131
Indexes

Edited by
CARL ROLLYSON
Baruch College, City University of New York

SALEM PRESS, INC.
Pasadena, California   Hackensack, New Jersey

All the essays in this set originally appeared in *Critical Survey of Drama,
Second Revised Edition*, 2003, edited by Carl Rollyson. Some new material
has been added.

∞ The paper used in these volumes conforms to the American National
Standard for Permanence of Paper for Printed Library Materials, Z39.48-1992
(R1997)

Library of Congress Cataloging-in-Publication Data

Notable playwrights / editor, Carl Rollyson.
   p. cm. – (Magill's choice)
  Includes bibliographical references and indexes.
  ISBN 1-58765-195-5 (set : alk. paper) – ISBN 1-58765-196-3 (vol. 1 : alk. paper) – ISBN 1-58765-197-1 (vol. 2 : alk. paper) – ISBN 1-58765-198-X (vol. 3 :
alk. paper)
  1. Drama–Bio-bibliography–Dictionaries. 2. Drama–Biography–Dictionaries. 3. Drama–History and criticism–Dictionaries. I. Rollyson, Carl E.
(Carl Edmund) II. Series.
  PN1625.N68 2005
  809.2'003–dc22

2004011762

First Printing

PRINTED IN THE UNITED STATES OF AMERICA

Contents – Volume 3

Complete List of Contents

Contents–Volume 1

Contents–Volume 2

Contents–Volume 3

NOTABLE
PLAYWRIGHTS

George Ryga

Born: Deep Creek, Alberta, Canada; July 27, 1932
Died: Summerland, British Columbia, Canada; November 18, 1987

Principal drama • *Indian*, pr. 1962 (televised), pb. 1962, pr. 1964 (staged); *Nothing but a Man*, pr., pb. 1966; *The Ecstasy of Rita Joe*, pr. 1967, pb. 1970; *Grass and Wild Strawberries*, pr. 1969, pb. 1971; *The Ecstasy of Rita Joe and Other Plays*, pb. 1971 (includes *Indian* and *Grass and Wild Strawberries*); *Captives of the Faceless Drummer*, pr., pb. 1971 (music and lyrics by Ryga); *Sunrise on Sarah*, pr. 1972, pb. 1973 (music by Ryga); *A Portrait of Angelica*, pr. 1973, pb. 1976; *A Feast of Thunder*, pr. 1973 (music by Morris Surdin); *Paracelsus and the Hero*, pb. 1974, pr. 1986; *Twelve Ravens for the Sun*, pr. 1975 (music by Mikis Theodorakis); *Ploughmen of the Glacier*, pr., pb. 1976; *Seven Hours to Sundown*, pr., pb. 1976; *Country and Western*, pb. 1976 (includes *A Portrait of Angelica*, *Ploughmen of the Glacier*, *Seven Hours to Sundown*); *Laddie Boy*, pb. 1978, pr. 1981; *Prometheus Bound*, pb. 1981 (adaptation of Aeschylus's play); *A Letter to My Son*, pr. 1981, pb. 1982; *Two Plays: "Paracelsus" and "Prometheus Bound,"* pb. 1982; *One More for the Road*, pr. 1985

Other literary forms • In addition to stage plays, plays for radio and television, poems, film scripts, and song lyrics, George Ryga wrote four novels and one fictionalized memoir of a journey through China. Ryga's first published novel, *Hungry Hills* (1963), is a story of a young man who returns to the cruel, barren prairie community that had exiled him three years earlier. Like many of Ryga's plays, *Hungry Hills* describes the suffering and isolation of the outcast whose social and spiritual alienation is further embittered by a "desperate climate which parch[es] both the soil and heart of man." Ryga's second novel, *Ballad of a Stone-Picker* (1966), tells of two brothers, one of whom stays to work on the family farm so that his younger brother can go to the university, where he becomes a Rhodes scholar; a revised edition was published in 1976. In *Night Desk* (1976), Ryga's third novel, the city (as always, in Ryga, a symbol of antilife) is given extended treatment. *In the Shadow of the Vulture* (1985), Ryga's fourth novel, is set in the desert at the Mexico-U.S. border and focuses on the hope and despair of immigrant laborers.

In a series of scenes narrated by a tough-talking Edmonton fight promoter, the city's grim and shabby underside is revealed. *Beyond the Crimson Morning: Reflections from a Journey Through Contemporary China* (1979) is based on Ryga's trip to China in 1976.

Achievements • In *The Ecstasy of Rita Joe*, George Ryga wrote one of Canada's best-known and most widely produced plays. On July 9, 1969, less than two years after its premier performance in Vancouver during Canada's centennial, *The Ecstasy of Rita Joe* was performed at the festival opening of the National Arts Centre in Ottawa. The play was next produced by the Fondation Nationale de la Comédie Canadienne, Montreal, in a French version by Gratien Gélinas, Quebec's leading dramatist. Adapted as a ballet by Norbert Vesak and produced by the Royal Winnipeg Ballet, *The Ecstasy of Rita Joe* was performed on tour in 1971 throughout Canada, the United States, and Australia. Ryga received additional acclaim on accepting the Edinburgh Festival Fringe Award for his play in 1974. Widely reprinted, *The Ecstasy of Rita Joe* has established itself as a classic of the Canadian dramatic repertoire.

As one of English Canada's major dramatists, Ryga received considerable recognition in a country in which artists, even those of his stature, have had to struggle to have their work officially acknowledged. In 1972, he was awarded a Canada Council Senior Arts Grant to work on *Paracelsus and the Hero*. In 1979 he was nominated for an ACTRA Award for the *Newcomers* television series, while also in 1979 and in 1980, he received the Frankfurt Academy of Performing Arts Award for *Ploughmen of the Glacier* (Ryga had a substantial foreign audience). In 1980 he was invited to serve as writer-in-residence at the University of Ottawa.

Biography • George Ryga grew up in what he has referred to as "the internal third-world of Canada"—the rugged, depression-ridden prairie land of northern Alberta. He was born in Deep Creek on July 27, 1932, the first child of George Ryga and Maria Kolodka, new immigrants from Ukraine. Though formally educated in a one-room schoolhouse, and only up to the eighth grade, Ryga read widely as a child while nurturing himself on the songs, myths, and folktales of his heritage. Ryga's Ukrainian background, the severe poverty in which he was reared, and the dominating reality of the northern landscape were all of enduring significance to his development as an artist. Of the land and language with which he grew up, Ryga commented:

> The language took the form of the land—uncompromising, hard, defiant—for three seasons of the year the long months of winter isolation made the desire for human contact a constant ache.

Having grown up beside a Cree reservation, Ryga soon discovered another kind of poverty from the one that he knew: the social and spiritual degradation of the indigenous community, alongside of whom Ryga would work as a laborer on his father's farm.

Ryga drew heavily from this experience in writing his first play, *Indian*, a play that Ryga described as a "milestone" in his development as a playwright. (The play was broadcast as part of the Canadian Broadcasting Corporation's *Quest* television series in November, 1962.) In an interview, Ryga discussed his experience:

> You know I grew up on the outskirts of a Cree reservation. The demoralization and degradation was about as total as any society can experience anywhere in the world. These people had been worked over by the Church; they had been worked over by the Hudson's Bay Co.; there was nothing left. There was no language left anymore. Even their heroes they picked up on from the dominant culture, like a chocolate-bar wrapper dropped in the street that's picked up as a piece of art and taken home and nailed on the wall.

Ryga's keen awareness of social injustice continued to develop throughout his teens and early twenties, a period of casual labor, artistic exploration, and deepening political commitment. The early to mid-1950's in particular saw Ryga performing political gestures of various kinds: In 1952, he wrote a controversial antiwar script for the Edmonton radio show *Reverie*; in 1953, he demonstrated in response to the Julius and Ethel Rosenberg trial; in 1955, he represented the Canadian peace movement at the World Peace Assembly in Helsinki, meeting the Chilean poet Pablo Neruda, the Turkish poet Nazim Hikmet, the soviet writer Ilya Ehrenberg, and other communist writers. In the same year, he traveled to Poland and Bulgaria. Though he left the Communist Party as a result of the Hungarian Revolution in 1956, Ryga claimed, in 1982, that "there has been no departure from the initial socialist commitment that I made a long time ago." In his plays, Ryga's "socialist commitment" emerges as a deep and abiding concern for the individual outcast, the person dispossessed economically, culturally, and spiritually who struggles to maintain dignity in the face of an impersonal system of domination, discrimination, and charity.

The early 1960's for Ryga marked the beginning of a great period of productivity and accomplishment. In 1960, he married Norma Lois Campbell, adopting her two daughters, Lesley and Tanya, and fathering, in 1961 and 1963, two sons, Campbell and Sergei. The early 1960's, moreover, saw Ryga coming to the theater via radio and television drama, where he had served his apprenticeship. Throughout the 1950's and into the early 1960's, Ryga had written short plays and stories for radio broadcasts in Edmonton. After the television production of *Indian* in 1962, Ryga turned to the stage, again with *Indian*, in 1964. There followed a period of major accomplishment, Ryga writing in succession *Nothing but a Man, The Ecstasy of Rita Joe, Grass and Wild Strawberries, Captives of the Faceless Drummer,* and *Sunrise on Sarah.* During the year that *A Portrait of Angelica* and *A Feast of Thunder* were produced, Ryga spent six months in Mexico working on *Paracelsus and the Hero,* and then, in 1976, he wrote two more plays, *Ploughmen of the Glacier* and *Seven Hours to Sundown,* both of which were produced that year. Also in 1976, Ryga traveled to China and later wrote his memoir of the journey, *Beyond the Crimson Morning: Reflections from a Journey Through Contemporary China* (1979).

On his own development as an artist, Ryga spoke of Edward Albee and Robert Burns, the Scottish poet, as having been major influences. Of Albee, Ryga commented:

> I credit a large part of the fact that *Indian* was written at all, to seeing *The Zoo Story* on television, and watching how that particular play was constructed. It was the freedom that Albee was exercising in departing from the traditions as then practiced, and taking theatre into a kind of arid area, which I found fascinating and which to a great extent I have used ever since.

Ryga had gone to Dumfries in 1955 to study Burns's poetry, and while there, he discovered drafts of unpublished manuscripts, learning much from them about the interconnections of poetry and music. In Burns's rural origins and in his artistic resistance to English culture, Ryga also recognized much with which to identify:

> I began to see . . . that the English dominance of Scotland, and Burns' contribution in retaining a semblance of language, and around that language developing a rallying point for Scotland's national aspirations, were translatable indirectly to the Canadian experience.

Ryga was a guest professor at the University of British Columbia, at Banff School of Fine Arts, and at Simon Fraser University. As an active member in the Association of Canadian Television and Radio Artists, and an honorary member of the British Columbia Civil Liberties Association, he brought his liberal ideas to the political format. The travelogue, *Beyond the Crimson Morning,* published in 1979, was one of his last published works. He died in Summerland, British Columbia, November 18, 1987, of undisclosed causes, at the age of fifty-five.

Analysis • George Ryga's achievements were fueled by his fierce, often embattled commitment to a national theater in Canada. From his earliest days as a dramatist,

Ryga resisted the imposition of British and American styles on the Canadian theater and sought to establish a living theater fully responsive to his own country's heterogeneous culture. By his own admission, however, Ryga had equivocal success in establishing such a theater in Canada: "I have known electrifying national prominence, and I have known a decade of exclusion from the theatres of my country. . . ." Nevertheless, Ryga's plays, which transform Canadian myth and experience into a vivid dramatic language, have been of major significance in the struggle to establish a national theater. He was a major dramatist who dug into his Canadian material and reached through to some universal truths.

Indian • In his first play, *Indian*, the dramatist compressed into one powerful act many basic materials of Canadian language, myth, and experience that he would develop in later plays. The play examines the poverty and despair of the variously named and ultimately anonymous "Indian," who elicits the intended guilt and sympathy from the members of the audience and who then rejects them violently in an outburst of rage, anguish, and guilt of his own. In the process, the play shatters the distorted and clichéd image of the native Canadians that has often been preserved in the Canadian consciousness.

Of the play's three characters, Indian, the boss Watson, and the Agent (a "comfortable civil servant" from the Department of Indian Affairs), it is the Agent who represents the "white man's" guilt over the Indians' degradation and who symbolizes the white man's attempts, primarily through impersonal charity and social welfare, to repair a tragic, structural flaw in Canadian society. Indian, however, is not interested in charity: "I want nothing from you—jus' to talk to me—to know who I am. . . ." In particular, Indian needs to tell of his brother, whom he was forced to kill in an act of mercy. The Agent, who is unable to conceive of Indian's essential humanity and who lacks, therefore, the emotional and moral strength to receive Indian's confession, is coerced, rather more violently than Samuel Taylor Coleridge's wedding guest in *The Rime of the Ancient Mariner* (1798), into hearing a story of great sin and suffering.

Against the Agent's cries of "No . . . no! This I don't understand at all," Indian describes how he killed his own brother (his brother had been trapped and left to die at the bottom of a well he was digging for a white "bossman," only to be finally rescued more dead than alive), how he "stole" his clothes, and how he allowed a "half-breed" to take the dead man's name so that he could collect the reservation subsidy on it ("All Indians same—nobody"). As he tells his story, the stereotyped image of the drunken and worthless Indian with which the play opened must be correlated with the profound humanity and existential integrity of the man who chose, at the cost of immense anguish, to save his own brother by murdering him:

> I . . . kill . . . my . . . brother! In my arms I hold him. He was so light, like small boy. I hold him . . . rock 'im back and forward like this . . . like mother rock us when we tiny kids. I rock 'im an' I cry . . . I get my hands tight on his neck, an' I squeeze an' I squeeze. I know he dead, and I still squeeze an' cry, for everything is gone, and I am old man now . . . only hunger an' hurt left now. . . .

Although the play is fundamentally realistic, its skillful compression of language, setting, and events produces powerful symbolic effects. The setting is a "flat, grey, stark non-country," a "vast empty expanse" that is at once the northern Albertan landscape and a spiritual wasteland, reminiscent of the elemental settings in Samuel

Beckett or T. S. Eliot. This simultaneous realism and symbolism in setting is matched on the levels of language and event, where the cadences of Indian dialect or the harsh hammer blows with which the play ends resonate with poetic force. The fusion of realism and symbolism at key points of *Indian* anticipates the more ambitious, sustained, and experimental techniques of *The Ecstasy of Rita Joe*, Ryga's more wide-ranging treatment of indigenous experience.

The Ecstasy of Rita Joe • The vibrant combination of dance, song, mime, recorded voices, and special lighting effects in *The Ecstasy of Rita Joe* signals Ryga's departure from the basic naturalism of *Indian*. Ryga dramatizes both the inner and the outer experience of Rita Joe by making use of a variety of impressionistic, expressionistic, and symbolic techniques. Thus, on a forceful and realistic groundwork he builds a poetic structure in which Rita's subjective experience and inevitable doom emerge in flashbacks, shadow plays, and interludes of music, mime, or dance.

The groundwork of the play is the basic tragedy of Rita's life and death. Having left her father, the reserve, and her sexual innocence behind, Rita comes to the city, where she becomes trapped in a closing circle of poverty, theft, and prostitution—until she is raped and murdered by three white men. (The Three Murderers shadow Rita's presence throughout the play until they emerge, clearly illuminated, to murder Rita and her lover Jamie at the end.) The play's poetic structure, however, transforms this linear, deterministic plot into a mythical, often allegorical elaboration of Rita's fate, whereby the murder of the Indian woman becomes the ecstasy and apotheosis of the martyr. The fusion of realism and symbolism is pure and lacks sentimentality. Appropriately, the play ends with the poignant words of Rita's sister Eileen, which focus on the human being at the heart of the myth: "When Rita Joe first come to the city—she told me. . . . The cement made her feet hurt."

The main action revolves around a recurring courtroom scene in which Rita stands accused—of vagrancy, prostitution, theft, and other crimes—before a sentimental and ineffectual Magistrate, symbol of white society's superficial understanding of Indian experience. By administering lectures and jail sentences, the Magistrate rests the blame for Rita's degradation and despair on Rita herself, evading whatever responsibility he might have both as a man and as an official representative of white society. He tries unsuccessfully to harmonize the image of a tiny Indian girl he once saw in the Cariboo country with the woman Rita, whom he accuses of carrying a venereal disease, a symbol of her permanent condemnation.

The courtroom scenes are touchstones of a present reality that Rita strives to evade via memories and fantasies. In these imaginative interludes, the people of her past and the materials of her oppressed spirit emerge. In one scene of dramatic counterpoint, her old dead father, David Joe, speaks beautifully of a dragonfly emerging from its shell while her lover, Jamie Paul, rails against the white oppressors and advocates violence against them. Torn by this conflict of generations, trapped between impossible alternatives of urban despair and powerlessness and an extinct pastoral majesty, Rita stands paralyzed and doomed. When she recalls scenes of warmth and inspiration, as when she and her sister Eileen comforted each other after a storm, the Three Murderers loom menacingly in the background. Memory, then, is fraught with pain and contains the seeds of her inevitable doom.

Other significant characters who appear out of Rita's past are a Teacher, a Priest, a Policeman, and a welfare worker, Mr. Homer, all of whom, as representatives of white society, stand as accusers of Rita Joe. Throughout, Rita's essential isolation is dramatized as she is torn violently from her memories by a court policeman or as she stands alone in a shaft of light, separated by a barrier of memory from her surroundings. Often, the dialogue assumes a contrapuntal rhythm as the characters talk across one another's meanings, each alone in a fading world.

As the play progresses, it becomes more and more dominated by Rita's imagination, which strains against the tragic inevitability of events. Increasingly, as she emerges from her memories and imaginings, the present reality assumes a more hallucinatory quality, shaped as it has become by Rita's disorientation, fear, hunger, and exhaustion. At times the boundaries of time and space, of inner and outer reality, vanish completely. In a scene that approaches the nightmarish intensity of the Circe episode of James Joyce's *Ulysses* (1922), all the testimonies of white authority—of Priest, Policeman, Teacher, Magistrate—fuse into one "nightmare babble" of perpetual condemnation. Out of this babble comes the searing cry of the Magistrate, a cry that is also the voice of Rita's self-accusation, the bitter acknowledgment of her forced betrayal of sexual innocence and Indian heritage:

> MAGISTRATE: Have you any boils on your back? Any discharge? When did you bathe last?
> *The Three Murderers appear, and circle Rita.*
> MAGISTRATE: Answer me! Drunkenness! Shoplifting! Assault! Prostitution, prostitution, prostitution, prostitution!

In *Indian*, the Agent represents the audience's point of view and dramatizes its violent discovery of Indian's complex and painful reality. In *The Ecstasy of Rita Joe*, the audience almost exclusively shares Rita's point of view, which accounts for the play's nonsequential, associative order, its blending of Rita's spirit and memory with the nightmare-present from which she struggles in vain to escape. The play inhibits a complete identification with Rita, however, by insistently recalling the members of the audience to their own identity. Before the play begins, for example, the players make their entrances in a "workmanlike and untheatrical way" with the houselights up, thus enforcing a sense of common reality and frustrating the audience's desire to escape into the suspension of disbelief that a darkened theater encourages.

Even when the lights are lowered and the play is long under way, the audience continues to be reminded of its status, sometimes rudely so. At one stunning moment, for example, Ryga calls for Jamie Paul to cross downstage and confront a member of the audience: "You know me? . . . You think I'm a dirty Indian, eh? Get outa my way!" At another equally uncomfortable moment, David Joe, Rita's father, gestures angrily toward the audience exclaiming, "And tell her what? . . . Of the animals there . . . who sleep with sore stomachs because . . . they eat too much?"

Structural among the play's alienating devices, however, is Rita's alter ego, the Singer, "a white liberal folklorist" who weaves the scenes together with wistful songs that bespeak her "limited concern and understanding of an ethnic dilemma." If the audience wishes to identify with Rita, it must simultaneously come to terms with the Singer, who sits, appropriately, off to the side and "turned away from the focus of the play." The Singer, consequently, serves as an alter ego of the audience as well. Thus, between the poles of intimacy and alienation, between the life and final ecstasy of Rita Joe and the superficial and sentimental songs of the Singer, the audience must steer in this most demanding of Ryga's plays.

Ploughmen of the Glacier • After *The Ecstasy of Rita Joe*, Ryga wrote several plays on subjects ranging from psychedelic culture to urban terrorism, small-town politics, and the Titan Prometheus. As might be expected, these plays use a wide variety of techniques, blending realism with myth, song, or dance while experimenting with both fluid and static settings. Among the plays Ryga wrote after 1967, however, *Ploughmen of the Glacier*, an exploration of the myth of the Canadian West, was his most profound. In *Ploughmen of the Glacier*, Ryga is a virtuoso who masters continuously the development of his materials, creating a play that is rich in character, language, and symbolism.

In the stage directions, Ryga called for a "possibly surrealistic" mountainside setting in which "all is staged and designed to highlight the elemental loneliness of the protagonists." Although the setting resembles that of *Indian* in its isolation and foreboding, the effect here is more dramatic as the Canadian Rockies loom unseen but felt in the background. The suggested mountainside functions in the play like the vast, mountainous range of the landscape painting: In both cases, the artist places human figures in the foreground of the vast scene to express human evanescence and isolation before nature's permanence and sublimity. At times, however, the lust and spirit of Ryga's characters succeed in dominating their surroundings.

The loneliness of the three protagonists is further reinforced by their distance from civilization. High on the mountain, the world below assumes a distant and obscure shape, formed only by the characters' infrequent allusion to the Gold Rush, the town, or the business "bandits" from Ontario. Thus isolated, the mountainside is free to open into abodes of myth, though its bearded, coughing men, moving about in clouds of real dust and speaking their raucous frontier language, suggest a particular history and region.

The action is structured on the periodic meeting of Volcanic and Lowery—the natural, elemental man and the bookish man of culture—who disguise their suppressed affection for each other in zealous, occasionally violent, and often bitter arguments about the best way to live. Their spirited and voluble antagonism is interrupted, however, on the entrance of Poor Boy, who wanders up and down the mountain with a pair of leaky water buckets in a futile attempt to hoard water against the coming fire. (Wandering through the scene playing his harmonica, Poor Boy pauses to speak wistfully and discontinuously about a dimly remembered Western legend.) As the play's Sisyphus, Poor Boy brings with him a whiff of the abyss that stops Volcanic and Lowery cold. From this prospect of madness and futility, Volcanic and Lowery avert their faces, infected by a doubt that leaves them spiritually exhausted though somehow closer as men. When Poor Boy leaves, however, they resume their argument. According to this rhythm of spirited argument, despair, and brief communion, the play progresses.

The play's bleak existentialism is substantially countered throughout by its lusty language and humor. Responsible for the finest displays of both, Volcanic is also the Old West personified, a symbol of its tireless energy. As his name suggests, he is at once flowing lava and petrified rock—a living fossil from another time. Like the West itself, he combines the grandeur of the pioneering imagination with its ignorance and brutality (Volcanic once shot a man who trespassed unknowingly on his land), and like most grand personifications, he is slightly absurd: For all Volcanic's dreams of wealth and talk of founding a city in his name, he, like Anse Bundren of William Faulkner's *As I Lay Dying* (1930), is dominated by the homely and pressing need for a set of false teeth. Nevertheless, Volcanic's vigorous speech achieves the force and resonance of poetry. When he rails against Lowery, he is at his best:

You're worn out by poverty . . . you depress me! . . . You're like a preacher in a whore-house. I want to dress up like a monkey to show the world I'm livin'. . . . I want to bleed myself . . . show God I can do without Him . . . that I can spill my life on the ground an' still have more left in me than men like you! . . . I want to smell out a claim an' go after it . . . all alone . . . just my body with a hammer an' chisel against the whole goddamned mountain! To eat what nobody's ever cooked for me . . . to stand on a cliff, pants aroun' my ankles . . . an' shake the sperm in me over the cliff into the val-ley . . . an' laugh to see a gull scoop down an' swallow it before it hits the ground . . . Hah! The seeds for children I could've had . . . eaten by a seagull!

An aged and failed editorialist and languid spokesman of civilization, Lowery is im-pelled periodically to climb the mountain to berate Volcanic and to assail him with issues from "down below"—from the society and culture of mankind that Lowery has increasingly come to doubt. Though he is attracted by Volcanic's tireless optimism and arrogant independence, he is also dumbfounded and deeply annoyed by it. Unable to live like Volcanic but no longer at home in civilization, Lowery is the most isolated and pathetic of the play's characters. Lacking the robust constitution of Volcanic or the single-minded purpose of Poor Boy, Lowery is alone between the frontier and society, living primarily with a painful memory of the beautiful woman with whom he declined to make love, so ashamed was he of his own nakedness.

The argument of Volcanic and Lowery continues until they die facing each other in their tracks. When they are finally still, Poor Boy comes on to deliver the eulogy for the dead whom he is already beginning to forget. As Poor Boy wanders off playing his har-monica, he will have yet another half-remembered tale to ponder as he carries his leaky water buckets up the mountain.

Other major works

LONG FICTION: *Hungry Hills,* 1963; *Ballad of a Stone-Picker,* 1966, revised 1976; *Night Desk,* 1976; *In the Shadow of the Vulture,* 1985.

TELEPLAYS: *The Storm,* 1962; *Bitter Grass,* 1963; *For Want of Something Better to Do,* 1963; *The Tulip Garden,* 1963; *Two Soldiers,* 1963; *The Pear Tree,* 1963; *Man Alive,* 1965; *The Kamloops Incident,* 1965; *A Carpenter by Trade,* 1967 (documentary); *Ninth Summer,* 1972; *The Mountains,* 1973 (documentary); *The Ballad of Iwan Lepa,* 1976 (documentary).

RADIO PLAYS: *Reverie,* 1952; *A Touch of Cruelty,* 1961; *Half-Caste,* 1962; *Masks and Shadows,* 1963; *Bread Route,* 1963; *Departures,* 1963; *Ballad for Bill,* 1963; *The Stone Angel,* 1965; *Seasons of a Summer Day,* 1975; *One Sad Song for Henry Doyle Matkevitch,* 1981.

NONFICTION: "Theatre in Canada: A Viewpoint on its Development," 1974; "Con-temporary Theatre and Its Language," 1977; "The Need for a Mythology," 1977; *Be-yond the Crimson Morning: Reflections from a Journey Through Contemporary China,* 1979; "The Artist in Resistance," 1982.

MISCELLANEOUS: *The Athabasca Ryga,* 1990 (collection); *Summerland,* 1992 (Ann Kujundzic, editor).

Bibliography

Boire, Gary. "Tribunalations: George Ryga's Postcolonial Trial 'Play.'" *Ariel* 22, no. 2 (April, 1991): 5-20. A "clumsily beautiful trial play," *The Ecstasy of Rita Joe* is com-pared with Margaret Atwood's novel *The Handmaid's Tale* (1986) and other anticolonial literature as a paradigm for examining the "encoding of class violence under the guise of social contract . . . [a] crucial feature of anti-colonial literatures."

Strong postmodern, semiotic deconstructionist look at "what postcolonial theorists call the reclamation of a world through irony."

Burgess, Patricia, ed. *Annual Obituary 1987.* Chicago: St. James Press, 1990. A good recapitulation of Ryga's themes, approaches to character, and patterns of composition during his career, along with an updated biography. "The lack of integration between land and people and between the individual and the group is the essential duality in Ryga's work," states the anonymous writer of this obituary. In his earlier life, before making a living as a writer, Ryga was concerned "with the degradation of human beings who are displaced and isolated, who lack a spiritual origin," a trait connected to Canadian life and society and one that informs Ryga's dramatic characterizations.

Carson, Neil. "George Ryga and the Lost Country." In *Dramatists in Canada: Selected Essays,* edited by William H. New. Vancouver: University of British Columbia Press, 1972. Discusses *The Ecstasy of Rita Joe.* Carson's opinion is that the play "establishes Ryga as the most exciting talent writing for the stage in Canada today." He believes that Ryga "rejects romantic and physical love, but does not preclude all meaningful human relationships."

Grace, Sherrill. "The Expressionist Legacy in the Canadian Theatre." *Canadian Literature,* no. 118 (Autumn, 1988): 47-58. This study of Ryga and Robert Gurik examines the non-naturalistic aspects of both writers. Mentions the influences of Edward Albee, Fyodor Dostoevski, Eugene O'Neill, Franz Kafka, and Bertolt Brecht. Details *The Ecstasy of Rita Joe,* especially the characters identified by function, and the fragmented structure.

Hoffman, James. *The Ecstasy of Resistance: A Biography of George Ryga.* Toronto: ECW Press, 1995. Describes major events in Ryga's life, especially those that relate to his writing. Bibliography and index.

Saddlemyer, Ann. "Crime in Literature: Canadian Drama." In *Rough Justice: Essays on Crime in Literature,* edited by M. L. Friedland. Toronto: University of Toronto Press, 1991. Ryga's *Indian* is discussed as drama that "involves the process of judgment, assigning responsibility for action, distinguishing truth from fiction."

Michael Zeitlin,
updated by Thomas J. Taylor

Jean-Paul Sartre

Born: Paris, France; June 21, 1905
Died: Paris, France; April 15, 1980

Principal drama • *Les Mouches*, pr., pb. 1943 (*The Flies*, 1946); *Huis clos*, pr. 1944, pb. 1945 (*In Camera*, 1946; better known as *No Exit*, 1947); *Morts sans sépulture*, pr., pb. 1946 (*The Victors*, 1948); *La Putain respectueuse*, pr., pb. 1946 (*The Respectful Prostitute*, 1947); *Les Jeux sont faits*, pr., pb. 1947 (*The Chips Are Down*, 1948); *Les Mains sales*, pr., pb. 1948 (*Dirty Hands*, 1949); *Le Diable et le Bon Dieu*, pr. 1951, pb. 1952 (*The Devil and the Good Lord*, 1953); *Kean: Ou, Désordre et génie*, pb. 1952, pr. 1953 (adaptation of Alexandre Dumas, *père*'s play; *Kean: Or, Disorder and Genius*, 1954); *Nekrassov*, pr. 1955, pb. 1956 (English translation, 1956); *Les Séquestrés d'Altona*, pr. 1959, pb. 1960 (*The Condemned of Altona*, 1960); *Les Troyennes*, pr., pb. 1965 (adaptation of Euripides' play; *The Trojan Women*, 1967)

Other literary forms • A philosopher by trade and training, Jean-Paul Sartre is best known as the principal exponent of existentialism, a philosophical attitude developed from the work of such earlier thinkers as Karl Marx, Edmund Husserl, and Sartre's older contemporary Martin Heidegger. Initially developed across such fictional texts as the early novel *La Nausée* (1938; *Nausea*, 1949) and the collected short stories of *Le Mur* (1939; *The Wall and Other Stories*, 1948),

Sartre's existentialism received full academic exposition in the massive *L'Être et le néant* (1943; *Being and Nothingness*, 1956). In the meantime, Sartre had discovered in the immediacy of theater a vehicle almost ideally suited to the expression of his ideas. Further experiments with prose fiction, somewhat less successful than his playwriting, resulted in the unfinished tetralogy *The Roads to Freedom* (1947-1950), which includes *L'Âge de raison* (1945; *The Age of Reason*, 1947), *Le Sursis* (1945; *The Reprieve*, 1947), and *La Mort dans l'âme* (1949; *Troubled Sleep*, 1950).

Sartre also achieved distinction with speeches and essays contained in the several volumes of the journal *Situations*, published from the 1940's through the 1960's, as well as with highly personal literary criticism devoted to such authors as Charles Baudelaire, Gustave Flaubert, and Jean Genet. In 1964, Sartre declined the Nobel Prize in Literature on grounds deemed both political and personal. His autobiographical essay *Les Mots* (*The Words*) had appeared earlier in that year to considerable critical acclaim.

Achievements • With the possible exception of his younger contemporary Jean Anouilh, Jean-Paul Sartre emerged as the most accomplished and noteworthy French playwright of the 1940's and early 1950's. Interested in the stage since childhood, Sartre soon found in the theater an ideal vehicle for his otherwise ponderous philosophical speculations on the nature of humankind and society. Indeed, the rapid spread and acceptance of Sartre's profound and challenging ideas can be almost entirely attributed to the success of his plays, in the best of which the complex is rendered not only simple but also visible and audible.

At times almost too close to such popular forms as melodrama to be considered literature, Sartre's characteristic dramatic style nevertheless provides for highly enter-

760

taining, accessible, and effective theater. Animated through rapid-fire dialogue exchanged among generally well-rounded and credible characters, Sartre's notions of truth and falsehood, of authentic and inauthentic behavior become both perceptible and memorable. In the best of his plays, most notably *The Flies* and *No Exit,* Sartre achieves the enviable goal of almost instantaneous communication with his audience. Perhaps even more remarkable, the strongest of his efforts remain valid as theater even without direct consideration of the ideas that they were written to express. In this respect, Sartre's achievement by far exceeds that of his erstwhile friend Albert Camus, an experienced actor and director whose efforts at playwriting failed, in general, to reach an audience secured in advance by the success of his essays and novels.

As a student and critic of the drama, with the best of his articles collected in *Situations* and elsewhere, Sartre advocated political commitment in the theater while stopping somewhat short of the "thesis drama," best exemplified by the work of Bertolt Brecht. In his own plays, Sartre, unlike Brecht, invites the participation and identification of his audience, even in the case of those characters who are to be weighed in the balance and found wanting. Indeed, such efforts as *The Flies, No Exit,* and *The Condemned of Altona* have managed to survive most post-Brechtian thesis dramas precisely because of Sartre's basically conventional, or Aristotelian, approach to character and plot.

Biography • Closely related on his mother's side to the Alsatian thinker and physician Albert Schweitzer, Jean-Paul Sartre was born in Paris on June 21, 1905. As he would later recall in *The Words,* Sartre grew up alongside his young, widowed mother in a household dominated largely by women who spoiled him, eventually provoking a virile reaction in his mature thought and prose style. After completing his secondary studies at the highly esteemed Lycée Henri IV, Sartre went on to the even more prestigious École Normale Supérieure as a student of philosophy. Failing in his initial attempt to gain the coveted, competitive *agrégation,* or secondary teaching credential, Sartre took the examination again in 1929 and was accepted. In the meantime, he had made the acquaintance of Simone de Beauvoir, a fellow philosophy student who was to remain his friend, companion, and occasional partner for life, although they never married.

During the 1930's, Sartre taught philosophy in *lycées* at Le Havre and elsewhere, and he also did some traveling before settling into the life of a professional thinker and writer. Around 1932, Sartre became ac-

Jean-Paul Sartre in 1964 (Library of Congress)

quainted with the eminent actor and director Charles Dullin, a member of the famous Cartel des Quatre that had revolutionized serious French drama during the 1920's. Although Sartre would not emerge as a dramatist for another decade or so, his abiding friendship with Dullin as early as his mid-twenties must be seen as a major influence on his life and career. During the Occupation, around the time of Sartre's first efforts at playwriting, Dullin hired Sartre as a lecturer on Greek drama in his School of Theatre Arts.

Actively involved in resistance to the Nazi Occupation after the fall of France in 1940 (and a brief period of incarceration as a prisoner of war), Sartre read widely, wrote extensively, and emerged, after the Liberation in 1944, as one of the most articulate and persuasive spokespeople of the postwar French Left, expressing his ideas in plays and novels as well as in essays. As founder and guiding spirit of the liberal periodical *Les Temps modernes*, Sartre expanded both his audience and his influence. It was this journal, for example, that served as Sartre's forum for his well-publicized break with Camus after the latter's publication of *L'Homme révolté* (1951; *The Rebel*, 1956).

Unable to find a satisfactory conclusion to his projected tetralogy of novels, Sartre, during the 1950's, continued writing essays and plays, beginning work also on the autobiographical project *The Words*. Although personally committed to Marxist theory, Sartre throughout his career shunned international communism as he did most other orthodoxies; still, he remained identified with what most foreigners considered to be the French Radical Left. After publication of *The Words*, Sartre devoted his attention almost exclusively to the life and work of Gustave Flaubert, in whom he found a most suitable context (or pretext) for his own reflections on philosophy, psychology, and art. By the time of Sartre's death in 1980, his work on Flaubert covered several thousand printed pages.

Analysis • Outside philosophical circles, it is likely that Jean-Paul Sartre's reputation will ultimately be determined by the success or failure of his theater. His works of literary criticism, impressive though they may be, lie somewhat outside the critical mainstream and are perhaps more profitably read either as essays or as philosophy. With the notable exception of the early *Nausea*, his novels, although well written and occasionally rewarding, fall far short of the communication established almost without apparent effort in the plays. The best of his plays, although somewhat superseded in fashion during the 1950's by the antirationalist efforts of Samuel Beckett, Eugène Ionesco, and the early Arthur Adamov, are still considered among the strongest and most effective dramatic efforts of the twentieth century.

Unlike most of the philosophers and other thinkers who, over the centuries, have attempted to write for the stage, Sartre was endowed with a basically theatrical imagination, heavily weighted toward the visual and psychological. In the strongest of his plays, the verbal element occurs as if spontaneously and by afterthought, the inevitable and hence quite plausible result of placing particular characters in a given situation. Language, instead of forming the basis of the action, arises from it as dialectic turns to dialogue. *No Exit*, in particular, was and remains a rousing piece of theater owing mainly to almost preverbal interaction among the ironically matched characters.

Although acquainted with Charles Dullin and other personalities of the Parisian stage from the early 1930's onward, Sartre did not attempt playwriting until 1940, when, as a prisoner of war, he saw the stage as a suitable vehicle for thinly veiled propaganda directed toward his fellow prisoners. The result was *Bariona*, ostensibly a

Christmas play about historical events surrounding the birth of Christ. Sartre's captors, predictably sidetracked by *Bariona*'s Roman characters and setting, allowed the play to be performed as planned.

The Flies • Sartre's earliest performed play, *The Flies*, brings forth in memorable, generally clear theatrical terms the distinctions between "essence" and "existence," *en-soi* and *pour-soi*, explained at great length in his contemporary treatise *Being and Nothingness*. Of all beings, Sartre maintains, only human beings are capable of creating themselves through continuous acts of choice, proceeding beyond mere essence (which humans share, at birth, with stones, plants, and animals) toward uniquely human existence. Those persons who refuse to choose or to accept responsibility for choices that they have already made are guilty of "bad faith" (*mauvaise foi*) and are indeed renouncing their truly human potential for existence in favor of subhuman, or at least nonhuman, essence or "definability" that is little more preferable than death. Indeed, as the prefigured Hell of *No Exit* makes even clearer, those who reject the anguish of choice for the comfort of convenient self-definition and labels are in fact already dead, insofar as their lives could be presumed to make a difference. Only after death, contends Sartre, should it be possible to take the measure of a human life; what it then "adds up to" is beyond progress or repair. Until that point, any effort to complete the phrase "I am . . ." with either a predicate adjective or a predicate noun is the mark of a person "in love with death" who has relinquished the privilege of existence. By contrast, those who "exist," in keeping with Sartre's apparent ideal, are too busy choosing their lives and are changing too rapidly for labels to be applied by themselves or by anyone else.

The Flies, conceived in part as a rebuttal to Jean Giraudoux's *Électre* (pr., pb. 1937; *Electra*, 1952), presents an Orestes who arrives in Argos quite unaware of his identity, only to choose the life and deeds of Orestes after weighing the evidence of Clytemnestra's crime against his own intentions. Intended also as a political statement, its topical import, thinly veiled by Sartre's then conventional use of antique characters and setting, *The Flies* portrays an Argive people crushed beneath the weight of a collective guilt, imposed on them from without by their self-serving and murderous rulers. Even Electra, perceived as a rebel in most prior retellings of the myth, is portrayed as inauthentic in her behavior: At the moment of crisis, she remains trapped in the acceptance (or perhaps even enjoyment) of an image of herself as seen by the usurpers. Only Orestes, having opted to define himself by choice alone, is capable of meaningful action.

Trading on a current vogue for Greek myth on the French stage, Sartre in *The Flies* managed both forceful anti-Nazi polemic and a reasonably effective presentation of his developing existentialist theories. Over the years since the play was first performed, even critics friendly to Sartre and to existentialism have perceived major flaws in the play that appear to have escaped notice for at least the first decade of its performed and published life; still, *The Flies* remains deservedly among the best-known and most frequently revived French plays.

No small part of the play's effectiveness derives from Sartre's confident use of imagery and language bordering frequently on crudity. The central image of predatory insects reflected in the play's title reverberates often throughout the dialogue, supported by complementary allusions to garbage, filth, and tender, vulnerable flesh. Taking as his real object of scorn the collective guilt that had haunted the French people since the fall of France in 1940, and the subsequent establishment of a collaborationist government at Vichy, Sartre in *The Flies* effectively exploits the murder of Agamemnon and the tyrannical rule of Aegistheus to draw parallels between the Argives and the French. In Sartre's version, Aegistheus and Clytemnestra have consolidated their rule by imposing on their subjects a collective guilt symbolized in a national tradition of mourning. At the start of the play, each subject, encouraged by the rulers, believes himself or herself to be vicariously guilty of Agamemnon's murder, having willed the event in advance; annually, on the anniversary of Agamemnon's death, ruled and rulers join in an act of ritual penance, groveling and fawning in gestures made vividly real by Sartre's pungent imagery and language. Such is the scene beheld by the young and callow Orestes, who arrives in Argos as the foreign student Philebus, accompanied by his tutor. It remains therefore for the disinterested, detached Philebus voluntarily to choose his identity as Orestes, delivering the Argive people from their collective guilt with two additional assassinations for which he alone will bear the blame and guilt.

Although managed perhaps as effectively as possible within the limits of legend, Sartre's portrayal of Orestes' choice constitutes one of the play's more fundamental and abiding weaknesses. Much as Sartre would have the audience accept Orestes as the archetypal existential hero, choosing his own existence above the comforting eventuality of essence, what remains at the play's end, even in "existential" terms, is the sum of his deeds, precisely those deeds attributed to Orestes by several thousand years of legend and theatrical experience. Considerably more effective is Sartre's presentation of Electra, a truly archetypal Sartrean coward who, at the moment of crisis, disastrously lacks the courage of her frequently spoken convictions. Long identified as a rebellious child who hates her mother and stepfather, Electra prefers the comfort of collective guilt to individual responsibility for their assassination. Almost equally effective is Sartre's evocation of Jupiter, a suitably decadent Roman deity who materializes in response to Orestes' repeated appeals for help from the Greek god Zeus. Displaying all the bonhomie of a corrupt political manipulator, Jupiter shows off his superhumanity with impressive parlor tricks, only to admit after Orestes' deeds that the gods are in fact inventions of mankind, powerless against truly free men.

At the very end of *The Flies*, Sartre's mixed metaphors run somewhat out of control as Orestes leaves Argos pursued by a horde of buzzing flies, defining himself by his current behavior as a curious blend of the Paraclete and the Pied Piper of Hamelin. Claiming that he has expiated the guilt of the Argives by taking the full burden on himself, he still refuses the additional burden of government. Self-defined as "a King with neither land nor subjects," Orestes then trudges, as it were, off into the sunset, leaving each of his putative subjects free to create his or her own destiny. Perhaps impressive as polemic, the ending of *The Flies* proves a bit too weak, on reflection, to carry the full burden of Sartre's existentialist exposition. No doubt confined within the restrictions of his chosen material, Sartre in *The Flies* still fails to provide the convincing illustration of human freedom that he appears to have had in mind. Notwithstanding, *The Flies* remains a perennially rousing and thought-provoking play, even when divorced from the historical context of its conception.

No Exit • With *No Exit*, first performed within fifteen months after *The Flies*, Sartre so far transcended his earlier effort as to prove that prior success to have been no accident. Here, unbound by the constraints of established legend, Sartre exercised his own freedom to bring forth an utterly human interpersonal hell for which physical death is no prerequisite. Although supposedly dead and hence incapable of changing the sum of their lives, the womanizer, lesbian, and nymphomaniac who find themselves locked uneasily together in the eternal torture of interdependence merely replicate the suffering endured, through implied consent, by those who consistently refuse to alter or even question their daily approach to life.

Pursuing the penchant for crude if apt imagery that had transformed Orestes' Furies into a horde of biting flies, Sartre, in *No Exit*, went even further to assure himself of an audience through his use of shock tactics, including explicit if still printable speech. Although some observers continue to see in the play a reasonably successful attempt at Camus's stated goal of "modern tragedy," Sartre's most perceptible method is that of melodrama as commonly interpreted, and practiced, by the producers of broadcast serials. *No Exit*, although often read in literature courses, might well be described as subliterary; on the stage, however, it remains both audacious and compelling.

The French title of *No Exit* is drawn from legal terminology (of which the British translation, *In Camera*, is no doubt a more faithful rendering than the American) to denote a trial or hearing conducted behind closed doors. *No Exit* is in all likelihood Sartre's one true dramatic masterpiece. Its action necessarily compressed into a single act of a little more than one hour's playing time, Sartre's second professional dramatic effort goes considerably further than *The Flies* toward illustrating the author's philosophy in memorable theatrical terms. Even without consideration of the ideas involved, *No Exit* remains one of the most effective and affecting plays to emerge from France in the twentieth century.

Intended as communication rather than as literature, *No Exit* achieves its remarkable effect at what might well be considered the level of soap opera, thanks in part to the brutal frankness of expression that Sartre had all but perfected in *The Flies*. Set in an imagined Hell that, by Sartre's own admission, need not be the afterlife, *No Exit* portrays the mutual torture of three individuals defined as "dead" by their individual resistance to change or even to self-interrogation. Within the terms of the play, the three principals are portrayed as physically dead as well; yet it is soon clear that such death has merely fixed and confined a reality of long standing. Even Inès, the strongest of the three main characters and the one among them who most clearly speaks for the playwright, remains condemned by her early and unquestioning acceptance of a label applied to her from without, by perceived public opinion.

Significantly, at least two of the three main characters of *No Exit* are little surprised to find themselves in Hell. Both Garcin and Inès have died violently; moreover, the conduct of their lives has led them to expect the worst. What they have not anticipated, however, is the precise nature of the place; Garcin, first to arrive, is somewhat nonplussed to find a Second Empire drawing room instead of a medieval torture chamber. As Inès will soon observe, however, whoever is in charge has decided to save on staff by having the "clients" torture one another themselves; indeed, the three eternal inhabitants of the overdecorated room have been diabolically well matched. Garcin, formerly a journalist, is a self-styled "tough guy" who believes himself to be in Hell because of the way he treated his long-suffering wife: On at least one occasion, he recalls, he brought his mulatto mistress into their home and had his wife serve them breakfast in bed. Inès, perhaps even tougher, admitted her lesbianism early in life and has since nourished few, if any, illusions. Only the third arrival, an incipient nymphomaniac and would-be socialite named Estelle, appears surprised to find herself in Hell; she is also the only member of the trio to have died from natural causes. Although Estelle has actually committed murder, her presence in Sartre's Hell derives rather from her passive, shallow, and, above all, unexamined life: Born poor, she married for money and became an unreflective snob. Inès, although sexually attracted to Estelle, despises her because she never had to work for a living; Inès, meanwhile, remains bitterly proud of her own long service as a postal clerk.

As the action progresses, it soon becomes clear that Garcin has the most to hide. As editor of a pacifist journal in Rio de Janeiro, he left for Mexico City as soon as World War II was declared; arrested for desertion, he was subsequently executed by a firing squad. Inès, considerably more honest with herself than Garcin has ever been, loses little time in exploiting Garcin's inner fears that he has died a coward's death, thus proving that he has lived a coward's life as well. Regardless of his hopes or motivations, the line has now been drawn, and his life adds up to nothing more or less than the sum of his proven actions. In the cold light of Inès' lucidity, Garcin stands all but revealed as a coward; his only hope, as it were, is to persuade Inès that he is a hero.

Inès, although no doubt the most exemplary of the three characters portrayed in *No Exit*, proves deserving of her fate because, although lucid, she has accepted without question the condemnation of society. Trading on the French expression *femme damnée* (literally, "damned woman") to denote a lesbian, Sartre here presents a woman who has allowed society's negative judgment of her sexual preference not only to dominate her life but also to define it. Most of Inès' life has indeed been spent living up (or down) to her bad name—disrupting marriages and causing suicides. Apparently, it has never occurred to her to choose any identity or existence other than that chosen for her by perceived public opinion.

Of the three characters, Estelle is deliberately portrayed as the least interesting, the object of mildly political satire insofar as she is a mindless, useless member of the bourgeoisie. For Estelle, the greatest torture to be found in Hell is the absence of mirrors, on which she has come to depend for confirmation of her essence. In one of the play's most effective conceits, Inès is able to manipulate Estelle completely by telling her that her lipstick is off-center or that she has a pimple on her chin. Only gradually does Estelle, a woman overfond of euphemisms, come to admit that she was guilty of drowning her love child, born of a relatively poor man who later committed suicide.

Outspoken not only in her preference for women but also in her parallel antipathy toward men, Inès provides the play with most of its perceptible action. As the most lucid of the trio, she is also the most emotional and the most articulate. Garcin's inept, halfhearted efforts to make love to Estelle elicit from Inès shrill cries of envy and denunciation. Estelle, meanwhile, proves resistant to Inès's amorous advances so long as there is a man in the room. Garcin, although attracted to Estelle, insists on her reassurance that he is not a coward, but Estelle remains too flighty and shallow to care whether he is a coward, "so long as he kisses well." When the door pops open unexpectedly, however, none of the characters leaves; each has by then become too dependent on the purely negative tensions that bind them together. Garcin, for example, "needs" Inès because she alone can understand him, her judgment an immovable object against which he must continually try his supposedly irresistible force.

Although, as Sartre concedes, the principals of *No Exit* need not be physically dead, the assumption of their demise allows for the inclusion of certain theatrical tricks that enhance the play's effectiveness. Being dead, the characters therefore cannot kill one another. As the conversation continues, moreover, it becomes increasingly evident that time in Hell has been somehow compressed (or perhaps stretched). Soon after their arrival, still somewhat attached to their lives, the characters can still see their erstwhile friends and surroundings; with time, however, their vision grows dimmer, and it soon becomes clear that each minute of their conversation is equivalent to several weeks on earth. At one point, for example, Garcin observes that his widow, alive at the start of the play, has been dead for about six months. By then, however, such details are quite without importance, as all three are well settled into the hell of mutual incomprehension that they have long since chosen through their actions.

Perennially popular with both professional and amateur theater groups, *No Exit* remains quite probably the most widely disseminated of Sartre's plays, its few flaws generally well concealed by the tightness and efficiency of its construction. Never again would Sartre the playwright express himself with such unerring aptness and economy, although at least two of his subsequent plays also give convincing dramatic form to his ideas.

Having discovered, with *No Exit*, the apparent secret of reaching and keeping an audience, Sartre continued to direct the remainder of his plays toward the same real or imagined public, with varying degrees of success. His next two plays, produced on a double bill in 1946, are deemed by most to have been failures and are seldom read or revived: *The Victors*, dealing with captured Resistance fighters during World War II, is an unconvincing blend of near-tragedy and melodrama; *The Respectful Prostitute*, incongruously set in an America that Sartre had not yet seen and based on the Scottsboro race trials of the 1930's, falls considerably short of Sartre's apparent intention of social satire with comic overtones. In both plays, however, Sartre's expressed thought remains consistent with his earlier and more successful dramatic efforts, stressing the difference between authentic and inauthentic behavior as exemplified in the individual character's perception between ends and means.

Dirty Hands • In 1948, Sartre undertook to combine the best of his approaches to theater with such existing conventions as the political thriller and the murder mystery. The result was *Dirty Hands* (also known as *Red Gloves*), later successfully filmed, an inversion of traditional procedure in that both victim and assassin are identified from the start. Consistent with Sartre's philosophy and general outlook, the suspense—and it can be considerable, provided that the play is competently directed—resides not in the identity but rather in the motive of the murderer, who himself participates in searching for the truth. A reluctant assassin at the very least, Hugo Barine must decide to his own satisfaction whether the shooting for which he has served time in prison was motivated by simple passion or by politics. Unsparing in its satire of expediency in leftist politics or indeed in any politics, *Dirty Hands* was interpreted by many contemporary observers, no doubt inaccurately, as Sartre's "anticommunist" play. In fact, *Dirty Hands* is both less and more than that, a philosophical play with strong psychological overtones, which, in a sense, simply happens to be about politics. Although perhaps excessive in length, *Dirty Hands* has proved over the years to be both less topical and more durable than was at first supposed, a powerful and memorable character study evoking the thin line between the psychological and social dimensions of the individual, here exemplified by the indulged, immature, and irresolute Hugo.

Dirty Hands remains one of Sartre's more noteworthy and satisfying efforts, a vigorous melodrama with undertones of both the comic and the tragic. Psychological rather than political in substance, *Dirty Hands* offers as its central character a considerably less-than-tragic hero, one who has committed murder without quite knowing why. Based in part on the known facts surrounding the assassination of Leon Trotsky in 1940, the murder of Hoederer was planned long in advance as a political act by members of his own party; the problem, however, derives from the party's ironic choice of an assassin. Hugo Barine, a pampered rich boy with strong radical leanings no doubt motivated by guilt, finds in the gruff, avuncular Hoederer a surrogate father figure to exceed his wildest dreams. For the longest time he cannot bring himself to kill the man, even as the party regulars grow increasingly impatient with his hesitation and plan an assault of their own. When at last Hugo does bring himself to kill Hoederer, his motives lie concealed beneath a tangled web of conflicting emotions, not the least of which is cuckoldry. In order to live with himself, however, Hugo must try to disentangle the web even after serving time in prison for the murder. By the time that Hugo regains his freedom, matters are complicated still further by the fact that Hoederer has been post-humously rehabilitated by the same political forces that engineered his death.

Exposed largely through flashbacks, the action of *Dirty Hands* involves a large cast of varied and interesting characters, ranging from the radical Olga (who probably loves Hugo but will not intervene to save his life) to the two inadvertently humorous hired thugs assigned to Hoederer as bodyguards. It is Hoederer himself, however, who emerges somewhat incongruously as the true hero of the play, one of the few truly decent and admirable characters in all of Sartre's theater. True to his character, he has done nearly all in his power to avoid romantic involvement with Hugo's wife, Jessica, who, without his knowledge, has volunteered to commit the murder herself so long as her husband refuses to do so.

With the possible exception of Hugo, Jessica is in all likelihood the most complex and fascinating character in *Dirty Hands*, although she often appears to have been cast by Sartre in the wrong play: Although her flirtatious and enigmatic behavior will provide one of the possible motivations for Hugo's act of murder, Jessica more often appears extraneous to the action, included more for her intrinsic interest than for her importance to the plot. Perhaps a borderline psychotic, Jessica is able to relate to her husband only during scenes of childish game playing that closely resemble *folies à deux*; such scenes, although they cast some doubt on Hugo's sanity, shed little light on his possible motivations.

Perhaps the major weakness of the play is that Hugo, for all his clinical interest as a psychological phenomenon, is simply not sufficiently interesting as a character to involve the spectator's interest in his possible thoughts as he pulls the trigger. His final, retrospective gesture of heroism—or suicide—thus strikes many audiences as either anticlimactic or gratuitous, robbing *Dirty Hands* of much of its apparently intended impact. Too particularized, and in a negative way, to be seen as Everyman, yet viewed too closely for Brechtian objectivity, the character of Hugo ultimately fails to bear the burden of exposition placed on his slender shoulders by an author then enamored of psychological case histories.

Heavily cut and adapted almost beyond recognition, *Dirty Hands* enjoyed a long, successful run in New York during the late 1940's as *Red Gloves*, an "anti-communist play by Jean-Paul Sartre." Sartre, believing his intentions to have been betrayed, protested vigorously, but the play went on to achieve a reputation perhaps ill-deserved. In the original French, *Dirty Hands* remains a better play than it at first may seem, but it is surely not a political play except to the extent that Sartre, like any effective satirist, casts aspersions on all sides.

The Devil and the Good Lord • Sartre's subsequent stage effort, *The Devil and the Good Lord*, is perhaps best remembered as the last play to be mounted by the eminent director Louis Jouvet, who died some two months after the play opened to somewhat mixed reviews. Perhaps overly ambitious both in theme and scope, *The Devil and the Good Lord* shares the historical setting and characters of Johann Wolfgang von Goethe's *Götz von Berlichingen mit der eisernen Hand* (pb. 1773; *Goetz of Berlichingen, with the Iron Hand,* 1799), which Sartre scrupulously avoided reading in order to guarantee, or prove, the authenticity of his own dramatic statement. Although considered by some critics to be among the author's finest dramatic efforts, Sartre's portrayal of Goetz and his uprising has generally failed to withstand the test of time and is seldom read or revived.

Kean • Somewhat more successful is *Kean,* adapted from Alexandre Dumas, *père*'s version of the British actor's life at the request of the French actor Pierre Brasseur, who had appeared in Jouvet's production of *The Devil and the Good Lord.* Couched, like the original, within the framework of a play-within-a-play, Sartre's adaptation successfully transforms the Romantic hero of Dumas into an anguished existentialist in search of his own authenticity. As interpreted by Brasseur, the play was not without its comic dimensions, and Sartre, thus encouraged, went on to attempt an original comedy for the first time since *The Respectful Prostitute.*

Nekrassov • The result was *Nekrassov,* a slight but generally successful satire of politics, the press, and the institution of celebrity. The protagonist, a petty criminal and confidence man named Georges de Valéra, endeavors to avoid capture by assuming the identity of one Nekrassov, a high-ranking Soviet politician who has mysteriously dropped out of sight. Abetted by the staff of a highly conservative evening newspaper, the fugitive plays his role of defector with consummate skill, only to find his authenticity compromised by right-wing political interests even after the real Nekrassov is discovered to have been sunning himself in the Crimea on a long-overdue vacation. Given the need for a Nekrassov who has defected to the West, de Valéra finds himself trapped in an unwelcome and increasingly uncomfortable role. For all its merits, *Nekrassov* nevertheless fell somewhat below the level of enlightened entertainment that audiences and critics alike had come to expect from Sartre, and in what turned out to be his last original play, Sartre appeared determined to offer something more.

The Condemned of Altona • *The Condemned of Altona,* first performed in 1959, ranks by any standard among Sartre's more impressive and memorable efforts, treading a thin line between realism and allegory in its evocation of contemporary history. The central character of the play is Franz von Gerlach, an erstwhile Nazi officer who has spent the postwar years in the apparent grip of madness, carefully hidden from view by his wealthy and influential family, while it is assumed by everyone else that he has died in Argentina. Determined to justify at all costs behavior that is now deemed abominable, Franz continually explains himself in taped addresses to the "tribunal of history," represented by hallucinated crabs on the ceiling that Franz sees as the future inhabitants of Earth. Like *Dirty Hands, The Condemned of Altona* is perhaps excessively long and somewhat confused in its plotting; yet it amply justifies the reputation that Sartre had earned with his earliest plays.

Sartre's last original play repays the spectator's attention with an ingenious, closely reasoned inquiry into the lessons of contemporary history. Although explicitly set in post-Nazi Germany, with strong topical allusions to the French presence in Algeria as well, *The Condemned of Altona,* like *Dirty Hands,* deals less with politics than with psychology. Franz von Gerlach, elder son of a wealthy shipbuilder, initially resists the Nazis with both his conscience and his deeds, until he learns to his chagrin that his inherited wealth renders true resistance impossible. Thereafter, he goes to war against the Allies with every expectation of meeting an early death in battle. Instead, he survives just long enough to inflict the torture of two captured Russian partisans and thereafter to become the Butcher of Smolensk, a full-fledged Nazi war criminal.

Believed dead, Franz has in fact spent the better part of fifteen years in the shelter of his family home, protected from the world (in all senses of the term) by an apparent wall of madness. The only member of the family who even sees him in his attic lair is his sister Leni, with whom he has long since conceived an incestuous relationship. Leni, whose personality has by now all but fused with his own, participates willingly in his delirium and nurtures his illusion that the war is still in progress, with Germany losing all its wealth and strength to the Allies. It is the elder von Gerlach's impending death from cancer that causes a long overdue rent in the antisocial fabric of Franz's isolation. Determined that he and his elder son should die together, the old man begins hatching desperate schemes to entice Franz out of hiding. In the main, these efforts involve his daughter-in-law Johanna, with whom the crafty old fellow correctly predicts that Franz will fall in love.

As the outside world begins to invade his life in the person of Johanna, it becomes increasingly clear to characters and spectator alike that Franz's insanity is largely willful, if indeed not totally feigned. As a basically decent man formed in a tradition of Protestant faith and practice, Franz simply cannot bring himself to admit that he has been the Butcher of Smolensk. Instead, he recites the "last messages of a dying Germany" to an imagined audience of crabs on the ceiling, taking care to tape his messages for posterity. Presumably, in Franz's semilucid consciousness, the inhuman crustaceans represent the future inhabitants of earth, successors to a humankind that is about to bungle its last chance. As in *Dirty Hands*, exposition occurs largely in vivid flashbacks, evolving toward a crisis in the present as Franz learns that the war is over and Johanna, who has just succeeded in fanning Franz's last latent spark of humanity, renounces him forever on learning the guilty secret of his past. The double suicide will then take place as old von Gerlach has planned it, with only his own body to be buried with funeral honors. After all, Franz has been "buried" for years under a headstone bearing his name in Argentina.

For all the unwieldiness and implausibility of its plot, *The Condemned of Altona* is, on balance, a rather more successful and satisfying play than *Dirty Hands*, owing in part to the generally credible and not-unsympathetic character of Franz. Indeed, the conflict between memory and ideals as one contemplates the unthinkable might well lead to madness, either willful or involuntary. In any event, Franz is a more dimensional and fully realized character than is Hugo Barine of *Dirty Hands*. Together with Johanna, the spectator, even as he finds Franz ultimately repellent, cannot fail to have found him more than a little fascinating as well. Aided by some of the most compelling dialogue that Sartre had written since *No Exit*, the play tends to linger in the spectator's mind, raising questions of guilt and innocence that can never truly be resolved. Indeed, suggests Sartre, the image of humankind in the mid-twentieth century is hardly preferable to that of the crabs on Franz von Gerlach's ceiling. Whether Sartre intended this play to be his last, it nevertheless closed his playwriting career on an impressive note approximating that of triumph.

The Trojan Women • By 1959, however, Sartre had all but lost interest in the stage as a vehicle for his thought and expression, preferring instead to practice the type of literary criticism that had occupied him earlier in his career. *The Trojan Women*, his adaptation of Euripides' *Trōiades* (415 B.C.E.; *The Trojan Women*, 1782), first performed in 1965, contains relatively few personal touches and was, in any case, his last attempt at writing for the stage.

Other major works

LONG FICTION: *La Nausée*, 1938 (*Nausea*, 1949); *L'Âge de raison*, 1945 (*The Age of Reason*, 1947); *Le Sursis*, 1945 (*The Reprieve*, 1947); *La Mort dans l'âme*, 1949 (*Troubled Sleep*, 1950; also known as *Iron in the Soul*; previous three novels collectively known as *Les Chemins de la liberté*, in English *The Roads to Freedom*).

SHORT FICTION: *Le Mur*, 1939 (*The Wall and Other Stories*, 1948).

NONFICTION: *L'Imagination*, 1936 (*Imagination: A Psychological Critique*, 1962); *Esquisse d'une théorie des émotions*, 1939 (*The Emotions: Outline of a Theory*, 1948); *L'Imaginaire: Psychologie phénoménologique de l'imagination*, 1940 (*The Psychology of Imagination*, 1948); *L'Être et le néant*, 1943 (*Being and Nothingness*, 1956); *L'Existentialisme est un Humanisme*, 1946 (*Existentialism*, 1947; also as *Existentialism and Humanism*, 1948); *Réflexions sur la question juive*, 1946 (*Anti-Semite and Jew*, 1948); *Baudelaire*, 1947 (English translation, 1950); *Qu'est-ce que la littérature?*, 1947 (*What Is Literature?*, 1949); *Situations I-X*, 1947-1975 (10 volumes; partial translation 1965-1977); *Saint-Genet: Comédien et martyr*, 1952 (*Saint Genet: Actor and Martyr*, 1963); *Critique de la raison dialectique, précédé de question de méthode*, 1960 (*Search for a Method*, 1963); *Critique de la raison dialectique, I: Théorie des ensembles pratiques*, 1960 (*Critique of Dialectical Reason, I: Theory of Practical Ensembles*, 1976); *Les Mots*, 1964 (*The Words*, 1964); *L'Idiot de la famille: Gustave Flaubert, 1821-1857*, 1971-1972 (3 volumes; partial translation *The Family Idiot: Gustave Flaubert, 1821-1857*, 1981, 1987); *Un Théâtre de situations*, 1973 (*Sartre on Theater*, 1976); *Les Carnets de la drôle de guerre*, 1983 (*The War Diaries of Jean-Paul Sartre: November, 1939-March, 1940*, 1984); *Le Scénario Freud*, 1984 (*The Freud Scenario*, 1985).

Bibliography

Anderson, Thomas C. *Sartre's Two Ethics: From Authenticity to Integral Humanity*. Chicago: Open Court, 1993. This work, while focusing on Sartre's ethics, provides an explanation of the themes that pervaded his dramatic works. Bibliography and index.

Bloom, Harold, ed. *Jean-Paul Sartre*. Phildelphia: Chelsea House, 2001. A collection of critical essays on Sartre, with an introduction by Harold Bloom. Bibliography and index.

Howells, Christina, ed. *The Cambridge Companion to Sartre*. New York: Cambridge University Press, 1992. A comprehensive reference work devoted to Sartre and his life, times, and literary works. Bibliography and index.

_____. *Sartre*. Modern Literatures in Perspective. New York: Longman, 1995. Editor Howells presents critical analyses of the literary works of Sartre. Bibliography and index.

Kamber, Richard. *On Sartre*. Belmont, Calif.: Wadsworth/Thomson Learning, 2000. Although this volume focuses on Sartre as philosopher, it explicates the thought and viewpoints that permeate his literary works. Bibliography.

McBride, William L., ed. *Existentialist Literature and Aesthetics*. Vol. 7 in *Sartre and Existentialism*. New York: Garland, 1997. This volume, part of a multivolume series on

Sartre and his philosophy, examines his literary works and how existentialism was expressed in them. Bibliography.

_____. *Sartre's Life, Times, and Vision du Monde*. Vol. 3 in *Sartre and Existentialism*. New York: Garland, 1997. This volume, one in a multivolume work on Sartre and existentialism, looks at his life, the times in which he lived and wrote, and his world-view. Bibliography.

Thody, Philip Malcolm Waller. *Jean-Paul Sartre*. New York: St. Martin's Press, 1992. An examination of Sartre as novelist, with some reference to his dramatic works.

Wardman, Harold W. *Jean-Paul Sartre: The Evolution of His Thought and Art*. Lewiston, N.Y.: Edwin Mellen, 1992. A critical examination of the literary works of Sartre that traces his philosophical development through his writings. Bibliography and index.

David B. Parsell

Friedrich Schiller

Born: Marbach, Württemberg (now in Germany); November 10, 1759
Died: Weimar, Sace-Weimar (now in Germany); May 9, 1805

Principal drama • *Die Räuber*, pb. 1781, pr. 1782 (*The Robbers*, 1792); *Die Verschwörung des Fiesko zu Genua*, pr., pb. 1783 (*Fiesco: Or, The Genoese Conspiracy*, 1796); *Kabale und Liebe*, pr., pb. 1784 (*Cabal and Love*, 1795); *Don Carlos, Infant von Spanien*, pr., pb. 1787 (*Don Carlos, Infante of Spain*, 1798); *Wallensteins Lager*, pr. 1798, pb. 1800 (*The Camp of Wallenstein*, 1846); *Die Piccolomini*, pr. 1799, pb. 1800 (*The Piccolominis*, 1800); *Wallensteins Tod*, pr. 1799, pb. 1800 (*The Death of Wallenstein*, 1800); *Wallenstein*, pr. 1799, pb. 1800 (trilogy includes *The Camp of Wallenstein*, *The Piccolominis*, and *The Death of Wallenstein*); *Maria Stuart*, pr. 1800, pb. 1801 (*Mary Stuart*, 1801); *Die Jungfrau von Orleans*, pr. 1801, pb. 1802 (*The Maid of Orleans*, 1835); *Die Braut von Messina: Oder, Die feindlichen Brüder*, pr., pb. 1803 (*The Bride of Messina*, 1837); *Wilhelm Tell*, pr., pb. 1804 (*William Tell*, 1841); *Historical Dramas*, pb. 1847; *Early Dramas and Romances*, pb. 1849; *Dramatic Works*, pb. 1851

Other literary forms • George Joachim Göschen in Leipzig published most of Friedrich Schiller's early work, including the early plays and the *Historischer Kalender für Damen* (1790, 1791), which included many of Schiller's essays and was his only bestseller during his lifetime. After *Don Carlos, Infante of Spain*, Schiller's plays were published by Johann Friedrich Cotta in Tübingen. Schiller's poems, reviews, and short stories appeared in literary journals such as the *Musenalmanach* (edited by Schiller), *Die Horen* (edited by Johann Wolfgang von Goethe and Schiller in Weimar), *Die Thalia*, and *Merkur*. Schiller's letters, published posthumously, not only are an indispensable key to the philosophical and historical background of his works, but also are autobiographical documents evocative of the man Schiller, his daily life, and his great gift for friendship. Schiller's collected works are available in several editions.

Achievements • Friedrich Schiller's audience might not have been ready to make the transition from the wildly emotional Sturm und Drang (storm and stress) of his first play, *The Robbers*, to the more philosophical and idealistic fervor of subsequent plays, but Schiller won them over with his ever more complex dramas. Schiller's work spans two literary periods, Sturm und Drang and classicism, and it paves the way for a third, Romanticism. At the same time, his work clearly has ties to the Enlightenment, with its emphasis on the perfectibility of humankind. In Schiller's work, German idealism attained its highest form. The lonely poet who wrote from his sickbed, however, never lost sight of the wishes of his audience. After his plays had accustomed later generations to his system of thought, Schiller became for them a poet of the people. He was acclaimed particularly by the middle class of the nineteenth century, which did not appear to notice the radical quality of freedom demanded by Schiller.

Schiller threw himself into his sources and settings, mostly historical, in order to demonstrate their true range and potential—what they might have been. His plays, showing his dialectical consciousness, express the struggle between reality and the ideal. His heroes are larger than life, their struggles overshadowing their time. The fiery younger generation was his first audience, but his idealism determined the intellectual horizon of the era. The romanticists turned away from Schiller's political idealism to pursue mysticism and the indefinable, but even among them, Friedrich Hölderlin and Novalis were profoundly influenced by Schiller. The German drama was dominated by Schiller's plays for almost a century, until the advent of naturalism. Then the theater of expressionism rediscovered the revolutionary passion and the power of Schiller's tragic pathos. Georg Kaiser and Bertolt Brecht, among others, brought Schiller's influence to bear on twentieth century drama.

Schiller equated the concept of patriotism with such ideals as truth, beauty, nobility, love, freedom, and

(Library of Congress)

immortality. He bound all these ideals with a religious sense of duty, as in his latter dramas, in which history appears as the fulfillment of a divine plan. Schiller was a subject of several absolute monarchs in a time of democratic and republican revolutions and reactionary wars and upheavals. He created, for the Germany that did not yet exist, a model of the political tragedy. In it the hero is seen not only as an energetic but also as a suffering human being, living out a metaphysical tragedy, a conflict between ideals and fate.

Schiller gave German literature basic concepts of structure, both of the art of tragedy and of aesthetics. The history of tragedy to the present day has been, to a great extent, a confrontation with Schiller.

Biography • The early years of Johann Christoph Friedrich von Schiller were deeply imprinted with the tyranny of two fathers. Johann Kaspar Schiller, barber-surgeon, military officer, and later, Royal Head Forester, ruled his family with an iron hand. Duke Karl Eugen, founder of a military academy for promising young men, considered himself the father of the talented boys he chose to attend the school. After two invitations, Johann Schiller no longer had any choice about sending his son, who had wanted to become a pastor, to the duke's academy.

The academy was strict in a sense of the word no longer meaningful today. Every moment of the day was organized. No boy had any time to himself, not even on the compulsory "pleasure" strolls. Army officers maintained discipline. Duke Karl had a discriminating eye for talented men; many of the teachers he brought to his new school were gifted. Professor Abel, for example, who taught Latin and Greek, expounded principles of the Enlightenment, particularly a quest for the ideal not dependent on religious conviction.

The duke's academy was unusual for its time because it admitted both Protestant and Roman Catholic boys. The atmosphere of religious tolerance, when combined with the secular idealism of the Enlightenment, tended to dilute the students' religious convictions, including Schiller's. Young Schiller was Professor Abel's finest student of Latin and Greek. He learned French partly to communicate with some of his fellow students from the French-speaking section of the Duchy of Württemberg. Soon, as the reputation of the school grew, boys began to appear from northern German areas, Switzerland, Scandinavia, and even from England.

Young Schiller studied law, but it was the duke's choice, not his, and after a few years, illness began making serious inroads into his accomplishments. As a result he was allowed to study medicine, including surgery. Anatomy classes never bothered Schiller, and it is possible that he escaped rigorous supervision because the military watchdogs were less vigilant in the dissection room. He was not permitted to visit his family more than one or two days a year. These ties were cut early; by age twelve, he was already at the academy.

By age twenty, Schiller had written one dissertation, which had been turned down as too speculative and theoretical, had seen himself relegated to another year at the academy to write another research paper, and had finished a manuscript of his first play, *The Robbers*, which was well in hand. The battle of sons against fathers, both in a political sense and in a familial sense, finds expression in this wildly emotional play. Above everything else, however, the protagonist is ruled by a morality that is not less strict for being his own, rather than society's. The play was written clandestinely, probably by candlelight late at night. Schiller kept it concealed, except from a few friends.

After presentation of a more technical dissertation, Schiller was graduated. Although he had every reason to expect favorable treatment from the duke, he was assigned a position as military surgeon, no higher than his unstudied father. Schiller was not well paid, was extremely restricted, and was bored. He borrowed money to publish *The Robbers* privately, the beginning of a lifetime of worry with creditors. He made several trips out of the country to Mannheim, to present his play for performance. Sometimes he traveled with official permission, sometimes not. The subject of his play was considered dangerously controversial in its contemporary context. Because Mannheim's censor might not have permitted it to be performed, Schiller had to rewrite the play as if it were happening in the 1400's, the end of the age of knighthood. Although Schiller had based his story on a contemporary robber chieftain, the theater director insisted that bands of marauders were simply not believable in eighteenth century Europe.

After the performance of *The Robbers* in Mannheim, Duke Karl Eugen forbade Schiller to publish anything further except medical research. Schiller fled the country, became a nearly penniless refugee in Mannheim until he was given a position of playwright for the theater, then contracted malaria and nearly died. His health, never robust, was permanently undermined. He was not able to fulfill some of the conditions of his contract, and the play he did complete, *Fiesco: Or, The Genoese Conspiracy*, puzzled the Mannheim audience with its political subtlety. They had been expecting more bombast. Schiller's contract was not renewed.

Schiller spent the next years, during the writing of *Cabal and Love* and *Don Carlos, Infante of Spain*, moving from the refuge of one set of friends to another, ever more deeply in debt, often despairing of finding a home. During this time he met Christian Gottfried Körner. Their letters offer insight into Schiller's life and thought. The friendship lasted for the rest of his life.

In 1787, Duke Karl August of Saxony-Weimar, impressed by Schiller's historical essays, called him to the new university at Jena and later knighted him for his accomplishments. Johann Wolfgang von Goethe, a high official in the duchy, had suggested that Schiller be named professor of history. He did not know Schiller, but as time passed Goethe and Schiller were to become working partners, inspiration for each other, and close friends. Schiller's and Goethe's works from this point bear the mark of each other's genius, as well as their own. Schiller's work also influenced Wilhelm von Humboldt, Heinrich von Kleist, Hölderlin, and Novalis. He was kindness itself to the visiting Madame de Staël, who "discovered" for the French, and ultimately for the rest of the world, the giants of German classicism, Schiller and Goethe.

During the Weimar years, Schiller was ill so often that he seemed to live in bed. The Wallenstein trilogy, *Mary Stuart, The Maid of Orleans, William Tell,* and the others were composed in the rare moments Schiller felt well enough to work. He had to stop lecturing at the university because his small store of energy would not permit it. At the age of forty-six he died, presumably of a combination of pneumonia and tuberculosis.

Analysis • It is not necessary to have studied Friedrich Schiller's theoretical writings or Immanuel Kant's *Kritik der reinen Vernunft* (1781; *Critique of Pure Reason,* 1838), which influenced him profoundly, to understand Schiller's works, but it is helpful to understand two concepts that are the source of tragic conflict in most of his plays: the concept of the "naïve" and of the "sentimental." For each word, a special sense is intended: "Sentimental" means reflective, analytical, conscious of oneself, intellectual; "naïve" means unselfconscious, natural, original, pure, unreflective. There can be sentimental modes of existence as well as sentimental art. In referring to people, Schiller used the terms "dignity" (roughly corresponding to sentimentality) and "grace" (naïveté). Homer's is an example of naïve art—that is, an outpouring of natural gifts. Eighteenth century art, with its conventions and rules, could only be sentimental. In terms of the artistic process, although the original act of creation is always naïve, it acquires a sentimental aspect as it is analyzed, structured, and contemplated by the artist. A naïve work of art is the outpouring of genius. A sentimental work of art has goals. Where a sentimental work of art has a moral, a naïve work of art is itself moral. Art is to be valued for its own sake and by its own rules. Schiller's essays *Briefe über die ästhetische Erziehung des Menschen,* 1795 (*On the Aesthetic Education of Man,* 1845), *Über Anmut und Würde* (1793; *On Grace and Dignity,* 1875), and *Über naïve und sentimentalische Dichtung* (1795; *On Naïve and Sentimental Poetry,* 1845), delineate this system of thought exemplified in the plays.

The Robbers • In Schiller's first play, *The Robbers,* critic Ilse Graham sees a version of the biblical Jacob and Esau conflict. The younger brother, who by virtue of his talent and charm has unintentionally stolen the father's affection, is tricked by the cunning, analytical older brother, and is eventually disinherited and disowned. Stunned, the younger brother takes charge of a group of marauders, looking to avenge social and political injustice in a very concrete manner. Meanwhile, the older brother uses the political power of feudalism to ruin the already weak father, while keeping the feared younger brother at bay. Although the robber chieftain makes a considerable effort to disclaim responsibility for his men's atrocities by holding himself aloof from scenes of carnage, his realization that he has become incurably tainted with moral degeneracy— that there is no way back—forms the central crisis of the play. In this moment of reflection on his actions, the robber chieftain crosses the boundary from naïve to sentimental. Like Hamlet, he contemplates suicide, but decides from pride in his own greatness to live out his bitter choice to the end: "I am my Heaven and my Hell." "Revenge is my trade." "Two such as I would bring down the whole structure of the civilized world."

Fiesco • The masks in Schiller's next play, *Fiesco*, are not confined to the operalike costume ball of the first scene. Andreas Doria, illegal dictator of Genua, is about to be toppled by another member of the hereditary oligarchy, a Machiavellian republican leader named Fiesco. Fiesco must be seen as an artist, rather than a politician, for he manipulates people much as a stage director moves actors. As the aesthetic mode of existence in which human genius can reach its full potential is possible only in the perfect freedom of play, Fiesco plays with his opponents, just as Schiller plays with the plot, drawing out the denouement with one complication after another. Fiesco, a sentimental artist in the sense of combining natural genius and reflection, is a charismatic villain with more than a hint of the subsequent century's Napoleon Bonaparte. If the robber chieftain's downfall was his naïve reaction—choosing outlawry—to a blow of fate, then Fiesco's downfall is his excessive commitment to sentimental artistry, playing with his own coup until at last he is murdered by a republican fellow-conspirator. Incredibly, the assassin rushes away from the scene to the side of the previous dictator. This is the last stroke of Schiller's "republican tragedy."

Cabal and Love • *Cabal and Love* includes many features of the comedy. Before Gotthold Ephraim Lessing's bourgeois tragedy *Miss Sara Sampson* (1755; English translation, 1933) and the subsequent *Emilia Galotti* (1772; English translation, 1786), only members of the nobility served as protagonists in tragedy. The middle classes were considered more suitable for comedy. Schiller, a lifelong believer in the aristocracy of art and intellect, rather than birth, brought a Shakespearean mixture of comic doings and tragic conflict to the stage in *Cabal and Love*. In this play, the potential of ideal love cannot be realized. Those who would pursue it are destroyed, on one level by their membership in diverse social classes, on another by their membership in the corrupt human race.

The play, retitled by the actor August Wilhelm Iffland, had been named after the main character, Luise Millerin, the first figure in Schiller's dramas to exemplify the *schöne Seele* (beautiful soul). Just as a naïve work of art is beautiful in and of itself, so the beautiful soul is the epitome of the naïve in a human life, a naturally pure and unspoiled being.

Cabal and Love contains some of Schiller's harshest social criticism. A despotic court conspires to deprive the lovers of any vestige of hope, seeking to destroy their vision of love and each other as well as to deprive them of the opportunity to marry. In another abuse of courtly power, the prince manages to pay for his latest gift of jewels to his mistress by selling many hundreds of young recruits to the English to be sent to fight in America. After the first few who protest are shot, their brains splashing on the pavement, the rest cheer, "Off to America! Hurrah!"

Don Carlos, Infante of Spain • The transitional play *Don Carlos, Infante of Spain* has an uneven plot, but is one of Schiller's most popular plays. "Geben Sie Gedankenfreiheit!" (give freedom of thought) a character demands of the startled King Philip of Spain in perhaps the most famous single line in all of German literature. As the scene develops, however, it becomes obvious that such a change would bring about the inevitable end of absolutism, and that on the other hand, anyone who became king would of necessity become a Philip.

It was not until the Wallenstein trilogy that Schiller showed that the unwillingness to act is a fateful action in itself. Thought by many to be Schiller's greatest work, the trilogy covers four days in the life of Wallenstein, duke of Friedland and supreme commander of the Imperial armies, during the Thirty Years' War (1618-1648). Having started his career as a naïve, naturally gifted military genius, Wallenstein was deposed as general for a period of time as a result of political conniving by the emperor and others. As things began to go badly for the Imperial armies in the so-called religious wars between Protestants and Roman Catholics, Wallenstein was recalled. At the time of his fall from power, however, the general became aware of the treachery and ungratefulness of the emperor in contrast to his own loyalty and incomparable achievements for the Roman Catholic side. All of this has taken place before the action of the trilogy: Wallenstein has already made the transition from naïve to sentimental. As Schiller depicts him in the drama, he relies on the counsel of the stars, broods on destiny, and negotiates with the Swedes (Protestants) to change his and his armies' allegiance, thus forcing the emperor to accept a compromised peace.

The Camp of Wallenstein • The calculating realist Wallenstein never appears in the first play, *The Camp of Wallenstein*, which shows the bright color and comedy of the military universe solely subject to, and dependent on, Wallenstein. In legends and anecdotes, the troops pay homage to their general, the charismatic god of the camp. Neither language, patriotism, nor religion can serve as a common point of allegiance for the camp, only Wallenstein.

Although Wallenstein's greatness is obvious, he is not a virtuous man. The intellectual, sentimental characteristics of the general come into sharp contrast with the naïve qualities of Max Piccolomini, a young officer who idolizes Wallenstein. For Max, the final judge of any matter is the heart, which in Schiller's works is the organ of religion as well as love, a direct connection with a divine realm.

The Piccolominis • In the second play, *The Piccolominis*, Wallenstein's downfall has been planned and ordered by the emperor. All that remains is to determine the manner of execution. At the same time Wallenstein, ignorant of approaching doom, is fully prepared to sacrifice the ideal love between two young people very dear to him, his daughter Thekla and Max Piccolomini, in order to arrange a politically propitious marriage for her. Max and Thekla, two beautiful souls, speak with the voice of the playwright in sadly prophesying the general's downfall at the end of the play. If *The Camp of Wallenstein* is a comedy, then *The Piccolominis*, with its plot exposition lacking fulfillment, is reminiscent of William Shakespeare's historical plays.

The Death of Wallenstein • *The Death of Wallenstein* is a tragedy. At the time he was working on the Wallenstein trilogy, Schiller translated a play by Jean Racine. He seems to have taken seriously literary journal editor Christoph Martin Wieland's call for German drama to adhere more closely to Aristotelian unities of time and place. Also, by this time Schiller and Goethe, with *Egmont* (1788; English translation, 1841) and *Don Carlos, Infante of Spain*, had established iambic pentameter as the meter of classical German tragedy.

Mary Stuart • *Mary Stuart*, containing a face-to-face confrontation never recorded in history between Elizabeth I and the Scottish queen, is also restricted in time and place, as in classical French tragedy. Schiller portrays the two queens as young women, Mary basically naïve—guilty of sexual transgressions and sins of impulsiveness—Elizabeth conniving and sentimental. Both love and are wooed by the same man, Leicester. Where enough humility and docility from Mary toward Elizabeth might have saved

Mary from her death sentence, the Scottish queen seizes the freedom to assert her integrity and pride. Some critics, including Ilse Graham, see the two queens as two halves of the same being or personality, neither able to function without the other.

The Maid of Orleans • "This play flowed from my heart," Schiller wrote in 1802 about *The Maid of Orleans*, "and it ought to speak to the hearts of the audience. It is not always true, unfortunately, that others have a heart." Where *The Death of Wallenstein* and *Mary Stuart* had demanded intellectual discipline from the playwright, the material concerning Joan of Arc also enjoyed his affection and sympathy. Goethe considered it Schiller's best play.

Although Schiller wrote *The Maid of Orleans* in Weimar, it opened in Leipzig, Berlin, and Hamburg. Duke Karl August of Saxony-Weimar thought the play ridiculous in comparison to Voltaire's satiric mock-epic poem *La Pucelle d'Orleans* (1755; *La Pucelle: Or, the Maid of Orleans*, 1785-1786). In addition, the only actress in Weimar suitable for playing the lead was the duke's mistress. The duke did not want her lack of qualifications for the role of a holy maiden to become the subject of gossip.

Schiller did not strive for an episodic style and frequent changes of scene, as did the romantic Ludwig Tieck in his *Leben und Tod der heiligen Genoveva* (pb. 1800, pr. 1807). Actually, Schiller missed the simplicity and structural unity of the *Mary Stuart* material. To convey the Joan of Arc material, Schiller had to let the demands of the plot determine the structure of the play, a procedure bringing him closer again to Shakespearean than to French models. Even so, Schiller felt free to let the Joan of his play differ from the historical Joan, probably most markedly in the manner of her death.

Instead of a witchcraft trial and a heretic's death at the stake, Schiller's Joan dies a victorious, glorious death from the wounds of battle. Schiller's Joan speaks more words of prophecy than the historical Joan, taking on some of the qualities of a heathen seeress. Saints Catharine and Margaret, who appeared to the historical Joan, are replaced by the repeated dream of the Virgin as Queen of Heaven. Where the historical Joan, although garbed in battle dress, limited herself to carrying a banner at the head of her troops, Schiller's Joan is commanded by God to kill the enemy mercilessly, and she does so with supernatural efficiency and cold-bloodedness. The English, typified by Montgomery, call her "terrible, dreadful."

Some critics saw in the play Schiller's intention to let the ideal qualities of form triumph over the violence of the plot in order to propel the audience into a sudden insight about the nature of beauty. Schiller used some techniques of the romantics in orchestrating the spoken voice, moving from dramatic speeches to lyric arias with their additional musical element, rhyme. There are iambic and folk-song stanzas, but also lines reminiscent of the classical hexameter and trimeter. Schiller must have called his tragedy "romantic" because of the presence of miracles and the story's proximity to medieval Christian mythology. The play also contains the motif of national liberation dear to the romantics.

Although Schiller's Joan is a heroic figure, she is not a sympathetic protagonist. She is characterized by a kind of inhuman heartlessness, required of her by God, but also proclaimed by her repeatedly. The pure and obedient shepherdess soon becomes an amazon, who even calls herself a pitiless spirit of terror. In the heat of battle she says, "My armor does not cover a heart. . . . Defend yourself; death is calling you. . . . Don't appeal to my sex; don't call me woman." She is in the human world, but not of it, her allegiance and activities forming a direct conduit from a supernatural realm. Indeed, *The Maid of Orleans*, according to some critics, shows the fate of the transcendent in the midst of a vain, impure, degrading world; its reconciliation with and return to its origin forms the culmination.

Schiller himself stated explicitly that the Joan of the last act and the shepherdess Joan of the prologue reflect each other. In 1801, he wrote in a letter to Goethe:

> I predict a good and proper effect for my last act; it explains the first act, and so the snake bites itself on the tail. Because my hero stands alone, quite deserted by the gods in her misfortune, quite free and independent, her worthiness for the role of prophet is demonstrated. The end of the fourth act is very theatrical, and the thundering *deus ex machina* will bring about the desired result.

The end of the fourth act, when the unprotesting Joan is cast out from the French army, is indeed theatrical, but also provides the point of departure for the process of tragedy: previous worldly adoration and internally, a steep fall. On the one side is the sumptuous coronation parade led by Joan with her banner of the Holy Virgin, on the other, the subsequent bitter accusations. Joan's speechlessness gives rise to the belief by all that the accusations are true, but Joan cannot deny that the enemy is in her heart—not the Devil but the Englishman Lionel. She is deeply conscious of her transgression against God, not in the form of witchcraft but in the form of love.

Seldom are Schiller's characters completely silent. Luise Miller in *Cabal and Love* is an example. Her silence might be seen as powerlessness at the beginning of the play, later the result of a forced oath to deny her love, and finally as an expression of helplessness. Joan is intransigent in her silence, which is emphasized by the clap of thunder from on high. Unfortunately, this sign from Heaven is just as subject to misinterpretation as Joan's speechlessness. Joan is mute as a sign of the fissure in her soul: She belongs neither in this world nor in the next. That is the tragic moment in this play, Joan's total isolation; not even those who love her and believe in her are able to break through it. Everyone believes that she is guilty of witchcraft, including her infatuated companion-in-exile. Thus, Joan remains uncanny—whether in love or hate—and inaccessible to other people, a figure from an alien world, yet human enough to awaken passion in others and succumb to it herself.

Joan's silence is also an indication that she accepts her downfall and humiliation as a just punishment for her transgression, although the nature of her sin is completely misunderstood by her human judges. The process of reflection by which she arrives at this point shows that the faculty of sentimentality is added to her previous naïveté, much the same as the sentimentality of Mary Stuart. Although not guilty of the crime with which she is charged, like Mary, Joan accepts the punishment to expiate another sin. Just as Mary Stuart receives absolution in the religious rites of the execution scene, so Joan, the outcast, finds her way back to God. By honoring and accepting her just punishment Joan again becomes God's prophet and messenger. Her love for Lionel cannot distract her from the immediacy of France's peril and her mission.

The final scene of the play is not one of martyrdom but of resplendence. Joan is not seen as a figure of Christian charity, but rather as a warrior as fierce and deadly as was Achilles. Schiller created her from many sources, not only from the historical Joan but also from Shakespeare, Greek antiquity, German classicism and romanticism, the Christian Middle Ages, and the Old Testament. Through Joan of Arc's glorious death, Schiller exalted the tragedy to a religious rite. Joan is immortal because art triumphs with her over earthly restrictions and imperfections, because humanity sees in her its own potential for transcendence.

Schiller's morality, like his characteristic victories over illness in order to create, had a Promethean cast. He was consistently moral to the point of impetuosity, trying to transform his bourgeois era into an age receptive to the demanding aesthetic values and radical idealism of his work. It seemed to him the duty of human beings surrounded by a materialist and rationalist environment, on an earth haunted by evil and lacking in religion, to rediscover divine values and concepts that had lain hidden, and to bring them out and to make them visible in a new way. The tragedy as religious celebration would serve this purpose. In tragedy, Schiller believed, ideals celebrate their purest triumph over the material world.

William Tell • If *William Tell* seems like a collection of clichés to people in the German-speaksing world, it is because this greatly beloved last play of Schiller's is perhaps the most quoted work of German literature. Schiller's lines have been repeated so often for so many decades and generations that they have become part of the German language, just as many lines of Shakespeare's *Hamlet, Prince of Denmark* (pr. c. 1600 1601) might hardly seem original to a speaker of English. Schiller's *William Tell* was originally performed March 17, 1804, under the personal direction of Schiller's great collaborator and friend, Goethe. So beloved did the play become that in a performance at the court of William II, emperor of Germany, the emperor and the entire audience stood during the oath-taking scene, repeating from memory with the actors the words of the pledge of allegiance of republican Switzerland. In this, Schiller's own favorite play, one sees that his realization of ideal humanity is the unity of nature and the psyche. Where the conflict of a natural drive (love) with heroic ideals nearly destroyed Joan of Arc in *The Maid of Orleans*, the unity of naïve and sentimental forces in the hero moves *William Tell* away from tragedy and into the realm of pageantry or ritual.

Other major works

LONG FICTION: *Der Verbrecher aus verlorener Ehre*, 1786 (*The Criminal, in Consequence of Lost Reputation*, 1841); *Der Geisterseher*, 1789 (*The Ghost-Seer: Or, The Apparitionist*, 1795).

POETRY: *Anthologie auf das Jahr 1782*, 1782; *Xenien*, 1796 (with Johann Wolfgang von Goethe); *Gedichte*, 1800, 1803; *The Poems of Schiller*, 1851; *The Ballads and Shorter Poems of Fredrick v. Schiller*, 1901.

NONFICTION: *Die Schaubühne als eine moralische Anstalt betrachtet*, 1784 (*The Theater as a Moral Institution*, 1845); *Historischer Kalender für Damen*, 1790, 1791; *Geschichte des dreissigjährigen Krieges*, 1791-1793 (3 volumes; *History of the Thirty Years' War*, 1799); *Über den Grund des Vergnügens an tragischen Gegenständen*, 1792 (*On the Pleasure in Tragic Subjects*, 1845); *Über das Pathetische*, 1793 (*On the Pathetic*, 1845); *Über Anmut und Würde*, 1793 (*On Grace and Dignity*, 1845); *Briefe über die ästhetische Erziehung des Menschen*, 1795 (*On the Aesthetic Education of Man*, 1845); *Über naïve und sentimentalische Dichtung*, 1795-1796 (*On Naïve and Sentimental Poetry*, 1845); *Über das Erhabene*, 1801 (*On the Sublime*, 1845); *Briefwechsel Zwischen Schiller und Goethe*, 1829 (*The Correspondence Between Schiller and Goethe*, 1845); *Aesthetical and Philosophical Essays*, 1845; *Schillers Briefwechsel mit Körner von 1784 bis zum Tode Schillers*, 1847 (*Schiller's Correspondence with Körner*, 1849).

MISCELLANEOUS: *Sämmtliche Werke*, 1812-1815 (12 volumes; *Complete Works in English*, 1870).

Bibliography

Graham, Ilse. *Schiller's Drama: Talent and Integrity*. London: Methuen, 1974. Graham provides an analysis of Schiller's plays, including *The Robbers* and *Mary Stuart*. He looks at both content and technique. Bibliography.

Hammer, Stephanie Barbé. *Schiller's Wound: The Theater of Trauma from Crisis to Commodity.* Detroit, Mich.: Wayne State University Press, 2001. Hammer examines Schiller's plays from a psychological standpoint, analyzing the thought behind them. Bibliography and index.

Miller, R. D. *A Study of Schiller's "Jungfrau von Orleans."* Harrogate, England: Duchy Press, 1995. Miller provides a close examination of Schiller's play about Joan of Arc, *The Maid of Orleans.* Bibliography and index.

Pugh, David. *Schiller's Early Dramas: A Critical History.* Rochester, N.Y.: Camden House, 2000. One volume in the series Studies in German Literature, Linguistics, and Culture: Literary Criticism in Perspective. Focuses on the early works of Schiller, their impact and controversies.

Reed, T. J. *Schiller.* New York: Oxford University Press, 1991. A biography of the German writer, which sheds light on his writing of dramas. Bibliography and index.

Sharpe, Lesley. *Friedrich Schiller: Drama, Thought, and Politics.* New York: Cambridge University Press, 1991. Part of the Cambridge Studies in German series, this scholarly study looks at Schiller's views and how they infused his drama and other works. Bibliography and index.

Fredericka A. Schmadel

Peter Shaffer

Born: Liverpool, England; May 15, 1926

Principal drama • *Five Finger Exercise*, pr., pb. 1958; *The Private Ear*, pr., pb. 1962 (one act); *The Public Eye*, pr., pb. 1962 (one act); *The Merry Roosters Panto*, pr. 1963 (music by Stanley Myers, lyrics by Lionel Bart); *The Royal Hunt of the Sun*, pr., pb. 1964; *Black Comedy*, pr. 1965, pb. 1967 (one act); *The White Liars*, pb. 1967, 1968 (one act; originally as *White Lies*, pr., pb. 1967); *Shrivings*, pb. 1973 (with *Equus*; originally as *The Battle of Shrivings*, pr. 1970); *Equus*, pr., pb. 1973; *Amadeus*, pr. 1979, pb. 1980; *The Collected Plays of Peter Shaffer*, pb. 1982; *Yonadab: The Watcher*, pr. 1985, pb. 1988; *Lettice and Lovage*, pr., pb. 1987; *The Gift of the Gorgon*, pr. 1992, pb. 1993

Other literary forms • Peter Shaffer began his writing career with a teleplay, *The Salt Land* (1955), and a radio play, *The Prodigal Father* (1955). Shaffer has also written several novels. With his twin brother, Anthony Shaffer, he wrote *The Woman in the Wardrobe* (1951), published in England under the collective pen name Peter Antony. The two brothers also collaborated on two more novels: *How Doth the Little Crocodile?* (1952), likewise issued under the pen name Peter Antony, and *Withered Murder* (1955), published under both authors' real names. Macmillan published *Withered Murder* (1956) and *How Doth the Little Crocodile?* (1957) in the United States, using the authors' real names. Shaffer also wrote the screenplays for *The Public Eye* (1972), *Equus* (1977), and *Amadeus* (1984), the last of which won the 1985 Academy Award for Best Screenplay Adaptation.

Achievements • Once Peter Shaffer settled on playwriting as a career, most of his plays succeeded on both sides of the Atlantic. *Five Finger Exercise*, his first work for the stage, earned the London *Evening Standard* Drama Award for 1958 and the New York Drama Critics Circle Award for Best Foreign Play of the season in 1960. The one-act comedies *The Private Ear* and *The Public Eye* sustained Shaffer's reputation as a skilled playwright, as did the exceptional pageantry of *The Royal Hunt of the Sun*. *Equus* won the Tony Award for Best Play of the 1974-1975 season, the New York Drama Critics Circle Award, the Outer Critics Circle Award, and the Los Angeles Drama Critics Award. With 1,207 performances on Broadway, *Equus* ranks among the top twenty-five longest-running plays in the history of New York theater. *Amadeus* again took the *Evening Standard* Drama Award, the Plays and Players Award, and the London Theatre Critics Award for Best Play. The New York production won the New York Drama Critics Circle Award and the Outer Critics Circle Award for 1981. The film version of *Amadeus* won eight Oscars in 1984, including Best Film and Best Adapted Screenplay. In 1987, Shaffer was honored with the title of Commander of the British Empire.

Biography • Peter Levin Shaffer was born to Orthodox Jewish parents, Jack and Reka Shaffer, in Liverpool, England, on May 15, 1926, with a twin brother, Anthony. Another brother, Brian, was born in 1929. Anthony is also a writer, author of the prize-winning play *Sleuth* (pr. 1970). Brian is a biophysicist.

A middle-class British family, the Shaffers moved to London in 1936. World War II brought several relocations, in part because of safety concerns and in part because of the demands of Jack Shaffer's real estate business. In 1942, Shaffer was enrolled in St. Paul's School in London. In 1944, the twin brothers were conscripted for duty in the coal mines, working first in Kent, then in Yorkshire. Shaffer entered Trinity College, Cambridge University, on a scholarship in 1947.

At Cambridge, Shaffer discovered his talent and taste for writing while editing a college magazine. Taking his degree in history in 1950, he sought employment with various publishers in England, to no avail. He moved to New York in 1951. From a brief stint as a salesperson in a Doubleday bookstore, he moved to a job in the acquisitions section of a branch of the New York Public Library. Shaffer returned to London in 1954 and worked for the music publisher Boosey and Hawkes for about a year. With the broadcast of his teleplay *The Salt Land* and his radio play *The Prodigal Father* in 1955, he decided to turn to writing as a full-time career.

The 1958 success of *Five Finger Exercise* at London's Comedy Theater in the West End brought Shaffer renown as a serious playwright. The play opened in New York in December, 1959, setting a pattern followed by most of his subsequent stage plays. His pair of one-act plays, *The Private Ear* and *The Public Eye*, opened in London in 1962 and in New York in 1963. The Christmas season of 1963 saw the production of *The Merry Roosters Panto* in London.

During 1964, Shaffer and Peter Brook worked on a film script of William Golding's *Lord of the Flies* (1954), but it was not used for the eventual film version of the novel. Shaffer's *The Royal Hunt of the Sun* opened at the National Theatre in Chichester, England, in July, 1964; in London in December of that year; and in New York in October of 1965. At the behest of Sir Laurence Olivier, the director of the National Theatre, Shaffer wrote *Black Comedy*. It played at Chichester in July, 1965, then in London, and was presented in tandem with *White Lies* in 1967. This second pair of one-act plays was staged again in London in 1968, by which time Shaffer had rewritten *White Lies* and retitled it *The White Liars*.

For Shaffer, the 1970's began with a lull: *The Battle of Shrivings* opened in London in February, 1970, but did not run for long. July, 1973, however, saw the London premiere of *Equus*, which in October, 1974, opened in New York for its remarkably long run. When Atheneum issued its edition of *Equus* in 1973, Shaffer included in it the book *Shrivings*, his revised version of *The Battle of Shrivings*, which had not survived onstage. In this general time period, Shaffer also developed the screenplay for the film version of *Equus*, which was released in 1977.

Finishing the 1970's with the highly successful *Equus*, Shaffer moved into the 1980's with the equally noteworthy *Amadeus*, which opened at the National Theatre, Chichester, in November, 1979, and subsequently opened in London. Shaffer revised his already very successful script during a run of the production in Washington, D.C., prior to its December, 1980, opening at New York's Broadhurst Theater. A film version was released in 1984 under the direction of Miloš Forman.

After the unsuccessful *Yonadab*, based on biblical themes, Shaffer returned to comedy with a star vehicle written for Maggie Smith, *Lettice and Lovage*, which received favorable reviews. Shaffer calls New York City home, despite his British citizenship and frequent returns to England.

Analysis • Writing for *Theatre Arts* in February, 1960, Peter Shaffer made a declaration of independence: "Labels aren't for playwrights." His independence shows in both his life and his art. Shaffer admits in a 1963 article in *Transatlantic Review*, "All art is autobiographical inasmuch as it refers to personal experience," but the adolescent torment in *Five Finger Exercise* and the passions he stages in other works stem from his personal experience only in a general sense. Shaffer does tell of seeing, hearing, or reading of events that trigger ideas for his plays. Seeing, in 1968 and 1969, pro- and anti-Vietnam War demonstrations in New York and watching the American people agonize over the war led him to write *Shrivings*. Still, he maintains a degree of distance between his personal life and his plays. John Russell Taylor sees in *Five Finger Exercise* the sort of detachment other critics agree is characteristic of Shaffer's work: "The playwright does not seem to be personally involved in his play.... This balance of sympathy in a dramatist . . . makes for effective drama."

Within the mainstream of theatrical tradition, Shaffer maintains his artistic independence, varying conventional form or shifting his approach to a theme in almost every play. *Five Finger Exercise* is a middle-class domestic drama written at a time when numerous domestic dramas were in vogue, but Shaffer did not repeat himself. He moved on to romantic triangles in his one-act plays, then to epic drama with *The Royal Hunt of the Sun*, to psychological drama in *Equus*, and to a historical play, *Amadeus*.

Sets of the earlier plays are realistic. *The Royal Hunt of the Sun, Equus,* and *Amadeus,* however, use impressionistic sets, rely on varying amounts of flashback technique, and employ varying amounts of coordinate action. Besides varying set types and play genres, Shaffer varies emphasis in theatrical appeal. Sounds or music are important secondary factors in *Five Finger Exercise, The Royal Hunt of the Sun,* and *Equus* and are central to the plots of *The Private Ear* and *Amadeus*. Seeing in silence is the proposed cure for a troubled marriage in *The Public Eye*, visual display is lavish in *The Royal Hunt of the Sun,* and the sight of characters groping and stumbling through the action as though in pitch dark makes *Black Comedy* a vivid farce.

Common trends • Given Shaffer's drive for fresh rendering of theatrical matter, various trends do appear in his plays. One such trait is cultural or ethnic variety. Possibly, being reared by Orthodox Jewish parents in nominally Protestant England sensitized him to the assets of ethnic identities and the liabilities of stereotypes. Whatever the reason, Shaffer commonly includes multicultural groupings of characters. *Five Finger Exercise* includes Louise, overly proud of her French ancestry, and Walter, the young German tutor who wants desperately to become a British subject. The protagonist of *The Public Eye*, Julian Christoforou, is Greek. To emphasize his foreignness, Christoforou was played in the film version by Topol, an Israeli actor. *Black Comedy* includes both an electrician and a prospective buyer of a young sculptor's art who are German. *Shrivings* includes an American secretary and an English poet who spends most of his time on the island of Corfu. *Amadeus* features an Italian composer in the Austrian court at Vienna, and the dialogue occasionally includes Italian and French exchanges.

Generally, Shaffer's northern European characters are identified with more rational or more placid behavior, while the Mediterranean characters are posed as more vivacious or romantic. Whatever the specific mix in a given play, each cultural alternative usually exposes a deficit in the *status quo* or brings a valuable influence to compensate for some perceived lack. The Greek private detective, Christoforou, is able to explain to the older, middle-class accountant that the young wife he suspects of infidelity really only needs some excitement in her life with her mate. Martin Dysart, the controlled, rational psychiatrist, tells of traveling each summer through Greece, yearning for the wild passion of the ancient festivals of Dionysus. Mozart, bored with writing opera according to the dominant Italian conventions, is glad for a commission from the Austrian King Joseph to write opera in German.

Despite the cosmopolitan flavor of Shaffer's work, his plays are consistently male-dominated. Significant conflicts tend to be between males. In *The Private Ear*, Tchaik loses Doreen to Ted. In *The Public Eye*, while following the wife is a major factor in the action, it is reported in dialogue between the two men. The wife does appear and interact with her husband and the detective, but she does not have equivalent exposure on-stage. *The Royal Hunt of the Sun*, *Equus*, and *Amadeus* all feature conflicts between males. Only in *White Lies*, one of Shaffer's less notable efforts, is there a female protagonist. While she achieves a moral victory in that she sees and tells the truth in the end, she is forced to return her fortune-telling fee to the belligerent male antagonist and thereby faces an ethical defeat. In rewriting *Shrivings*, Shaffer strengthened the conflict by removing Sir Gideon Petrie's wife altogether, leaving the American secretary, Lois Neal, as the sole female party in a struggle primarily among men.

Significantly, Shaffer's strongest plays have usually included either more female characters or more active female characters than have the less successful plays. Even in their activity, however, the women may not be wholly ideal types. Louise in *Five Finger Exercise* is a domineering mother. Her daughter Pamela is aware of the family politics but is never permitted significant access to the actual struggles played out among the older members of the family, since she is only fourteen. *Black Comedy* features young Brindsley contending with Carol, his current and very superficial fiancée, on the night his former lover, Clea, returns. His upstairs neighbor, Miss Furnival, helps build the farce as a typical middle-aged spinster getting tipsy during the action, but she remains a convenient comic stereotype. All three women are actively involved in the plot, and all three have considerable dialogue. The protagonist, though, is a male.

Equus and *Amadeus*, Shaffer's strongest works, include women as supporting characters. Dysart turns several times to Hester Salomon for emotional support during the course of *Equus*. Wise and compassionate, she is the most wholesome of Shaffer's female characters. Constanze Mozart, too, is a support for her husband in *Amadeus* and is the only woman in the play who has a speaking role. The few others onstage are seen but not heard.

Because Shaffer is a twin, Jules Glenn suggests that his various pairs of male characters embody the conflicts and complementary satisfactions typical of twins. Although none of the character-pairs is portrayed as biological twins in the plays, their roles often have parallel aspects. Two men are involved with a single woman in *The Private Ear*, *The Public Eye*, and *White Lies*; two men in *Equus*, Martin Dysart and his patient Alan Strang, are inadequate in their sexual relationships with women. In *Amadeus*, both Mozart and Salieri have affairs with Katherina Cavalieri. *The Royal Hunt of the Sun* features two men who claim the role of a god.

Role of self-disclosure • The key to an overview of Shaffer's work is his talent for revelation of character through self-disclosure. *Five Finger Exercise*, conventional in many respects, is outstanding for its characters' multiple levels of self-disclosure, from Stanley, who rants without understanding, to Walter, who understands both the Harringtons' needs and his own and attempts suicide when fulfillment of his needs seems impossible. Shaffer's other plays take their depth and texture from this technique, if not their basic purpose. Self-disclosure is the major structural pattern for *The*

Royal Hunt of the Sun, Equus, and *Amadeus,* each of which is presented by a narrator recalling past events. Similarly, Shaffer's choice of themes as his craft matures leads to a progressive revelation of the human condition. Clive, Shaffer's first stage protagonist, searches for individual identity and independence. Protagonists in the one-act plays, both the serious and the comic, are generally reaching for satisfactory relationships with other individuals. Leading characters in the major serious plays probe the ambitions, ideals, and institutions of humankind in the world at large.

Shaffer's comments on *The Royal Hunt of the Sun* reveal a salient concern obvious in that play and others overtly dealing with worship: He is disturbed that "man constantly trivializes the immensity of his experience" and "settles for a Church or Shrine or Synagogue . . . and over and over again puts into the hands of other men the reins of oppression. . . ." Even his earliest play, though portraying domestic rather than political or religious struggles, shows that revelation of character, the self-disclosure essential to informed, mature relationships, makes the individual human being vulnerable to another's control.

Five Finger Exercise • Dennis A. Klein observes that "there is not one happy marriage in all of Shaffer's plays . . . and the prototype is the marriage between Louise and Stanley Harrington." Clive Harrington, the protagonist of *Five Finger Exercise,* is his mother's pet; he is also the target of his father's criticism because he lacks "practical" or "useful" interests. Struggling for identity and independence, Clive is never safe in the family bickering. Agreeing with Stanley that the new tutor is a needless expense draws reproach from Louise. Admitting that he is writing a review of a performance of the Greek play *Electra* triggers one more paternal lecture on the really useful pursuits in life. Clive shows contradictory responses to Walter Langer, the young German whom his mother has hired as the family tutor. Clive needs and wants the contact with an understanding, mature role model. At the same time, he is jealous of his mother's attraction to Walter, and therefore opposes Walter's efforts to become part of the Harrington family.

Home from Cambridge, Clive drinks to avoid parental control. Walter advises him to get out on his own but declines to travel with him during the coming holidays. Seeing Louise cradle Walter's head in her arms during a tender moment, Clive reports to Stanley that the two were engaged in lovemaking. Warmed by Walter's Continental graces—he is fluent in French, plays classical music on the piano and on his phonograph, and brings her wildflowers—Louise enjoys toying with the young man in somewhat the same fashion as she toys with Clive. When Walter makes it clear that he esteems her as a mother, though, Louise urges Stanley to fire Walter for being "a bad influence on Pamela."

Stanley, although he doubts that Clive's accusation is true, resents Walter's advice to Clive and uses the claim of an illicit relationship as a reason for dismissal. The lie is a very versatile weapon. It can help rid Stanley of the unwanted cost of the tutor and simultaneously serve vengeance on the young German for counseling Clive to leave home. It will punish Louise for her affectations. It will embarrass Clive—due vengeance for the boy's lack of filial piety—and weaken Clive's relationship with his mother, a bond Stanley could never match in his attempts at fathering and could never before attack so severely. Though he still understands his family no better than before, Stanley can dominate them all in one stroke.

Clive is shocked that the lie he told in private becomes his father's bludgeon in public. He realizes that his capacity to injure others is as great as that of his parents. Walter, who has opened himself to Clive and Louise in his bid for acceptance as a family member, cannot tolerate the betrayal, the victimization, resulting from his vulnerability. Walter's suicide attempt shows Clive the need for all the Harringtons to change: "The courage. For all of us. Oh God—give it."

The Royal Hunt of the Sun • Pairs of one-act plays bracket Shaffer's epic drama *The Royal Hunt of the Sun,* which turns squarely to the issue of worship in both institutional and individual dimensions. Old Martin, the narrator, tells of his youthful adventure as page boy to Pizarro, conqueror of Peru. To Young Martin, Pizarro is a hero to worship. To the priests Valverde and De Nizza, military conquest is a necessary evil that will bring the Incas the good of institutional Christianity. To Estete, the Royal Overseer, Pizarro's personal ambition and the blessings of the Church are the necessary tools for advancing the dominion of King Carlos and thus for increasing his personal status within the king's domain. Pizarro takes the noble justifications of Church and State and the outright greed of his soldiers as the means for attaining personal glory. A hard man, he warns Young Martin never to trust him: He will surely betray anyone and anything in his drive for fame.

Atahuallpa, god-king of the Incas, believes the approaching Pizarro must be the White God of ancient legend returning as foretold. Estete declares to the Inca general, Challcuchima, that the Spanish come in the names of King Carlos of Spain and of Jesus Christ, the Son of God. Challcuchima insists that it is he who comes to them in the name of the Son of God—Atahuallpa, Son of the Sun. The two leaders are fascinated with each other. When cautioned against blasphemy in this duel of rank, Pizarro exclaims, "He is a God: I am a God."

Young Martin's faith in his hero and their cause is challenged when the Spanish massacre three thousand unarmed Inca warriors and capture Atahuallpa. Hernando de Soto gives the boy the stock rationale for the "huntsmen of God": "There must always be dying to make new life." Young Martin replaces a treacherous native translator for Pizarro and Atahuallpa and witnesses their growing kinship. The thirty-three-year-old Inca ruler learns Spanish and swordsmanship from his sixty-year-old captor. In return, Atahuallpa teaches Pizarro Inca songs and dances as the subdued empire collects gold to ransom its god-king.

Once the ransom is paid, Pizarro demands that Atahuallpa pledge that the Spanish will have safe passage out of Peru. He refuses, and Pizarro's officers insist that Atahuallpa must die. Though he himself has found no special meaning in his mother Church, Pizarro persuades the Inca to accept Christian baptism. Without it, he would be burned to ashes. The god-king does not fear death; he believes his Father Sun will resurrect him. By accepting the rites of the Spanish Church, he earns death by strangulation and will leave a body to be restored.

There is no resurrection. Pizarro, however, weeps for his personal loss for the first time in his life and takes solace in the humanistic observation that at least Atahuallpa and he will be buried in the same earth under the same sun.

For Young Martin, Pizarro's betrayal of Atahuallpa is the end of faith: "Devotion never came again." Thus, Shaffer poses the high personal cost of trusting individuals and institutions further than they merit. The conquest was possible because Church and State accepted each other as justifications for destroying competing systems—and both fed on human greed and ambition. The Inca empire fell because its supreme ruler was convinced of his own divinity and was fascinated by the invader's claim of equal status. He never ordered a significant counterattack.

Equus • Shaffer gives a macrocosmic study of worship through the conflict of whole systems in *The Royal Hunt of the Sun*, with glimpses of the personal cost of faith in such systems in the lives of Atahuallpa, Pizarro, and Young Martin. *Equus*, by contrast, provides a detailed microcosmic study of the elements of worship. Seventeen-year-old Alan Strang has blinded six horses in the stable where he works. Hester Salomon, a magistrate and friend of psychiatrist Martin Dysart, brings the boy to Dysart for treatment. The psychoanalyst uncovers, little by little, the attitudes and symbols Alan has fashioned into a mysterious personal religion—worship of Equus, the horse-god.

Alan Strang is more than the average troubled adolescent of the usual domestic drama. He is the most isolated, most disturbed of all Shaffer's characters. The son of a printer and former schoolteacher, Alan is practically illiterate. His father forbids television in the home, so Alan sneaks off to watch Westerns at the neighbors' house. An avowed atheist, Frank Strang considers the religious instruction Dora gives to Alan just so much "bad sex." Dora, for her part, assures Alan that God sees him everywhere; she has read the Bible to him often. Alan especially enjoyed passages from Job and Revelation that refer to the strength and power of horses. Not wanting to interfere with her son, Dora allowed him to have a graphic poster of Christ being flogged by Roman centurions even though she believed it was a little "extreme." After an argument over religion, Frank once stormed into Alan's room and ripped the poster off the wall. Alan was devastated. A few weeks later, Frank gave Alan a picture of a horse, which Alan hung in the same spot at the foot of his bed. Frank once observed Alan chanting a genealogy, haltering himself with string, and beating himself with a coathanger before the horse picture. Frank never discussed sex with his son; Dora did so only in generalities that linked it with the love of God.

Shaffer opens both the first and second acts of *Equus* with Dysart pondering what the horse might want of Alan, and why, of all the things in the world "equal in their power to enslave . . . one suddenly strikes." When Dysart questions the propriety of "curing" Alan, whose exotic worship is "the core of his life," Hester Salomon assures the doctor that the boy must be relieved of his pain and helped to normal living. Expert in his profession, Dysart knows what he must do in order to lead the minds of troubled children into normal patterns, but he is himself led back to the borders of the rational, sensing something vital beyond: "that boy has known a passion more ferocious than I have felt in any second of my life. . . . I envy it."

The self-disclosure integral to Shaffer's drama, which built the dialogue and plot of *Five Finger Exercise* and which became a structural device as well via the narrator in *The Royal Hunt of the Sun*, rises to full force in *Equus*. Dysart is both narrator and protagonist. He relates the numerous episodes that present and then unravel the mystery of Alan's attack on the horses. Through his speeches to the audience about the plot and through his confidences shared with Hester Salomon as the protagonist within the action, Dysart exposes his own character, just as he exposes Alan's. Shaffer's use of games—which appears in the follow-the-leader ploy of *The Public Eye*, the pretended shock-treatment scene of *Shrivings*, and so on—is important in *Equus* as well. As Dysart elicits one disclosure after another from Alan, the boy extracts significant answers from Dysart in return. The methods of revelation become more intimate as the plot advances. Alan at first sings commercials when Dysart asks questions. He later divulges information via tape recordings. He finally responds in direct encounters, first with resistance, then relying on supposed hypnosis, and finally under the pretended use of a truth drug that allows him to reenact the events of the night he attacked the horses.

Alan had been out with Jill Mason, who suggested a tryst in the stable—the Holy of Holies for Equus. Alan's worship was so exclusive that his god blocked intimacy with any other. Caught between passion for another human being and passion for his horse-god—which, like his mother's God, could see him everywhere—Alan struck out to blind the god who thwarted his relationship with Jill Mason.

Martin Dysart concludes that he can lead Alan into a normal existence, but it will probably be a drab, routine life. He himself remains drawn to the nonrational source of human passion: "I need—more desperately than my children need me—a way of seeing in the dark." His need is marked with a remnant of the worship he is taking away from Alan; "There is now, in my mouth, this sharp chain. And it never comes out."

For Pizarro, the late attraction of a meaningful, dominating force appeared and died with Atahuallpa, a confident believer in an alien faith, but a faith with numerous parallels to the Christian tradition familiar to the conquistador. Pizarro had used his own religious heritage as a weapon for so long that he could only hope for meaning among a new set of symbols enlivened by a personal contact with the god-king the symbols supported. Martin Dysart's relationship with his patient also draws him into confrontation with passionate worship. The motion from Pizarro to Dysart, however, is an ideological step from a protagonist who concludes that human beings make their own gods to one who can destroy a god and still sense some force beyond human reason that endures regardless of whether the belief-system of a given worshiper is destroyed. Shaffer's next protagonist steps further into premises consistent with those of the Judeo-Christian tradition.

Amadeus • Antonio Salieri continues Shaffer's trend of self-disclosing characters by serving as both narrator and protagonist of *Amadeus*. Old Martin and Young Martin in *The Royal Hunt of the Sun* give the narrator's view and the more passionate view of Pizarro's page, respectively, and are cast as separate characters who both may be onstage at once. Dysart serves as narrator and protagonist in turn for *Equus*, not needing a distinction in age for the separate facets of the character, because the story Dysart tells took place in the recent past. His explanations and deliberations unify the flow of cinematic scenes, which include recent events retold from Dysart's viewpoint and flashbacks to some more distant events in Alan's past. Salieri, too, serves as both narrator and protagonist, but he must bridge a temporal gap of decades, as must Old Martin. Shaffer keeps Salieri a single character, similar to Dysart, but has Salieri change costume onstage and specify the shifts in time—covering two different eras in his life through changes in the character before the eyes of the audience. The transitions are yet one more method for effecting character revelation without simply repeating a narrative technique.

Salieri is Shaffer's first protagonist to operate so nearly within traditional premises of religious devotion. Salieri interacts with a God anthropomorphic enough to respond to his prayers—but a deity shaped by the Salieri family's mercantile values. In his youth, Salieri knelt "before the God of Bargains" and prayed to be a composer. In return, he would live virtuously, help other musicians, and "honor God with much music." Mozart's appearance in Vienna threatens the established Salieri's self-esteem. Mozart the man is rash, vulgar, and obnoxious. For all the faults of the man, however, Salieri hears the voice of God in some of Mozart's music. He prays for such inspiration in his own work, since "music is God's art," but to no avail.

Salieri's star voice pupil, Katherina Cavalieri, sings the lead in Mozart's opera *The Abduction from the Seraglio* and has an affair with him as well. A jealous Salieri considers seducing Mozart's fiancée, Constanze, in revenge. Mozart marries Constanze, despite his father's objections, and struggles to support himself and his wife. Constanze Mozart approaches Salieri for help in securing an appointment for her husband. Salieri nearly exacts her virtue as the price for any assistance, but in the musical scores she has brought to further her husband's cause, Salieri has seen Absolute Beauty. He recognizes his own mediocrity and rages at his God, "To my last breath, I shall block You on earth as far as I am able!"

Narrator Salieri introduces act 2 as his "battle with God" in which "Mozart was the battleground." Salieri soon breaks his vow of virtue. Although he turns away a resentful offer of an interlude with Constanze, he takes Katherina Cavalieri as his mistress. Breaking his vow to help fellow musicians, he hinders Mozart's career whenever possible. He recommends that Mozart not be appointed to tutor the Princess Elizabeth. He does suggest that Mozart be appointed chamber composer after the death of Christoph Gluck—but at one tenth the former salary. Salieri is determined to "starve out the God." As Mozart thinks through the plot of *The Magic Flute*, Salieri raises the notion of using the rites and ideals of the Masonic order in the opera. The two composers were among many notables in Vienna who belonged to the lodge. As all the rituals and doctrines are to be kept secret, Mozart's stage parallels of Masonic practices alienate the very lodge brothers who have helped him to find what work he can get.

Alone and ailing, Mozart begs God for time to complete his *Requiem Mass*. He asks Salieri to speak for God and to explain the continual suffering of his adult years. Salieri declares, "God does not love! He can only use!"

Salieri lives to see Mozart's music come into vogue after the composer's death. His own music dies before he does. He takes this as his punishment; "I must survive to see myself become extinct." His claim to be Mozart's murderer is his last attack on God. If his fame cannot last, perhaps his infamy can. Even so negative a grasping for glory proves vain: No one really believes him.

Salieri's actions are reminiscent of those of the ancient Hebrew heroes who were held to covenants with their God. Salieri's assertion that his virtue merits blessing while Mozart's vices deserve punishment echoes a plaint recurrent in the Psalms. The pattern of Israel's God favoring the unworthy or the unlikely candidate for leadership—the naïve Gideon, the young shepherd David, and so on—also has its reflex in *Amadeus* as the esteemed court composer finds the voice of God in the music of an immature, foulmouthed upstart. In a sense, Salieri also is a failed Cain. Jealous of God's favor to Mozart regardless of all of Salieri's musical and moral efforts, the aging narrator cannot even secure for himself the name of murderer. The biblical Cain bore a mark to signify his archetypal fratricide. Salieri cannot even invent the curse for himself. His God of Bargains wins the battle. Salieri gets no more and no less than he asked for when the bargain was struck, and he is punished for failing to keep his part of the covenant.

Thus, the trend of character revelation begun in the Harrington household persists. The issues of self-control versus domination by authority are broached from varying perspectives, institutional and individual, as Shaffer moves from a protagonist searching for self, through others searching for meaningful relationships with individuals, to characters exploring the human being's relationship to the structures and forces of the world at large. From *The Royal Hunt of the Sun* to *Shrivings* (which probes the limits of secular humanism as thoroughly as other plays challenge aspects of traditional religion) and on through *Equus* and *Amadeus*, Shaffer's protagonists become more overtly self-revealing and steadily more concerned with a focused search for meaning. Shaffer's mature use of a character's personal disclosures culminates in the award-winning cinematic narratives of *Equus* and *Amadeus*, in which there is a great passion to pursue, and in which the revelation of character shapes form, theme, and technique all at once.

The Gift of the Gorgon • *The Gift of the Gorgon* combines naturalism of plot and dialogue with highly imaginative staging. Through the use of lighting, screens, and a wall that can part centrally into halves, one set becomes half a dozen or so locales. The action takes place during the years 1975 to 1993. The role of the playwright and the plays he or she writes is combined with elements of Greek mythology and the contemporary phenomenon of terrorism. *The Gift of the Gorgon* opened to mixed reviews in December 1992. Peter Hall, who directed the play, praised Shaffer for undertaking such a bold, ambitious task at his age (Shaffer was sixty-six years of age at the time). Hall asserts that most dramatists in their sixties are content to sit and collect their royalties.

The setting is a villa on the Greek island of Thera but often becomes England during scenes of recollection. The protagonist is Edward Damson, a once successful but now reclusive English playwright. He has Anglicized his name from Damsinski, that of his father, a whining, bigoted Russian émigré. Edward's wife is the former Helen Jarvis, whose father is a liberal Cambridge professor, a prominent member of the Peace League. Helen was a promising classical scholar until she gave up her own pursuits to devote herself totally to her husband and his career. Edward despises academic critics. Ironically, that is what his illegitimate son, Philip—never acknowledged by him—has become. As the play opens, Edward has recently died, and Philip has traveled to Thera to learn more about the father he never met. Helen is at first unwilling but does eventually review the Damson's eighteen-year relationship in a series of flashbacks. One of Edward's curious practices over those years was communicating with his wife through unpublished dramatic scenes he would leave on her pillow or in his desk where she would find them. In these scenes, Perseus, the Greek hero, represents Edward, and Athena, the goddess of wisdom, represents Helen. Early in their relationship, Athena-Helen empowers Perseus-Edward to slay the Gorgon, a monster so horrible that the beholder is turned to stone. The Gorgon represents Edward's initial inability to complete a play without his wife's inspiration.

Edward is a man of extremes, violent in language if not in behavior. The rational Helen persuades him to tone down violent scenes in his plays *Icons* and *Prerogative*, which become great successes. Later, after Edward has come to believe that Helen is more stultifying than inspiring, he writes a play, *I.R.E.*, about an Irish terrorist and a mother whose child he has killed. In the climactic scene (against which Helen has strongly recommended), the mother ritually murders the terrorist, then dances around his bloody corpse. The audience is repulsed, the play fails, and Edward exiles himself to Thera for the last five years of his life. There, he drinks, hangs about bars with pretty young tourists, and abuses Helen through total neglect. Eventually, the couple experiences something of a role reversal. The once pacific Helen writes a scene and leaves it in her husband's desk. In the scene, Athena tongue-lashes a cowering Perseus, concluding with the accusation that Perseus himself has become the Gorgon. Edward appears contrite but plots to have his wife deal him a mortal blow. The scene mimics Clytemnestra's murder of her husband, Agamemnon, in his bath in the classical tragedy, an act that Edward has earlier characterized as totally justified. He persuades Helen to give him a ritually cleansing shower, but he secretes a razor blade in the soap with which she will scrub his body. Philip, who has worshiped his father from afar, is forced to face the reality of his life and death.

As usual, Shaffer explores a moral subject, in this case vengeance in conflict with an all-encompassing forgiveness. He skillfully merges the classical and the contemporary. The choice of Helen's name is suggestive of classical restraint. Edward's surname (which he has consciously chosen, changing it from Damsinski) is evocative of his fate. The same is true for Philip, who has taken his father's name, as Edward complains, without permission. The play is almost fiendishly clever and ambiguous, so that at the final curtain the audience may ask: Just *what* is the gift of the Gorgon, and just *who* is the Gorgon?

Other major works

LONG FICTION: *The Woman in the Wardrobe*, 1951 (as Peter Antony; with Anthony Shaffer); *How Doth the Little Crocodile?*, 1952 (as Peter Antony; with Anthony Shaffer); *Withered Murder*, 1955 (with Anthony Shaffer).

SCREENPLAYS: *The Public Eye*, 1972; *Equus*, 1977; *Amadeus*, 1984.

TELEPLAYS: *The Salt Land*, 1955; *Balance of Terror*, 1957.

RADIO PLAY: *The Prodigal Father*, 1955; *Whom Do I Have the Honour of Addressing?*, pr. 1989.

Bibliography

Beckerman, Bernard. "The Dynamics of Peter Shaffer's Drama." In *The Play and Its Critic: Essays for Eric Bentley*, edited by Michael Bertin. Lanham, Md.: University Press of America, 1986. A structural study, especially of *Equus*, by one of the best dramatic critics of the twentieth century. Examines Shaffer's "binary form . . . the tendency of plays to be a sequence of scenes between two characters" in his work. This essay was originally given in 1983, in Shaffer's presence, at the Modern Language Association (MLA) convention in New York.

Cooke, Virginia, and Malcolm Page, comps. *File on Shaffer*. London: Methuen, 1987. An indispensable source of information in the Methuen series format. Contains brief comments, play by play (not including, however, *Lettice and Lovage*), and Shaffer's own comments on his methods of work, sedulous rewrites, film adaptations, and more. The production dates and publication information are more accessible here than in Eberle Thomas's work (below).

Gianakaris, Constantine J., ed. *Peter Shaffer: A Casebook*. New York: Garland Press, 1991. Volume 10 in the Casebooks on Modern Dramatists Series. Consists of a collection of essays on the playwright's work.

Klein, Dennis A. *Peter Shaffer*. Rev. ed. New York: Twayne, 1993. A combination of biographical and critical information.

Plunka, Gene A. *Peter Shaffer: Roles, Rites, and Rituals in the Theatre*. Rutherford, N.J.: Fairleigh Dickinson University Press, 1988. Disappointing in the absence of coverage of later plays but strong on *The Royal Hunt of the Sun*, *Equus*, and *Amadeus*. This work is part sociology and part mythology, and it is fed by an interview with the playwright in 1986. It contains occasional insights but is generally too scholarly to get at the essence of Shaffer's examination of the ways of God to humankind.

Taylor, John Russell. *Peter Shaffer*. London: Longman, 1974. A brief but provocative essay on Shaffer's contributions through *Equus*. Taylor sees detachment in this work and "a tendency to analyze emotions without too far engaging himself in them as a dramatist." He concludes, however, that "there is no guessing what he can do next, but it seems inevitable that it will be grand and glorious," a foresight of *Amadeus* and *Lettice and Lovage*. Select bibliography.

Thomas, Eberle. *Peter Shaffer: An Annotated Bibliography.* New York: Garland, 1991. A
    thorough checklist of work on Shaffer, from full-length studies (four) to dissertations
    and theses (six), to individual studies of plays through *Lettice and Lovage.* The intro-
    duction outlines the scope of the book and notes the paucity of biographical infor-
    mation on this private playwright, "the most widely produced and most popular of
    England's playwrights during the post-World War II era." A general chronology fol-
    lows, but exact production information is found at each play's entry. Page-number
    index.
Trussler, Simon, et al., eds. *File on Shaffer.* Methuen Writer-Files series. Westport,
    Conn.: Methuen, 1988. A concise (eighty-eight-page) treatment of the plays through
    Lettice and Lovage.

*Ralph S. Carlson,
updated by Thomas J. Taylor
andPatrick Adcock*

William Shakespeare

Born: Stratford-upon-Avon, England; April 23?, 1564
Died: Stratford-upon-Avon, England; April 23, 1616

Principal drama • *Henry VI, Part I,* wr. 1589-1590, pr. 1592, pb. 1623; *Edward III,* pr.
c. 1589-1595, pb. 1596; *Henry VI, Part II,* pr. c. 1590-1591, pb. 1594; *Henry VI, Part III,*
pr. c. 1590-1591, pb. 1595; *Richard III,* pr. c. 1592-1593, pb. 1597; *The Comedy of Errors,*
pr. c. 1592-1594, pb. 1623; *The Taming of the Shrew,* pr. c. 1593-1594, pb. 1623; *Titus
Andronicus,* pr., pb. 1594; *The Two Gentlemen of Verona,* pr. c. 1594-1595, pb. 1623; *Love's
Labour's Lost,* pr. c. 1594-1595 (revised 1597 for court performance), pb. 1598; *Romeo
and Juliet,* pr. c. 1595-1596, pb. 1597; *Richard II,* pr. c. 1595-1596, pb. 1600; *A Midsummer Night's Dream,* pr. c. 1595-1596, pb. 1600; *King John,* pr. c. 1596-1597, pb. 1623; *The
Merchant of Venice,* pr. c. 1596-1597, pb. 1600; *Henry IV, Part I,* pr. c. 1597-1598, pb.
1598; *The Merry Wives of Windsor,* pr. 1597 (revised c. 1600-1601), pb. 1602; *Henry IV,
Part II,* pr. 1598, pb. 1600; *Much Ado About Nothing,* pr. c. 1598-1599, pb. 1600; *Henry V,*
pr. c. 1598-1599, pb. 1600; *Julius Caesar,* pr. c. 1599-1600, pb. 1623; *As You Like It,* pr. c.
1599-1600, pb. 1623; *Hamlet, Prince of Denmark,* pr. c. 1600-1601, pb. 1603; *Twelfth
Night: Or, What You Will,* pr. c. 1600-1602, pb. 1623; *Troilus and Cressida,* pr. c. 1601-
1602, pb. 1609; *All's Well That Ends Well,* pr. c. 1602-1603, pb. 1623; *Othello, the Moor of
Venice,* pr. 1604, pb. 1622 (revised 1623); *Measure for Measure,* pr. 1604, pb. 1623; *King
Lear,* pr. c. 1605-1606, pb. 1608; *Macbeth,* pr. 1606, pb. 1623; *Antony and Cleopatra,* pr. c.
1606-1607, pb. 1623; *Coriolanus,* pr. c. 1607-1608, pb. 1623; *Timon of Athens,* pr. c. 1607-
1608, pb. 1623; *Pericles, Prince of Tyre,* pr. c. 1607-1608, pb. 1609; *Cymbeline,* pr. c. 1609-
1610, pb. 1623; *The Winter's Tale,* pr. c. 1610-1611, pb. 1623; *The Tempest,* pr. 1611, pb.
1623; *The Two Noble Kinsmen,* pr. c. 1612-1613, pb. 1634 (with John Fletcher); *Henry
VIII,* pr. 1613, pb. 1623 (with Fletcher).

Other literary forms • William Shakespeare's primary reputation is based upon his
status as the foremost playwright of the English language. He also produced a highly respected body of poetry, however, and his sonnets in particular are frequently included
as appendices to collections of his dramatic works. In addition to the sonnets, Shakespeare wrote several other major poems, including *Venus and Adonis* (1593) and *The
Rape of Lucrece* (1594).

Achievements • Few dramatists can lay claim to the universal reputation achieved
by William Shakespeare. His plays have been translated into many languages and
performed on amateur and professional stages throughout the world. Radio, television, and film versions of the plays in English, German, Russian, French, and Japanese
have been heard and seen by millions of people. The plays have been revived and reworked by many prominent producers and playwrights, and they have directly influenced the work of others. Novelists and dramatists such as Charles Dickens, Bertolt
Brecht, William Faulkner, and Tom Stoppard, inspired by Shakespeare's plots, characters, and poetry, have composed works that attempt to re-create the spirit and
style of the originals and to interpret the plays in the light of their own ages. A large and

flourishing Shakespeare industry exists in England, America, Japan, and Germany, giving evidence of the playwright's popularity among scholars and the general public alike.

Evidence of the widespread and deep effect of Shakespeare's plays on English and American culture can be found in the number of words and phrases from them that have become embedded in everyday usage: Expressions such as "star-crossed lovers" are used by speakers of English with no consciousness of their Shakespearean source. It is difficult to imagine what the landscape of the English language would be like without the mountain of neologisms and aphorisms contributed by the playwright. Writing at a time when English was quite pliable, Shakespeare's linguistic facility and poetic sense transformed English into a richly metaphoric tongue.

Working as a popular playwright, Shakespeare was also instrumental in fusing the materials of native and classical drama in his work. *Hamlet, Prince of Denmark*, with its revenge theme, its ghost, and its bombastic set speeches, appears to be a tragedy based on the style of the Roman playwright Seneca, who lived in the first century C.E. Yet the hero's struggle with his conscience and his deep concern over the disposition of his soul reveal the play's roots in the native soil of English miracle and mystery dramas, which grew out of Christian rituals and depicted Christian legends. The product of this fusion is a tragedy that compels spectators and readers to examine their own deepest emotions as they ponder the effects of treacherous murder on individuals and the state. Except for Christopher Marlowe, the predecessor to whom Shakespeare owes a considerable debt, no other Elizabethan playwright was so successful in combining native and classical strains.

Shakespearean characters, many of whom are hybrids, are so vividly realized that they seem to have achieved a life independent of the worlds they inhabit. Hamlet stands as the symbol of a man who, in the words of the famous actor Sir Laurence Olivier, "could not make up his mind." Hamlet's name has become synonymous with excessive rationalizing and idealism. Othello's jealousy, Lear's madness, Macbeth's ambition, Romeo and Juliet's star-crossed love, Shylock's flinty heart—all of these psychic states and the characters who represent them have become familiar landmarks in Western culture. Their lifelikeness can be attributed to Shakespeare's talent for creating the illusion of reality in mannerisms and styles of speech. His use of the soliloquy is especially important in fashioning this illusion; the characters are made to seem fully rounded human beings in the representation of their inner as well as outer nature. Shakespeare's keen ear for conversational rhythms and his ability to reproduce believable speech between figures of high and low social rank also contribute to the liveliness of action and characters.

In addition, Shakespeare excels in the art of grasping the essence of relationships between husbands and wives, lovers, parents and children, and friends. Innocence and youthful exuberance are aptly represented in the fatal love of Romeo and Juliet; the destructive spirit of mature and intensely emotional love is caught in the affair between Antony and Cleopatra. Other relationships reveal the psychic control of one person by another (of Macbeth by Lady Macbeth), the corrupt soul of a seducer (Angelo in *Measure for Measure*), the twisted mind of a vengeful officer (Iago in *Othello*), and the warm fellowship of simple men (Bottom and his followers in *A Midsummer Night's Dream*). The range of emotional states manifested in Shakespeare's characters has never been equaled by succeeding dramatists.

These memorable characters have also been given memorable poetry to speak. In fact, one of the main strengths of Shakespearean drama is its synthesis of action

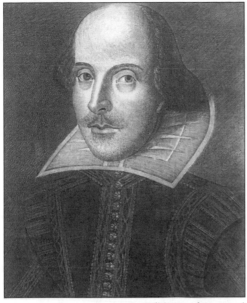

(Library of Congress)

and poetry. Although Shakespeare's poetic style is marked by the bombast and hyperbole that characterize much of Elizabethan drama, it also has a richness and concreteness that make it memorable and quotable. One need think only of Hamlet's "sea of troubles" or Macbeth's daggers "unmannerly breech'd with gore" to substantiate the imagistic power of Shakespearean verse. Such images are also worked into compelling patterns in the major plays, giving them greater structural unity than the plots alone provide. Disease imagery in *Hamlet, Prince of Denmark*, repeated references to blood in *Macbeth*, and allusions to myths of children devouring parents in *King Lear* represent only a few of the many instances of what has been called "reiterated imagery" in Shakespearean drama. Wordplay, puns, songs, and a variety of verse forms, from blank verse to tetrameter couplets—these features, too, contribute to the "movable feast" of Shakespeare's style.

In a more general sense, Shakespeare's achievement can be traced to the skill with which he used his medium—the stage. He created certain characters to fit the abilities of certain actors, as the role of Falstaff in the *Henry IV* and *Henry V* plays so vividly demonstrates. He made use of every facet of the physical stage—the trapdoor, the second level, the inner stage, the "heavens"—to create special effects or illusions. He kept always before him the purpose of entertaining his audience, staying one step ahead of changes in taste among theatergoers. That both kings and tinkers were able to find in a Shakespearean play something to delight and instruct them is testimony to the wide appeal of the playwright. No doubt the universality of his themes and his deep understanding of human nature combined to make his plays so popular. These same strengths generate the magnetic power that brings large audiences into theaters to see the plays today.

Biography • William Shakespeare was born in Stratford-upon-Avon, Warwickshire, England, descended from tenant farmers and landed gentry. His traditional birth date, April 23, 1564, is conjectural. Baptism was on April 26, so April 23 is a good guess—and a tidy one, since that date is also St. George's Day as well as the date of Shakespeare's own death.

One of Shakespeare's grandfathers, Richard Shakespeare of Snitterfield, rented land from the other, Robert Arden of Wilmcote. Shakespeare's father, John, moved to nearby Stratford-upon-Avon, became a prosperous shop owner (dealing in leather goods) and municipal officeholder, and married his former landlord's youngest daughter, Mary Arden. Thus Shakespeare—the third of eight children but the first to survive infancy—was born into a solidly middle-class family in a provincial market town. During Shakespeare's infancy, his father was one of the town's leading citizens. In 1557, John Shakespeare had become a member of the town council and subsequently held such offices as constable, affeeror (a kind of assessor), and chamberlain (treasurer). In 1568, he became bailiff (mayor) and justice of the peace.

As the son of a municipal officer, the young Shakespeare was entitled to a free education in the town's grammar school, which he probably entered around the age of seven. There, he studied Latin grammar, literature, rhetoric and logic for between eight and ten hours a day, six days a week. William Lily's largely Latin text, *A Short Introduction of Grammar* (1527), was the staple of the course, but Shakespeare also read Cicero, Plautus, Terence, Vergil, and Ovid. Many of these authors influenced the playwright's later work; Ovid in particular was a favorite source of material, used in such plays as *A Midsummer Night's Dream* and *Romeo and Juliet*. Shakespeare probably knew very little of other languages, although he does exhibit an understanding of French in such plays as *Henry V* and *All's Well That Ends Well*. (The sources for most, if not all, of the plays existed in English translations published during Shakespeare's lifetime.)

When Shakespeare was a teenager, his family fell on hard times. His father stopped attending town council meetings in 1577, and the family's fortunes began to decline. Matters were not improved in 1582 when Shakespeare, at the age of eighteen, hastily married Anne Hathaway, the daughter of a farmer from the nearby village of Shottery. She was eight years his senior and pregnant at the time of the wedding. The child, Susanna, was born in May, 1583. In 1585, the couple also became the parents of twins, Hamnet and Judith. (It is interesting to note that by 1670, the last of Susanna's descendants died, thereby ending the Shakespeare family line.)

There is no evidence concerning Shakespeare's activities between 1585 and 1592. Legend asserts that he was forced to leave Stratford in order to escape punishment for poaching deer on the estate of Sir Thomas Lucy, one of Stratford's leading citizens. Another popular story has Shakespeare taking a position as schoolmaster at the grammar school, where he supposedly improved his Latin. None of these accounts can be substantiated by fact, yet they continue to seduce modern readers and playgoers. One intriguing suggestion is that Shakespeare joined a troupe of professional actors that was passing through Stratford in 1587. This company, called the Queen's Men, may have been in need of a new performer, since one of their members, William Knell, had been murdered in a brawl with a fellow actor. Whatever his path may have been, however, by 1592, Shakespeare was working as an actor and playwright in London.

When Shakespeare arrived in London, he found the dramatic theater dominated by a group known as the University Wits: John Lyly, George Peele, Thomas Lodge, Robert Greene, Thomas Nashe, and Christopher Marlowe. Shakespeare learned his art by imitating these Oxford and Cambridge men, but for him they were a difficult group to join. They looked down on most actors and on those playwrights, such as Thomas Kyd, who had not attended a university. Shakespeare offended on both counts, and Robert Greene expressed his resentment in the posthumously published book *Greene's Groatsworth of Wit Bought with a Million of Repentance* (1592), which included a famous warning to three fellow "gentlemen" playwrights:

> Yes, trust them [the players] not: for there is an upstart crow, beautified with our feathers, that with his *Tiger's heart wrapt in a player's hide*, supposes he is as well able to bombast out a blank verse as the best of you: and being an absolute *Johannes Factotum*, is in his own conceit the only Shake-scene in a country.

Greene's literary executor, Henry Chettle, later published an apology for this slur on Shakespeare, with its pun on his name and its parody of a line from *Henry VI, Part III*. On meeting him, Chettle found Shakespeare's "demeanor no less civil than he, excellent in the quality he professes. Besides, divers of worship have reported his uprightness of dealing, which argues his honesty, and his facetious grace in writing, that approves his art."

Shakespeare's early plays—notably the *Henry VI* plays—achieved a measure of success, but his greatest early popularity came from two long narrative poems, *Venus and Adonis* (1593) and *The Rape of Lucrece* (1594). Shakespeare wrote these two poems during the two years that the plague closed down the London theaters. He dedicated the poems to a patron, the young Henry Wriothesley, third earl of Southampton, who may have granted him a substantial monetary reward in return. In any event, when the theaters reopened in 1594, the acting companies were almost decimated financially, but Shakespeare was in a position to buy or otherwise acquire a one-tenth interest in one of the newly reorganized companies, the Lord Chamberlain's Men. Henceforth, Shakespeare earned money not only from the plays he had written or in which he acted but also from his share of the profits of every company performance.

Shakespeare continued as both member and shareholder of this essentially stable company until he retired from the stage in 1611 or 1612. In part because of the popularity of Shakespeare's plays and in part because of the strong support of Elizabeth and James I, the company achieved considerable financial success. The company was able to stop renting theaters and built its own, the Globe, in 1599. In 1603, they were renamed the King's Men by King James himself. The company also began performing most of the plays of Ben Jonson, who ranked second only to Shakespeare and who excelled at satiric comedy, thus increasing their profits.

Shakespeare remained in close contact with his family in Stratford-upon-Avon throughout his career, and he used his newfound wealth to change their status as well. By 1596, he was able to purchase a coat of arms for his father, and in the next year, he acquired New Place, the second-best house in Stratford. Indeed, he made the Shakespeares into one of the leading families in the area. In 1596, however, they became a family bereaved, when Hamnet Shakespeare died at the age of eleven.

The degree of prominence and success achieved by Shakespeare in his lifetime was unusual for someone in a profession that was not highly regarded in Renaissance England. Actors and playwrights were in fact regarded as entertainers whose companions were bearbaiters, clowns, and jugglers. Confirmation of this fact comes from evidence that some public theaters were used both for plays and for bearbaiting and bullbaiting. After 1590, moreover, the playhouses had to be constructed in the Bankside district, across the Thames from London proper. City fathers afraid of plague and opposed to public entertainments felt that the Bankside, notorious for its boisterous inns and houses of prostitution, was the fitting locale for "playing" of all kinds. Indeed, theatrical productions were not regarded as high art; when plays were published, by the company or by individual actors, apparently no effort was made to correct or improve them. Shakespeare himself never corrected or took to the printer any of the plays attributed to him. Poetry was valued as true literature, and there is considerable evidence that Shakespeare hoped to become a recognized and respected poet like Sir Philip Sidney or Edmund Spenser. Despite the immense popularity of his early poems, however, Shakespeare eventually chose to become a public entertainer.

Shakespeare continued to write poetry alongside his drama. At about the time he composed *Romeo and Juliet* (pr. c. 1595-1596, pb. 1597) and *Richard II* (pr. c. 1595-1596, pb. 1600), he probably also began his great sonnet sequence, not published until 1609. The 154 sonnets, tracing a friendship with a young man, sometimes called the "Fair Youth," and a romance with a "Dark Lady," raise the question of how Shakespeare lived when he was away from Stratford, where his wife and children presumably remained. The young man might be a patron—perhaps Southampton, though other names have also been proposed—and the Dark Lady strictly imaginary, created to overturn the sonnets' trite Petrarchan conventions. Other speculations favor a more personal interpretation, seeing an actual *ménage à trois* of the poet, the Fair Youth, and the Dark Lady. All the questions raised by the sonnets remain open, and the only evidence about how Shakespeare spent his spare time in London indicates that he sometimes frequented taverns (notably the Mermaid) with his fellow playwrights and players.

The company to which he belonged was relatively small—fifteen or twenty players at most. The actors were generally well known to the audience, and their particular talents were exploited by the playwrights. Richard Burbage, the manager of Shakespeare's company for many years, was renowned for his skill in acting tragic parts, while William Kemp and Robert Armin were praised for their talents as comic actors. Shakespeare composed his plays with these actors in mind, a fact borne out by the many comedies featuring fat, drunken men such as Sir John Falstaff (of the *Henry IV* and *Henry V* plays) and Sir Toby Belch (of *Twelfth Night*). Shakespeare could not compose his works for an ideal company; he suited his style to the available talent.

Because his company was underwritten to some degree by the government, Shakespeare and his fellows were often called on to perform at court: 32 times during Elizabeth's reign and 177 times under James I. The king and queen did not venture to the Theatre or the Globe to mingle with the lower classes, depending instead on the actors to bring their wares to them. *Macbeth* was written as a direct compliment to James I: Banquo, the brave general treacherously murdered by the villainous hero, was one of James's ancestors. Shakespeare had to change the facts of history to pay the compliment, but the aim of pleasing his and the company's benefactor justified the change.

There were no women actors on Shakespeare's stage; they made their appearance when Charles II returned to the throne in 1660. Young boys (eleven to fourteen years old) played the female parts, and Shakespeare manipulated this convention with considerable success in his comedies, where disguises created delightful complications and aided him in overcoming the problem of costuming. The lady-disguised-as-page device is worked with particular effect in such plays as *As You Like It*, *Twelfth Night*, and *Cymbeline*.

Because there were few actors and sometimes many parts, members of the company were required to double (and sometimes triple) their roles. The effect of this requirement becomes evident when one notes that certain principal characters do not appear in consecutive scenes. One should likewise remember that performance on the Elizabethan stage was continuous; there was no falling curtain or set change to interrupt the action. No scenery to speak of was employed, although signs may have been used to designate cities or countries and branches may have been tied around pillars to signify trees. The absence of scenery allowed for a peculiar imaginative effect. A place on the stage that had been a throne room could within a few seconds become a hovel hiding its inhabitants from a fierce storm. Shakespeare and his contemporaries could thereby demonstrate the slippery course of Fortune, whose wheel, onstage and in real life, might turn at any moment to transform kings into beggars.

The apronlike stage jutted out into an area called "the pit," where the "groundlings," or those who paid the lowest admission fee (a penny), could stand to watch heroes perform great deeds. The octagon-shaped building had benches on the two levels above the pit for customers willing to pay for the privilege of sitting. Although estimates vary, it is now generally believed that the Globe could accommodate approximately twenty-five hundred people. The design of the stage probably evolved from the model of innyards, where the traveling companies of actors performed before they took up residence in London in the 1570's. On either side of the stage were two doors for entrances and exits and, at the back, some kind of inner stage behind which actors could hide and be discovered at the right moment. A trapdoor was located in the middle of the apron stage, while above it was a cupola-like structure that housed a pulley and chair. This chair could be lowered to the stage level when a *deus ex machina* (literally, a "god from a machine") was required to resolve the action. This small house also contained devices for making sound effects and may have been the place from which the musicians, so much a part of Elizabethan drama, sent forth their special harmonies. The little house was called "the heavens" (stars may have been painted on its underside), while the trapdoor was often referred to as "hell." For Shakespeare's Globe audience, then, the stage was a world in which the great figures of history and imagination were represented doing and speaking momentous things.

In 1608, the King's Men purchased an indoor theater, the Blackfriars, which meant that the company could perform year-round. This theater was located within the city proper, which meant that a somewhat more sophisticated audience attended the plays. Seating capacity was approximately seven hundred; there was no pit to stand in, and there is some evidence that the stage machinery was more elaborate than the equipment at the Globe. Some historians therefore argue that the plays written after 1608—*Cymbeline; Pericles, Prince of Tyre; The Winter's Tale; The Tempest*—were composed especially for performance at the Blackfriars. These tragicomedies or romances teem with special effects and supernatural characters, and this emphasis on spectacle differentiates them from Shakespeare's earlier comedies. Although such a theory is attractive, at least a few of these plays were also performed at the supposedly "primitive" Globe.

Along with the Blackfriars, the King's Men acquired the services of two playwrights who wrote for it, the collaborators Francis Beaumont and John Fletcher. With their light, witty comedy and melodramatic tragicomedy, represented by such plays as *The Knight of the Burning Pestle* (pr. 1607), *Philaster: Or, Love Lies A-Bleeding* (pr. c. 1609), and *A King and No King* (pr. 1611), Beaumont and Fletcher introduced a new "cavalier" style into Renaissance English drama that ultimately eclipsed even Shakespeare's popularity and perhaps hurried his retirement.

By 1608, Shakespeare had achieved the fame and recognition for which he had no doubt hoped. He was in a position to reduce his output to one or two plays per year, a schedule that probably allowed him to spend more time in Stratford with his family. In 1607, his elder daughter had married Dr. John Hall, the local physician, and in 1608, with the birth of their daughter, Elizabeth, Shakespeare became a grandfather. In 1611, he left London for Stratford, returning from time to time to see plays performed at both theaters and possibly to engage in collaborative efforts with new playwrights such as John Fletcher. His last play, *Henry VIII*, was a collaboration with Fletcher; it was produced on June 29, 1613, a fateful day for the Globe. A spark from one of the cannon shot off during the performance set the thatched roof on fire and burned the building to the ground.

On February 10, 1616, Shakespeare's thirty-one-year-old daughter, Judith, married Thomas Quiney, a member of another prominent Stratford family. On March 25, 1616, Shakespeare made out his last will and testament, leaving most of his estate to Susanna, a substantial amount of money to Judith, and his "second best bed" to his wife, Anne. He died on April 23, 1616, and was buried in Holy Trinity Church, Stratford-upon-Avon.

In 1623, Shakespeare's surviving partners in the King's Men, John Heminge and Henry Condell, published a collection of his plays now known as the First Folio. The portrait included in the First Folio depicts Shakespeare with a short mustache, large, staring eyes, and an oval face accentuated by his high, balding forehead and the remaining hair that almost covers his ears. The bust erected above his grave is similar, except that he has a goatee and the balding has progressed further. The First Folio portrait resembles a soulful intellectual, while the Stratford bust suggests a prominent burgher.

Analysis • The two portraits of Shakespeare portray the two parts of his nature. On one hand, he possessed immense intellectual curiosity about the motives and actions of people. This curiosity, plus his facility with language, enabled him to write his masterpieces and to create characters who are better known than some important figures in world history. On the other hand, reflecting his middle-class background, Shakespeare was himself motivated by strictly bourgeois instincts; he was more concerned with acquiring property and cementing his social position in Stratford than he was with preserving his plays for posterity. If his partners had not published the First Folio, there would be no Shakespeare as he is known today: still acted and enjoyed, the most widely studied and translated writer, the greatest poet and dramatist in the English and perhaps any language.

Besides his ability to create a variety of unforgettable characters, there are at least two other qualities that account for Shakespeare's achievement. One of these is his love of play with language, ranging from the lowest pun to some of the world's best poetry. His love of language sometimes makes him difficult to read, particularly for young students, but frequently the meaning becomes clear in a well-acted version. The second quality is his openness, his lack of any restrictive point of view, ideology, or morality. Shakespeare was able to embrace, identify with, and depict an enormous range of human behavior, from the good to the bad to the indifferent. The capaciousness of his language and vision thus help account for the universality of his appeal.

Shakespeare's lack of commitment to any didactic point of view has often been deplored. Yet he is not entirely uncommitted; rather, he is committed to what is human. Underlying his broad outlook is Renaissance Humanism, a synthesis of Christianity and classicism that is perhaps the best development of the Western mind and finds its best expression in his work. This same generous outlook was apparently expressed in Shakespeare's personality, which, like his bourgeois instincts, defies the Romantic myth of the artist. He was often praised by his fellows, but friendly rival and ferocious satirist Ben Jonson said it best: "He was, indeed, honest, and of an open and free nature," and "He was not of an age, but for all time."

The history plays • William Shakespeare began his career as a playwright by experimenting with plays in the three genres—comedy, history, and tragedy—that he would perfect as his career matured. The genre that dominated his attention throughout his early career, however, was history. Interest in the subject as proper stuff for drama was no doubt aroused by England's startling victory over Spain's vaunted navy, the Armada, in 1588. This victory fed the growing popular desire to see depictions of the critical intrigues and battles that had shaped England's destiny as the foremost Protestant power in Europe.

This position of power had been buttressed by the shrewd and ambitious Elizabeth I, England's "Virgin Queen," who, in the popular view, was the flower of the Tudor line. Many critics believe that Shakespeare composed the histories to trace the course of destiny that had led to the emergence of the Tudors as England's greatest kings and queens. The strength of character and patriotic spirit exhibited by Elizabeth seem to be foreshadowed by the personality of Henry V, the Lancastrian monarch who was instrumental in building an English empire in France. Because the Tudors traced their line back to the Lancastrians, it was an easy step for Shakespeare to flatter his monarch and please his audiences with nationalistic spectacles that reinforced the belief that England was a promised land.

Whatever his reasons for composing the history plays, Shakespeare certainly must be seen as an innovator of the form, for which there was no model in classical or medieval drama. Undoubtedly, he learned much from his immediate predecessors, however—most notably from Christopher Marlowe, whose *Edward II* (pr. c. 1592) treated the subject of a weak king nearly destroying the kingdom through his selfish and indulgent behavior. From Marlowe, Shakespeare also inherited the idea that the purpose of the history play was to vivify the moral dilemmas of power politics and to apply those lessons to contemporary government. Such lessons were heeded by contemporaries, as is amply illustrated by Elizabeth's remark on reading about the life of one of her predecessors: "I am Richard II."

Shakespeare's contribution to the history-play genre is represented by two tetralogies (that is, two series of four plays), each covering a period of English history. He wrote two other plays dealing with English kings, *King John* and *Henry VIII*, but they are not specifically connected to the tetralogies in theme or structure. *Edward III*, written sometime between 1589 and 1595, is, on the other hand, closely related to the second tetralogy in theme, structure, and history. Edward III is the grandfather of Richard II, and his victories in France are repeated by Henry V. Muriel Bradbrook has pointed out the structural similarities between *Edward III* and *Henry V*. Like the second tetralogy as a whole, *Edward III* deals with the education of the prince. King Edward, like Prince Hal, at first neglects his duties and endangers the realm by placing personal pleasure above his country's needs. The Countess of Salisbury begins his education in responsibility, and Queen Philippa completes the process by teaching him compassion. By the end of the play, Edward has become what Shakespeare calls Henry V, "the mirror of all Christian kings."

Henry VI, Part I • The first tetralogy concerns the period from the death of Henry V in 1422 to the death of Richard III at the Battle of Bosworth Field in 1485. Although he probably began this ambitious project in 1588, Shakespeare apparently did not compose the plays according to a strict chronological schedule. *Henry VI, Part I* is generally considered to have been written after the second and third parts of the Henry story; it may also have been a revision of another play. Using details from Raphael Holinshed's *Chronicles of England, Scotland, and Ireland* (1577) and Edward Hall's *The Union of the Two Noble and Illustre Families of Lancaster and York* (1548)—his chief chronicle sources for the plays in both tetralogies—Shakespeare created in *Henry VI, Part I* an episodic story of the adventures of Lord Talbot, the patriotic soldier who fought bravely to retain England's empire in France. Talbot fails and is defeated primarily because of a combination of intrigues by men such as the Bishop of Winchester and the indecisiveness of young King Henry VI.

Here, as in the other history plays, England appears as the central victim of these human actions, betrayed and abandoned by men attempting to satisfy personal desires at the expense of the kingdom. The characters are generally two-dimensional, and their speeches reveal the excesses of Senecan bombast and hyperbole. Although a few of the scenes involving Talbot and Joan of Arc—as well as Talbot's death scene, in which his demise is made more painful by his having to witness a procession bearing his son's corpse—aspire to the level of high drama, the play's characters lack psychological depth, and the plot fails to demonstrate the unity of design that would mark Shakespeare's later history plays. Joan's nature as a strumpet-witch signals the role of other women characters in this tetralogy; Margaret, who will become England's queen, helps to solidify the victory that Joan cleverly achieves at the close of *Henry VI, Part I.* Henry V's French empire is in ruins and England's very soul seems threatened.

Henry VI, Part II • *Henry VI, Part II* represents that threat in the form of what might be called "civil-war clouds." The play focuses on the further degeneration of rule under Henry, whose ill-considered marriage to the French Margaret precipitates a power struggle involving the two houses of York and Lancaster. By eliminating wise Duke Humphrey as the chief protector of the king, Margaret in effect seizes control of the throne. In the meantime, however, a rebellion is broached by Jack Cade, the leader of a group of anarchist commoners.

This rebellion lends occasion for action and spectacle of the kind that is lacking in *Henry VI, Part I.* It also teaches a favorite Shakespearean lesson: The kingdom's "children" cannot be expected to behave when their "parents" do not. Scenes involving witchcraft, a false miracle, and single combat seem to prove that the country is reverting to a primitive, chaotic state. Though the uprising is finally put down, it provides the excuse for Richard, duke of York, and his ambitious sons to seize power. York precipitates a vengeful struggle with young Clifford by killing his father; in response, Clifford murders York's youngest son, the earl of Rutland. These murders introduce the theme of familial destruction, of fathers killing sons and sons killing fathers, which culminates in the brutal assassination of Prince Edward.

Henry VI, Part III • As *Henry VI, Part III* begins, England's hopes for a strong successor to weak King Henry are dashed on the rocks of ambition and civil war. When Henry himself is murdered, one witnesses the birth of one of Shakespeare's most fascinating villain-heroes, Richard, duke of Gloucester. Although Richard's brother Edward becomes king and restores an uneasy peace, Shakespeare makes it clear that Richard will emerge as the political force of the future. Richard's driving ambition also appears to characterize the Yorkist cause, which, by contrast with the Lancastrian, can be described as self-destructive on the biblical model of the Cain and Abel story. While one is made to see Richard's wolfish disposition, however, Shakespeare also gives him a superior intellect and wit, which help to attract one's attention and interest. Displaying touches of the irony and cruelty that will mark his behavior in *Richard III,* Richard declares at the close of *Henry VI, Part III:* "See how my sword weeps for the poor king's death."

Richard III • In order to present Richard as an arch-villain, Shakespeare was obliged to follow a description of him that was based on a strongly prejudiced biographical portrait written by Sir Thomas More. More painted Richard as a hunchback with fangs, a beast so cruel that he did not flinch at the prospect of murdering the young princes. To More—and to Shakespeare—Richard must be viewed as another Herod; the imagery of the play also regularly compares him to a boar or hedgehog, beasts that know no restraint. Despite these repulsive features, Richard proves to be a consummate actor, outwitting and outperforming those whom he regards as victims. The most theatrical scene in the play is his wooing of the Lady Anne, who is drawn to him despite the knowledge that he has killed her husband (Prince Edward) and father-in-law, whose corpse she is in the process of accompanying to its grave. Many of the audacious wooing tricks used in this scene suggest that one of the sources for Richard's character is the Vice figure from medieval drama.

Richard III documents the breakneck pace and mounting viciousness of Richard's course to the throne. (Steeplechase imagery recurs throughout, culminating in the picture of Richard as an unseated rider trying desperately to find a mount.) He arranges for the murder of his brother Clarence, turns on former supporters such as Hastings and Buckingham, whom he seemed to be grooming for office, and eventually destroys the innocent princes standing in his path. This latter act of barbarism qualifies as a turning point, since Richard's victories, which have been numerous and easily won, now begin to evaporate at almost the same rate of speed.

While Richard moves with freedom and abandon from one bloody deed to another, he is hounded by the former Queen Margaret, who delivers curses and prophecies against him in the hope of satisfying her vengeful desires. She plays the role of a Senecan fury, even though her words prove feeble against her Machiavellian foe. Retribution finally comes, however, in the character of the Lancastrian Earl of Richmond, who defeats Richard at Bosworth Field. On the eve of the battle, Richard's victims visit his sleep to announce his fall, and for the first time in the play, he experiences a twinge of conscience. Unable to respond by confessing and asking forgiveness, Richard fights fiercely, dying like a wounded animal that is finally cornered. With Richmond's marriage to Elizabeth York, the Wars of the Roses end, and England looks forward to a prosperous and peaceful future under Henry Richmond, founder of the Tudor line.

King John • Whether Shakespeare wrote *King John* in the period between the first and second tetralogies is not known, but there is considerable support for the theory that he did. In the play, he depicts the career of a monarch who reigned into the thirteenth century and who defied papal authority, behavior that made him into something of a Protestant hero for Elizabethans. Shakespeare's John, however, lacks both the dynamism and the charisma of Henry V; he is also guilty of usurping the throne and arranging for the death of the true heir, Arthur.

This clouded picture complicates the action and transforms John into a man plagued by guilt. Despite his desire to strengthen England and challenge the supremacy of Rome, John does not achieve either the dimensions of a tragic hero or the sinister quality of a consummate villain; indeed, his death seems anticlimactic. The strongest personality in the play belongs to Faulconbridge the Bastard, whose satiric commentary on the king's maneuvering gives way to patriotic speeches at the close. Faulconbridge speaks out for Anglo-Saxon pride in the face of foreign challenge, but he has also played the part of satirist-onstage throughout much of the action. Something of the same complexity of character will be seen in Prince Hal, the model fighter and king of the second tetralogy.

In *King John*, Shakespeare managed only this one touch of brilliant characterization in an otherwise uninteresting and poorly constructed play. He may have been attempting an adaptation of an earlier chronicle drama.

Richard II • Shakespeare began writing the second tetralogy, which covers the historical period from 1398 to 1422, in 1595. The first play in this group was *Richard II*, a drama which, like the *Henry VI* series, recounts the follies of a weak king and the consequences of these actions for England. Unlike Henry, however, Richard is a personage with tragic potential; he speaks the language of a poet and possesses a self-dramatizing talent. Richard invites his fall—the fall of princes, or *de casibus virorum illustrium*, being a favorite Elizabethan topic that was well represented in the popular *A Mirror for Magistrates* (first published under Elizabeth I in 1559, although printed earlier under Queen Mary)—by seizing the land of the deceased John of Gaunt to pay for his war preparations against Ireland. This dubious act brings Henry Bolingbroke, Gaunt's son, rushing back from France, where he had been exiled by Richard, for a confrontation with the king. The result of their meeting is Richard's sudden deposition—he gives up the crown almost before he is asked for it—and eventual death, which is so movingly rendered that many critics have been led to describe this as a tragedy rather than a political play.

Such a reading must overlook the self-pitying quality in Richard; his actions rarely correspond to the quality of his speech. Yet there has been little disagreement about Shakespeare's achievement in advancing the history-play form by forging a world in which two personalities, one vacillating, the other resourceful, oppose each other in open conflict. *Richard II* likewise qualifies as the first play in which Shakespeare realizes the theme of the fall by means of repeated images comparing England to a garden. Richard, the gardener-king, has failed to attend to pruning; rebels, like choking weeds, grow tall and threaten to blot out the sun. Because Bolingbroke usurps the crown and later arranges for Richard's death, however, he is guilty of watering the garden with the blood of England's rightful—if foolish—ruler. The result must inevitably be civil war, which is stirringly prophesied by the Bishop of Carlisle as the play draws to a close: "The blood of English shall manure the ground,/ And future ages groan for this foul act."

Henry IV, Part I • The civil strife that Carlisle predicted escalates in *Henry IV, Part I*. Bolingbroke, now King Henry IV, is planning a crusade in the midst of a serious battle involving rebels in the north and west of Britain. This obliviousness to responsibility is clearly motivated by Henry's guilt over the seizing of the crown and Richard's murder. It will take the courage and ingenuity of his son, Prince Hal, the future Henry V, to save England and to restore the order of succession that Shakespeare and his contemporaries saw as the only guarantee of peaceful rule. Thus, *Henry IV, Part I* is really a study of the rise of Hal, who in the opening of the play appears to be a carefree time waster, content with drinking, gambling, and carousing with a motley group of thieves and braggarts led by the infamous coward Sir John Falstaff. Using a kind of Aristotelian mode of characterization, Shakespeare reveals Hal as a balanced hero who possesses the wit and humanity of Falstaff, without the debilitating drunkenness and ego, and the physical courage and ambition of Henry Hotspur, the son of the earl of Northumberland and chief rebel, without his destructive choler and impatience.

The plot of *Henry IV, Part I* advances by means of comparison and contrast of the court, tavern, and rebel worlds, all of which are shown to be in states of disorder. Hal leaves the tavern world at the end of the second act with an explicit rejection of Falstaff's fleshly indulgence; he rejoins his true father and leads the army in battle against the rebels, who are unable to organize the English, Welsh, and Scottish factions of which they are formed. They seem to be leaderless—and "fatherless." Above all, Hal proves capable of surprising both his own family and the rebels, using his reputation as a madcap to fullest advantage until he is ready to throw off his disguise and defeat the bold but foolish Hotspur at Shrewsbury. This emergence is nicely depicted in imagery associated by Hal himself with the sun (punning on "son") breaking through the clouds when least suspected. Falstaff demonstrates consistency of character in the battle by feigning death; even though Hal allows his old friend to claim the prize of Hotspur's body, one can see the utter bankruptcy of the Falstaffian philosophy of self-preservation.

Henry IV, Part II • In *Henry IV, Part II*, the struggle against the rebels continues. Northumberland, who failed to appear for the Battle of Shrewsbury because of illness, proves unable to call up the spirit of courage demonstrated by his dead son. Glendower, too, seems to fade quickly from the picture, like a dying patient. The main portion of the drama concerns what appears to be a replay of Prince Hal's reformation. Apparently Shakespeare meant to depict Hal's acquisition of honor and valor at the close of *Henry IV, Part I*, while *Part II* traces his education in the virtues of justice and rule. Falstaff is again the humorous but negative example, although he lacks the robustness in sin that marked his character in *Part I*. The positive example or model is the Lord Chief Justice, whose sobriety and sense of responsibility eventually attract Hal to his side.

As in *Part I*, Shakespeare adopts the structure of a medieval morality play to depict the rejection of the "bad" angel (or false father) and the embracing of the "good" one (or spiritual father) by the hero. The banishment of Falstaff and his corrupt code takes place during the coronation procession. It is a particularly poignant moment—to which many critics object, since Hal's harshness seems so uncharacteristic and overdone—but this scene is well prepared for by Hal's promise, at the end of act 2 in *Part I*, that he would renounce the world and the flesh at the proper time. The example of Hal's father, whose crown Hal rashly takes from his pillow before his death, demonstrates that for the king there can be no escape from care, no freedom to enjoy the fruits of life. With the Lord Chief Justice at his side, Hal prepares to enter the almost monklike role that the kingship requires him to play.

Henry V • It is this strong and isolated figure that dominates *Henry V*, the play that may have been written for the opening of the Globe Theatre. Appropriately enough, the Chorus speaker who opens the play asks if "this wooden O" can "hold the vasty fields of France," the scene of much of the epic and episodic action. Hal shows himself to be an astute politician—he outwits and traps the rebels Scroop, Cambridge, and Grey—and a heroic leader of men in the battle scenes. His rejection of Falstaff, whose death is recounted here in tragicomic fashion by Mistress Quickly, has transformed Hal's character into something cold and unattractive. There is little or no humor in the play. Yet when Hal moves among his troops on the eve of the Battle of Agincourt, he reveals a depth of understanding and compassion that helps to humanize his character. His speeches are masterpieces of political rhetoric, even though

Pistol, the braggart soldier, tries to parody them. "Once more into the breach, dear friends, once more . . ." introduces one of the best-known prebattle scenes in the language.

With the defeat of the French at Agincourt, Hal wins an empire for England, strengthening the kingdom that had been so sorely threatened by the weakness of Richard II. Both tetralogies depict in sharp outline the pattern of suffering and destruction that results from ineffective leadership. In Henry VII and Henry V, one sees the promise of peace and empire realized through the force of their strong, patriotic identities. At the close of *Henry V*, the hero's wooing of Katherine of France, with its comic touches resulting from her inability to speak English, promises a wedding that will take place in a new garden from which it is hoped humankind will not again fall. The lesson for the audience seems to be that under Elizabeth, the last Tudor monarch, England has achieved stability and glory, and that this role of European power was foreshadowed by the victories of these earlier heroes. Another clear lesson is that England cannot afford another civil war; some capable and clearly designated successor to Elizabeth must be chosen.

Henry VIII • Shakespeare's last drama dealing with English history, a probable collaboration with Henry Fletcher, is *Henry VIII*, which is normally classed with romances such as *The Tempest* and *Cymbeline*. It features none of the military battles typical of earlier history plays, turning instead for its material to the intrigues of Henry's court. The play traces the falls of three famous personages, the duke of Buckingham, Katherine of Aragon, and Cardinal Wolsey. Both Buckingham and Queen Katherine are innocent victims of fortune, while Wolsey proves to be an ambitious man whose scheming is justly punished. Henry seems blind and self-satisfied through much of the play, which is dominated by pageantry and spectacle, but in his judgment against Wolsey and his salvation of Cranmer, he emerges as something of a force for divine justice. The plot ends with the christening of Elizabeth and a prophecy about England's glorious future under her reign. Shakespeare's audience knew, however, that those atop Fortune's wheel at the close—Cranmer and Anne Bullen, in particular—would soon be brought down like the others. This last of Shakespeare's English history plays, then, sounds a patriotic but also an ironic note.

The comedies • Of the plays that are wholly or partly attributed to Shakespeare, nearly half have been classified as comedies. In addition, many scenes in plays such as *Henry IV, Part I* and *Romeo and Juliet* feature comic characters and situations. Even in the major tragedies, one finds scenes of comic relief: the Porter scene in *Macbeth*, the encounters between the Fool and Lear in *King Lear*, Hamlet's inventive punning and lugubrious satire. There can be little doubt that Shakespeare enjoyed creating comic situations and characters and that audiences came to expect such fare on a regular basis from the playwright.

The Comedy of Errors • In his first attempt in the form, *The Comedy of Errors*, Shakespeare turned to a source—Plautus, the Roman playwright—with which he would have become familiar at Stratford's grammar school. Based on Plautus's *Menaechmi* (*The Twin Menaechmi*, 1595), the comedy depicts the misadventures of twins who, after several incidents involving mistaken identity, finally meet and are reunited. The twin brothers are attended by twin servants, compounding the possibilities for humor growing out of mistaken identity.

Considerable buffoonery and slapstick characterize the main action involving the twins—both named Antipholus—and their servants. In one hilarious scene, Antipholus of Ephesus is turned away from his own house by a wife who believes he is an impostor. This somewhat frivolous mood is tempered by the presence of the twins' father in the opening and closing scenes. At the play's opening, Egeon is sentenced to death by the Duke of Ephesus; the sentence will be carried out unless someone can pay a ransom set at one thousand marks. Egeon believes that his wife and sons are dead, which casts him deep into the pit of despair. By the play's close, Egeon has been saved from the duke's sentence and has been reunited with his wife, who has spent the many years of their separation as an abbess. This happy scene of reunion and regeneration strikes a note that will come to typify the resolutions of later Shakespearean comedy. Providence appears to smile on those who suffer yet remain true to the principle of family.

Shakespeare also unites the act of unmasking with the concept of winning a new life in the fifth act of *The Comedy of Errors*. Both Antipholus of Syracuse, who in marrying Luciana is transformed into a "new man," and Dromio of Ephesus, who is freed to find a new life, acquire new identities at the conclusion. The characters are, however, largely interchangeable and lacking in individualizing traits. Types rather than full-blown human beings people the world of the play, thus underscoring the theme of supposing or masking.

Shakespeare offers a gallery of familiar figures—young lovers, a pedantic doctor, a kitchen maid, merchants, and a courtesan—all of whom are identified by external traits. They are comic because they behave in predictably mechanical ways. Dr. Pinch, the mountebank based on Plautus's *medicus* type, is a good example of this puppetlike caricaturing. The verse is designed to suit the speaker and occasion, but it also reveals Shakespeare's range of styles; blank verse, prose, rhymed stanzas, and alternating rhymed lines can be found throughout the play. This first effort in dramatic comedy was an experiment using numerous Plautine elements, but it also reveals, in the characters Egeon and Emilia, the playwright's talent for humanizing even the most typical of characters and for creating life and vigor in stock situations.

The Taming of the Shrew • In *The Taming of the Shrew*, Shakespeare turned to another favorite source for the theme of transformation: Ovid's *Metamorphoses* (c. 8 C.E.; English translation, 1567). He had already used this collection for his erotic poems *Venus and Adonis* and *The Rape of Lucrece*; now he plundered it for stories about pairs of lovers and the changes effected in their natures by the power of love. In *The Taming of the Shrew*, he was also improving on an earlier play that dealt with the theme of taming as a means of modifying human behavior.

Petruchio changes Kate's conduct by regularly praising her "pleasant, gamesome" nature. By the end of the play, she has been tamed into behaving like a dutiful wife. (Her sister Bianca, on the other hand, has many suitors, but her father will not allow Bianca to marry until Kate has found a husband.) The process of taming sometimes involves rough and boisterous treatment—Petruchio withholds food from his pupil, for example—as well as feigned madness: Petruchio whisks his bride away from the wedding site as if she were a damsel in distress and he were playing the role of her rescuer. In the end, Kate turns out to be more pliant than her sister, suggesting that an ideal wife, like a bird trained for the hunt, must be instructed in the rules of the game.

Shakespeare reinforces the theme of transformation by fashioning a subplot featuring a drunken tinker named Christopher Sly, who believes he has been made into a lord during a ruse performed by a fun-loving noble and his fellows. The Sly episode is not resolved because this interlude ends with the play's first scene, yet by employing this framing device, Shakespeare invites a comparison between Kate and Sly, both of whom are urged to be "better" than they thought they were.

The Two Gentlemen of Verona • *The Two Gentlemen of Verona* takes a comic tack that depends less on supposing than on actual disguise. Employing a device he would later perfect in *As You Like It* and *Twelfth Night,* Shakespeare put his heroine Julia in a page's outfit in order to woo her beloved Proteus.

The main theme of the comedy is the rocky nature of love as revealed in male friendship and romantic contest. Valentine, Proteus's friend, finds him to be fickle and untrue to the courtly code when Proteus tries to force his affections on Silvia, Valentine's love. Although Proteus deserves worse punishment than he receives, he is allowed to find in Julia the true source of the romantic love that he has been seeking throughout the play. These pairs of lovers and their clownish servants, who engage in frequent bouts of punning and of horseplay, perform their rituals—anatomizing lovers, trusting false companions—in a forest world that seems to work its magic on them by bringing about a happy ending.

As in the other festive comedies, *The Two Gentlemen of Verona* concludes with multiple marriages and a mood of inclusiveness that gives even the clowns their proper place in the celebration. The passion of love has led Proteus (whose name, signifying "changeable," symbolizes fickleness) to break oaths and threaten friendships, but in the end, it has also forged a constant love.

Love's Labour's Lost • After this experiment in romantic or festive (as opposed to bourgeois) comedy, Shakespeare next turned his hand to themes and characters that reflect the madness and magic of love. *Love's Labour's Lost* pokes fun at florid poetry, the "taffeta phrases [and] silken terms precise" that typified Elizabethan love verses. There is also a satiric strain in this play, which depicts the foiled attempt of male characters to create a Platonic utopia free of women. The King of Navarre and his court appear ludicrous as, one by one, they violate their vows of abstinence in conceits that gush with sentiment. Even Berowne, the skeptic-onstage, proves unable to resist the temptations of Cupid.

As if to underscore the foolishness of their betters, the clowns and fops of this comic world produce an interlude featuring the Nine Worthies, all of whom overdo or distort their roles in the same way as the lover-courtiers have distorted theirs. (This interlude was also the playwright's first attempt at a play-within-a-play.) When every Jack presumes to claim his Jill at the close, however, Shakespeare deputizes the princess to postpone the weddings for one year while the men do penance for breaking their vows. The women here are victorious over the men, but only for the purpose of forcing them to recognize the seriousness of their contracts. Presumably the marriages to come will prove constant and fulfilling, but at the end of this otherwise lighthearted piece, Shakespeare interjects a surprising note of qualification. Perhaps this note represents his commentary on the weight of words, which the courtiers have so carelessly—and sometimes badly—handled.

A Midsummer Night's Dream • In *A Midsummer Night's Dream,* Shakespeare demonstrates consummate skill in the use of words to create illusion and dreams. Although he again presents pairs of young lovers whose fickleness causes them to fall out of, and then back into, love, these characters display human dimensions that are missing in the character types found in the earlier comedies. The multiple plots concern not only the lovers' misadventures but also the marriage of Duke Theseus and Hippolyta, the quarrel between Oberon and Titania, king and queen of the fairy band, and the bumbling rehearsal and performance of the play-within-a-play *Pyramus and Thisbe* by Bottom and his companions. All of these actions illustrate the themes of love's errant course and of the power of illusion to deceive the senses.

The main action, as in *The Two Gentlemen of Verona*, takes place in a wood, this time outside Athens and at night. The fairy powers are given free rein to deceive the mortals who chase one another there. Puck, Oberon's servant, effects deception of the lovers by mistakenly pouring a potion in the wrong Athenian's eyes. By the end of the play, however, the young lovers have found their proper partners, Oberon and Titania have patched up their quarrel, and Bottom, whose head was changed into that of an ass and who was wooed by the enchanted Titania while he was under this spell, rejoins his fellows to perform their tragic and comic interlude at the wedding reception. This afterpiece is a burlesque rendition of the story of Pyramus and Thisbe, whose tale of misfortune bears a striking resemblance to that of Romeo and Juliet. Through the device of the badly acted play-within-the-play, Shakespeare instructs his audience in the absurdity of lovers' Petrarchan vows and in the power of imagination to transform the bestial or the godlike into human form. In design and execution, *A Midsummer Night's Dream*, with its variety of plots and range of rhyme and blank verse, stands out as Shakespeare's most sophisticated early comedy.

The Merchant of Venice • *The Merchant of Venice* shares bourgeois features with *The Taming of the Shrew* and *The Two Gentlemen of Verona*, but it has a much darker, near-tragic side, too. Shylock's attempt to carve a pound of flesh from the merchant Antonio's heart has all the ingredients of tragedy: deception, hate, ingenuity, and revenge. His scheme is frustrated only by the superior wit of the heroine Portia during a trial scene in which she is disguised as a young boy judge. Requiring Shylock to take nothing more than is specified in his bond, while at the same time lecturing him on the quality of mercy, Portia's speeches create the elements of tension and confrontation that will come to epitomize the playwright's mature tragedies. With the defeat and conversion of Shylock, the pairs of lovers can escape the threatening world of Venice and hope for uninterrupted happiness in Belmont, Portia's home.

Venice, the scene of business, materialism, and religious hatred, is contrasted with Belmont (or "beautiful world"), the fairy-tale kingdom to which Bassanio, Antonio's friend, has come to win a fair bride and fortune by entering into a game of choice involving golden, silver, and leaden caskets. Though the settings are contrasted and the action of the play alternates between the two societies, Shakespeare makes his audience realize that Portia, like Antonio, is bound to a contract (set by her dead father) which threatens to destroy her happiness. When Bassanio chooses the leaden casket, she is freed to marry the man whom she would have chosen for her own. Thus "converted" (a metaphor that refers one back to Shylock's conversion), Portia then elects to help Antonio, placing herself in jeopardy once again. Portia emerges as Shakespeare's first major heroine-in-disguise, a character-type central to his most stageworthy and mature comedies, *Twelfth Night* and *As You Like It*.

Much Ado About Nothing • *Much Ado About Nothing* likewise has a dark side. The main plot represents the love of Claudio and Hero. Hero's reputation is sullied by the melodramatic villain Don Juan. Claudio confronts his supposedly unfaithful partner in the middle of their wedding ceremony, his tirade causing her to faint and apparently expire. The lovers are later reunited, however, after Claudio recognizes his error. This plot is paralleled by one involving Beatrice and Benedick, two witty characters who in the play's beginning are set against each other in verbal combat. Like Claudio and Hero, they are converted into lovers who overcome selfishness and pride to gain a degree of freedom in their new relationships. The comedy ends with the marriage of Claudio and Hero and the promise of union between Beatrice and Benedick.

A central comic figure in the play is Dogberry, the watchman whose blundering contributes to Don Juan's plot but is also the instrument by which his villainy is revealed. His behavior, especially his hilariously inept handling of legal language, is funny in itself, but it also illustrates a favorite Shakespearean theme: Clownish errors often lead to happy consequences. Like Bottom in *A Midsummer Night's Dream*, Dogberry and his men are made an important part of the newly transformed society at the end of the play.

As You Like It • *As You Like It* and *Twelfth Night* are widely recognized as Shakespeare's wittiest and most stageworthy comedies; they also qualify as masterpieces of design and construction. In *As You Like It*, the action shifts from the court of Duke Frederick, a usurper, to the forest world of Arden, the new "court" of ousted Duke Senior. His daughter Rosalind enters the forest world in disguise, along with her friend Celia, to woo and win the young hero Orlando, forced to wander by his brother Oliver, another usurping figure. Although his florid verses expressing undying love for Rosalind are the object of considerable ridicule, Orlando earns the title of true lover worthy of Rosalind's hand. She proves successful in winning the support of the audience by means of her clever manipulation of Orlando from behind her mask. His inept poetry and her witty commentary can be taken "as we like it," as can the improbable conversions of Oliver and Duke Frederick that allow for a happy ending.

Two characters—Touchstone, the clown, and Jacques (pronounced JAYK weez), the cynical courtier—represent extreme attitudes on the subjects of love and human nature. Touchstone serves as Rosalind's protector and as a sentimental observer, commenting wistfully and sometimes wittily on his own early days as a lover of milkmaids. Jacques, the trenchant commentator on the "Seven Ages of Man," sees all this foolery as further evidence, along with political corruption and ambition, of humankind's fallen state. He remains outside the circle of happy couples at the end of the play, a poignant, melancholy figure. His state of self-centeredness, it might be argued, is also "as we like it" when our moods do not identify so strongly with youthful exuberance.

Twelfth Night • *Twelfth Night* also deals with the themes of love and self-knowledge. Like *As You Like It*, it features a disguised woman, Viola, as its central figure. Motifs from other earlier Shakespearean comedies are also evident in *Twelfth Night*. Viola and Sebastian are twins (a motif found in *The Comedy of Errors*) who have been separated in a shipwreck but, unknown to each other, have landed in the same country, Illyria. From *The Two Gentlemen of Verona*, Shakespeare took the motif of the disguised figure serving as page to the man she loves (Duke Orsino) and even playing the wooer's role with the woman (Olivia) whom the duke wishes to marry. Complications arise when Olivia falls in love with Viola, and the dilemma is brought to a head when Orsino threatens to kill his page in a fit of revenge. Sebastian provides the ready solution to this dilemma, but Shakespeare holds off introducing the twins to each other until the last possible moment, creating effective comic tension.

The play's subplot involves an ambitious and vain steward, Malvolio, who, by means of a counterfeited letter (the work of a clever servant named Maria), is made to believe that Olivia loves him. The scene in which Malvolio finds the letter and responds to its hints, while being observed not only by the theater audience but also by an audience onstage, is one of the funniest stretches of comic pantomime in drama. When Malvolio attempts to woo his mistress, he is thought mad and is cast in prison. Although he is finally released (not before being tormented by Feste the clown in disguise), Malvolio does not join the circle of lovers in the close, vowing instead to be revenged on all those who deceived him. In fact, both Feste and Malvolio stand apart from the happy company, representing the dark, somewhat melancholy clouds that cannot be dispelled in actual human experience. By this stage in his career, Shakespeare had acquired a vision of comedy crowded by elements and characters that would be fully developed in the tragedies.

The Merry Wives of Windsor • *The Merry Wives of Windsor* was probably composed before Shakespeare reached the level of maturity reflected in *As You Like It* and *Twelfth Night*. Legend suggests that he interrupted his work on the second history cycle to compose the play in two weeks for Queen Elizabeth, who wished to see Falstaff (by then familiar from the history plays) portrayed as a lover. What Shakespeare ended up writing was not a romantic but instead a bourgeois comedy that depicts Falstaff attempting to seduce Mistress Ford and Mistress Page, both wives of Windsor citizens. He fails, but in failing he manages to entertain the audience with his bragging and his boldness. Shakespeare may have been reworking an old play based on a Plautine model; in one of Plautus's plays, there is a subplot in which a clever young man (Fenton) and his beloved manage to deceive her parents in order to get married. This is the only strain of romance in the comedy, whose major event is the punishment of Falstaff: He is tossed into the river, then singed with candles and pinched by citizens disguised as fairies. Critics who see Falstaff as the embodiment of Vice argue that this punishment has symbolic weight; his attempted seduction of honest citizens' wives makes him a threat to orderly society. Regardless of whether this act has a ritual purpose, the character of Falstaff, and the characters of Bardolph, Pistol, and Justice Shallow, bear little resemblance to the comic band of *Henry IV, Part I*. In fact, *The Merry Wives of Windsor* might be legitimately seen as an interlude rather than a fully developed comedy, and it is a long distance from the more serious, probing dramas Shakespeare would soon create.

All's Well That Ends Well • *All's Well That Ends Well* and *Measure for Measure* were composed during a period when Shakespeare was also writing his major tragedies. Because they pose questions about sin and guilt that are not satisfactorily resolved, many critics have used the terms "dark comedies" or "problem plays" to describe them. *All's Well That Ends Well* features the familiar disguised heroine (Helena) who pursues the man she loves (Bertram) with skill and determination.

The play differs from the earlier romantic comedies, however, because the hero rejects the heroine, preferring instead to win honor and fame in battle. Even though Helena is "awarded" the prize of Bertram by the King of France, whom she has cured of a near-fatal disease, she must don her disguise and pursue him while undergoing considerable suffering and hardship. In order to trap him, moreover, she must resort to a "bed trick," substituting her body for that of another woman whom Bertram plans to seduce. When Bertram finally assents to the union he bears little resemblance to comic heroes such as Orlando or Sebastian; he could be seen in fact as more a villain (or perhaps a cad) than a deserving lover. The forced resolution makes the play a "problem" for many critics, but for Shakespeare and his audience, the ingenuity of Helena and the multiple marriages at the close probably satisfied the demands of romantic comedy.

Measure for Measure • *Measure for Measure* has at the center of its plot another bed trick, by which a patient and determined woman (Mariana) manages to capture the man she desires. That man, Angelo, is put in the position of deputy by Duke Vincentio at the opening of the action. He determines to punish a sinful Vienna by strictly enforcing its laws against fornication; his first act is to arrest Claudio for impregnating his betrothed Juliet. When Isabella, Claudio's sister, who is about to take vows as a nun, comes to plead for his life, Angelo attempts to seduce her. He asks for a measure of her body in return for a measure of mercy for her brother. Isabella strongly resists Angelo's advances, although her principled behavior most certainly means her brother will die. Aided by Vincentio, disguised as a holy father, Isabella arranges for Mariana to take her place, since this woman is in fact Angelo's promised partner. Thus, Angelo commits the deed that he would punish Claudio for performing. (Instead of freeing Claudio, moreover, he sends word to have him killed even after seducing his "sister.")

Through another substitution, however, Claudio is saved. In an elaborate judgment scene, in which Vincentio plays both duke and holy father, Angelo is forgiven—Isabella being required by the duke to beg for Angelo's life—and marries Mariana. Here, as in *All's Well That Ends Well*, the hero proves to be an unpunished scoundrel who seems to be in fact rewarded for his sin, but the biblical "Judge not lest ye be judged" motivates much of the action, with characters finding themselves in the place of those who would judge them and being forced to display mercy. Some critics have argued that this interpretation transforms Duke Vincentio into a Christ figure, curing the sins of the people while disguised as one of them. Whether or not this interpretation is valid, *Measure for Measure* compels its audience to explore serious questions concerning moral conduct; practically no touches of humor in the play are untainted by satire and irony.

The tragedies • For about four years following the writing of *Measure for Measure*, Shakespeare was busy producing his major tragedies. It is probably accurate to say that the problem comedies were, to a degree, testing grounds for the situations and characters he would perfect in the tragedies. These tragedies include the famous *Romeo and Juliet*, *Julius Caesar*, *Hamlet, Prince of Denmark*, *Othello, the Moor of Venice*, *King Lear*, and *Antony and Cleopatra*. His earliest—and clumsiest—attempt at tragedy was *Titus Andronicus*.

Titus Andronicus • The plot of *Titus Andronicus* no doubt came from the Roman poet Ovid, a school subject and one of the playwright's favorite Roman authors. From Seneca, the Roman playwright whose ten plays had been translated into English in 1559, Shakespeare took the theme of revenge: The inflexible, honor-bound hero seeks satisfaction against a queen who has murdered or maimed his children. She was acting in retaliation, however, because Titus had killed her son. Titus's rage, which is exacerbated by the rape and mutilation of his daughter Lavinia, helps to classify him as a typical Senecan tragic hero. He and the wicked queen Tamora are oversimplified characters who declaim set speeches rather than engaging in realistic dialogue. Tamora's lover and accomplice, the Moor Aaron, is the prototype of the Machiavellian practitioner that Shakespeare would perfect in such villains as Iago and Edmund. While this caricature proves intriguing, and while the play's structure is more balanced and coherent than those of the early history plays, Titus's character lacks the kind of agonizing introspection shown by the heroes of the major tragedies. He never comes to terms with the destructive code of honor that convulses his personal life and that of Rome.

Romeo and Juliet • With *Romeo and Juliet,* Shakespeare reached a level of success in characterization and design far above the bombastic and chaotic world of *Titus Andronicus.* Based on a long narrative and heavily moralized poem by Arthur Brooke, this tragedy of "star-crossed lovers" excites the imagination by depicting the fatal consequences of a feud between the Veronese families of Montague and Capulet. Distinguished by some of Shakespeare's most beautiful poetry, the style bears a strong resemblance to that of the sonnets: elaborate conceits, classical allusions, witty paradoxes, and observations on the sad consequences of sudden changes of fortune. Some critics have in fact faulted the tragedy because its plot lacks the integrity of its poetry; Romeo and Juliet come to their fates by a series of accidents and coincidences that strain credulity. The play also features abundant comic touches provided by the remarks of Romeo's bawdy, quick-witted friend Mercutio and the sage but humorous observations of Juliet's nurse. Both of these "humor" characters (character types whose personalities are determined by one trait, or "humor") remark frequently, and often bawdily, on the innocent lovers' dreamy pronouncements about their passion for each other.

With the accidental murder of Mercutio, whose last words are "A plague on both your houses!" (referring to the feuding families), the plot accelerates rapidly toward the catastrophe, showing no further touches of humor or satire. The tireless Friar Lawrence attempts, through the use of a potion, to save Juliet from marrying Paris, the nobleman to whom she is betrothed, but the friar proves powerless against the force of fate that seems to be working against the lovers. Although it lacks the compelling power of the mature tragedies, whose heroes are clearly responsible for their fate, *Romeo and Juliet* remains a popular play on the subject of youthful love. The success of various film versions, including Franco Zeffirelli's 1968 feature film, with its teenage hero and heroine and its romantically moving score, proved that the play has a timeless appeal.

Julius Caesar • At least three years passed before Shakespeare again turned his attention to the tragic form. Instead of treating the subject of fatal love, however, he explored Roman history for a political story centering on the tragic dilemma of one man. In *Julius Caesar,* he could have dealt with the tale of the assassination of Caesar, taken from Plutarch's *Bioi paralleloi* (c. 105-115 C.E.; *Parallel Lives,* 1579), as he did with material from English history in the chronicle dramas he had been writing in the 1590's. That is, he might have presented the issue of the republic versus the monarchy as a purely political question, portraying Caesar, Brutus, Cassius, and Antony as pawns in a predestined game. Instead, Shakespeare chose to explore the character of Brutus in detail, revealing the workings of his conscience through moving and incisive soliloquies. By depicting his hero as a man who believes his terrible act is in the best interest of the country, Shakespeare establishes the precedent for later tragic heroes who likewise justify their destructive deeds as having righteous purposes.

The tragic plot is developed by means of irony and contrast. Cassius, jealous of Caesar's achievements, seduces Brutus into taking part in the conspiracy by appealing to his idealism. This political naiveté stands in sharp contrast to Antony's Machiavellianism, which is so brilliantly demonstrated in his crowd-swaying funeral oration ("Friends, Romans, countrymen, lend me your ears . . ."). Antony's transformation from playboy to power broker displays Shakespeare's belief that the historical moment shapes the natures of great men. Caesar appears to be a superstitious, somewhat petty figure, but in typical fashion, Shakespeare makes his audience see that, just as the conspirators are not free of personal motives such as jealousy, so Caesar is not the cold and uncompromising tyrant they claim he is. With the visit by Caesar's ghost to Brutus's tent on the eve of the final battle at Philippi, Shakespeare foreshadows the ultimate revenge of Caesar in the character of his grandson, Octavius, who emerges as a strong personality at the close of the play. Brutus and Cassius quarrel before the end, but they nevertheless achieve a kind of nobility by committing suicide in the Roman tradition. For Brutus, the events following the assassination demonstrate the flaw in his idealism; he could not destroy the spirit of Caesar, nor could he build a republic on the shifting sand of the populace. In *Julius Caesar*, one witnesses a tragedy that is both politically compelling and morally complex.

Hamlet, Prince of Denmark • Although the revenge theme is an important part of *Julius Caesar*, it dominates the action of *Hamlet, Prince of Denmark*. Learning from his father's ghost that Claudius, the new king, is a brother-murderer and a usurper, the hero sets out passionately to fulfill his personal duty by destroying the villain-king. Like Brutus, however, Hamlet is a reflective man, given to "saucy doubts" about the veracity of the ghost, about the effect on his soul of committing regicide, and about the final disposition of Claudius's soul. As a result, Hamlet delays his revenge—a delay that has preoccupied audiences, readers, and critics for centuries.

Numerous reasons have been proposed for the delay: Hamlet is melancholic; his morality does not condone murder; he is a coward; he is secretly envious of Claudius for murdering his "rival" for his mother's affections. These explanations, while appealing, tend to shift attention away from other, equally significant elements in the play. Hamlet's soliloquies illustrate the range of Shakespearean blank verse and provide the means for exploring character in detail. The play's trap motif can be seen to represent effectively the doomed, claustrophobic atmosphere of the play. Indeed, those who deliberatively set traps in the play—Polonius, Claudius, Laertes, and Hamlet—find that those traps snap back to catch the "inventor." Hamlet's relationships with Ophelia and with Gertrude amply reveal his self-destructive belief that his mother's marriage to Claudius has tainted his own flesh and transformed all women into strumpets.

Throughout the action as well, one becomes aware that Shakespeare is using the theatrical metaphor "All the world's a stage" to illustrate the way in which deceit and corruption can be masked. In another sense, Hamlet's behavior is that of a bad actor, one who either misses his cues (as in the accidental murder of Polonius) or fails to perform when the audience expects action (as in his behavior following the play-within-the-play). There is a good deal of reflection on death and disease in *Hamlet, Prince of Denmark* as well; the hero's preoccupation with these images seems to mirror the sickness of the state and of his own enterprise. When Hamlet finally acts, however, he does so in the role of an avenger and scourge. He murders Claudius after the king has arranged for Laertes to slay him in a duel and after the queen has fallen dead from a poisoned drink intended for Hamlet. With Hamlet's death, the kingdom reverts to the control of young Fortinbras, whose father Hamlet's father had killed in another duel. Though Fortinbras stands as a heroic figure, one cannot help but observe the irony of a situation in which the son, without a struggle, inherits what his father was denied.

Troilus and Cressida • In *Troilus and Cressida*, one encounters another kind of irony: satire. This strange play, which may have been composed for a select audience, possibly of lawyers, was placed between the histories and tragedies in the First Folio. The dual plot concerns the political machinations among the Greeks during their siege of Troy and the tortured love affair between Troilus and the unfaithful Cressida.

There are no epic battles in the play; indeed, the murder of Hector by a band of Achilles' followers might easily be viewed as cowardly or ignominious at best. Much of the political action consists of debates: Hector argues eloquently that Helen should be sent back to Menelaus; Ulysses produces many pithy arguments urging the reluctant Achilles to fight. Many of these scenes, moreover, end in anticlimax, and action is often frustrated. Throughout, Thersites, the satirist-onstage, bitterly attacks the warring and lecherous instincts of men; even the love affair between Troilus and Cressida seems tainted by the general atmosphere of disillusion. Although the two lovers share genuine affection for each other, one cannot ignore the truth that they are brought together by Pandarus and that their passion has a distinctly physical quality.

When Cressida proves unable to resist the advances of Diomedes, Troilus becomes a cuckold like Menelaus; his bitterness and misogyny push one toward Thersites' assessment that the "argument" of the war "is a whore and a cuckold." Still it is possible to see tragic dimensions in the characters of both Hector and Troilus—one the victim of treachery in war, the other the victim of treachery in love.

Timon of Athens • Although probably written after the other major tragedies, *Timon of Athens* shares a number of similarities with *Troilus and Cressida*. Here again is an ironic vision of humanity, this time in a social rather than martial setting. That vision is expanded by the trenchant comments, usually in the form of references to sexual disease, of Apemantus, another cynical choric commentator.

Timon appears to be a tragic rather than misanthropic figure only if one sees him as the victim of his idealistic reading of humankind. When those on whom he has lavishly bestowed gifts and money consistently refuse to return the favor, Timon then becomes a bitter cynic and outspoken satirist. This exploding of a naïve philosophy or political idea, with its attendant destructive effect on the believer, would seem to be the basis for tragedy in a character such as Brutus or Hamlet, but even Hamlet fails to achieve the degree of misanthropy that typifies Timon's outlook. Although he is loyally followed to the end by his servant Flavius, he dies alone and not as a result of someone else's direct attack. One cannot say that the hero acquires a larger view of humanity or of himself as the result of his experience; he simply seems to swing from one extreme view to its opposite.

A comparison of Timon with more sympathetic "railers" such as Hamlet and Lear shows how narrow and shallow are his character and the dimensions of the play. The fragmented nature of the text has led some critics to question Shakespeare's authorship, but it is probably closer to the truth to say that this was an experiment that failed.

Othello, the Moor of Venice • An experiment that clearly succeeded is *Othello, the Moor of Venice*, an intense and powerful domestic tragedy. Based on an Italian tale by Giambattista Giraldi Cinthio, the story concerns a Moor, a black man who is made to believe by a treacherous, vengeful ensign that his new Venetian bride has cuckolded him with one of his lieutenants, Cassio. In a rage, the Moor suffocates his bride, only to discover too late that his jealousy was unfounded. Rather than face the torture of a trial and his own conscience, he commits suicide as he bitterly accuses himself of blindness.

In its simple outline, this story has the appearance of a crude melodrama, but Shakespeare brilliantly complicates the play's texture through skillful manipulation of scenes, characters, and language. He also creates a world with two distinct symbolic settings: Venice and Cyprus. In Venice, Othello shows himself to be a cool, rational captain, deserving of the respect he receives from the senators who send him to Cyprus to defend it from the Turks. Once Othello is on the island, however, Iago begins to chip away at the hero's veneer of self-control until he transforms him into a terrifyingly destructive force.

Iago's success depends not only on his close contact with Othello on the island but also on the generally held opinion that he, Iago, is an "honest man." He is thus able to manipulate all the central characters as if he were a puppeteer. These characters share information with Iago that he later uses to ensnare them in his web, as when Desdemona begs him to find some way to reinstate Cassio in Othello's favor. Iago is especially adept at using the handkerchief Othello gave to Desdemona but which she dropped while trying to ease her husband's headache. When Iago's wife Emilia dutifully hands her husband this handkerchief, he easily makes Othello believe that Desdemona gave it to Cassio as a love token. Although some critics have ridiculed Shakespeare for depending so heavily on one prop to resolve the plot, they fail to note the degree of psychological insight Shakespeare has displayed in using it. The handkerchief represents Othello's wife's honor and his own. She has given both away, in Othello's mind, as if they were trifles.

This play features a hero whose reason is overwhelmed by the passion of jealousy— "the green-eyed monster," in Iago's words. This theme is realized through numerous sea images, by which Shakespeare likens Othello's violent reaction to a storm or tidal wave that drowns everything in its path. Like Shakespeare's other great villains, Iago is a supreme individualist, acknowledging no authority or power beyond himself. That this attitude was a copy of the fallen angel Satan's would not have escaped the attention of Shakespeare's audience, which no doubt interpreted the plot as a replay of the Fall of Man. It may be especially important to perceive Iago as another Satan, since commentators have suspected the sufficiency of his motive (he says he wants revenge because Othello passed over him in appointing Cassio as his lieutenant). The extreme evilness of Iago's nature and the extreme purity of Desdemona's have led others to claim that Shakespeare was simply intent on fashioning a contemporary morality play for his audience. Such a reading tends to simplify what is in fact a thoroughgoing study of the emotions that both elevate and destroy humankind. As Othello discovers before his suicide, he was one "who loved not wisely but too well"; one might observe ironically that it was Iago, and not Desdemona, whom he loved "too well."

King Lear • If Othello's tragedy results from the corrosive disease of jealousy, the hero of *King Lear* suffers from the debilitating effects of pride and self-pity. When the play opens, he is in the process of retiring from the kingship by dividing his kingdom into three parts, basing his assignment of land on the degree of affection mouthed by each of the three daughters to whom he plans to assign a part. Cordelia, his youngest and favorite, refuses to enter into this hollow ceremony, and Lear responds by suddenly and violently banishing her. Left in the hands of his evil and ambitious daughters

Goneril and Regan, Lear quickly discovers that they plan to pare away any remaining symbols of his power and bring him entirely under their rule.

This theme of children controlling, even destroying, their parents is echoed in a fully developed subplot involving old Gloucester and his two sons, Edmund and Edgar. With Cordelia and Edgar cast out—the former to live in France, the latter in disguise as Poor Tom—Lear and Gloucester suffer the punishing consequences of their sins. Lear runs mad into a terrible storm, accompanied by the Fool, a witty and poignant commentator on the unnaturalness of his master's decision. There, Lear goes through a "dark night of the soul" in which he sees for the first time the suffering of others whom he has never regarded. Gloucester, who is also lacking insight into the true natures of his sons, is cruelly blinded by Regan and her husband and cast out from his own house to journey to Dover. On the way, he is joined by his disguised son, who helps Gloucester undergo a regeneration of faith before he expires. Cordelia performs a similar task for Lear, whose recovery can be only partial, because of his madness. After Cordelia is captured and killed by the forces of Edmund, whose brother conquers him in single combat, Lear, too, expires while holding the dead Cordelia in his arms.

This wrenching ending, with its nihilistic overtones, is only one of the elements that places this play among the richest and most complex tragedies in English. Lear's blindness, which is expertly represented in image clusters dealing with sight and insight, leads to cataclysmic suffering for his family and the state. More than any other Shakespearean tragedy, *King Lear* also succeeds in dramatizing the relationship between the microcosm, or little world of humankind, and the macrocosm, or larger world. One sees how the breakdown of the king's reason and control leads to the breakdown of control in the state and in nature. At the moment when Lear bursts into tears, a frightening storm breaks out, and civil war soon follows. Images of human suffering and torture likewise crowd the action, the most compelling of which is the representation of the hero tied to a "wheel of fire" and scalded by his own tears as the wheel turns.

The Wheel of Fortune emblem is clearly evoked by this image, revealing Shakespeare's purpose of depicting the king as another fallen prince brought low by his own mistakes and by the caprice of the goddess. That Lear has created the circumstances of his own fall is underscored by the antic remarks of his companion the Fool, the choric speaker who early in the play tries to keep Lear's mind from cracking as he comes to realize how wrong was the banishment of Cordelia. The Fool speaks in riddles and uses barnyard analogies to make the point that Lear has placed the whip in the child's hand and lowered his own breeches. Gloucester must learn a similar lesson, although his dilemma involves a crisis of faith. Lear must strip away the coverings of civilization to discover "unaccommodated man," a discovery he begins to make too late. Just as he realizes that Cordelia represents those qualities of truth and compassion that he has been lacking, she is suddenly and violently taken from him.

Macbeth • *Macbeth* treats the *de casibus* theme of the fall of princes, but from a different perspective. Unlike Lear, Macbeth is a usurper who is driven to kill King Duncan by the witches' prophecy, by his own ambition, and by his wife's prompting. Once that deed is done, Macbeth finds himself unable to sleep, a victim of conscience and guilt. Although Lady Macbeth tries to control his fears, she proves unsuccessful, and her influence wanes rapidly. Evidence of this loss of power is Macbeth's plot to kill Banquo, his fellow general, to whom the witches announced that he would be the father of kings. During the climactic banquet scene, Duncan's ghost enters, invisible to the other guests, to take Macbeth's place at the table; when the host reacts by raging and throwing his cup at the specter, the celebration is broken up and the guests scatter. Immediately, Macbeth rushes to the witches to seek proof that he is invincible. They tell him that he will not be conquered until Birnam Wood comes to Dunsinane and that no man born of woman can kill him. They also show him a procession of eight child-kings, all of whom represent Banquo's descendants, including the last king, who is meant to be James I. (This procession has helped many critics to conclude that *Macbeth* was written as an occasional play to honor James, who became the company's protector in 1603.)

Seeking to tighten his control of Scotland and to quiet his conscience, Macbeth launches a reign of terror during which his henchmen kill Lady Macduff and her children. Macduff, exiled in England with Duncan's son Malcolm, learns of this vicious deed and spearheads an army that returns to Scotland to destroy the tyrant. In the final battle, which commences with the attacking army tearing down branches from trees in Birnam Wood to camouflage its advance, Macbeth discovers that his nemesis, Macduff, "was from his mother's womb/ Untimely ripped." Thus standing alone (Lady Macbeth commits suicide) and defeated, Macbeth represents himself as a "poor player" who has had his moment onstage and is quickly gone. This use of the theatrical metaphor looks back to the world of *Hamlet, Prince of Denmark* at the same time that it underscores the villain-hero's role as an impostor king.

Macbeth is also depicted as a Herod figure (recalling Richard III) when he murders the innocent children of Macduff in an obsessive fit brought on by the realization that he is childless and heirless. Two strains of imagery reinforce this perception, featuring recurring references to blood and to children. When Macbeth kills Duncan, he describes his blood as "gilding" his flesh, suggesting that the king is God's anointed representative on earth. Shakespeare also depicts Macbeth's nemesis as a bloody child; this image hints at the strength-in-innocence theme that dominates the latter part of the play. That is, as Macbeth grows into the "man" that Lady Macbeth claimed he should be, he becomes more destructive and less humane, the caricature of a man. Macduff, on the other hand, in tears over the brutal murder of his wife and children, emerges as a stronger and more compassionate man because he has shown himself capable of deep feeling. The bloody-babe image might also be defined as a Christ emblem, with the attendant suggestion that Macduff comes to free the land from a tyrant's grasp by spreading a philosophy of goodness and mercy. If the play was written to honor James I, it might also be argued that the comparison between his reign and that of Christ was intended. Whatever the intention of these image patterns, they help one to trace the transformation in Macbeth's character from battlefield hero to usurping tyrant, a transformation brought about by the powerful motive of ambition.

Antony and Cleopatra • Written soon after *Macbeth, Antony and Cleopatra* again traces the complex psychological patterns of a male-female relationship. Like Lady Macbeth, Cleopatra appears to control and direct the behavior of her man, Antony, but as the play progresses, she, too, begins to lose power. Unlike Lady Macbeth, Cleopatra outlasts her love, gaining from Antony's death the spirit and stature of rule that was not evident throughout much of the play. Indeed, most of the action involves quarrels between these two mature but jealous and petulant lovers as they struggle to escape the harsh political world created by Octavius Caesar, Antony's rival.

Angered by Antony's reveling in Egypt and later by his desertion of Caesar's sister Octavia, whom Antony married only to buy time and an unsteady truce, Octavius begins to move against Antony with a powerful army and navy. During a first encounter between the two forces, in which Antony foolishly decides to fight at sea and also depends on Cleopatra's untested ships, Antony leaves the field in pursuit of the retiring Cleopatra. Angered by her withdrawal and his own alacrity in following her, Antony rages against his "serpent of old Nile" and vows to have nothing further to do with her, but Cleopatra's pull is magnetic, and Antony joins forces with her for a second battle with Caesar. When a similar retreat occurs and Antony finds Cleopatra apparently arranging a separate peace with one of Caesar's representatives, he has the messenger beaten and sent back to Octavius with a challenge to single combat. These wild and desperate moves are commented on by Enobarbus, associate of Antony and choric voice. After the threat of single combat, Enobarbus leaves his master to join forces with Octavius. (Overcome by remorse, however, Enobarbus dies on the eve of battle.)

Believing that Cleopatra has killed herself, Antony decides to commit suicide and calls on his servant Eros to hold his sword so that he can run himself on it. Instead, Eros kills himself, and Antony must strike the blow himself. Still alive, he is carried to the monument where Cleopatra has decided to take up residence. There, Antony expires, "a Roman, by a Roman/ Valiantly vanquished." Almost immediately, Cleopatra's character seems to change into that of a noble partner; her elegant speeches on Antony's heroic proportions are some of the most powerful blank verse in the play. It is also clear that she intends to escape Octavius's grasp, knowing that he intends to parade her and her children before a jeering Roman crowd. Putting on her royal robes and applying the poison asps to her breast, Cleopatra hurries off to join her lover in eternity.

This complicated story is brilliantly organized by means of placing in balance the two worlds of Rome and Egypt. While Rome is presented as a cold, calculating place, reflective of the character of Octavius, Egypt stands out as a lush paradise in which the pursuit of pleasure is the main business of the inhabitants. This contrast is particularly telling because Antony's status as a tragic hero depends on one's seeing him as caught between the two worlds, at home in neither, master of neither. Water and serpent imagery dominate the play, creating a picture of Cleopatra as a Circe figure or a spontaneously generated creature that has seduced the once heroic Antony. Although this is the Roman view of the "gypsy" queen, Shakespeare requires his audience to appreciate her infinite variety. She is beautiful and playful, demanding and witty, cool and explosive. On the other hand, the assessment of Octavius as a puritanical, unfeeling man of destiny is also oversimplified; his reaction to Antony's death reveals genuine emotion. At the close of the play, one realizes that Antony and Cleopatra's vast empire has been reduced to the size of her monument—Caesar must attend a while longer to make this discovery himself. Antony and Cleopatra, however, have found a world of love that Octavius could never enter, and the tragedy is as much concerned with tracing the boundaries of that empire as it is with marking the triumphs of Octavius.

Coriolanus • While reading the story of Antony and Cleopatra in Plutarch's *Parallel Lives*, to which the play reveals a number of similarities, Shakespeare found another Roman figure whose career he saw as appropriate matter for tragedy: Coriolanus. Composed in the period between 1607 and 1608, *Coriolanus* dramatizes the career of a general in Republican Rome. He proves to be a superhuman figure in battle, earning his name by single-handedly subduing the town of Corioles and emerging from its gates covered in blood. (This birth image has a mixed meaning, since the blood is that of his victims.)

Unfortunately, Coriolanus refuses to humble himself before the Roman plebeians, whom he despises, as a requirement for holding the office of consul. Indeed, many of his bitter comments about the fickleness and cowardice of the populace remind one of characters such as Thersites and Apemantus. Such contempt and condescension make it hard to identify with Coriolanus, even though one is made aware that the Roman crowd is set against him by the jealous and ambitious tribunes, Brutus and Sicinius. Driven by his pride and anger, Coriolanus challenges the citizens' rights and is subsequently banished. He then joins forces with his former enemy Aufidius, and the two of them lead an army to the very gates of Rome. Coriolanus's mother comes out to plead with her son to spare Rome—and his family—in the most emotional scene of the play. Deeply moved by his mother's arguments, Coriolanus relents and urges his companion to make peace with their enemy.

Aufidius agrees but awaits his opportunity to ambush his partner, whom he regards as a lifelong enemy. In a masterstroke of irony, Coriolanus is brought down by the citizens of the very town—Corioles—that he conquered in acquiring his name. Because the play is so heavily laden with swatches of Coriolanus's vitriol and instances of irony such as the final one, it is difficult to classify this tragedy with those in which the heroes present richly complex characters. If Hamlet, Othello, Macbeth, and Lear possess tragic flaws, those flaws are only a part of their complicated makeup. Coriolanus, on the other hand, can be understood only in terms of his flaw, and the character and play are therefore one-dimensional.

There is little argument, however, that Shakespeare's tragedies constitute the major achievement of his career. These dramas continue to appeal to audiences because their stories are intriguing; because their characters are fully realized human beings, if somewhat larger than life; and because their poetic language is metaphorically rich. Shakespeare possessed a profound insight into human nature and an ability to reveal what he found there in language unequaled in its power and beauty.

The romances • In the later years of his career, Shakespeare returned to writing comedy of a special kind: tragicomedy or romance. The four plays usually referred to as "the romances" are *Pericles, Cymbeline, The Winter's Tale,* and *The Tempest.* Three of these portray situations in which fathers are separated from daughters, then are rejoined through some miraculous turn of fortune. The plays also involve travel to exotic locales by the heroes and heroines, and, except for *The Tempest,* they portray events which occur over a span of many years. Sharp contrasts between court and pastoral settings vivify the theme of nature as the ideal teacher of moral values. In *Pericles, Cymbeline,* and *The Winter's Tale,* the plots move inexorably toward tragedy, but through some form of intervention by Providence—or in some cases, by the gods themselves—happiness is restored and characters are reunited. All the plays witness the power of faith as instrumental in the process of regeneration; the loyal counselor or servant is a regular character type in the plays. The general outlook of the romances is optimistic, suggesting that humankind is indeed capable of recovering from the Fall and of creating a new Paradise.

Pericles • *Pericles* recounts the adventures of a good king who seems hounded by fortune and forced to wander through the Mediterranean. The plot is faintly reminiscent of that of *The Comedy of Errors,* suggesting that Shakespeare was returning to tested materials from his earliest comedies. During a storm at sea, Pericles' wife, Thaisa, apparently dies in childbirth and is set ashore in a coffin. He then leaves his daughter Marina in the care of a scheming queen, who tries to have her murdered. Instead, Marina is captured by pirates and eventually is sold to a brothel owner. After many years of lonely sojourning, Pericles is finally reunited with his daughter; later, through the offices of a doctor figure named Cerimon, they find Thaisa in the temple of Diana at Ephesus, where she has been resting for years. Throughout, the sea represents both a threatening and a peaceful force; Marina's name points to the theme of the sea as a great restorative power. She "cures" her father aboard a ship.

Cymbeline • *Cymbeline*, set in ancient Britain, recounts the misfortunes of its characters against the background of the Roman invasion of England. The tragicomedy has strong patriotic overtones, but it does not qualify as a history play such as those in the two tetralogies. The play depicts the moral education of Posthumus, the hero, whose desire to marry Imogen, Cymbeline's daughter, is frustrated by his low birth. While in exile in Italy, Posthumus brags to an Italian acquaintance, Iachimo, that his beloved would never consider deceiving him. Thus challenged, Iachimo visits Imogen's room while she sleeps and, through a clever ruse involving a ring and a birthmark, convinces Posthumus that he has slept with her. As a result of numerous plot turns, one of which calls for Imogen to disguise herself as a page, the two lovers are finally reunited when Iachimo confesses his sin.

Comingled with this strain of plot is another involving two sons of Cymbeline who have been reared in the rugged world of caves and mountains by an old counselor banished by the king. (He originally kidnapped the boys to seek revenge against Cymbeline.) In a climactic scene brought about by the Roman invasion, the mountain-men heroes are reunited with their father and sister, whom all believed was dead. So complex is the plot that many readers and audiences have found the play confusing and sometimes unintentionally humorous. The characters are not fully developed, and it is difficult to determine just what is the central story. Here, too, spectacle overpowers dialogue and characterization, with little or no attention paid to plausibility. Shakespeare seems preoccupied with demonstrating the healthfulness of pastoral life, the patriotic spirit of Englishmen, and the melodramatic quality of evil. Clearly, this agenda of themes and values places one in a comic world that is distinct from the one that typifies the mature comedies.

The Winter's Tale • In *The Winter's Tale*, Shakespeare again explores the motif of the daughter separated from her father, but in this play, the father, King Leontes, must be seen as a potentially tragic figure. His jealousy leads him to accuse his wife, Hermione, of unfaithfulness with his friend and fellow king Polixenes. When Leontes confronts her, even after consultation of the oracle indicates her honesty, she faints and apparently expires. Leontes banishes the child Perdita, who is his daughter but whom he refuses to acknowledge because of his suspicions, and the third act ends with a loyal servant depositing the baby on the shore of Bohemia to be favored or destroyed by Fortune. (A bear pursues and kills the servant, thus destroying any link between Leontes' court and the baby.)

Perdita, "the lost one," is found and reared by a shepherd. As sixteen years pass, she grows into a kind of pastoral queen, revealing those traits of goodness and innocence that Shakespeare associates with the Golden Age. When Polixenes repeats Leontes' sin by banishing his son Florizel for falling in love with a lowly shepherdess, the couple, with the help of a rejected servant still loyal to Leontes, returns to Sicilia to seek the aid of the now repentant king. Through a series of revelations and with the help of the old shepherd, Perdita's identity is discovered. She and Florizel are married, and the two kings are reunited in friendship. As a final tour de force, Hermione, who has been hidden away for the whole time by another loyal servant, comes to life as a statue supposedly sculpted by a famous artist. As in the other romances, some divine force has obviously been operating in the affairs of humans to bring about this happy reunion of families, friends, and countries.

The Winter's Tale comes closer than the earlier romances to a realistic treatment of emotion, with all of its destructive possibilities, and to a more nearly honest vision of the pastoral world. Autolycus the clown, for example, pretends to be nothing other than a successful thief, "a snapper-up of unconsidered trifles."

The Tempest • *The Tempest* is the only romance in which father and daughter are together from the beginning. It also possesses the only plot that observes the classical unities of time and place. Many commentators believe that the play represents Shakespeare's greatest dramatic achievement, blending together beautiful verse, richly realized characters, and the moving wonders of the imagination. There can be no question that *The Tempest* is a refined and elevating statement of the themes of Providence and of order and degree. Prospero, the duke of Milan, exiled by his usurping brother Antonio, vows to punish both Antonio and his chief supporter, King Alonso. The two are aboard a ship sailing near the island on which Prospero and his daughter Miranda reside. Using magical power and the aid of a spirit named Ariel, Prospero apparently wrecks the ship, saving all the voyagers but supposedly drowning Ferdinand, Alonso's son. Once on the island, the party is tormented by disorienting music and distracting sights, especially when Prospero's brother Antonio attempts to persuade Alonso's brother Sebastian to kill him and seize the crown. Another rebellion is attempted by Caliban (his name an anagram for "cannibal"), the half-human, half-bestial servant of Prospero.

Both rebellions fail, but instead of punishing his victims further, Prospero, moved by the compassion displayed by Ariel, decides to give up his magic and return to civilization. The decision proves crucial, since Prospero was on the verge of becoming a kind of Faust, forgetting his identity as a man. When he acknowledges Caliban, "this thing of darkness," as his own, one realizes that this gesture betokens an internal acceptance of the passions as a legitimate part of his nature. Instead of revenging himself on Alonso, Prospero allows Ferdinand to woo Miranda in a mood and manner that recall Eden before the Fall. It should also be noted that Prospero creates a marriage masque featuring Iris, Ceres, and Juno, at the close of which he delivers the famous "Our revels now are ended" speech. Some critics claim that Prospero's words constitute Shakespeare's farewell to the stage, but there is considerable evidence that he continued to write plays for at least another year.

The Two Noble Kinsmen • *The Two Noble Kinsmen* was probably one of the plays composed during that period. It is not included in the First Folio (published 1623). It appeared in print in 1634 and bearing a title page ascribing the comedy to John Fletcher and William Shakespeare. Although collaboration was common among Elizabethan and Jacobean playwrights, it was not a form of composition in which Shakespeare regularly engaged. Because *Henry VIII* was also most likely a collaborative effort, there seems to be compelling evidence that Shakespeare was enjoying a state of semiretirement during this period. Based on Geoffrey Chaucer's "The Knight's Tale" (from his *Canterbury Tales*), *The Two Noble Kinsmen* depicts the love of Palamon and Arcite for Emilia in a polite and mannered style that can easily be identified with Fletcher's other work. The play is similar to the other romances in its emphasis on spectacle. It opens with a magnificent wedding ceremony before the Temple of Hymen, and there are excursions to the shrines of Mars and Diana as well. However, there are no scenes of regeneration involving fathers and daughters, no emphasis on the forgiveness of sin. If this was Shakespeare's last play, it shows him returning to old sources for oft-told tales; his interest in developing new comic forms had obviously waned.

On the whole, the romances represent a more sophisticated but less playful and inventive style than that of the character-oriented comedies, such as *Twelfth Night* and *Much Ado About Nothing*. They are the work of a playwright at the height of his powers, and they perhaps reveal the issues with which Shakespeare came to grapple in his later years: familial relationships, faith and redemption, and the legacy of each generation to its successors.

Other major works

POETRY: *Venus and Adonis*, 1593; *The Rape of Lucrece*, 1594; *The Passionate Pilgrim*, 1599 (miscellany with poems by Shakespeare and others); *The Phoenix and the Turtle*, 1601; *A Lover's Complaint*, 1609; *Sonnets*, 1609.

Bibliography

Bloom, Harold. *Shakespeare: The Invention of the Human.* New York: Riverhead, 1998. A drama-by-drama analysis of William Shakespeare's plays, focusing on character development and the playwright's contribution to the modern understanding of the human experience.

Brown, John Russell. *Shakespeare: The Tragedies.* New York: Palgrave, 2001. A study of the tragedies in chronological order.

Danson, Lawrence. *Shakespeare's Dramatic Genres.* New York: Oxford University Press, 2000. Danson's scholarly study examines Shakespeare's philosophy and how it was demonstrated in his dramas. Bibliography and index.

De Grazia, Margreta, and Stanley Wells, eds. *The Cambridge Companion to Shakespeare.* New York: Cambridge University Press, 2001. This work provides an extensive guide to Shakespeare's life and works.

Dobson, Michael, and Stanley Wells, eds. *The Oxford Companion to Shakespeare.* Oxford, England: Oxford University Press, 2001. An encyclopedic treatment of the life and works of Shakespeare.

Draper, Ronald P. *Shakespeare, the Comedies.* New York: St. Martin's Press, 2000. Draper provides an analysis of the playwright's comedies. Bibliography and index.

Duncan-Jones, Katherine. *Ungentle Shakespeare: Scenes from His Life.* London: Arden Shakespeare, 2001. Duncan-Jones portrays Shakespeare as a man influenced by the political, social, and literary climate in which he found himself. She also examines speculative stories such as his love for a Dark Lady. Bibliography and index.

Holderness, Graham. *Shakespeare: The Histories.* New York: St. Martin's Press, 2000. Holderness examines the historical plays of Shakespeare and the historical events on which they were based. Bibliography and index.

Honan, Park. *Shakespeare: A Life.* 1999. Reprint. New York: Oxford University Press, 1999. Honan's life of Shakespeare shuns the mythology that has grown up around the playwright and places him in the context of his age.

Kermode, Frank. *Shakespeare's Language*. New York: Farrar Straus & Giroux, 2000. Between 1594 and 1608, Kermode argues, the language of Shakespeare's plays was transformed, acquiring a new complexity that arose out of the playwright's increasingly successful attempts to represent dramatically the excitement and confusion of thought under stress.

McConnell, Louise. *Dictionary of Shakespeare*. Chicago: Fitzroy Dearborn, 2000. A basic reference.

McLeish, Kenneth, and Stephen Unwin. *A Pocket Guide to Shakespeare's Plays*. London: Faber and Faber, 1998. This concise guide summarizes the plots and characters of Shakespeare's plays, providing an easy reference.

Marsh, Nicholas. *Shakespeare, the Tragedies*. New York: St. Martin's Press, 2000. Marsh analyzes the tragedies of Shakespeare, providing study guides. Bibliography and index.

Proudfoot, Richard. *Shakespeare: Text, Stage, and Canon*. London: Arden Shakespeare, 2001. A study of Shakespeare's plays, with emphasis on their stage history and how they were produced. Bibliography and index.

Richards, Jennifer, and James Knowles, eds. *Shakespeare's Late Plays: New Readings*. Edinburgh: Edinburgh University Press, 1999. A collection of essays focusing on the playwright's later plays, including *The Winter's Tale*, *The Tempest*, and *The Two Noble Kinsmen*. Bibliography and index.

Southworth, John. *Shakespeare, the Player: A Life in the Theatre*. Stroud, England: Sutton, 2000. A biography that focuses on the dramatist as a member of the theater, writing for the theater in collaboration with the theater company.

Thomson, Peter. *Shakespeare's Professional Career*. New York: Cambridge University Press, 1992. Thomson examines the theatrical world of Elizabethan England to illuminate William Shakespeare's life and writings.

Wells, Stanley. *Shakespeare: A Life in Drama*. New York: W. W. Norton, 1995. A critical introduction to William Shakespeare's life and work.

Wilson, Ian. *Shakespeare: The Evidence: Unlocking the Mysteries of the Man and His Work*. London: Headline, 1993. Wilson draws on documents discovered during the excavation of the site of the Globe Theatre to delve into the mysteries surrounding Shakespeare's life, including authorship of his plays, his sexuality, his religion, and the curse he set on his own grave.

Robert F. Willson, Jr.,
additional material by Harold Branam,
updated by John R. Holmes and Joseph Rosenblum

Ntozake Shange

Paulette Williams

Born: Trenton, New Jersey; October 18, 1948

Principal drama • *for colored girls who have considered suicide/ when the rainbow is enuf,* pr., pb. 1975; *A Photograph: Still Life with Shadows; A Photograph: A Study in Cruelty,* pr. 1977 (revised as *A Photograph: Lovers in Motion,* pr. 1979, pb. 1981); *Where the Mississippi Meets the Amazon,* pr. 1977 (with Thulani Nkabinde and Jessica Hagedorn); *From Okra to Greens: A Different Kinda Love Story,* pr. 1978, pb. 1985; *Black and White Two Dimensional Planes,* pr., 1979; *Spell #7: Geechee Jibara Quik Magic Trance Manual for Technologically Stressed Third World People,* pr. 1979, pb. 1981; *Boogie Woogie Landscapes,* pr. 1979, pb. 1981; *Mother Courage and Her Children,* pr. 1980 (adaptation of Bertolt Brecht's play); *Three Pieces,* pb. 1981; *Betsey Brown,* pr. 1991 (based on her novel); *The Love Space Demands: A Continuing Saga,* pb. 1991, pr. 1992; *Plays: One,* pb. 1992; *Three Pieces,* pb. 1992

Other literary forms • Ntozake Shange's three genres—plays, poems, and novels— so overlap that one might say she has invented a new genre, which she has named the "choreopoem." She has published several volumes of poetry, including *Nappy Edges* (1978), parts of which were included in her 1975 play *for colored girls who have considered suicide/ when the rainbow is enuf; Natural Disasters and Other Festive Occasions* (1979); *A Daughter's Geography* (1983); *Ridin' the Moon in Texas: Word Paintings* (1987); and *I Live in Music* (1994). Among her novels are *Sassafrass, Cypress, and Indigo* (1982) and *Betsey Brown* (1985). She has gathered writings about her work from 1976 to 1984 into *See No Evil: Prefaces, Essays, and Accounts, 1976-1983* (1984), the study of which is essential to an understanding of her art.

Shange has also distinguished herself as a director, of both her own work and that of others, notably Richard Wesley's *The Mighty Gents* in 1979. In 1980, Shange adapted Bertolt Brecht's *Mutter Courage und ihre Kinder* (1941; *Mother Courage and Her Children,* 1941), changing the scene from mid-seventeenth century Europe to post-Civil War America, making the protagonist an emancipated slave doing business with the army oppressing the Western Indians, and changing the language to black English.

Achievements • Ntozake Shange's work embodies a rich confusion of genres and all the contradictions inherent in a world in which violence and oppression polarize life and art. These polarizations in Shange's work both contribute to her artistry and complicate it. She has been criticized and praised for her unconventional language and structure, for her almost religious feminism, and for her stand on black/white and male/female issues. Her first play, *for colored girls who have considered suicide/ when the rainbow is enuf,* produced in 1976 by Joseph Papp's New York Shakespeare Festival, was honored in that year by the Outer Critics Circle, which consists of those who write about the New York theater for out-of-town newspapers. That play also received Obie and Audelco Awards as well as Tony and Grammy Award nominations in 1977. Shange's 1980 adaptation of Bertolt Brecht's *Mother Courage and Her Children* won one of

the *The Village Voice*'s Obie awards.
Among her many other awards are a
Los Angeles Times Book Prize for Po-
etry and a Pushcart Prize.

(Jules Allen)

Biography • Ntozake Shange (pronounced "En-to-zaki Shong-gay")
was born Paulette Williams in Trenton, New Jersey, on October 18,
1948, daughter of a surgeon and a
psychiatric social worker and educa-
tor. She grew up surrounded by music, literature, art, and her parents'
prominent friends, among them
Dizzy Gillespie, Chuck Berry, and
W. E. B. Du Bois, as well as Third
World writers and musicians. Her
ties with her family were strong; she
also was close to her family's live-in
black maids. She was graduated from Barnard College with honors in 1970, then received a graduate degree at the University of Southern California in Los Angeles.

While in California, she began studying dance, writing poetry, and participating in
improvisational works (consisting of poems, music, dance, and mime) at bars, cabarets, and schools. These gradually grew into *for colored girls who have considered suicide/
when the rainbow is enuf*, which she carried across the country to perform in workshops
in New York, then at the Public Theatre, and eventually on Broadway. The contrasts
between her privileged home and education and the realities of the lives of black
women led her, in 1971, to change her name legally from what she called the "slave
name" of Paulette Williams to Ntozake Shange, meaning "she who comes with her
own things" and "she who walks like a lion" in Xhosa (Zulu). Her two failed marriages,
her suicide attempts, and her contact with city violence resulted in an anger that found
its outlet in her poems. During the late 1970's, she lived in New York City, but she later
moved to Houston, Texas, with her daughter, Savannah. She has taught and lectured at
many colleges and universities, including Mills College in Oakland California; The
State University in Rutgers, New Jersey; the University of California, Berkeley; the
University of Houston; Rice University; Yale University; Howard University; and
New York University.

Her work with Emily Mann on the script version of *Betsey Brown* brought her into
prominence among feminists and experimental theaters. Working under the auspices
of the New York Shakespeare Festival, the two women brought the play into its production form through a series of staged readings, workshops, and tryouts, and their collaboration techniques were the subject of forums among dramaturges in 1990.

Shange's poetic "reading/performance" piece *The Love Space Demands*, in which she
reads her own work (accompanied by guitarist Billie Patterson), was performed in New
Jersey at the Crossroads Theatre and in San Francisco at the Hansberry Theatre in
1992.

Analysis • In Ntozake Shange's introduction to the volume *Three Pieces*, she makes
this statement about drama:

as a poet in american theater/ i find most activity that takes place on our stages over-
whelmingly shallow/ stilted & imitative. that is probably one of the reasons i insist on
calling myself a poet or writer/ rather than a playwright/ i am interested solely in the
poetry of a moment/ the emotional & aesthetic impact of a character or a line.

Her plays have evoked a range of critical responses commensurate with their unconventional nature. Should her work be characterized as poetry or drama, prose or
poetry, essay or autobiography? Her choreopoems, made up of poetry, drama, prose,
and autobiography, are unified by a militant feminism in which some critics have seen
a one-sided attack on black men. Others, however, point out the youthful spirit, flair
with language, and lyricism that carry her plays to startling and radical conclusions.
Her style and its seeming contradictions, such as the use of both black English and the
erudite vocabulary of the educated, are at the heart of her drama. Influenced by their
method of development—public poetry reading in bars, cafés, schools, Off-Off-Broadway theaters—the plays are generally somewhere between a poetry reading and a
staged play.

First among the contradictions or contrasts is her blending of genres: Her poems
shade into drama, her dramas are essentially verse monologues, and her novels incorporate poetic passages. Second, her language varies radically—on a single page and even
in a single phrase—from black dialect ("cuz," "wanna," "awready," "chirren") to the
language of her middle class upbringing and education ("i cant count the number of
times i have viscerally wanted to attack deform n maim the language that i waz taught
to hate myself in/"). In the published texts of her poetry, plays, and essays, in addition
to simplified phonetic spellings, she employs the slash instead of the period and omits
capitalization. Many recordings of her work are available, and these provide the lis-
tener with a much fuller sense of the dynamic quality of her language in performance.

Shange's bold and daring use of language, her respect for people formerly given little value, and her exploration of the roles of black men and women have opened a new
dimension in theater. Her blendings of poetry, music, and dance bring theater back to
its origins and simultaneously blaze a trail toward the drama of the future.

for colored girls who have considered suicide/ when the rainbow is enuf ·
Shange's first dramatic success, *for colored girls who have considered suicide/ when the rainbow is enuf,* is the recital, individually and in chorus, of the lives and growth of seven
different black women, named according to their dress colors: "lady in red," "lady in
blue," "lady in orange," "lady in brown," "lady in yellow," "lady in purple," and "lady
in green." The term "colored girls" in the title evokes a stereotype of black women yet
also contains a germ of hope for the future (the "rainbow," both of color and of eventual salvation).

These seven stylized figures are representative voices of black women, and they express their fury at their oppression both as women and as blacks. The first segment
shows high school graduation and the social and sexual rite of passage for "colored
girls" in the working-class suburbs. Some of the women who have been cruelly disappointed in relationships with men discuss their spiritual quests. A black woman pretends to be Puerto Rican so that she can dance the merengue in Spanish Harlem. A
woman breaks up with her lover by returning to him his plant to water. The scenes become more somber, portraying rape, abuse, city dangers, and abortion. Ties with a
more heroic black past appear in "Toussaint," while the glamorized prostitute evicts
her lover from her bed. The women begin to analyze their predicaments and to assert

their independence in segments entitled "somebody almost walked off wid alla my stuff" and "pyramid," in which three women console one another for the actions of the faithless lover whom they share. In the brutal culminating scene, a crazed Vietnam veteran, Beau Willie Brown, abuses his woman Crystal and kills their infant children, dropping them from a window.

The recurrent motif of the recitation is the thwarting of dreams and aspirations for a decent life by forces beyond one's control: war, poverty, and ignorance. There is, however, a saving grace. Toward the end of the play, the seven women fall into a tighter circle of mutual support, much like a religious "laying on of hands" ceremony, in which they say, "i found god in myself/ & i loved her/ i loved her fiercely." Their bitter pain, shown throughout the dramatic episodes, turns into a possibility of regeneration. Thus, the play is a drama of salvation for women who do not receive their full value in society.

Though it was a landmark in the emergence of new black women playwrights, *for colored girls who have considered suicide/ when the rainbow is enuf* has been criticized for its lack of discussion of black traditions in religion, family, and ordinary work, and for its omissions of both black literary and political history and the influence of whites. Its style, considered as an attack on language, part of blacks' "enslavement," has also been criticized. Later plays, however, include these elements in a constantly enriching network of allusions.

A Photograph • In *A Photograph*, a set of meditations and sketches involving an ideal black woman named Michael and her lover Sean, a failed photographer, Shange explores her idea of art—"the poetry of a moment"—as well as representative stages of the African American experience. Photography, dance, and drama are shown to be art forms that capture meaningful moments and present them to viewers and readers so that they might behold and understand the essence and the value of art and life. The young professionals that reside in or pass through Sean's San Francisco apartment-studio are shown to examine the psychological factors that impede and that motivate them and other African Americans.

The five figures of this piece are representative of other aspects of black life than those put forward in her first play. Nevada, a lawyer and lover-supporter of Sean, the struggling artist, sets herself above other "common" African Americans: Her family, she boasts, "was manumitted in 1843/ [when] yall were still slaves/ carrying things for white folks . . . /" The upwardly mobile Earl, also a lawyer, former lover of Claire and long-time friend of Sean, pleads Nevada's case to Sean when the latter rejects her. Claire is a dancer who dances seductively for Sean as he photographs and then ravishes her. Michael is a dancer and the woman Sean comes truly to love as she shares herself and her ideas of art and of the African experience with him.

Early in the drama Sean tells Michael, "i'm a genius for unravelling the mysteries of the darker races/. . . i know who we are." After he rejects Nevada and is rejected by her, Sean reveals his insecurities as a son, a man, an African American, and an artist. The self- and race-assured artist Michael challenges her temporarily broken lover. Sean soon responds to this and to a poetic story danced and told by Michael with his own story and assurances.

yes. that's right. me. i'ma be it. the photographer of all time. look out ansel/ . . . i can bring you the world shining grainy focused or shaking/ a godlike phenomenon/ sean david . . . i realize you're not accustomed to the visions of a man of color who has a gift/ but fear not/ I'll give it to ya a lil at a time. i am only beginning to startle/ to mesmerize and reverse the reality of all who can see. I gotta thing bout niggahs/ my folks/ that just wont stop/ & we are so correct for the photograph/ we profile all the time/ styling/ giving angle & pattern/ shadows & still life. if somebody sides me cd see the line in niggahs/ the texture of our lives/ they wda done it/ but since nobody has stepped forward/ here I am . . .

Sean seems obviously representative of Shange the artist in his coming-into-his-own response to Michael, who is yet another representative of Shange the artist. This choreopoem seems a particularly significant statement made by Shange, poet and writer: She, like Sean, presents "the contours of life unnoticed" and she, like Michael, speaks "for everybody burdened."

Boogie Woogie Landscapes • After examining the identity of isolated young black women in *for colored girls who have considered suicide/ when the rainbow is enuf* and of couples in *A Photograph*, Shange concentrates on one woman's visions, dreams, and memories in *Boogie Woogie Landscapes*, which was first produced as a one-woman poetry piece in 1978 and then cast as a play in 1979, with music and dance. Layla, a young black woman, entertains in her dreams a series of nightlife companions who exemplify her perceptions of herself and her memories. "Layla" in Arabic means "born at night,"and the entire drama exists in Layla's nighttime subconscious. Layla's dreams of Fidel Castro's Cuba, of primitive cruelties to African women, and of rock and roll and blues interweave with her feelings about growing up, family, brothers and sisters, parents, maids (some of which appear later in Shange's semiautobiographical novel *Betsey Brown*).

Spell #7 • Shange's 1979 play *Spell #7*, like her first play, is structured like a highly electric poetry reading, but this time the cast is mixed male and female. A huge blackface mask forms the backdrop for actors and actresses of an imitation old-time minstrel show, where actors did skits, recited, and joked, all under the direction of a Mr. Inter locutor. The actors come offstage, relax at an actors' bar, and gradually remove their masks, revealing their true selves. Lou, the "practicing magician," reveals that his father gave up his role as magician when a colored child asked for a spell to make her white. The actors tell each other and the audience tall stories. One of these involves a child who thought blacks were immune to dread diseases and disease-ridden passions such as polio and pedophilia. She is disillusioned when, as an adult, she finds that blacks not only can but also do hurt one another, so she buys South African gold

to remind the black people that it cost a lot for us to be here
our value/ can be known instinctively
but since so many black people are having a hard time not being like white folks
i wear these gold pieces to protest their ignorance
their disconnect from history.

Another woman loves her baby, which she names "myself," while it is in the womb but kills it after it is born. Still another girl vows to brush her "nappy" hair constantly so that she can toss it like white girls. By these contrasts and by wry lists and surprising parallels, Shange shows the pain and difficulty, as well as the hopefulness, of being black. Lou refers to the spell that caused his father to give up magic as he (Lou) casts the final spell of Spell #7:

aint no colored magician in his right mind
gonna make you white
cuz this is blk magic you lookin at
& i'm fixin you up good/ fixin you up good & colored
& you gonna be colored all yr life
& you gonna love it/ bein colored

The others join him in celebration of "bein colored"; but the minstrel mask drops down and Lou's final words contain anger as well as celebration:

crackers are born with the right to be
alive/ i'm making ours up right here
in yr face/ & we gonna be
colored & love it

From Okra to Greens • Shange's *From Okra to Greens* draws together and expands on the themes of her earlier theater pieces. The discovery by the lovers Okra and Greens of the beauty and strength—the god—within the individual is like that of the women who populate *for colored girls who have considered suicide/ when the rainbow is enuf.* Similarly, the lovers' discovery of what is sacred—of the fullness and color of life versus the "skinny life" of black and white—is the goal of Layla in *Boogie Woogie Landscapes*, of the actors in *Spell #7*, and of the artists of *A Photograph*. The love between two fully realized human beings, like that experienced by Sean and Michael in *A Photograph*, is fully expanded on in this two-character drama of Okra and Greens. The theme of the responsibility of the artist touched on by Sean and by Michael is also fully developed by the poets Okra and Greens.

In the opening scenes of *From Okra to Greens*, Greens speaks of Okra's plight as single black woman as Okra acts/dances the role. This scene is reminiscent of Sean and Michael speaking in unison about Sean's and then Michael's art in the final scene of *A Photograph* and Ross's talking while Maxine acts out the role that the two are creating together, on the spot, in *Spell #7*. In *From Okra to Greens*, as in her other choreopoems, Shange turns her dramatic poetry into staged drama. She presents verbatim much of the poetry of her collection *A Daughter's Geography*. Although her feminist protests are dramatized in this play as in *for colored girls who have considered suicide/ when the rainbow is enuf* and in *Boogie Woogie Landscapes*, here her feminist protest is given voice by the male character Greens. That both Okra and Greens are poets allows them to have an understanding of one another and of the roles forced on too many African American women and men as well as an understanding of the role that human beings *should* play in the world.

Okra first dances as "the crooked woman" as Greens speaks, showing his and society's distorted view of black women. Okra's dance reflects both her pain and her potential strength and beauty. As the two come together, Greens admits his own crookedness in telling Okra that before their encounter he had not known "what a stood/up straight man felt like." Together the two characters create and present portraits of "some men" who degrade women (as they are encouraged to do by the patriarchy). Once married, the two continue their dialogue, which includes their consideration of one another and of the sociopolitical climate in which they and, later, their daughter, must reside.

Shange's *Okra and Greens* celebrates, as do Sean and Michael in *A Photograph*, the richness of African American life. Her love story extends to the poor of not only her own country but also the world. Okra pleads for the return of Haitian liberators Dessalines, Petion, and L'Ouverture with their visions of "*la liberte, l'egalite, la frater-nite.*" As in her other theater pieces, Shange calls here, too, for the return of American visionaries, among them W. E. B. Du Bois.

As the hope of the world's visionaries is shown to have dimmed, so the relationship between the lovers Okra and Greens dims momentarily. Abandoned by Greens, Okra says that "the moon cracked in a ugly rupture." Joined once more, the two encourage each other and others to "rise up" and to "dance with the universe." This story of the love between two poets is a love song to a universe in sad need of hope.

The refrain of *Boogie Woogie Landscapes*, that "we dont recognize what's sacred any-more," is revealed in *From Okra to Greens* in the portrait of the "pretty man" whose pretty floors are covered with the kind of rug that "little girls spend whole/ lives tying." Lack of recognition of the sacred is a theme repeated throughout the work. However, the love between Okra and Greens and their hope for their daughter and for the op-pressed peoples of the world shows recognition of the sacred is possible for aware, thinking, and caring individuals. The memory of other visionaries also shows the po-ets' and others' recognition of the sacred. It is clear here and throughout her writing that Shange would have her audience recognize the sacred in themselves and in others and do their part in telling the story—in spreading the word—and in fighting for lib-erty, equality, and fraternity for all.

Betsey Brown and **The Love Space Demands** • In 1991, Shange adapted her novel *Betsey Brown* into a play. The semiautobiographical work tells the story of a thirteen-year-old African American girl growing up in a middle-class household in 1950's St. Louis. *The Love Space Demands*, a loosely connected series of poems and monologues Shange herself performs with musical accompaniment, revolves around sexual rela-tions in the age of AIDS (acquired immune deficiency syndrome).

Other major works

LONG FICTION: *Sassafras: A Novella*, 1976; *Sassafras, Cypress, and Indigo*, 1982; *Betsey Brown*, 1985; *Liliane: Resurrection of the Daughter*, 1994.

POETRY: *Nappy Edges*, 1978; *Natural Disasters and Other Festive Occasions*, 1979; *A Daughter's Geography*, 1983, 1991; *From Okra to Greens: Poems*, 1984; *Ridin' the Moon in Texas: Word Paintings*, 1987; *I Live in Music*, 1994.

NONFICTION: *See No Evil: Prefaces, Essays, and Accounts, 1976-1983*, 1984; *If I Can Cook, You Know God Can*, 1998.

EDITED TEXT: *The Beacon Best of 1999: Creative Writing by Women and Men of All Colors*, 2000.

Bibliography

Brown-Guillory, Elizabeth. *Their Place on the Stage: Black Women Playwrights in America.* New York: Greenwood Press, 1988. A good study of Shange, along with Alice Childress and Lorraine Hansberry. Analyzes *for colored girls who have considered sui-cide/ when the rainbow is enuf* at considerable length, as well as the 1979 trilogy, *Spell #7, Boogie Woogie Landscapes*, and *A Photograph.*

Effiong, Philip Uko. *In Search of a Model for African American Drama: A Study of Selected Plays by Lorraine Hansberry, Amiri Baraka, and Ntozake Shange.* New York: University Press of America, 2000. Analyzes the historical and sociopolitical considerations that determine the choices made by each dramatist. Considers the ritualization of black theater by each dramatist.

Lester, Neal A. *Ntozake Shange: A Critical Study of the Plays.* New York: Garland, 1995. Lester examines critically Shange's contributions to the American stage, suggests aspects of her work for further study, and contextualizes Shange's drama within appropriate literary traditions. A thorough and insightful study of Shange's *for colored girls who have considered suicide/ when the rainbow is enuf, Spell #7, A Photograph, Boogie Woogie Landscapes,* and *From Okra to Greens.*

Russell, Sandi. *Render Me My Song: African American Women Writers from Slavery to the Present.* New York: St. Martin's Press, 1990. Supplies a list of Shange's work up to *Betsey Brown.* Good biography and comments on the "choreopoem" format. Discusses the trilogy of plays ending with *A Photograph* and examines Shange's version of Bertolt Brecht's *Mother Courage and Her Children.* Puts Shange in context with Alexis DeVeaux, Rita Dove, and Toni Cade Bambara, writers using blues styles fed by oral traditions, of which *for colored girls who have considered suicide/ when the rainbow is enuf* is exemplary.

Shange, Ntozake, and Emily Mann. "The Birth of an R&B Musical." Interview by Douglas J. Keating. *Inquirer* (Philadelphia), March 26, 1989. Follows the story of how Emily Mann and Shange took Shange's *Betsey Brown* from book to stage, in a long interview with both playwrights to mark the opening of the play at the Forum Theater in Philadelphia, as part of the American Music Theater Festival.

Sommers, Michael. "Rays of Hope in a Sky of Blues." Review of *The Love Space Demands* by Ntozake Shange. *Star-Ledger* (Newark, N.J.), March 12, 1992. This appreciative review of *The Love Space Demands* provides an insightful overview of how Shange takes her poetry to the stage. Sommers finds the work "[a] very accessible, dramatically gripping and altogether handsomely-done theater piece."

"*Spell #7* Takes Us on Magical Trip." Review of *Spell #7* by Ntozake Shange. *Times* (Washington, D.C.), May 9, 1991. This descriptive review of *Spell #7* places the piece in the context of a continuing struggle of black women for a dignified place in society: "After all the tribulations and outpourings of feeling, the lingering message is one of racial pride."

Anne Mills King,
updated by Thomas J. Taylor
and Judith K. Taylor

George Bernard Shaw

Born: Dublin, Ireland; July 26, 1856
Died: Ayot St. Lawrence, Hertfordshire, England; November 2, 1950

Principal drama • *Widowers' Houses*, wr. 1885-1892, pr. 1892, pb. 1893; *Mrs. Warren's Profession*, wr. 1893, pb. 1898, pr. 1902; *The Philanderer*, wr. 1893, pb. 1898, pr. 1905; *Arms and the Man*, pr. 1894, pb. 1898; *Candida: A Mystery*, pr. 1897, pb. 1898; *The Devil's Disciple*, pr. 1897, pb. 1901; *The Man of Destiny*, pr. 1897, pb. 1898; *You Never Can Tell*, pb. 1898, pr. 1899; *Captain Brassbound's Conversion*, pr. 1900, pb. 1901; *Caesar and Cleopatra*, pb. 1901, pr. 1906; *The Admirable Bashville*, pr. 1903, pb. 1909 (based on Shaw's novel *Cashel Byron's Profession*); *Man and Superman*, pb. 1903, pr. 1905; *How He Lied to Her Husband*, pr. 1904, pb. 1907; *John Bull's Other Island*, pr. 1904, pb. 1907; *Major Barbara*, pr. 1905, pb. 1907; *Passion, Poison, and Petrifaction*, pr., pb. 1905; *The Doctor's Dilemma*, pr. 1906, pb. 1911; *The Interlude at the Playhouse*, pr., pb. 1907 (playlet); *Getting Married*, pr. 1908, pb. 1911; *Press Cuttings*, pr., pb. 1909; *The Shewing up of Blanco Posnet*, pr. 1909, pb. 1911; *The Fascinating Foundling*, wr. 1909, pb. 1926, pr. 1928; *The Glimpse of Reality*, wr. 1909, pb. 1926, pr. 1927; *The Dark Lady of the Sonnets*, pr. 1910, pb. 1914; *Misalliance*, pr. 1910, pb. 1914; *Fanny's First Play*, pr. 1911, pb. 1914; *Androcles and the Lion*, pr. 1912 (in German), pr. 1913 (in English), pb. 1916; *Overruled*, pr. 1912, pb. 1916; *Pygmalion*, pb. 1912, pr. 1914 (in English), pr. 1913 (in German); *Beauty's Duty*, wr. 1913, pb. 1932 (playlet); *Great Catherine*, pr. 1913, pb. 1919; *Heartbreak House*, wr. 1913-1919, pb. 1919, pr. 1920; *The Music Cure*, pr. 1914, pb. 1926; *The Inca of Perusalem*, pr. 1916, pb. 1919; *O'Flaherty, V.C.*, pr. 1917, pb. 1919; *Augustus Does His Bit*, pr. 1917, pb. 1919; *Annajanska, the Bolshevik Empress*, pr. 1918, pb. 1919; *Back to Methuselah*, pb. 1921, pr. 1922; *Jitta's Atonement*, pr. 1923, pb. 1926; *Saint Joan*, pr. 1923, pb. 1924; *The Apple Cart*, pr. 1929, pb. 1930; *Too True to Be Good*, pr. 1932, pb. 1934; *How These Doctors Love One Another!*, pb. 1932 (playlet); *On the Rocks*, pr. 1933, pb. 1934; *Village Wooing*, pr., pb. 1934; *The Six Men of Calais*, pr. 1934, pb. 1936; *The Simpleton of the Unexpected Isles*, pr., pb. 1935; *Arthur and Acetone*, pb. 1936; *The Millionairess*, pr., pb. 1936; *Cymbeline Refinished*, pr. 1937, pb. 1938 (adaptation of William Shakespeare's *Cymbeline*, act 5); *Geneva*, pr. 1938, pb. 1939; *In Good King Charles's Golden Days*, pr., pb. 1939; "The British Party System," wr. 1944 (playlet); *Buoyant Billions*, pb. 1947, pr. 1948 (in German), pr. 1949 (in English); *Shakes Versus Shaw*, pr. 1949, pb. 1950; *Far-Fetched Fables*, pr., pb. 1950; *The Bodley Head Bernard Shaw: Collected Plays with Their Prefaces*, pb. 1970-1974 (7 volumes)

Other literary forms • Although George Bernard Shaw is generally thought of as a dramatist, he wrote a considerable amount of nondramatic prose. He completed, for example, several novels before turning to the stage, and even though none of them is likely to be remembered for its own sake, all show Shaw's gift for witty dialogue. His *The Intelligent Woman's Guide to Socialism and Capitalism* (1928), written for his sister-in-law, is one of the clearest expositions of socialism or communism ever written. *The Quintessence of Ibsenism* (1891), *The Perfect Wagnerite* (1898), and *The Sanity of Art* (1908) are representative of his criticism in drama, music, and art, respectively. The prefaces to his plays—some of which are longer than the plays they preface and which often explain little about the plays themselves—are brilliantly written criticisms of everything from the four Gospels to the contemporary prison system.

Other notable Shaw works include *Fabian Essays in Socialism* (1889), *The Common Sense of Municipal Trading* (1904), *Dramatic Opinions and Essays* (1907), *The Adventures of the Black Girl in Her Search for God* (1932), and several collections of letters: *Letters to Miss Alma Murray* (1927), *Ellen Terry and Shaw* (1931), *Correspondence Between George Bernard Shaw and Mrs. Patrick Campbell* (1952), *Collected Letters* (1965-1988, 4 volumes; Dan H. Laurence, editor), and *The Nondramatic Literary Criticism of Bernard Shaw* (1972; Stanley Weintraub, editor).

Achievements • George Bernard Shaw came to an English theater settled into the well-made play, a theater that had not known a first-rate dramatist for more than a century. The pap on which its audiences had been fed, not very different from television fare today, provided a soothing escape from the realities of the working world. Instead of fitting himself to this unreal mold, Shaw offered reality in all its forms: social, political, economic, and religious. He was a didact, a preacher who readily acknowledged that the stage was his pulpit. In startling contrast to his contemporary Oscar Wilde and Wilde's fellow aesthetes, Shaw asserted that he would not commit a single sentence to paper for art's sake alone; yet he beat the aesthetes at their own artistic game. Though he preached socialism, creative evolution, the abolition of prisons, and real equality for women, and railed against the insincerity of motives for war, he did so as a jester in some of the finest comedy ever written. He had no desire to be a martyr and insisted that, though his contemporaries might merely laugh at his plays, "a joke is an earnest in the womb of time." The next generation would get his point, even if the current generation was only entertained.

Many of the next generations have gotten his point, and Shaw's argument—that he who writes for all time will discover that he writes for no time—seems to have been borne out. Only by saying something to the age can one say something to posterity. Today, evolution and creationism and Shaw's ideas on creative evolution and the Life Force remain timely issues. In Shaw's own day, as Dan Laurence points out, Henri Bergson changed the dramatist's Life Force into the *élan vital* four years after Shaw wrote of it in *Man and Superman*, and Pierre Teilhard de Chardin's evolutionary ideas, so appealing to moderns, about the movement of the "noosphere" toward an omega man, show the timeliness of Shaw's evolutionary theory that humankind is in the process of creating a God. Shaw's condemnation of the prison system as a vindictive, not a rehabilitative force, matches the widespread concern with the ineffectiveness of that system today. His struggle for the genuine equality of women with men before the law also gives his work a surprisingly contemporary thrust. Shaw brought serious themes back to the trivialized English stage, creating a body of drama that left him second to none among twentieth century dramatists.

Biography • George Bernard Shaw was born in Dublin, Ireland, at No. 3 Upper Synge Street on July 26, 1856. The house still stands, though the address became 33 Synge Street, and the residence is marked by the surprisingly understated plaque, "Bernard Shaw, author of many plays, was born in this house." Shaw's father was a cheerful drunk, and the son's loss of faith in the father might have affected his faith in general. In any event, though he was baptized into the Church of Ireland, he became a lifelong scoffer at organized religion while always remaining a profoundly religious thinker.

Shaw's mother and sister were fine singers and eventually left Shaw's father to move in with the eccentric music teacher, George Vandeleur Lee. From Lee, Shaw himself learned the voice control that would later stand him in good stead as a public debater. He also learned a great deal from respected uncles: From one, a curate at St. Bride's in Dublin, he learned Latin; another, a ship's surgeon, taught him that the Bible was the greatest pack of lies ever invented.

Shaw left secondary school because of boredom. The Latin he had learned early put him too far ahead of his classmates to make the instruction profitable, and by the time the others caught up, he had lost interest and formed poor study habits. He worked for a firm of land agents before finally leaving Ireland when he was nineteen years old, joining his mother and Vandeleur Lee in London.

For a time after arriving in London, Shaw wrote music criticism that Lee had been commissioned to write but turned over to Shaw. Shaw was later to write music criticism (under the pen name "Corno di Bassetto") that qualified him, in the judgment of W. H. Auden and other observers, as the finest music critic ever. By the time he was twenty-three years old, Shaw was convinced that he could not return to office work, and he began a career as a novelist. He wrote five novels, none of which was immediately published, although later, all but the first novel would find publishers.

Around 1884, Shaw made the acquaintance of William Archer at the British Museum. The meeting launched Shaw on his career as a critic, first as an art critic, then as a music critic (as mentioned above), and finally as a drama critic for more than three years for the *Saturday Review.*

(© The Nobel Foundation)

While Shaw was a struggling novelist and critic, he became a vegetarian and a socialist; both of these causes were to color his writing for the rest of his life. The conversion to vegetarianism came when he was twenty-five years old and under the influence of Percy Bysshe Shelley's Idealism. His conversion to socialism came somewhat later, probably through the influence of a lecture by Henry George and subsequent reading of Karl Marx. In 1884, Shaw helped Beatrice and Sidney Webb found the Fabian Society, a socialist organization later joined by H. G. Wells. When Shaw's nervousness made him stumble badly during a lecture on John Stuart Mill for the society, he determined to make a public speaker of himself by promptly planting his soapbox for socialism in Hyde Park. Considering the extraordinary public speaker and debater Shaw became, it is hard to believe that he began as a young man who was so shy he could not visit a friend without pacing up and down the street trying to gain courage to ring the door bell.

In 1892, the Independent Theatre was about to open and needed plays. Shaw quickly finished *Widowers' Houses*, which he had begun seven years earlier with William Archer. The noted drama critic, however, decided Shaw was no playwright and was never to change his mind. Although Shaw had accepted Archer's opinion at first, he gave the play a second try and began a career that was to continue until 1950.

When Shaw was awarded the Nobel Prize in Literature in 1925, he refused it at first, but, on learning he could donate the money to a fund for popularizing Scandinavian literature, he accepted the award and gave the money away. This award marked the high point of his career, though he was still to write seventeen plays. In September, 1950, Shaw, who seemed on the way to becoming the ageless superman he proclaimed, fell from an apple tree he was pruning. He died in November of that year, of complications stemming from that injury. His ashes were mingled with his wife's and spread on his garden.

Analysis • A religious thinker, George Bernard Shaw saw the stage as his pulpit. His major interest was to advance the Life Force, a kind of immanent Holy Spirit that would help to improve and eventually perfect the world. Shaw believed that to help in this conscious purpose, human beings must live longer in order to use their intellectual maturity. They must be healthier, without the debilitating force of poverty, and—most important—they must be interested in purpose, not simply pleasure. As the giraffe could develop its long neck over aeons because of a need to eat from the tops of trees, so can human beings, with a sense of purpose, work toward the creation of healthier, longer-lived, more intelligent individuals.

According to Shaw, evolution is not merely haphazard but is tied to will. Human beings can know what they want and will what they know. Certainly, individuals cannot simply will that they live longer and expect to do so. Such desire might help, but it is the race, not the individual, that will eventually profit from such a common purpose. Ultimately, Shaw believed, this drive toward a more intelligent and spiritual species would result after aeons in human beings' shucking off matter, which had been taken on by spirit in the world's beginning so that evolution could work toward intelligence. When that intelligence achieves its full potential, matter will no longer be necessary. Humankind is working toward the creation of an infinite God.

Shaw's plays are not restricted to such metaphysics. They treat political, social, and economic concerns: the false notion that people help criminals by putting them in jail or help themselves by atonement (*Major Barbara, Captain Brassbound's Conversion, The Simpleton of the Unexpected Isles*), the need for tolerance (*On the Rocks, Androcles and the Lion*), the superstitious worship of medicine and science (*The Philanderer, The Doctor's Dilemma*), the superiority of socialism to capitalism (*Widowers' Houses, The Apple Cart, The Inca of Perusalem*), the evils of patriotism (*O'Flaherty, V.C., Arms and the Man*), the need for a supranational state (*Geneva*), the necessity for recognizing women's equality with men (*In Good King Charles's Golden Days, Press Cuttings*), and so on. Nevertheless, all of Shaw's efforts to question social and political mores were subsumed by his religious purpose. All were meant to help free the human spirit in its striving toward the creation of a better and more intelligent person, the creation of a superman, the creation, finally, of a God.

Arms and the Man • In 1894, two years after completing his first play, Shaw wrote *Arms and the Man*. Although lighter and less complex than later plays, it is typical of the later plays in that Shaw uses comedy as a corrective—a corrective, as Louis Crompton effectively puts it, that is intended to shame the audience *out* of conformity, in contrast to Molière's, which is intended to shame the audience *into* conformity.

The year is 1885. Bulgaria and Serbia are at war, the Serbs have just been routed, and the play opens with one of the Serbs' officers, Captain Bluntschli, climbing through the window of a Bulgarian house. The house belongs to Major Petkoff, and Raina Petkoff lies dreaming of her lover, a dashing Byronic hero, Sergius Saranoff, who has led the cavalry charge that routed the Serbs. Bluntschli comes into her room, gun in hand, but persuades her not to give him away, more because a fight will ensue while she is not properly dressed than for any fear she has of being shot.

Bluntschli turns out to be Saranoff's opposite. He is a practical Swiss who joined the Serbs merely because they were the first to enlist his services, not because he believed either side to be in the right. When the Bulgarian soldiers enter the house and demand to search Raina's room, she hides Bluntschli on impulse. After the soldiers' departure, he describes for Raina the recent battle in which some quixotic fool led a cavalry charge of frightened men against a battery of machine guns. All were trying to rein in their horses lest they get there first and be killed. The Serbs, however, happened not to have the right ammunition, and what should have been a slaughter of the Bulgarians turned out to be a rout of the Serbs. Yet for his irresponsible foolishness, this "Don Quixote" is sure to be rewarded by the Bulgarians. When Raina shows Bluntschli the picture of her lover, and Saranoff turns out to be "Quixote," Bluntschli is duly embarrassed, tries to cover by suggesting that Saranoff might have known in advance of the Serbs' ammunition problem, but only makes it worse by suggesting to this romantic girl that her lover would have been such a crass pretender and coward as to attack under such conditions.

This is Shaw's first ridicule of chivalric notions of war. The viewpoint is corroborated in the next act by Saranoff when he returns disillusioned because he has not been promoted. He did not follow the scientific rules of war and was thus undeserving. Saranoff has discovered that soldiering is the cowardly art of attacking mercilessly when one is strong and keeping out of harm's way when weak.

In this second act, which takes place at the war's end only four months later, the audience is treated to some satire of Victorian "higher love," which Saranoff carries on with Raina before more realistically flirting with her maid, Louka. Later, in a momentary slip from his chivalric treatment of Raina, Saranoff jokes about a practical Swiss who helped them with arrangements for prisoner exchange and who bragged about having been saved by infatuating a Bulgarian woman and her mother after visiting the young woman in her bedroom. Recognizing herself, Raina chides Saranoff for telling such a crass story in front of her, and he immediately apologizes and reverts to his gallant pose.

Finally in act 3, after Bluntschli has returned for an overcoat and Saranoff discovers that Raina and her mother were the women who saved the Swiss, Saranoff challenges Bluntschli to a duel. Bluntschli, however, will not return the romantic pose and calls Saranoff a blockhead for not realizing that Raina had no other choice at gunpoint. When Saranoff realizes that there is no romance in fighting this prosaic shopkeeper, he backs off. Bluntschli wins Raina's hand, Saranoff wins Louka's, and all ends happily. Yet at the very point at which the audience might expect the play to use its romantic, well-made plot to criticize romanticism, Shaw again changes direction by showing his antihero Bluntschli to be a romantic. To everyone's consternation, Saranoff's in particular, Bluntschli points out that most of his problems have been the result of an incurably romantic disposition: He ran away from home twice as a boy, joined the army rather than his father's business, climbed the balcony of the Petkoff house instead of sensibly diving into the nearest cellar, and came back to this young girl, Raina, to get his coat when any man his age would have sent for it. Thus, Shaw uses *Arms and the Man* not only to attack romanticism about war or love but also to assert the importance of knowing and being true to oneself, to one's life force. It matters little whether Bluntschli is a romantic. He knows and is true to himself. He does not pose and does not deceive himself, as do Saranoff and Raina.

Only one who is true to himself and does not deny himself can attune himself to the Life Force and help advance the evolutionary process. Although Saranoff changes his career when he renounces soldiering, he does so because he was not justly rewarded for his dashing cavalry charge. He does not abandon his habitual self-deception. Even his marriage to the servant girl, Louka, has something of the romantic pose about it; it is rebellious. Raina's marriage to Bluntschli has more potential; at least she has come to see her own posing.

Although the play seems light when set beside the later, more complex triumphs, Shaw's "religious" purpose can be seen here at the beginning of his career. It will be better argued in *Man and Superman* and more fully argued in *Back to Methuselah,* but the failure of the latter, more Utopian work shows that Shaw's religious ideas most engaged his audience when they were rooted in the social, political, or economic criticism of his times, as they were in *Arms and the Man.*

Candida • A year after *Arms and the Man,* Shaw wrote *Candida,* his version of Henrik Ibsen's 1879 play, *Et dukkehjem* (*A Doll's House,* 1880). *Candida* showed that, while Shaw was as much a proponent of equality as was his early mentor, he saw women's usual familial role from an opposite perspective. As Ibsen saw it, women suffer in marriage from being treated like children; a wife is denied the larger responsibilities that are the province of her husband. As a consequence, the wife's personal maturity is arrested. She becomes, in a word, a doll. Shaw did not think this the usual marital paradigm; his view of marriage included a husband who does tend to see himself as the dominant force in the family, but the wife is seldom the petted child that Ibsen's Nora is. Much more frequently, she is like Candida, the real strength of the family, who, like her husband's mother before her, allows her husband to live in a "castle of comfort and indulgence" over which she stands sentinel. She makes him master, though he does not know it. Men, in other words, are more often the petted, indulged children, and women more often the sustaining force in the family.

Candida is set entirely in St. Dominic's Parsonage, and the action is ostensibly a very unoriginal love triangle involving the parson, James Morell, his wife, Candida, and a young poet, Eugene Marchbanks. The originality comes from the unique twist given this stock situation. Morell is a liberal, aggressive preacher, worshiped by women and by his curate. Marchbanks is a shy, effeminate eighteen-year-old, in manner somewhat reminiscent of a young Percy Bysshe Shelley, and he is possessed too of Shelley's inner strength, though this is not immediately apparent. The young poet declares to Morell his love for Candida, Morell's beautiful thirty-three-year-old wife. The self-assured Morell indulges the young man and assures him that the whole world loves Candida; his is another version of puppy love that he will outgrow. The ethereal Marchbanks cannot believe that Morell thinks Candida capable of inspiring such trivial love in him.

He is able, as no one else is, to see that Morell's brilliant sermons and his equally brilliant conversation are nothing but the gift of gab; Morell is an inflated windbag. Marchbanks forces Morell to see himself in this way, and Morell shows that the poet has hit home when he almost throttles him.

Morell broaches the subject of Marchbanks's love to Candida, at the young man's insistence, and Candida assures her husband that she already knows Eugene is in love with her. She is surprised, however, to find Morell upset by it. Nevertheless, the two foolish men force a crisis by making Candida choose between them. When she plays their game and asks what each has to offer, Morell offers his strength for her defense, his honesty for her surety, his industry for her livelihood, and his authority and position for her dignity. Eugene offers his weakness and desolation.

Candida, bemused that neither offers love and that each wishes to own her, acknowledges that the poet has made a good offer. She informs them that she will give herself, because of his need, to the weaker of the two. Morell is desolate, but Eugene is, too, since he realizes that Candida means Morell. Eugene leaves with the now famous "secret in his heart." The secret the poet knows is that he can live without happiness, that there is another love than that of woman—the love of purpose.

The twist Shaw gives the standard triangle, then, is not merely that the effeminate young poet is stronger than the commanding figure of Morell, but also that Candida is stronger than both. Morell is clearly the doll in this house. Even so, to identify Shaw with Marchbanks, as his fine biographer Archibald Henderson does, makes little sense. Marchbanks is an aesthete like Wilde or the young William Butler Yeats, and the poetic sentiments he expresses to Candida sound very like Shelley's *Epipsychidion*. Shaw, who did not share Shelley's rapture about romantic love and who liked aestheticism so little that he swore he would not face the toil of writing a single sentence for art's sake alone, clearly cannot be confused with Marchbanks. He has more in common with Morell, who is socialistic and industrious. It is Morell who voices Shaw's sentiments when he tells Marchbanks that people have no more right to consume happiness without producing it than they have to consume wealth without producing it. The character in this play who comes closest to Shaw, however, is Candida herself. Much stronger than Ibsen's Nora, she is the only character who does not deceive herself. Morell does not realize that he needs to be coddled in order to play his role as a dynamic, liberal clergyman. Only at the play's end and with Candida's help, does Marchbanks discover the truth she has known all along.

Candida is subtitled *A Mystery*, and, though Shaw is treating a dramatic convention with humor, there is perhaps a more serious sense in which he uses the subtitle: There is some mystery involved in the ties that bind people together in marriage. In the climactic scene, in which Candida is made to choose between the two men, a traditional dramatist might have demonstrated the lover to be a cad and have thrown him out. A more romantic dramatist would have shown the husband to be a tyrant and had the wife and lover elope. Shaw chooses neither solution. He has the wife remain with the husband, but not because the lover is a cad or because she owes it to her husband contractually or for any of the standard reasons Morell offers, but because he needs her and she loves him. In this mystery about what binds partners in marriage, Shaw seems to suggest that it is not the contract, still less any ideal of purity, but simply mutual love and need.

What connects *Candida* with *Arms and the Man*, as well as with the later plays, is the demand that persons be true to themselves. Morell taught Candida to think for herself, she tells him, but it upsets him when that intellectual independence leads to conclusions different from his own. Candida will not submit to Christian moralism any more than she will to poetic romanticism. If there is any salvation for Marchbanks, it is that he has learned from Candida the secret that lies hidden in his heart: He is not dependent on happiness or on the love of a woman. In becoming aware of this, he has the potential to be a true artist, one attuned to purpose and not to self-indulgence. Thus, the play leads to the more lengthy dramatization of the struggle between the philosopher-artist and the woman-mother that is evident in *Man and Superman.*

Man and Superman • *Man and Superman* promotes Shaw's philosophy of the Life Force more explicitly than do any of his previous plays. Indeed, much of the play is given to discussion, particularly during the long dream sequence in act 3; Shaw never thought that a play's action need be physical. The dynamics of argument, of intellectual and verbal exchange, were for Shaw much more exciting than conventional action.

The drama originated in a suggestion by Arthur Bingham Walkley that Shaw write a Don Juan play. After all, did not Shaw suffer as a playwright from an excess of cerebration and a lack of physicality? Surely, Walkley reasoned, the subject of the amours of Don Juan would force him off his soapbox and into the boudoir. In response to this challenge, Shaw wrote a much more cerebral play than he had ever written before. In his lengthy "Epistle Dedicatory" to Walkley, Shaw explains why. The essence of the Don Juan legend is not, like Casanova's, that its hero is an "oversexed tomcat." Rather, its essence lies in Juan's following his own instincts rather than law or convention.

The play is as diffuse and difficult to stage as *Candida* is concise and delightful to produce. Most of the difficulty has to do with the lengthy Don Juan in Hell dream sequence during act 3, which causes the play to run more than four hours. More often than not, the sequence has been separated from the play. Not until 1964, in fact, when the Association of Producing Artists staged the play at New York City's Phoenix Theatre was the entire play produced in the United States.

As the delightful first act opens, Ann Whitefield has lost her father, and everyone is waiting to learn from the will who her guardian will be. Roebuck Ramsden, close friend of her father and self-styled liberal, is the leading candidate and is at the moment lecturing Ann's young suitor, Octavius, on his friend, Jack Tanner, who is not fit to be seen with Octavius, much less with Ann. Tanner has scandalized this Victorian liberal by his newly published "The Revolutionist's Handbook," whose entire text Shaw appends to the play. "The Revolutionist's Handbook" is a didact's device for getting across some of the ideas that would have been unpalatable in the play, as when Tanner argues (here without opposition) that the Life Force would be served better if people were given more freedom in mating. That is to say, people who might not be compatible as marriage partners might nevertheless produce the finest offspring.

When Tanner appears, the audience is delighted by his wit. He good-humoredly but repeatedly scandalizes Ramsden, particularly when he announces that he and Ramsden have been named joint guardians of Ann. Tanner is not eager to undertake his role; he knows how manipulative Ann can be, but he does not yet recognize what even his chauffeur could have told him: Ann has designs on him and not on his friend, Octavius. Ann is in the grip of the Life Force, which drives all women in their capacity as mothers to want to reproduce, and she implicitly knows that Tanner would be the proper father for her offspring, not the romantic but spiritually flabby young Octavius.

Tanner, however, is Shaw's philosopher-artist and, as such, Tanner knows that he must flee the stifling bliss of marriage and domesticity to pursue his own purpose—something that Marchbanks learned at the end of *Candida*.

When Tanner learns of Ann's designs, he flees to Spain. Here, he and his chauffeur are captured by a group of brigands led by an Englishman named Mendoza. While captive, Tanner dreams the lengthy dream that constitutes the Don Juan in Hell scene. The scene is a brilliant debate involving Don Juan (looking like John Tanner), the Devil (looking like Mendoza), Doña Ana (looking remarkably like Ann Whitefield), and Ana's father, Don Gonzalo (looking like Roebuck Ramsden). The debate centers on the relative merits of Heaven and Hell. Doña Ana, "a good Catholic," is astonished to find herself a newcomer to Hell and has to have it explained to her that some of the best company are here. One can go to Heaven if he or she wishes, but one must remember that the gulf between the two is really a matter of natural inclination or temperament. Hell is a place for those in whom enjoyment predominates over purpose, desires over reason, the heart over the head, the aesthetic over the ideological, and romance over realism.

Don Juan is about to depart for Heaven because he is sick of the Devil's cant about the aesthetic values, the enjoyment of music, the pleasures of the heart. An eternity of enjoyment is an intolerable bore. He wishes not to enjoy life but to help it in its struggle upward. The reason Juan went to Hell to begin with was that he thought he was a pleasure-seeker, but he has discovered, as Shaw indicates in the dedicatory epistle, that his amours were more a form of rebellion than of pleasure-seeking. Realizing that he is temperamentally a philosophical man, who seeks to learn in contemplation the inner will of the world, to discover in invention the means of achieving that will, and to follow in action those means, he prefers Heaven.

The dream sequence is also concerned with woman's maternal role in advancing the Life Force. If it seems, at first glance, that the ardent feminist who authored *Candida* has here turned his coat and relegated women to a merely sexual role, it must be remembered that for the moment Shaw is speaking only of one side of woman. When Ana corrects Don Juan's view of woman's mind, he points out to her that he speaks not of woman's whole mind but only of her view of man as a separate sex. Only sexually is woman's nature a contrivance for perpetuating its highest achievement. She too can be the philosopher-artist attuned to the work of advancing the Life Force. Thus, two ways of achieving the inner will of the world are open to her.

In the fourth and final act, having awakened from his dreams, Tanner shows that he is not yet as forceful as his ancestor, Don Juan, when he gives in to Ann's superior force and agrees to marry her. Ironically, the romantic Octavius is the one who resigns himself to bachelorhood.

The play, then, is a philosophical comedy whose theme is that the Life Force is dependent on man and woman if it is to move creation upward. A man or woman possessed of a sense of purpose must attune himself or herself to the Life Force, since the only true joy lies in being used for its purposes, in being willing to burn oneself out and heap oneself on the scrap pile at the end without any promise of a personal reward. Although a number of critics see Tanner as the epitome of Shavian man, Tanner does capitulate to Ann. He lacks the fiber of Don Juan, who realizes the boredom of a life of pleasure. Indeed, Marchbanks of *Candida* is more truly Shavian than Tanner.

Notwithstanding Shaw's overt didacticism in this play, he is true to his belief that, like the Ancient Mariner, he must tell his tale entertainingly if he is to hold the attention of the wedding guest. Consequently, he claims full responsibility for the opinions of Don Juan but claims equal responsibility for those of the other characters. For the dramatic moment, each character's viewpoint is also Shaw's. Those who believe there is an absolutely right point of view, he says in the "Epistle Dedicatory," usually believe it is their own and cannot, in consequence, be true dramatists.

Major Barbara • In *Major Barbara*, published not long after *Man and Superman*, Shaw's dramatic means of advancing his theory of the Life Force was to assert that poverty was the world's greatest evil. What critics, even astute ones such as G. K. Chesterton, thought materialistic in Shaw, the author would insist was spiritual. Only with money could one save one's soul.

Major Barbara opens in the home of Lady Britomart Undershaft, whose estranged millionaire husband has been invited to the house for the first time since the children, now adults, were toddlers. Her purpose in inviting this scandalous old atheist to her house is to get more money for her daughters, Barbara and Sarah, who are about to marry. Moreover, she would like Andrew Undershaft to break the ridiculous custom of having the Undershaft munitions business go to an orphan and instead give it to his own son, Stephen. When Undershaft meets his family, he is favorably impressed by Barbara, who is a major in the Salvation Army, and by Adolphus Cusins, her suitor, who is a professor of Greek. He recognizes that Stephen is hopelessly inept and that Charles Lomax, Sarah's young man, is less pompous than Stephen but no less foolish. Barbara invites her father to West Ham so that he might see the constructive work of the Salvation Army, and he agrees, provided that she come to see his munitions plant at Perivale St. Andrews. Thus, the play's structure is neatly determined, with a second act at West Ham and a third at Perivale St. Andrews.

In act 2, Barbara shows her father the Salvation Army's good work, only to learn from her father and the Army's Commissioner, Mrs. Baines, the painful fact that the Army—like all religious organizations—depends on contributions from whiskey distillers and munitions owners such as her father. When Barbara is told that the Army could not subsist without this "tainted" money, she realizes that she is not changing the essential condition of the poor but simply keeping them alive with a bowl of soup; she is helping the capitalists justify themselves with conscience money. She thus serves capital rather than God.

When in act 3 the family visits the munitions factory, Undershaft surprisingly reveals the existence of a model socialist community at Perivale St. Andrews. Though Undershaft lives off the need of people to conduct war, he accepts that need and uses it to destroy society's greatest evil, poverty. In his community, all men work, earn a decent wage, and can thus turn to matters of the soul, such as religion, without being bribed to do so. Since Barbara has come to realize that religious organizations exist by selling themselves to the rich, she decides to get Peter Shirley a job rather than feed him and ask him to pray in thanksgiving at West Ham. She herself joins her father's model village, especially since Cusins is conveniently discovered to be an orphan and the ideal person to inherit the munitions factory.

Shaw's lengthy preface to the play sets out a good deal of his ethical philosophy: Poverty is the worst evil against which man struggles; religious people should work for the betterment of the one world they have and not turn from it for a vision of private bliss in the hereafter. The world will never be bettered by people who believe that they can atone for their sins and who do not understand that their misdeeds are irrevocable. While society should divide wealth equally, no adult should receive his allowance unless he or she produces by personal exertion more than he or she consumes. Society should not punish those guilty of crime, especially by putting them in prisons that render them worse, but neither should it hesitate to put to death anyone whose misconduct is incorrigible, just as people would not hesitate to destroy a mad dog.

Though these ideas are familiar to Shavians, and though most of them are fleshed out in the play itself, *Major Barbara* may first take a reader by surprise. Can the pacifist and socialist Shaw be making a hero of a capitalist who makes his living on the profits of warfare? It is not enough to answer that the capitalist uses his capital to create an ideal socialist community; for this, Shaw could have chosen a banker. On the contrary, he deliberately chooses a munitions manufacturer because the irony helps make his point. However horrid warfare is, it is not so horrid as poverty. Undershaft tells Barbara and Cusins in the final act that poverty is the worst of crimes, for it blights whole cities, spreads pestilence, and strikes dead any souls within its compass. Barbara cannot save souls in West Ham by words and dreams, but if she gives a West Ham ruffian thirty-eight shillings a week, with a sound house in a handsome street and a permanent job, she will save his soul.

When Barbara turns from the Salvation Army to Undershaft's community at Perivale St. Andrews, she is not giving up religion. She is turning, Shaw would have it, from a phony religion dependent on a bribe to the poor and on the maintenance of inequitable present conditions, to a genuine religion that will bring significant social change. Her conversion is completely consistent with her character. When her father asks her to tell Cusins what power is, she answers that before joining the Salvation Army, she was in her own power and, as a consequence, did not know what to do with herself. Once she joined the Army, she thought herself in the power of God and did not have enough time for all that needed to be done. Undershaft helps her to transfer this commitment to a more realistic cause, which will genuinely improve the lot of the poor, but a cause that is still essentially spiritual.

Because Undershaft sees his work in the same light as Barbara sees hers, he can insist that he is not a secularist but a confirmed mystic. Perivale St. Andrews is driven by a will of which he is a part. Thus, once again, Shaw's hero is chosen because he is attuned to the Life Force. It matters little that he is a munitions maker. In *Saint Joan*, the heroine is a saint, yet she is chosen not as a representative of Christian orthodoxy but because she was mystic enough to see that she served a will greater than her own.

In *Major Barbara*, Shaw also makes use of a host of lesser characters to dramatize his political, moral, and ethical theories. When Stephen Undershaft is asked by his father what he is able to do in life, so that Undershaft can give him a fair start, he makes it evident that he is capable of nothing, except—he asserts defensively—of knowing the difference between good and evil, something he implies his father does not know. With this, Undershaft has great fun. Stephen knows nothing of law, of business, of art, or of philosophy, yet he claims to know the secret that has baffled philosophers for ages. Because Stephen knows nothing but claims to know everything, Undershaft declares him fit for politics. To this remark, Stephen takes exception; he will not hear his father insult his country's government. Undershaft once again, however, reflects Shaw's conviction that big business rules government when he sputters, "The government of your country! I am the government of your country."

Peter Shirley, rather than Barbara, provides the real contrast with Undershaft. Barbara shares her father's "heavenly" temper, his sense of purpose. The Army shares with him the recognition that it needs money. Peter Shirley, the unemployed visitor at

West Ham, plays Lazarus to Undershaft's Dives, as Shaw puts it. Because the majority of the world believes that an "honest" poor man such as Shirley is morally superior to a "wicked" rich one such as Undershaft, the misery of the world continues. It is significant that when Undershaft gives Shirley a job, the man is unhappy.

Bill Walker, who beats up an old woman visiting the West Ham shelter and then a young woman member of the Army itself, tries to atone by having himself beaten up in turn by a professional boxer, Todger Fermile. Such a grotesque instance of atonement is no more grotesque than any other attempt at atonement, Shaw believes, and both Barbara and Cusins agree with Undershaft that one cannot atone for evil; one does good only by changing evil ways. It can be argued, as in the case of many other Shavian criticisms of Christianity, that Shaw did not understand the Christian doctrine. Perhaps, however, he understood *de facto* Christianity all too well.

Adolphus Cusins also plays a significant role in the drama, certainly the most significant after those of Undershaft and Barbara, and he eventually takes over the munitions factory. A man of greater intelligence and more humane sympathies than Undershaft, he may be the hope for the Life Force taking a significant step forward. Undershaft repeatedly refers to this professor of Greek as "Dionysius," which suggests in Cusins a capacity to stand outside himself to achieve union with the Life Force. Clearly, Undershaft invites him to make war on war when he turns over the munitions works to him.

Major Barbara is perhaps freighted with too much paradox to do its job convincingly. Certainly, act 1 is sparkling comedy as Undershaft meets his family without knowing who is who. Moreover, the contrast between Undershaft's "gospel" and Barbara's is convincingly set forth. Act 2 is occasionally excellent comedy, and comedy fused with meaning, as when Barbara deals with the bully Bill Walker, but Walker's part becomes a bit too obtrusive a vehicle for attacking atonement, and Undershaft's demonstration of how all religious organizations exist by selling themselves to the rich is somewhat more asserted than dramatized. Perhaps the concluding act is the least successful, since Barbara's and Cusins's conversion is necessarily hurried to preserve the unities, and Shaw has difficulty making his Utopia convincing, a difficulty he later experienced more keenly in *Back to Methuselah*. To do Shaw justice, he acknowledged that, while one can know that the Life Force is driving upward, one cannot know precisely how. Thus, attempts to dramatize future points of progress in creative evolution present insuperable obstacles.

Saint Joan • More than in *Major Barbara* and perhaps more than in *Man and Superman*, Shaw found in *Saint Joan* a fit medium to dramatize his major religious ideas. He had intended to write a play about Christ, but he was not permitted to portray divinity on the English stage. Yet no play by Shaw succeeds more unobtrusively in carrying his ideas about the Life Force. As captivating a play as *Major Barbara* is, Undershaft has straw men with whom to do battle, and, though such was not the case in *Man and Superman*, Shaw needed for his purposes the lengthy dream sequence that has made the play so difficult to stage. *Candida* might be a more perfectly structured play, but it does not carry so much of Shaw's mature philosophy. Among Shaw's major dramas, then, *Saint Joan* is perhaps the finest blend of matter and form.

Saint Joan is divided into six scenes and an epilogue. In the first scene, Joan appeals to Robert de Baudricourt for horse and armor to aid in the siege of Orleans and to see to the coronation of the Dauphin. Although he at first scoffs at this request, made through his servant, when faced with Joan, he is persuaded by the strength of her person, as everyone else is. In scene 2, the courtiers try to dupe her and pretend that Gilles de Rais is the Dauphin. Not taken in, she carries the Dauphin, too, by her force of persuasion and convinces this weakling that he, too, has a divine mission that he must be strong enough to accept. In scene 3, Joan joins Dunois, the leader of the French forces, and under their combined leadership, France enjoys a series of victories. In scene 4, the Earl of Warwick and the Bishop of Beauvais plan Joan's eventual execution. The Englishman wants her dead for obvious military reasons; the Frenchman, because she is a dangerous heretic. In scene 5, she is told to give up fighting, that there is no need for more victories. She is told to let the English have Paris. Her sense of destiny, however, convinces her that the English must be driven from French soil.

In scene 6, Joan has been arrested. She is given by the Inquisition what Shaw considers a fairer trial than is available to defendants today. She finally recants what the clergymen consider her heresy, but when told that she must remain forever in prison as punishment for her spiritual offenses, she tears up her recantation and goes to the stake under Warwick's authority. The epilogue gets the play back into the comic frame and allows Joan and the rest of the cast of characters to appear twenty-five years later before Charles, now King, and discuss the Church's recent reversal in favor of Joan. There is even a time-shift of several centuries, to the year 1920, so that Joan's canonization can be mentioned. Yet the epilogue ultimately suggests that, were she to return to France in the twentieth century, Joan would again be put to death by the very people who now praise her.

The greatness of *Saint Joan* lies in its scrupulous dramatization of a universal problem. The problem of how one reconciles the dictates of the individual conscience with the demands of authority is one without easy solutions, whether the individual stands against ecclesiastical, civil, military, or familial authority. The sympathy Shaw extends to Joan in declaring her one of the first "Protestant" saints he extends also to the Inquisitors, who, he asserts, tried Joan more fairly than they themselves were later tried when the judgment on Joan was reversed.

Shaw's fairness is evident in scene 4, for example, when Peter Cauchon makes clear to the Earl of Warwick that, even though both men want Joan captured, they differ in every other respect. Cauchon, Bishop of Beauvais, does not believe that Joan is a witch and will not allow Warwick to get rid of her on this trumped-up charge. Joan is a heretic, much more dangerous than a witch, but he would prefer to save her soul. She is a pious and honest girl who, through pride, is caught up in the Devil's mighty purpose: to wrack the Church with discord and dissension—the same purpose for which the Devil used John Huss and John Wycliffe. If a reformer will not finally effect reform within the pale of Church authority, every crackpot who sees visions will be followed by the naïve populace, and the Church will be wrecked beyond repair.

These arguments are completely familiar to the present age, in which soldiers are told they must obey commanding officers who order the extinction of noncombatants. Can one obey such orders? Yet there surely must be obedience to authority, despite doubts about its wisdom, or there will be anarchy. Humankind has come no closer to finding a solution to the tensions between individual conscience and authority than it had in Joan's day, and it is that insoluble problem that forces audiences to move beyond easy condemnation of the Inquisition and equally easy sanctification of Joan.

Critics have often objected to Shaw's epilogue on the ground that Joan's tragedy is trivialized by it, yet the epilogue is necessary for Shaw's theme: that from the same elements, the same tragedy would come again. The trial at which Joan's judges were judged and she was exonerated was a much more unscrupulous affair than was Joan's trial. Ladvenu, who had been the most sympathetic of those who tried Joan, tells King Charles that the old trial was faultless in every respect except in its unjust verdict, while the new trial is filled with perjury and corruption yet results in a just verdict. Charles, who is concerned only about his having been crowned by a woman who was considered a witch and a heretic, and who is relieved now by having his reign validated, asserts that no matter what the verdict, were Joan brought back to life, her present admirers would burn her within six months.

In his preface, Shaw argues that there was no inconsistency in the Church's reversal on Joan. Although the Roman Catholic Church does not defer to private judgment, it recognizes that the highest wisdom may come to an individual through private revelation and that, on sufficient evidence, the Church will eventually declare such an individual a saint. Thus, many saints have been at odds with the Church before their canonization. In fact, Shaw contends, had Francis of Assisi lived longer, he might have gone to the stake, while Galileo might yet be declared a saint. Thus, the epilogue helps dramatize the complexity inherent in Joan's struggle with the Church.

In none of the plays discussed—perhaps nowhere else in his canon, with the possible exception of *Caesar and Cleopatra*—does Shaw present an example of a character in the grip of the Life Force so convincingly as he does in the character of Joan. Bluntschli is an amusing soldier-adventurer; Marchbanks, a callow poet; Tanner, a failed revolutionary; and Undershaft, a munitions maker who has built a socialist community. Joan is both a Christian and a Shavian saint. She is caught up in a sense of purpose to a degree none of Shaw's other characters is. *Saint Joan*, then, is the culmination of Shaw's art. Although other plays might embrace more of his standard literary and philosophical obsessions, none takes his most central obsessions, those relating to the Life Force and creative evolution, and fleshes them out with such dramatic integrity.

Other major works

LONG FICTION: *Cashel Byron's Profession*, 1886; *An Unsocial Socialist*, 1887; *Love Among the Artists*, 1900; *The Irrational Knot*, 1905; *Immaturity*, 1930.

SHORT FICTION: *The Adventures of the Black Girl in Her Search for God*, 1932.

NONFICTION: *The Quintessence of Ibsenism*, 1891; *The Perfect Wagnerite*, 1898; *The Common Sense of Municipal Trading*, 1904; *Dramatic Opinions and Essays*, 1907; *The Sanity of Art*, 1908 (revised from 1895 serial publication); *Letters to Miss Alma Murray*, 1927; *The Intelligent Woman's Guide to Socialism and Capitalism*, 1928; *Ellen Terry and Shaw*, 1931; *Everybody's Political What's What*, 1944; *Sixteen Self Sketches*, 1949; *Correspondence Between George Bernard Shaw and Mrs. Patrick Campbell*, 1952; *The Matter with Ireland*, 1961; *Platform and Pulpit*, 1961 (Dan H. Laurence, editor); *Collected Letters*, 1965-1988 (4 volumes; Laurence, editor); *An Autobiography, 1856-1898*, 1969; *An Autobiography, 1898-1950*, 1970; *The Nondramatic Literary Criticism of Bernard Shaw*, 1972 (Stanley Weintraub, editor); *Shaw: Interviews and Recollections*, 1990 (A. M. Gibbs, editor); *Bernard Shaw's Book Reviews*, 1991 (Brian Tyson, editor).

EDITED TEXT: *Fabian Essays in Socialism*, 1889.

MISCELLANEOUS: *Works*, 1930-1938 (33 volumes); *Short Stories, Scraps, and Shavings*, 1932; *Works*, 1947-1952 (36 volumes).

Bibliography

Davis, Tracy C. *George Bernard Shaw and the Socialist Theatre*. Westport, Conn.: Greenwood Press, 1994. Davis examines Shaw's belief in socialism and how it affected and was demonstrated in his dramatic works. Bibliography and index.

Dukore, Bernard Frank. *Shaw's Theater.* Gainesville: University Presses of Florida, 2000. Part of the Florida Bernard Shaw series, this volume explores the production of Shaw's dramatic works. Bibliography and index.

Holroyd, Michael. *The Search for Love, 1856-1898.* Vol. 1 in *Bernard Shaw.* New York: Random House, 1988. In this superb beginning to his authoritative biography, Holroyd describes Shaw's Irish origins and trials of following his mother to London. His journalistic and musical career is interwoven with various love affairs, culminating in marriage in 1898. Sensitive analyses of political and aesthetic ideas are balanced with insights into early drama. Includes illustrations, a bibliographic note, and an index.

_____. *The Pursuit of Power, 1898-1918.* Vol. 2 in *Bernard Shaw.* New York: Random House, 1989. Describes the complicated interrelationships of Shaw's middle plays (from *Caesar and Cleopatra* to *Heartbreak House*) with ethics, politics, economics, medicine, religion, and war. The popularity of his drama is explained and analyzed, while the sophistication of his personality is narrated through his friendships with such persons as G. K. Chesterton, H. G. Wells, and Mrs. Patrick Campbell. Illustrations, index.

_____. *The Lure of Fantasy, 1918-1950.* Vol. 3 in *Bernard Shaw.* New York: Random House, 1991. The final volume covers Shaw's drama from *Saint Joan,* with late plays such as *Geneva* and *In Good King Charles's Golden Days* receiving balanced attention. Also surveys Shaw's films from his plays, including *Pygmalion* and *Major Barbara.* Shaw's interest in communism and the Soviet Union receives attention, as does his criticism of American culture. Illustrations, bibliographic note, and index.

Innes, Christopher, ed. *The Cambridge Companion to George Bernard Shaw.* New York: Cambridge University Press, 1998. This reference work in the Cambridge series provides an in-depth look at Bernard Shaw's life, works, and philosophy. Bibliography and index.

Larson, Gale K., ed. *Shaw: Volume 21 in the Annual Bernard Shaw Series.* University Park: Pennsylvania State University Press, 2001. This collection of essays is part of an annual series that examines various aspects of Shaw. This volume contains essays on Shaw's stagecraft, Shaw's and Mark Twain's revisions of Genesis, and Shaw in Sinclair Lewis's writings. Bibliography.

Lenker, Lagretta Tallent. *Fathers and Daughters in Shakespeare and Shaw.* Westport, Conn.: Greenwood Press, 2001. Lenker examines the fathers and daughters portrayed in the plays of William Shakespeare and Shaw. Bibliography and index.

Henry J. Donaghy,
updated by Richard D. McGhee

Sam Shepard

Samuel Shepard Rogers VII

Born: Fort Sheridan, Illinois; November 5, 1943

Principal drama • *Cowboys*, pr. 1964 (one act); *The Rock Garden*, pr. 1964, pb. 1972 (one act); *Up to Thursday*, pr. 1964; *Chicago*, pr. 1965, pb. 1967; *Dog*, pr. 1965; *Icarus's Mother*, pr. 1965, pb. 1967; *Rocking Chair*, pr. 1965; *4-H Club*, pr. 1965, pb. 1971; *Fourteen Hundred Thousand*, pr. 1966, pb. 1967; *Melodrama Play*, pr. 1966, pb. 1967; *Red Cross*, pr. 1966, pb. 1967; *La Turista*, pr. 1966, pb. 1968; *Cowboys #2*, pr. 1967, pb. 1971; *Forensic and the Navigators*, pr. 1967, pb. 1969; *The Unseen Hand*, pr., pb. 1969; *Operation Sidewinder*, pb. 1969, pr. 1970; *Shaved Splits*, pr. 1969, pb. 1971; *The Holy Ghostly*, pr. 1970, pb. 1971; *Back Bog Beast Bait*, pr., pb. 1971; *Cowboy Mouth*, pr., pb. 1971 (with Patti Smith); *The Mad Dog Blues*, pr. 1971, pb. 1972; *Nightwalk*, pr., pb. 1972 (with Megan Terry and Jean-Claude van Itallie); *The Tooth of Crime*, pr. 1972, pb. 1974; *Action*, pr. 1974, pb. 1975; *Geography of a Horse Dreamer*, pr., pb. 1974; *Little Ocean*, pr. 1974; *Killer's Head*, pr. 1975, pb. 1976; *The Sad Lament of Pecos Bill on the Eve of Killing His Wife*, pr. 1975, pb. 1983; *Angel City*, pr., pb. 1976; *Curse of the Starving Class*, pb. 1976, pr. 1977; *Suicide in B Flat*, pr. 1976, pb. 1979; *Buried Child*, pr. 1978, pb. 1979; *Seduced*, pr. 1978, pb. 1979; *Tongues*, pr. 1978, pb. 1981; *Savage/Love*, pr. 1979, pb. 1981; *True West*, pr. 1980, pb. 1981; *Fool for Love*, pr., pb. 1983; *A Lie of the Mind*, pr. 1985, pb. 1986; *States of Shock*, pr. 1991, pb. 1992; *Simpatico*, pr. 1994, pb. 1995; *Plays,* pb. 1996-1997 (3 volumes); *When the World Was Green*, pr. 1996, pb. 2002 (with Joseph Chaikin); *Eyes for Consuela*, pr. 1998, pb. 1999; *The Late Henry Moss*, pr. 2000, pb. 2002

Other literary forms • Sam Shepard has written a number of screenplays, including the ill-fated *Zabriskie Point* (1970) for Michelangelo Antonioni and the award-winning *Paris, Texas* (1984). He also wrote and directed *Far North* (1988) and *Silent Tongue* (1994). Shepard has also written poetry and short fiction, in *Hawk Moon: A Book of Short Stories, Poems, and Monologues* (1973) and *Motel Chronicles* (1982), and recorded the major events of Bob Dylan's Rolling Thunder Revue tour in a collection of essays titled *Rolling Thunder Logbook* (1977).

Achievements • Sam Shepard is one of the United States' most prolific, most celebrated, and most honored playwrights. Writing exclusively for the Off-Broadway and Off-Off-Broadway theater, Shepard has nevertheless won eleven Obie Awards (for *Red Cross, Chicago, Icarus's Mother, Forensic and the Navigators, La Turista, Melodrama Play, Cowboys #2, The Tooth of Crime, Curse of the Starving Class, Buried Child,* and *Fool for Love*). In 1979, he received a Pulitzer Prize for *Buried Child*. His screenplay for Wim Wenders's film *Paris, Texas* won the Palme d'Or at the Cannes Film Festival, and Shepard himself received an Oscar nomination for his portrayal of Colonel Chuck Yeager in *The Right Stuff* (1983). *A Lie of the Mind* was named the outstanding new play of the 1985-1986 season by the Drama Desk. In 1998 Public Broadcasting Service's (PBS) *Great Performances* devoted an hour-long TV program to Shepard's life and plays.

Biography • Born Samuel Shepard Rogers VII, on an army base in Fort Sheridan, Illinois, on November 5, 1943, Sam Shepard's early years were marked by repeated moves from one place to another: South Dakota, Utah, Florida, Guam, and eventually Southern California. Shepard's father was severely wounded during World War II, became an alcoholic, and progressively withdrew from the family until he became a desert-dwelling, storytelling recluse. Shepard recalls that his mother, Jane Schook Rogers, would fire her army-issued Luger pistol at the Japanese soldiers sneaking out of the jungle on Guam in the years following World War II. After Shepard's father retired from the army, the family moved to an avocado ranch in the San Bernardino valley in Southern California, where Shepard spent his adolescent years. In 1962, Shepard joined a barnstorming acting company with a religiously based repertory, the Bishop's Repertory Company. When the company reached New York, Shepard, nineteen years old, dropped out of the company and into the Lower East Side bohemian lifestyle, busing tables at the Village Gate, dabbling with acting, doing drugs, and running the streets with Charles Mingus, Jr., an old California friend.

In 1964, the twin bill of Shepard's first two plays, the original *Cowboys* and *The Rock Garden*, premiered at one of Off-Off-Broadway's most important theaters, Theater Genesis, and Shepard's career was launched. Shepard wrote prolifically for the Off-Off-Broadway theater during the last half of the 1960's, gaining recognition and critical acclaim with each play, many of which contained made-to-order parts for his girlfriend, Joyce Aaron. By 1967, Shepard had gathered three Obie Awards, produced his first full-length play, and could boast of plays being produced on the West Coast, in New York, and in London. In 1969, Shepard married O-Lan Johnson (they had one son, Jesse Mojo), the actress who played the eponymous Oolan in *Forensic and the Navigators*.

The following year, however, brought many difficulties for Shepard: *Operation Sidewinder* was produced at the Vivian Beaumont Theater at New York's Lincoln Center, but the frustrations posed by an expensive Broadway production and the generally unfavorable reaction to the play prompted Shepard to return to Off-Off-Broadway. Further, Shepard's romance with the emerging rock star Patti Smith severely taxed his nascent domestic life. Finally, losing patience with the New York theater scene, Shepard and his family moved to London in 1972. On his return to the United States in 1976, Shepard joined Bob Dylan on his Rolling Thunder Revue Tour and then moved to San Francisco, where he began working with Joseph Chaikin and the Magic

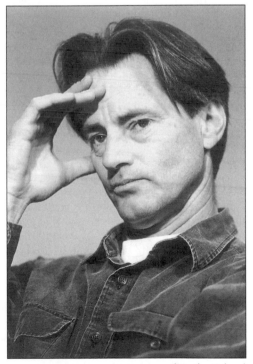

(Martha Holmes)

Theatre. The move to California also marked the beginning of Shepard's career as a film star; his portrayal of Colonel Chuck Yeager in *The Right Stuff* earned for him an Oscar nomination. While on the set of the film *Frances* (1982), Shepard met Jessica Lange; they later bought a ranch together in New Mexico and subsequently moved to Virginia and later to Minnesota. Shepard and Lange had two children together.

Analysis • Nearly all Sam Shepard's plays examine the functions (and dysfunctions) of the relationships between individuals that constitute either family structures or social structures that approximate family structures—close friendships or tight-knit business alliances. The conflict between the two halves of what can be considered a single unit (brother and brother, father and son, husband and wife, boyfriend and girlfriend) as they struggle either for supremacy or for survival amid surrounding pressures can be found at the core of most of Shepard's plays. Further, his principal characters tend not only to be alienated from their immediate circumstances but also to be victimized by their drive toward a destructive self-isolation. The wake of devastation left by figures who are incapable of bridging the abysses they have created shapes the central conflict in many of Shepard's plays.

The pulsating rhythms of those conflicts can be tracked through Shepard's unique use of dramatic language. Instead of the series of natural exchanges between characters found in plays constructed on the principle of mimetic realism, the language in Shepard's plays reflects his extensive musical background. His dialogue ranges from realistic banter to highly metaphoric and figurative speech, to the beat and patter of rock and roll, to free-form, yet highly complex, jazz-like improvisational riffs. Characters frequently disrupt the flow of the dialogue with abrupt shifts in voice (such as Hoss's switch from the street talk of a rock and roll star to the argot of an old Delta blues singer in *The Tooth of Crime*), sudden shifts in character (such as Chet's and Stu's metamorphosis from modern urban cowboys to old-time prospectors in *Cowboys #2*), or unexpected irruptions into convoluted soliloquies that arrest the flow of the action (such as Wesley's recollection of his drunken father's return in *Curse of the Starving Class*). Even when it is primarily realistic, the plays' language is highly figurative, establishing a layer of metaphoric significance that points toward each play's thematic center.

The settings of Shepard's plays also contribute figurative significance to their dominant themes. The action often unfolds against a backdrop composed of commonplace materials such as bathtubs, old wrecked cars, kitchen tables, refrigerators, living-room sofas, hotel beds, children's bedrooms, or hospital rooms, but these articles suggest an environment that is primarily metaphoric, not realistic. Shepard uses the icons of American pop culture to represent the mythic landscape of the American psyche, thereby demonstrating how personal identity is so often assembled out of the bits and pieces of the social iconography that dominates American culture. His figurative settings also underscore the predominant tensions dramatized, as in *Curse of the Starving Class*, where the lack of food in the refrigerator represents the lack of love and nurture in the family. Because Shepard is primarily interested in depicting figurative conflicts and actions, he is free to draw on a wide variety of materials in the physical setting, as well as the dialogue, in order to create his mythic landscapes. Hence, Shepard's plays are filled with borrowings from, and allusions to, what he sees as the core of the United States' mythology: rock and roll and country-western music, Hollywood and films of all kinds (Westerns in particular), the trappings of middle-class suburbia, the physical geography of the West (the desert in particular), science fiction, and the conflict between generations that shredded American society and culture during the Vietnam era.

Although Shepard has spoken of his personal aversion for the 1960's and early 1970's, the pulsing beat of his scintillating dramatic language, the resonant depth of the mythic images that permeate his plays, and the unwavering intensity of the conflicts that give his plays an unmatched toughness all have their ultimate source in the turmoil both caused and embraced by the sex-drugs-and-rock-and-roll generation. The center of Shepard's work moves steadily and inexorably toward a distinctly American version of the domestic drama defined by his predecessors Henrik Ibsen, Anton Chekhov, and Eugene O'Neill, but the conflicts between siblings, husbands and wives, or parents and children are consistently played out against the backdrop of the icons that created the American national identity during the Vietnam era: cowboys, rock and roll music, Hollywood films, middle-class suburbia, science fiction, and the West. It is Shepard's consistent ability, however, to use the particular to suggest the universal that indicates his greatness. In a play written by Shepard, the foreground and shading of a conflict between father and son will inevitably be couched in terms of rock music, cars, gunfights, and liquor, but the outline of that conflict is as old and as evocative as Sophocles' *Oidipous Tyrannos* (c. 429 B.C.E.; *Oedipus Tyrannus*, 1715).

One-act plays • Shepard's earliest extant play, *The Rock Garden*, sketches many of the themes that resonate throughout his work. In the first of the play's three scenes, Shepard defines the estrangement between generations: A Boy and a Girl sit in silence, sipping milk, while a Man, absorbed in his magazine, ignores them. In the second scene, the Boy signals his alienation from the mother figure (the Woman) by donning more and more clothing, which metaphorically suggests the barriers erected between the family members. The third scene repeats this figurative action, with the mother replaced by the father figure, the Man, who bores his son almost to death. Finally, the Boy shatters the superficial complacency of the relationships with a graphic and intensely personal recounting of his sexual preferences and prowess. Thus, the rock garden metaphorically defines this typical Shepardian family: sterile, arid, and empty.

Most of the one-act plays that Shepard wrote for the Off-Off-Broadway theater during the 1960's explore themes that emerged in *The Rock Garden*. *Chicago* examines the dynamics of isolation. The alienation of Stu—who reposes in a bathtub naked from the waist up but wearing jeans and tennis shoes—from the other cast members cannot be overcome by the figurative barriers that Stu creates through his active imagination. In *4-H Club*, three men, Joe, John, and Bob, take turns imposing improvised antics on the other two; in *Red Cross*, Jim, a tourist infested with crab lice, imposes imaginative scenarios on two women: Carol (Jim's girlfriend) and a hotel maid. All three plays present characters who are markedly alienated from their selves and their surroundings; moreover, Shepard suggests that the imposition of personal desires on others leads typically to irreversible alienation. *Cowboys #2* is perhaps Shepard's best depiction of the ability of the imagination to assert a separate reality, as Chet and Stu, two urban cowboys, take turns imposing imaginative vistas on each other. For example, Chet assumes the voice and posture of an Old West prospector and addresses Stu as Mel, who plays along. The two urban cowboys and old-time prospectors rollick through a number of fanciful incidents: calisthenics, a rainstorm, an Indian attack, a descant on the decay of the modern West, and a trek across the desert. The play suggests that the imaginative world is just as "real" as the actual world.

In a series of plays from the late 1960's to the early 1970's, Shepard explores isolation and alienation by employing metaphoric sets, characterizations, and actions. *Icarus's Mother* depicts a conflict between five metaphorically "grounded" characters and a jet pilot—a transcendent Icarus figure. When the two females (Jill and Pat) respond to the pilot sexually, the pilot reacts sexually, looping, rolling, climbing, and finally plunging to an explosive climax in the ocean. The play suggests that sexual desire is both irresistible and destructive, that permanent transcendence is not possible, and that males and females cannot communicate successfully. *Forensic and the Navigators* examines the American antiwar movement of the 1960's. Two would-be revolutionaries, Forensic (whose name suggests talk but no action) and Emmet, ineptly attempt to chart out a revolutionary action. When the radicals' hideout is suddenly invaded by California Highway Patrol-like exterminators, the fundamental distinctions between the revolutionaries and the forces of oppression progressively disintegrate, since neither side is capable of significant action.

La Turista • Shepard's first full-length play, *La Turista*, examines the inexorable decay of American society. Set in a Mexican hotel room for the first act, *La Turista* depicts the inability of two middle-class Americans, Kent and Salem, to overcome their cultural and spiritual sickness, symbolized by the dysentery they have contracted. Kent and Salem's internal malaise contrasts sharply with the vitality of the Mexican Boy, who symbolizes both the underdeveloped nations' peoples exploited by American materialism and the son caught in an Oedipal conflict with his father. Moreover, Kent's symbolic role as the epitome of American cultural dominance is undercut by Kent's ironic attack on the obsessions that have made the United States irrecoverably weak. After Kent faints on seeing the Boy in bed with Salem, the remainder of the first act consists of an attempt to revive Kent (who is described as dead), which involves a Witch Doctor, his son, and sacrificial chickens.

The second act of *La Turista* duplicates the first in action, although it employs a separate metaphorical structure. Set in a drab American hotel room, Kent's revival continues. The Witch Doctor and the Boy from the first act enter, dressed now like country doctors from the Civil War era. Kent's disease is the result of a psychological and emotional starvation endemically linked to the structure of the typical American family. Kent and the Doctor become enmeshed in a mutually imposed *Frankenstein* scenario that recalls the father/son conflicts of the first act with Kent in the role of monster/son and the Doctor as the creator/father. As the imaginative play reaches its peak, Kent transforms into the monster and escapes his repressive society by crashing through the upstage wall, leaving a cutout of his body. *La Turista* compellingly suggests that the barren American family and its disposable society are incurably diseased structures that produce generation after generation of monsters.

The Unseen Hand and **Operation Sidewinder** • *The Unseen Hand* and *Operation Sidewinder* also explore unresolvable conflicts. *The Unseen Hand*, a cross between a science-fiction adventure and a television Western, pits Willie the Space Freak and the Morphan brothers (a trio of Old West outlaws) against the High Commission of Nogoland with its powerful Unseen Hand, a force that squeezes the mind. The conflict unfolds on a stage cluttered with the detritus of the American consumer society (symbolized by the play's setting: Azusa, everything from A to Z in the United States). Nogoland and Azusa are but two different names for the tyrannizing force of established culture that opposes those who seek true freedom. Willie's ability to escape the

Unseen Hand's power seems to be a qualified endorsement of revolutionary action. *Operation Sidewinder*, Shepard's big-budget Broadway production, develops the structure sketched in *The Unseen Hand.*

The plot brings together a group of revolutionaries consisting of Mickey Free (an Indian), a hippie known as the Young Man (who symbolizes all the impatience, violence, and frustrations of American youths during the 1960's and 1970's), and Blood (a Black Panther type), all of whom struggle against the forces of political oppression led by a Central Intelligence Agency goon (Captain Bovine), a mad scientist (Dr. Vector), and Dr. Vector's gigantic and deadly missile/computer shaped like a sidewinder rattlesnake. When Mickey Free liberates Honey, the play's only significant female, by cutting off the Sidewinder's head, the action suggests that violent political confrontation can lead to true liberation, but the remainder of the play does not fulfill that promise.

Shepard uses satiric language and irony to undercut the pretentiousness of both the anti-establishment and the establishment. Only Mickey Free's desire to use the Sidewinder's head as a source of spiritual renewal provides a viable alternative to the sterile and debilitating social mythologies embraced by both the revolutionaries and the establishment. The play ends with a pyrotechnic encounter between a group of Desert Tactical troops who futilely discharge their machine guns into Mickey Free, the Young Man, Honey, and a group of Hopi Indians who are caught up in the spirituality of the snake dance and have thereby achieved a higher level of existence. Although the play preaches too much, *Operation Sidewinder* is perhaps Shepard's most hopeful offering, suggesting that the futility of political and generational conflict can at last be transcended.

Geography of a Horse Dreamer • Although *Geography of a Horse Dreamer* is on the surface a play about a group of gamblers who are trying to squeeze information from Cody, an artistically minded young man with the ability to dream the winners of horse or dog races, it is really an extended metaphor that reproaches the tendency of a culture to treat its most gifted artists like disposable goods, demanding that they produce more and more until the artists themselves are consumed. Cody's abilities steadily wither, since he cannot meet the demands of the Mafia-like gangsters, until he is liberated from them by his shotgun-wielding brothers from the West in a violent scene at the play's end.

Angel City • *Angel City* also examines the role of the artist in society. Rabbit, a filmscript fixer, is hired by a motion-picture studio to repair the script of the company's latest big-budget disaster film. The line between films and the "real," however, is a tenuous distinction in *Angel City*. Miss Scoons, the type of the vacuous American female, desires beyond all else to become the people she sees on the silver screen since she believes their lives to be more "real" than hers. Further, the great disaster that Rabbit is supposed to script becomes the cataclysm that destroys both the world without and the world within the play; *Angel City*'s apocalyptic ending suggests that the American film industry, and the mythology it creates, are primary sources of the United States' cultural and spiritual corruption.

The Tooth of Crime • *The Tooth of Crime* is best described as a rock-and-roll gunfight between a top-of-the-charts but aging rocker, Hoss, and his up-and-coming rival, Crow. Set in a stylized future where rockers mark out territory through acts of violence much like members of rival gangs stake out their turf, *The Tooth of Crime* examines the dynamics by which males relate to one another when establishing their fundamental identities. As Hoss and Crow square off in the musical battle that dominates the play's second act, it becomes clear that Hoss and Crow, like so many of Shepard's other male characters, are locked into the battle of identity that pits father against son. Hoss quickly recognizes that "father" and "son" are locked into a generational cycle in which the younger will inevitably usurp the place of the elder, and the play's conclusion, in which Crow takes possession of Hoss's entourage, goods, and status, suggests that father and son are locked in an endless cycle in which the younger generation is doomed to repeat patterns of its forebears.

Curse of the Starving Class • The cyclical pattern etched into the relationship between the generations provides the dominant structure for what have been called Shepard's "family" plays: *Curse of the Starving Class, Buried Child, True West, Fool for Love,* and *A Lie of the Mind.* The "curse" in *Curse of the Starving Class* is quite clearly the curse of generational repetition: Children inevitably duplicate the actions of their parents. The natures of the parents are planted within the psyches of the children and emerge in actions that emphasize the familial curse passed down from generation to generation. Weston, the father, recalls the poison of his father's alcoholism; Wesley, the son, provides a chilling account of Weston's drunken attack on the home's locked front door; and in the third act, Wesley dons Weston's discarded clothes and admits that his father's essence is beginning to control him. Ella, the mother, passes on to her daughter Emma the curse of menstruation as well as the mother's desire to escape her family.

The curse of starvation is overtly symbolized by the perpetually empty refrigerator, which underscores the family's physical, emotional, psychological, and spiritual starvation. Further, the curse of denial pervades all the play's relationships and colors almost every action. Clearly beset from within, this typical Shepardian family is also beset from without by those forces that Shepard believes threaten the mythic (and therefore true) West: the march of progress that wants to destroy the natural world and replace it with shopping malls, freeways, and tract housing developments. There is, obviously, no salvation for this family. Weston runs off to Mexico with the money he has received from the sale of the farm; Emma is blown up in Weston's car by thugs who are looking to extort money from Weston; Ella refuses to acknowledge what happens right in front of her and repeatedly addresses Wesley as Weston; Wesley completes the transformation into his father by adopting his father's attitudes and behaviors. The anecdote that Ella and Wesley jointly tell to close the play becomes the play's second great symbol: An eagle and a tomcat, tearing at each other in a midair struggle, crash to earth. Like that pair of animals, there is no salvation or escape that awaits the family in *Curse of the Starving Class*, only inevitable destruction.

Buried Child • Shepard's vision of the family in *Buried Child* is even darker; long and deeply buried familial secrets constitute the hereditary curse in Shepard's Pulitzer Prize winner. The family patriarch, Dodge, spends all of his time wrapped in an old blanket on the sofa, staring at the television. His wife, Halie, speaks at her husband (not to him) of trivial matters when she is not busy soliciting the local clergyman, Father Dewis. Their eldest son, Tilden, is a burned out and mentally defective semimute who brings armload after armload of corn onto the stage. The second son, Bradley, had one leg cut off by a chain saw and now spends most of his time wrestling with Dodge for control of the blanket and television set or threatening to cut Dodge's hair.

In a series of statements that recalls the pattern of denial that occurs in *Curse of the Starving Class,* Dodge refuses to acknowledge that Bradley is his own son, claiming that his flesh and blood are buried in the backyard. To complicate matters, Halie frequently mentions yet another son, Ansel, who (according to Halie and Halie alone) was a hero and basketball star. Into the midst of this dysfunctional home comes Vince, Tilden's son, who wants to reestablish his family ties, and Shelly, Vince's girlfriend. Tilden, however, refuses to recognize Vince, claiming that the son he once had is now dead and buried.

The denial of family connections suggests both the physical and the emotional rejection that pervades the home in *Buried Child.* On a physical level, the dead child refers to Halie and Tilden's incestuously conceived child who was killed by Dodge and buried in the field behind the house. Metaphorically, the dead child represents all the children in the family, all of whom are dead to their father and mother and to one another. Unable to gain recognition from any of his progenitors, Vince stomps out one evening and goes on an alcoholic binge, leaving Shelly at the mercy of Bradley, who menaces her sexually. When Vince returns the next morning, thoroughly drunk, his open violence provides Halie and Dodge with the clue to Vince's identity, once again suggesting that behavior is mechanically passed from generation to generation. When Dodge dies, Vince proclaims himself the family's new patriarch just as Tilden enters carrying the exhumed body of the buried child. The play's highly equivocal ending juxtaposes the hope symbolized by the rebirth of a new generation against despairing images of denial, disease, and death.

True West • *True West* explores the conflict between two brothers: Lee, a reclusive and violent thief who has been living in the Mojave desert, and Austin, a suburban Yuppie and screenwriter. Austin is trying to close a motion-picture deal with a Hollywood movie mogul, Saul Kimmer, but when Kimmer hears Lee's impromptu outline for a motion picture about two cowboys chasing each other across the plains of Texas, Kimmer decides to drop Austin's project and develop Lee's. *True West,* in addition to analyzing the fate of the artist in a manner that recalls *Angel City* and *Geography of a Horse Dreamer,* questions which version of the West is indeed true. Lee claims that the desert, with its brutally harsh environment that forces its denizens to live by their wits and strength, is the true West, while Austin claims that suburban California, with its shopping malls, highways, and tract housing, constitutes the real West. Further, the numerous references to famous Western films suggest that the only true West is Hollywood's West.

The pressure of Kimmer's decision to pursue Lee's screenplay causes the brothers to switch roles: Austin, responding to Lee's taunts, steals a variety of toasters from the neighbors; Lee slaves over the typewriter roughing out the dialogue. The reversal of roles indicates the fundamental similarities that bind the brothers. On the abrupt return of their Mother from Alaska, (who, showing rare good sense for a Shepardian mother, claims to recognize nothing and immediately leaves), Lee and Austin square off in a physically violent but unresolved confrontation. *True West* not only questions the mythology that defines the American West but also probes the violence spawned by the fundamental psychological and behavioral equivalence of family members.

Fool for Love • Shepard also examines the equivalency of siblings in *Fool for Love,* replacing the brother-brother conflict of *True West* with a love/hate relationship between half-brother and half-sister, Eddie and May. Reared in different towns by different mothers, Eddie and May meet, fall in love, and begin their incestuous relationship before discovering that they share the same father, the Old Man. Although the friction dramatized in Eddie and May's emotional and sexual relationship points toward Shepard's signature characterization of men and women as two opposite animals who cannot coexist, *Fool for Love* also examines how the same event is often shaped and reshaped by different individuals to create widely divergent memories and understandings of what happened. Eddie and May do not share the same recollection of their meeting and cannot come to terms with the implications of their relationship; moreover, none of their stories agrees with versions of the same incidents told by the Old Man, who at times seems to be Eddie's and May's mental projection but who at other times seems to be an independent character. Despite her attempt to establish a different lifestyle with Martin, the new man in her life, May is as inextricably bound to Eddie as he is to her. Even though Eddie leaves at the end of the play and May believes that he is not coming back, the play suggests that the audience has witnessed but one episode in a continually repeating cycle in which Eddie and May are victimized by their repetitive actions just as surely as Wesley and Weston were by theirs in *Curse of the Starving Class.*

A Lie of the Mind • *A Lie of the Mind* explores the dysfunctional structure of the American family as well as the delusions that individuals impose on others and themselves. Beaten nearly to death by her husband Jake, Beth creates lies of the mind—fictions that permit her to survive. The play suggests that each character assembles a personal reality in his or her mind. For example, Jake's mother, Lorraine, blocks out the pain of being abandoned by her husband by pretending indifference; Beth's father, Baylor, hides from his family by erecting a facade of the crusty frontier hunter; Jake represses all of his memories of the race in Mexico that led to his father's death. Further, *A Lie of the Mind* suggests that the "two opposite animals," the male and the female, even when yoked together by an irresistible and consuming love, are torn apart by the violence of their fundamental incompatibility. Both Beth and Jake are trapped by their love—neither can be complete without the other—and their obsessive need to be reunited thrusts Beth into delusions of marriage and propels Jake to Montana to find Beth. Their drive for reunification, however, at last proves futile. After kissing Beth, Jake exits into the darkness, and Beth compulsively turns to Jake's wounded brother, Frankie. *A Lie of the Mind* suggests that the American family, like Beth, is fundamentally crippled.

States of Shock • *States of Shock* is a heavily symbolic exercise in antiwar sentiment that pits a demented, saber-waving colonel against Stubbs, a wheelchair-bound armed-services veteran (who still has a conspicuously large and bloody hole in his chest) in a battle over the symbols and myths that permeate and define large-scale war. Set in a thoroughly American family restaurant, *States of Shock* exposes all the contradictions that surround the concept of war in post-Vietnam America without offering any more than the violence of the inevitable collisions.

Simpatico • *Simpatico* concerns two Californian friends, Carter and Vinnie, who fifteen years earlier had used Vinnie's wife Rosie to blackmail Ames, a horse racing official, into overlooking a race track scam involving look-alike horses. Carter and Rosie then ran off to Kentucky together where they became wealthy. Vinnie uses photographs of Rosie with Ames to extort money from Carter, who returns to California to retrieve the photographs. As in *True West*, the main characters undergo role reversals during the play's progress. Carter becomes an alcoholic ne'er-do-well while Vinnie shaves, puts on a suit, and flies to Kentucky to seek his fortune.

Eyes for Consuela • *Eyes for Consuela* is based on the short story, "The Blue Bouquet," by Octavio Paz. Henry, a middle-class American whose marriage has disintegrated, flees to a decrepit hotel in a Mexican jungle. There he meets a philosophical Mexican bandit Amado, who threatens to cut out Henry's blue eyes as a gift to his wife Consuela. Henry insists that his eyes are brown, not blue, but this does not impress Amado. Throughout two acts the men argue, drink tequila, and trade life histories, as Amado contends that Henry's despair is an example of anxiety caused by the complexity of American civilization.

The Late Henry Moss • *The Late Henry Moss* begins with two brothers, Ray and Earl, sharing a whiskey bottle and memories of their father, who lies dead in the bed behind them. Ray sets out to discover how his father died by interrogating everyone who knows anything about his last day. The story is told in flashbacks as Ray interviews the taxi driver who took Henry Moss on a fatal fishing trip; Esteban, a kindly next-door neighbor; and Conchalla, a sensuous Mexican woman who shared a drinking binge with Henry.

Other major works

SHORT FICTION: *Cruising Paradise*, 1996; *Great Dream of Heaven: Stories*, 2002.

SCREENPLAYS: *Me and My Brother*, 1969 (with Robert Frank); *Zabriskie Point*, 1970; *Ringaleevio*, 1971; *Renaldo and Clara*, 1978; *Paris, Texas*, 1984 (with L. M. Kit Carson); *Fool for Love*, 1985 (adaptation of his play); *Far North*, 1988; *Silent Tongue*, 1994.

NONFICTION: *Rolling Thunder Logbook*, 1977.

MISCELLANEOUS: *Hawk Moon: A Book of Short Stories, Poems, and Monologues*, 1973; *Motel Chronicles*, 1982 (poetry and short fiction); *Joseph Chaikin and Sam Shepard: Letters and Texts, 1972-1984*, 1989.

Bibliography

Auerbach, Doris. *Shepard, Kopit, and the Off-Broadway Theater*. Boston: Twayne, 1982. One of the first important academic analyses of Shepard's plays, Auerbach's book provides a valuable analysis of Shepard's work as Off-Broadway drama. Auerbach also provides extensive information on the directors, actors, and theatrical spaces that made up the Off-Broadway theater during the 1960's and 1970's.

Bottoms, Stephen J. *The Theatre of Sam Shepard: States of Crisis*. Cambridge, England: Cambridge University Press, 1998. Along with a thorough examination of Shepard's plays, Bottoms presents an impartial comparison of Shepard's work with that of other leading contemporary dramatists. Contains detailed chronology and bibliography.

DeRose, David J. *Sam Shepard*. New York: Twayne, 1992. DeRose provides a brief overview of Shepard's life and work, analyzing his theatrical and thematic goals. Includes an annotated bibliography of secondary sources and a detailed list of important play reviews.

Hart, Lynda. *Sam Shepard's Metaphorical Stages*. Westport, Conn.: Greenwood Press, 1987. Hart argues that Shepard's plays from *Cowboys #2* to *A Lie of the Mind* are influenced by techniques developed by the Theater of the Absurd, particularly by the work of Samuel Beckett, Antonin Artaud, and Eugène Ionesco. The book contains a brief chapter on Shepard's work for the television and film industries as well as a pithy biography and an extensive bibliography.

King, Kimball, ed. *Sam Shepard: A Casebook*. New York: Garland, 1988. This collection of essays written mostly by academics approaches Shepard's work from many angles and demonstrates the range of response the plays evoke. The casebook includes a solid annotated bibliography and a piece by Patrick Fennel that identifies and discusses Shepard's unperformed and unpublished works.

Marranca, Bonnie, ed. *American Dreams: The Imagination of Sam Shepard*. New York: Performing Arts Journal Publications, 1981. A compendium of essays written by academics, directors, and actors, this volume is a good introduction to Shepard's early work for the Off-Broadway theater. A number of short pieces by Shepard himself round out the volume, including Shepard's influential short essay, "Language, Visualization, and the Inner Library."

Mottram, Ron. *Inner Landscapes: The Theater of Sam Shepard*. Columbia: University of Missouri Press, 1984. Perhaps the best sustained examination of Shepard's plays, Mottram's biographical analysis offers many insightful readings of Shepard's work by comparing incidents in the plays to parallel episodes from Shepard's life or to stories from *Hawk Moon* or *Motel Chronicles* with similar characters or incidents. Mottram also includes a brief chronology of Shepard's work to 1985.

Gregory W. Lanier,
updated by Milton Berman

Richard Brinsley Sheridan

Born: Dublin, Ireland; October 30, 1751
Died: London, England; July 7, 1816

Principal drama • *The Rivals*, pr., pb. 1775; *St. Patrick's Day: Or, The Scheming Lieutenant*, pr. 1775, pb. 1788; *The Duenna: Or, The Double Elopement*, pr. 1775, pb. 1776 (libretto; music by Thomas Linley the elder and Thomas Linley the younger, and others); *A Trip to Scarborough*, pr. 1777, pb. 1781 (adaptation of Sir John Vanbrugh's *The Relapse*); *The School for Scandal*, pr. 1777, pb. 1780; *The Critic: Or, A Tragedy Rehearsed*, pr. 1779, pb. 1781; *Pizarro: A Tragedy in Five Acts*, pr., pb. 1799 (adaptation of August von Kotzebue's *Die Spanier in Peru*); *Complete Plays*, pb. 1930; *Plays*, pb. 1956 (L. Gibbs, editor); *The School for Scandal and Other Plays*, pb. 1998 (Michael Cordner, editor)

Other literary forms • Richard Brinsley Sheridan's other literary efforts, all minor, include the early poems "Clio's Protest" and "The Ridotto of Bath," published in *The Bath Chronicle* (1771); a youthful translation, *Love Epistles of Aristaenetus* (1771), in collaboration with Nathaniel Brassey Halhed; and later occasional verses in connection with the theater—such as prologues and epilogues to other writers' plays—the most important being "Verses to the Memory of Garrick, Spoken as a Monody" (1779). Of far greater significance, especially to biographers and historians, are Sheridan's speeches in Parliament, collected in five volumes (1816), and his letters, collected in three volumes, entitled *The Letters of Richard Brinsley Sheridan* (1966). Unfortunately, his speeches are preserved only in summary or imperfect transcript.

Achievements • Richard Brinsley Sheridan was the best playwright of eighteenth century England, a time of great actors rather than great playwrights. Judged on theatrical rather than strictly literary merit, Sheridan also ranks with the best English writers of comedy: William Shakespeare, Ben Jonson, William Congreve, Oscar Wilde, George Bernard Shaw. Until the era of Wilde and Shaw, only Shakespeare's plays had held the stage better than Sheridan's.

Of Sheridan's plays, *The School for Scandal*, a comedy of manners, is universally acclaimed as his masterpiece. Also applauded are *The Rivals*, another comedy of manners; *The Duenna*, a comic opera; and *The Critic*, a burlesque. The two comedies of manners have fared better over time than have the two more specialized works, perhaps because their attractions are apparent even in printed form and perhaps because changes of taste have gone against the specialized works. The topical allusions in *The Critic* are mostly lost on modern audiences, and *The Duenna* affronts modern sensibilities with episodes of anti-Catholicism and anti-Semitism. In Sheridan's own opinion, his best piece of work was act 1 of *The Critic*.

In recent times, Sheridan's reputation has waned: His "artificial" comedies lack the high seriousness that the modern age demands. Yet the basis of his appeal remains: effective theater embodied in smooth traditional plots, stock characters fleshed out by Sheridan's observations of his time, and some of the wittiest dialogue ever written. Sheridan has never been known for the originality of his plots and characters, some of which can be traced through Shakespeare and Jonson all the way back to Roman comedy, but—like Shakespeare and Jonson—he had the assimilative genius to transform the old into something lively and new. Revolving around a trickery motif, chronicling the age-old battles of the sexes or the generations, culminating in a marriage or marriages, his plots still entertain with their well-paced intrigues and discoveries. Onto the old stocks he grafted such memorable characters as Mrs. Malaprop, Joseph Surface, Lady Teazle, and Sir Fretful Plagiary. One reason why Sheridan does not seem dated is his language, a distinctly modern prose idiom, supple, utilitarian, informal, expressing the hopeful coherence of the early modern era.

Sheridan's achievement is even more impressive when one considers that he wrote all of his plays (except for the adaptation of *Pizarro*) during a period of five years when he was in his mid-twenties and during a period of severe restrictions on the theater. The upper- and upper-middle-class establishment controlled the theater with an iron grip through limitations on the number of theaters, official censorship, and the unofficial censorship of its tastes. No play could be presented that did not satisfy the political and social assumptions of the ruling classes. It is remarkable that, under these restrictions, Sheridan could get away with saying as much as he did.

Biography • In eighteenth century Great Britain, Richard Brinsley Sheridan's lot was pretty much cast when he was born into a genteelly poor Irish theatrical family. All of these social disadvantages, however, worked to his advantage in the theater. Being Irish has given numerous British writers of comedy special insight into the vices and follies of their fellow Britons, as well as the rhetorical skills to air their observations. Being in a theatrical family was obviously an advantage for the aspiring playwright. Finally, being genteelly poor sparked his ambitions with both positive and negative charges. Combined, these factors made Sheridan acutely aware of the disparity between his personal worth and his actual place in society—always a great aid to developing a sense of comic incongruity.

Although lacking wealth and social position, Sheridan's family was both well educated and talented. Both his father and mother were children of scholarly clergymen. On being graduated from Trinity College, Dublin, Sheridan's father, Thomas, already a playwright, entered the theater as an actor and soon advanced to manager. Sheridan's mother, the former Frances Chamberlaine, wrote novels and plays. After initial prosperity, the family of six (Richard was the third son) ran into hard times when a minor political indiscretion—reminiscent of an indiscreet sermon that ruined his own father—forced Thomas out of his position. He suppressed some antigovernment lines in a play, thus antagonizing the Irish public. After two years of acting in London, Thomas tried to reestablish himself in Dublin, but without success. Taking his family with him, he returned to England, where, moving from place to place, he pursued an impecunious existence as actor, author, editor, lecturer on elocution, and projector of ambitious undertakings.

After attending Sam Whyte's Seminary for the Instruction of Youth in Dublin, Richard was entered into Harrow School, despite the family's precarious financial situation. How precarious that situation was became evident when, to escape creditors, the rest of the family fled to France, where they lived for several years and where Frances Sheridan died. Left behind at Harrow, Sheridan, lonely and destitute, suffered the abuse heaped on him by his well-bred schoolmates and masters. The unhappy scholar later maintained that he learned little at Harrow.

When his family returned to London, Sheridan, by then a young man, rejoined them. There his education continued informally, and it was completed when, in the fall of 1770, the family moved to Bath, where the father presented entertainments and tried to establish an academy of oratory. The favorite spa of eighteenth century England, Bath gave young Sheridan a closeup study of *le beau monde*, the fashionable world later depicted in his comedies of manners. He managed to join this scene on the basis of few credentials except a ready wit and charm. In Bath, he also met young Elizabeth Ann Linley, a great beauty and singing member of the musical Linley family, which sometimes collaborated with the Sheridans on entertainments. Elizabeth's public performances brought her the unwanted attentions of numerous suitors, most notably one Thomas Mathews. The boorish Mathews importuned her so closely that, to escape him, Elizabeth (already the subject of a racy play, Samuel Foote's *The Maid of Bath*, 1771) ran away to France—accompanied by Richard Brinsley Sheridan as her protector. After a few weeks, the couple returned, Sheridan fought two duels with Mathews, and, on April 13, 1773, Sheridan and Elizabeth were married.

With this background, Sheridan wrote his plays. He and Elizabeth settled in London, where the need to make a living turned him, like his father, toward the theater. In 1775, he took London by storm, presenting three plays, the first (*The Rivals*) reflecting his recent romantic past. By 1780, however, his playwriting career was over. Although he owned a managing interest in Drury Lane Theatre, he was beginning a distinguished career in Parliament, which consumed much of his efforts.

Sheridan's long service in Parliament has no bearing on his playwriting (aside from the fact that it stopped) but much on his reputation. A liberal Whig, Sheridan sympathized with the American and French revolutions and supported such programs as Roman Catholic emancipation. A principled politician, he could not be bribed despite his constant need for money to pay for elections and entertaining. An independent thinker, he sometimes bucked his own party. Such a man was obviously dangerous, especially when he was also such a powerful speaker. Therefore, the leaders of his party used his powers but never allowed him to become a leader. Sheridan even became an adviser and a friend to the prince of Wales, later George IV, but it was the snobbish prince who led the establishment's strategy against the upstart Sheridan. That strategy was to depict Sheridan as an unreliable lightweight—a strategy dictated at first by Sheridan's background and later by his drinking and debts.

When Drury Lane Theatre burned in 1809, Sheridan's debts drained his resources so that he lacked sufficient funds to win an election in 1812, and his political and princely associates swiftly fell away. Although he died in poverty, he was honored with a lavish funeral in Westminster Abbey, attended by scores of solemn dignitaries and peers of the realm. He is buried in the Poets' Corner of Westminster Abbey.

Analysis • "Poor Sherry," said the prince of Wales, a line echoed by other noble contemporaries of Richard Brinsley Sheridan and even by Sheridan's admirer Lord Byron. Unhappily, the verdict of the prince of Wales and his crowd still represents the official response to Sheridan, coloring understanding of his plays with an *argumentum ad hominem*. This official line runs something as follows: "Poor Sherry was motivated by overwhelming vanity and self-interest. That is why he entered the theater and why he left the theater to enter politics. A poor Irish actor's son, he always wanted to hobnob with the rich and powerful, to be part of *le beau monde*, whose attitudes he reflects in his plays. There was something calculating, something insincere and insubstantial, about the fellow. Same thing about his plays." This is the establishment Sheridan safely tucked away in the Poets' Corner.

There is also, however, an antiestablishment Sheridan—the penniless child suffering at Harrow, the spirited young man dueling for his girl, the member of Parliament sympathizing with the American and French revolutions, whose servants in his plays are smarter than their masters. True, Sheridan's leading characters are usually gentry or better, and Sheridan usually exhibits the doings of *le beau monde*. In addition, he does not issue a clarion call for revolution and the institution of a republic. He was working within the restrictions of accepted traditions, theatrical tastes, and official censorship. Within those restrictions, however, he exhibited *le beau monde* as vain, money-grabbing, and scandalmongering. As a playwright, Sheridan enjoyed the satisfaction of seeing the fashionable world pay and applaud to see itself pilloried.

Sheridan lived in the midst of what one of his characters calls "a luxurious and dissipated age," but the people enjoying the luxuries and dissipations were standing on the heads of a mass of poor people. He could not attack the upper classes directly, even though they offered big targets for satire. In particular, their illusions about themselves, their pretensions of nobility and gentility, made them vulnerable. Sheridan knew a whoring society when he saw one, and he satirized its illusions and pretensions relentlessly.

Sheridan's satire is milder in tone, however, than that of cynical Restoration comedy or the savage attacks Alexander Pope and Jonathan Swift could deliver. The tone of Restoration comedy harks back to the dark, stinging satire of Ben Jonson, who presented the world as little better than a zoo. Such satire incorporates the conservative vision of the Great Chain of Being, wherein human nature is permanently flawed, half angel, half animal. The animal side must be cynically accepted or flogged into good behavior by Church, State, and satirists. Sheridan's satire is more optimistic, softened by the influence of the sentimental mode that grew up in the eighteenth century as the main competitor of the satiric mode, especially in the novel and drama.

Originating in Nonconformist religious thought and maturing in Romanticism, sentimentalism rested on the revolutionary doctrine that human nature is essentially good. Stressing empathy and the humane emotions, sentimentalism was susceptible to hypocrisy. It also had a devastating effect on drama: Tragedy turned into melodrama, and comedy turned to provoking sympathetic tears. The two most notorious examples of sentimental literature, Henry Mackenzie's novel *The Man of Feeling* and Richard Cumberland's play *The West Indian* both came out in 1771, just before Sheridan began writing. Like his fellow countryman Oliver Goldsmith, Sheridan accepted the underlying doctrine of sentimentalism but reacted against its excesses. Not unnaturally, Goldsmith and Sheridan thought comedy ought to provoke laughter.

To produce "laughing comedy," Sheridan returned to the witty, satiric comedy of manners of the Restoration, but without the Restoration cynicism and sexual license. Whereas the Restoration offered refinement and style as a substitute for goodness, Sheridan still believed in its possibilities. The result is a warmly human balance similar to that in Henry Fielding's novels. As William Hazlitt said of *The School for Scandal,* "it professes a faith in the natural goodness, as well as habitual depravity, of human nature." Human frailties are laughed at and, if acknowledged, usually forgiven. Among prominent failings is hypocrisy, and anyone too good is suspect. Most of all, empathy has become a sense of participation—the author's and the audience's—in the vices and follies of humankind. This laugh of recognition is perhaps Richard Brinsley Sheridan's greatest gift to "high seriousness."

The Rivals • Sheridan's first play, *The Rivals,* reflects his own experiences—his life in Bath, his elopement with Elizabeth Linley, his duels—but it is not strictly autobiographical. Nor was it only a *succès de scandale*, although being the talk of the town proba-bly helped Sheridan at the time. Rather than seeing parallels to Sheridan's life in *The Rivals*, modern audiences are more likely to notice parallels to Shakespeare's plays, for Sheridan drew unashamedly not only on his own experiences but also on his predeces-sors' work. These two seams in the play reveal Sheridan's apprentice patchings, but what is amazing is that he sewed them all up so well. When the play failed in its first performance, Sheridan revised it within a few days and turned *The Rivals* into one of the great English comedies of manners.

Set in the fashionable resort town of Bath, *The Rivals* concerns the efforts of Captain Jack Absolute, "son and heir to Sir Anthony Absolute, a baronet of three thousand a year," to win the hand of Miss Lydia Languish, an heiress who "could pay the national debt." Miss Languish, however, entertains romantic notions of marrying only for love: She is determined to wed a penniless suitor who will elope and live with her in blissful poverty. To humor her fantasies, Captain Absolute pretends to be Beverley, "a half-pay ensign." His wooing is further complicated by the opposition of Mrs. Malaprop, Lydia's battle-ax guardian aunt; and by two rivals, bumbling country squire Bob Acres and duelist Sir Lucius O''Trigger (whose love letters are actually being delivered to Mrs. Malaprop by the maid, Lucy). The final complication is the appearance of Sir An-thony with news of an arranged marriage for Jack. After a heated confrontation be-tween father and son, this complication proves to be the resolution of the plot: The young lady intended for Jack Absolute is Miss Lydia Languish. The discovery of Beverley's true identity alienates Lydia, but she is brought around when Jack's life is threatened by a duel with the rivals. Averted at the last moment, the threatening duel also persuades Julia Melville to forgive Mr. Faulkland, Jack's friend, for doubting her love.

Drawn out too long, Mr. Faulkland's almost psychotic behavior mars the tone of the play, but his fantasies of doubt correspond to Lydia's fantasies of romance, perhaps pointing up the theme that a good marriage must be rooted in reality: true love and a solid bank account. The other characters provide a display of diverse human nature. Reminiscent of Shakespeare's Sir Andrew Aguecheek, the cowardly suitor Acres con-trasts with the equally ridiculous O'Trigger, whose name describes his ready disposi-tion. Lydia's whims and Sir Anthony's commands typify the ludicrous demands that sweethearts and fathers can make, and Mrs. Malaprop's comical misuse of words ("a nice derangement of epitaphs") epitomizes the cavalier misunderstanding of reality that the characters exhibit.

The play is full of notable examples of human illusion—O'Trigger's "honor," Sir Anthony's parental authority, Bob Acres's "polishing" (that is, new clothes, hairdo, dancing lessons, and swearing), Mrs. Malaprop's vanity, Faulkland's doubts, and Lydia's romance. Their illusions make them easy marks for one another and for the streetwise servants. To manipulate them, one simply plays up to their fantasies. For ex-ample, Jack is "Beverley" to Lydia, a dutiful son to Sir Anthony, and a flatterer to Mrs. Malaprop. All the characters with illusions are worthy of study, but perhaps the most important are Mrs. Malaprop, Faulkland, and Lydia.

On the periphery of the action, Mrs. Malaprop is symbolically at the play's center. She provides a simplified example of how illusion works. Her funny misuse of words, symbols of reality, epitomizes the break with reality. She thinks her big words make her, as O'Trigger says, "a great mistress of the language," "the queen of the dictionary," or, as Jack says, a leader in "intellectual accomplishments, elegant manners, and unaf-fected learning." The reality is summed up in Jack's intercepted letter: "I am told that the same ridiculous vanity, which makes her dress up her coarse features, and deck her dull chat with hard words which she don't understand, does also lay her open to the grossest deceptions from flattery and pretended admiration." To Sir Lucius O'Trigger, she is "Delia," a female counterpart of romantic Beverley. When Sir Lucius sees the real thing, however, he turns her down—as do Jack and Acres. Clinging to her illusions, Mrs. Malaprop stomps off the stage, huffing that "men are all barbarians."

The illusions of Faulkland and Lydia are essentially overreactions of the young to the sterile social order represented by Mrs. Malaprop and the older generation: Their illusions are examples of sentimentalism, the gross exaggeration of feeling that Goldsmith and Sheridan deplored. Faulkland is a man of sensibility, but unfortunately, as he notes, love "urges sensibility to madness." His "too exquisite nicety" leads him constantly to question and torture Julia, a "mild and affectionate spirit" any man would be lucky to find. The least suggestion can send him into paroxysms of doubt: Jack and even the "looby" Acres are able to play on his sensibility at will. He is, as he finally admits, a "fool." Lydia's overreaction contrasts with that of Faulkland, but she would agree with him that "when *Love* receives such countenance from *Prudence*, nice minds will be suspicious of its birth." Fed by sentimental novels, her overheated mind throws prudence to the wind. Jack easily deceives her by playing her romantic games and speaking the language of the novels she has read. Thinking to outwit and shock her relatives, she is shocked to discover herself "the only dupe at last." The young lady who had hoped for a "sentimental" elopement with all the trimmings must settle for being "a mere Smithfield bargain." Actually, she gets more than she bargained for: When confronted by the reality of a truly romantic situation—men dueling to the death over her—she comes to her senses.

The illusions of all these characters in *The Rivals* say something about the society in which they live. First, being born in the upper strata apparently encourages illusions about oneself: Only wealth and privilege could create a Mrs. Malaprop. Second, to sustain those illusions apparently requires a lot of lying and deceiving. Third, with all the lying and deceiving, it becomes difficult to find anything genuine—hence the hard search of Faulkland and Lydia for true love. That Sheridan himself sought the genuine is suggested by his repeated use throughout the play of the word "sincerity," apparently a quality he found in short supply in eighteenth century England.

The Duenna • Musically untalented, Sheridan wrote the comic opera *The Duenna* in collaboration with his father-in-law and brother-in-law (both named Thomas Linley) and probably with the help of his wife. Despite this piecemeal method of composition, the completed opera was an immense success. In particular, the opera is a testimony to Sheridan's patchwork skill and to the talented Linleys, whose tunes were hummed about London streets. Typically, however, the words of the songs are bland, and so are the opera's stock characters, some of whom are almost indistinguishable from one another. Of all Sheridan's works, *The Duenna* most requires performance, since it depends so much on acting, spectacle, and music (twenty-seven songs in all).

Set in Seville, *The Duenna* features not one but two pairs of lovers thwarted by tyrannical parents. Donna Louisa's father has arranged an unsuitable match for her, notwithstanding her love for Don Antonio, and Donna Clara's father and stepmother are forcing her into a convent, even though she is loved by Don Ferdinand. Both young ladies run off and, assisted by bribed nuns and priests (the latter also drunk), marry their lovers in a convent. Louisa tricks her father, Don Jerome, with the help of her governess, old Margaret the Duenna. When Don Jerome vows "never to see or speak to"

Louisa until she marries his choice, Louisa and the Duenna trade places, and the penniless old Duenna marries Louisa's intended, Isaac Mendoza, a rich Jew who has never seen Louisa and who thinks he is adding to his coffers.

Like most of Sheridan's works, *The Duenna* offers sparkling intrigue and dialogue. Here again, a female servant masterminds the plotting, but to a great extent the fathers and the villain outsmart themselves. The scheming Mendoza, recently converted to Christianity and hence standing "like the blank leaves between the Old and New Testament," is well known for being "the dupe of his own art." Of the characters, only the ugly Duenna, the obnoxious Mendoza, and the drunken priest Father Paul stand forth with any distinction, and they are stereotypes.

The broad strokes of the stock characters and action do provide simplified versions of some of Sheridan's themes. For example, the hypocritical nuns and priests show, as Louisa notes, that "in religion, as in friendship, they who profess most are ever the least sincere"—a forewarning of Joseph Surface in *The School for Scandal*. Louisa herself seems of two minds on the relationship of love and wealth. Early in the opera, she sings that she loves Don Antonio "for himself alone," since he has no wealth. Later in the play, faced with the prospect of being disinherited, she changes her tune: "There is a chilling air around poverty that often kills affection that was not nursed in it. If we would make love our household god we had best secure him a comfortable roof."

At least Louisa's aims are different from her father's, who sets forth his marriage as a proper example: "I married her for her fortune, and she took me in obedience to her father, and a very happy couple we were. We never expected any love from one another, and so we were never disappointed." Such cold-blooded reasoning is a reminder of how often, in Sheridan's plays, the older and younger generations are at odds on the subject of marriage. The two views presuppose radically different ideas not only of marriage but also of personality and society: The vital difference is between valuing someone "for her fortune" and "for himself alone." Thus, in Sheridan's plays, the struggle within the family is a microcosm of the larger struggle between the old and new order in society. There is no doubt about which side Sheridan took, as his own father opposed his marriage to Elizabeth Ann Linley (old Thomas had the absurd notion that the Sheridans were too good for "musicians").

Another theme in *The Duenna* revolves around the idea of "seeing." There are a number of observations on how subjective states, especially love, affect one's seeing, especially of the beloved. The merging of subject and object here, encouraged perhaps by eighteenth century empathy, foreshadows Romantic "seeing," wherein what is observed takes its coloring from the imagination. *The Duenna* also contains a number of warnings about such "seeing": Don Jerome gets so angry that he does not recognize his daughter posing as the veiled Duenna, and Don Ferdinand gets so jealous he does not recognize his beloved dressed as a nun. In the opera's most philosophical song, however, Don Jerome gets the final word on "seeing":

> Truth, they say, lies in a well,
> Why, I vow I ne'er could see;
> Let the water-drinkers tell,
> There it always lay for me;
> For when sparkling wine went round,
> Never saw I falsehood's mask;
> But still honest truth I found
> In the bottom of each flask.

He seems to say that people need their illusions, or at least their opiates.

Possibly Don Jerome was speaking for Sheridan, since the opium of entertainment is precisely what Sheridan provided in *The Duenna*. The first English comic opera to use specially composed music, *The Duenna* was a forerunner of the operettas by W. S. Gilbert and Sir Arthur Sullivan and the Broadway musical, which by now have institutionalized sentimental "seeing."

The School for Scandal • If *The Rivals* shows the fashionable world on vacation, *The School for Scandal* shows it back home in London, working hard to "murder characters" and "kill time." If the duelist O'Trigger is deadly, he is nothing to this school of piranhas, which renders "a character dead at every word." The difference between vacation and work is precisely the difference in tone, theme, and achievement between *The Rivals* and *The School for Scandal*. No seams or weaknesses obtrude in *The School for Scandal*, the title of which sums up the play's prevailing imagery and unity.

The play begins with a marvelous expository device: The "scandalous college" is in session, headed by its "president," Lady Sneerwell. As the pupils gather—Snake, Joseph Surface, Mrs. Candour, Crabtree, Sir Benjamin Backbite—the audience hears juicy bits of scandal about the president and each pupil. The key information is that Sir Peter Teazle has a pack of trouble. The Surface brothers, to whom Sir Peter is "a kind of guardian," are competing for Maria, Sir Peter's rich ward. Joseph, the older brother, is a scheming knave who, with "the assistance of his sentiment and hypocrisy," passes for a paragon of virtue, while Charles is "the most dissipated and extravagant young fellow in the kingdom." Joseph enjoys the favor of Sir Peter, and Charles, that of Maria. During a recess, Sir Peter is also shown having fits with his young wife. Country-bred Lady Teazle has blossomed into a London woman of fashion, even joining Lady Sneerwell's group and carrying on a flirtation with Joseph. The scandalmongers, however, have linked her to Charles.

The Surfaces are unmasked when Sir Oliver Surface, a rich uncle, returns from many years in the East Indies and puts the brothers to the test. Posing as a moneylender, Sir Oliver observes Charles's dissipation, even purchases the family portraits from him—but forgives the young man when Charles will not part with the portrait of dear Uncle Oliver. Charles also sends some of the money to old Stanley, a poor relation in distress, but when Sir Oliver, posing as Stanley, applies to Joseph, he is given the brush-off. In a famous scene, Joseph is also discovered hiding Lady Teazle behind a screen and Sir Peter Teazle in a closet, where each has heard an earful. The screen symbolizes Joseph's character and the nature of the society in which he flourishes, and the closet suggests where Sir Peter has been hiding. The truth comes out, however—confirmed by the confessions of Snake—and the people have to live with it. Now the centerpiece of a raging scandal, stodgy Sir Peter mellows; Lady Teazle and Charles will reform; Joseph's punishment is being "known to the world"; and Snake hopes his good deeds will not spoil his professional reputation. Meanwhile, the audience, schooled by a master, has been treated to a delightful exposition of illusion and reality in society.

Sheridan exposes a shallow society in which appearances rule: It is not what you are but what you appear to be that counts; reputation is all. The main proponent of this philosophy—still not entirely discredited even in modern society—is the well-spoken Joseph Surface, whose hypocrisy illustrates another danger inherent in sentimentalism. Actually, the talented Joseph represents both types prominent in his society: the hypocrite, who manipulates appearances to enhance his own reputation, and the scandalmonger, who manipulates appearances to tear down the reputations of others (as Joseph shows, the two callings go together). Behind facades of gentility, both types feel free to indulge their basest instincts. For example, the motives acknowledged by scandalmongers include bitterness over being slandered oneself, personal spite, impersonal malice, fun, and following the fashion, though the dullness of their lives is also a factor. They have nothing better to do than sit around and gossip about other people's lives, with perhaps a touch of envy. As Lady Teazle makes clear, these "are all people of rank and fortune." They represent a society rotten at the core.

Luckily, this decadent society includes a saving remnant that is not fooled by appearances. There is the faithful old servant Rowley, who believes in the goodness of a reprobate's heart. There is crusty Sir Oliver, who is sickened by scraps of morality and who believes that a man is not sincere if he has not made any enemies. There is Lady Teazle, whose personal development through the play marks the course of the plot. At first she is drawn to the world of appearances, of high fashion and rich furnishings, of the circle of scandalmongers and Joseph. Her turning point comes when Joseph suggests that she go to bed with him, literally and figuratively. She returns to her country wisdom and rejects him. When the screen is pulled down and she is caught in Joseph's quarters, she refuses to second his story and dubs him "Good Mr. Hypocrite." Thereafter, she withdraws from the "scandalous college" and turns over a new leaf.

Finally, there is Charles, the reprobate himself. His regeneration is harder to believe than Lady Teazle's, but Sheridan shrewdly keeps him offstage until halfway through the play, by which time he contrasts favorably with Joseph and the scandalmongers. Although dissolute and bankrupt, Charles has two important qualities that Joseph lacks: benevolence and honesty. Unlike the hypocritical Joseph Surface, Charles Surface is exactly what he appears to be. His loss of reputation has, in fact, freed him to be himself, and his experience has prepared him to see himself and others clearly. He is given the two main symbolic gestures in the play: pulling down the screen and selling off the family portraits. Symbolically, he attacks both the pretensions of his society and their hereditary basis. Charles's auction of the family portraits now seems merely funny, but the mockery involved in "knocking down" one's ancestors "with their own pedigree" was probably a shock to the eighteenth century system, even though Sheridan softened the revolutionary gesture by keeping it in the family.

The Critic • In the tradition of *The Rehearsal* (pr. 1671) by George Villiers, duke of Buckingham, and Henry Fielding's *Tom Thumb: A Tragedy* (pr. 1730), Sheridan's *The Critic* is a burlesque, a type of comedy especially popular in eighteenth century England. *The Critic* provides an engaging and informative survey of the theatrical world in Sheridan's time. Despite its many topical references, the play also has potential for revival in the contemporary age of self-conscious art, in which burlesque is a staple of television comedy. The topical references, in fact, would reverberate with a certain irony, since it appears from *The Critic* that things have not changed all that much in the theater.

Act 1 opens on a breakfast scene, where the critic Mr. Dangle holds court, entertaining all sorts of solicitations. This day there appear Mr. Sneer, another critic; Sir Fretful Plagiary, a vain playwright (based on Richard Cumberland); Mr. Puff, an advertising writer who has authored a play; and Signor Pasticcio Ritornello and a chorus of Italian girls come for audition (the scene probably gives some insight into the Sheridan household). Repartee, malice, and dissimulation fly around the table, in the manner of theatrical shoptalk, with Mrs. Dangle occasionally clearing the air in straightforward language.

In the other two acts, Dangle and Sneer attend a rehearsal of Puff's play, a wretched tragedy entitled *The Spanish Armada*. Again there is much opportunity for satire. Puff has given the actors permission "to cut out or omit whatever they found heavy or unnecessary to the plot"; thus, the play is very brief. Brief as it is, it is a smashing parody of the kind of tragedy written in Sheridan's time, full of clumsy exposition, bombastic verse, stilted characters, and improbable, sensational events, ending with a triumphant sea battle and a procession of all the English rivers accompanied by George Frederick Handel's water music and a chorus.

The faked feelings of the actors in the play-within-the-play are reminders that theater is the essence of illusion, and the framing action of *The Critic* is a reminder of how theater people are often caught up in the illusion. To Mr. Dangle, the theater is more important than the real world: When he reads "the news," it is the theatrical news rather than the news of the impending French invasion. He is such a stargazer because he considers himself a moving force in the theatrical world, as he tells Mrs. Dangle: "You will not easily persuade me that there is no credit or importance in being at the head of a band of critics, who take on them to decide for the whole town, whose opinion and patronage all writers solicit, and whose recommendation no manager dares refuse!" Representing a commonsense point of view, Mrs. Dangle is a counterweight to the vanity that is such an occupational hazard for theatrical (and literary) people. At regular intervals, she tells Mr. Dangle that he is ridiculous: "Why should you affect the character of a critic?" and "Both managers and authors of the least merit laugh at your pretensions. The Public is their Critic."

The real critic in the play is the play itself, as the double meaning in the title indicates. Taking a hard look at the eighteenth century theater, *The Critic* first notes the ideal: "the stage is 'the mirror of Nature.'" The statement is a reminder of how theatrical illusion, and art in general, can paradoxically arrive at the truth. The theater (and art), however, can also go astray, as it did in Sheridan's time. First there is comedy, which strayed into two sorts: "sentimental" comedy, which contains "nothing ridiculous in it from the beginning to the end," and "moral" comedy, which treats "the greater vices and blacker crimes of humanity." To her discredit, Mrs. Dangle prefers the former sort, and Mr. Sneer defends the latter: "The theatre, in proper hands, might certainly be made the school of morality; but now, I am sorry to say it, people seem to go there principally for their entertainment." As for what was happening to tragedy, Mr. Puff's *The Spanish Armada* is sufficient example. Choosing Mr. Puff to be the featured author was an inspired symbolic stroke: as a master of "puffing" (advertising) who commands the language of "panegyrical superlatives," the ability to exaggerate or even invent reality ("to insinuate obsequious rivulets into visionary groves"), he truly represents the spirit of the age in the theater.

Sheridan's remaining plays little enhance his literary reputation, but they do reveal a great deal about his political and social attitudes. The plays are *St. Patrick's Day*, a two-act comedy; *A Trip to Scarborough*, an adaptation of Sir John Vanbrugh's comedy *The Relapse* (pr., pb. 1696); and *Pizarro*, an adaptation of August von Kotzebue's tragedy *Die Spanier in Peru* (1794).

Pizarro • *Pizarro* is an embarrassing reminder of the kind of tragedy which Sheridan parodied in *The Critic*. Treating the depredations of European invaders against the noble Incas, the play gives evidence of Sheridan's antipathy to colonial oppression (it echoes his speeches in Parliament against British rule in India) and his ability to satisfy the growing popular taste for romantic melodrama. In its day, *Pizarro* was a tremendous box-office success.

St. Patrick's Day • Like *Pizarro, St. Patrick's Day* was probably a vehicle for specific actors. The short farce also satisfied the requirements of an afterpiece, a slighter work presented after the main play. Full of scheming and disguising, it dramatizes Lieutenant O'Connor's winning of Miss Lauretta Credulous over the opposition of her father, Justice Credulous, who hates Irishmen and soldiers. Aside from its lighthearted action, *St. Patrick's Day* is notable for its Irish sentiments and its sympathy for the lot of poor soldiers (in Sheridan's time, often Irishmen).

A Trip to Scarborough • *A Trip to Scarborough*, a much more substantial work, was adapted from *The Relapse*, a favorite Restoration comedy. In his adaptation, Sheridan trimmed the plot and cleaned up the sexual innuendo of the original. The adaptation has many features similar to those of Sheridan's other comedies of manners —in particular, an intrigue centering on assumed identity and rivalry between two brothers for a rich heiress. In the course of the intrigue, the penniless Tom Fashion triumphs over his older brother, Lord Foppington, "an ungrateful narrow-minded coxcomb." Furthermore, Lord Foppington is roughly handled by the father-in-law, Sir Tunbelly Clumsy, a jovial Yorkshireman whose personality and household (Muddymoat Hall) are in a tradition stretching to Emily Brontë's *Wuthering Heights* (1847) and Charles Dickens' *Nicholas Nickleby* (1838-1839).

The humbling of a lord in *A Trip to Scarborough* is another example of the antiestablishment Sheridan, a side that the official pronouncements have preferred not to mention. Yet it is as much a part of Sheridan as his inspired ability to write entertaining comedy. A subversive element in eighteenth century Britain, Sheridan was constantly chipping away at the illusions and pretensions of the old order and interjecting stirrings of the egalitarianism that was sweeping away the old order elsewhere. His attack on primogeniture, at the heart of the old system, is typical:

LORD FOPPINGTON: . . . Nature has made some difference 'twixt me and you.

TOM FASHION: Yes—she made you older.

Something of a transitional figure in British drama, Sheridan looked back to Restoration comedy for his inspiration, but his social attitudes looked forward to George Bernard Shaw. During the long barren stretch of two hundred years between Restoration comedy and Shaw, Sheridan preserved the comic spirit in British drama largely through the force of his talent.

Other major works

POETRY: "Clio's Protest," 1771; "The Ridotto of Bath," 1771; *A Familiar Epistle to the Author of the Heroic Epistle to Sir William Chambers,* 1774; "Epilogue to *The Rivals,*" 1775; "Epilogue to *Semiramis,*" 1776; "Verses to the Memory of Garrick, Spoken as a Monody," 1779; "Epilogue to *The Fatal Falsehood,*" 1779; "Prologue to *Pizarro,*" 1799; "Lines by a Lady of Fashion," 1825.

NONFICTION: *Speeches of the Late Right Honourable Richard Brinsley Sheridan (Several Corrected by Himself),* 1816 (5 volumes); *The Letters of Richard Brinsley Sheridan,* 1966 (3 volumes; C. J. L. Price, editor).

MISCELLANEOUS: *The Plays and Poems of Richard Brinsley Sheridan,* 1928, 1962 (3 volumes; R. Compton Rhodes, editor).

Bibliography

Ayling, Stanley. *A Portrait of Sheridan.* London: Constable, 1985. More than two hundred pages on Sheridan's life and work. Ayling offers glimpses of Sheridan's true nature, including the unflattering views on the theater expressed in his letters. The treatment of the early plays is rather brief. Includes some comments on the management of the Drury Lane in later chapters.

Davision, Peter, ed. *Sheridan: Comedies.* Basingstoke, England: Macmillan, 1986. A casebook for the two best-known plays, plus discussions of *The Critic* and *A Trip to Scarborough.* Contains an introductory section on Sheridan's family, his orations, his life and letters; general commentary on Restoration comedy and Sheridan's plays; and final sections on each of the four plays with commentaries by William Hazlitt, Max Beerbohm, George Bernard Shaw, Sir Laurence Olivier, and numerous others. Bibliography and index.

Hare, Arnold. *Richard Brinsley Sheridan.* Windsor, England: Profile Books, 1981. Sketches the major details about Sheridan's life and family. Pays brief attention to the theatrical milieu but analyzes the plays, including some relatively minor ones. Complemented by a select bibliography and a portrait from a pastel by John Russell.

Kelly, Linda. *Richard Brinsley Sheridan: A Life.* London: Sinclair-Stevenson, 1997. The biography looks at Sheridan as both dramatist and legislator. Bibliography and index.

Morwood, James. *The Life and Works of Richard Brinsley Sheridan.* Edinburgh: Scottish Academic Press, 1985. Morwood believes that Sheridan's career as a writer and theatrical manager is inseparable from his private and political life. Makes a fresh effort to evaluate Sheridan's political career and to create a balanced assessment of his thirty-two years as manager of the Drury Lane. Several illustrations, bibliography, index.

Morwood, James, and David Crane, eds. *Sheridan Studies.* New York: Cambridge University Press, 1995. A collection of essays on Sheridan as a dramatist and member of Parliament. Includes a bibliography and index.

O'Toole, Fintan. *A Traitor's Kiss: The Life of Richard Brinsley Sheridan, 1751-1816.* New York: Farrar, Straus and Giroux, 1998. This biography covers Sheridan's earlier years and his plays as well as his later life in Parliament. Also describes his romantic life. Bibliography and index.

Worth, Katharine. *Sheridan and Goldsmith.* New York: St. Martin's Press, 1992. Worth compares and contrasts the writings of Oliver Goldsmith and Sheridan. Bibliography and index.

Harold Branam,
updated by Howard L. Ford

Neil Simon

Born: Bronx, New York; July 4, 1927

Principal drama • *Come Blow Your Horn*, pr. 1960, pb. 1961; *Little Me*, pr. 1962, revised pr. 1982 (music by Cy Coleman, lyrics by Carol Leigh; adaptation of Patrick Dennis's novel); *Barefoot in the Park*, pr. 1963, pb. 1964; *The Odd Couple*, pr. 1965, pb. 1966; *Sweet Charity*, pr., pb. 1966 (music and lyrics by Coleman and Dorothy Fields; adaptation of Federico Fellini's film *Nights of Cabiria*); *The Star-Spangled Girl*, pr. 1966, pb. 1967; *Plaza Suite*, pr. 1968, pb. 1969; *Promises, Promises*, pr. 1968, pb. 1969 (music and lyrics by Hal David and Burt Bacharach; adaptation of Billy Wilder and I. A. L. Diamond's film *The Apartment*); *Last of the Red Hot Lovers*, pr. 1969, pb. 1970; *The Gingerbread Lady*, pr. 1970, pb. 1971; *The Comedy of Neil Simon*, pb. 1971 (volume 1 in *The Collected Plays of Neil Simon*); *The Prisoner of Second Avenue*, pr., pb. 1971; *The Sunshine Boys*, pr. 1972, pb. 1973; *The Good Doctor*, pr. 1973, pb. 1974 (adaptation of Anton Chekhov's short stories); *God's Favorite*, pr. 1974, pb. 1975 (adaptation of the biblical story of Job); *California Suite*, pr. 1976, pb. 1977; *Chapter Two*, pr. 1977, pb. 1979; *They're Playing Our Song*, pr. 1978, pb. 1980 (music by Marvin Hamlisch, lyrics by Carole Bayer Sager; adaptation of Patrick Dennis's novel); *The Collected Plays of Neil Simon*, pb. 1979 (volume 2); *I Ought to Be in Pictures*, pr. 1980, pb. 1981; *Fools*, pr., pb. 1981; *Brighton Beach Memoirs*, pr. 1982, pb. 1984; *Biloxi Blues*, pr. 1984, pb. 1986; *Broadway Bound*, pr. 1986, pb. 1987; *The Odd Couple*, pr. 1985, pb. 1986 (female version); *Rumors*, pr. 1988, pb. 1990; *Jake's Women*, pr. 1990, pb. 1991; *Lost in Yonkers*, pr., pb. 1991; *The Collected Plays of Neil Simon*, pb. 1991 (volume 3); *Laughter on the 23rd Floor*, pr. 1993, pb. 1995; *London Suite*, pr. 1994, pb. 1996; *Three from the Stage*, pb. 1995; *Proposals*, pr. 1997, pb. 1998; *The Dinner Party*, pr. 2000; *45 Seconds from Broadway*, pr. 2001

Other literary forms • In addition to his plays, Neil Simon has written numerous scripts for motion pictures. Among these are *After the Fox* (1966, with Cesare Zavattini), *The Out-of-Towners* (1970), *The Heartbreak Kid* (1972), *Murder by Death* (1976), *The Goodbye Girl* (1977), *The Cheap Detective* (1978), *Seems Like Old Times* (1980), *Max Dugan Returns* (1983), *The Lonely Guy* (1984), and *The Slugger's Wife* (1985). He has also adapted dozens of his plays to the screen, from *Barefoot in the Park* (1967) to *I Ought to Be in Pictures* (1982) and *Biloxi Blues* (1988). Along with his brother, Simon wrote during the 1940's and 1950's for a variety of television shows, including *The Phil Silvers Show* (1948), *The Tallulah Bankhead Show* (1951), *The Sid Caesar Show* (1956-1957), and *The Garry Moore Show* (1959-1960). His teleplays include *Broadway Bound* (1992), *Jake's Women* (1996), and *The Sunshine Boys* (1997). Simon published *Rewrites: A Memoir* in 1996, adding a second autobiographical volume, *The Play Goes On: A Memoir*, in 1999.

Achievements • Neil Simon has established himself as a leading American playwright of the late twentieth century. As a master of domestic comedy and one-line humor, his popular appeal was established early in his career. Though considered

873

by some to be lighter or less serious because of his comedic talents, as his career progressed, Simon infused his comedy with greater amounts of social relevance, auto-biographical inspiration, and dramatic depth. Many of his plays explore the thin line that separates comedy from pathos, provoking audiences to laugh through their tears. His plays focus on character and personal relationships in primarily middle-class, urban settings in the United States. Nevertheless, the stories he dramatizes are about basic human problems and aspirations, and his plays have proven to have universal appeal.

Simon has been the recipient of numerous awards and honors. They include two Emmy Awards for his work in television in 1957 and 1959; a Tony Award for Best Author for *The Odd Couple* in 1965, and another for *Biloxi Blues* in 1985; a New York Drama Critics Circle Award in 1983 for *Brighton Beach Memoirs*; a New York State Governor's Award in 1986; and a Pulitzer Prize in Drama and a Tony Award for Best Play for *Lost in Yonkers*, both in 1991. In 1993 President Bill Clinton hosted Simon at the White House when Simon received Kennedy Center Honors.

Biography • Marvin Neil Simon was born in the Bronx, New York, on July 4, 1927. His father, Irving, was a salesman in Manhattan's garment district; his mother, Mamie, worked at Gimbel's department store. The family moved to Washington Heights in northern Manhattan when Simon was young. The family's life was not always tranquil. Irving was an errant husband who occasionally abandoned the family altogether, leaving Mamie, a frustrated and bitter woman, alone to deal with Neil and his older brother, Danny. Eventually, the parents were divorced, and Neil went to live with relatives in Queens. From an early age, he exhibited a quick wit and an active imagination. He earned the nickname "Doc"—which stayed with him into adult life—because of his penchant for imitating the family doctor. He loved films and sometimes was asked to leave the theater for laughing too loud. In high school, Simon was sometimes ostracized as a Jew, an experience that would later inform his work. That changed, however, when he joined the baseball team and became a star center fielder. Meanwhile, he and his brother began collaborating on comedy material that they sold to stand-up comics and radio announcers. Simon was graduated from DeWitt Clinton High School in 1944 at the age of sixteen.

He entered New York University under the U.S. Army Air Force Reserve program and was sent to basic training in Biloxi, Mississippi, and then to Lowry Field, Colorado. Throughout his military career, he continued to hone his writing skills, reading favorite authors such as Mark Twain and Robert Benchley and writing for military newspapers. Discharged in 1946, Simon took a job in the mail room at Warner Bros. in New York, where Danny worked in the publicity department. The brothers were soon hired to write for Goodman Ace of the Columbia Broadcasting System (CBS), and over the next decade they provided material for such television comedians as Tallulah Bankhead, Jackie Gleason, Carl Reiner, and Red Skelton. During the summers of 1952 and 1953, they wrote sketches for the professional acting company at Camp Tamiment in Pennsylvania, some of which were featured on Broadway several years later. At Camp Tamiment, Simon fell in love with a young actress named Joan Baim, and the couple was married on September 30, 1953. Five years later, Joan gave birth to a daughter, Ellen; a second daughter, Nancy, was born in 1963.

In 1956, Danny Simon moved to California to be a television director. Neil stayed in New York and wrote for Phil Silvers's *Sergeant Bilko*, Sid Caesar's *Your Show of*

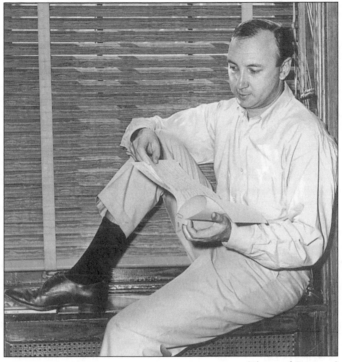

(Library of Congress)

Shows, and *The Garry Moore Show.* He also adapted Broadway plays for television, including Lorenz Hart and Richard Rodgers's musical *Dearest Enemy* (pr. 1925). By the later 1950's, however, he wanted more independence than television writing could offer. He began writing a play of his own. For three years, he wrote and revised, as many as fifty times, his first full play. *Come Blow Your Horn* was optioned by twenty-five producers before it was finally staged in 1960 at the Bucks County Playhouse in New Hope, Pennsylvania. A greatly improved version opened on Broadway the following February. The play received positive notice, and, in 1962, Simon's book for the musical *Little Me* reinforced his growing reputation. It was his third full script, however, *Barefoot in the Park,* that firmly established him on the American stage. It ran for four years, with a total of 1,532 performances. In 1965, Simon had a second smash hit with *The Odd Couple,* which ran for two years and earned for him his first Tony Award.

Over the next decade, Simon's work was characteristically prodigious, with a new play appearing every year or two. While the plays were not all unqualified successes, Simon's popularity continued to rise. At the same time, he accrued a list of screenplay credits. Many were adaptations of his own plays; others were original screenplays or adaptations of other people's works. These films helped spread his notoriety beyond primarily urban, middle-class theater audiences to a wider range of viewers. Despite his popular success, however, Simon was still regarded by serious critics as a lightweight scenarist writing for laughs.

In 1972, Simon faced a harrowing personal tragedy. His wife, Joan, was diagnosed with cancer. Simon nursed her through fifteen agonizing months until she succumbed to the disease in 1973. After twenty years of happy marriage, the loss affected him deeply. Later that year, Simon met an actress named Marsha Mason. The two had a whirlwind romance and within weeks were husband and wife. While never rediscovering the deep passion he had known with Joan, Simon enjoyed a good marriage with Mason that lasted nine years.

In 1974, Simon received a special Tony Award for his contributions to the American theater. His plays continued to appear regularly, and on the screen he scored with such films as *The Goodbye Girl* and *The Cheap Detective*. In 1983, he received a singular honor: The Nederlander Organization renamed a Broadway theater after him.

In the mid-1980's, the trilogy composed of *Brighton Beach Memoirs*, *Biloxi Blues*, and *Broadway Bound* showed a more serious, mature, and openly autobiographical Simon. The three plays garnered many awards, including a Tony Award for *Biloxi Blues* as best play of 1985. *Lost in Yonkers* received even more praise, winning the 1991 Pulitzer Prize in Drama and the Tony Award for best play. Most important, critics began to take Simon seriously as a respectable dramatist.

His third marriage came in 1987, to Diane Lander, a former actress and model. Though divorced in 1988, the couple remarried in 1990, and Simon adopted Lander's daughter Bryn. In 1998 Simon divorced Lander a second time. Marrying for a fifth time, he wedded actress Elaine Joyce shortly after divorcing Lander.

By the 1990's, through four decades of diligent writing, Simon had developed great skill and technique. He divided his time between homes in Manhattan and Bel Air, California, and wrote methodically for seven hours every day. Behind each play that reached fruition, Simon had another ten beginnings that had been put aside, and many more ideas not yet even committed to paper. Nevertheless, with the prodigious output already behind him, he has claimed his position in the history of American theater.

Analysis • Neil Simon's plays have so set the standard for American domestic comedy that they almost form a subgenre in themselves. His work is certainly marked by a distinct style and mastery of certain principles of comic writing. Though the mood, subject matter, and focus of his writing have developed over the years, the Neil Simon signature can still be read throughout.

His plays tend to be domestic comedies focusing on family life and relationships. Almost all are set in New York City and, explicitly or not, depict the concerns and values of middle-class, Jewish family life, writers and show business people, and Americans in touch with the liberal movements of the 1960's and 1970's. As a keen observer of contemporary life, Simon fills his plays with recognizable topical references and details. Dealing with such themes as marriage, divorce, sexual liberation, and intergenerational conflict, his work effectively chronicles late twentieth century American lifestyles and values.

Coming as Simon did from a training ground in stand-up comedy and television writing, he is technically expert at coining and structuring one-line jokes. One-liners are not restricted to token "comic" characters; rather, they are distributed among all the characters in his plays. Furthermore, Simon is skilled at connecting the jokes and embedding them in the texture of the conflict in a way that reinforces the integrity of a scene. The jokes serve rather than divert the flow of action; they inform characterization rather than reduce characters to mere mouthpieces for the author's wit. Simon supports his quick humor with characters who are clearly delineated, defined not only by their backgrounds, tastes, idiosyncrasies, and language but also by their larger objectives and outlooks on life. They are drawn with eccentricity and excess, but with sympathy and warmth as well. The tendency toward stereotypes and caricatures that Simon sometimes indulged early in his career gradually disappeared as he honed his craft.

Creating rich characters, Simon serves them well by carefully structuring his plays to maximize the potential for both conflict and humor. Knowing that the line between tragedy and comedy is a thin one, he heightens the stakes of his characters' desires. Indeed, many a Simon play, drained of its wit, could easily be transformed into serious high drama, with situations worthy of Henrik Ibsen or August Strindberg. The people of Simon's plays are frustrated, sometimes nearly neurotic; they take their problems head-on and search earnestly for solutions. Like William Shakespeare, Simon lets the meaning of his plays inhabit the surface, so there is rarely a deep subtext to unearth. As his characters are generally intelligent and perceptive, they police one another against emotional subterfuge. Unlike Shakespeare, however, Simon does not utilize subplots but rather provides a single, clear conflict to propel the action.

Through more than two dozen plays and nearly as many film scripts, Simon became the wealthiest dramatist in history and the most-produced playwright on the contemporary American stage behind Shakespeare. More important, in addition to his supremacy over the popular American theater, his devotion to craft, hard work, simplicity, honesty, and diligence as a playwright have secured him a primary position in its literary annals.

Simon's techniques are clearly evident in his first two major successes, *Barefoot in the Park* and *The Odd Couple*. Both plays are simply constructed, consisting of four scenes in three acts, taking place in a single locale within a span of several weeks, and built on the conflict between two distinctly defined characters.

Barefoot in the Park • *Barefoot in the Park* is about newlyweds Paul and Corie Bratter. The young lawyer and his wife are moving into their first New York apartment, a living space too small, cold, dilapidated, expensive, and high up to induce peaceful living. In the first scene, they take inventory of their new home, amid visits from Corie's well-intentioned mother from New Jersey and a flamboyant older gentleman from the upstairs apartment. Corie hatches a plan to make a match between Mother and the exotic Mr. Velasco.

The second scene is the dinner gathering, pitting Mother's tender stomach against Velasco's gourmet hors d'oeuvres, Corie's enthusiasm against Paul's reluctance, and the foursome against a cold apartment and a catastrophic kitchen. In the third scene, the group returns from a dinner out, Mother leaves with Velasco, and Corie and Paul become embroiled in a fight that ends in a decision to divorce. In facing the challenges of the apartment and the evening, the newlyweds have come to believe that they have nothing in common. Paul considers his wife irrational and irresponsible; she thinks that he is a stuffed shirt incapable of enjoying life.

In the final scene, Mother is unaccounted for, divorce plans proceed apace, and Corie and Paul are miserable. Ultimately, Mother appears, no worse for wear from a night at Velasco's, and Paul and Corie discover the importance of surrender and compromise. She recognizes her need for order, he relaxes enough to take a walk "barefoot in the park," and they both realize the depth of their love.

From the start, Simon creates a situation rife with possibilities. The setting offers opportunities for visual jokes and offstage action: For example, there are ongoing references to the six-flight ascent to the apartment. As newlyweds adapting to a new home, job, and lifestyle, Corie and Paul are portrayed in the midst of major upheaval. The stolid Mother and the splendiferous Velasco are great foils for each other and for the younger couple as well. Furthermore, in Corie and Paul, Simon creates protagonists whose personalities, often in harmony, easily become diametrically opposed through their responses to difficult circumstances.

The Odd Couple • Even more than in *Barefoot in the Park*, the conflict in Simon's next play, *The Odd Couple*, is built squarely on the collision of opposites. Oscar Madison is a divorced sportswriter living alone, who hosts five friends for a weekly poker game, including his good friend Felix Ungar. (During his childhood, Simon's mother used to run poker games in the family home for extra income.) In the first scene, Felix, usually quite punctual, arrives hours late in emotional distress, with the horrific news that his wife kicked him out. Oscar invites Felix to become his roommate, and the "odd couple" is formed.

Simon established Felix's sensitive and fastidious nature in the opening scene, so it is no surprise when, in the second scene, two weeks later, Felix is driving the slovenly Oscar crazy with his devotion to detail and cleanliness. Their relationship is implicitly a send-up of marriage in an age of rising divorce rates and precarious gender roles. The bachelor life is clearly threatened by Felix's uxoriousness. To break the tension and salve their solitude, Oscar suggests a double date with their upstairs neighbors, the Pigeon sisters. Felix reluctantly agrees.

In the third scene, Cecily and Gwendolyn Pigeon come downstairs for dinner, straight out of an Oscar Wilde drawing room. As in *Barefoot in the Park*, however, the menu is sabotaged by circumstance, and, instead of succumbing to the double seduction that Oscar envisions, the Pigeons both take sisterly pity on the heartbroken Felix. The failed date precipitates a climactic conflagration between the two men, and, as in *Barefoot in the Park*, the only solution seems to be separation.

In the final scene, amid a cold war of silence and anger, Oscar and Felix vent their rage and passion, coming to understand that their conflict reflects an unhappy combination of personality types and the larger tragedies of failed marriages and solitary middle age. These themes reappear time and again in Simon's work—the distance between people, the effects of time on relationships, and the different ways that men and women deal with emotion. In the end, Oscar and Felix reach a mutually respectful peace, forged of patience, humility, and a willingness to laugh.

Other early plays • The formula established by these early comedies provides the basis for many of the plays that followed. In 1966, Simon wrote the book for *Sweet Charity*, a Bob Fosse musical based on the Federico Fellini film *Nights of Cabiria* (1957). In *The Star-Spangled Girl*, he pitted liberal journalists against an old-fashioned southern belle. Both of these pieces met mixed response. Years later, Simon called *The Star-Spangled Girl* "simply a failure," a play "where I did not have a clear visual image of the characters in my mind as I sat down at the typewriter." Nevertheless, with the opening of *The Star-Spangled Girl*, Simon could claim the singular distinction of having four plays running simultaneously on Broadway.

In 1968, Simon tried something new: a series of three one-act plays set in the same hotel room. The result, *Plaza Suite*, is vintage Simon with an added bittersweetness. The first piece focuses on a stale marriage and a revelation of infidelity; the second, on high school flames reuniting in midlife; and the third, on a bride's wedding day jitters and what they bring out in her parents' marriage. That same year, Simon wrote the book for *Promises, Promises,* a Burt Bacharach-Hal David musical version of the 1960 film *The Apartment.*

Mid-career plays • A mid-career Simon focused on the romantic woes of a middle-aged man in his next play, *Last of the Red Hot Lovers.* Then came *The Gingerbread Lady,* dealing with the subject of alcoholism; *The Prisoner of Second Avenue,* about the nervous breakdown of a man caught in the vertigo of urban life; and *The Sunshine Boys,* depicting the deteriorating relationship of a pair of old comedians. These plays signaled an attempt by Simon to move into issue-oriented material with a more serious tone. While still striking with characteristic wit and receiving popular acclaim, he sometimes overindulged in sentiment and high seriousness. Some critics lambasted the attempt and urged him to stay on familiar, lighter terrain.

In 1972 and 1973, during the period of his wife's illness and death, Simon's writing reflected his personal tragedy. *The Good Doctor* was his adaptation of the tragicomic stories of Russian dramatist Anton Chekhov. More penetrating was *God's Favorite,* a modern reworking of the biblical story of Job, in which a man challenges God and the universe to help him understand the extremity of his sufferings. It was Simon's attempt to find solace and peace through his writing.

California Suite • *California Suite,* a Pacific Coast retake of the *Plaza Suite* concept, appeared in 1976. Like its predecessor, and much of the intervening work, it takes a more sophisticated approach to relationships and social situations. It consists of four short plays set in a two-room suite at the Beverly Hills Hotel. The first and third have definite pathos beneath their comic gloss; the second and fourth are lighter and broader.

The second of the four pieces is about Marvin and Millie, a husband and wife from Philadelphia who have come to Los Angeles for a nephew's Bar Mitzvah. Marvin arrived a night early and returned to the suite to find a gift from his brother waiting for him: a prostitute. It is the next morning, and Millie arrives; the other woman, however, is still drunk and asleep in the bed, and for most of the play, Marvin scrambles to conceal her inert form. Eventually, he confesses his sin to Millie, and they face the crisis with equal guilt and stoicism. The play runs on frantic energy, physical comedy, and the audience's discrepant awareness of the other woman's presence.

The fourth play is also built on physical comedy emerging from a situation that is out of control. Mort and Beth and Stu and Gert are two couples from Chicago who have taken a three-week vacation together. Best friends at the start, their rapport has steadily eroded. At last, an accidental injury on the tennis court unleashes torrents of accumulated hostility; the feuding then triggers a series of freak accidents, a veritable comedy of mishaps. The barroom brawl-like mayhem ends in unresolved pandemonium. Simon here displays his ability to bring together one-liners, character conflict, and physical comedy into an orchestrated whole.

Set against these two lighter plays are the first and third pieces. In the first, a divorced couple negotiate where their daughter will live for her last year of high school. Billy and Hannah are both brashly intelligent and piercingly sarcastic. What begins as a brittle, venomous battle of words and wits subtly evolves into a deep struggle for pride and control. Knowing each other all too well, they ultimately bring their hopes, fears, and even some of their long-abandoned love into the open. While the characters use humor as a weapon throughout, their true feelings are always evident, and Simon allows and validates their enduring anger. Ultimately, a deal is struck, but the tone and outcome make it clear that there are no winners in this struggle.

The same is true of the third piece, in which a British actress and her husband have come to Hollywood for the Academy Awards. Dividing the action into two scenes, Simon contrasts their hopeful harmony before the ceremony with their bitter and drunken divisiveness after it. Diana has not won the coveted Oscar but instead has made a fool of herself at the ensuing parties. At the heart of her recklessness is a deep dissatisfaction with her marriage. Her husband, Sidney, an unassuming antiques dealer, is a "bisexual homosexual," and his flirtation with a young actor over dinner has brought dangerous issues to the surface. In the end, Sidney will hold, soothe, and probably make love to Diana, but it is evident that the connection is only temporary. That they can come together at all is a sign of hope, but Simon allows no illusions about the sacrifices they are making and the evanescence of their union.

This mix of pieces and tones, all still focused on relationships, marriages, sex, and love, bespeaks an unapologetic honesty that cannot be found in Simon's earlier work. Indeed, in 1979, Simon said that he believed the third play of *California Suite* was his best and most honest writing.

Autobiographical works • While parts of his earlier plays are drawn loosely from personal experience, by the late 1970's Simon was ready to take on autobiographical material more directly. *Chapter Two* was the first play in this direction. It tells the story of a recently widowed man who meets and falls in love with a woman, a story the playwright had known firsthand several years before. During this period, he also wrote a second version of *The Odd Couple*, this time with two women in the leading roles (produced and published a decade later); the book for a Marvin Hamlisch-Carole Bayer Sager musical called *They're Playing Our Song*, a play called *I Ought to Be in Pictures*, about a screenwriter and his daughter; and *Fools*, a comic fable based on a Ukrainian folktale. This last was Simon's only unequivocal flop.

Brighton Beach Memoirs • The real breakthrough came with *Brighton Beach Memoirs*, which, with *Biloxi Blues* and *Broadway Bound*, forms Simon's acclaimed autobiographical trilogy. In these plays, the playwright's own past is clear and unmistakable. The plays center on Eugene Morris Jerome, a teenage writer and baseball enthusiast growing up in Brighton Beach, New York, in the 1940's. Eugene has an older brother, unhappily married parents, and great aspirations. These aspirations lead him to chronicle his family's trials and tribulations, and his writings become a vehicle for narrating and commenting on the action directly to the audience. As Eugene is representative of the young Simon, his direct address offers an intimacy between playwright and audience that Simon had never before attempted or allowed.

In the trilogy, Simon also effectively explores dramatic structure. "I really made a quantum leap in *Brighton Beach* as a playwright," Simon said in 1985, "because it was the first full-bodied play I had ever written, in terms of dealing with a group of people as individuals and telling all their stories." Before, he would focus on a central character or conflict; now, though Eugene was the connecting thread, Simon was portraying a more integrated and balanced world. In *Brighton Beach Memoirs*, Eugene's adolescent fascination with his cousin Nora, his aunt Blanche's quandary over reestablishing her independence, his older brother Stanley's moral crisis at work, Nora's dreams of a show business career, her sister Laurie's fragile health, and Jack and Kate Jerome's precarious marriage and difficult economic straits are all woven together into a delicate tapestry of events and emotions. The play, suffused with characteristic wit but a deeper sense of poignancy, won the New York Drama Critics Circle Award, the first truly critical recognition of Simon's work.

Biloxi Blues • *The New York Times* critic Frank Rich wrote that he would love to see a "chapter two" to *Brighton Beach Memoirs*, so Simon decided to continue Eugene's story. *Biloxi Blues* takes place at an army training camp in Biloxi, Mississippi, no doubt the camp that Simon had attended four decades earlier. It is one of his few plays set outside New York City and one of the few that feature a group of strangers. Like its predecessor, it balances the stories of several characters. Simon introduces Arnold Epstein, a tender Jewish youth with a will of steel; Sergeant Toomey, a career military man facing his mortality and determined to make soldiers of the last group assigned to him; Wykowski and Selridge, the company bullies; and Carney and Hennesey, who bring other colors of adolescence to the complete picture. Outside the barracks, there are Rowena, the weekend prostitute who takes Eugene's virginity, and Daisy, the lovely schoolgirl who wins his heart.

The play gains steady momentum through a variety of means: the rigors of training, the competitive banter of the barracks, the young men's unrelenting fears and hormones, the often blatant bigotry and anti-Semitism, the lurking suspicions of homosexuality, and the implicit challenges to pride and manhood. In the climactic scene, Simon distills all the play's themes into a tense confrontation between the old soldier Toomey and the unwilling hero Epstein, in a way that seals the play's uncanny, but human, logic.

In *Biloxi Blues*, Eugene again takes the audience into his confidence, sharing his process of maturing as both man and writer. The one-liners are ever-present, but the world of the play is darkened by the shadow of World War II, establishing a type of meaningful historical context that is unseen in Simon's work before the trilogy. The fourteen scenes, spanning months and moving through a variety of settings, are also unusual for Simon. *Biloxi Blues* is a rite-of-passage play, and Simon treats the inherent issues—adolescence, manhood, fear, sexuality, separation—with deep warmth, sensitivity, and subtlety.

Broadway Bound • *Broadway Bound* completed the trilogy in 1986. Eugene is back in Brighton Beach, and the tapestry interweaves his fledgling career, writing comedy with his brother Stanley, with the quickly unraveling threads of his parents' marriage. Past and family are inescapable even as the future looks bright, and, when their homegrown skit actually comes across the radio waves, Eugene and Stanley learn an important lesson about the dangers of mixing humor and autobiography. It is no doubt an issue that had crossed the playwright's mind as well.

In *Broadway Bound*, Eugene still narrates and comments, and audiences who followed him through the first two plays can appreciate his ripening maturity. The most powerful scene of the play is remarkably simple: Eugene dances with his mother, Kate, amid the disarray of the kitchen and her crumbling marriage, to her lyrical reminiscences of a girlhood infatuation with a dashing celebrity and a magical night when she danced with him. The intimacy of the story embarrasses even Eugene, a fact that he candidly confesses to the audience. The Oedipal implications of the scene magnify both the young man's coming-of-age and his mother's life of pain and frustration. By using details taken directly from his own youth, Simon frankly investigates his filial memories and feelings, and the result is powerful. The writing shows a level of dramatic achievement of which the author of *Come Blow Your Horn* could only have dreamed.

The trilogy was followed by *Rumors*, Simon's first attempt at all-out farce, and *Jake's Women*, a whimsical play about a writer and the women who populate his mind. *Jake's Women* endured many rewrites and an aborted out-of-town trial before finally coming to Broadway, a process that testified to Simon's power and diligence as a playwright.

Lost in Yonkers • In 1991, continuing in the spirit of the trilogy, *Lost in Yonkers* appeared on Broadway. Portraying the sojourn of two boys with their brusque grandmother and eccentric aunt and uncle, it earned Simon critical praise, his second Tony Award for best play, and a prestigious Pulitzer Prize in Drama. The play continues in the spirit of the Brighton Beach trilogy, but with less sense of nostalgia as Simon wrings comedy from the anguish of five deeply disturbed people. Critic David Richards noted that "Were it not for his [Simon's] ready wit and appreciation of life's incongruities, *Lost in Yonkers* could pass for a nightmare."

As in the trilogy, there are two young boys, clearly based on Simon and his older brother, but the other characters and the action are inventions. The place is the apartment over Kurnitz's Kandy Store in Yonkers, where Grandma Kurnitz lives with her thirty-five-year-old, brain-damaged daughter Bella. Grandma Kurnitz's experiences with anti-Semitism as a child in Germany convinced her that to succeed in this world you must be hard as steel. Ignoring her four surviving children's emotional life, she rigidly disciplined them.

The time is 1942, and son Eddie has come to beg his mother to take in his two boys while he travels as a salesman. Having borrowed from loan sharks to pay the medical bills of his recently deceased wife, he desperately needs to earn money. Grandma reluctantly agrees. Following his mother's advice to be hard, a second son, Louie, became a small-time gangster and now comes home to hide from the associates he has cheated. An older daughter Gert also stops by; she suffers from a breathing problem whenever she visits her mother and cannot finish a sentence without gasping for breath.

The emotional center of the play is the struggle of Bella to fashion a life of her own, against the opposition of her mother. Bella falls in love with a mentally retarded movie theater usher and is determined to marry him, despite the grim disapproval of her mother and the skepticism of her siblings, but the usher is too timid to leave the protection of his parents and the romance fails. At the play's end Eddie returns to claim his sons, and Bella asserts herself. She tells her mother she is going to the movies with a new girlfriend who likes her. Further, the girlfriend has a brother, and Bella plans to invite them both for dinner later that week.

Later plays • Simon continued to send new plays to Broadway, though none repeated the critical or monetary success of *Lost in Yonkers*. *Laughter on the 23rd Floor*, based on Simon's years as a writer for Sid Caesar's television shows, portrays activities in the writers' room as eight conflicting personalities and egos struggle to put together a new comic script every week. *London Suite* echoes *Plaza Suite* and *California Suite* with four one-act dramas, this time taking place in an elegant London hotel. *Proposals*, set in the 1950's at a summer cottage in a resort area of eastern Pennsylvania, revolves around the disagreements between a retired businessman, his former wife, his daughter, and his daughter's various boyfriends, one of whom is the son of a Mafia baron. *The Dinner Party* occurs in a private room at an expensive Parisian restaurant as six diners explore the various reasons their marriages have failed. *45 Seconds from Broadway* takes its title from the time needed to walk from theaters to a coffee shop, familiarly known as the Polish Tea Room, that is a favorite hangout of theater folk. Ten actors exchange banter and good-natured insults with each other and the restaurant's owners.

Other major works

SCREENPLAYS: *After the Fox*, 1966 (with Cesare Zavattini); *Barefoot in the Park*, 1967; *The Odd Couple*, 1968; *The Out-of-Towners*, 1970; *Plaza Suite*, 1971; *The Last of the Red Hot Lovers*, 1972; *The Heartbreak Kid*, 1972; *The Prisoner of Second Avenue*, 1975; *The Sunshine Boys*, 1975; *Murder by Death*, 1976; *The Goodbye Girl*, 1977; *California Suite*, 1978; *The Cheap Detective*, 1978; *Chapter Two*, 1979; *Seems Like Old Times*, 1980; *Only When I Laugh*, 1981; *I Ought to Be in Pictures*, 1982; *Max Dugan Returns*, 1983; *The Lonely Guy*, 1984; *The Slugger's Wife*, 1985; *Brighton Beach Memoirs*, 1987; *Biloxi Blues*, 1988; *The Marrying Man*, 1991; *Lost in Yonkers*, 1993; *The Odd Couple II*, 1998.

TELEPLAYS: *Broadway Bound*, 1992; *Jake's Women*, 1996; *London Suite*, 1996; *The Sunshine Boys*, 1997.

NONFICTION: *Rewrites: A Memoir*, 1996; *The Play Goes On: A Memoir*, 1999.

Bibliography

Henry, William A., III. "Reliving a Poignant Past." *Time*, December 15, 1986, 72-78. Henry describes the success of the play *Broadway Bound* and its biographical sources, and includes in-depth material about Simon's marriages, lifestyle, writing habits, and older brother Danny. Compares Simon's life with its fictional parallels, especially in *Broadway Bound*.

Johnson, Robert K. *Neil Simon*. Boston: G. K. Hall, 1983. In this thoughtful and penetrating study, Johnson examines Simon's career and output through 1982, providing thorough synopses, analysis, and criticism of both plays and screenplays. Includes a chronology, a select bibliography, notes, and an index.

Konas, Gary, ed. *Neil Simon: A Casebook*. New York: Garland, 1997. Seven scholarly articles examine the influence of Simon's Jewish heritage and compare his work with that of other dramatists. Four essays discuss recurrent patterns in Simon's plays. The volume closes with two Simon interviews.

Koprince, Susan. *Understanding Neil Simon*. Columbia: University of South Carolina Press, 2002. Offering a guide to Simon's work, Koprince provides an overview of Simon's career and an in-depth analysis of his major plays. Includes bibliography and index.

McGovern, Edythe. *Not-So-Simple Neil Simon: A Critical Study*. Van Nuys, Calif.: Perivale Press, 1978. McGovern examines twelve of Simon's earliest plays with an even, theoretical, scholarly tone, occasionally tending toward unqualified praise. The slim volume includes a preface by the playwright, a list of characters from the plays, twenty-two production photographs, and seven illustrations by renowned Broadway caricaturist Al Hirschfeld.

Richards, David. "The Last of the Red Hot Playwrights." Review of *Lost in Yonkers*, by Neil Simon. *The New York Times Magazine*, February 17, 1991, 30. Celebrating Simon's success with *Lost in Yonkers*, this reviewer describes the play and production and profiles the playwright. The article brings together personal and professional material, using quotes from Simon, his family members, and actors associated with his plays. Personal and in-depth, with nine photographs.

Simon, Neil. "The Art of Theater X." Interview by James Lipton. *The Paris Review* 34 (Winter, 1992): 166-213. A chatty, revealing interview. The first half of the interview is largely given to discussion of how Simon became a playwright and the strong autobiographical elements in his work: "I think my greatest weakness is that I can't write outside my own experience." Other topics include the "almost invisible line" between comedy and tragedy and the gradually darkening vision of Simon's plays, which he sees as a movement toward greater truthfulness. Simon's ongoing enthusiasm for theater is clear; he concludes, "Every time I write a play it's the beginning of a new life for me."

Barry Mann,
updated by Milton Berman

Stephen Sondheim

Born: New York, New York; March 22, 1930

Principal drama • *West Side Story*, pr. 1957, pb. 1958 (lyrics; music by Leonard Bernstein; book by Arthur Laurents); *Gypsy*, pr. 1959, pb. 1960 (lyrics; music by Jule Styne; book by Laurents); *A Funny Thing Happened on the Way to the Forum*, pr., pb. 1962 (lyrics and music; book by Larry Gelbart and Burt Shevelove); *Anyone Can Whistle*, pr. 1964, pb. 1965 (lyrics and music; book by Laurents); *Do I Hear a Waltz?*, pr. 1965, pb. 1966 (lyrics; music by Richard Rodgers; book by Laurents); *Candide*, pr. 1974, pb. 1976 (lyrics with Richard Wilbur and John Latouche; music by Bernstein; book by Hugh Wheeler); *Company*, pr., pb. 1970 (lyrics and music; book by George Furth); *Follies*, pr., pb. 1971 (lyrics and music; book by James Goldman); *The Frogs*, pr. 1974, pb. 1975 (lyrics and music; book by Shevelove); *A Little Night Music*, pr., pb. 1973 (lyrics and music; book by Wheeler); *Pacific Overtures*, pr. 1976, pb. 1977 (lyrics and music; book by John Weidman); *Sweeney Todd: The Demon Barber of Fleet Street*, pr., pb. 1979 (lyrics and music; book by Wheeler); *Marry Me a Little*, pr. 1980 (lyrics and music; book by Craig Lucas and Norman René); *Merrily We Roll Along*, pr. 1981, pb. 1982 (lyrics and music; book by Furth); *Sunday in the Park with George*, pr. 1983, pb. 1986 (lyrics and music; book by James Lapine); *Into the Woods*, pr. 1987, pb. 1988 (lyrics and music; book by Lapine); *Assassins*, pr. 1990, pb. 1991 (lyrics and music; book by Weidman); *Passion*, pr., pb. 1994 (lyrics and music; book by Lapine); *Getting Away with Murder*, pr. 1995, pb. 1997 (with Furth); *Gold!*, pr. 2002 (lyrics and music; book by Weidman; originally pr. 1999 as *Wise Guys*)

Other literary forms • Stephen Sondheim wrote a film script, *The Last of Sheila* (1973), with Anthony Perkins. He has composed music for films as well. He wrote the scores for *Stavisky* (1974) and *Reds* (1981) and songs for *Dick Tracy* (1990) and *The Birdcage* (1996). However, Sondheim's reputation is based primarily on his music and lyrics for Broadway-style musicals.

Achievements • Stephen Sondheim was the most critically acclaimed figure in American musical theater during the last three decades of the twentieth century. Sondheim has won the Tony Award for Best Original Score five times, more than any other individual. These awards were for *Follies* (1972), *A Little Night Music* (1973), *Sweeney Todd* (1979), *Into the Woods* (1988), and *Passion* (1994). In 1971 only, separate Tonys were awarded for score and lyrics, and Sondheim won both for *Company*. Numerous plays on which Sondheim has collaborated have won Tony Awards and New York Drama Critics Circle Awards for Best Musical; these awards were not presented specifically to Sondheim. *Sunday in the Park with George* won the 1985 Pulitzer Prize in Drama.

Sondheim turned down the National Medal of Arts in 1992 in protest because the National Endowment for the Arts, the granting agency, had canceled some of its more controversial grants. He accepted that award in 1997.

Biography • Stephen Joshua Sondheim was born on March 22, 1930, in New York City, the only child of Herbert and Janet Fox Sondheim. His parents owned a clothing company and were both very involved in the business. The Sondheims separated when Stephen was ten, and he attended military school for two years and then attended the George School, a prep school. He was an exceptional student who had skipped two grades and who showed an early talent for music.

In the early 1940's, Sondheim and his mother became close friends with the family of Oscar Hammerstein II, one of the leading figures in musical theater at the time. Sondheim and the Hammersteins' son were close in age, and Sondheim even spent a summer with the family at their home in Bucks County, Pennsylvania. Janet Sondheim bought a house near the Hammersteins' home where her son lived during his adolescence. Stephen Sondheim asked Hammerstein to read a musical he wrote as a teenager at the George School; Hammerstein critiqued the piece, giving Sondheim valuable training in writing for musical theater. He also hired Sondheim to work on the set of one of his plays.

Sondheim attended Williams College; initially, he majored in English but changed to music. During his college years, he pursued a training program devised by Hammerstein to learn musical theater; the plan involved writing four plays. The first step was to set a play he liked to music, the second was to fix the flaws in a play and set it to music, the third was to write a musical based upon a nondramatic source, and the fourth was to write an original work. After graduation, Sondheim studied music in New York City with Milton Babbitt, an avant-garde composer. As part of his studies, he performed in-depth analyses of classical works; his seriousness about music would be apparent in the complexity of his later compositions.

Sondheim's first big break was as a lyricist for *West Side Story*; he followed by writing lyrics for *Gypsy*. He finally got to write both music and lyrics for *A Funny Thing Happened on the Way to the Forum*, which opened in 1962. Sondheim's reputation and success continued to grow such that he became a central figure in musical theater.

Sondheim's most serious romantic involvement has been with Peter Jones, with whom he exchanged wedding rings in 1994.

Analysis • The most critically acclaimed writer of music and lyrics for Broadway-style musicals in the late twentieth century, Stephen Sondheim has advanced the sophistication of the musical form through his experimentation with content and musical style. One of American musical theater's contributions to drama is the integration of spoken words and music within a production. The majority of Sondheim's lyrics make sense only when sung by the character for whom they are written. Much popular American music earlier in the century came from musical theater. With the exception of "Send in the Clowns" from *A Little Night Music*, Sondheim's songs have not enjoyed popularity, in large part because their meaning is so specific to the dramatic context for which they were written.

The sophistication of Sondheim's compositions has also been an important element in elevating critical assessment of the musical theater genre, which has often been dismissed as pure entertainment rather than serious drama. Sondheim's musical influences range from classical, as seen in the Gregorian chant motif in the score of *Sweeney Todd*, to Asian motifs in *Pacific Overtures*, to contemporary popular music from musical theater and film.

Sondheim's drama, as well, is notable for the range of its sources and themes. For example, *A Funny Thing Happened on the Way to the Forum* is a farce based on the works of the Roman playwright Plautus, *Pacific Overtures* is styled after Japanese Kabuki theater, and *Sunday in the Park with George* draws on the life and work of French Impressionist painter Georges Seurat. Although collaborative work and drawing on pre-existing sources for materials is within the tradition of musical theater, Sondheim's multiple references are also consistent with the practice of postmodernist writers of self-consciously borrowing from existing works. Musical theater, and Sondheim's works in particular, epitomize the postmodernist tendency to reinterpret earlier forms for contemporary uses.

A Funny Thing Happened on the Way to the Forum • Based on plays written by the Roman playwright Plautus, *A Funny Thing Happened on the Way to the Forum* is a farce, with the plot centering on men lusting for beautiful prostitutes and plot twists deriving from coincidences and mistaken identities.

The show's bawdy content and farcical nature pushed the limits of musical theater. The drama is framed as a play-within-a-play, a theatrical device that allows a play to be self-conscious about itself and its intentions. Beginning with the chorus of Greek drama, a tradition has long existed in the theater of voices external to the drama offering commentary on the events. However, most twentieth century drama presents characters going about their business as if unaware of the audience. The framing of Sondheim's drama both ties the play to its classical sources and invites the audience to adopt, despite the lighthearted subject matter, a critical attitude toward the work, as the play offers an explanation of itself as comedy with details about what that means.

A Little Night Music • *A Little Night Music* is a romantic comedy that draws on the conventional comedic topic of mismatched lovers trying to find their true loves. The idea originally began with a desire by Sondheim and others to make a musical from Jean Anouilh's play *L'Invitation au château* (pr. 1947; *Ring Round the Moon*, 1950). When Anouilh declined an adaptation of his play, Sondheim viewed films with similar plots including Jean Renoir's 1939 *Rules of the Game* and Ingmar Bergman's 1956 *Smiles of a Summer Night*.

The themes and mood of the play draw from a long theatrical tradition, evoking, for example, William Shakespeare's *A Midsummer Night's Dream* (pr. c. 1595-1596), which also portrays mismatched lovers seeking their true loves on a magical evening. In proper comedic form, *A Little Night Music* ends with the lovers properly matched.

Beyond the follies and maneuvering of the lovers, the theme of youth and age is important to both the play's meaning and its structure. Most of the action takes place at the country house of an old woman who, with her young granddaughter, watches the action. The grandmother teaches her young charge that a summer night smiles three times: at the young who know nothing, the fools who know too little, and the old who know too much. The primary plot could occur without the older and younger characters, but they deepen the drama's scope by showing the lovers' plots as part of a stage of life between youth and age.

The musical opens with a quintet of characters who are not part of the main story but who perform lyrics both at the beginning and later in the show that comment on the play's main action. This use of choruslike characters serves to distance the audience from identification with the main characters because of the obvious artifice involved. This distancing evokes an intellectual or critical response from the audience.

Sweeney Todd • *Sweeney Todd* blurs the boundaries between musical theater and opera and has, in fact, been performed by various opera companies. The play retells a story about a mass murderer originally written for the stage in the nineteenth century, rewritten by contemporary British playwright Christopher Bond, and finally set to music by Sondheim. The play presents the challenges of portraying murders onstage without disgusting the audience or resorting to slapstick. Further, although the nineteenth century sources were not notable for their psychological subtlety, Sondheim's version seeks to offer insight into the mind of the deranged killer. Beyond the psychological intrigue, the musical explores the themes of revenge and justice. Despite these serious themes, the drama contains significant, albeit black, humor. Todd's accomplice, Mrs. Lovett, bakes the meat from the corpses into pies that she sells in her shop.

The play's significant accomplishment is its ability to interweave tragedy and comedy as well as sophistication and base humor within a musical score that draws on sources ranging from Gregorian chant to contemporary, popular music.

Sunday in the Park with George • Inspired by the life and work of Georges Seurat, especially the painting *Un Dimanche Après-Midi à l'île de la Grande Jatte* (*A Sunday Afternoon on the Island of La Grande Jatte*), *Sunday in the Park with George* explores what it means to be an artist and the relationship between life and art. In the musical's first act, the people in the painting go about their lives as George sketches them. For example, his pregnant girlfriend Dot decides to marry the baker Louis, and two young women pursue an attractive soldier. At the end of the act, as the characters argue among themselves, the painter stops them and arranges them into the poses and positions for his picture. The dual statement is that the piece of art hides the tensions of life, and at the same time, the artwork turns ordinary life into something beautiful.

The second act continues to explore the meanings of art as Seurat's daughter and her grandson George attend an opening for the grandson's artwork. In contrast to his grandfather, who was focused solely on his artistic vision and never sold a painting, the younger George works the crowd of art patrons and critics, seeking funding for his work. As the play ends, he has decided to move on to new projects rather than repeating variations of his current work. His great-grandmother practiced writing in a book that has been passed down, and George reads from it some of his grandfather's favorite words about art, including order, design, and tension. The grandfather is able, through this medium, to instruct his grandson on the importance of following his own artistic vision.

Other major works

SCREENPLAY: *The Last of Sheila,* 1973 (with Anthony Perkins)
TELEPLAY: *Evening Primrose,* 1966 (lyrics and music)

Bibliography

Banfield, Stephen. *Sondheim's Broadway Musicals.* Ann Arbor: University of Michigan Press, 1993. A very thorough study of Sondheim's work, this book is particularly useful in its discussions of his music. Although perhaps at times too technical for the typical reader, this book provides much valuable information on Sondheim's life and his musicals. Sondheim himself reviewed the manuscript before publication.

Block, Geoffrey. "Happily Ever After: *West Side Story* with Sondheim." In *Enchanted Evenings: The Broadway Musical from "Show Boat" to Sondheim.* New York: Oxford University Press, 1997. This chapter places Sondheim in the context of the musical theater, arguing that his work is the culmination of the form's development since the late 1920's. The earlier chapters provide a useful history of musical theater.

Goodhart, Sandor, ed. *Reading Stephen Sondheim: A Collection of Critical Essays.* New York: Garland, 2000. The essays in this volume, written by literary critics, treat Sondheim with the seriousness afforded other twentieth century playwrights. The essays range from general treatments to explorations of specific features of the plays.

Gordon, Joanne. *Art Ain't Easy: The Achievement of Stephen Sondheim.* Carbondale: Southern Illinois University Press, 1990. Gordon argues for the recognition of Sondheim and musical theater as art rather than merely as escapist entertainment. This study notes many connections between Sondheim's works and works considered high art. Gordon's analysis of the musical qualities of Sondheim's numbers is thorough.

Secrest, Meryle. *Stephen Sondheim: A Life.* New York: Delta, 1998. This full-length biography is based primarily on interviews with Sondheim's friends and associates. It describes not only the events of Sondheim's life but also the history of each of the musicals on which Sondheim worked, including the inspiration for the story, the process the collaborators went through to see the project to production, and the critical and audience response to the play.

Zadan, Craig. *Sondheim and Company.* 2d ed. New York: Da Capo, 1994. This book provides analysis and history of each of Sondheim's musicals. Its many photographs offer a good sense of the style of the productions as well as the process of their preparation. A useful appendix lists who worked on the various productions, provides Broadway performance histories, and lists nonmusical projects in which Sondheim participated.

Joan Hope

Sophocles

Born: Colonus, Greece; c. 496 B.C.E.
Died: Athens, Greece; 406 B.C.E.

Principal drama • *Aias*, early 440's B.C.E. (*Ajax*, 1729); *Antigonē*, 441 B.C.E. (*Antigone*, 1729); *Trachinai*, 435-429 B.C.E. (*The Women of Trachis*, 1729); *Oidipous Tyrannos*, c. 429 B.C.E. (*Oedipus Tyrannus*, 1715); *Ēlektra*, 418-410 B.C.E. (*Electra*, 1649); *Philoktētēs*, 409 B.C.E. (*Philoctetes*, 1729); *Oidipous epi Kolōnōi*, 401 B.C.E. (*Oedipus at Colonus*, 1729); *Sophocles: The Plays and Fragments with Critical Notes, Commentary, and Translation in English Prose*, pb. 1897 (7 volumes)

Other literary forms • In addition to his plays, Sophocles also wrote paeans and elegies. Fragments exist of a paean to the god Asclepius, of an ode to the historian Herodotus, and of an elegy to the philosopher Archelaus. An apparently complete epigram addressed to the poet Euripides also survives. According to ancient tradition, Sophocles wrote a literary treatise in prose, *On the Chorus*. Unfortunately, this work, which may have discussed the tragedian's increase in the size of the chorus, is lost.

Achievements • Sophocles' dramatic career, which intersects both Aeschylus's and Euripides' periods of production, was noted in antiquity for several important theatrical innovations, and his plays have experienced a remarkably constant popularity beginning in his own lifetime and continuing into the present. Perhaps no other playwright has had as great an influence on both ancient and modern concepts of the dramatic art.

Like Aeschylus, Sophocles acted in his own plays. His performances as a ball-playing Nausicaa and as a lyre-playing Thamyras in lost plays were well known in the fifth century. Sophocles is said by ancient sources, however, to have been the first playwright to have abandoned the practice of acting in his own works. It is now impossible to determine whether this change, which became the norm among later Greek tragedians, was a true Sophoclean innovation, the result of, as the sources state, Sophocles' own weakening voice, or was rather the result of a general trend toward increasing specialization in later fifth century B.C.E. tragedies.

Sophocles is also said to have increased the size of the tragic chorus from twelve to fifteen members and to have added a third actor. If Aeschylus's *Oresteia*, produced in 458 B.C.E., can be used as chronological evidence, the former innovation had not yet become the rule by 458, but the latter change had most certainly been introduced by that date. All the surviving plays of Sophocles make use of three actors, but the size of the chorus in a given play is rarely easy to document. The introduction of the third actor was the final evolutionary stage in the development of Greek tragedy, which probably had its origins in a choral song to which one, two, and, finally, three actors were added. With the use of three actors, Sophocles was able to concentrate dramatic attention on the actors and the spoken dialogues and agons or "debates" for which his plays are noted. Sophocles' mastery of dialogue is especially evident in his prologues, which almost always begin not with the static, expository monologues of Euripides, but with dramatic, plot-advancing dialogues, such as the bitter exchange between Antigone and Ismene at the beginning of *Antigone*.

In general, Sophocles accomplishes this development of the actor's role in tragedy without neglecting the choral portions of the play. Sophocles' interest in the chorus is suggested not only by the tradition that he wrote a prose treatise on the chorus and increased its size, but also by the extant plays themselves. While the choruses of Sophocles' tragedies do not have the central importance of such Aeschylean choruses as those in *Hiketides* (463 B.C.E.?; *The Suppliants*, 1777) and *Eumenides* (English translation, 1777; one of three parts of *Oresteia*, 458 B.C.E.), nevertheless, several Sophoclean odes, such as the "Ode to Man" in *Antigone* and the Colonus ode in *Oedipus at Colonus*, are among the most beautiful in Greek tragedy. Sophocles also shows himself able to manipulate dramatic mood through the tone of his odes, as in *Ajax*, when he places a joyful song just before disaster. Only in *Philoctetes*, which has only one true choral ode, does a work of Sophocles exhibit the diminished choral role common in Greek tragedy of the last decades of the fifth century B.C.E.

Two other innovations attributed in antiquity to Sophocles suggest that the playwright was interested in the visual as well as the verbal effects of drama. The ancient biography on the life of Sophocles states that he designed boots and staffs for both actors and the chorus, and in *De poetica* (c. 334-323 B.C.E.; *Poetics*, 1705), Aristotle says that Sophocles invented scene painting. In general, however, the extant plays show little of the spectacular stagecraft found in both Aeschylus and Euripides. The closest Sophocles comes to Aeschylus's use of ghosts is the supernatural disappearance of Oedipus in *Oedipus at Colonus*, and he employs the favorite Euripidean technique of the *deus ex machina* only once, in *Philoctetes*.

Modern scholars often state that Sophocles was responsible for the abandonment of connected tragic trilogies in favor of thematically independent plays, a conclusion based on the tenuous assumption that all mid-fifth century B.C.E. productions of three tragedies and one satyr play were connected in theme. Another possible interpretation of the scanty ancient evidence on trilogies is that connected trilogies were an Aeschylean experiment that few, if any, later tragedians repeated. Sophocles' composition *Telepheia*, usually considered to be his only connected trilogy, may not have been a connected group at all. Not even the names of the plays that made up *Telepheia* are known, and there is no evidence that the *-eia* ending signifies a connected trilogy in fifth century B.C.E. terminology, despite the *-eia* ending in *Oresteia*.

Although it is unlikely, then, that Sophocles was an innovator in the production of unconnected trilogies, several of his individual plays do possess another distinctive structural feature, diptych composition. Composed of two nearly independent parts or with two separate main characters, *Ajax*, *Antigone*, and *The Women of Trachis* all divide neatly into two parts, with the departures or deaths of Ajax, Antigone, and Deianira, respectively. Only Euripides' *Alkēstis* (438 B.C.E.; *Alcestis*, 1781) approaches the two-part structure of these Sophoclean plays, the "disunity" of which has been noted by both ancient and modern critics. Yet dipytch form appears to have been an intentional feature of these tragedies, perhaps even a Sophoclean experiment made in response to the Aeschylean connected trilogy. This Sophoclean form is based not on structural disunity but rather on structural flexibility and demonstrates a general deemphasis on the need for single central characters that is notable not only in Sophocles but also in extant Greek tragedy in general. Sophocles' *Oedipus Tyrannus*, with its nearly exclusive attention to the fate of a single character, is rather the exception than the rule in this respect.

(Library of Congress)

The esteem in which Sophocles' work was held in the fifth century B.C.E. is evident from such contemporary evidence as Aristophanes' *Batrachoi* (405 B.C.E.; *The Frogs,* 1780), in which praise of the late Sophocles as "good-natured while alive and good-natured in Hades," is clearly comic understatement, and Phrynichus's *Muses,* produced in the same year, in which Sophocles is described as "a prosperous and clever man who wrote many good tragedies." This fifth century B.C.E. respect for Sophocles was intensified in the fourth century B.C.E., under the influence of Aristotle, whose high praise of Sophoclean tragedy in *The Poetics* has shaped all subsequent critical approaches, not only to Sophocles but also to tragedy in general. Aristotle, for whom Sophoclean tragedy, and specifically *Oedipus Tyrannus,* was an ideal tragedy, particularly admired Sophocles' dramatic development of character and quoted the playwright as saying that "he [Sophocles] made men as they ought to be; Euripides as they are."

Along with the works of Aeschylus and Euripides, Sophocles' plays were widely adapted by Roman tragedians in the second and first centuries B.C.E., but Seneca's *Oedipus* (c. 40-55 C.E.; English translation, 1581) is the only extant Roman imitation of Sophocles. Seneca follows closely the plot of Sophocles' *Oedipus Tyrannus,* but with a typically Roman overemphasis on Teiresias's rites of prophecy and with a compressed version of Oedipus's discovery of his true identity that pales beside its Sophoclean source. Seneca's play also lacks the great mood of irony for which Sophocles is justly famous.

The role of Sophoclean tragedy in the history of ideas would be incomplete without mention of Sophocles' influence on the philosophy of Georg Wilhelm Friedrich Hegel in the nineteenth century and on the psychological theories of Sigmund Freud in the twentieth century. In his *Ästhetik* (1835; *The Philosophy of Fine Art,* 1920), Hegel praised *Antigone* for its ideal tragic form—that is, its dramatic reconciliation of conflicting positions, which conformed well with the Hegelian concept of dialectics, of thesis-antithesis-synthesis. In *The Interpretation of Dreams* (1900), Freud cited *Oedipus Tyrannus* as an expression of a child's love of one parent and hatred of the other, the psychic impulse that Freud came to call the "Oedipus complex."

Despite such influence outside the theater, it is on Sophocles' tragic art, and in particular on his skilled use of character development, dialogue, and dramatic irony, that his reputation has justly rested for more than two thousand years.

Biography • The main events of Sophocles' life are known from several ancient sources, including inscriptions and especially an Alexandrian biography that survives in the manuscript tradition. Although it is difficult at times to distinguish fact from anecdote in these sources, even the fiction is a useful gauge of Sophocles' image and reputation in antiquity.

Sophocles' lifetime coincides with the glorious rise of Athenian democracy and Athens's naval empire and with the horrors of the Peloponnesian War. Born a generation later than Aeschylus and a generation earlier than Euripides, Sophocles won dramatic victories over both of these playwrights. He was born c. 496 B.C.E. to Sophilus, a wealthy industrialist and slave owner from the Athenian *deme* of Colonus. Although Sophocles generally avoids personal references in his plays, his love for his native Colonus is evident in his last work, *Oedipus at Colonus*, and especially in the famous Colonus ode of that play.

Sophocles received a good education. According to ancient sources, as a youth he won competitions in wrestling and in music. His music teacher, Lamprus, was known for his epic and conservative compositions, for which he was ranked in his day with the great lyric poet Pindar. Sophocles himself is said to have been chosen to lead the victory song with lyre after the Athenian sea victory at Salamis in 480 B.C.E.

The patriotism of Sophocles was well known in antiquity. In the ancient biography, he is called *philathenaiotatos*, "a very great lover of Athens," and, unlike both Aeschylus and Euripides, he is said never to have left his native city for the court of a foreign king. Sophocles was also unlike his fellow dramatists in that he held public office several times: In 443/442 B.C.E., he was *Hellenotamias*, a financial overseer of the Delian League in Athens; in 441/440, he was general along with Pericles in the Samian Revolt. Sophocles may have been general again, around 427, this time with Nicias; and in 413, he was elected *proboulos*, a member of a special executive committee formed after the Sicilian disaster.

No clear conclusions concerning the dramatist's political sentiments can be derived from Sophocles' political career, especially since fifth century Athenian democracy often survived on noncareer appointments from among its citizens. There are several hints in Sophocles' biography, however, of links with the pro-Spartan and aristocratic circle of the Athenian statesman Cimon: Plutarch says that Sophocles won his first dramatic victory in 468 B.C.E., when, as requested, Cimon and his nine fellow generals took the place of judges chosen by lot for the tragic competition. Sophocles, as general in 441/440, is said to have visited the poet Ion of Chios, a close friend of Cimon. Sophocles wrote an elegy, of which fragments survive, to another member of Cimon's circle, the philosopher Archelaus of Miletus. Finally, Sophocles is also connected with Polygnotus, the famous painter and friend of Cimon who is said to have made a well-known portrait of Sophocles holding a lyre. On the other hand, Sophocles may have also been a friend of Pericles, the great Athenian statesman and Cimon's political rival, with whom Sophocles was general in 441/440 B.C.E.

It may be that Sophocles attempted to separate his probable friendship with Cimon from his civic duty and patriotic sentiments. At the least, this evidence shows that Sophocles was not politically detached, but rather, very much involved in the political and intellectual life of his day. The ancient biography mentions that Sophocles established a *thiasos*, or religious guild, in honor of the Muses. Other members of this intellectual group are unknown, but it may have included Sophocles' good friend, the historian Herodotus, whom the dramatist occasionally used as a source and to whom he wrote an ode.

Sophocles won his first dramatic victory in 468 B.C.E. by defeating Aeschylus, probably with a group that included a *Triptolemus*, now lost. Whether this was Sophocles' first dramatic competition is not known, but it is recorded that the playwright went on to win twenty-three more victories, to earn second place many times, and third place never. With four plays in each production, this means that ninety-two out of Sophocles' approximately 124 dramas won for him first prizes. This great contemporary success contrasts strikingly with the career of Euripides, who won first place only five times. Sophocles did not compete in 467 B.C.E. but probably won second place against Aeschylus's Danaid trilogy in 463 (?).

Unfortunately, no plays from Sophocles' earliest years survive. The earliest extant play is probably *Ajax*, from the early 440's B.C.E. In his *Ethika* (after c. 100; *Moralia*, 1603), Plutarch distinguishes three periods of Sophoclean style: a "weighty" period with Aeschylean similarities; a "harsh and artificial stage"; and a final group "most suited to express character and best." No extant plays, except perhaps *Ajax*, belong to the first two periods. Because the categories themselves, with their progression toward increasing worth, are obviously peripatetic in origin, it is doubtful that these periods can be accepted as reliable statements about Sophoclean drama.

In 441 B.C.E., Sophocles probably produced *Antigone*, for which he may have won first prize, since the *hypothesis*, or ancient introduction, to this play states that the dramatist was elected general in 441/440, based on the merit of *Antigone*. The Athenian democracy of that period was perfectly capable of making political appointments on such an apolitical basis. Other ancient sources imply that Sophocles saw no military action as general in the Samian Revolt that year but that he did travel to Ionia with the Athenian fleet.

Sophocles was certainly back in Athens in 438 B.C.E., when he won first prize with unknown plays against an Euripidean group which included *Alcestis*. The dating of *The Women of Trachis* is perhaps the most fiercely debated of all extant Sophoclean tragedies, but the stylistic and thematic similarities of this play to the firmly dated *Alcestis* make possible at least an approximate dating of *The Women of Trachis* to the period between 435 and 429.

In 431, Sophocles, competing with an unknown group of plays, came in second to the dramatist Euphorion, Aeschylus's son. Euripides came in third in that year with *Mēdeia* (431 B.C.E.; *Medea*, 1781). Sophocles made no production at the Greater Dionysia of 428. *Electra* is another play that is difficult to date accurately, but based on its links with Euripides' *Ēlektra* (413 B.C.E.; *Electra*, 1782), Sophocles' play can at least be dated to the decade beginning 420 B.C.E., except for the year 415, when it is known that Sophocles made no production. Only the last two extant plays are firmly dated: *Philoctetes*, which won for him first prize in 409 B.C.E., and *Oedipus at Colonus*, produced posthumously in 401 B.C.E. by Sophocles' grandson of the same name, which also won for him first prize.

In addition to his patriotism, Sophocles was also noted for his piety. Specifically, he is linked with the cult of the healing god Asclepius, whose cult the dramatist helped establish in Athens in 420 B.C.E. Sophocles' paean to Asclepius was quite famous in antiquity and still survives in fragments. Sophocles was a priest of the hero Halon, who was ritually connected with Asclepius and under whose epithet, Dexion or "Receiver," Sophocles was honored posthumously. Such associations with public cults, however, were distinct in fifth century B.C.E. Athens from intellectual belief, and the classical view of Sophocles as calm, pious, and moderate has come to be questioned by such modern scholars as C. H. Whitman, who notes that the extant tragedies exhibit little of that blind piety that tradition links with the dramatist. Sophocles' true religious sentiments are lost behind the poetic veil of his tragedies.

There are indications in ancient sources that Sophocles had a troubled family life in his old age. The playwright had two sons: Iophon by Nicostrata and Ariston by the Sicyonian woman Theoris. Iophon was a dramatist in his own right and even competed against his father at least once. Less is known about Ariston, except that his son, Sophocles, was so favored by the grandfather that Iophon brought a lawsuit to have the old man made a legal ward of his son on the grounds of senility. Sophocles, speaking in his own defense at the trial, is said to have stated: "If I am Sophocles, I am not insane; if I am insane, I am not Sophocles." When Sophocles concluded by reciting lines from *Oedipus at Colonus*, his work in progress, the case was dismissed.

In March of 406 B.C.E., at the *proagon*, or preview to the Greater Dionysia, Sophocles dressed a chorus in mourning for the recent death of Euripides. This appearance at the *proagon* is evidence for a Sophoclean production in that year, but Sophocles must have died shortly after the dramatic festival, because in Aristophanes' *The Frogs*, produced in early 405, Sophocles is mentioned as already dead. Despite Sophocles' advanced age, the ancient sources still sought to embellish his death with several spurious causes: that he choked on a grape (like Anacreon), that he became overexerted while reciting *Antigone*, or that he died for joy after a dramatic victory. More reliable is the report that Sophocles' family was granted special permission from the Spartan general Lysander to bury the dramatist in his family plot on the road to Decelea, where the Spartans maintained a garrison. Death thus spared Sophocles from witnessing the complete collapse of the Athenian empire and the submission of Athens to Sparta in 405 to 404 B.C.E.

Analysis • The textual transmission of Sophocles is remarkably similar to that of Aeschylus, with a first complete ancient edition by the Athenian orator Lycurgus in the late fourth century B.C.E. and a definitive Alexandrian edition by Aristophanes of Byzantium in the second century B.C.E. A school selection of the seven extant tragedies was made sometime after the second century C.E. and was reedited by the late fourth century rhetorician Salustius. The plays may have survived the medieval period in only one manuscript, although this has been debated. The present text was extensively revised in the fourteenth century by several Byzantine scholars, including Planudes, Thomas Magister, and Triclinius. The plays reached the West in the fifteenth century, and the first printed edition of Sophocles was the Aldine edition of Venice (1502).

The *Life of Sophocles* devotes a lengthy paragraph to describing the playwright's links with the epic poetry of Homer, and scholars of all periods have continued to note Sophoclean imitation of Homeric subject matter and language. Sophocles achieved his greatest success in the art of character development and especially in the depiction of the hero, for which he owes a major debt to Homer. Many Sophoclean characters, including nearly all the *dramatis personae* of *Ajax* and the Odysseus of *Philoctetes*, are derived from Homeric sources at least in part, but even where Sophocles treats a subject not directly handled by Homer, such as the stories of Oedipus and Antigone, the poetic techniques of Homer and Sophocles intersect in their methods of character development, in the types of characters depicted, and especially in their focus on the heroic qualities of particular individuals.

Even Aristotle recognized the importance of character development to Sophoclean studies. In his *Poetics*, he frequently cited Sophocles' Oedipus as the ideal tragic character and stated that "Sophocles is the same kind of imitator as Homer, for both imitate characters of a higher type." Much modern scholarship, too, has been devoted to a study of Sophocles' technique of character development and of the "Sophoclean hero." In particular, the works of C. H. Whitman and of B. M. W. Knox have both helped to clarify the characteristics of the Sophoclean hero and to show his affinities with the Homeric hero. It is impossible to analyze a Sophoclean play without studying Sophocles' character development and without taking into account the Aristotelian and later interpretations of the Sophoclean hero that have molded a modern understanding of this dramatist and his work. At the same time, such an analysis must not lose sight of Sophocles' other dramatic skills, such as his mastery of dialogue and his use of the chorus, both of which complement the development of Sophocles' main characters.

The Theban plays • Sophocles' so-called Theban plays have always been considered the center of his corpus. Although *Antigone, Oedipus Tyrannus,* and *Oedipus at Colonus* do not form a connected trilogy and, indeed, represent productions spanning a period of forty years, these plays project many consistencies of style and character development that suggest some continuity in Sophoclean dramatic art. The story of the unfortunate house of Laius was a popular theme of fifth century B.C.E. Greek tragedy, but except for Aeschylus's *Hepta epi Thēbas* (467 B.C.E.; *Seven Against Thebes,* 1777) and Euripides' *Phoinissai* (c. 410 B.C.E.; *The Phoenician Women,* 1781), which are extant, far too little is known about any of these lost plays to judge their relationship to the Sophoclean versions. The misfortunes of the house of Laius, including Oedipus's destiny to kill his father and marry his mother as well as the mutual fratricide of his sons, were mentioned by Homer, and several epics on this Theban cycle are known to have survived past the fifth century B.C.E. Knowledge of these epics is scanty, but Sophoclean innovations in this mythic cycle may include the blinding of Oedipus, the dramatic use of a local Athenian legend concerning the death of Oedipus in Sophocles' native *deme* of Colonus, and the development of the story of Antigone.

Antigone • *Antigone* concerns the events after the deaths of her brothers Eteocles and Polyneices and her decision to bury Polyneices despite the decree of Creon, the new ruler of Thebes, that the body remain unburied as a lesson to traitors. Sophocles begins the play with a dramatic prologue in which Antigone announces her decision to her sister Ismene, asks for her help and is refused, and finally determines in anger to act alone. This scene between the sisters, which Sophocles later skillfully imitated in *Electra,* demonstrates Sophocles' ability to employ action to develop his characters. Absent are the long, choral, narrative beginnings of Aeschylus's *Persai* (472 B.C.E.; *The Persians,* 1777) and *Agamemnon* (*Agamemnōn,* 1777; one of three parts of *Oresteia,* 458 B.C.E.), and the expository prologues of Euripides. Within one hundred lines of dialogue, Sophocles not only has significantly advanced the action but also has vividly depicted Antigone's character. Antigone's stubbornness, isolation, and strong sense of self-righteous nobility are well developed in this scene and help to define not only her character but also that of the Sophoclean hero in general. Much like the Homeric hero, especially Achilles, the Sophoclean hero projects *arete,* an untranslatable Greek word implying a "pattern of virtue." *Arete* sets the hero apart from other people and is inevitably self-destructive through its greatness. Thus, from the outset, Antigone is determined to face death for what she believes to be the noble course of action.

By contrast to the gloom of the prologue, the parodos, or choral entrance song, is a jubilant victory song celebrating the end of the siege of Thebes by Polyneices and is a striking example of Sophoclean manipulation of mood through choral passages. The chorus in Sophocles is usually considered to be a mouthpiece for the playwright's own views, but the interest in dramatic effect that Sophocles demonstrates in this chorus and others should be sufficient warning against reading such direct authorial intrusion into the dramatic text. Therefore, the chorus's Aeschylean sentiments in the parodos, that an insolent—that is, hubristic—Polyneices has been justly punished by Zeus, cannot necessarily be applied to Antigone's situation or to Sophocles' belief. Rather, the Sophoclean chorus tends to speak in character and with little extradramatic insight. *Antigone*'s chorus of elders express their own views in the parodos, views that serve as an excellent dramatic transition from Antigone in the prologue to Creon in the next scene.

In the first episode, Sophocles once again moves events along swiftly while developing character, this time that of Creon. Hardly has Creon finished his long and self-revealing inaugural address as ruler of Thebes and announced his decree concerning Polyneices, than a messenger arrives to report that this decree has already been disobeyed. Hegel used Creon's insistence in this scene on the primacy of the state and positive law over the individual to argue that the meaning of *Antigone* lay in the inevitable resolution or synthesis of Creon's conflict with Antigone, who stands for the right of the individual and the family and for the superiority of divine law. This interpretation of *Antigone*, however, is Hegelian, not Sophoclean, for there is no real synthesis in *Antigone*. Rather, there is a constant affirmation of the righteousness of the heroine that is evident even in this first episode, in which the messenger's suggestion that certain bizarre circumstances surrounding Polyneices' burial may hint at divine complicity is roundly rejected by Creon. Divine sanction for Antigone's action is inherent in the ancient Greek belief that all human corpses must be buried, a law to be challenged only under pain of punishment by the gods.

The choral ode that follows, often called the "Ode to Man," is probably the most famous ode of Sophocles, if not of all Greek tragedy. With its thematic links with Homer's *Odyssey* (c. 725 B.C.E.; English translation, 1614) and Aeschylus's *Choëphoroi* (*Libation Bearers*, 1777; one of three parts of *Oresteia*, 458 B.C.E.), as well as its philosophical connections with Protagoras and other thinkers of that time, this ode is a poetic statement of the wonder of humankind, of the ability of the human intellect to surmount the limitations of nature, and of the dangers inherent in such a powerful intelligence. Application of this ode to the dramatic events of *Antigone* is ambiguous. Clearly, the chorus is thinking of the unknown lawbreaker who buried Polyneices and whose deeds are a good example of humankind's dangerous intellect. As early as Homer, a hero's greatness had led to self-destruction, and this is no less true of Antigone. On the other hand, later events in the play will prove the relevance of the chorus's words as well to Creon, whose decree has dishonored the "sworn right of the gods." The multiplicity of interpretations that can be applied to this ode enhances its dramatic value and emphasizes once again Sophocles' skilled use of the chorus.

The "Ode to Man" also illustrates the power of Sophocles' so-called diptych structure and shows the futility of searching for a single main character in this or several other Sophoclean plays. Antigone and Creon complement each other. Antigone could not be Antigone without Creon, who, like Antigone, possesses some of the qualities of a Sophoclean hero, including stubbornness, isolation, and a self-righteous nobility. Creon's encounter with his son Haemon in the third episode is particularly revealing of the king's character. The scene is a brilliant combination of set speeches by both Creon and Haemon followed by rapid and emotional stichomythia, or line-by-line interchange, between father and son. This dialogue reveals Creon's stubborn inability to yield to reason and a lack of understanding of and isolation from his son Haemon that lead inevitably to disaster.

Haemon's appearance in the play may have been another Sophoclean innovation in the myth. As Creon's son and Antigone's fiancé, Haemon serves an an excellent illuminator not only of Creon's but also of Antigone's character. Sophocles does not present Haemon's relationship to Antigone in a romantic manner; the two are certainly not "lovers" in the modern sense because they never meet onstage. If the manuscript attribution of line 572 to Ismene is correct, Antigone never even speaks of her betrothed. Rather, Haemon's loyalty for Antigone, even unto death, serves as another, and perhaps the most vivid, proof of the heroine's isolation from all human contact in pursuit of her noble goal.

Antigone ends as quickly as it began, with a decision to free Antigone forced on Creon by the seer Teiresias, but not before it is too late. In rapid succession, the suicides of Antigone, Haemon, and his mother, Eurydice, are announced, and Creon returns in the exodos, or last scene, as a broken man. It is Creon, not Antigone, who comes closest to fitting the requirements of an Aristotelian tragic hero, with a peripeteia, or "fall," caused by hamartia, a "tragic flaw." Like both Xerxes in *The Persians* and Agamemnon in the first play of *Oresteia*, Creon's hamartia may be a form of faulty thinking that is punished by the gods. (Creon himself realizes this and uses the word "hamartemata.") By contrast, Antigone has no true peripeteia; while she does die, she dies as a Sophoclean hero in the glory and isolation of her self-conscious nobility. An Aristotelian tragic hero can thus be found in this play, but only at Antigone's expense.

Oedipus Tyrannus • *Oedipus Tyrannus* concerns an earlier stage in the same myth, with the discovery by Oedipus, Antigone's father, that he has fulfilled a Delphic oracle by unwittingly killing his father, Laius, and marrying his mother, Jocasta. The play is perhaps better known by its Latin title, *Oedipus Rex* or *Oedipus the King*, but the Greek title, while probably not Sophoclean (fifth century B.C.E. playwrights apparently did not title their plays, which were usually identified by their first lines), is more dramatically accurate. Technically, the Greek word *tyrannos*, means not a "harsh ruler" but an "unconstitutional" one. At the beginning of the play, Oedipus, having gained power by solving the Sphinx's riddle, rules Thebes as a true *tyrannos*; yet, dramatic events prove that Oedipus is also Thebes's true *basileus* or "king" because he is really the son of the late King Laius.

This irony in Oedipus's situation is the focus of the drama, which was so admired by Aristotle for its depiction of peripeteia caused directly by anagnorisis or "recognition." Sophocles further developed this irony, if not by actually inventing the blinding of Oedipus (who does not blind himself in Homer), then by using the theme of sight and blindness to great dramatic effect in the famous scene with Teiresias, in which the blind prophet is forced by Oedipus to contrast his own true knowledge with the ruler's ignorance; Teiresias tells Oedipus: "You have eyes but cannot see in what evil you are." In an ironic sense, then, the action of the play is directed toward an Oedipus, who sees with his eyes but not with his mind, becoming like Teiresias, who sees with his mind but not with his eyes. *Oedipus Tyrannus* is a true tragedy of discovery.

Many of the same dramatic skills found in *Antigone* can also be seen in *Oedipus Tyrannus*. In this play, too, Sophocles combines rapid action and dialogue with careful character development. One striking difference between *Antigone* and *Oedipus Tyrannus*, however, is structural: *Oedipus Tyrannus* lacks the diptych form and vacillation between two main characters that are found in *Antigone*. Rather, *Oedipus*

Tyrannus is focused entirely on Oedipus and the development of his personality. This development is accomplished through a series of dialogues between Oedipus and most of the other *dramatis personae*, beginning in the prologue and not ending until Oedipus learns the fatal truth of his identity in the fourth episode. In these scenes, the qualities of a Sophoclean hero are again and again revealed in Oedipus: in his heroic intransigence, his determination to discover the murderer of Laius and his own identity, in his sense of nobility and self-worth, in his angry alienation from all who try to help. Oedipus's own heroic nature—like that of Antigone—leads him on to self-destruction.

Aristotle's admiration of *Oedipus Tyrannus* as the ideal tragedy has, in a sense, been a Trojan horse for this play, because it has directed too much scholarly attention to Aristotle's interpretation of the play, an interpretation that is more Aristotle's reaction to Plato's prohibition of tragedy in *Politeia* (388-368 B.C.E.; *Republic*, 1701) than it is a close reading of *Oedipus Tyrannus*. Aristotle sought to counter Plato's objections to tragedy by making Oedipus into a morally satisfying character, by seeing in Oedipus a man, neither outstandingly virtuous nor evil, who falls into misfortune through hamartia. By doing this, Aristotle has created several thorny questions for the play: Does Oedipus really have a tragic flaw? Could he have acted any differently and still have been himself? Finally, is Oedipus of only average virtue?

The Sophoclean answer to all these questions could only have been negative. Oedipus is not an ordinary person. He is the solver of the Sphinx's riddle and a man of superior intelligence. He is a man of outstanding virtue. In short, he is a Sophoclean hero. To have acted other than he did would have meant a denial of his heroic identity, a denial of himself. This heroic firmness is a remarkably constant theme in the Sophoclean corpus. It can be found in the suicide of Ajax, in the desperate love of Deianeira, in the civil disobedience of Antigone, in the inquest of Oedipus the *tyrannus*, in the hatred of Electra, in the suffering of Philoctetes, and in the mysterious death of Oedipus at Colonus. Sophocles' primary contribution to the history of drama, then, is his masterful focus on character development, and, in particular, his portrayal of the unyielding hero.

Bibliography

Budelmann, Felix. *The Language of Sophocles: Communality, Communication, and Involvement*. New York: Cambridge University Press, 2000. A scholarly study of the language used in Sophocles' works. Bibliography and indexes.

Daniels, Charles B. *What Really Goes on in Sophocles' Theban Plays*. Lanham, Md.: University Press of America, 1996. Daniels examines Sophocles' Theban plays with reference to Greek mythology. Bibliography and index.

Kirkwood, Gordon MacDonald. *A Study of Sophoclean Drama: With a New Preface and Enlarged Bibliographical Note*. Ithaca, N.Y.: Cornell University Press, 1994. A scholarly look at the tragedies of Sophocles. Bibliography and indexes.

Pucci, Pietro. *Oedipus and the Fabrication of the Father: "Oedipus Tyrannus" in Modern Criticism and Philosophy*. Baltimore, Md.: The Johns Hopkins University Press, 1992. A study of Sophocles' works that focuses on the Oedipus character. Bibliography and index.

Segal, Charles. *Oedipus Tyrannus: Tragic Heroism and the Limits of Knowledge*. 2d ed. New York: Oxford University Press, 2001. A close examination of the role of heroes in Sophocles' tragedies, particularly Oedipus in *Oedipus Tyrannus*. Bibliography and index.

_____. *Sophocles' Tragic World: Divinity, Nature, Society.* Cambridge, Mass.: Harvard University Press, 1995. The tragedies of Sophocles are analyzed in respect to religion, nature, and society. Bibliography and indexes.

_____. *Tragedy and Civilization: An Interpretation of Sophocles.* Norman: University of Oklahoma Press, 1999. In this work, Segal examines Sophocles' major plays as well as the role of Greek mythology and civilization in his works. Bibliography and indexes.

Van Nortwick, Thomas. *Oedipus: The Meaning of a Masculine Life.* Norman: University of Oklahoma Press, 1998. A scholarly study of the Oedipus character, particularly in *Oedipus Tyrannus* and *Oedipus at Colonus.* Bibliography and index.

Thomas J. Sienkewicz

Wole Soyinka

Born: Ijebu Isara, near Abeokuta, Nigeria; July 13, 1934

Principal drama • *The Swamp Dwellers*, pr. 1958, pb. 1963; *The Invention*, pr. 1959 (one act); *The Lion and the Jewel*, pr. 1959, pb. 1963; *Camwood on the Leaves*, pr. 1960, pb. 1973 (radio play); *A Dance of the Forests*, pr. 1960, pb. 1963; *The Trials of Brother Jero*, pr. 1960, pb. 1963; *The Strong Breed*, pb. 1963, pr. 1964; *Three Plays*, pb. 1963; *Five Plays*, pb. 1964; *Kongi's Harvest*, pr. 1964, pb. 1967; *The Road*, pr., pb. 1965; *Madmen and Specialists*, pr. 1970, revised pr., pb. 1971; *The Bacchae*, pr., pb. 1973 (adaptation of Euripides' play); *Jero's Metamorphosis*, pb. 1973, pr. 1975; *Collected Plays*, pb. 1973-1974 (2 volumes); *Death and the King's Horseman*, pb. 1975, pr. 1976; *Opera Wonyosi*, pr. 1977, pb. 1980 (adaptation of Bertolt Brecht's play *The Three-Penny Opera*); *Requiem for a Futurologist*, pr. 1983, pb. 1985; *A Play of Giants*, pr., pb. 1984; *Six Plays*, pb. 1984; *A Scourge of Hyacinths*, pr. 1990, pb. 1992 (radio play); *From Zia, with Love*, pr., pb. 1992; *The Beatification of Area Boy: A Lagosian Kaleidoscope*, pb. 1995, pr. 1996; *Plays: Two*, pb. 1999

Other literary forms • Wole Soyinka is not only a dramatist but also a poet, novelist, and critic. His poetry has appeared in several collections, including *Idanre and Other Poems* (1967), *Poems from Prison* (1969), *A Shuttle in the Crypt* (1972), and *Mandela's Earth and Other Poems* (1988). The long poem *Ogun Abibiman*, connecting Yoruba mythology with African liberation, was first published in 1976. Soyinka has also written a few short stories as well as *The Interpreters* (1965) and *Season of Anomy* (1973), two novels. He has also translated the Yoruba novel of D. O. Fagunwa, *Forest of a Thousand Daemons: A Hunter's Saga* (1968). His most famous piece of criticism is *Myth, Literature, and the African World* (1976). In addition, Soyinka has produced two autobiographical works– *"The Man Died": Prison Notes of Wole Soyinka* (1972), a memoir of his prison experiences, and *Ake: The Years of Childhood* (1981), a dramatic and imaginative re-creation of his early life– and a memoir to his father, *Isarà: A Voyage Around "Essay"* (1989).

Achievements • In spite of frequent criticism of his obscure and difficult style, Wole Soyinka is generally regarded as a major literary figure in the contemporary world; by some he is considered to be the most sophisticated writer to emerge in Anglophone Africa. He has achieved success in the three major forms—poetry, fiction, and drama— and in the drama, for which he is best known, his range extends from broad farce and satire to tragedy. If he seems obscure, it is usually because of the density of the text: the constant reliance on imagistic and rhythmic expression and on the ever-present mythic and metaphysical dimension. An ambitious and experimental writer, he invites close textual analysis. His success as a dramatist extends to the practical arts of acting and directing. He has been the prime mover in the establishment of theater companies and the encouragement of the theatrical arts in Nigeria.

Behind all this literary activity lies Soyinka's loyalty to traditional Yoruba culture. He has had the intellectual capacity to understand and adapt it to his own needs and to the needs of his country. This has, perhaps inevitably, led him into the political arena, since his primary concern for human freedom is based largely on the identity of Ogun, the dynamic god of Yoruba mythology. Ogun is not necessarily the god of all

901

Nigerian society. Soyinka is one of those rare writers of genius whose productions appeal both to the professional critic and to the general public. Soyinka's social consciousness has given his works a moral force that has made him a leader among political activists in Africa. His plays are translated into French and have been produced in Africa's Francophone countries. His influence on African theater has been tremendous, and the fear of Soyinka's revolutionary themes has led at least one African country to ban his plays.

Soyinka was awarded the Nobel Prize in Literature in 1986. Other prizes include the Jock Campbell Award for Fiction in 1968, the John Whiting Drama Prize in 1966, and his first prize at the Dakar Negro Arts Festival in 1960.

(© The Nobel Foundation)

Biography • Akinwande Oluwole Soyinka was born July 13, 1934, at Abeokuta in Western Nigeria. His mother was a strong-willed businesswoman; his father, a school supervisor. Soyinka is a member of the Yoruba tribe whose culture is dominant in Western Nigeria. He has studied Yoruban mythology and theology as a scholar, and he has developed a theory of tragedy from Yoruban culture and has used it as the basis and inspiration of his fiction, poetry, and drama. His works are filled with its gods and spirits and its rituals and festivals. The traditional leader, the Oba, retains his spiritual and moral authority. The Yoruba language influences Soyinka's rhythmic and imagistic English style. Soyinka's formal education, however, has been basically Christian and European. Biblical and literary echoes pervade his work. Still, he considers himself African, writing for an African audience. He defends his eclecticism as the right of any artist and insists that even his representation of Yoruba culture is necessarily and justifiably personal.

Soyinka's primary and secondary education was in Nigeria. He attended St. Peter's School in Aké, Abeokuta (1938-1943), Abeokuta Grammar School (1944-1945), and Government College in Ibadan (1946-1950). His undergraduate preparation began at University College, Ibadan (later the University of Ibadan), where he studied from 1952 to 1954 with such future notables as Chinua Achebe and Christopher Okigbo. He then went to the University of Leeds in England, where he received his bachelor of arts degree with honors in English in 1957. He was later to receive an honorary degree from Leeds in 1973. His academic career began four years after graduation. He received a Rockefeller Research Fellowship to the University of Ibadan (1961-1962) and became lecturer at the University of Ife (1962-1964). In 1969, he became drama director, and he soon established a drama department and an acting company at the University of Ibadan. He has held various university academic posts, including a visiting professorship at Yale University in 1981, and has also delivered papers at academic meetings and published critical reviews and articles.

As early as his high school days, Soyinka was writing sketches for presentation and, soon after, clever comedies for the radio. At Leeds, he concentrated on the dramatic component in his course work. His career as a dramatist actually began when he became a play reader at the Royal Court Theatre in London, where some of his own early work was performed. Believing that special skills were necessary for the performance of his Nigerian plays, after his return to Lagos in 1960, he organized two theater companies: the Masks Company (1960) in Lagos and the Orison Theatre Group (1964) in Ibadan. Since then, he has argued that the best place for such companies, to ensure that they remain nonpolitical, is the university campus.

This insistence on political nonalignment points to a final aspect of Soyinka's life—his social commitment. He has continually spoken out on public issues and, as a result, has risked the constant displeasure of existing authorities and institutions; he was detained in prison during the Biafran War, from August, 1967, to October, 1969. Even his early work contains political themes, but the Biafran War and his prison experiences have made his subsequent work more explicitly committed to social justice. He lived in exile from Nigeria for five years (1970-1975). His plays of those years and afterward, produced both abroad and at home, exhibit a political pessimism and employ varying degrees of political rhetoric, from subtle, intricate, metaphysical exploration to overt, satirical attack in public forums and over the radio. The dominant theme in his drama, as well as in his poetry and fiction, is individual human freedom, with its capacity for creation and destruction. Soyinka's own life is an example of that exertion of will, the responsibility of the individual to understand, reinterpret, and act on his or her cultural surroundings.

Given the political climate of Nigeria since 1993, Soyinka frequently led the exile's life, shuttling back and forth between the United States and Europe. Some reforms after 1998 have allowed him to return intermittently to his country. He continues his outspoken criticism of repressive regimes.

Analysis • For Wole Soyinka, art and morality are inseparable. This does not mean simply that sensitivity to beauty is a good indicator of moral awareness, though that is strongly suggested in *A Dance of the Forests*. What is more to the point is that the primary obligation of art is to tell the truth: That obligation implies exposure and denunciation of falsehood. Even in Soyinka's broad farces—for example, the two plays that feature the prophet Jero—the object is not entertainment for its own sake but satire against any religious, social, or political leader who makes a mockery of human freedom. Soyinka also insists—with an eye on the romantic notion of negritude—that human beings have a dual nature whether they be African or Western; that is, they have destructive as well as creative urges. Part of his purpose as an artist is to expose the self-serving idealization of primitive African virtue; the problems in contemporary Africa may exist in a context of Western colonial oppression, but moral responsibility lies within the individual person as much as in the cultural milieu.

What is special about the moral content of Soyinka's drama is its metaphysical dimension, based on his own personal rendering of Yoruba myth. It assumes a continuum between the worlds of the dead, the living, and the unborn. That continuum is made possible by a fourth realm, which, in *Myth, Literature, and the African World*, Soyinka calls "the fourth stage," a realm that links the living with their ancestors and with the future. The myth of Ogun, the god who risked the dangers of the abyss and created a road from the spiritual to the human world, is the key to an understanding of all Soyinka's work, including his drama. The worship of Ogun is a ritual repetition of the god's feat. Yoruba drama, in a comparison that Soyinka himself makes, thus resembles Greek drama in its ritual essence and its origin. Ogun is the Yoruba counterpart of Dionysus. To emphasize its ritual nature, Soyinka incorporates in his drama elements of dance, music, mime, and masquerade. Characters are not merely actors playing a role—which in itself has ritual suggestions—but, in moments of high tension, are symbolically possessed by a god. The central actions are variations of rites of passage, with transformation or death-rebirth being the central archetypal pattern. Soyinka's most frequently used term for the terrifying experience of the numinous fourth stage is "transition." In some plays, the transition experience is artificial or incomplete, or it is parodied (the Jero plays); in others, it is the most pervasive theme.

Soyinka has a remarkable ability to combine the dramatic and theatrical device of peripeteia with the metaphysical experience of transition. The peripeteia, or climactic event of the play, is at the same time as the moment of divine possession. Generally, the plays move from ordinary realism to ritual enactment, with the nonverbal elements of dance, song, and masquerade receiving increasing prominence as the climax approaches. Thus, for Soyinka, drama is a serious matter. He may say in a facetious moment that it must be primarily entertainment, but in fact he treats it not only as a social and moral force but also as an act of human freedom and a ritual reenactment of human beings' relationship to divinity.

Early plays • Among Soyinka's early plays, *A Dance of the Forests* is the most ambitious; it is also the most complex treatment of the chthonic, or underworld, realm of gods and spirits of transition. Even in Soyinka's earliest major play, *The Swamp Dwellers*, the sensitive protagonist, Igwezu, appears as an outcast from ordinary society, as one who has returned from a confrontation with the gods and is not yet able to deal with the compromising and capricious worlds of society and nature. His climactic decisions are those of a man dazed by his revolutionary experiences. The wise old Beggar (an incarnation of the god?) cannot persuade him to turn his knowledge to account. *The Lion and the Jewel*, a comic rendition of society, presents the archetype of transition in at least two ways: through a parody of transformation as the ridiculous country schoolteacher, Lakunle, imagines his passage from bachelor to husband, and through the real rite of passage experienced by the heroine, Sidi, from maiden to wife.

A Dance of the Forests • *A Dance of the Forests*, as the title itself suggests, is in another world entirely. All the action is set in the forest, a universal symbol of the unknown, of the mysterious secrets of nature. It relies heavily on ritual, with its accompanying music, mime, dance, and masquerade. In the forest are representatives of the three other realms—the ancestors from the past, the living, and spiritual projections of posterity—as well as the gods and spirits who participate in and organize an extraordinary ritual to bridge the abyss between them.

A Dance of the Forests was written for the Nigerian independence celebrations in 1960, represented in the play as the Gathering of the Tribes. The principal human figures, Adenebi, Rola, and Demoke, have left the public festivities and sought the solitude of the forest. They are all guilty of some crime, hence uneasy in public, though the degree of their awareness varies considerably. Adenebi remains a lost soul because he cannot admit his guilt, even to himself. Rola, a prostitute, and Demoke, an artist who has just murdered his rival, at first, like Adenebi, try to hide their shame, but eventually they face the truth about themselves as human beings and achieve redemption. This is the essential plot of the play; it requires that these three characters—especially Demoke, as the central figure on whom the climax turns—pass from the ordinary world of the living to the world of the dead and the gods—that is, that they enter the "fourth stage." The first people they meet are Dead Man and Dead Woman, who have come in answer to the summons of the tribes. These ancestors turn out to be not the glorious heroes of Africa's imaginary past but fallen human beings who led unsatisfactory lives. They are accusers rather than celebrators of humankind.

Part 1 ends with some of the townspeople trying, through divination, ritual proverbs, dance and song, and a smoking, air-polluting lorry, to chase them away. Early in part 1, the three human protagonists also meet the Supreme Deity, called in the play Forest Head and temporarily disguised as an ordinary man named Obaneji. He guides them to the appointed place for the ritual Welcome of the Dead, which he has decided to hold in the forest because human society has refused to acknowledge the two dead guests as true ancestors out of their past.

Part 2 depicts a conflict between the forces of chance, retribution, and destruction, represented by the god Eshuoro, and the creative forces, represented by the god Ogun and his human agent, Demoke. It is a spiritual conflict that takes place in the realm of transition, symbolically rendered by the swamplike setting deep in the forest. The actual conflict between Eshuoro and Demoke is preceded by an elaborate Welcome of the Dead. Forest Head, in Prospero-like fashion, stages a drama that re-creates the crucial event in the lives of Dead Man and Dead Woman. Dead Man, a warrior in the court of Mata Kharibu three centuries earlier, had defied the order of his ruler and refused to fight a senseless war. His punishment was emasculation and slavery, which he had to endure in two subsequent incarnations. What he wants now is rest. Forest Head is sympathetic, but Eshuoro is not. Dead Woman was Dead Man's pregnant wife, who, overcome by grief, committed suicide and hence doomed her unborn child to the fate of an *abiku*, an infant that dies repeatedly in childbirth.

This scene, designed to arouse fear and pity for the suffering in human life, especially of those whose motives are pure, becomes in the hands of Eshuoro, an uninvited guest who appears in disguise as the Questioner of the Dead, further evidence of the weakness and sinfulness of human nature. The scene also includes two other figures, previous incarnations of Rola and Demoke as Madame Tortoise, the archetypal prostitute, and the Court Poet, who along with the Warrior resists her charms. What the scene also suggests, therefore, is the ever-recurring cycle of human history, and what follows is a dramatic and symbolic investigation of the question: Do human beings have the freedom and the will to change the pattern? Again it is Eshuoro who attempts to control the inquisition.

Up to this point, the three human protagonists have remained in the background (partly through dramatic necessity, since Rola and Demoke are actors in the flashback), but now the magic of Forest Head concentrates on their redemption. He insists that he cannot change anything himself; he can only provoke self-awareness. Thus, he designs a spiritual projection of the future but remains a passive observer. Significantly, the three humans are masked and become possessed by the spirits who speak through them. Having lost their identities, they enter totally the abyss of transition. The spirit voices from the intangible void are purposely obscure in their dire warnings. Scattered among them are the cries of Half-Child, whom Forest Head has meanwhile taken from the womb of Dead Woman. Its voice, too, is a voice of the future; it wants a full existence with a living mother.

With Eshuoro directing the action, the future of humankind appears desolate, but Eshuoro's power is not absolute. The play's climactic events, couched as they are in symbolic mime and dance, have elicited numerous interpretations. Eshuoro appears bent on separating Half-Child from its mother, as though a reunion would mean salvation. Demoke becomes a principal actor (once Forest Head has restored his consciousness), as he attempts to protect the child. With Ogun's help, he succeeds in returning the child to the mother, but Eshuoro emits a shout of victory even at this, suggesting perhaps that Demoke's act may save the child but place his own life in jeopardy, for he is taking on the responsibility of changing the pattern of history. A ritual scene follows in which Eshuoro forces Demoke, a "sacrificial basket" on his head, to climb the totem that Demoke had carved for the tribal festivities. Eshuoro then sets fire to the totem in order to kill both the artist and his creation, but his vengeance is foiled by Ogun, who catches the falling Demoke.

These scenes, depicting the saving of the child and of Demoke himself, are symbolically taking place within the unconscious and are a resolution to Demoke's particular problem and to the central issue raised by the play. As the tribe's carver, Demoke occupies a vital position. Without his art, ritual contact with the gods is impossible, yet in the act of carving the totem he had through jealousy flung his assistant and rival to his death. The incident reflects Soyinka's insistence on the creative and destructive tendencies in humankind. How can Demoke atone for his crime? The play dramatizes his inner acceptance of his human nature, his admission of guilt, and his redemption through the saving of Half-Child. Soyinka seems to suggest that all salvation is essentially personal and must follow the path of self-awareness, confession, and risk—a rite of passage across the abyss that separates human beings and the gods. The public celebration at the Gathering of the Tribes is pointless and meaningless, even hypocritical, because it denies the realities of the past and the destructive, darker side of human nature. The play thus offers both a tragic vision of life and hope for the future through the courageous acts of individual people. It also identifies the artist as the key provoker of self-awareness. Like Demoke, he is closest to the abyss; he possesses "fingers of the dead."

The Strong Breed and **Kongi's Harvest** • Between *A Dance of the Forests* in 1960 and *The Road* in 1965, Soyinka devoted his energies to the writing of his first novel, *The Interpreters*, but he did complete two plays, *The Strong Breed* and *Kongi's Harvest*, both of which present a young man taking the responsibilities of the community on his own shoulders. In *The Strong Breed*, Eman first tries to deny the very fact of ritual atonement, especially his own inherited role as the "carrier" of tribal guilt; eventually, however, he plays out this role in another tribe with such obsession that he pays for his rebellion with his life. Daodu, in *Kongi's Harvest*, assumes the Hamlet-like role of avenger as he challenges the authority of the usurping President Kongi, forcing him in the climactic scene to face the horrors of death, of the abyss, which in his egotism he had ignored. In both plays, the myth of transition clearly remains the key to self-awareness.

The Road • These two plays were followed by *The Road*, Soyinka's first drama centered on the danger to human sanity posed by contact with the chthonic realm. The setting of *The Road* differs significantly from that of *A Dance of the Forests*. The latter takes place entirely within the realm of passage—symbolically the forest—and hence is essentially an inner experience; in contrast, *The Road* takes place in society—although a very specialized and symbolic segment of it—and is mainly concerned with the effects of death on social behavior. The vision of *A Dance of the Forests* is, broadly speaking, tragic, but with a comic ending: Demoke receives both atonement and a sobering projection of the future. *The Road*, on the other hand, maintains a comic atmosphere through most of its scenes but ends on a tragic note; it actually contains every conceivable dramatic mode, from satire and realism to Symbolism and the absurd. Like *A Dance of the Forests*, it is a complex, multifaceted, and ambiguous play.

Structurally, *The Road* proceeds in a manner similar to *A Dance of the Forests*, from the ordinary to the ritualistic. Throughout, Soyinka maintains a tension between the practical world of survival and the spiritual world of essences, between the self and the other. Samson is a realist. He always retains contact with the ordinary world and fulfills the role of mirror or "narrator" even though he never steps out of his role as character. He is the reference point by which one measures the psychological states and obsessions of the other characters. In part 1, he remains onstage and controls the action until the final scene, when Professor, the epitome of obsession with death and the other major figure in the play, takes over the action.

The same pattern emerges in part 2, in which Samson and Professor are usually onstage together and in which the balance gradually shifts in the direction of ritual. The setting for the play is a kind of rundown truck stop. Samson is a "tout" for the truck driver Kotonu, who has recently given up his job for psychological reasons that the play gradually makes clear. Professor, a former lay reader in the adjacent church, now runs the truckers' rest stop, which doubles as a spare-parts shop and headquarters of his Quest for the meaning of Death. He holds his own communion every evening for his followers and hangers-on. Murano, his assistant and palm-wine tapster, symbol of the transition stage and Professor's best hope for enlightenment, leaves every morning and returns in the evening with wine for the ritual service.

The play deals with one day in the lives of these characters, a day made decisive by two recent occurrences that bring Professor's Quest to its crisis. In part 1, the occurrences are merely suggested; part 2 contains their reenactment as past merges with present. Kotonu and Samson narrowly missed being killed in an accident on the road; a truck passed them and then fell through a rotted portion of a bridge. Though Samson viewed the near miss stoically, Kotonu was so disturbed by the thought of death that he has given up driving, much to the displeasure of Samson, whose main preoccupation throughout the play is to restore Kotonu to his common sense. To this end, Samson solicits the aid of Professor, who has hired Kotonu to manage the spare-parts store. Samson insists that Kotonu's genius is in driving, not in scavenging parts off wrecked vehicles and selling them. Professor, however, is sympathetic with Kotonu's sudden concern with death.

The second incident is even more significant. Kotonu and Samson were involved in a hit-and-run accident in which they "killed" a man masquerading as Ogun (the "guardian of the road") in a ritual ceremony; he was in the *agemo* phase, in transition from the human to the divine essence. They hid the body in the back of the truck and carried it to the truck stop, where Professor found it. This victim is the Murano of the play, in dumb suspension between life and death and, hence, supposedly in possession of secrets that Professor is after. The incident intensified Kotonu's withdrawal, especially since he was required to don Murano's bloody mask to escape capture by the other celebrants. Thus, Kotonu himself symbolically became the god Ogun in the rite of passage. The reenactment of these scenes, together with several others in which Samson mimics Professor or recalls past incidents, dramatizes the impact of death on the living and structurally prepares for the final ritual act.

One other significant event has also recently occurred. Usually Professor leaves every morning for his tour of the road and, like Murano, does not return until evening. On this particular day, he has broken that pattern after coming upon a wreck and finding a road sign with the word "Bend" on it, which he takes to be symbolic. He returns to his headquarters more absentminded than usual and then departs in a daze. Part 1 ends at noon with a funeral service for the victims of the accident at the bridge, and with the return of Murano, confused by the organ music that usually calls him back in the evening. The day is clearly ominous. Murano is almost "killed" as a thief by one of the hangers-on.

The communion service at the end of part 2 is the culmination of the various "performances" during the play that have become progressively more intense. The policeman, Particulars Joe, is at the truck stop in search of the hit-and-run victim, whom no one has as yet identified as Murano. The identification soon becomes clear as Murano discovers the Mask he had worn, puts it on, and begins the dance that is to continue until Professor's closing speech. Everyone at the communion, already intoxicated by the wine, senses the power of the moment, the traditional reenactment of the rite of passage from human to divine. Murano is becoming possessed by the god Ogun. Professor hopes to use the moment to gain secret knowledge of death without dying himself. Salubi, to retain his sanity, wants to leave. Say Tokyo Kid, apparently the Eshuoro figure, symbolic of retribution and destruction, skeptical of such ritual behavior, challenges Murano and, during the struggle, stabs Professor with a knife passed to him by Salubi. Murano, completely possessed by the god, hurls Say Tokyo Kid to his death. Professor ends the play with a sermon to his followers, enjoining them to imitate the Road by lying in wait and treacherously destroying the unsuspecting traveler.

The key figure in this play is Professor, but he is such a strange composite that the play remains an ambiguous statement. He is an archetypal character, or rather a composite of archetypes. He is Faust, Falstaff, Jesus, and Don Quixote mixed up in a bundle of conflicting motives. Like Falstaff, he insists on the survival instincts in human nature. Like Faust, he challenges the gods to achieve knowledge denied to the descendants of Adam. He has messianic fantasies, but he is maddened by his preoccupation with death as surely as Don Quixote's romance with literature blinds him to ordinary reality.

It is as though the mind of Professor has become a chaotic image of the chthonic realm that he so desperately searches out but that he as a human being cannot understand. He never learns that the road of his daily wanderings on which his drivers make their living is not a real substitute for the Road that Ogun traveled to make contact with the human. Whereas Demoke in *A Dance of the Forests* undergoes the transition experience but retains his human perspective, Professor becomes obsessed with the realm itself and intellectualizes himself out of human society. To a large extent he is a comic figure—the proverbial absentminded professor—but the ambivalent messianic-Machiavellian Quest gives him a certain magnificent dimension and elevates his flaw to the hubris of classical tragedy.

The Trials of Brother Jero and **Jero's Metamorphosis** • The chaotic misdirection of *The Road*—and, indeed, of much of Soyinka's work in the 1960's, with its motifs of political chicanery, moral inertia, and death in modern Nigeria—anticipated the horrors of the Biafran War at the end of the decade. The war and Soyinka's two-year detention in prison did not, in fact, drastically change his philosophical approach to his craft, but they did intensify his concerns. *The Trials of Brother Jero*, for example, written before the war, is political and social satire, but Jero as the trickster is essentially a comic figure mixing farce and wit. The political caricature who undergoes a mock transformation in the final scene is more ridiculous than dangerous. In a companion piece, however, *Jero's Metamorphosis*, written after the war, the ritual transformation of the beach prophets into an Apostolic Salvation Army is a thinly veiled attack on a military regime that has, as the play reiterates, made public execution a national spectacle. Jero, dressed in his general's uniform, sitting underneath his own portrait as the curtain falls, is a sinister threat to moral sanity.

Madmen and Specialists • The very subject of *Madmen and Specialists*, written soon after Soyinka's release from prison, is the war's devastating effect on every phase of human life. Its central character, Bero, is hubris itself in his absolute denial of the essence of Yoruba culture: the continuity of life, the gods, the ancestors, and humankind's responsibility toward the future. He renders meaningless the realm that links human beings with the gods, and he violates the primary law of existence—return to nature as much as or more than is taken from it—and reduces people to organisms.

The Bacchae • Soyinka's willingness to undertake an adaptation of Euripides' *Bakchai* (405 B.C.E.; *The Bacchae*, 1781) thus comes as no surprise: It, too, deals with a madman in defiance of the gods and of the basic rhythms of human society and human nature. Dionysian possession and retribution are the closest thing in Western culture to the worship of Ogun among the Yoruba: *The Bacchae*, like *Madmen and Specialists*, constitutes a warning to militaristic oppression. In all three of these postwar plays, the motif of death, the numinous realm of passage, has retained its central place within the philosophical and dramatic structure; it has simply taken on added significance and urgency because of the realities through which Soyinka has had to live. Death has become part of a greater political commitment and a deeper pessimism.

Death and the King's Horseman • The new commitment and tone are nowhere more evident than in *Death and the King's Horseman*, a play that addresses the failure of the older generation to preserve intact the traditional Yoruba culture and that pessimistically depicts the attempt of their children to undertake the responsibility. According to Yoruba custom, when a king dies, his horseman must, at the end of the thirty days of mourning, commit suicide and join him in the passage to the underworld; otherwise, the king remains in the passage, subject to evil forces. Soyinka builds his play around the king's horseman, Elesin Oba, whose weakness of will breaks the age-old formula and places the entire society in danger of extinction. As with the other plays, much of the action is ritual, and, as is common in Soyinka, the climactic scenes combine dramatic peripeteia with divine possession and entrance into the transition phase. The structure also reflects the clash of African and Western cultures, a theme common in African literature but rather rare in Soyinka; the scenes alternate between Nigerian and British settings. Soyinka insists in a prefatory note that the British presence is only accidental: Elesin's failure is not imposed from without but is self-inflicted.

　　Soyinka organizes the play with his usual economy. All the action takes place within the span of a few hours. Act 1 presents Elesin's procession through the market just at closing time, on the way to his own death. He and his Praise Singer chant his fate. His love of the market as a symbol of earthly activity and life, however, suggests his ambivalence toward his role, and when he sees a beautiful young girl and arranges with Iyaloja, her future mother-in-law and leader of the market women, to marry and enjoy this maiden as his last earthly act, his eventual failure to carry out his appointed role is almost certain. Both Iyaloja and the audience, however, yield temporarily to Elesin's sophistic arguments. He insists that this is not mere sexual indulgence but a mingling of the "seeds of passage" with the life of the unborn; he deceives himself and his audience with poetic fancies and beautiful language. Iyaloja grants him the gift of the girl but warns him of his responsibility. His poetic fancy will not become a reality unless he dies.

In act 2, the scene changes to the home of the British District Officer, Simon Pilkings, and his wife, Jane; the accompanying music changes from sacred chant and rhythm to the tango. The *egungun* mask, used in Ogun worship to represent divine possession, has been turned into a costume for the masquerade later that evening. Here, Soyinka presents ritual suicide through the eyes of the supercilious Pilkings, who rejects Yoruba culture as barbaric; Jane is more sympathetic but still uncomprehending. Simon arranges for Amusa, a Nigerian sergeant in his employ, to arrest Elesin and prevent the completion of the ritual.

Act 3 begins with a comic scene in which the market women and their daughters turn Sergeant Amusa's duty into a mockery and send him packing back to his white superior. This moment of hilarious triumph gives way to what appears to be the climactic scene of the play, Elesin's emergence from his wedding chamber and his hypnotic dance of possession as he symbolically enters the abyss of transition.

This sacred event is replaced again by the artificiality of British custom, as act 4 begins with a mime at the masquerade ball, with the prince of Wales (having come to Nigeria as a gesture of courage and solidarity during World War II) and his entourage dressed in seventeenth century costume, dancing to a Viennese waltz and admiring Pilkings's demonstration of the *egungun* dance movements and vocal accompaniments. When he learns that Amusa has failed in his mission, Pilkings departs for the market to halt the suicide. Meanwhile, Jane has a long discussion with Elesin's son, Olunde, who has just returned from studying medicine in England to oversee his father's ritual burial. Jane is shocked that Olunde still clings to barbaric customs in spite of his Western education; in turn, Olunde suggests the greater barbarism of world wars, and there is no meeting of minds. The act closes with the unexpected return of Pilkings with Elesin. Olunde, who had assumed with absolute confidence that his father had completed the ritual obligation, senses immediately the cosmic reversal of roles, represented onstage by the father on his knees begging forgiveness from his son and the son judging the father.

Act 5 sees Elesin in chains imprisoned at the Residency. Iyaloja and the other market women bear the body of Olunde to his cell. She condemns Elesin for forcing his son to die in his place, thus reversing the cycle of nature. At the sight of his son, Elesin strangles himself with his chain and enters the abyss, though perhaps too late to satisfy the demands of the gods. What is especially significant about this scene is Elesin's second attempt to conceal the truth from himself. In act 2, he had refused to face his excessive love of life, his inability to leave the world of pleasure to the young.

Now, in his conversation with Iyaloja before his recognition of his son, Elesin is denying responsibility for his failure of will. He blames the tempting touch of young flesh and mentions Iyaloja's own complicity in the temptation; he blames especially Pilkings for his abrupt intervention. His most significant statement, however, is his self-serving appeal to the cultural situation. The power and influence of British culture, he says, caused him to question the loyalty of his own gods, and he came to doubt the validity of the ritual itself. The play ends with a dirge over the deaths of Olunde and

Elesin, but also, perhaps, over the death of a culture. Iyaloja and Olunde have completed the ritual as best they could, but she is not sure whether the son's death will satisfy the gods. The question remains, whether the younger generation of Nigerians will be able to save the civilization that their parents, in self-indulgence, doubt, and cowardice, have abandoned.

A Play of Giants and **Requiem for a Futurologist** • Two satirical plays of the 1980's, *A Play of Giants* and *Requiem for a Futurologist*, insist that neither the political leaders nor the people have emerged from the chaos. In the first, set in New York City, Field-Marshal Kamini (a thinly disguised Idi Amin of Uganda) is a con artist who leads three other heads of state in a hostage-taking, blackmailing, terrorist challenge against the United Nations. It is an all-out, farcical attack on the worship of power by those who wield it and those who submit to it. In the second play, the con artist is an opportunistic servant, Alaba, who uses various disguises to "overthrow" his master, Dr. Godspeak, a well-known prophet or "futurologist," by convincing the public and the doctor himself that he is dead. At Godspeak's "death," Alaba becomes the futurologist, a reincarnation of the famous French astrologer Nostradamus, who can use his supposed powers to exploit a gullible population. In Kamini and Alaba, Soyinka thus metamorphoses once again the Jero of the 1960 play. Nigeria—and the world—still plays the grotesque, exhausting, and futile game of the quack and the dupe.

Plays of the 1990's • Three plays written in the 1990's, *From Zia, with Love, A Scourge of Hyacinths*, and *The Beatification of Area Boy: A Lagosian Kaleidoscope*, are Soyinka's direct responses to the military dictators and irresponsible government of Nigeria. For his critical portrayals, Soyinka paid an additional four years (1993 to 1998) of self-imposed exile. During that period, he taught and traveled in the United States and England.

Both *From Zia, with Love* and *A Scourge of Hyacinths* were originally written as radio plays. Each grew out of real situations. Whether parodying the dictatorship of General Sani Abachu by comparing life under him to living in a prison in *From Zia, with Love* or likening the destruction of civil liberties to an invasion of water hyacinths in *A Scourge of Hyacinths*, Soyinka used his position as a world-respected writer to protest and was charged with treason for his efforts.

The Beatification of Area Boy • *The Beatification of Area Boy* shows the suffering of the average Nigerian at the hands of both the military and corrupt politicians. Soyinka's protagonist is Sanda, a university dropout, who is the leader of a group of small-time vendors on Broad Street in Lagos, the capital. This one-act play, written in 1995, combines many of Soyinka's writing strengths with his political determination. He uses the setting of the streets of modern Lagos to illustrate the huge disparities in the lives of Nigerians and to show that while at one time the country's problems may have been imposed on it by outsiders, usually Western powers, current difficulties are primarily indigenous, rooted in the corruption and greed of the Nigerian military and political parties.

The title is taken from the name given to the Area Boys, or young men who operate more or less like gang leaders in specific, assigned turf in Lagos, basically conning and blackmailing wealthy businesspeople and tourists. Their quasi-director and the play's protagonist is Sanda. What becomes quickly apparent is that Sanda and all the other

characters hustling on the street really have no other choice. The corruption and brutality in the country have made it all but impossible for them to have legitimate jobs
and the chance at a better life.

Soyinka's sympathy for the ordinary Nigerian is obvious because the characters ex-
ude charm and warmth and care for each other in addition to exhibiting a realistic assessment of their situation and the powers that persecute them. On this busy street,
working from their humble stalls, exists a community of people like Mama Put, who
sells food; Judge, a vagrant; Barber; Cyclist; Boyko; Sanda; and Sanda's former girlfriend Miseyi, although she is actually from a well-connected family. The police, military officers, and a military governor use their considerable positions and thugs against
these people, who are merely trying to survive. A public wedding and the bride's last-
minute rejection of the groom force a showdown between the street people and the
military and political powers. Despite a serious skirmish complete with gunshots and
beatings, the street people escape to try another day, showing that Soyinka still har-
bors hope for his country.

Soyinka's considerable skill at presenting song and dance in his plays is evident in
The Beatification of Area Boy. For example, upset because the Area Boys have overcome
some of his soldiers, a screeching military officer belts out a tune entitled, "DON'T
TOUCH MY UNIFORM!!!" Another song example is "Maroko," which describes a
"wretched shanty town." Both are funny despite the pathetic and miserable situations
being described.

Other major works

LONG FICTION: *The Interpreters,* 1965; *Season of Anomy,* 1973.

POETRY: *Idanre and Other Poems,* 1967; *Poems from Prison,* 1969; *A Shuttle in the Crypt,*
1972; *Ogun Abibiman,* 1976; *Mandela's Earth and Other Poems,* 1988; *Early Poems,* 1997.

NONFICTION: *"The Man Died": Prison Notes of Wole Soyinka,* 1972 (autobiography);
Myth, Literature, and the African World, 1976; *Aké: The Years of Childhood,* 1981 (autobiog-
raphy); *Art, Dialogue, and Outrage,* 1988; *Ìsarà: A Voyage Around "Essay,"* 1989; *The Credo
of Being and Nothingness,* 1991; *Wole Soyinka on "Identity,"* 1992; *Orisha Liberated the Mind:
Wole Soyinka in Conversation with Ulli Beier on Yoruba Religion,* 1992; *"Death and the Kings'
Horseman": A Conversation Between Wole Soyinka and Ulli Beier,* 1993; *Ibadan: The
Penkelemes Years: A Memoir, 1946-1965,* 1994; *The Open Sore of a Continent: A Personal
Narrative of the Nigerian Crisis,* 1996; *The Burden of Memory, the Muse of Forgiveness,* 1999;
Seven Signposts of Existence: Knowledge, Humour, Justice, and Other Virtues, 1999; *Conversa-
tions with Wole Soyinka,* 2001 (Biodun Jeyifo, editor).

TRANSLATION: *Forest of a Thousand Daemons: A Hunter's Saga,* 1968 (of D. O. Fagunwa's novel *Ogboju Ode Ninu Igbo Irunmale*).

Bibliography

Gates, Henry Louis, Jr., ed. *In the House of Oshugbo: Critical Essays on Wole Soyinka.* London: Oxford University Press, 2002. This large collection of essays includes analyses of specific plays, biographical information, comparative studies involving contemporary writers such as Bertolt Brecht and James Joyce, and discussions of
literary theory, the art of writing, and Yoruba culture.
Jeyifo, Biodun, ed. *Conversations with Wole Soyinka.* Jackson: University Press of Mississippi, 2001. The first book to feature recorded interviews of Soyinka. Interviewers
include Henry Louis Gates, Jr., Anthony Appiah, and Biodun Jeyifo. These interviews help clarify what are called the obscurities in Soyinka's most difficult plays.

_____. *Perspectives on Wole Soyinka.* Jackson: University Press of Mississippi, 2001. This collection of critical essays covers three decades. Its major contribution is analyzing Soyinka's work using many kinds of contemporary schools of critical theory from feminism to recuperated phenomenology. Also discussed are his postcolonial politics and aestheticism.

Jones, Eldred Durosimi. *The Writing of Wole Soyinka.* 3d ed. Portsmouth, N.H.: Heinemann, 1988. This introductory survey of Soyinka's works opens with a background essay on the author. Subsequent essays deal with individual texts under the general chapter headings "Autobiography," "Plays," "Poetry," and "Fiction." Essays on thirteen plays follow a summary-commentary format, approaching them as individual, literary texts, but with some cross-referencing, a few production and theatrical notes, and occasional attention to stylistic development. Includes a biographical outline and a brief bibliography.

Lindfors, Bernth, and James Gibbs, eds. *Research on Wole Soyinka.* Lawrenceville, N.J.: Africa World Press, 1992. These essays represent a wide variety of critical methodologies applied to Soyinka's works, including linguistics and structural, textual, and cultural interpretations.

Maja-Pearce, Adewale, ed. *Wole Soyinka: An Appraisal.* Portsmouth, N.H.: Heinemann, 1994. This book is a collection of essays primarily by African writers. Topics include Soyinka's fiction, poetry, and drama, as well as the African culture from which he writes. His Noble lecture is the lead entry. An interview with Soyinka is also presented.

Okome, Onookome. *Ogun's Children: The Literature and Politics of Wole Soyinka Since the Nobel Prize.* Lawrenceville, N.J.: Africa World Press, 2002. An analysis of Soyinka that focuses on his work since receiving the Nobel Prize.

Wright, Derek. *Wole Soyinka Revisited.* New York: Twayne, 1992. This introductory study of Soyinka includes critical studies of his works, biographical information, and a chronology of his life and works.

Thomas Banks,
updated by Judith Steininger

Tom Stoppard

Tomas Straussler

Born: Zlin, Czechoslovakia; July 3, 1937

Principal drama • *A Walk on the Water,* pr. 1963 (televised; revised and televised as *The Preservation of George Riley,* 1964; revised and staged as *Enter a Free Man,* pr., pb. 1968); *The Gamblers,* pr. 1965; *Rosencrantz and Guildenstern Are Dead,* pr. 1966, pb. 1967; *Tango,* pr. 1966, pb. 1968 (adapted from the play by Sławomir Mrożek); *Albert's Bridge,* pr. 1967 (radio play), pr. 1969 (staged), pb. 1969; *The Real Inspector Hound,* pr., pb. 1968 (one act); *After Magritte,* pr. 1970, pb. 1971 (one act); *Dogg's Our Pet,* pr. 1971, pb. 1976 (one act); *Jumpers,* pr., pb. 1972; *Travesties,* pr. 1974, pb. 1975; *Dirty Linen and New-Found-Land,* pr., pb. 1976; *The Fifteen-Minute Hamlet,* pr. 1976, pb. 1978; *Every Good Boy Deserves Favour,* pr. 1977, pb. 1978 (music by André Previn); *Night and Day,* pr., pb. 1978; *Dogg's Hamlet, Cahoot's Macbeth,* pr. 1979, pb. 1980; *Undiscovered Country,* pr. 1979, pb. 1980 (adapted from Arthur Schnitzler's play *Das weite Land*); *On the Razzle,* pr., pb. 1981 (adaptation of Johann Nestroy's play *Einen Jux will er sich machen*); *The Real Thing,* pr., pb. 1982; *The Dog It Was That Died, and Other Plays,* pb. 1983; *The Love for Three Oranges,* pr. 1983 (adaptation of Sergei Prokofiev's opera); *Rough Crossing,* pr. 1984, pb. 1985 (adaptation of Ferenc Molnár's play *Play at the Castle*); *Dalliance,* pr., pb. 1986 (adapted from Arthur Schnitzler's play *Liebelei*); *Hapgood,* pr., pb. 1988; *The Boundary,* pb. 1991 (with Clive Exton); *Arcadia,* pr., pb. 1993; *The Real Inspector Hound and Other Entertainments,* pb. 1993; *Indian Ink,* pr., pb. 1995; *The Invention of Love,* pr., pb. 1997; *The Seagull,* pr., pb. 1997 (adaptation of Anton Chekhov's play); *Plays: Four,* pb. 1999; *Plays: Five,* pb. 1999

Other literary forms • In addition to composing plays and occasionally adapting the dramas of others, Tom Stoppard has written several short stories, radio plays, teleplays, screenplays, and the novel *Lord Malquist and Mr. Moon* (1966). He prides himself on his versatility, eschewing the notion of the dedicated author plowing a lonely furrow and sacrificing almost all other concerns on the altar of high art. Instead, as he told an interviewer in 1976:

> I've got a weakness . . . for rather shallow people who knock off a telly play and write a rather good novel and . . . interview Castro and write a good poem and a bad poem and . . . every five years do a really good piece of work as well. That sort of eclectic, trivial person who's very gifted.

Stoppard's novel *Lord Malquist and Mr. Moon* is "rather good." It is an exuberant farce that uses a collage of literary styles and allusions ranging from those of Joseph Conrad to Oscar Wilde, and from James Joyce to T. S. Eliot. Lord Malquist is a modern-day earl who seeks to sustain the dandyish refinements of his eighteenth century ancestors. His hired diarist, Mr. Moon, is a pathetically ineffectual man obsessively nursing a homemade bomb. Where the imperious and selfish Malquist anticipates such later dramatic characters as Sir Archibald Jumper of *Jumpers,* the confused, Prufrockian Moon models for the rebuffs experienced by the same text's George Moore. Malquist sums up what seems to be the novel's thesis when he declares, "since we cannot hope for order, let us withdraw with style from the chaos."

Achievements • Tom Stoppard's dramaturgy has a uniquely wide appeal in the contemporary theater because he often manages to combine comedy with social concern, farce with moral philosophy, and sometimes absurdism with naturalism. He and Harold Pinter, beginning in the 1960's, came to be considered the English-speaking world's leading playwrights. Both owe a large debt to Samuel Beckett and exhibit a willingness to experiment with theatrical forms. Pinter's sparse language, pauses, and silences, however, contrast sharply with Stoppard's free-flowing fountains of verbal play and display. Moreover, Pinter's carefully guarded characters and often baffling, static plots could not differ more from Stoppard's accessible people and vividly detailed, fast-paced action sequences. His plays have won Tony and Olivier awards. The film of *Rosencrantz and Guildenstern Are Dead* won the Golden Lion at the Venice film festival in 1990. In 1999 *Shakespeare in Love,* for which he wrote the screenplay, won seven Academy awards and three Golden Globes. In 1997 Stoppard became the first British playwright to be knighted since Terence Rattigan.

Stoppard's work is postmodernist in its self-conscious artfulness and intricate game playing. He loves to confound his audience with abrupt shifts of time and convention, unreliable narrations, and surprising twists of plot. His eclectic borrowings fuse high and low culture, invading the texts of William Shakespeare, George Bernard Shaw, Wilde, Joyce, Eliot, and many more to combine them with "whodunit" thrillers, journalistic techniques, music-hall comedies, and popular love songs.

The leading debate among Stoppard's critics is whether his works are too frivolous and waggish to be taken seriously and whether, despite his eye for striking situations and ear for witty talk, he is no more than an ingenious but juvenile sprinter, too short-winded to complete the potential of his promising situations. His supporters insist that Stoppard is able to fuse his fertile comic sense with intellectual substance. They find his vision of life mature and profound as he dramatizes such concerns as free will versus fate (*Rosencrantz and Guildenstern Are Dead*), moral philosophy (*Jumpers*), art versus politics (*Travesties*), totalitarianism (*Every Good Boy Deserves Favour*), the press's freedoms and responsibilities (*Night and Day*), and married love (*The Real Thing*). They assert that Stoppard's career has shown an increasing commitment to ethical humanism and freedom of conscience while his dramatic craft has forged a rare compact between high comedy and the drama of ideas.

Biography • Tomas Straussler was born on July 3, 1937, in the town of Zlin, Czechoslovakia, since renamed Gottwaldov. He was the youngest of two sons of a physician, Eugene Straussler, and his wife, Martha. Stoppard's parents were Jewish, although Stoppard did not know this until much later in life. Their religious background caused the family to move to Singapore in early 1939, on the eve of the German invasion of their homeland. In 1942, all but the father moved again, to India, just before the Japanese invasion, in which Dr. Straussler was killed. In 1946, Martha Straussler married Kenneth Stoppard, a major in the British army who was stationed in India. Both children took their stepfather's name when the family moved to England later that year. Demobilized, Kenneth Stoppard prospered as a machine-tool salesperson.

Despite this globe-trotting background—in one interview he called himself "a bounced Czech"—Stoppard has spoken and written in English since the age of five. His first school in Darjeeling, India, was an English-language, American-run institution. He attended preparatory schools in Nottingham and Yorkshire, leaving at the age of seventeen after having completed his "A" levels. In 1954, he began working as a local journalist in Bristol, rejoicing in the life of a newspaper reporter for the next six years. He did not consider becoming a playwright until the late 1950's, when a new breed of English dramatists, led by John Osborne and Arnold Wesker, asserted themselves on the London stage. Simultaneously, a new breed of actors emerged, prominent among them Peter O'Toole, whose blazing performances for the Bristol Old Vic repertory company definitively turned Stoppard to the theater.

In July, 1960, Stoppard wrote *The Gamblers*—a one-act clumsily derived from Beckett's *En attendant Godot* (pb. 1952, pr. 1953; *Waiting for Godot*, 1954)—which was unsuccessfully staged in Bristol in 1965. Later in 1960, he composed his first full-length play, *A Walk on the Water*. Considerably rewritten and retitled *Enter a Free Man*, it was staged in London in 1968 after *Rosencrantz and Guildenstern Are Dead* had established Stoppard as a major playwright. In 1962, Stoppard moved to a London suburb and became the drama critic of a new magazine, *Scene*, which folded after eight months. Fortunately, he had begun by then a steady career as a writer of radio plays for the British Broadcasting Corporation (BBC).

With the aid of a Ford Foundation grant, he wrote, in 1964, a one-act version of *Rosencrantz and Guildenstern Are Dead*, which he rewrote and expanded for the Royal Shakespeare Company in 1965, then for the Oxford Theatre Group in 1966, which performed it at that year's Edinburgh Festival. An enthusiastic review in *The Observer* caused Laurence Olivier to buy the play for his National Theatre, which staged it in 1967. Critical acclaim showered on this production, which continued in the National Theatre's repertoire for an unprecedented three and a half years.

In 1965, Stoppard married Jose Ingle; they became the parents of two sons, Oliver and Barnaby. They were divorced in 1972, and the same year, Stoppard married Dr. Miriam Moore-Robinson, a physician and television personality, with whom he had two sons, William and Edmond.

After the worldwide success of *Rosencrantz and Guildenstern Are Dead*, Stoppard not only has produced a number of one-act and full-length dramas but also has adapted the plays of several European writers. He has written film scripts as well as radio and television plays. He has directed several stage plays, usually but not always his own, and has supervised the filming of *Rosencrantz and Guildenstern Are Dead*. In 1983, he adapted Sergei Prokofiev's *The Love for Three Oranges* for the Glyndebourne Opera.

Although he had known that one or two of his grandparents were Jewish, Stoppard learned in 1994 that, in fact, all of his grandparents were Jewish and all were killed by the Nazis. His adopted father's anti-Semitism became public when he asked Stoppard in 1996 to stop using the name Stoppard because the playwright had been working for the cause of Russian Jews. In 1999 he wrote an article entitled "On Turning Out to Be Jewish" in which he discusses how these discoveries fundamentally altered his sense of self.

Analysis • Tom Stoppard's dramaturgy reveals a cyclical pattern of activity. He tends to explore certain subjects or techniques in several minor works, then creates a major play that integrates the fruits of his earlier trial runs. Thus *Rosencrantz and Guildenstern Are Dead* explores the dialectic of individual freedom opposed to entrapment, which such earlier plays as *A Walk on the Water* had rehearsed.

Stoppard's major theatrical work in the late twentieth century, *Hapgood, Arcadia, Indian Ink*, and *The Invention of Love* show a depth to his characters and ideas that did not exist in his earlier work. Unlike his early plays, which were often described by critics as being too academic, his later work demonstrates Stoppard's discovery of lyricism. Although just as complex intellectually, these later plays are equally about ideas and emotions and present fully realized characters, rather than the witty, though ultimately shallow ones that populate his work before *The Real Thing*. Despite greater emphasis on developed characters, these late plays still manage to tackle concepts as diverse and complex as Heisenberg's uncertainty principle (in *Hapgood*), chaos theory (in *Arcadia*), colonialism (in *Indian Ink*), and classicism (in *The Invention of Love*). Stoppard has already earned an honored place in the ranks of England's playwrights. Like Wilde, his ferocious wit and intellectual acuity dazzle audiences; like Shaw, he stylishly explores intellectual and emotional dilemmas; and like Beckett, his comedy is sometimes bathed in pain and sadness. Altogether, Stoppard is an immensely talented, uniquely unclassifiable writer who invites his public to discover the humaneness of plays and the glory of the English language's density and richness.

Rosencrantz and Guildenstern Are Dead • In *Rosencrantz and Guildenstern Are Dead*, Stoppard assumes the audience's close knowledge of Shakespeare's *Hamlet, Prince of Denmark* (pr. c. 1600-1601, pb. 1603). In the Elizabethan tragedy, Rosencrantz and Guildenstern are two former schoolmates of Hamlet who have been summoned to Elsinore by King Claudius to probe the puzzling behavior of the prince. Hamlet soon intuits that they have become Claudius's spies. When Claudius has them accompany Hamlet on the ship to England, Hamlet discovers the King's letter ordering his execution. He coolly substitutes his escorts' names for his in the letter and shrugs off their consequent deaths as resulting from their dangerous trade of espionage.

From a total of nine scenes in *Hamlet, Prince of Denmark* involving Rosencrantz and Guildenstern, Stoppard incorporates six, omits two, and distributes the other in scenes wholly devised by him. Stoppard's Ros and Guil know that they have been summoned to Elsinore but can remember nothing more of their past. They are two bewildered young men playing pointless games (such as coin flipping) in a theatrical void, while the real action unfolds off stage. They are adrift in a predetermined plot, bumbling Shakespeare's lines on the occasions when the palace intrigue sweeps their way. Just as Beckett's Vladimir and Estragon engage in mock-philosophizing disputations and vain recollections as they await Godot, so Ros and Guil pursue frequent speculations about their past, their identity, and the baffling world around them.

Stoppard has here constructed an absurdist drama that owes its largest debts to Franz Kafka and Beckett. His Ros and Guil are unaccountably summoned to a mysterious castle where, between long periods of waiting, they receive cryptic instructions that eventually lead to their deaths. They remain uncertain whether they are the victims of chance or fate, mystified by events that are within the boundaries of their awareness but outside the circumference of their understanding.

Like Beckett's Vladimir, Ros is the one who worries and protects; like Beckett's Estragon, Guil is the one who feels and follows. Beckett's world is, however, considerably bleaker than Stoppard's. He offers no comforting irony behind his characters' somber metaphysical flights, while Stoppard's buffoonery is humane. He presents his coprotagonists as likable though confused and frightened strangers in a world somebody else seems to have organized.

Stoppard's literary borrowings include a generous slice of Eliot's poetry, as Ros and Guil imitate Prufock in their roles as attendants and easy tools, playing insignificant parts in a ferociously patterned plot featuring mightier powers. This sympathy for the ineffectual underdog is a constant in Stoppard's dramatic world, as he demonstrates, over and over, his compassionate concern for decent people shouldered aside and manipulated by more brutal peers. Is *Rosencrantz and Guildenstern Are Dead* an immensely entertaining but ultimately shallow exercise, or is it a brilliant transposition of Shakespeare's universe to Beckett's absurdist world? Most critics and large audiences have cast their votes in favor of this erudite, witty, crackling clever drama.

Jumpers • A second group of Stoppard's plays dramatizes the conflict between a protagonist's wish to know and the many difficulties that frustrate this desire, such as the limitations of human perceptions, the frequent deceptiveness of one's senses, and the complexity of ethical choices in a world in which guidance is either uncertain or unavailable. Plays belonging to this category include such one-acts as *After Magritte* and the radio play *Artist Descending a Staircase* (1972), as well as Stoppard's two most ambitious, full-length dramas, *Jumpers* and *Travesties*.

Jumpers is a kaleidoscopic work, part bedroom farce, part murder mystery, part political satire, part metaphysical inquiry, and part cosmic tragedy, creating new configurations of ideas and themes from each angle of vision. Stoppard's hero is George Moore, a work-obsessed, seedy, middle-aged professor of moral philosophy, whose name is identical with that of the great English thinker who wrote *Principia Ethica* (1903). George's career has ground to a halt because his adherence to absolute values—beauty, goodness, God—makes him odd man out in a university dominated by logical positivists who hold that value judgments cannot be empirically verified and are therefore relative and meaningless.

George's main adversary is Sir Archibald Jumper, vice chancellor of the university, who is authoritative in a staggering number of roles: He holds degrees in medicine, philosophy, literature, and law, and diplomas in psychiatry and gymnastics. He is organizer of the Jumpers—a combination of philosophical gymnasts and gymnastic philosophers—all members of the Radical Liberal Party that Archie also heads. The Radical Liberals embody Stoppard's satiric vision of socialism in action. Having just won an election—which they may have rigged—they have taken over the broadcasting services, arrested all newspaper owners, and appointed a veterinary surgeon Archbishop of Canterbury.

The female principal in the George-Archie struggle is represented by George's beautiful but aptly named wife, Dotty. She is a neurotic musical-comedy star, many years younger than her husband, who retired from the stage after having suffered a nervous breakdown because she believed that the landing of a human being on the Moon had eliminated that planet as a source of romance and thousands of songs. In an ironic reversal of the selflessly heroic British Antarctic Expedition of 1912, Dotty sees, on her bedroom television set, a fight for survival between the damaged space capsule's commander, Captain Scott, and his subordinate officer, Oates. To reduce the weight load, Scott kicks Oates off the capsule's ladder, thereby condemning him to death. Pragmatism has sacrificed moral values—an indictment of logical positivism's slippery ethics. George and Archie are not only philosophic but also erotic rivals. While Dotty has barred her husband from her body—and he makes little effort to overcome her resistance—she is available at all hours to Archie, who visits her in the mornings in her bedroom and is her doctor and psychiatrist and presumably her lover, leaving her room "looking more than a little complacent."

In the first scene, as the Jumpers tumble in the Moores' apartment to celebrate the Rad-Lib victory, a bullet suddenly kills one of them. He turns out to be Duncan McFee, a logical positivist who was scheduled to debate with George at a symposium the next day. Dotty is left whimpering with the corpse, while George, concentrating on composing his lecture, knows nothing of the killing, so that he and his wife talk at cross-purposes while the body hangs behind her bedroom door, always unseen by him. Stoppard parodies the whodunit formula by having Inspector Bones bumble the murder investigation. The resourceful Archie persuades Bones to drop the case by having Dotty trap him in an apparently compromising position. At the close of act 2, McFee is revealed as probably the victim of George's vengeful secretary, who had been McFee's mistress and had learned that he was married and planned to enter a monastery.

Holding together the frequently delirious action is the shabby but lovable person of George, shuffling distractedly between his study and Dotty's bedroom, preparing his case against Archie's cynical materialism, which insists that observability has to be a predicate of all genuine knowledge. He does his best—and clearly advocates Stoppard's position—to defend a God in whom he cannot wholly bring himself to believe, so as to support his adherence to moral and aesthetic standards, which he considers a necessary basis for civilization.

The condescending Archie dismisses George as no more than the local eccentric: "[He] is our tame believer, pointed out to visitors in much the same spirit as we point out the magnificent stained glass in what is now the gymnasium." George is less mocked by Stoppard as bumbler and clown than he is admired as a fragmented culture's last humanist, clinging with mad gallantry to lasting values.

In *Jumpers*, Stoppard has written his best play. It is not only a swiftly paced farce and mystery but also a brilliantly humane comedy about the only animal in the cosmos trapped in the toils of an overdeveloped consciousness: the human being. The ultimate mystery, *Jumpers* suggests, is the meaning of life. The work constitutes Stoppard's richest and most brilliant exploration of ethical concerns.

Artist Descending a Staircase • In *Artist Descending a Staircase*, a radio play, Stoppard undertook what he has called "a dry run" of *Travesties*. *Artist Descending a Staircase* uses a continuous loop of recording tape to involve the audience with three artists engaged in an inquiry into the meaning of art. A more striking bond, between *Jumpers* and *Travesties*, has been summarized by Stoppard in an interview:

> *Jumpers* and *Travesties* are very similar plays. . . . You start with a prologue which is slightly strange. Then you have an interminable monologue which is rather funny. Then you have scenes. Then you end up with another monologue. And you have unexpected bits of music and dance, and at the same time people are playing ping-pong with various intellectual arguments.

Travesties • *Travesties* is aptly named. In one of those travesties of probability, the writer James Joyce, the Romanian poet Tristan Tzara, and the Russian revolutionary Vladimir Ilich Ulyanov (who assumed the name of Lenin) were all living in Zurich in 1917: the Irishman working on *Ulysses*, the Romanian helping to set off the Dadaist explosion, and the Russian planning the Armageddon of the Bolshevik Revolution. Stoppard uses his literary license to have the trio interact, and adds, as his protagonist, a British consular official, Henry Carr, historically a minor clerk but promoted by the author to head the British consulate, while the name of the real consul in Zurich—Bennett—is assigned to Carr's butler. Old Carr, like Beckett's Krapp, replays the spool that contains his past.

The play's plot is both a pastiche and a travesty of Oscar Wilde's great comedy *The Importance of Being Earnest* (pr. 1895, pb. 1899). Stoppard discovered that Joyce had been the business manager of an amateur theatrical company that had staged Wilde's work in Zurich in 1918 and had cast Carr in one of the leading roles as Algernon Moncrieff. This prompted Stoppard not only to have his Carr also echo Algernon but also to double Tzara as Wilde's Jack Worthing, Bennett as Wilde's manservant Lane, and to name his romantic interests Gwendolen and Cecily to mirror Wilde's Gwendolen and Cecily. Rather surprisingly, Joyce intermittently becomes Lady Bracknell; after all, his middle name, Augusta, corresponds to Bracknell's first.

Travesties is a tour de force of spirited language and convoluted situations that fuses Wilde's high comedy of manners with Shavian dialectic, Joycean fiction, Epic theater, Dadaist spontaneity, music-hall sketches, and limerick word-games. Underneath the bouncy mattress of witty farce is a hard board: Stoppard's lust for ideas. He takes a piercingly cross-eyed look at those movers and shakers of everything that is not nailed down: artists and revolutionaries. The drama revolves four views on art through its ironic prism: Tzara represents Dadaist antiart; Joyce advocates the formalist tradition of art that emphasizes its long-meditated artifice; Lenin subordinates art to an instrument of state policy; and Carr holds a Philistine suspicion of the artist as an ungrateful drone.

In an interview, Stoppard declared himself particularly pleased with a scene, late in act 1, in which Tzara and Joyce confront each other on several levels: Joyce quizzes Tzara along the lines of the catechism chapter involving Bloom and Dedalus in *Ulysses*; Lady Bracknell quizzes Jack about his eligibility for her niece's hand; Tzara informs the audience about the nature of Dadaism; and Joyce affirms the mission of art to shape the ephemeral fragmentation of life into quasi-eternal objects.

Tzara may be the play's most attractive personality. He is not only a Romanian eccentric but also a sardonic social critic and an irreverent deconstructionist of platitudinous slogans. Stoppard has Tzara demand the right both to create a poem out of words jumbled in his hat and to urinate in different colors. Stoppard's Joyce is eloquent in his devout allegiance to the religion of art but less convincing as a shamrock-jacketed spouter of limericks and scrounger of money.

The characterization of Lenin, encountered in the public library but never in Carr's drawing room, proves most problematic. While the artists and bourgeoisie play, he acts, preparing to depart for Russia. His admirer, the librarian Cecily, opens the second act with an earnest lecture on Marxism, interrupted only by Carr's wooing of her. Lenin does not participate in any parallel pairing with Wilde's play—his political weight negates travesty except, perhaps, that his role as Cecily's instructor faintly resembles Miss Prism's. Theatrically, Stoppard's shift from the high-spirited merriment of act 1 to the solemn opening of act 2 is audacious and controversial; some critics have demurred at the drastic undercutting of comic momentum, since it upsets the audience's assumption that the play is made up of the blurred and unreliable recollections of a senile Henry Carr.

Carr is shocked by Tzara's and Lenin's demands that society should be transformed. He tells Tzara, who has expressed sympathy for Lenin's ideas, "You're an amiable bourgeois . . . and if the revolution came you wouldn't know what hit you. . . . Multicoloured micturition is no trick to these boys, they'll have you pissing blood." Yet Carr, while inveighing against artists as self-centered and hostile, also insists that an individual artist's freedom is the most reliable test of a society's freedom.

In the play's coda, old Carr concludes that he learned these lessons from his Zurich experiences: One should be a revolutionary; if not, one should be an artist; and then there is a third lesson—which he cannot recall. Carr may well be a travesty of the sentiments of the public at large, trying to make sense of the meaning of history and the nature of art—and usually failing to do so.

In *Travesties*, Stoppard has composed a witty test whose laughs may outweigh the moral force of its ideas. "In the future," he told Ronald Hayman in June, 1974, "I must stop compromising my plays with this whiff of social application. . . . I should have the courage of my lack of convictions." Yet most of Stoppard's plays after *Travesties* show a marked increase in his political concerns and the deepening of his social conscience.

Dirty Linen and New-Found-Land • In *Dirty Linen and New-Found-Land*, Stoppard for the first time takes an unequivocal political stance, opposing any absolute right of the press to wash any and all linen in the glare of trash journalism's exposures. Even politicians, the play contends, are entitled to their confidential lives, as long as their private conduct does not handicap their public performance.

Starting in 1975 with his participation in a protest march against the mistreatment of Soviet dissidents, Stoppard has consistently voiced, both on and off the stage, his outrage at totalitarian violations of human rights. He has particularly befriended and championed the Czech playwright and later statesman Václav Havel, who is in significant ways his mirror image: Havel was born nine months before Stoppard, shares Stoppard's perspectives of absurdism and penchant for wordplay as well as Czech nativity, but he has consistently committed his work as well as his person to social causes, while Stoppard's recognition of social responsibilities has been intermittent. Both playwrights value as their highest goods freedom of expression and individualism.

Every Good Boy Deserves Favour • In *Every Good Boy Deserves Favour*, Stoppard created what he termed "a piece for actors and orchestra." With music by André Previn and a setting in a psychiatric prison in the Soviet Union, the work uses for its title a mnemonic phrase familiar to students of music because the initial letters, EGBDF, represent in ascending order the notes signified by the black lines of the treble clef. This play-oratorio is a sharply ironic, point-blank attack on the ways in which Soviet law is perverted to stifle dissent. The work is unfortunately flawed by Stoppard's and Previn's self-contradictory uses of the orchestra: On one hand, it evokes a totalitarian society based on a rigid notion of harmonious order in which improvisation and nonconformity are forbidden; on the other hand, the orchestra seeks to offer a lyrical and humane commentary on the action. The text fails to resolve these opposing purposes.

A far more accomplished attack on the suppression of individual freedom is Stoppard's teleplay *Professional Foul* (1977), dedicated to Havel. The text explores the same ethical problems posed in *Jumpers* and is one of Stoppard's most impressive works.

Night and Day • Although *Every Good Boy Deserves Favour* and *Professional Foul* represent ambitious advances in Stoppard's dramaturgy, *Night and Day* is a disappointing sidestep into a naturalism that none of Stoppard's previous plays has embraced. He does continue his new role as a didact, opposing any force that might inhibit the untrammeled passage of information, whether it be a union-closed shop or venal media tycoons or a totalitarian state. The drama takes place in a convulsed African country, possibly Uganda, which is agitated by a rebellion against a despotic government led by equally despotic officers. The play's serious concerns, however, are often obscured by stylish posturing and excessive verbal sparks that subvert the serious circumstances of the action. As a result, the text toys with difficult subjects, trivializing them in a manner reminiscent of Noël Coward's flip cleverness.

The Real Thing • In *The Real Thing*, Stoppard again harks back to Coward (as well as Wilde) for an exercise in love among the leisured classes, in which aristocrats of style spend their time polishing epigrams and tiptoeing into one another's penthouse souls. This play, however, also has a heart, throbbing with the domestic passion to which even an intellectual playwright, the protagonist Henry, can succumb. Henry has an affair with his good friend's wife, Annie; they fall in love, divorce their spouses, and marry. They are happy for two years, but Annie takes Henry's complaisance for complacence and has trysts with other men. Henry discovers howling-wolf pain in his cuckoldry before he and Annie realize that their marriage is, for better and worse, the real thing.

As so often in his dramatic practice, Stoppard mines his play with parallel phrases and repeated allusions. Yet this time his characters do more than skate on brittle surfaces. They suffer recognizable pain in the throes of romance, sharp darts of regret and ardor, frustration and anguish as they find themselves betrayed and rejected by those they love. This time, Stoppard has created recognizable people as well as flashed the laser beams of his intellect.

Hapgood • More than five years after *The Real Thing*, and after a series of adaptations, Stoppard wrote *Hapgood*, first performed in London in 1988 and subsequently revised for its American tour. Stoppard was inspired by quantum mechanics and the discovery that light consists of particles and waves. He took his fascination with physics' duality and applied it to *Hapgood*, in the form of dual human nature, that is, double agents and double dealings—or, more specifically, espionage. The principal character, Hapgood (also code-named Mother), is a female spy who has been ordered by the Central Intelligence Agency to get rid of a double agent who has been serving the Soviet government. The kind but at the same time merciless Hapgood carries out her mission amid thrilling scenes of kidnappings that are not exactly what they seem to be, double agents who may actually be triple or even quadruple agents, and sexual delusions, in a cerebral drama unequivocally demonstrating its author's love of paradox.

Indian Ink • Between screenplays, adaptations, and original dramas, Stoppard wrote perhaps one of his best works, the 1991 radio play *In the Native State*, which he later adapted for the stage as *Indian Ink*. Like other writers fascinated with British imperialism and India, such as E. M. Forster, Stoppard deals here with the ambiguous theme of India's gaining of independence or, as it can also be seen, India's losing its status as a territory of the British Empire. *In the Native State* is also about the Anglo-Indian taboo of sexual relations between British women and Indian men.

While on a visit to India, the young poet Flora Crewe has her portrait painted by Nirad Das, an Indian artist. Das, however, has painted two portraits of Crewe: a "proper" one and a nude, the latter remaining in the possession of his son. The nude represents the "more Indian" side of Nirad Das, which is exactly how Crewe wants him to be, for if he anglicized himself she would despise him, since he would be attempting to bring the bloodlines closer together and eventually erase the distinction between ruler and ruled.

Arcadia • Although after *The Real Thing* Stoppard began devoting most of his time to screenplays and to adapting other writers' dramas, his 1993 play *Arcadia*, which was produced after a break of five years, was greeted with enthusiasm among theater critics, who saw the play returning Stoppard to the stage world.

In *Arcadia*, Stoppard again manages to throw his audience into confusion with sudden shifts from one time period to another; he also continues his experiment of borrowing authentic literary figures, such as Lord Byron, whom spectators find here involved in a murder mystery, one requiring a certain level of intellectual gymnastics on their part.

Arcadia is set in 1809 in the garden room of a beautiful country house in Derbyshire, England. The play's two principal characters, Thomasina Coverly, a thirteen-year-old pupil of Lord Byron's contemporary Septimus Hodge, and Bernard Nightingale, a detective/academic, are separated in time by 180 years. Nightingale, who visits the Coverly house in the 1990's, has as a motive a desire to expose a scandal that occurred in the country house and that involved Lord Byron. According to Nightingale, the fictional poet Ezra Chater, whom Byron criticized in *English Bards and Scotch Reviewers*, is shot following an erotic meeting in the country house. The supposed shooting of Chater, his fictitiousness (as viewers discover that he is Nightingale's invention), and the insinuated quarrel between him and Lord Byron are only some of the mysteries that engage spectators into becoming detectives.

The Invention of Love • Stoppard's last play written in the twentieth century, *The Invention of Love*, is also one of his most ambitious. The play is a memory play again based on a real-life writer: A. E. Housman, poet and classics scholar of the late nineteenth and early twentieth centuries. It begins with Housman's arrival in Hades upon his death in 1936. As he travels down the river Styx with Charon, the ferryman, he remembers/encounters/relives important moments in his life, particularly those that involve Moses Jackson, the man Housman loved unrequitedly throughout his entire life. Here again Stoppard plays with the audiences' perception of time, showing both the young Housman and the old, even allowing them to interact at the ends of both acts.

Stoppard parallels the life of Housman with the life of Oscar Wilde, his contemporary. Where Wilde acted on his homosexual tendencies, ultimately leading to his imprisonment, Housman repressed his own leanings. Rather than simply being a play about denial of love, Stoppard uses Housman to question the nature of many types of love, including brotherly, scholarly and physical. When Housman encounters Wilde in Hades the two discuss the differences between artist and scholar, as well as the two types of love that can be created by these two types of men. *The Invention of Love* is Stoppard's most complex musings on the nature of love, time, life, and death. It is arguably his densest, and most rewarding, work at the time of its first performances.

Other major works

LONG FICTION: *Lord Malquist and Mr. Moon*, 1966.

SCREENPLAYS: *The Engagement*, 1970; *The Romantic Englishwoman*, 1975 (with Thomas Wiseman); *Despair*, 1978 (adaptation of Vladimir Nabokov's novel); *The Human Factor*, 1979 (adaptation of Graham Greene's novel); *Brazil*, 1986; *Empire of the Sun*, 1987 (adaptation of J. G. Ballard's novel); *The Russia House*, 1990 (adaptation of John Le Carré's novel); *Rosencrantz and Guildenstern Are Dead*, 1990; *Billy Bathgate*, 1991 (adaptation of E. L. Doctorow's novel); *Medicine Man*, 1992; *Vatel*, 1997 (translation and adaptation of Jeanne LaBrune's screenplay); *Shakespeare in Love*, 1998; *Enigma*, 1999.

TELEPLAYS: *A Separate Peace*, 1966; *Teeth*, 1967; *Another Moon Called Earth*, 1967; *Neutral Ground*, 1968; *The Engagement*, 1970; *One Pair of Eyes*, 1972 (documentary); *Boundaries*, 1975 (with Clive Exton); *Three Men in a Boat*, 1975 (adaptation of Jerome K. Jerome's novel); *Professional Foul*, 1977; *Squaring the Circle*, 1984; *The Television Plays, 1965-1984*, 1993; *Poodle Springs*, 1998.

RADIO PLAYS: *The Dissolution of Dominic Boot*, 1964; *M Is for Moon Among Other Things*, 1964; *If You're Glad I'll Be Frank*, 1965; *Where Are They Now?*, 1970; *Artist Descending a Staircase*, 1972; *In the Native State*, 1991; *Stoppard: The Plays for Radio, 1964-1991*, 1994.

NONFICTION: *Conversations with Stoppard*, 1995.

TRANSLATION: *Largo Desolato*, 1986 (of Václav Havel's play).

Bibliography

Billington, Michael. *Stoppard the Playwright*. London: Methuen, 1987. Long the drama critic of *The Guardian*, Billington, who writes from a leftist perspective, admires Stoppard's eloquence but mistrusts his conservative ideas. Still, Billington praises *The Real Thing* and expresses his hopes that Stoppard will increase his passion for both people and causes.

Brassell, Tim. *Tom Stoppard: An Assessment*. New York: St. Martin's Press, 1985. Brassell's study is detailed, elegantly written, and learned. He applies a considerable knowledge of modern drama as well as philosophy.

Gusso, Mel. *Conversations with Stoppard*. New York: Limelight Editions, 1995. A collection of interviews between *New York Times* drama critic Gusso and the playwright that covers the time from 1972 to 1995 when the playwright's *Indian Ink* was about to open in London. Presents Stoppard's own erudite thoughts on his work.

Hayman, Ronald. *Tom Stoppard*. London: Heinemann, 1977. Hayman's compact text is chiefly valuable for two highly revealing interviews conducted in 1974 and 1976.

Kelly, Katherine E., ed. *The Cambridge Companion to Tom Stoppard*. Cambridge, England: Cambridge University Press, 2001. Provides essays on all things Stoppard, including an in-depth biography, as well as scholarly criticism on his plays, radio plays, and screenplays. Also contains a very extensive bibliography.

Rusinko, Susan. *Tom Stoppard*. Boston: Twayne, 1986. Mainly summarizes the views of other critics and reviewers. Its chief service is an extended bibliography of secondary as well as primary sources.

Whitaker, Thomas. *Tom Stoppard*. New York: Grove Press, 1983. Whitaker's text is succinct, perceptive, and smoothly worded. He stresses the performance aspects of Stoppard's plays, often commenting on particular productions that he has seen.

Gerhard Brand,
updated by Matthew J. Kopans

August Strindberg

Born: Stockholm, Sweden; January 22, 1849
Died: Stockholm, Sweden; May 14, 1912

Principal drama • *Fritänkaren*, pb. 1870; *I Rom*, pr., pb. 1870; *Den fredlöse*, pr. 1871, pb. 1876 (*The Outlaw*, 1912); *Hermione*, pb. 1871; *Anno fyrtioåtta*, wr. 1876, pb. 1881; *Mäster Olof*, pb. 1878, pr. 1890 (*Master Olof*, 1915); *Gillets hemlighet*, pr., pb. 1880; *Herr Bengts hustru*, pr., pb. 1882; *Lycko-Pers resa*, pr., pb. 1883 (*Lucky Peter's Travels*, 1912); *Fadren*, pr., pb. 1887 (*The Father*, 1899); *Marodörer*, pr. 1887; *Fröken Julie*, pb. 1888, pr. 1889 (*Miss Julie*, 1912); *Kamraterna*, pb. 1888, pr. 1905 (with Axel Lundegård; *Comrades*, 1912); *Fordringsägare*, pb. in Danish 1888, pr. 1889, pb. 1890 (*Creditors*, 1910); *Hemsöborna*, pr. 1889, pb. 1905 (adaptation of his novel); *Paria*, pr. 1889, pb. 1890 (*Pariah*, 1913); *Den starkare*, pr. 1889, pb. 1890 (*The Stronger*, 1912); *Samum*, pr., pb. 1890 (*Simoom*, 1906); *Himmelrikets nycklar, eller Sankte Per vandrar på jorden*, pb. 1892, pr. 1929 (*The Keys of Heaven*, 1965); *Moderskärlek*, pb. 1893, pr. 1894 (*Mother Love*, 1910); *Bandet*, pb. in German 1893, pb. 1897, pr. 1902 (*The Bond*, 1960); *Debet och kredit*, pb. 1893, pr. 1900 (*Debit and Credit*, 1906); *Första varningen*, pr., pb. 1893 (*The First Warning*, 1915); *Inför döden*, pr., pb. 1893 (*In the Face of Death*, 1916); *Leka med elden*, pb. 1893, pr. in German 1893, pr. 1897 (*Playing with Fire*, 1930); *Till Damaskus, forsta delen*, pb. 1898, pr. 1900 (*To Damascus I*, 1913); *Till Damaskus, andra delen*, pb. 1898, pr. 1916 (*To Damascus II*, 1913); *Advent, ett mysterium*, pb. 1899, pr. 1915 (*Advent*, 1912); *Brott och Brott*, pb. 1899, pr. 1900 (*Crime and Crime*, 1913; also known as *There Are Crimes and Crimes*); *Erik XIV*, pr., pb. 1899 (English translation, 1931); *Folkungasagan*, pb. 1899, pr. 1901 (*The Saga of the Folkungs*, 1931); *Gustav Vasa*, pr., pb. 1899 (English translation, 1916); *Gustav Adolf*, pb. 1900, pr. 1903 (English translation, 1957); *Carl XII*, pb. 1901, pr. 1902 (*Charles XII*, 1955); *Dödsdansen, första delen*, pb. 1901, pr. 1905 (*The Dance of Death I*, 1912); *Dödsdansen, andra delen*, pb. 1901, pr. 1905 (*The Dance of Death II*, 1912); *Engelbrekt*, pr., pb. 1901 (English translation, 1949); *Kaspers fet-tisdag*, pr. 1901, pb. 1915; *Kristina*, pb. 1901, pr. 1908 (*Queen Christina*, 1955); *Midsommar*, pr., pb. 1901 (*Midsummertide*, 1912); *Påsk*, pr., pb. 1901 (*Easter*, 1912); *Ett drömspel*, pb. 1902, pr. 1907 (*A Dream Play*, 1912); *Halländarn*, wr. 1902, pb. 1918, pr. 1923; *Kronbruden*, pb. 1902, pr. 1906 (*The Bridal Crown*, 1916); *Svanevit*, pb. 1902, pr. 1908 (*Swanwhite*, 1914); *Genom öknar till arvland, eller Moses*, wr. 1903, pb. 1918, pr. 1922 (*Through Deserts to Ancestral Lands*, 1970); *Gustav III*, pb. 1903, pr. 1916 (English translation, 1955); *Lammet och vilddjuret: Eller, Kristus*, wr. 1903, pb. 1918, pr. 1922 (*The Lamb and the Beast*, 1970); *Näktergalen i Wittenberg*, pb. 1904, pr. 1914 (*The Nightingale of Whittenberg*, 1970); *Till Damaskus, tredje delen*, pb. 1904, pr. 1916 (*To Damascus III*, 1913); *Brända tomten*, pr., pb. 1907 (*After the Fire*, 1913); *Oväder*, pr., pb. 1907 (*Storm*, 1913); *Pelikanen*, pr., pb. 1907 (*The Pelican*, 1962); *Spöksonaten*, pb. 1907, pr. 1908 (*The Ghost Sonata*, 1916); *Abu Casems tofflor*, pr., pb. 1908; *Bjälbo-Jarlen*, pr., pb. 1909 (*Earl Birger of Bjälbo*, 1956); *Riksföreståndaren*, pb. 1909, pr. 1911 (*The Regent*, 1956); *Siste riddaren*, pr., pb. 1909 (*The Last of the Knights*, 1956); *Stora landsvägen*, pb. 1909, pr. 1910 (*The Great Highway*, 1954); *Svarta handsken*, pb. 1909, pr. 1911 (*The Black Glove*, 1916); *Hellas: Eller, Sokrates*, pb. 1918, pr. 1922 (*Hellas*, 1970); *Toten-Insel: Eller, Hades*, pb. 1918 (*Isle of the Dead*, 1962); *Six Plays*, pb. 1955; *Eight Expressionist Plays*, pb. 1965

Other literary forms • August Strindberg wrote nearly two dozen novels, many of which are autobiographical; several volumes of short stories and poems; and more than twenty book-length essays, including writings about the history of Sweden, philosophy, religion, language, and dramatic theory. In addition to the individual Swedish- and English-language editions of Strindberg's work, translated selections appear in *The Strindberg Reader* (1968), edited by Arvid Paulson, and *Inferno, Alone and Other Writings* (1968), edited by Evert Sprinchorn.

Achievements • Tremendously influential in both Europe and the United States, August Strindberg was begrudgingly praised by Henrik Ibsen as one who would be greater than he, and more generously lauded half a century later by Eugene O'Neill as the writer to whom the American playwright owed his greatest debt. Although Strindberg wrote some seventy dramatic pieces, he is best known outside his native Sweden for a small number of plays that represent the range of his achievement. Of these, *The Father*, *Miss Julie*, *A Dream Play*, and *The Ghost Sonata* have earned for Strindberg his stature alongside Ibsen, Anton Chekhov, and George Bernard Shaw as a seminal figure in the first stage (1880-1920) of modern drama.

Strindberg's intensity and versatility are generally considered as much a product of his own neuroses as of his literary genius. The turbulent male-female relationships that his plays portray are commonly accepted as the playwright's expression of his own ambivalent feelings toward women, just as his treatment of the class conflict would seem to have its impulse in his domestic position as "the son of a servant." His late, expressionistic plays, written after a period of intense despair and nonproductivity, reflect the emphasis on atonement that characterizes Strindberg's later writing.

Aside from the provocative autobiographical content of his work, however, Strindberg's achievement rests on his perfection of the naturalistic form, his extension of that form into an imaginative forum for modern psychology, and his movement from dramatic realism to expressionism.

Most of Strindberg's plays that were translated into English and published early in the century are no longer in print. There are, however, a number of more recent translations that have appeared in collections, including, among others, Elizabeth Sprigge's *Six Plays* (1955), Arvid Paulson's *Eight Expressionist Plays* (1965), and the translations of Strindberg's drama by Walter Johnson.

Biography • Born in Stockholm on January 22, 1849, Johan August Strindberg was the fourth child of twelve born to Ulrika Eleonora Norling, formerly a waitress, and Carl Oscar Strindberg, a shipping agent. Strindberg's early life was spent in poverty, in the aftermath of his father's bankruptcy. When he was thirteen, his mother died, and his father married a housemaid. In 1867, Strindberg entered the University of Uppsala, where he studied, intermittently, until 1872, only to leave the university without a degree. In 1869, during one of his respites from university life, he tried acting at the Royal Theater and completed an acting course at the Dramatic Academy, though with little promise of success on the stage. By the following year, Strindberg had turned to playwriting, returned to the university, and had a modest theatrical success with the production of *I Rom* by Runa, a local literary club. The play had been preceded by several other dramatic efforts, and its production encouraged Strindberg to begin work on *Master Olof*, a play about the Swedish religious reformer Olaus Petri, on which Strindberg was to work for nearly a decade. When he left the university, Strindberg worked as a journalist in Stockholm. In 1874, following a second unsuc-

cessful attempt at acting, he took
a position at the Royal Library in
Stockholm, which he retained for
eight years as he continued writing
plays.

In 1875, Strindberg met the first
of his three wives, Siri von Essen,
who was married at the time to
Baron Carl Gustaf Wrangel. The actress divorced her husband following an attempted suicide by Strindberg and, late in 1877, married the
man who had been a frequent guest
in their home. The marriage lasted
until 1891, producing three children
(a fourth, born two months after the
wedding, did not live). During this
period, Strindberg wrote a number
of naturalistic plays that reflected
the class and gender struggles that
were to characterize his best-known
work.

Though reasonably secure in his
reputation among Swedish writers,

(Courtesy of the D. C. Public Library)

Strindberg became disillusioned with the theater when *Herr Bengts hustru* (Sir Bengt's
wife), a play he wrote in response to Ibsen's *Et dukkehjem* (pr., pb. 1879; *A Doll's
House*, 1880), with his wife in the lead role, failed in production, and he and Siri entered
the period of their lives that critics have called "the wander years." From 1883 through
1891, the pair traveled extensively, settling at various times in France, Switzerland,
Bavaria, and, in 1889, again in Sweden. Following their divorce, Strindberg continued
his nomadic life, moving to Berlin, Paris, London, Lund, and, finally, back to Stockholm. Strindberg was particularly creative during the wander years, publishing a
short story collection in two volumes, entitled *Giftas I* and *Giftas II* (1884, 1886;
Married, 1913), a historical novel, two autobiographical works, and three naturalistic
dramas, two of which, *The Father* and *Miss Julie*, are among the most successful of his
plays.

Immediately after the divorce, Strindberg entered a six-year period during which
his literary achievements were nearly nonexistent. Distraught over a blasphemy trial
centering on statements made in his short-story collection and deeply disturbed by his
suspicions concerning Siri's infidelity, Strindberg married Frida Uhl, an Austrian journalist whom he met in Berlin. A year and a half later, in 1894, the couple were divorced, with Frida taking custody of their infant daughter.

For the next three years, Strindberg endured poverty and humiliation and suffered
fantastic visions and unfounded fears. Displaying the classic symptoms of paranoia, he
entered the torment about which he was to write in *Inferno* (1897; English translation,
1912). It was a time during which he experimented with alchemy, hypnotism, and
black magic. He surfaced from his Inferno a self-styled religious man, practicing a hy-
brid of Roman Catholicism and Swedenborgianism and working on the first play in
the allegorical Damascus trilogy.

In Stockholm, Strindberg met a young actress, Harriet Bosse, and, despite nearly thirty years difference in their ages, married her. During a separation from Harriet, Strindberg began writing his expressionistic *A Dream Play*, with intentions of having his wife play the Daughter of Indra. In 1903, however, after only two years of marriage, Harriet left with their infant daughter, apparently unable to accommodate Strindberg's excessive jealousy.

In 1907, Strindberg became codirector, with August Falck, of the Intimate Theater, founded especially for the production of Strindberg's "chamber plays." The theater closed three years later, and in 1912 Strindberg died of stomach cancer. Though the Swedish writer did not have the honor of receiving the prestigious Nobel Prize, he was awarded the Anti-Nobel Prize—fifty thousand crowns through public subscription— two months before his death.

Analysis • Because August Strindberg's drama falls into two distinct periods, separated by the years of his personal Inferno, it is easy to generalize about his work. The pre-Inferno plays are naturalistic in form and are insistently concerned with sexual and class struggles bringing to the philosophy of naturalism a psychological realism that validates his characters as among the most excitingly credible in modern drama. The post-Inferno plays reflect Strindberg's experience with mysticism and a variety of religions, along with his preoccupation in later life with guilt, expiation, and reconciliation. These plays are important especially for the ways in which they extend the boundaries of dramatic form, introducing expressionism and Symbolism into the mainstream of world drama.

Strindberg's early plays reflect the literary preoccupation of the time with the philosophy of naturalism, which holds forces beyond the control of the individual will responsible for human behavior yet also poses the question of individual choice. The resulting complexity of character allowed Strindberg to approach with renewed intensity the two conflicts that for him both personally and artistically were never resolved.

Though Strindberg's work was published as early as 1869, *The Father*, produced and published in 1887, is considered the first of his great naturalistic plays. In that play, as in a number of others that followed, Strindberg dramatizes a major concern of his life and work: the eternal power struggle between men and women. Laura stands as a prototypical Strindbergian woman: immensely powerful and in control yet perhaps not so by design. The play does not clarify whether Laura's triumph over her husband is the consequence of malevolent cunning or of an innocent but nevertheless destructive wielding of a natural female power. That same power is evident in the relationship between Miss Julie and Jean in *Miss Julie*, in which the sexual encounter between mistress and servant is initiated through Julie's aggression, though here the male ultimately achieves superiority as Julie endures postcoital humiliation and finally commits suicide. A concurrent struggle in *Miss Julie*, which is a second preoccupation of Strindberg, is that between the classes. Julie may be seduced to her death by Jean, but she reestablishes class honor, whereas the intimidated servant reverts to subservience.

Strindberg's personal conflicts were to expand during the Inferno period and were reflected in the religious and historical plays produced between 1897 and 1901. In those years, the playwright turned to mysticism and allegory, as in the Damascus trilogy. During this period, he also devoted considerable attention to Swedish history, dramatizing the lives of its people and several of its kings in such plays as *The Saga of the*

Folkungs, Gustav Vasa, Gustav Adolf, and *Carl XII.* In *The Dance of Death I* and *The Dance of Death II,* he confirmed that his obsession with the battle of the sexes was still alive.

Strindberg's most interesting work, however, comes with his later plays, which attempt to capture the dream form in drama. In both *A Dream Play* and *The Ghost Sonata,* his two most successful efforts, the playwright violates the laws of causality and logic, creating a fluid and subjective sequence of events that is dominated by the vision of an implied dreamer. In *A Dream Play,* the Daughter of Indra visits Earth and both observes and participates in the activities of those she encounters. In *The Ghost Sonata,* a young student passes through several rooms in a symbolic house en route to an encounter with a symbolic hyacinth girl. In the earlier play, the recurrent lament of the Daughter of Indra is, "Humankind is to be pitied," reflecting the deep sadness of the playwright, who had been through several religious conversions and had himself seen the condition of humankind. In *The Ghost Sonata,* a similar pessimism prevails but is redeemed in that play by a final tone of reconciliation. A statue of Buddha in the inner room suggests the religious preoccupation and the need to reconcile good and evil that characterizes Strindberg's post-Inferno plays.

The Father • Strindberg once remarked that he did not know whether *The Father* was an invention or a reflection of his own life. The play, in which a man is driven mad by doubts concerning his parenthood, was written at a time when Strindberg's marriage to Siri von Essen was near collapse. Like the Captain in *The Father,* Strindberg was haunted by the knowledge that a man can never know with certainty that he is his child's father, as his suspicions of Siri developed into an obsession with whether he had fathered their first child, born two months after the wedding.

The sexual power struggle that takes place between husband and wife when the two disagree on the future of their daughter, Bertha, forms the dramatic center of the play. Determined to have her way, Laura, the Captain's wife, devises ways of undermining her husband's credibility and confidence. Her goal is to have the Captain certified insane so that he loses his legal claim to their daughter. Her method is psychological torment: Only she, not he, can know whether Bertha is his natural child. Made suspicious by her suggestion, the Captain becomes obsessed with the need to know, devising biological, experiential, and literary tests to affirm his paternity, only to be driven to madness by the impossibility of knowing. In the final tableau, the straitjacketed Captain, surrounded by the women in the household, lies helpless at the nurse's breast, repudiating his child, then falling in a fatal stroke; his wife, embracing Bertha, cries, "My child! My own child!"

Laura's manipulations are not less effective than those of an Iago, and she emerges as uncontested champion in this domestic duel of wills. Yet the play—and she herself—question how conscious her manipulations have been. Moments before the Captain's defeat, Laura claims that she never meant for any of this to happen, that she never thought through her behavior to its consequence. Allusions throughout the play to Omphale and to other women in classical literature suggest that for Strindberg, Laura represents a prototypical evil, a curiously innocent power that is uniquely and naturally feminine. Laura achieves control less by design than by instinct.

In a letter to Friedrich Nietzsche, Strindberg reported the reaction to the production of his play: One woman died, another miscarried, and most of the audience ran from the theater, bellowing. Strindberg's hyperbole, though obviously intended to be frivolous, nevertheless reflects the excitement generated by this highly personal but powerful portrayal of women and of marriage.

Miss Julie • The best known of Strindberg's plays, *Miss Julie* takes place on a midsummer eve in Sweden. In the absence of her father, a nobleman, the twenty-five-year-old Julie, a member of Strindberg's degenerate, emancipated "third sex," initiates a psychological battle with Jean, the valet, that culminates in his sexual triumph. The battle, however, is a social conflict as well, and, in a dramatic suicide-seduction scene, Julie regains her social honor, leaving Jean to tremble at the return of her father, the count. Throughout their encounter, the sexual and social lines separating the two shift, as each lives out the respective dreams of rising and falling that unify the work's images and give dramatic design to the play.

Jean's dream is one of aspiration: He is lying under a tree in a thick and darkened wood; he wants to climb to the top of the tree to look out over the brightly lit landscape and rob a bird's nest of its golden eggs. Despite persistent climbing, however, he never arrives at the first branch, much less the top. When Jean was younger, he once found himself in a compromising position. A servant who had no business being in the gentry's outhouse (the Turkish pavilion), Jean avoided discovery by leaving through the sewer, only to surface to spy Julie, in pink dress and white stockings, standing in the fields. Since that time, he has been symbolically cleansing himself of the dirt and excrement that characterize his servile status, hoping to become proprietor of a Swiss hotel and, eventually, a Rumanian count.

Julie's dream is one of degradation and fall. She is on top of a pillar, longing to descend to the ground, but she does not have the courage to jump. The daughter of an aristocratic father and a common but feminist mother, Julie has developed a hostility toward men (she forces her fiancé to jump over her slashing whip) and an attraction to the servant class. At the Midsummer Eve's festivity, both she and Jean find occasion to act out their perversities and temporarily realize their dreams.

Jean's aspiration and Julie's desire to fall meet in an offstage sexual consummation, signaled onstage by the crescendo of the sounds of the reveling peasants. When the couple emerge from Jean's bedroom, it is clear that Jean is in control. Just as Julie had flaunted her superiority before the sexual act, Jean flaunts his now, ruthlessly abusing the younger woman by refusing to be tender and by calling her a whore. Yet any sense of triumph or defeat is neutralized by the couple's awareness of the consequences of their act; the two plan their departure for Switzerland, Jean to start his hotel, Julie to escape her shame.

Julie reappears in traveling clothes, a smudge of dirt on her face, her pet bird in hand. Asserting his masculine strength, Jean refuses to let Julie take the bird along, decapitating it as Julie expresses a brutal death wish for the entire male sex. Recovering from the fantasy that allowed her hope, she urges Jean to seduce her into killing herself. Jean's dream of self-advancement dissipates as Julie, in her willingness to die to atone for the sacrifice of her honor, endorses an aristocratic principle of reputation and personal integrity that the servant cannot understand. Julie's social victory is affirmed when Jean flinches at the sound of the bell announcing the count's return.

In his preface to the play, Strindberg identifies the factors that were responsible for Julie's tragic fate, including her parents' and her fiancé's characters, the mood of the Midsummer Eve, the urgency of the sexually aroused Jean, Julie's "monthly indisposition," chance, and other biological and environmental conditions. Strindberg's analysis of Julie's behavior reflects the extent to which the playwright incorporated into the play the naturalistic philosophy first given literary expression by novelist Émile Zola. As Strindberg himself notes in the preface, however, *Miss Julie* also includes a psychological dimension that implies Julie's complicity in her fate.

Because it articulates the philosophy of naturalistic drama and suggests both the psychological and the expressionistic, Strindberg's preface has become one of the most widely reprinted statements of modern dramatic theory. Similarly, *Miss Julie*, as the dramatic representation of that theory, and as an emotionally and intellectually engaging play as well, has become an acknowledged masterpiece of world drama.

A Dream Play • An example of Strindberg's post-Inferno work, *A Dream Play* replaces the causal structure of the early naturalistic plays with a loosely constructed series of events that approximate the form of a dream. Though seemingly random, spontaneous, and formless, the action of the play is carefully contrived to re-create the unconscious and reveal inner truth. *A Dream Play* is an astonishing foray into expressionistic drama that testifies to Strindberg's quest for a form to accommodate the polyphonic thinking that characterizes his later work.

A Dream Play has a cast of thirty-nine, as well as a sizable number of walk-on performers. Its central character is the supernatural Daughter of Indra, who visits Earth both as an observer and as a participant. As emissary of her father, she is to report back to him on whether human complaint is justified; as a result of her sojourn, she concludes that humankind is to be pitied.

The Daughter of Indra's earthly enterprise first brings her in contact with an imprisoned officer, whom she frees from punishing labor, and then with the officer's family, whom she observes as the mother, preparing for death, saddens her husband by offering a servant the shawl that he once gave her. The Daughter of Indra's preliminary judgment is that humankind is to be pitied, but that love conquers all.

In an alley leading to the opera house, the Daughter of Indra witnesses the disappointments of auditioning opera singers, who tell their troubles to the doorkeeper, who wears the mother's shawl. Roses in hand, the officer awaits Miss Victoria, who never appears. In the alley, there is a locked door with a cloverleaf cutout that presumably shields the mysteries of life, but a court order is needed to open it.

In a lawyer's office, a white-faced divorce attorney, sitting in the stench of crime, prompts the Daughter of Indra's judgment. The office is transformed into a church, where a commencement ceremony, presided over by four deans of the faculties, is in progress. When the lawyer steps forward to receive his laurels, he receives only a crown of thorns. Unable to understand the cries for mercy that surround the lawyer or the tears dropping to the pavement, the Daughter of Indra offers to marry the lawyer to test the redemptive power of love, marriage, and home.

Yet in the next scene, she is a poor, tired housewife, cooking over a hot stove while the baby screams. Announcing that he now has his degree, the lawyer offers to take his wife to Fairhaven, where the world is more pleasant. By mistake, however, they wind up in Foulstrand, a contemporary inferno, to be greeted by the Quarantine Master and an assortment of miserable people. A dragon boat arrives with newlyweds at the helm, but the blissful couple kill themselves. At Fairhaven, strains of a Johann Sebastian Bach toccata and a waltz conflict to ruin the dance, while at a Mediterranean resort, two men shovel coal in the heat, complaining of their misfortune.

Finally, at Fingal's Cave, or Indra's Ear, the Daughter of Indra again encounters the poet whom she first met at Foulstrand, and here she invokes the Kingdom of Heaven and speaks of what she has learned, asking, with the poet, why humankind must be so miserable. Though much time has passed since her descent to Earth, a telescoping now takes place that transports the Daughter of Indra back to the opera house and the cloverleaf stage door. She listens as the deans of the faculties quarrel over whether it should be opened, then watches as it swings ajar to reveal nothing.

The Daughter of Indra returns to the Growing Castle that had appeared on her descent and prepares to return to the ethereal world. As she offers her assessment of the divided nature of humankind, promising to carry the world's lamentations to her father's throne, the Castle bursts into flame, revealing a wall of human faces in despair, and, finally, a chrysanthemum. The Daughter of Indra departs, leaving behind the poet, the one visionary capable of articulating the coexistence of misery and joy that is the story of humankind.

Influenced by Indian religion and Oriental philosophy, Strindberg envisions the world in this play as a mirage, caught in the eternal conflict between spirit and form. In a diary entry made two days before he completed the play, Strindberg equated love with sin, remarking on the paradox that the world (if it exists at all) exists through sin, making life an endless vacillation between "the pleasures of love and the agony of penance." *A Dream Play* remained unproduced for five years after it was published in 1902, finally seeing production during the same year in which *The Ghost Sonata* was published.

The Ghost Sonata • *The Ghost Sonata* is one of Strindberg's chamber plays, so named for their intimacy, their lyricism, and their simplicity of theme. Like chamber music, the chamber plays were designed for small audiences, particularly those at Strindberg's Intimate Theater. Like *A Dream Play*, *The Ghost Sonata* is abstract in form, presenting a series of images suggestive of a dream.

The dominant consciousness in the play is a student named Arkenholz, who progresses through the symbolic episodes of the dream until he acquires understanding, at which point the dream ends through his awakening. While he is in the dream, Arkenholz is poet-seeker, possessing exceptional acuity of perception. He is limited, however, by an equally powerful, ambivalently evil old man named Hummel, who guides Arkenholz into a house in which strange and symbolic characters reside. In the deepest room of the house is the Hyacinth Girl, the vision of beauty and love that the student cannot resist.

Arkenholz's mythic quest begins at the facade of the building, where he encounters a milkmaid and Hummel, an old man in a wheelchair who tells him that by sitting through a Richard Wagner opera he will gain entrance to the house. Excited by Arkenholz's fondness for the house, Hummel identifies its inhabitants: the colonel who beats his wife; the marble statue of the colonel's wife, who is now a mummy; the Lady in Black; the dead consul; the decrepit fiancé, who is mad; the caretaker's wife; and, in the Hyacinth Room, the Girl.

Once inside, the student observes the unnatural coterie in the Round Room, where he witnesses Hummel's inhumane treatment of the colonel and hears of a network of sexual relationships as the residents of the house gather for their ritual supper. The student pauses for introductions to the mummy, who comes out of her closet squawking like a parrot, and to the marble statue of her youthful form, while Hummel, who has fathered the woman's child, hangs himself in the closet. Without his guide, Arkenholz continues his journey into the timeless world of the Hyacinth Room, in which the clock that stood prominently on the mantle in the Round Room and strikes to signal the last minutes of the old man's life is replaced by a statue of the Buddha.

The Hyacinth Girl turns out to be an emaciated woman, drained of her strength by a vampire cook who boils the nourishment out of the meat, but the student is awed by her beauty. When she hears that Arkenholz wants to marry her, the Hyacinth Girl reveals the secrets of the house, transforming his vision of innocence and beauty into a lamentation, then a plea for redemption. As the student begins to awaken from his dream, he speaks of what he has learned, reconciling the woe that he has discovered and the innocence in which he had believed.

A "world of intimations," suggestively inviting its readers into its seemingly strange but curiously familiar landscape, *The Ghost Sonata* is a richly evocative vision of guilt and expiation, of innocence and evil, that extends to all humankind. Strindberg claimed that writing the play was a painful experience, that he hardly knew himself what he had written, but that he felt in it the sublime.

Other major works

LONG FICTION: *Från Fjärdingen och Svartbäcken*, 1877; *Röda rummet*, 1879 (*The Red Room*, 1913); *Jäsningstiden*, 1886 (*The Growth of the Soul*, 1914); *Hemsöborna*, 1887 (*The Natives of Hemsö*, 1959); *Tschandala*, in Danish 1889, in Swedish 1897; *I havsbandet*, 1890 (*By the Open Sea*, 1913); *Le Plaidoyer d'un fou*, 1893 in German, 1895 in Swedish (*A Madman's Defense*, 1912, also known as *The Confession of a Fool*); *Inferno*, 1897 (English translation, 1912); *Ensam*, 1903 (*Alone*, 1968); *Götiska rummen*, 1904; *Svarta fanor*, 1907; *Taklagsöl*, 1907; *Syndabocken*, 1907 (*The Scapegoat*, 1967); *Författaren*, 1909.

SHORT FICTION: *Giftas I*, 1884; *Svenska öden och äventyr*, 1882-1892; *Giftas II*, 1886 (*Married*, 1913; also known as *Getting Married*, 1973; includes *Giftas I* and *Giftas II*); *Utopier i verkligheten*, 1885; *Skärkarlsliv*, 1888; *Legender*, 1898 (*Legends*, 1912); *Fagervik och Skamsund*, 1902 (*Fair Haven and Foul Strand*, 1913); *Sagor*, 1903 (*Tales*, 1930); *Historiska miniatyrer*, 1905 (*Historical Miniatures*, 1913).

POETRY: *Dikter och verkligheter*, 1881; *Dikter på vers och prosa*, 1883; *Sömngångarnätter på vakna dagar*, 1884.

NONFICTION: *Gamla Stockholm*, 1880; *Det nya riket*, 1882; *Svenska folket i helg och söcken, krig och fred, hemma och ute eller Ett tusen år av svenska bildningens och sedernas historia*, 1882; *Tjänstekvinnans son: En s äls utvecklingshistoria*, 1886 (4 volumes; *The Son of a Servant: The Story of the Evolution of a Human Being*, 1966, volume 1 only); *Vivisektioner*, 1887; *Blomstermalningar och djurstycken*, 1888; *Bland franska bönder*, 1889; *Antibarbarus*, 1896; *Jardin des plantes*, 1896; *Svensk natur*, 1897; *Världshistoriens mystik*, 1903; *Modersmålets anor*, 1910; *Religiös renässans*, 1910; *Folkstaten*, 1910-1911; *Tal till svenska nationen*, 1910-1911; *Världsspråkens rötter*, 1910; *Oppna brev till Intima Teatern*, 1911-1912 (*Open Letters to the Intimate Theater*, 1959); *Zones of the Spirit: A Book of Thoughts*, 1913.

Bibliography

Carlson, Harry Gilbert. *Out of "Inferno": Strindberg's Reawakening as an Artist*. Seattle: University of Washington Press, 1996. A study of the change in Strindberg's literary works after his publication of *Inferno*. Bibliography and index.

Ekman, Hans-Göran. *Strindberg and the Five Senses: Studies in Strindberg's Chamber Plays*. Somerset, N.J.: Transaction, 2000. A critical analysis of Strindberg's chamber plays, with particular emphasis on the five senses. Bibliography and index.

Marker, Frederick J., and Christopher Innes, eds. *Modernism in European Drama: Ibsen, Strindberg, Pirandello, Beckett: Essays from Modern Drama*. Buffalo, N.Y.: University of Toronto Press, 1998. A collection of essays from *Modern Drama* published between 1963 and 1994 on modernism in the dramatic works of Strindberg, Henrik Ibsen, Luigi Pirandello, and Samuel Beckett. Bibliography and index.

Martinus, Eivor. *Strindberg and Love.* Charlbury, Oxford, England: Amber Lane Press, 2001. A study of Strindberg's relations with women, including how it manifested in his literary works. Bibliography and index.

Robinson, Michael. *Studies in Strindberg.* Norwich: Norvik Press, 1998. A critical analysis and interpretation of the literary works of Strindberg. Bibliography and index.

Robinson, Michael, and Sven Hakon Rossel, eds. *Expressionism and Modernism: New Approaches to August Strindberg.* Vienna: Edition Praesens, 1999. A collection of papers from the Thirteenth International Strindberg Conference, Linz Austria, October, 1997, and one essay from the Internationale Strindberg-Tage, Vienna, October, 1997, that examine the literary works of Strindberg. Bibliography and index.

Törnqvist, Egil. *Strindberg's "The Ghost Sonata" from Text to Performance.* Amsterdam: Amsterdam University Press, 2000. An in-depth analysis of Strindberg's *The Ghost Sonata.* Bibliography and index.

June Schlueter

John Millington Synge

Born: Rathfarnham, Ireland; April 16, 1871
Died: Dublin, Ireland; March 24, 1909

Principal drama • *When the Moon Has Set,* wr. 1900-1901, pb. 1968; *Luasnad, Capa, and Laine,* wr. 1902, pb. 1968; *A Vernal Play,* wr. 1902, pb. 1968; *The Tinker's Wedding,* wr. 1903, pb. 1908, pr. 1909; *In the Shadow of the Glen,* pr. 1903, pb. 1904 (one act); *Riders to the Sea,* pb. 1903, pr. 1904 (one act); *The Well of the Saints,* pr., pb. 1905; *The Playboy of the Western World,* pr., pb. 1907; *Deirdre of the Sorrows,* pr., pb. 1910; *The Complete Plays,* pb. 1981

Other literary forms • John Millington Synge's nondramatic works—autobiographical sketches, essays, reviews, and diaries—document the proposition that his dramatic career began with his response to William Butler Yeats's advice to abandon Paris for Ireland's remote regions. Synge's observations of the lives of the country people of Aran, Connemara, Kerry, and Wicklow indicate that until he lived in these repositories of folk tradition, he had not found either theme or style. The diaries and essays from these visits report Synge's compilation of dramatic incidents, details of local color, images, and turns of speech, and show an understanding of that way of life that encompassed its dialect, character, and fatalism. Although these accounts show an acute eye for the dramatic, they have less-than-scientific reliability, permeated as they are with Synge's nature mysticism, his brooding remove from social engagement, and his lack of sympathy with the religious traditions of the people. Synge's direct, precise prose is chiefly valuable as a record of the sources for his plays and of his developing creative consciousness.

With a few exceptions—"In Kerry," "Queens," and "Danny"— Synge's poetry merits the same judgment. Ironic, romantic, and morbid, it is rich with Celtic and folk reference. It also shows, however, the influence of various European poets—François Villon, Giacomo Leopardi, Petrarch—whose works Synge translated. There is some evidence that Synge's direct idiom contributed to Yeats's abandonment of romantic idealism after 1902.

Synge's photographs (*My Wallet of Photographs,* 1971) are valuable documents of turn-of-the-century life on the Irish seaboard. His *Letters to Molly* (1971) and *Some Letters of John M. Synge to Lady Gregory and W. B. Yeats* (1971) are equally valuable in coming to an appreciation of Synge's personal and business struggles in his final and more creative years.

Achievements • The Irish Literary Renaissance was the result of the collective efforts of diverse talents in the fields of translation, folklore, fiction, poetry, and drama. Under the leadership of the Olympian William Butler Yeats, the movement counted the folklorist Douglas Hyde, the novelists James Joyce and George Moore, the translator and dramatist Lady Augusta Gregory, and the poet and editor George Russell (whose pseudonym was Æ) among its contributors. These writers shared the desire for the establishment of a national literature that would express what they considered distinctive about the Irish imagination. Each contributed to the dramatic literature presented on the stage of the Abbey Theatre, but John Millington Synge is the only one of this group whose contribution lies mainly in the drama. Indeed, Synge is generally regarded as the most distinguished dramatist of the Irish Literary Renaissance.

This reputation rests on the output of his final seven years: six plays, two of which, *Riders to the Sea* and *The Playboy of the Western World,* are masterpieces. These plays in particular exhibit the characteristic qualities of intense lyric speech drawn from the native language and dialects of Ireland, romantic characterization in primitive settings, and dramatic construction after the classics of European drama. Three central theses dominate Synge's work: the enmity between romantic dreams and life's hard necessities, the relationship between human beings and the natural world, and the mutability of all things. These plays are the expressions of a complex personality, formed by Synge's early musical training, his alienation from his own Anglo-Irish roots, his love for the landscapes and country people of Ireland, the tension between romantic impulse and realistic imperatives, and his persistent morbidity and personal loneliness.

Synge has had considerable influence in shaping the style and themes of subsequent Irish dramatists, such as George Fitzmaurice and M. J. Malloy, and some influence outside Ireland, most notably in the work of Federico García Lorca and Eugene O'Neill.

Biography • Edmund John Millington Synge was born April 16, 1871, in Rathfarnham, County Dublin, the youngest of the five children of a comfortable Anglo-Irish Protestant family. His schooling was mostly private until, at the age of seventeen, he entered Trinity College, Dublin, where he won prizes in Irish and Hebrew even though he put most of his energy into the study of the piano, violin, and flute. During his youth, he developed a strong reaction to his mother's religiosity and an enthusiasm for the antiquities and natural beauty of the Irish countryside. He went to Germany in 1893 to study music but the following year abandoned his plans to move to Paris and attend lectures in European language and literature at the Sorbonne. Instead, he traveled through Germany, Italy, and France between 1894 and 1896. He wrote some poetry and dramatic fragments, gave lessons in English, and studied French and Italian, returning during the summers to Dublin, where he furthered his interests in the Irish language and Irish antiquities.

In December, 1896, Yeats encountered Synge in Paris and discerned a literary talent in search of a subject. He advised Synge to go to the Aran Islands off the Atlantic coast of Ireland, where the people spoke Irish and still led lives free of modern

(Library of Congress)

convention. Synge complied, and for a portion of each summer from 1898 to 1902, he lived among the fisherfolk and recorded his observations with notebook and camera.

Yeats continued to write dramatic sketches and literary reviews and edited his notes under the title *The Aran Islands* (1907). His first plays, *When the Moon Has Set,* written in prose, and *A Vernal Play* and *Luasnad, Capa, and Laine,* written in verse—although apprenticeship works—exhibit fragmentary characteristics of his mature work. This maturity came rapidly, for during the summer of 1902, he wrote *Riders to the Sea* and *In the Shadow of the Glen* and began *The Tinker's Wedding. Riders to the Sea* was the first of Synge's plays to be published (October, 1903), but *In the Shadow of the Glen* was the first to be produced on the stage—by the Irish National Theatre Society (October, 1903). An acrimonious public debate over the play's depiction of Irish life followed this production, a debate to which its author contributed little. When *Riders to the Sea* was produced, Synge's reputation improved, especially following the London presentation of the two plays in March, 1904.

When the Abbey Theatre opened in December of 1904, Synge was appointed literary adviser and later director, along with Lady Augusta Gregory and W. B. Yeats. The following February, *The Well of the Saints* was produced there, though it was poorly received. Meanwhile, Synge was visiting Counties Kerry, Galway, and Mayo and was working on his masterpiece, *The Playboy of the Western World.* As he drafted and revised this play throughout 1906, a romantic relationship was growing with Molly Allgood (known on stage as Máire O'Neill), the Abbey actress who played the role of Pegeen Mike in the first production, on January 26, 1907. The play offended Irish sensibilities, provoking a week of riots and a bitter public debate over the play and freedom of expression on the stage. Again, Synge took little part in the argument, leaving the burden of defending his work to Yeats.

Synge commenced his last play, *Deirdre of the Sorrows,* which is based on a story of the Sons of Usnach from the Ulster cycle of Celtic tales, during 1907. During this same year, the symptoms of Hodgkin's disease, which had first manifested themselves in 1897, reappeared. The resultant operations interfered with Synge's revisions of the play, caused the postponement of his wedding, and failed to arrest the disease. He died on March 24, 1909. In January, 1910, *Deirdre of the Sorrows* was first performed, with Molly Allgood in the title role.

Analysis • When, in 1893, John Millington Synge was choosing between musical and literary careers, two seminal documents were published that would profoundly affect his decision and form the character of his subsequent work. These were Stopford Brooke's lecture "The Need of Use of Getting Irish Literature into the English Tongue," and Douglas Hyde's *Love Songs of Connaught* (1893). Brooke's lecture identified four tasks essential to the development of an Irish national literature: the translation of ancient Irish texts, the molding of the various mythological and historical cycles into an imaginative unity, the treatment in verse of selected episodes from these materials, and the collection of folk stories surviving in the Irish countryside. Some of these tasks had already been undertaken, but none had an impact on the developing revival to equal that of Hyde's slim volume of the same year. He showed that the living song tradition in the Irish Gaelic-speaking areas was rich, complex, and sensitive; that a strong link with an ancient cultural tradition still persisted; and that a translation of these songs into Hiberno-English opened new avenues of expression to the literary artist.

By the early 1890's, Yeats was already committed to some of the tasks outlined by Brooke, and he also greeted Hyde's work enthusiastically. Yeats wrote in an 1893 issue of *The Bookman*: "These poor peasants lived in a beautiful if somewhat inhospitable world, where little has changed since Adam delved and Eve span. Everything was so old that it was steeped in the heart, and every powerful emotion found at once noble types and symbols for its expression." When Yeats encountered Synge in Paris three years later, it was with these principles and sentiments that he persuaded him to abandon the French capital for the Aran Islands. The plays that resulted do indeed constitute a distinguished translation of folk and heroic materials to the modern stage.

Synge set himself not only against the mystical excesses of the Irish writers of his time but also against the intellectual drama of Henrik Ibsen and George Bernard Shaw and produced works of narrow but intense passion. Synge's plays realize, more successfully than those of any of his contemporaries, Yeats's dictum that Irish writers should seek their form among the classical writers, but their language at home.

Riders to the Sea • *Riders to the Sea* was the first play Synge wrote, and it draws most heavily and directly on his experience of life on the Aran Islands; many of the details, along with the main incident on which the play is based, can be found in the journals Synge kept during his visits there. It was Synge's first successful use of Hiberno-English to serve his own dramatic and poetic purposes, and it is regarded by most commentators as one of the finest short plays in that literature.

The action of the play is simple and highly compressed. An old woman of the Aran Islands, Maurya, has lost her husband, father-in-law, and four sons to the sea. She now awaits news of the fate of Michael, another son, as her last and youngest son, Bartley, prepares to make the crossing to Galway with two horses. Maurya's two daughters have just received a bundle of clothes which they identify as those of Michael. As the young women attempt to keep the news from her, she attempts to dissuade Bartley from the hazardous journey—in vain, for just as Bartley must play the provider's part, Maurya's timeworn experience has taught her to anticipate the truth. While her daughters find confirmation of Michael's death in the bundle of clothes, Maurya sees a vision of what is about to happen: Bartley's drowning. As the daughters tell Maurya of Michael's death, the neighbors carry in Bartley's body. The play climaxes with Maurya's lament for these and all her menfolk, ending with a prayer for all the living and the dead.

Although it requires less than thirty minutes to perform, the play encompasses a succession of moods and a universe of action. By contrasting the young women's particular, objective attitudes (their preoccupation with the physical evidence of Michael's death) with Maurya's subjective, universal, even mystical, consciousness (her forgetting the blessing and the nails, and her visionary experience), Synge establishes a pattern of dramatic ironies. Maurya's feelings in regard to the external action of the play, moreover, are seen to evolve from a subdued disquiet, to a higher anxiety, to a visionary sympathy with her last two sons, and finally to a threnody of disinterested compassion for the mothers and sons of all humankind. Maurya is, therefore, not only a credible individual character but also an archetypal figure: She is cast among domestic details yet is inattentive to them because her awareness of commonality and community eventually obscures particular concerns. Only her indomitable attitude in those eloquent, passionate speeches offers a nearly adequate human response to the implacable antagonist, the sea.

The sea that surrounds the bare islands is both the islanders' source of sustenance and their principal natural enemy; in the play, it insistently reminds the characters that, contend with it or not, they are doomed. Synge has carefully selected the domestic details to develop his themes—the bread, the nets, boards, knife, rope, and knot—details which establish a practical and symbolic relationship between the smaller and larger worlds of action, onstage and offstage, practical and moral. Other elements in the play act as religious or mystical allusions: the apocalyptic horses, the fateful dropped stitches, the ineffectual young priest, the omens in the sky and in the holy well. Many aspects of the setting—the door, the colors, the blessing—repeat and reverse themselves as images of the life-and-death ritual that sets Maurya and the sea against each other again and again. Maurya's maternal mysticism is solemnly expressed by her prayers, blessings, gestures, litanies, and pitiful elegy for the cavalcade of death.

Although Maurya's speeches are interlaced with Christian invocation, her response to the catastrophe does not, at its most profound depths, derive from conventional Christian feelings. Maurya confronts a system of natural elements that confounds all human aspirations, and her response is in the tradition of characters from grand tragedy. Thus Synge has written a play that combines elements from Greek tragedy (it reminded Yeats of the plays of Aeschylus), the attitudes of primitive Gaelic society (its fatalism and impersonality), and the modern world, with its nihilism and cultivation of a sense of the absurd. There has been considerable argument over the compatibility of these ethics with one another, but there is no disagreement over the intensity and complexity of the emotions engendered by the play, whether read or staged.

In the Shadow of the Glen • Synge's second produced play, *In the Shadow of the Glen* (written under the title *The Shadow of the Glen*) is set in the Wicklow Mountains south of Dublin, a remote area familiar to Synge, in which he had a cottage and about which he had written several essays gathered under the title *In Wicklow* (1910). The play shows the influence of Ibsen's *Et dukkehjem* (pr., pb. 1879, *A Doll's House*, 1880), but its direct source is "An Old Man's Story," which Synge had heard from the Aran Island storyteller Pat Dirane; it is found in Synge's prose work *The Aran Islands*. The question of the play's origin is significant because it was immediately attacked for its depiction of an unfaithful wife and its unfair portrayal of Irishwomen. Synge unquestionably took considerable liberty with his raw materials—drawing, for example, on an episode from Petronius's *Satyricon* (c. 60 C.E.; *The Satyricon*, 1694), "The Widow of Ephesus"—and the result was an original, concise, complex comedy.

A "Tramp" is admitted to a lonely cottage by one Nora Burke, whose husband is laid out as if for a wake. Conversation between the two reveals that Nora has been living unhappily with her relatively well-off but aged husband, a situation that has led to a number of dalliances with other men, including the now deceased Patch Darcy. Nora then exits to rendezvous with another young man, Michael Dara, leaving the Tramp to maintain the wake. The Tramp, however, is soon shocked to find that Nora's husband, Dan Burke, is feigning death in order to trap his wife and either bring her to heel or eject her from his house. No sooner has the Tramp agreed to cooperate with Dan's scheme than Nora returns with Michael Dara. The pair discuss their prospects of marriage now that Nora is apparently free. Suddenly Dan springs from the bed to confront the pair. Michael Dara backs off immediately, and Nora is left to face her husband alone; at this point, the Tramp reintroduces himself with renewed eloquence, offering Nora a romantic life with him outside material security. This appeal finally releases Nora's imaginative energies, and she departs with him, leaving Dan Burke and Michael Dara to share a bottle of whiskey.

In the Shadow of the Glen offered the first explicit treatment of sexual frustration on the modern Irish stage; at the same time, the play's symbolic setting and the rich imagery of its language enlarge its reference to register a protest against the constraints of time and space (represented by the mists moving up and down the Wicklow glen). Synge sympathizes with Nora and identifies with the Tramp, the two developing characters in the play, in opposition to their static counterparts, Dan Burke and Michael Dara. The Tramp's sympathetic nature and colorful talk awaken hitherto untapped imaginative reserves in Nora, so that the surroundings of mountain mist and road become reinvested with their primary magic. The play thus dramatizes Synge's central preoccupations: the conflict between actuality and human aspirations, the awareness of human mutability, and human beings' intimate relation with the natural world.

In the Shadow of the Glen dramatizes life-and-death issues in many ways, both literally and metaphorically, and on different levels of seriousness and comedy: Daniel Burke appears dead but rises twice. His ploy is to test the convention of life (his wife's fidelity) with the perspective of death, and he succeeds in exposing it as illusory. The audience begins with a conventional view of death; proceeds, after Dan's first resurrection (through the sharing of his vantage point, but not his point of view), to a seriocomic view of life; and ends, after his second resurrection, with a romantic sharing of the Tramp's vantage point and point of view on both life and death. As its sympathies shift, the audience proceeds from an ironic view of Nora's infidelity to an ironic view of Dan's righteousness. The first revelation is that the conventional phenomena of death are deceptive; the final revelation is that the conventional phenomena of life are equally deceptive. The playgoer begins by believing Dan to be dead in body and ends by believing him dead in soul. These ambiguities and shifts in the plot are reflected in the language and imagery of the play, which propose states of animality, madness, and age as relative conditions between life and death.

It is clear, for example, that Nora's memories of Patch Darcy condition her response to the Tramp, and as the play progresses, the connections between these two male figures multiply, as do the associations of the Tramp with death. Thus, as the image of Patch Darcy (his life-in-death counterpart), the Tramp is at once the antagonist of Dan and Michael, death-in-life counterparts. The Tramp is, in an important sense, the ghost of Patch Darcy, for he is the counterpart, in Nora's consciousness, of her dead lover. She seems to recognize the affinity, at first dimly but with sufficient clarity at the end to follow her Patch into the mists on the mountainside to romance, and probably to madness and death. Thus, the Tramp, as Patch Darcy revenant, is Nora's shadow of the Wicklow glen. By a combination of poetic language, naturalistic action, and farce, the play transforms its source into a small triumph, preparing the way for Synge's greatest achievement, *The Playboy of the Western World.*

The Playboy of the Western World • *The Playboy of the Western World* originated in a story, recorded in 1898, about a man named Lynchenaun "who killed his father with the blow of a spade when he was in a passion" and, with the aid of the people of Inishmaan, evaded the police to escape eventually to the United States. When later (1903-1905) Synge visited Counties Kerry and Mayo, he gathered further materials for this work: observations of the lonely landscapes of the western seaboard, the moodiness and rebellious temperament of the people, and their religiosity, alcoholism, and fanciful language. For the next two years, he worked steadily on the play under five successive titles, almost twenty scenarios, and a dozen complete drafts, before it was finally produced on January 26, 1907.

The play develops the Lynchenaun story into that of Christy Mahon, a timorous Kerry farmboy who has fled north from the scene of his parricide to a lonely stretch of the coastline of Mayo. There he happens on a remote public house where he tells his story. The villagers give him refuge, and as he is called on to retell his story to a succession of curious neighbors, his embellishments become more colorful, and his self-confidence grows in proportion to the hyperbole. The villagers respond to these accounts with increasing admiration, so that Christy is soon regarded as a hero for his passionate deed. He strikes fear in the men and desire in the women, especially in the daughter of the house, Pegeen Mike. She rejects her fiancé, the pious Shawn Keogh, for Christy's attentions, which she seeks to retain against the competition of the village women, especially the Widow Quin. All this attention drives Christy to further heights of eloquence—especially in the love scene with Pegeen—and to feats of athletic skill at the village sports.

These triumphs, however, are rudely deflated by the appearance of another, older Kerryman, with a bandaged head: Christy's father, very much alive. He exposes Christy as a coward and a liar, and the crowd, Pegeen included, immediately rejects their erstwhile champion. Christy has been changed, however, and to prove his father wrong and regain his reputation and Pegeen's affections, he attacks his father again, this time laying him low "in the sight of all." Christy, however, has misjudged the effect of such an action on the villagers, who distinguish between the admirable "gallous story" and the shocking "dirty deed," and they capture Christy to bring him to justice. He is disillusioned with all of them and threatens indiscriminate vengeance, whereupon his father again revives, recognizes Christy's newfound character, and invites him back to Kerry as master of the house. Christy agrees, and they depart, casting aspersions on the "villainy of Mayo and the fools in here." Too late, Pegeen realizes that she has lost a true champion.

The play provoked immediate outrage among the Dublin audiences: They considered it an insult to national pride, to Roman Catholicism, and to common decency. Among a people hoping for a fair, if not positive, treatment in support of their long-standing grievance against British rule, the play was a cruel disappointment. For his part, Synge refused to tone down the play's oaths and irreverent allusions, even when appealed to privately by the actors and by his fellow Protestants Yeats and Lady Gregory. The protests, in fact, turned into a full-scale riot with Christy's reference to "a drift of chosen females standing in their shifts," which was considered an intolerable obscenity. In the week that followed, the police protected the stage and players from nightly attack, Yeats defended the freedom of the stage in public debate, Synge himself granted an unfortunate interview to the press, and the newspapers were full of acrimonious argument. In retrospect, it is not difficult to understand why a Dublin audience, sensitive to signs of religious and ethnic derogation, should react so vehemently to the work of a son of the landed class produced at the "national" theater and composed of such an original blend of Rabelaisian humor, lyricism, romance, and exaggeration.

In his preface to the play, Synge anticipates a hostile reaction by praising the "popular imagination that is fiery and magnificent, and tender" that he found among the people of the remote regions. He proposes that the language and images are authentic, "that the wildest sayings and ideas in this play are tame indeed compared with the fancies one may hear in any little hillside cabin." Although it is true that Synge's sources—in plot, language, and characterization—are sound, the combination here, more than in his other works, is uniquely his own. Just as the action and characterization lack normal constraints, so, too, is the language compressed and heightened.

The distinctive language of *The Playboy of the Western World* derives from several sources: the Hiberno-English dialects of the West of Ireland, vestiges of Tudor English still found in Ireland, popular sermons, and Synge's own penchant for musical, rhythmic prose. Chief among these is the influence of Irish Gaelic syntax, vocabulary, and idiom, with its rich lode of religious and natural imagery. This convention is particularly effective at the romantic climax in act 3, although it can sound parodic in scenes of less excitement. Even so, Synge's particular artistic use of local dialect is considerably more flexible and expressive than the comparable experiments of Lady Gregory or Yeats.

In this dialect, Synge found an ideal vehicle for his own passionate vision of the lonely outsider. Christy is the poet whose creative gifts are only superficially appreciated by a convention-bound society; Christy not only invests the language with new zest and daring but also unknowingly transforms himself, by the same process of imaginative energy, from a cowering lout into a master of his destiny. His transformation begins as the people of Mayo trust his story and continues as he realizes his own narrative skills; it is completed when, with full moral awareness, he strikes his father down a second time. His father is the first to recognize the new Christy; Pegeen Mike does so, too, but for her it is too late; for the rest, the episode is no more than a subject for gossip.

Christy's path to his apotheosis comes only after an erratic journey of surges and reversals; *The Playboy of the Western World* is exuberant comedy in its action as well as in its language and characterization. It contains moments of farce, satire, tragicomedy, and the mock heroic. As Ann Saddlemyer's standard edition shows, Synge's revisions were vigorous and meticulous, act 3 giving him the most difficulties; some of these difficulties—Pegeen's motivations and the resolution of the Widow Quin's role—arguably remain unresolved. For all of its difficulties, however, this act achieves brilliant closure and includes perhaps the finest dramatic writing to come from the Irish theater.

The power of *The Playboy of the Western World* rests on more than its verbal pyrotechnics and comic structure; as many critics have argued, it exhibits features of the scapegoat archetype, the Oedipus myth, and the Messiah theme. It has relationships with Irish folk legend, with the early Irish Ulster cycle of heroic tales, and with Ibsen's *Peer Gynt* (1867). Whatever the relevance of these sources or analogues to an appreciation of this great play, the play's qualities derive from the happy collaboration of Synge's instinctive sense of the dramatic and the quality of his material. He describes it thus to an admirer: "The wildness and, if you will, the vices of the Irish peasantry are due, like their extraordinary good points of all kinds, to the *richness* of their nature—a thing that is priceless beyond words."

Deirdre of the Sorrows • In his unfinished last play, *Deirdre of the Sorrows*, Synge was in the process of making a new departure. He found that the challenge of writing on a heroic theme from the Ulster cycle presented fresh difficulties, which he took satisfaction in solving. It is generally conceded that his version humanizes the legend: It is more realistic than the versions by Æ and Yeats, with which it is often compared.

Other major works

NONFICTION: *The Aran Islands,* 1907; *In Wicklow,* 1910; *The Autobiography of J. M. Synge,* 1965; *Letters to Molly: John Millington Synge to Máire O'Neill, 1906-1909,* 1971 (Ann Saddlemyer, editor); *My Wallet of Photographs,* 1971 (Lilo Stephens, introducer and arranger); *Some Letters of John M. Synge to Lady Gregory and W. B. Yeats,* 1971 (Saddlemyer, editor); *The Collected Letters of John Millington Synge*, 1983-1984 (2 volumes; Saddlemyer, editor).

MISCELLANEOUS: *Plays, Poems, and Prose*, 1941; *Collected Works*, 1962-1968 (Ann Saddlemyer and Robin Skelton, editors).

Bibliography

Casey, Daniel J. *Critical Essays on John Millington Synge*. New York: G. K. Hall, 1994. These essays by Synge scholars cover topics such as Synge's use of language, his poems, and most of his plays, including *The Well of the Saints* and *The Tinker's Wedding* as well as the more famous *The Playboy of the Western World*. Bibliography and index.

Gerstenberger, Donna Lorine. *John Millington Synge*. Rev. ed. Boston: Twayne, 1990. A basic biography and critical evaluation of Synge's works. Bibliography.

Kiely, David M. *John Millington Synge: A Biography*. New York: St. Martin's Press, 1995. Kiely covers the life of this complex and difficult dramatist. Bibliography and index.

Krause, Joseph. *The Regeneration of Ireland: Essays*. Bethesda, Md.: Academica Press, 2001. This scholarly work focuses on the intellectual life of Ireland in the late nineteenth and early twentieth centuries, focusing on Synge's life and works. Bibliography and index.

McCormack, W. J. *Fool of the Family: A Life of J. M. Synge*. New York: New York University Press, 2000. McCormack draws on previously unpublished material in his depiction of Synge, which places the dramatist in the context of the cultural changes taking place around him.

McDonald, Ronan. *Tragedy and Irish Writing: Synge, O'Casey, Beckett*. New York: Palgrave, 2001. McDonald examines the treatment of tragedy in Irish literature, focusing on the works of Synge, Sean O'Casey, and Samuel Beckett. Bibliography and index.

Watson, George J. *Irish Identity and the Literary Revival: Synge, Yeats, Joyce, and O'Casey*. 2d ed. Washington, D.C.: Catholic University of America Press, 1994. Watson looks at the historical and sociological developments taking place in Ireland while Synge, W. B. Yeats, James Joyce, and Sean O'Casey were writing and the influence these events had on their works. Bibliography and index.

Cóilín D. Owens,
updated by Peter C. Holloran

Terence

Publius Terentius Afer

Born: Carthage; c. 190 B.C.E.
Died: En route from Greece; 159 B.C.E.

Principal drama • *Andria*, 166 B.C.E. (English translation, 1598); *Hecyra*, 165 B.C.E. (*The Mother-in-Law*, 1598); *Heautontimorumenos*, 163 B.C.E. (*The Self-Tormentor*, 1598); *Eunuchus*, 161 B.C.E. (*The Eunuch*, 1598); *Phormio*, 161 B.C.E. (English translation, 1598); *Adelphoe*, 160 B.C.E. (*The Brothers*, 1598)

Other literary forms • Terence is remembered only for his plays.

Achievements • Latin literature took an important step in its development when Terence arrived on the scene. Although Plautus had done much to improve the Latin tongue and to refine the stage, he was hindered in his efforts by an audience lacking in culture. It was otherwise with Terence. In the interval that separated Plautus and Terence, a society of literary men had grown up at Rome, and their tastes were dominated by admiration of Greek literature and culture. It was in this circle that Terence moved and formed his literary aspirations and ideals. As a result, his main purpose differed from that of Plautus, who aimed at securing the applause of the people. Instead, Terence directed his efforts especially toward the attainment of elegance and correctness of expression and toward symmetry in the elaboration of his plots. Terence believed that the best way to obtain these results and the surest method for building up a national literature was a faithful reproduction of Greek works. Accordingly, he set himself the task of Hellenizing Roman comedy more completely, and by a close imitation of his Greek models, he succeeded in combining with the refined Latin of the cultivated class much of the flexibility, delicacy, and smoothness of the Attic idiom.

Biography • Publius Terentius Afer (Terence) is said to have been a native of Carthage and to have been brought in his childhood to Rome as a slave. There he was educated as a free man, by Terentius Lucanus, the senator, by whom he was afterward set free. Although originally a slave, Terence cannot have been a prisoner of war because there was no war between Rome and Carthage during his lifetime. He may, however, have fallen into the hands of a slave-dealer at Carthage because many of the native African tribes were subject to the Carthaginians. In Carthage, there must have been enslaved *Afri* whose children were in bondage with their parents. The children of such parents were often sold into foreign lands, and it is easy to conceive how Terence, if born at Carthage under these or similar circumstances, may have been sold by a slave-dealer to Lucanus at Rome. Such an explanation of his origin and deportation to Rome is justified in part by his cognomen Afer, which points to his being of other than Phoenician blood. Had Terence been of Phoenician origin, the last of his three names would more naturally have been Poenulus, since the Carthaginians were commonly distinguished from the Africans and it was customary to give names to slaves to indicate the nation to which they belonged. On receiving his freedom, Terence would have added to his praenomen, Publius, the Gentile name of his master (Terentius), which then would become his nomen, while as cognomen he might retain the title of "the African" (Afer) as a mark of particular distinction.

Terence's personal attractions and intellectual gifts, which had helped him to obtain his freedom, were the cause also of his permanent reception within the aristocratic circle of younger literary men at Rome. Terence probably became known to these men while he was still a member of his master's household. This circle included many of the nobility who were mainly responsible for introducing into Roman life Greek culture and refinement.

Among the noble young men who were friends of Terence and members of the same literary circle was Scipio Africanus the Younger; it was he who gave his name to what has since been known as the Scipionic circle of literati, a small group of people who made Greek literature their special study and Greek refinement and education their standard. It was the men of this class and character whom Terence especially endeavored to please with his comedies. He seems to have been indifferent to the general public.

Reportedly, when Terence submitted his first play to the aediles for production, he was told to obtain the opinion of Caecilius, who was then an established author. Going to Caecilius's house, where a dinner was in progress, Terence sat at the side of the room and began reading his play aloud. Soon he was invited to join the guests on the couches, where he finished reading it to great applause.

Having gained the support of Caecilius and Scipio and other members of the literary and aristocratic class at Rome, he was able to repel the attacks of his enemies, who, moved by jealousy, brought against Terence the unfounded charge of plagiarism—or more exactly, hypocrisy—in representing as his own compositions dramas that were written at least in part by his noble friends. The truth appears to be that Terence read his compositions aloud to his literary friends and employed, independently and according to his choice, their criticisms and suggestions.

After producing six comedies between 166 and 160 B.C.E., Terence went to Greece, probably for the purpose of studying Greek life and institutions, which, according to his habit, he portrayed in his comedies. In 159 B.C.E., he died, just as he was about to return to Rome with translations, which he had made in Greece, of a number of Menander's plays. Accounts vary as to the place and manner of his death. One story relates that he was lost at sea off the island of Leucas while on his way to Italy and that his translations per-

(Library of Congress)

ished with him. Another account reports that he died at Stymphalus in Arcadia, after
having lost his baggage and manuscripts in a shipwreck.

Analysis • Terence's literary activity displayed itself wholly in the production of
palliatae, plays that are fundamentally Greek and are representations of Greek habits,
morals, and customs. The name *palliatae* comes from the *pallium*, a Greek cloak worn
by the actor. It is clear that Terence deliberately tried not to break the Greek illusion.
The characters must have seemed distinctly foreign to the Roman audience to such an
extent that sometimes it appears that the only truly Latin element in his plays is the language. He based all of his plays on the Greek New Comedy; his favorite model was
Menander, on whose plays four of Terence's are based (*Andria, The Self-Tormentor, The
Eunuch*, and *The Brothers*). The remaining two (*Phormio* and *The Mother-in-Law*) are
based on originals by the later writer Apollodorus.

Terence's use of the Greek plays led to an accusation of *contamnatio* (contamina-
tion). Normally, the use of a Greek original meant the closest possible adherence to it.
Terence, contrary to the artistic usage of the time, used parts and materials drawn from
more than one Greek model in the construction of a play. Terence countered the
charge in the prologues of several plays, most notably in *Andria*. It is now generally accepted that the charge was malicious and inspired by the jealousy of his enemies.

All six of Terence's plays tend to be conservative and more staid than those of
Plautus. The scene is always "a street in Athens"; the characters are the standard old
man, young man, courtesan, and slave; the chief variation is the more frequent introduction of the elderly married lady, and of the young couple already married when the
play begins. The parasite, when he appears in *Phormio* and *The Eunuch*, has been elevated from the status of buffoon to that of an intelligent man-about-town; similarly the
pimp, when he appears in *Phormio* and *The Brothers*, is much more the businessman
than the scoundrel.

Terence's plays show almost no clowning and no slapstick. Nearest to rowdy foolishness are the scenes in *The Eunuch* in which a braggart soldier, in the company of his
parasite and an "army" consisting of two or three ragged numbskulls, lays siege to the
house of a prostitute. The plays are nearly perfect in form; every scene is functional
and serves to forward the action of the plot or to provide necessary elaboration on
some character trait. There are no wasted scenes, introduced merely for comic diversion; indeed, there is hardly a wasted word. There are no immoral scenes, no drunken
revels, few remarks that even smack of impropriety, let alone of obscenity, and no violence at all. Action on stage is quiet and rarely undignified. That the plays move
smoothly, gracefully, and rapidly is a tribute to the skill with which they were put together; for all their quietness, they never lose the fast action that is the essence of
Terence's comedy.

Terence's plays move on a higher moral level than Plautus's. In every one of the six,
there is a "recognition" of one sort or another; in every one, except for *The Mother-in-
Law* in which the characters are already married when the story begins, the hero and
heroine properly end by becoming husband and wife. In *Andria, The Self-Tormentor*,
and *Phormio*, a long-lost daughter is found and recognized. In *The Eunuch*, the girl turns
out to be the sister of a proper Athenian citizen. In *The Mother-in-Law* and *The Brothers*,
the girls had been foolish enough to go out on the streets at night in the course of a
wildly sexual festival and had been raped by unknown young men. In *The Mother-in-
Law*, the young man in question has subsequently married the girl he raped, without
realizing who she was. His self-righteous anxiety on discovering that she was already

pregnant, presumably by some man other than himself, causes the complications that Terence sets out to solve. In *The Brothers*, the young man has acknowledged his act and has promised to marry the girl, even though she is poor and of a lower class. The suspicion on the part of the girl's mother that the young man is about to renege on his promise forms one of the problems that this intricate play tries to solve.

In all of his plays, Terence is a thoroughly gentle and tactful poet, never overly forceful or blatant. Still, through all of his plays runs a persistent note of social criticism, directed particularly at the position of slaves and of women in Greek and Roman society. There is not a single slave or female character who is not decent, honorable, resourceful, and intelligent. This is certainly not the result of inadvertence, nor can it be brushed aside as simple sentimentality. It is rather Terence's way of arraigning ancient society for the heartless indifference that it commonly demonstrated toward its slave population and for the hypocritical and specious reasoning with which it handled prostitutes. Terence, perhaps because he himself had been a slave, shows sympathy toward them, and this gains for him respect for his understanding and courage. Terence's plays, as documents of human nature, are not much better than Plautus's, but where Plautus saw in other people chiefly an opportunity for creating an amusing situation, Terence viewed humanity with affection and regard.

The Brothers • The critical consensus has been that *The Brothers* is Terence's masterpiece. First, it is a serious comedy because it deals with the theme of education and works out the consequences of opposing theories in ways that are simultaneously logical and amusing. Second, it is a tour de force of double plotting hardly equaled in drama: There are two systems of upbringing; two young products thereof, with their two love affairs, as well as the two brothers of the older generation who are the cause of it all. Last, in spite of the play's clever plot, its characters remain complex.

Although the plot elements of all the plays are conventional and repetitive, they form no more than a base on which Terence erects a remarkably varied set of stories, which hold the attention of the audience not only by unfolding a tale but even more by the sympathetic presentation of an interesting set of human problems and by a remarkable, gentle, unobtrusive, yet persistent note of social criticism.

The Eunuch • A good example of a conventional play of New Comedy is *The Eunuch*. The play presents two stories. In the primary plot, the young man has lost his position as lover of a courtesan to a braggart soldier. The courtesan hopes to regain possession of a young Athenian girl who had been like a sister to her and who has been lost to her for many years. By coincidence, the young girl has turned up in the soldier's possession. Once the problem of getting the young girl back has been solved, the courtesan is presumably ready to take the young man back as her lover.

The chief interest of the play centers on its subplot, in which the Athenian girl herself is the central figure, even though she appears on the stage briefly and speaks no lines. The young man's brother falls in love with her and substitutes himself for a eunuch who was given to the courtesan by the young man. The "eunuch" and the Athenian girl make love, and the other slaves wonder wide-eyed how a eunuch managed it. In the meantime, the Athenian girl is recognized as the sister of an Athenian citizen, and after disentangling the identity of the brother from that of the eunuch, he (the brother) is engaged to the girl. The play comes very near to being foolish; it is certainly the least interesting of all of them, yet it is said to have been the most popular and Terence's greatest success in his lifetime. One reason may be that it is the most lively and vivid of Terence's plays; although it is noted for its bawdy scenes, its vulgarity is greatly minimized by Terence's tasteful treatment.

Phormio • *Phormio* has a double plot somewhat better balanced than that of *The Eunuch*. There are two love affairs, one concerned with the love of the young man Antipho for an orphan girl, Phanium, who never appears on the stage, and the other with the passion of Phaedria, the second young man, for the usual courtesan. By a series of clever tricks, the parasite Phormio succeeds in getting Antipho married to Phanium and obtaining the money that Phaedria needs to purchase his ladylove. At the end of the play, Phanium turns out to be an Athenian citizen, in fact, the daughter of Phaedria's father Chremes, who is cajoled into letting Phaedria keep his courtesan.

Aside from *The Brothers*, *Phormio* has earned more praise than any other Terentian comedy. It is more comical than the others; the handling of the improbable plot is masterly; the characters, as is usual with Terence, are complex and sympathetic; and in a variation on a theme, it is interesting to see the parasite rather than the slave carry the burden of intrigue.

Andria • *Andria* is the closest of all Terence's plays to a tender love story and probably the best known of all of his plays. The play centers on the usual love-of-young-man-for-long-lost-daughter theme. The conflict is occasioned by the young man, Pamphilus, and his determination to keep the girl whom he has married without his father's consent and without adequate proof of her citizenship. Pamphilus has to withstand the equally strong determination of his father, Simo, to separate the couple, not so much because he disapproves of the girl, Glycerium, as because of Simo's hurt that a son of his flouted both Athenian law and custom by, apparently, marrying a noncitizen.

In the end, Glycerium turns out to be a citizen, in fact, the daughter of Simo's old friend, Chremes. The story might be quite commonplace except for the curious way in which the character of a dead woman, Chrysis, pervades it. She is the true "woman from Andros." She came to Athens a penniless orphan, tried with courage and persistence to earn an honest living, but, finding this too difficult, dropped into the less happy but more prosperous trade of the prostitute, and died just before the story of the play opens. Her courage, kindness, generosity, and devotion to Glycerium makes the whole play shine and gives it a human warmth and sympathy that would not be possible otherwise.

Interest inevitably centers on the slave Davus, who considerably outdoes his master in matters of intelligence and sheer manliness. Davus is clever, quick, and resourceful. He has a buoyant spirit that even the abuse of slavery cannot break. More than that, he never loses his human dignity; he may be a slave, but he is nevertheless a man.

The Self-Tormentor • Terence apparently believed that there is no one right way to rear sons, and this is confirmed in *The Self-Tormentor*. The bewildered and self-pitying father in this play, with his foolish attempts to punish himself for what he perceives as a mistake in bringing up his son, represents Terence's opinion of fathers. The play once again involves two fathers. One is Menedemus, whose son Cinia has joined the Persian army because his love for a poor woman, Antiphila, has shamed his father. The other is Chremes whose son Clitipho has as a mistress a prostitute, Bacchis. The plot centers on the attempts of the young men to obtain their respective ladyloves. *The Self-Tormentor* is usually considered a less successful *The Brothers*. Its theme is similar and its characterization almost as good. Terence is thought to have started weaving more threads here than he could effectively manage; the general pattern, even when completed, is hard to follow. There is one unique feature in the plot: In this play, the recognition scene adds to the complication rather than leading to the denouement.

The Mother-in-Law • The remaining play, *The Mother-in-Law*, had a curious history. On the first two occasions when it was presented, the audience walked out before the play was over to go and see, on one occasion, a tightrope walker, and on the other, a gladiatorial exhibition. Only on the third attempt did the play succeed in holding the audience until the final curtain. This original bad luck has been at least in part responsible for the generally low rating that the play still enjoys. Actually, it tells an unusual story and tells it remarkably well. The plot concerns a young man who has raped a girl during a religious festival and later has married her without knowing that she was this same person, only to be greatly distressed on discovering that she was pregnant, apparently by some other man. The resolution of this tangle comes about through a variation of the recognition device: A ring, pulled from the girl's finger by the young man in the act of raping her and later presented by him to his mistress, a prostitute, is produced by the prostitute at the critical moment and establishes the identity of the young man's wife.

The role of the prostitute immediately attracts the attention of the audience; generous and sympathetic courtesans are not unknown in the comedy of Terence, but this one is the only one who deliberately, and out of sheer kindness and generosity, engages in an act that must inevitably and permanently sever her from her former lover. The young man, too, presents an interesting variant, for unlike other young men in Roman comedy who seem to have had mothers only through biological necessity, this one is devoted to his mother—so much so, in fact, that he considers her happiness more important than his wife's.

Bibliography

Forehand, Walter. *Terence.* Boston: Twayne, 1985. A basic biography of Terence with literary criticism of his works. Includes some general discussion of Latin drama. Bibliography and index.

Goldberg, Sander M. *Understanding Terence.* Princeton, N.J.: Princeton University Press, 1986. Goldberg provides a brief biography of Terence along with analysis of his works and of Latin drama in general.

Snowden, Frank M., Jr. *Blacks in Antiquity: Ethiopians in the Greco-Roman Experience.* Cambridge, Mass.: Belknap Press of Harvard University Press, 1970. The author examines the role of blacks in the Greek and Roman worlds.

Sutton, Dana Ferrin. *Ancient Comedy: The War of the Generations.* New York: Maxwell Macmillan International, 1993. This study of ancient comedy looks at Terence, Menander, and Plautus. Bibliography and index.

Shelley P. Haley

Michel Tremblay

Born: Montreal, Canada; June 25, 1942

Principal drama • *Le Train*, pr. 1964 (televised), pb. 1990; *Cinq*, pr. 1966, pb. 1971 (English translation, 1976; includes *Berthe, Johnny Mangano and His Astonishing Dogs*, and *Gloria Star*); *Les Belles-sœurs*, pr., pb. 1968 (English translation, 1973; also as *The Guid Sisters*, 1988); *En pièces détachées*, pr. 1969, pb. 1970 (revision of *Cinq*; *Like Death Warmed Over*, 1973; also as *Broken Pieces* and *Montreal Smoked Meat*); *La Duchesse de Langeais*, pr. 1969, pb. 1970 (English translation, 1976); *Demain matin, Montréal m'attend*, pr. 1970, pb. 1972 (musical); *À toi, pour toujours, ta Marie-Lòu*, pr., pb. 1971 (*Forever Yours, Marie-Lou*, 1972); *Les Paons*, pr. 1971; *Hosanna*, pr., pb. 1973 (English translation, 1974); *Bonjour, là, bonjour*, pr., pb. 1974 (English translation, 1975); *Surprise! Surprise!*, pr. 1975, pb. 1977 (English translation, 1976); *La Duchesse de Langeais, and Other Plays*, pb. 1976 (includes *La Duchesse de Langeais*, *Berthe, Johnny Mangano and His Astonishing Dogs*, *Gloria Star*, and *Surprise! Surprise!*); *Les Héros de mon enfance*, pr., pb. 1976 (musical; music by Sylvain Lelièvre); *Sainte-Carmen de la Main*, pr., pb. 1976 (*Saint Carmen of the Main*, 1978); *Damnée Manon, Sacrée Sandra*, pr., pb. 1977 (English translation, 1979); *Les Socles*, pb. 1979 (*The Pedestals*, 1979); *L'Impromptu d'Outremont*, pr., pb. 1980 (*The Impromptu of Outrement*, 1981); *Les Anciennes Odeurs*, pr., pb. 1981 (*Remember Me*, 1984); *Albertine en cinq temps*, pr. 1985, pb. 1986 (*Albertine in Five Times*, 1986); *Le Vrai Monde?*, pr., pb. 1987 (*The Real World?*, 1988); *La Maison suspendue*, pr., pb. 1990; *Nelligan*, pr., pb. 1990 (libretto; music by Andre Gagnon); *Théâtre: Volume 1*, pb. 1991; *Marcel poursuivi par les chiens*, pr., pb. 1992 (*Marcel Pursued by the Hounds*, 1992); *En circuit fermé*, pb. 1994; *Messe solenelle pour une pleine lune d'été*, pr., pb. 1996 (*Solemn Mass for a Full Moon in Summer*, 2000); *Encore une fois, si vous le permettez*, pr., pb. 1998 (*For the Pleasure of Seeing Her Again*, 1998); *L'État des lieux*, pr., pb. 2002

Other literary forms • Although Michel Tremblay is best known for his drama, he is also the author of a number of short stories, film scripts, and television plays; in addition, he translated into French Aristophanes' *Lysistratē* (411 B.C.E.; *Lysistratē*, 1837), Paul Zindel's *And Miss Reardon Drinks a Little* (pr. 1967, pb. 1972) and *The Effect of Gamma Rays on Man-in-the-Moon Marigolds* (pr. 1965, pb. 1971), four short plays by Tennessee Williams, and Dario Fo's *Mistero buffo: Giullarata popolare* (pr. 1969, pb. 1970; *Mistero Buffo: Comic Mysteries*, 1983). He has also published a number of novels, including *La Grosse Femme d'à côté est enceinte* (1978; *The Fat Woman Next Door Is Pregnant*, 1981); *Thérèse et Pierrette à l'École des saintes-anges* (1980; *Thérèse and Pierrette and the Little Hanging Angel*, 1984); *Le Cœur découvert* (1986; *The Heart Laid Bare*, 1989; also as *Making Room*, 1990), and *Hotel Bristol: New York, NY* (1999). In 1990, Tremblay wrote and published the libretto for an opera, *Nelligan*, which was produced the same year.

Achievements • Michel Tremblay is part of a new generation of playwrights that emerged in Quebec during the 1960's and 1970's, a time of profound political and cultural change for this province. Led by Tremblay, these writers saw as their primary task the liberation of Quebec culture from the shackles of foreign domination. With very few exceptions, the theater of Quebec to the mid-twentieth century had never treated issues genuinely French-Canadian; it was a theater enslaved to the thematic, stylistic, and linguistic control of "mother" France. With the opening of Tremblay's *Les Belles-sœurs*, at the Théâtre du Rideau Vert in Montreal on August 28, 1968, a new and autonomous Québécois theater was born.

Significant partly for its thematic focus on the realities of the working class of Quebec, *Les Belles-sœurs* is the first play to be written in the distinctive French of Tremblay's people–*joual*. A peculiar mixture of Anglicanisms, Old French, neologisms, and standard French, *joual* (from the Québécois pronunciation of the French word *cheval*) is the popular idiom of Quebec and especially of Montreal's working class. To the French and to Quebec's cultural elite, *joual* was a bastard tongue, emphasizing the pitiful nature of Quebec culture. To Tremblay, however, *joual* was a symbol of identity, a language not to be silenced but to be celebrated for its richness and for its distinctive flavor. To discuss Tremblay's greatest achievements is thus not simply to focus on the fact that he has become Canada's leading playwright, that his enormous creative output in the areas of theater, literature, film, and television has won for him international fame, that he has influenced the development of Canadian drama, and that he has won countless awards for his work. Though all of this is true, it is also important to recognize him as a cultural leader with a commitment to articulate and grapple with the problems of an oppressed community.

Tremblay has accumulated a long list of literary prizes and distinctions. Among the most important are his being named a Chevalier de l'Ordre des Arts et des Lettres de France; his *Albertine in Five Times* brought him the Chalmers Prize in 1986; in 1988, Tremblay received the Prix Athanase-David for his work as a whole; in 1989, he received the Grand Prix du Livre de Montréal for *Le Premier Quartier de la lune* (*The First Quarter of the Moon*, 1994), a prose work. Tremblay was named Chevalier de l'Ordre national du Québec in 1991. In 1994, he was given the Molson Prize for Lifetime Achievement in the Arts. In 1999, Tremblay received a Governor-General's Award. A controversy developed when some Quebec nationalists expected him to refuse the award. However, Tremblay accepted it—announcing for the first time, however, that he had refused the Order of Canada award in 1990. Tremblay won two prizes, the Chalmers Award and a Dora Mavor Moore Award, for *For the Pleasure of Seeing Her Again*.

Biography • Michel Tremblay was born in east-end Montreal on June 25, 1942, the youngest child of a working-class family. His family lived in a small seven-room house with two other families, and Tremblay remembers distinctly the first voices of his life: women who would speak candidly to one another about their lives and who would censor nothing in front of the young child. Indeed, these are the voices sounded in many of his plays, especially *Les Belles-sœurs*. In 1955, he won a scholarship to a school for gifted children; his innate distaste for the cultural elite soon caused him to return to the public schools.

Tremblay speaks of his adolescence as a time of personal anguish, a time when writing became his primary channel of expression. Moreover, as a young man he became obsessed with television: "It was the only theatre I knew." In 1959, he took a job as a linotype operator and during this period wrote his first television play, *Le Train*, for which he eventually won first prize in the 1964 Radio-Canada Contest for Young Authors. It is also in 1964 that he met André Brassard, who became one of his closest friends, his principal collaborator, and the director of many of the premier performances of his plays. His publishing career began in 1966 with a book of short stories,

Contes pour buveurs attardés (*Stories for Late Night Drinkers*, 1978). In the same year, he submitted his first full-length play, *Les Belles-sœurs* (written in 1965), to the Dominion Drama Festival, but the revolutionary piece was rejected. Two years later, however, it was produced, with great success, at the Théâtre du Rideau Vert in Montreal and later in Paris.

The years following 1968 marked a creative and prolific period for Tremblay. For English-speaking Canadians, however, Tremblay was not so widely publicized, partly because of the playwright's desire to restrict his work to his French compatriots. It was only after 1976, the year the Separatists' Parti Québécois under René Lévesque took power in the provincial House, that Tremblay opened his work to the English-speaking world. After 1976, translations of his plays appeared, productions abounded, and Tremblay emerged as Canada's leading playwright, recognized as such in both North America and Europe. That he has achieved international acclaim testifies to the fact that his work is as universal in meaning as it is specific to contemporary Quebec life.

In the late 1980's, Tremblay's work became increasingly autobiographical with such plays as *The Real World?* and *For the Pleasure of Seeing Her Again* and the series of autobiographical novels, *Chroniques du Plateau-Mont-Royal*. In 1989 he added *Le Premier Quartier de la lune* to the series, and *Un Objet de beauté* (*A Thing of Beauty*, 1998) was published in 1997. He has also written the memoirs *Les Vues animées* (1995; *Bambi and Me*, 1998) and *Douze coups de théâtre* (1992; *Twelve Opening Acts*, 2002).

In general, Tremblay is so productive in so many artistic genres—musical theater, opera, fiction, painting, and film among them—that an observer may find it difficult to keep track of what Tremblay has done and is doing. His career is certainly one of the richest in literary history.

Analysis • Antecedents in the history of dramatic literature help to characterize the plays of Michel Tremblay. The playwright himself cites as most influential the ancient Greek tragedians on one hand and Samuel Beckett on the other. The influence of the ancient playwrights shows itself most notably in Tremblay's repeated use of choruses and in the rhythmic precision of his work. Indeed, much of his theatrical power stems from a native musical sensibility that informs the structure of his plays. Like the Greeks, Tremblay writes dramatic pieces that operate, at least in part, as rhythmic scores for performance; his plays abound with overlapping voices and interwoven monologues, and possess a rhythm so peculiar to the language and intonations of the Québécois that there is often as much power in how his characters speak as there is in what they say.

Beckett's influence on Tremblay manifests itself in the specific context in which Tremblay places his characters and in the way those characters grapple with the struggles of life. Tremblay celebrates the notion that, despite the seeming despair of Beckett's figures, there is a beauty in their struggle to face and accept their lives: "I never read or see a Beckett play without experiencing a lift." His appreciation of Beckett is significant; although Tremblay's characters seem trapped in the underbelly of culture, in seedy nightclubs, confined apartments, in a world of whores, pimps, and transvestites, or trapped even in their own social roles and family relationships, still there is a sense of uplift in their struggles and in the courage they find in themselves.

Les Belles-sœurs • Stylistically, Tremblay's dramas are eclectic, not only when looked at as a body of work, but also within single plays. In *Les Belles-sœurs*, for example, he creates a realistic setting, utilizes realistic dialogue, and then counters that realism with stylized elements reminiscent of the Theater of the Absurd. The premise of the play is simple: Fifteen women of the neighborhood gather to help Germaine Lauzon paste a million Blue Chip stamps in booklets for a contest she has won. The women of the title ("the sisters-in-law" or "the beautiful sisters," an ambiguity in French that accounts for the original title maintained in translation) gossip as they paste. When Germaine is not looking, however, the women secretly steal the stamps. This ostensible, realistic line of the story unfolds in a dynamic relationship with stylized, isolated monologues spoken by the women to express the more honest, individual problems of their miserable, trapped lives: Marriage, family, and sex—the basis of their worlds—have achieved a level of banality that seems to reduce all of life to sheer endurance.

Perhaps the clearest example of the juxtaposition of styles comes at the end of the play. Germaine discovers the thieves, throws them out of her home, and feels a profound sense of loneliness and isolation. She falls to her knees to pick up the stamps that scattered on the floor during the chaos of discovering the theft. At that moment, Tremblay breaks out of the realistic structure once again. From off stage the women begin to sing a chorus of "O Canada," while simultaneously a rain of stamps falls from the ceiling. The stylized "shower" of prosperity is parallel to Germaine's windfall of stamps at the beginning of the play. Yet the playwright creates his final image as a self-consciously artificial construct, an image that contrasts with the conventionally realistic form used at the outset. Like a Euripidean *deus ex machina*, Tremblay's rain of stamps is a theatrical joke; humanity is in turmoil and has reached an impasse within the realistic conventions of the play. The playwright's ending undercuts that impasse, however, and, with a broad satirical gesture, he clarifies the source of the problem itself; the values of the Canadian middle class have their price.

The family cycle • The body of Tremblay's dramatic work possesses a remarkable consistency both in theme and in focus. His *dramatis personae* are the underprivileged, the people on the fringe of society, people who live in disguise. His plays also have a striking similarity of context; indeed, in the bulk of his work, he examines two specific worlds. On one hand, he looks at the family, at the home, and at the nature of the individual within the family construct. On the other hand, he looks to a horrifying world external to the family: the world of the Main in Montreal, with its host of transvestites, whores, and pimps, all set against a backdrop of "gambling joints, cabarets, lights and noise." In the words of André Brassard, "The Main is the Kingdom of the marginals . . . the underprivileged and forgotten part of the proletariat . . . the underlayer of society." The Tremblay opus can thus be examined to a large degree in two major cycles: the family cycle and the Main cycle. The two worlds do intersect at points, creating a potent juxtaposition. Indeed, when considered as a whole, Tremblay's work is interesting not only because of his investigation into these two separate worlds but also because of his ability to show how those worlds mirror each other. In effect, the two cycles intersect to illuminate the "family" of the Main and the "underbelly" of the home.

Like Death Warmed Over • *Like Death Warmed Over*, the first play of the family cycle, was actually written, in its original version, before *Les Belles-sœurs* but published and performed at a later date. It unfolds in four loosely connected episodes. The play begins in the inner courtyard of an east-end Montreal tenement on a sweltering summer afternoon. For the chorus of neighbors, the single point of interest is the window across the way—the home of Robertine, her daughter Hélène, Hélène's husband, Henri, and their daughter Francine. The neighbors are fascinated with the peculiar and unsavory domestic battles in Robertine's home. They offer a detailed description of the troubled family and its history as they wait for Hélène to come home, for the "show" of the evening to begin.

The middle two episodes tell the story of Hélène, how she spends her time slinging smoked meat in a cheap restaurant on Papineau Street after having lost her job in a bar on the Main. She gets drunk, returns to the bar, only to have the frustrations of her life become that much more glaring as she confronts the figures of her past. The final episode takes place back in Robertine's living room. Hélène comes home, verbally abuses Henri (who spends all of his time watching cartoons on television) and Robertine, and gives the neighbors the "show" for which they have waited. Toward the end, Claude, the retarded brother, returns home for a visit after escaping from his sanatorium. He wears "sunglasses and speaks English" and believes that doing so gives him ultimate power: It makes him invisible. In Tremblay's world, the madman overturns his alienation to make it an illusory source of strength. Claude's presence thus provides a sharp contrast to the feeling of humiliation and powerlessness among the other members of the family. Typically, the play ends in a series of stylized monologues in which the family members express their despair. They repeat a refrain in unison during this final section, a refrain that sums up their despondency and languor: "There's not a goddamn thing I can do."

Forever Yours, Marie-Lou • Although *Like Death Warmed Over* is a play about failure and ultimate despair in family relationships, Tremblay's next play in the family cycle, *Forever Yours, Marie-Lou*, presents the attempt of two sisters, Carmen and Manon, to find refuge from the traumas of family life. In this play, two conversations transpire simultaneously, one between Marie-Louise and her husband, Leopold, and the other between their daughters Carmen and Manon. The two conversations take place in the family home, but ten years apart. Carmen and Manon (in the 1970's) recall the past, ten years earlier, when their parents and younger brother Roger died in a car accident. Manon, a religious zealot, believes her father Leopold was responsible for the accident, an act of suicide and filial murder. Carmen denies this account, although her rejection is undermined when Leopold (in the action of the 1960's) threatens Marie-Louise with that very scenario.

Structurally, the play is a quartet of interweaving voices as each level of action comments on the other through a powerful theatrical juxtaposition. Each character has complaints about the others, each feels abused, each feels as if life has dealt him or her an unfair blow. In the turbulence of the marriage, Marie-Louise turns to religion and Leopold to his drinking and television. The daughters, too, have their share of trouble, not only as products of their repressive and abusive home but also as individuals who must cope with the tragic past. Carmen has turned to the Main and to singing in cabarets. Manon has, on the other hand, withdrawn entirely into a lonely life of religious fanaticism. The two women have clearly gone in opposite directions, but it is evident that they are both striving to find shelter from the traumas of the family.

While Marie-Louise and Manon hide in an existence of religious repression, and Leopold in an escape into alcohol and boredom that finally erupts in the violence of murder and suicide, Carmen achieves a degree of liberation from her repressive past. This is evident only when one realizes that the core of Tremblay's play is the collision of real human needs with the religious and social constructs that make the fulfillment of those needs impossible. That Carmen turns to the Main is perhaps only a limited alternative, another subculture with its own restrictions. Yet, within the context of the play, Carmen's choice is the most fruitful; she has at least discovered a part of herself that opens the way toward personal creativity. This notion is the center of the play in which she next appears: *Saint Carmen of the Main*, a play in which issues of the family and the Main intersect in a subtle but provocative way.

Saint Carmen of the Main • In this later play, Carmen is returning from a stay in Nashville, where she has been sent to improve her yodeling technique; the play opens with the chorus (the people of the Main) celebrating her return. Indeed, her education away from the Main was more than simply a time to improve technique: Carmen comes back as a leader of the people, as their voice; it is a voice expressed through her new lyrics and songs that relate directly to the concerns of the community. Carmen's journey from repression to release is a model of realized human potential and gives her strength to speak for others. Despite the ecstasy of the people over their newfound leader, however, Carmen must face her antagonists: the cabaret owner Maurice, who wants her to sing the "old songs," and Carmen's rival, Gloria, who fights for her "rightful place." When he challenges Carmen, Maurice articulates the political question of the play, a question that perhaps haunts the playwright himself: "All right. Let's say they take our advice. Let's say they smarten up, they wake up and they get mad. Then what? It's fine to wake people up, but once they're awake, what do you do with them?"

Shortly after her performance at the cabaret, Carmen is brutally murdered; she is denounced as a lesbian so that the crime may be pinned on her innocent dresser, Harelip. "The lights go out completely on the Choruses"; the sun is down, the fire of awakening quelled. This is a play about the possibility of awakening, of fighting repression, of the change that can come about when human beings are acknowledged for their strengths. Carmen has found that strength within herself and is a beacon for the people. Yet the figures of the status quo—threatened for reasons both political and financial—end the triumph of humanity that lit the world for an instant.

Bonjour, là, bonjour • If in the story of Carmen, Tremblay suggests that personal strength can come only from a freedom discovered outside the repressive home, then in *Bonjour, là, bonjour*, he explores the act of personal acceptance within the family itself. Again, this play is inspired by musical principles; there are thirty-one sections entitled "solo," "duo," "trio," and so forth, up to "octuor," depending on the number of voices involved in a given episode.

The central figure in *Bonjour, là, bonjour*, Serge, is a young man who has just returned from a three-month stay in Paris, where he has tried to deal with his love for his sister Nicole. Though the odds are against him, Serge breaks through the oppressive structures of his family life to assert his integrity and express his love both to Nicole and to his aging and deaf father, Gabriel. Serge must defend himself against the invasion of his relatives (two spinster aunts and three sisters other than Nicole), who try to use his vitality to serve their needs. Once he sees past moral taboo to admit fully his incestuous love, he is able to triumph and communicate with his father. Like Carmen, in her relationship to the people of the Main, Serge becomes a figure who releases his father from a suffocating life. He invites his father to live with him and Nicole and, in the end, finds the strength to shout the words "I love you" into Gabriel's deaf ears.

The Main cycle • The plays of the family cycle are clearly parables of the political and cultural repression Tremblay sees within Quebec culture. Like Tremblay's characters, the Québécois must begin a long journey to self-acceptance. Still, there is another "family" Tremblay explores: the family of the Main. In the Main cycle, he focuses on the individual desperately trying to find himself in a chaotic and frightening world, a world in which the search for identity is no less difficult, nor alienation less painful, than it is within the home. Perhaps most indicative of his concern is the recurring transvestite figure, whose multiple personas epitomize the alienation of the individual in the Main.

Tremblay began his investigation of the Main in three short plays written early in his career: *Berthe, Johnny Mangano and His Astonishing Dogs,* and *Gloria Star.* The three plays function as a trilogy and were originally part of the collection entitled *Cinq,* written in 1966. The trilogy examines the individual's alienation from the self by focusing on the collision of one's dreams and fantasies of fame and glory with the stark realities of a boring and desperate life. Tremblay once again works toward a stylized ending to the trilogy in which he communicates how dreams of success and perfection are the offspring of artifice; the playwright makes this abundantly clear in a surrealistic conclusion of theatrical make-believe.

La Duchesse de Langeais • *La Duchesse de Langeais,* a piece in which the past of an aging transvestite unravels in monologue, is the next play of the Main cycle and represents Tremblay's first treatment of this sexually complex figure. The Duchesse is a human being who is desperately alone. She speaks of how she became the Duchesse, "the biggest faggot ever," how she envisions herself as a "woman of the world," how she spent her life whoring for hundreds of men, how she was sexually abused as a child by her cousin Leopold (later to appear in *Forever Yours, Marie-Lou*), and how she entered a life of obsessive sexual activity from the age of six.

The theme of alienation operates on many levels in *La Duchesse de Langeais.* She is a transvestite locked in a sexually ambiguous role. She is aware of her age and feels a frightening sense of attenuation in her life. She has a history of being a female impersonator, trapped in a Pirandellian disparity between the roles performed and the actress/actor underneath. Yet the monologue itself attests her alienation in a more immediate way. Is there any possibility of verifying the past she describes? Is she merely creating a fiction for the audience? Is she creating the fiction for herself? Indeed, reality and illusion are so disconnected in this play that it is impossible to verify much. Tremblay (the primary illusion-maker) communicates through this onslaught of unverifiable information the pain and suffering that accompanies the life of one lost in a labyrinth of insubstantiality and artifice.

Hosanna • *Hosanna,* on the other hand, probes deeper into the tensions of the multiple roles of the transvestite and female impersonator. The play takes place in the early hours of the morning in the confined and oppressive apartment of Hosanna, a transvestite whose original name is Claude, and "her" lover Cuirette ("Leatherette" in French, but also suggesting the English "Queerette"), whose original name is Raymond. Hosanna has returned from a night of humiliation and ridicule, a night that will ultimately lead her to a painful acceptance of self.

Hosanna and Cuirette represent two extremes. The former is a highly effeminate drag queen whose excessive perfume, makeup, jewels, and clothing constitute her mask. The latter is a "leather-man," who has grown too fat for the clothes that once expressed his exaggerated machismo image; nevertheless, his leather jacket, motorcycle, and tough persona are all the accoutrements through which he defines himself. The first act deals with the tensions and collisions of the relationship, the inability of the two individuals to recognize each other's needs and, more important, to recognize and accept themselves for who they are. When the second act begins, Hosanna is alone; she tells the story of how the people of the cabaret (including the Duchesse) played a practical joke on her, how they faked plans for a costume party for which they were all to dress as famous women in history. For weeks, Hosanna prepares her role as Elizabeth Taylor playing Cleopatra; when she arrives, however, everyone at the club is dressed in a Cleopatra costume—"Everyone made up better than me!" She tries to keep her composure, even through the taunting repetition of the chant that haunts the audience as much as Hosanna herself: "Hosanna, Hosanna, Hosanna, Ho!"

The event is enough to shock Hosanna into a state of self-reflection and to force her to confront the mask she wears. Cuirette, who is absent for most of the second act in a frustrated sexual escapade, and who had been privy to the joke played on Hosanna, returns home to shed his own mask and to be with the one he loves. It is, thus, Raymond and Claude present at the last moment of the play, not Cuirette and Hosanna. In the end, Tremblay shows two human beings who have begun the difficult journey involved with the abandonment of self-hatred. Raymond and Claude must accept who they are, together and as individuals.

Damnée Manon, Sacrée Sandra • The theme of reconciliation with the self dominant in the Main cycle is also at the core of *Damnée Manon, Sacrée Sandra*. (The literal English translation would be "doomed Manon, holy Sandra," but is finally inadequate because of the ambiguous implication of *sacrée* in French, a word with meanings both sacred and profane. Indeed, this ambiguity is precisely what this conceptually complex piece is about.) Manon, the religious sister from *Forever Yours, Marie-Lou*, and Sandra, the transvestite cabaret owner from *Hosanna*, are the characters of the drama. Tremblay again creates a double action by juxtaposing two monologues. The double action eventually moves to a single point that articulates the place in which the sacred and profane meet. Moreover, the play ends with the kind of theatrical self-consciousness that informs much of the playwright's work: Both characters realize that they are the invention of the same author. As Manon comes to recognize the erotic nature of her religious devotion and Sandra the obsessive religiosity of her sexual escapades, the playwright himself seems to imply a reconciliation of seeming opposites within himself. He is the creator of both characters; indeed, as an individual, he, too, embodies both the sacred and profane.

The Impromptu of Outrement • Tremblay wrote three major plays after 1979: *The Impromptu of Outrement, Remember Me*, and *Albertine in Five Times*. In these plays, he plucks his characters out of the Main and places them back in a domestic context. In *The Impromptu of Outrement*, Tremblay presents four sisters who were brought up in a middle-class Montreal suburb, Outrement, and who are meeting for the occasion of Yvette's birthday. The party has become an annual custom, a time for a little "impromptu." The real purpose of their meeting, however, is to have a chance to lash out against one another, to complain about one another's lives, to scream about one another's failures and life choices. Ultimately, however, it is an occasion when they feel disgust with who they are; the sisters mirror to one another what they deem ugliest in themselves. The play is Tremblay's version of Anton Chekhov's *Tri sestry* (pr., pb. 1901, revised pb. 1904; *The Three Sisters*, 1920), a work that explores the torture of languishing potentiality, of the trap of the middle class, of unrealized dreams and bourgeois isolation.

Remember Me • *Remember Me* examines two men who are meeting long after the end of their relationship of seven years. Each man has continued with his career and with other relationships; each, however, feels the burden of his own mediocrity and a profound discontent with life. Like *The Impromptu of Outrement*, therefore, *Remember Me* centers on the individual who feels disenfranchised from his own potential; both plays demonstrate how middle-class promise quickly turns to mundane routine. In addition, by focusing on four women in one play, and two homosexual men in the other, Tremblay makes a clear statement about the frustrations minorities feel with the false promises of acceptance in bourgeois society.

Albertine in Five Times • *Albertine in Five Times* is a play about the life of one woman at five different points in her life. Tremblay presents the fragmented individual in many of his dramas, but this time he exploits his art to realize all pieces simultaneously. In this play, Tremblay pursues his preoccupation with self-alienation by grappling with the problem of the ever-changing self in time; as in Beckett's *Krapp's Last Tape* (pr., pb. 1958), *Albertine in Five Times* creates a picture of the individual estranged from the past and from the self that has emerged over time. Nevertheless, the play provides a moving portrait of the stages of one woman's struggle. Like so many of Tremblay's characters, Albertine, though desperate, does struggle; the search for identity is the most challenging task for any individual. Tremblay celebrates the courage of his characters, and of the Québécois themselves; he celebrates their strength to look at themselves and begin the long journey to freedom.

The Real World? • Almost all Tremblay's plays since the mid-1980's have to do, in one way or another, with the family—in particular, how troubled characters fit into their families and how members of those families respond to threat from within or without. Another important theme in the plays of this period is artistic creation—its sources and its problems. *The Real World?* focuses on both of these concerns.

This piece deals with a young playwright whose first drama features characters named after his father, mother, and sister—the sources of his inspiration. As the play's characters look more and more like their models, Claude, the writer, is troubled by what he is doing. He wonders if he has the right to plunder his private life and to invade the lives of his family members in order to create. And, as the title suggests, where does a writer draw the line between what is fact and what is imagined? Clearly, this subject is of importance to Tremblay, and he has said that he and Claude have shared the same concerns.

La Maison suspendue • *La Maison suspendue* presents a couple, Jean-Marc and Mathieu, who come to spend a summer vacation with Mathieu's son, Sébastien, in a log cabin in the Laurentian Mountains. The cabin has been in Jean-Marc's family for three generations, and when he opens the front door, he takes off on a discovery of his roots.

The couple finds that the cabin contains vibrations of fiddler-tale teller Josaphat-le-violon who had a son by his sister, Victoire. In 1950, the home witnesses the trials of Edouard, who fantasizes his ambiguous sexuality while living with his sister, Albertine, who rejects such fantasies. Jean-Marc, who has had to deal with his own sexual identity, reconciles his identity and his new family with the figures from the past.

Marcel Pursued by the Hounds • In *Marcel Pursued by the Hounds*, the protagonist is fifteen-year-old Marcel—who is subject to hallucinations that suspend him between dream and reality. He hopes to makes things better by living with his sister, Thérèse, but it may be too late: He seems hopelessly trapped by imagination, even madness. The play is a form of dialogue between Marcel and Thérèse, in which other characters constitute a kind of Greek-tragedy chorus. The ultimate point is the extent to which people's childhood games and fantasies come back to haunt them in their adult lives—which are full of the dangers and cruel realities that people did not recognize when they were children.

Solemn Mass for a Full Moon in Summer • The form of *Solemn Mass for a Full Moon in Summer* resembles that of *Marcel Pursued by the Hounds*. The title of this play is an accurate one: *Solemn Mass for a Full Moon in Summer* is an incantatory rite, in which the voices of the characters—Isabelle, Yannick, Jeannine, Louise, Rose, Mathieu, Gaston, Mireille, Yvon, Gérard, and the Widow—mingle in a liturgical drama. All the characters complain about their lives, yet they try hard to not succumb to bitterness. Instead, they long for some kind of self-liberation—and when the summer moon appears, a solution, hope, and consolation seem possible.

For the Pleasure of Seeing Her Again • *For the Pleasure of Seeing Her Again* is a short play but one of Tremblay's most moving works. It is an extended conversation between the Narrator (a stand-in for Tremblay himself) and Nana (who represents the playwright's late mother). The play contains wonderfully funny reminiscences by both the Narrator and his mother—about growing up in Montreal and Saskatchewan, about oddball family members, about Tremblay's choice of career and his mother's ambivalent attitude toward the latter. However, the tone takes a deeply somber turn near the play's end, when Nana tells about the cancer that she carried for a time, the pain, and her death. The finale features an angel descending to take Nana to Heaven.

L'État des lieux • *L'État des lieux* is, on one hand, a riotous comedy and on the other, an investigation into such subjects as aging, failure, and artistic energy. It all begins when soprano Patricia Pasquetti has a crisis during the final scene of Richard Strauss's *Salome*. Before a packed house, Patricia hits a grotesquely false note. It is not surprising that Patricia's life starts to fall apart. Through the sympathetic eyes of her longtime accompanist, the audience sees Patricia struggle for a while in Paris before returning home to Quebec's L'Ile des Soeurs. Once she gets home, Patricia takes out her disappointment on her daughter, who is an actress. Mother accuses daughter of lacking creative élan. However, Patricia's own mother—another actress—intervenes. She knows firsthand how artists decline with age—but she also knows the immense power of artistic freedom that transcends aging.

Other major works

LONG FICTION: *La Cité dans l'œuf*, 1969 (*The City in the Egg*, 1999); *C't'à ton tour, Laura Cadieux*, 1973; *Le Cœur découvert*, 1986 (*The Heart Laid Bare*, 1989; also as *Making Room*, 1990); *Le Cœur éclaté*, 1993; *La Nuit des princes charmants*, 1995; *Quarante-quatre minutes, quarante-quatre secondes*, 1997; *Hotel Bristol: New York, NY*, 1999; *Chroniques du Plateau-Mont-Royal*, 2000 (series of six novels including: *La Grosse Femme d'à côté est enceinte*, 1978 [*The Fat Woman Next Door Is Pregnant*, 1981]; *Thérèse et Pierrette à l'École des saintes-anges*, 1980 [*Thérèse and Pierrette and the Little Hanging Angel*, 1984]; *La Duchesse et le roturier* 1982 [*The Duchess and the Commoner*, 1999]; *Le Premier Quartier de la lune*, 1989 [*The First Quarter of the Moon*, 1994]; *Des nouvelles d'Édouard*, 1984 [*News from Edouard*,

2000]; and *Un Objet de beauté*, 1997 [*A Thing of Beauty*, 1998]); *L'Homme qui entendait siffler une bouilloire*, 2001.

SHORT FICTION: *Contes pour buveurs attardés*, 1966 (*Stories for Late Night Drinkers*, 1978); *Manoua*, 1966.

SCREENPLAYS: *Françoise Durocher, Waitress*, 1971; *Backyard Theatre*, 1972; *Il était une fois dans l'est*, 1974; *Parlez-nous d'amour*, 1974.

TELEPLAYS: *Trois Petits Tours*, 1969; *En pièces détachées*, 1971; *Le Soleil se lève en retard*, 1975; *Bonheur d'occasion*, 1977; *Les Belles-sœurs*, 1978.

NONFICTION: *Douze coups de théâtre*, 1992 (memoir; *Twelve Opening Acts*, 2002); *Un Ange cornu avec des ailes de tôle*, 1994 (memoir); *Les Vues animées*, 1995 (memoir; *Bambi and Me*, 1998); *Pièces à conviction: Entretiens avec Michel Tremblay*, 2001 (interviews).

TRANSLATIONS: *Lysistrata*, 1964 (of Aristophanes' play); *L'Effet des rayons gamma sur les vieux garçons*, 1970 (of Paul Zindel's play *The Effect of Gamma Rays on Man-in-the-Moon Marigolds*); *Et Madame Roberge boit un peu*, 1971 (of Paul Zindel's play *And Miss Reardon Drinks a Little*); *Mistero buffo*, 1973 (of Dario Fo's play); *Mademoiselle Marguerite*, 1975 (of Roberto Athayde's play *Apareceu a Margarida*); *Oncle Vania*, 1983 (with Kim Yaroshev-skaya; of Anton Chekhov's play); *Le Gars de Quebec*, 1985 (of Nikolai Gogol's play *Revizor*).

Bibliography

Anthony, G., ed. *Stage Voices: Twelve Canadian Playwrights Talk About Their Lives and Work*. Garden City, N.Y.: Doubleday, 1978. Canadian playwrights, including Tremblay, discuss their plays and their lives. Index.

David, Gilbert, and Pierre Lavoie, eds. *Le Monde de Michel Tremblay*. Montreal: Cahiers de Théâtre Jeu, 1993. Presents a series of studies relevant to Tremblay's entire body of work from *Les Belles-sœurs* to *Marcel Pursued by the Hounds*. In French.

Godin, Jean-Cléo, and Laurent Mailhot, eds. *Théâtre Québecois II*. Montreal: Biblio-thèque Québecoise, 1988. A collection of essays on theater in Quebec. In French.

Massey, Irving. *Identity and Community: Reflections on English, Yiddish, and French Litera-ture in Canada*. Detroit, Mich.: Wayne State University Press, 1994. Provides a sec-tion containing criticism and interpretation of Tremblay's works. Bibliography and index.

Usmiani, Renate. *Michel Tremblay*. Vancouver: Douglas & McIntyre, 1982. An analysis of Tremblay's works and discussion of his life. Bibliography.

_____. *The Theatre of Frustration: Super Realism in the Dramatic Work of F. X. Kroetz and Michel Tremblay*. New York: Garland, 1990. A comparative study of the realism in the works of Tremblay and Franz Xaver Kroetz. Bibliography and index.

Lorne M. Buchman,
updated by Gordon Walters

Luis Miguel Valdez

Born: Delano, California; June 26, 1940

Principal drama • *The Theft*, pr. 1961; *The Shrunken Head of Pancho Villa*, pr. 1965, pb. 1967; *Las dos caras del patroncito*, pr. 1965, pb. 1971; *La quinta temporada*, pr. 1966, pb. 1971; *Los vendidos*, pr. 1967, pb. 1971; *Dark Root of a Scream*, pr. 1967, pb. 1973; *La conquista de México*, pr. 1968, pb. 1971 (puppet play); *No saco nada de la escuela*, pr. 1969, pb. 1971; *The Militants*, pr. 1969, pb. 1971; *Vietnam campesino*, pr. 1970, pb. 1971; *Huelguistas*, pr. 1970, pb. 1971; *Bernabé*, pr. 1970, pb. 1976; *Soldado razo*, pr., pb. 1971; *Actos*, pb. 1971 (includes *Las dos caras del patroncito*, *La quinta temporada*, *Los vendidos*, *La conquista de México*, *No saco nada de la escuela*, *The Militants*, *Vietnam campesino*, *Huelguistas*, and *Soldado razo*); *Las pastorelas*, pr. 1971 (adaptation of a sixteenth century Mexican shepherd's play); *La Virgen del Tepeyac*, pr. 1971 (adaptation of *Las cuatro apariciones de la Virgen de Guadalupe*); *Los endrogados*, pr. 1972; *Los olivos pits*, pr. 1972; *La gran carpa de los rasquachis*, pr. 1973; *Mundo*, pr. 1973; *El baille de los gigantes*, pr. 1973; *El fin del mundo*, pr. 1975; *Zoot Suit*, pr. 1978, pb. 1992; *Bandido!*, pr. 1981, pb. 1992, revised pr. 1994; *Corridos*, pr. 1983; *"I Don't Have to Show You No Stinking Badges!,"* pr., pb. 1986; *Luis Valdez—Early Works: Actos, Bernabé, and Pensamiento Serpentino*, pb. 1990; *Zoot Suit and Other Plays*, pb. 1992; *Mummified Deer*, pr. 2000

Other literary forms • Although Luis Miguel Valdez is known primarily for his plays, his writing on Chicano culture has had a significant impact. In a number of essays initially in the 1960's and 1970's ("Theatre: El Teatro Campesino," "Notes on Chicano Theatre," and several others), he elaborated an aesthetic based on what he believed to be the special features of Chicano reality: bilingualism, *mestizaje* (mixed race), and cultural disinheritance. Valdez's commitment to Chicano nationalism is reflected in two important works of nontheatrical writing—*Aztlan: An Anthology of Mexican American Literature* (1972; coedited with Stan Steiner), whose lengthy introduction recounts the history of the Chicano people as the original inhabitants of "Aztlan" (the contemporary American Southwest), and *Pensamiento Serpentino: A Chicano Approach to the Theatre of Reality* (1973), which explores the influence of Aztec and Mayan spirituality on Chicano art and thought. It is in this latter book that all of Valdez's published poetry can be found.

Achievements • Without Luis Miguel Valdez, the Chicano theater would not exist in its present vibrant form. At the age of twenty-five, in the fields of rural California, without financial backing and using farm laborers as actors, Valdez single-handedly created a movement that has since become international in scope, leading to the founding of Chicano theater troupes from Los Angeles, California, to Gary, Indiana. Although not usually mentioned in the company of revered American playwrights of his generation, such as Sam Shepard, David Mamet, and Richard Foreman, he is in many ways as distinguished and as well known internationally, both in Europe and in Latin America.

In one respect especially, Valdez has accomplished what no other American playwright has: the creation of a genuine workers' theater, completely indigenous and the work of neither university intellectuals nor producers of a commercialized "mass cul-

961

ture." He has made "serious" drama popular, political drama entertaining, and ethnic drama universal.

Valdez has won acclaim in two parallel but distinct artistic communities. If his early career fits neatly within the contours of the cultural nationalism of the Civil Rights movement (whose Chicano forms in the American Southwest are perhaps less well known than the African American forms of the South), he found a hearing also in more established circles. One of the original organizers for the United Farm Workers Union, a tireless propagandist for Chicano identity, and a founder of an annual cultural festival in Fresno, California, he has also been a founding member of the California Arts Council. In addition to this, he served on a congressional subcommittee of the National Endowment for the Arts and on the board of directors of the Theatre Communications Group, and he acted in teleplays and films based on his own work. Winning an honorary Obie Award in 1968 for his work on the West Coast, he appropriately was the first, ten years later, to produce a Chicano play on Broadway, the highly acclaimed *Zoot Suit.*

He cannot, however, be seen simply as a major playwright. His fortunate position as a public figure at the first serious outbreak of Chicano nationalism, in the mid-1960's—which he helped articulate and which helped articulate him—makes him also an emblematic representative of American cultural politics, especially as it regards the important (and often forgotten) Latino community.

Crucial in this respect is his groundbreaking book, *Aztlan,* which brings together writings from the pre-Columbian period to the late twentieth century, sketching a picture of Chicanos as a distinct people with a long tradition and an active history. Valdez's passionate commitment to Chicano nationalism must be seen as a driving force of his art. If *Aztlan* defiantly underlines the uniqueness of the Chicano in an alienating landscape of oppressive Anglo institutions, his next book, *Pensamiento Serpentino,* emphasizes the evils of artificially separating peoples on the basis of race and culture; it argues for a common North American experience in a spirit of forgiveness and mutual cooperation and derives its moral approach to contemporary social problems from Aztec and Mayan teachings.

The rarity of someone from Valdez's background and interests finding so distinctive a public voice cannot be underestimated. Nevertheless, his greatest work is probably the legacy he leaves to Chicano culture itself. The Centro Campesino Cultural, a nonprofit corporation he founded in Del Rey, California, in 1967, became a clearinghouse for Chicano artists around the country and operated film, publishing, and musical recording facilities for their use. Inspired by the success of El Teatro Campesino, many other groups have come into being. Some of the most important are Teatro Urbano, Teatro de la Esperanza, El Teatro de la Gente, and El Teatro Desengañó del Pueblo. It is the pioneering work of Valdez that has allowed these vital regional theaters to operate in a coordinated and organized fashion under a national network known as TENAZ (Teatro Nacional de Aztlan), a direct offshoot of the Centro Campesino Cultural.

Biography • Luis Miguel Valdez was born on June 26, 1940, in Delano, California, the second of ten brothers and sisters. His father and mother were migrant farmworkers. Already working in the fields by the age of six, Valdez spent his childhood traveling to the harvests in the agricultural centers of the San Joaquin Valley. Despite having little uninterrupted early schooling, he managed to win a scholarship to San Jose State College in 1960.

Soon after his arrival at college, he won a regional playwriting contest for his first one-act play, *The Theft*. Encouraged by his teachers to write a full-length work, Valdez complied with *The Shrunken Head of Pancho Villa*, which was promptly produced by the San Jose State drama department. Graduating with a bachelor's degree in English in 1964, Valdez spent the next several months traveling in Cuba; on his return, he joined the San Francisco Mime Troupe under Ron Davis, where he worked for one year, learning from the troupe's *commedia dell'arte* techniques, which he was later to adapt in new ways.

Partly as a result of the sense of solidarity that he gained from his experiences while in Cuba, Valdez returned home to Delano, where the United Farm Workers Union was then being formed under the leadership of César Chávez. Amid a strike for union recognition, the union officials responded enthusiastically to Valdez's offer to create an educational theater group. Using volunteer actors from among the strikers, he formed El Teatro Campesino in 1965. Traveling on a flatbed truck from field to field, the troupe produced a series of one-act political skits dubbed *actos* (actions, or gestures), performing them in churches, storefronts, and on the edges of the fields themselves.

Enormously successful, the plays soon won outside attention and led to a United States tour in the summer of 1967. Later that year, Valdez left the fields to found the Centro Campesino Cultural in Del Rey, California. Similar recognition followed, with an Obie Award in New York in 1969 for "creating a workers' theater to demonstrate the politics of survival" and an invitation to perform at the Theatre des Nations festival in Nancy, France—one of four tours to Europe between 1969 and 1980. Later in 1969, Valdez and the troupe moved to Fresno, California, where they founded an annual Chicano theater festival, and Valdez began teaching drama at Fresno State College.

The Centro Campesino Cultural relocated once again in 1971 to San Juan Bautista, a small rural California town, where it would stay for the next several years, rooting itself in the community and transforming its dramaturgy to reflect local concerns—particularly through its adaptations of earlier devotional drama dating from the Spanish occupation. El Teatro Campesino there underwent a fundamental transformation. Living more or less in a commune, the group began increasingly to emphasize the spiritual side of their work, as derived not only from the prevalent Christianity of the typical Chicano community but also from their own newfound Aztec and Mayan roots. This shift from the agitational *actos* to a search for spiritual solutions was met with anger by formerly admiring audiences at the Quinto Festival de los Teatros Chicanos in Mexico City in 1974.

From its base in San Juan Bautista, the Centro Campesino Cultural continued to flourish, touring campuses and communities on a yearly basis; giving financial support, training, and advice to other theater troupes; and hosting visitors such as English director Peter Brook, who brought his actors from the International Centre of Theatre Research in 1973. After a career of refusing to participate in the commercial theater, Valdez determined finally, in 1978, to try reaching a middle-class audience. The result was *Zoot Suit*, a polished, full-length dance-musical based on the Sleepy Lagoon murder trial of 1943. It premiered at the Mark Taper Forum in Los Angeles in 1978 and ran for eleven months. The play opened at the Wintergarden Theatre on Broadway in 1979 but was forced to close after a month because of bad reviews. A film version of the play was made in 1981. In 1985, *Soldado razo* and *Dark Root of a Scream* were performed for the first time in New York at the Public Theatre as part of a Latino theater festival.

Valdez brought Tony Curiel into El Teatro Campesino in 1985 to help run the company. Valdez's play *"I Don't Have to Show You No Stinking Badges!"* (a famous line from the 1948 film *The Treasure of the Sierra Madre*) was coproduced with the Los Angeles Theatre Center in 1986. The film *La Bamba* (1987), written and directed by Valdez, was the first major release to celebrate the urban Hispanic youth lifestyle.

In 1991, a trio of *actos* from earlier El Teatro Campesino projects were presented in Dallas at the South Dallas Cultural Center; reviewers noted that they remained "remarkably fresh and quick-witted." *Soldado razo*, a 1970's play of protest about Chicano involvement in the Vietnam War, was revived in San Jose, California, in 1991.

El Teatro Campesino began the process of restructuring in 1988, learning to work more independently of Valdez, although his commitment to it remained substantial. On July 29, 1990, in a retrospective in the *Los Angeles Times* in celebration of Valdez's fiftieth birthday ("Luis Valdez at Fifty: The Rage Has Cooled"), the playwright, firmly established in Hollywood, admitted: "I couldn't turn around and kiss the teatro good-bye . . . without ruining my chances in Hollywood . . . my roots would dry up. I need to be true to what I set out to do."

In 2001, in a keynote address for the American Society for Theatre Research, with a new play in production and a forthcoming anthology, Valdez reaffirmed his commitment to El Teatro Campesino, Chicano Theatre, politicization and his work.

Analysis • Luis Miguel Valdez's genius was to reach an audience both Chicano and working-class, not only with political farces about strikers, "scabs," and bosses in a familiar street-theater concept but also by incorporating the popular theatrical forms of Latin America itself: the *carpas* (traveling theater shows), *variedades* (Mexican vaudeville), *corridos* (traditional Mexican folk ballads), and others. It is a unique combination to which Valdez added his own distinctive forms. Appraising Valdez's work is, however, different from appraising that of most other playwrights of his stature. By political conviction and by necessity, much of his dramatic work is a collective product. Although he has always been El Teatro Campesino's major creative inspiration and although entire passages from the collective plays were written by him alone, Valdez's drama is largely a joint project under his guidance—a collective political and religious celebration.

The starting point for all of Valdez's work is his evocation of what he calls *la plebe, el vulgo*, or simply *La Raza*, that is, the Chicano people. It is from this outlook that the first *actos* were created—a genre very close to the Brechtian *Lehrstück* (teaching piece), with its episodic structure, its use of broad social types, its indifference to all but the most minimal of props and scenery, and its direct involvement of the audience in the solving of its dramatized social problems. In Valdez's words, the *actos* "must be popular, subject to no other critics except the pueblo itself, but it must also educate the pueblo toward an appreciation of *social change*, on and off the stage."

According to various accounts, the form was first developed in a Delano storefront, where Valdez had assembled his would-be performers from among the strikers. He hung signs around their necks that read: *huelguista* (striker), *esquirol* (scab), and *patroncito* (little boss) and then simply asked them to show what had happened that day on the picket line. After some hesitation, the actors performed an impromptu political play, alive with their own jargon and bawdy jokes and inspired by the passions of the labor dispute within which they found themselves.

Valdez's theatrical vision is inseparable from the conditions under which he founded El Teatro Campesino in the farmworkers' strike of 1965. Born in struggle, his early plays all have a vitality, directness, and urgency that cannot be divorced from their lasting appeal. His achievement blossoms finally with his successful incorporation of the deep cultural roots of the Chicano nation, which are found in the religious imagery of the *indio* past. Both facets of his career have been widely copied by other Chicano directors and playwrights and admired widely outside the Chicano community as well.

Las dos caras del patroncito • One exemplary early *acto* is *Las dos caras del patroncito* (the two faces of the boss), in which a typical undocumented worker, recruited fresh from Mexico by a California landowner in order to scab on the strike, exchanges roles with his *patroncito*. Dressed in a pig mask and speaking in an absurd Texas drawl, the *patroncito* playfully suggests that he temporarily trade his own whip for the *esquirol*'s pruning shears. The two quickly assume the inner reality of these symbolic outward forms. The climactic moment occurs when the owner removes his mask, at which point the *esquirol* has the revelation that worker and boss look (and therefore are) the same. Calling now for help, the boss is mistaken by the police for a troublemaker and is hauled off-stage, shouting for César Chávez and declaring his support for *La huelga* (the strike). The social tensions and contradictions of this role-reversal are central to all the *actos*. If the boss is brought down to a vulnerable stature and the worker is shown to be capable of leadership, there is no simplistic identification of one or the other as totally good or evil.

Bernabé • In the next stage of his career, Valdez explored the legends and myths of the Chicano's *indio* past. *Bernabé* is perhaps Valdez's most fully realized *mito* (myth play). The hero is a thirty-one-year-old village idiot who has never had sexual relations with a woman. At the same time, he is a symbolic embodiment of the Chicano who possesses what Valdez calls "divinity in madness." After a series of taunts by the village toughs and an embarrassing encounter with Consuela, the local prostitute, Bernabé flees to a favorite hiding place in the countryside, where he has dug a gravelike hole in which he frequently masturbates in a kind of ritual copulation with *La Tierra* (the earth).

The climactic scene occurs when the elemental surroundings take on the forms of an Aztec allegory. *La Luna* (the moon) appears dressed as a *pachuco* (an urban Chicano zoot-suiter), smoking marijuana and acting as a go-between for his sister *La Tierra*, who then enters in the costume of a Mexican revolutionary camp follower (the proverbial "Adelita"). In the interchange, *La Tierra* questions the extent of Bernabé's love for her—whether he is "Chicano" enough to kill and to die for her. It is precisely his status as *loco* (crazy) that gives him the courage finally to say yes, and *El Sol* (the sun), as father, is pleased. As if mimicking the sacrifices to the Aztec sun god, Huitzilopochtli, Bernabé offers his physical heart to *La Tierra* and immediately ceases being the village idiot he was before, buried now within the earth but living on as a lesson to his people.

Valdez was to refine further this allegorical (and less immediately political) approach to Chicano identity in his plays throughout the 1970's, particularly in *La gran carpa de los rasquachis* (the great tent of the underdogs) and *El fin del mundo* (the end of the world), which further developed the use of the Mexican *corrido* (musical ballad), the split-level staging designed to evoke a mythical and suprahistorical realm of action, and the traditional images from Latino religious drama—particularly the *calavera* (skeleton) costume. In *El fin del mundo*, his play had become a full-scale allegorical ballet—a great dance of death.

Zoot Suit • With his first deliberate turn to the commercial theater in 1978, Valdez incorporated the *mito, acto,* and *corrido* in the unlikely framework of a play about the urban Chicano of the 1940's. *Zoot Suit*—filled with stylized scenes from the Los Angeles barrio—was a drama about a celebrated murder trial and the racist hysteria surrounding it. A panorama of American life of the time, the play deliberately adopted many of the outward features of the "professional" theater, while transforming them for its purposes. It displayed immense photographic projections of newspaper headlines, slickly choreographed dances and songs, and the overpowering central image of the narrator himself, dressed in a zoot suit—the mythical *pachuco.* To an extent greater than in any other of his plays, the work addressed Americans as a whole, reviving for them a historical moment of which they had never been aware and bringing them face-to-face with their latent prejudices.

"I Don't Have to Show You No Stinking Badges!" • Valdez's most celebrated play concerns a middle-class Chicano family's attempts to blend into the American cultural mainstream. The family's parents, Buddy and Connie Villa, are middle-aged bit-part actors who play stereotyped Latino roles in television and films; their son, Sonny, is a law student who disapproves of his parents' work, which he finds demeaning. The play's mixture of the themes of generational and cultural conflict drew wide praise, and the work confirmed Valdez's standing as an important contemporary dramatist.

Mummified Deer • *Mummified Deer* is Valdez's first play after a gap in playwriting of almost fifteen years. It reaffirms his status as the "father of Chicano drama" and continues his exploration of his heritage through the juxtaposition of ritual and realism. The play takes its inspiration from a newspaper article Valdez read concerning the discovery of a sixty-year-old fetus in the body of an eighty-four-year old woman. According to scholar Jorge Huerta, in his unpublished paper, "For Valdez the mummified fetus became a metaphor for the Chicanos' Indio heritage, seen through the lens of his own Yaqui blood." A Yaqui deer dancer serves as the alter-ego to the old woman, Mama Chu, and is visible only to her. A present-day narrative is established, and the gathering of Mamu Chu's relatives around the old woman provides the play's central image. The play's major dramatic action, however, operates in the historical/fictional past. Through the representation of Cajeme, the deer dancer, Valdez deftly divides his characters' philosophies into two distinct camps—revolutionaries and colonizers. The deer dancer "is, to Mama Chu, above all, a son, a man, a symbol of freedom, purity and preconquest liberation," according to actress Alma Martinez, who originated the role of Mama Chu. When Mama Chu dies, "Cajame dances to a climax at the foot of the bed. With his deer head up in triumph, he collapses, lifeless," thus commenting on the past versus the present, cultural heritage versus assimilation.

Other major works

SCREENPLAYS: *Zoot Suit,* 1982; *La Bamba,* 1987.

TELEPLAYS: *Fort Figueroa,* 1988; *La Pastorela,* 1991; *The Cisco Kid,* 1994.

EDITED TEXT: *Aztlan: An Anthology of Mexican American Literature,* 1972 (with Stan Steiner).

MISCELLANEOUS: *Pensamiento Serpentino: A Chicano Approach to the Theatre of Reality,* 1973.

Bibliography

Broyles-Gonzales, Yolanda. *El Teatro Campesino: Theater in the Chicano Movement.* Austin: University of Texas Press, 1994. This study uses previously unexamined materials such as production notes and interviews with former ensemble members to demystify the roles Valdez and El Teatro Campesino played in the development of a Chicano theatre aesthetic. Broyles-Gonzales employs a cultural studies methodology and reexamines the company in terms of class, race, and gender. Provides an "alternative reading" to the accepted El Teatro Campesino narrative.

Elam, Harry J., Jr. *Taking It to the Streets: The Social Protest Theatre of Luis Valdez and Amiri Baraka.* Ann Arbor: University of Michigan Press, 2001. Noted African American Theatre scholar Harry Elam explores the political, cultural, and performative similarities between El Teatro Campesino and Baraka's Black Revolutionary Theater. An intriguing examination of the political theater of these two marginalized groups, Chicanos and African Americans, and their shared aesthetic.

Flores, Arturo C. *El Teatro Campesino de Luis Valdez.* Madrid: Editorial Pliegos, 1990. This five-chapter study examines the importance, gradual development, theoretical considerations, touring, and "return to identity," and the "steps to commercialization (1975-1980)" represented by *Zoot Suit.* A strong study with a bibliography. In Spanish.

Huerta, Jorge A. *Chicano Theatre: Themes and Forms.* Ypsilanti, Mich.: Bilingual Press, 1982. This well written and well-illustrated study begins with Valdez's experiences in Delano in 1965. It contains an excellent immediate description with dialogue of these first energies and is written in the present tense for immediacy and energy. Provides some discussion of the beginnings of the San Francisco mime troupe and strong description of the *actos* and their literary history in Europe. Highly descriptive and lively. Valuable bibliography and index.

_____. "Labor Theatre, Street Theatre, and Community Theatre in the Barrio, 1965-1983." In *Hispanic Theatre in the United States,* edited by Nicolas Kanellos. Houston: Arte Publico Press, 1984. Placed at the end of a longer study of Hispanic theater history, this essay takes on more importance by indicating that Valdez's contribution belongs in a continuum of history. Under the wing of César Chávez's farm labor union, the playwright used the workers in a manner reminiscent of Clifford Odets's *Waiting for Lefty* (pr., pb. 1935). Good on contemporaries of El Teatro Campesino; strong bibliography.

Kanellos, Nicolas. *Mexican American Theater: Legacy and Reality.* Pittsburgh: Latin American Literary Review Press, 1987. Begins with an examination of Valdez's transformation from director of El Teatro Campesino, in league with the rural farm worker, to the urban commercial playwright of *Zoot Suit* in 1978, "an attempt at addressing a mass audience on a commercial basis." Cites Valdez's contribution to the "discernible period of proliferation and flourishing in Chicano theatres" from 1965 to 1976, then moves on to examine other offshoots of the impulse.

Morales, Ed. "Shadowing Valdez." *American Theatre* 9 (November, 1992): 14-19. An excellent essay on Valdez, his followers, his film plans, his shelved Frida Kahlo project (he was criticized for casting an Italian American in the role of Kahlo), and later productions in and around Los Angeles, with production stills. Includes an essay entitled "Statement on Artistic Freedom" by Valdez, in which he defends his nontraditional casting: "My first objective is to create mutual understanding between Americans and Mexicans, not to provoke more mistrust and suspicion."

Orona-Cordova, Roberta. "*Zoot Suit* and the Pachuco Phenomenon: An Interview with Luis Valdez." In *Mexican American Theatre: Then and Now*, edited by Nicolas Kanellos. Houston: Arte Publico Press, 1983. The opening of the film version of *Zoot Suit* in 1982 prompted this interview, in which Valdez reveals much about his motives for working, his view of Chicano literature and art, and his solutions to "the entrenched attitude" that will not allow Chicano participation in these industries. Much on Pachuquismo from an insider's point of view.

Pottlitzer, Joanne. *Hispanic Theater in the United States and Puerto Rico: A Report to the Ford Foundation.* New York: Ford Foundation, 1988. This volume provides a brief history to 1965 and discusses the Hispanic theater during the upheaval of the Vietnam War. Also examines the theater's activities and budget and pays homage to the inspiration of El Teatro Campesino and Valdez. Supplemented by an appendix and survey data.

Timothy Brennan,
updated by Thomas J. Taylor,
Robert McClenaghan, and Anne Fletcher

Lope de Vega Carpio

Born: Madrid, Spain; November 25, 1562
Died: Madrid, Spain; August 27, 1635

Principal drama • *Los comendadores de Córdoba*, wr. 1596-1598, pb. 1609; *El nuevo mundo descubierto por Cristóbal Colón*, wr. 1596-1603, pb. 1614 (*The Discovery of the New World by Christopher Columbus*, 1950); *El mayordomo de la duquesa de Amalfi*, wr. 1599-1606, pb. 1618 (*The Majordomo of the Duchess of Amalfi*, 1951); *El anzuelo de Fenisa*, wr. 1602-1608, pb. 1617; *La corona merecida*, wr. 1603, pb. 1620; *La noche toledana*, wr. 1605, pb. 1612; *Los melindres de Belisa*, wr. 1606-1608, pb. 1617; *El acero de Madrid*, wr. 1606-1612, pb. 1618 (*Madrid Steel*, 1935); *Castelvines y Monteses*, wr. 1606-1612, pb. 1647 (English translation, 1869); *La niña de plata*, wr. 1607-1612, pb. 1617; *Peribáñez y el comendador de Ocaña*, wr. 1609-1612, pb. 1614 (*Peribáñez*, 1936); *La buena guarda*, wr. 1610, pb. 1621; *Las flores de don Juan, y rico y pobre trocados*, wr. 1610-1615, pb. 1619; *El villano en su rincón*, wr. 1611, pb. 1617 (*The King and the Farmer*, 1940); *Fuenteovejuna*, wr. 1611-1618, pb. 1619 (*The Sheep Well*, 1936); *Lo cierto por lo dudoso*, wr. 1612-1624, pb. 1625 (*A Certainty for a Doubt*, 1936); *El perro del hortelano*, wr. 1613-1615, pb. 1618 (*The Gardener's Dog*, 1903); *El caballero de Olmedo*, wr. 1615-1626, pb. 1641 (*The Knight from Olmedo*, 1961); *La dama boba*, pb. 1617 (*The Lady Nit-Wit*, 1958); *Amar sin saber a quién*, wr. 1620-1622, pb. 1630; *El mejor alcalde, el rey*, wr. 1620-1623, pb. 1635 (*The King, the Greatest Alcalde*, 1918); *Los Tellos de Meneses I*, wr. 1620-1628, pb. 1635; *El premio del bien hablar*, wr. 1624-1625, pb. 1636; *La moza de cántaro*, wr. 1625-1626, pb. 1646?; *El guante de doña Blanca*, wr. 1627-1635, pb. 1637; *El castigo sin venganza*, pb. 1635 (based on Matteo Bandello's novella; *Justice Without Revenge*, 1936); *Las bizarrías de Belisa*, pb. 1637; *Four Plays*, pb. 1936; *Five Plays*, pb. 1961

Other literary forms • Lope de Vega Carpio was an incredibly prolific writer. In addition to his plays, which number in the hundreds, he wrote poems, such as *La Dragontea* (1598; Drake the pirate), *El Isidro* (1599), *La hermosura de Angélica* (1602; Angélica's beauty), *Jerusalén conquistada* (1609; Jerusalem regained), and *La gatomaquia* (1634; *Gatomachia*, 1843). He also wrote several prose works, including *La Arcadia* (1598), *El peregrino en su patria* (1604; *The Pilgrim: Or, The Stranger in His Own Country*, 1621), *Los pastores de Belén* (1612; the shepherds of Bethlehem), *Novelas a Marcia Leonarda* (1621; stories for Marcia Leonarda), and *La Dorotea* (1632). His *Égloga a Claudio* (1637; eclogue to Claudio), published after his death, contains autobiographical and critical material on his life and work.

Achievements • Lope de Vega Carpio, "the father of Spanish theater," is generally credited with establishing the norms for the drama of Spain's Golden Age and is recognized as one of its most accomplished dramatists as well as its most prolific. His *El arte nuevo de hacer comedias en este tiempo* (1609; *The New Art of Writing Plays*, 1914), presented to a Madrid literary society, sets out the norms that Lope de Vega followed in writing his dramas. These norms are not entirely original with him but represent instead his synthesis of a long process of development in which many dramatists participated. It is significant, however, that once this style of theater received Lope de Vega's endorsement, it became fixed in the Spanish canon. Thus, *The New Art of Writing Plays* provides a fairly accurate description of most Spanish drama from that time until the death of the last great Golden Age dramatist, Pedro Calderón de la Barca, in 1681.

The full extent of Lope de Vega's dramatic production remains unknown and is the subject of scholarly debate. He is the undisputed author of 316 surviving full-length plays and the probable or reputed author of many more. In 1609, in *The New Art of Writing Plays*, he claimed to have authored 483 dramas, and, toward the end of his life, he elevated that number to 1,500. His first biographer, Juan Pérez de Montalbán, who was also a close friend, credited him with more than 1,800 dramatic works. Both sources, however, are suspect. Lope de Vega is certainly not noted for his modesty,

(Library of Congress)

and there is some evidence indicating that he never intended the figures he cited to be taken literally; Pérez de Montalbán's biography is an exaggerated encomium that deliberately suppresses the various scandalous incidents in Lope de Vega's life that would have damaged his reputation. Therefore, more cautious critics have suggested that Lope de Vega's total dramatic production probably did not exceed 800 full-length plays.

Lope de Vega also produced a number (estimates run as high as 400, a tenth of which remain) of *autos sacramentales*—short, allegorical, religious dramas that were used in the Corpus Christi celebrations. His contribution to this genre, however, has been overshadowed by that of Calderón.

Biography • Lope Félix de Vega Carpio was born in Madrid on November 25, 1562, to Félix de Vega Carpio and Francisca Fernández Flores, humble Asturian (northern Spanish) parents, who had moved to Madrid less than a year earlier. Very little is known about his childhood and early youth. His biased biographer, Pérez de Montalbán, claims that Lope de Vega studied at the prestigious Jesuit school the Colegio Imperial de San Pedro y San Pablo, but court records indicate that he studied at the smaller Colegio de los Teatinos. He attended the University of Alcalá de Henares (as did Miguel de Cervantes, Calderón, and Tirso de Molina), and he may have studied at the University of Salamanca as well. He enlisted in the armed forces in 1583 and fought in the Azores.

On returning to Madrid, Lope de Vega engaged in a love affair with Elena Osorio, the married daughter of a theater manager for whom he wrote plays. This affair lasted until 1587, when Elena (apparently at her parents' instigation) rejected him in order to establish a liaison with a wealthier man. Lope de Vega reacted violently, circulating anonymous poetry in which he insulted Elena and her family. He was consequently accused and convicted of criminal libel and was sentenced to eight years of exile from Madrid. It was apparently at this time that he recorded in *La Dorotea* his impressions of this, the first of many amorous affairs that were subsequently reflected in his writing; this novel, however, was not published until 1632.

During his exile, which he apparently violated on several occasions, Lope de Vega lived first in Valencia and then in Toledo, where he was in the service of the duke of Alba. In 1588, he was married by proxy to Isabel de Urbina (the Belisa of his poetry), by whom he had a daughter, Antonia, and who died giving birth to another, Teodora, in 1594. Neither daughter lived to maturity. In the same year as his marriage, Lope de Vega may also have participated in the ill-fated expedition of the Spanish Armada against England.

Lope de Vega returned to Madrid in 1596 and was indicted the same year for concubinage with Antonia Trillo de Armenta, a wealthy widow in her early thirties who was noted for her easy virtue. Shortly afterward, he began a more lasting (until 1608) affair with Micaela de Luján, an actor's wife, whom he referred to in his writings as Lucinda or Camila Lucinda. In 1598, apparently motivated by the promise of a huge dowry (which he never received), he married Juana de Guardo, the daughter of a wealthy fish and meat merchant. Through his writings, he managed to maintain two households, moving both wife and mistress with him to Seville and Toledo before finally returning to Madrid. Both Juana and Micaela bore him children. Those born to Micaela were baptized in the name of her husband until his death in 1603; those born afterward were listed in the baptismal registry as being of unknown parents. Only two of his children by Micaela lived to maturity: One, a son named Lope Félix, joined the armed forces and died in a pearl-hunting expedition toward the end of his father's life; the other, a daughter, Marcela, became a nun at the age of sixteen. Lope's wife, Juana, bore him three daughters and a son before her death in 1613; of these children only one, a daughter, Feliciana, reached maturity.

On a visit to Madrid in 1605, Lope de Vega met Luis Fernández de Córdoba, the twenty-three-year-old duke of Sessa, and established with him a friendship that was as remarkable as it was enduring. The duke used Lope de Vega to write letters to his paramours and prevailed on him to give him letters that he had written to his own mistresses—at least one of whom the duke may have shared. Because of the duke's fondness for Lope de Vega and his penchant for collecting anything that the writer's pen had produced, a substantial amount of Lope de Vega's correspondence as well as the manuscripts of a number of his plays have survived to the present.

In 1614, a year after his second wife's death, Lope de Vega decided to enter the priesthood. His religious vocation, however, did not involve a conversion to chastity. He had already replaced Micaela with another mistress, a friend of hers and, like her, married and an actress, Jerónima de Burgos. Jerónima—whom he called *la señora Gerarda* ("Mrs. Gerarda") in his letters to the duke of Sessa—was with Lope de Vega when he was ordained in Toledo, and she continued to live with him until he rejected her because of her increasing obesity and her chronic alcoholism. He then engaged in a brief but passionate fling with Lucía de Salcedo, whom he refers to as *la loca* ("the crazy girl").

The last great love of Lope de Vega's life was Marta de Nevares (Amarilis in his writing), the wife of the highly unattractive (if Lope de Vega's description of him can be trusted) Roque Hernández de Ayala, the scribe who copied Lope de Vega's plays for the duke of Sessa. A daughter, Antonia Clara, was born to Marta in 1617 and was baptized as the daughter of Hernández, though it was common knowledge that Lope de Vega was her father. After a number of difficulties—including an attempt by Hernández to have Lope de Vega killed—Marta obtained a separation decree from her husband. He appealed but died suddenly, leaving both Marta and Lope de Vega ecstatic.

A few years later, when Marta began to lose her sight, Lope de Vega was seized by the fear that her misfortune was divine retribution for their sin. As he grew increasingly repentant, scourging himself every Friday, new calamities arrived. Marta lost her sight completely and suffered periodic bouts of insanity, from which she recovered only briefly before her death in 1632; Lope Félix drowned during a pearl-hunting expedition; and Antonia Clara was abducted by a Madrid nobleman. Lope de Vega continued to write in spite of these misfortunes and produced some of his most admirable works in the final years of his life. He died on August 27, 1635, and was buried in the Church of Saint Sebastian in Madrid after an elaborate nine-day funeral arranged by the duke of Sessa.

Analysis • The theater of Lope de Vega Carpio is so varied that it eludes generalizations. Indeed, its rich variety is probably its most defining trait, and it would seem that Lope de Vega intended this to be so. Commenting in *The New Art of Writing Plays* on his decision to mix comic and tragic elements in the same drama, he noted that this choice is based on his imitation of nature, which is beautiful because of its variety. Their diverseness explains why virtually all of Lope de Vega's plays are referred to as *comedias*, or "comedies." This designation does not mean that his plays are not often serious. Indeed, they frequently concern subjects (such as rape, murder, and political intrigue) that can scarcely be treated humorously.

The designation "comedy" implies only that the plays are not tragedies; they usually end with a restoration of order rather than a catastrophe, and their principal characters are generally common people rather than the nobility whom classical norms deemed appropriate for tragedy. Moreover, humor is an important element in all of Lope de Vega's plays, no matter how serious they are. Even those few that are designated tragedies include a buffoonlike character known as a *gracioso* ("funny one"), usually a servant, whose lack of dignity provides occasion for laughter in spite of the generally serious tone of these works.

By mixing comic and tragic elements in the same work, Lope de Vega was intentionally ignoring the classical dramatic precepts established by Aristotle and Horace. He also deliberately disregarded the classical unities, which sought to limit a play's setting to a single place and decreed that its action should occur in a single day. For all these reasons, Lope de Vega's drama (and Spanish Golden Age drama in general) bears a closer resemblance to the theater of Elizabethan England than to the more classically oriented theater of seventeenth century France. His theater differs from its English counterparts in other ways, however, such as following a three-act rather than a five-act format and employing polymetric verse.

In *The New Art of Writing Plays*, Lope de Vega recommended accommodating the verse form used in each passage to the material being treated—a principle based on Spanish poetic tradition. Therefore, Lope de Vega recommended that exposition be written in one of the two standard verse forms used for narrative poetry: Normal exposition may be handled in the popular *romance* or ballad form, but special cases should be rendered in the more elegant Italianate *octava real*, used for the polished epic poetry of the day. Lope de Vega also recommended accommodating each character's speech to his station and to the material being treated, using figurative language in key discussions, for example, while rendering everyday conversations in more prosaic speech.

In spite of its varied nature, Lope de Vega's theater is characterized by a few constants. Among these are an interest in nature, an affection for the common people, an ability to discover poetic beauty in the everyday life of sixteenth and seventeenth century Spain, a penchant for reflecting his own experiences in his drama, and—above all—an abiding interest in the theme of honor or reputation. Lope de Vega recommended this theme in *The New Art of Writing Plays* because of its ability to elicit a strong emotional response from the audience, and he followed his own recommendation by including this theme in the overwhelming majority of his plays, where his treatment of it ranges from the humorous to the tragic.

Peribáñez • Probably no play illustrates all that is typical of Lope de Vega better than does *Peribáñez*, a drama about a common Spanish farmer who kills the noble commander of the town's military forces in order to defend his wife (and his own honor) against the commander's unwelcome advances—and who is pardoned by King Enrique III for this offense. Much of the play's appeal is its poetic treatment of life in the town of Ocaña, where Peribáñez and his wife live. The play's opening scene shows a simple and joyful wedding celebration in Peribáñez's house following his marriage to Casilda, and other scenes concern the town's celebration of its patron saint's day and farm laborers who sing in the fields as they work.

Not only do these scenes paint an appealing picture of rural Spanish life, but also they advance the play's action. The town's commander passes by the wedding celebration and—appropriately, for a man who cannot control his passions—is thrown from his horse, so that he must be taken to recuperate in Peribáñez's house, where he sees Casilda. The scenes centering on the celebration of the patron saint's day and the singing farm laborers similarly contribute to the play's development. It is because of his involvement in the preparations for the festival of San Roque that Peribáñez is obliged to visit Toledo and accidentally sees there a portrait of Casilda, which the commander has ordered painted surreptitiously. He learns of the commander's attempt to seduce Casilda and of her refusal when, on returning from Toledo, he overhears a song that the farm laborers have composed celebrating the incident.

Probably the most discussed passage in the play is a statement by a minor character, Belardo—a name that Lope de Vega frequently used as a pseudonym for himself—that he has taken refuge in the Church. Because *Peribáñez* was first published in 1614, the same year that Lope de Vega became a priest, some critics have believed that this passage is a reflection of that event. The current consensus, however, is that the play was written four years earlier and that this passage actually reflects Lope de Vega's joining the Congregation of the Calle del Olivar in 1610. A far more interesting reflection of Lope de Vega's life can be found in the play's evocation of the biblical story of David and Bathsheba when the commander has Peribáñez sent to war (just as David did Uriah) so that he may satisfy his lust for his subject's wife. Lope de Vega evoked the story of David in many of his works, and it is likely that he felt a special affinity for this biblical king whose great sin was lust and who enjoyed divine forgiveness for that sin. In this light, it is interesting to note that Lope de Vega has the commander, who is stabbed by Peribáñez, live long enough to receive absolution, but that the commander's servant and Casilda's treacherous friend Inés—both of whom are motivated by greed—are not so fortunate.

The most noteworthy aspect of the play is its treatment of the theme of honor. In the commander's opinion, honor is the prerogative of the nobility. This view was probably a commonly held one at the time of the play's composition. Therefore, Peribáñez is obliged to defend his slaying of the commander on the grounds that, when the commander ordered him to fight the Moors, he also made him a knight—thereby endowing him with honor and the obligation to defend it. It is clear, however, that in the author's view, the common man possesses honor and dignity as an inalienable birthright, and it is significant that the play closes with the king's pronouncement that his pardoning of Peribáñez is not an act of grace but of justice.

The Sheep Well • The right of the common man to defend his honor was a popular theme that reappeared in the work of Lope de Vega's followers as well as in several other plays by Lope de Vega himself. Probably the most notable of these is his most frequently anthologized work, *The Sheep Well*, which is based on a rebellion that occurred in 1476 in the Spanish town of Fuente Ovejuna ("Sheep Well"). Like *Peribáñez*, this play dramatizes the murder of a town's military commander. In the case of *The Sheep Well*, however, the commander's offense is against the entire town. The commander believes that all of the town's women are obligated to satisfy his sexual appetite, and it is thus appropriate that his death occurs because of the united action of the entire populace rather than at the hands of a single individual.

Initially, *The Sheep Well* may impress a modern reader as a rather disjointed work in which several independent episodes—the town's vindication of its honor, the love and marriage of two of the town's young people, and the war between Queen Isabel and her half sister Juana—are not satisfactorily united into an aesthetically pleasing whole. Closer inspection, however, reveals that Lope de Vega has established a thematic unity based on a proper understanding of love and of the relationship between love and harmony. He thus carefully develops in the play a connection between the broken political order in Spain and in Fuente Ovejuna and a perverted understanding of love as appetite, and he shows that the restoration of this broken harmony depends on a self-sacrificing love evident in the willingness of the citizens to risk their individual security because of their love for their neighbors.

As with *Peribáñez*, much of the charm of *The Sheep Well* comes from its poetic portrayal of the simple townspeople and of their customs and festivals. By including music and dancing in these and by having this music interrupted by the commander, Lope de Vega emphasizes even in these scenes the central theme of the relationship between love and harmony. This theme is based largely on the Neoplatonic view of love that had become popular in Spain during the sixteenth century.

The King, the Greatest Alcalde • A third important play revolving around the common man's right to honor and a nobleman's abuse of that right is *The King, the Greatest Alcalde*, which dramatizes the abduction, during her wedding, of an attractive peasant girl, Elvira, by a nobleman, Don Tello. In this case, Elvira's intended husband, Sancho, does not avenge his honor himself but relies instead on King Alfonso VII, whom he implores to send a mayor. Rather than do this, the king comes himself. On learning that Don Tello has already raped Elvira, the king commands him to marry her and endow her with half his estate and then has Tello put to death for his offense. Elvira, with her lost honor thus restored by her marriage to the man who raped her, is then able to marry Sancho and to bring to her marriage a large dowry. This ending inevitably seems unconvincing to modern readers, and it is unlikely that any amount of discussion could change this impression. However, seventeenth century Spanish audiences apparently found it quite satisfactory, and various other plays of this period end in a similar manner.

The King and the Farmer • It is clear that in Lope de Vega's view, society functions best if it is a harmonious whole in which each member assumes a place appropriate to his station. Plays such as *Peribáñez, The Sheep Well,* and *The King, the Greatest Alcalde,* show how the social balance is broken when aristocrats abuse their position of authority. *The King and the Farmer* gives a contrasting and complementary view by illustrating the presumption of a peasant, Juan Labrador ("John Worker"), who fails to recognize his dependence on the aristocracy. Living in a comfortable rural world in which nature's bounty seems to respond generously to all human needs, Juan is proud of his isolation from the court and presumes to build, before his death, his tomb, which he inscribes with the boast that he lived and died without having seen the king. The folly of this boast becomes evident when the king visits Juan's town on a hunting trip, sees the tomb, and visits Juan without revealing his identity. Juan receives him hospitably but in a series of comic scenes issues to him a series of arrogant commands, which the king obligingly obeys before eventually revealing his identity.

Although this play is one of Lope de Vega's most curious works, its main point seems evident enough: In spite of their apparent isolation from each other, the world of the court and the world of the peasant (the worlds of government and of the people) are mutually dependent. The marriage at the end of the play between Juan's daughter Lisarda and Otón, the king's marshal, is an expression of this complementary relationship.

Los melindres de Belisa • The theme of honor, which is treated seriously in *Peribáñez, The Sheep Well,* and *The King, the Greatest Alcalde,* is handled in a humorous manner in *Los melindres de Belisa* (the caprices of Belisa). This work is typical of a genre referred to as *comedias de capa y espada* or cape and sword plays, a name derived from the costume worn by the actors playing the leading male roles. These plays have complicated plots revolving around the courtship of one or more sets of middle-class youths who devise ingenious measures to overcome the obstacles to their love. The young people frequently resort to deceptions or disguises that lead to a confusion of identities and threaten to cause a loss of honor, but cape and sword plays inevitably have happy endings each involving at least one wedding. Though duels are frequently an ingredient of these plays, they are never serious, merely contributing an additional element to the prevailing atmosphere of confusion and misunderstanding.

Thus, in *Los melindres de Belisa,* it is Felisardo's and his sweetheart Celia's mistaken belief that Felisardo has killed a man in a duel, which causes them to hide in their friend Elisio's house and to disguise themselves as slaves. As is usual in cape and sword plays, their seemingly logical deception backfires, and they are seized by the authorities as payment of a debt that Elisio owes the mother of the flighty and finical Belisa, who has rejected many suitors because she can find none refined enough for her. Ironically, this finical girl and her widowed mother both fall in love with Felisardo, whom they believe to be a slave, and Belisa's brother Don Juan falls in love with Celia. In a treatment that pokes fun at the hypocrisy underlying the Spanish concept of honor, Lope de Vega has each family member express outrage when he or she suspects that one of the others may damage the family's reputation by loving a social inferior.

The Lady Nit-Wit • *The Lady Nit-Wit* is a relatively simple cape and sword play that lacks the disguises and the intricate complications of *Los melindres de Belisa*. Nevertheless, it has most of the standard ingredients of the genre, including a humorous duel that ends harmlessly when the two contenders realize that each of them prefers the girl whom the other is supposed to be courting. This ironic treatment of dueling is typical of the tone of the entire play, which dramatizes a scheme by which the supposedly stupid Finea outsmarts her brilliant sister Nise in order to win Nise's suitor for herself. The play also shows how Finea—so naïve and illiterate in the beginning that she requests help from her father in deciphering a love letter that her sister's suitor has smuggled to her—is transformed by love into an intelligent and discreet person. The theme that love could change people for the better is part of the same Neoplatonic tradition, which, as has been noted, provided the background for understanding *The Sheep Well*.

Las bizarrías de Belisa • Lope de Vega cultivated the cape and sword drama all his life. Written the year before he died, *Las bizarrías de Belisa* continues to be typical of the genre. The plot concerns Belisa's contest—involving various misunderstandings—with her rival Lucinda for the affection of Don Juan de Cardona (who is involved twice in dueling in the course of the play). The work closes with a passage in which Lope de Vega addresses the public through Belisa, informing them that the author's desire to serve them caused him to leave retirement to write this play. Because of this statement, critics believed until recently that this was the last play he wrote. Though that conclusion has been questioned, it is probable that Lope de Vega himself expected that this would be the case. Therefore, throughout the play, he mixes references to the phoenix (evoking his own nickname "the Phoenix of Spain") and the swan (who, according to tradition, sings before his death).

The Gardener's Dog • Because one of its principal characters, the Countess Diana, belongs to the nobility rather than the middle class, *The Gardener's Dog* is not a cape-and-sword play in the strictest sense. It is generally linked with this genre, however, because it treats humorously an ingenious scheme that allows two lovers—the countess and her secretary Teodoro—to overcome the obstacle to their love caused by their differing social stations. This obstacle is a serious one, and the countess struggles with it through most of the play, refusing to recognize openly her love for Teodoro but refusing also to allow him to marry one of her servants. Her behavior is thus like that of the proverbial dog in the manger, who neither eats nor allows others to eat.

The solution to Teodoro's and Diana's dilemma is provided by Teodoro's servant, the *gracioso* Tristán, who devises a scheme that convinces everyone that Teodoro is the lost son of a wealthy nobleman, Ludovico—and who begs the audience in the last lines of the play not to reveal Teodoro's secret. This request emphasizes the artificiality of the play, and it is possible that this is Lope de Vega's way of underscoring the artificiality of the restricting social conventions of his day. It is also possible that the audience might have felt threatened by the play's violation of its social conventions had it not been reminded that this was only fiction after all.

The Knight from Olmedo • Though he wrote very few tragedies, two of Lope de Vega's finest works belong to this genre. The first of these, *The Knight from Olmedo*, dramatizes the murder of the protagonist, Alonso, a handsome and courageous knight, by Rodrigo, a man whose life Alonso saves but who is his rival for the love of Inés. The play establishes tragic expectations from the beginning by evoking in its title a well-known song (sung in the last act) about the murder of a knight described as "the flower of Olmedo" (Alonso's birthplace) and "the glory of Medina" (the town in which Alonso courted Inés), and these expectations are reinforced by parallels between the play's action and passages in the song describing the knight from Olmedo as being warned by ghosts of the danger that awaits him. In spite of this, much of the first part of the play strikes the modern reader, who is unfamiliar with the song evoked by the title, as being inappropriately light for tragedy—evidence that Lope de Vega is following his customary practice of mixing tragic and humorous elements in the same work.

Alonso's employment of the witch Fabia's services in order to win Inés led a number of critics to interpret this play moralistically and to view the protagonist's death as a form of divine punishment. This reading has been corrected, however, and the current view of the play recognizes it as a poetic evocation of the thanatos-eros theme—of the inherent connection between love and death.

Justice Without Revenge • Another tragedy, *Justice Without Revenge*, is more consistent in its tone than *The Knight from Olmedo* and is generally acknowledged as the equal of the great tragic dramas of the ancient Greeks and of William Shakespeare. Because of its tragic tone, it is probably the least typical of all of Lope de Vega's plays, but one still finds among its characters the customary *gracioso* (whose jokes are in this case often related to the play's serious theme). Lope de Vega's abiding interest in nature is also evident in a number of passages that extol—perhaps ironically—the virtues of rural life.

The play's plot, taken from a novella by Matteo Bandello, concerns a scheme by which the Italian duke of Ferrara tricks his illegitimate son Federico into unwittingly murdering Casandra, the duke's young bride, with whom Federico has had an adulterous affair. The duke then has Federico put to death for killing his stepmother. Because of its bloody and startling denouement, this play is typical of the Senecan tragic style that was popular in Spain and sought to dazzle or amaze the audience with the spectacular. It is also typical of a peculiarly Spanish genre referred to informally as the "wife-murder play," because it dramatizes a husband's need to defend his honor by murdering his wife. Calderón is a more noted writer of this type of drama, but Lope de Vega had experimented with it as early as 1596-1598, when he wrote *Los comendadores de Córdoba* (the commanders of Cordoba). However, until the composition of *Justice Without Revenge* in the final years of his life, he did not produce a masterpiece in the genre, and it is probable that the work's tragic tone reflects the author's own circumstances at the time he wrote it.

The most striking feature of *Justice Without Revenge* is its ambiguity, which is not limited to the dialogue but also extends to the characters and the theme. For this reason, the play has been the subject of many conflicting interpretations, in which scholars have tried to assign the blame for the final catastrophe to one or another of the characters. As with *The Knight from Olmedo*, however, it is probably best to avoid moralistic interpretations of this work. Rather, the play's ambiguity seems designed to evoke the ultimate ambiguity of life, and all three of the main characters seem caught in a dilemma for which they are not entirely responsible. The work's basically pessimistic tone is attenuated, however, by a complex series of images in which Lope de Vega—apparently now taking his religious vocation seriously—evokes the Christian doctrine of the Atonement. Thus, even in his final, despairing years, he was unable to view life without hope.

Other major works

LONG FICTION: *La Arcadia*, 1598; *El peregrino en su patria*, 1604 (*The Pilgrim: Or, The Stranger in His Own Country*, 1621); *Los pastores de Belén*, 1612; *Novelas a Marcia Leonarda*, 1621; *La Dorotea*, 1632.

POETRY: *La Dragontea*, 1598; *El Isidro*, 1599; *La hermosura de Angélica*, 1602; *Rimas*, 1602; *El arte nuevo de hacer comedias en este tiempo*, 1609 (*The New Art of Writing Plays*, 1914); *Jerusalén conquistada*, 1609; *Rimas sacras*, 1614; *La Circe*, 1621; *La filomena*, 1621; *Triunfos divinos*, 1625; *La corona trágica*, 1627; *Laurel de Apolo*, 1630; *Amarilis*, 1633; *La gatomaquia*, 1634 (*Gatomachia*, 1843); *Rimas humanas y divinas del licenciado Tomé de Burguillos*, 1634; *Filis*, 1635; *La Vega del Parnaso*, 1637.

NONFICTION: *Égloga a Claudio*, 1637.

Bibliography

Fox, Diane. *Refiguring the Hero: From Peasant to Noble in Lope de Vega and Calderón*. Penn State Studies in Romance Literature series. University Park: Pennsylvania State University Press, 1991. Fox examines the image of the hero and class status in the works of Lope de Vega and Pedro Calderón de la Barca. Bibliography and index.

McKendrick, Melveena. *Playing the King: Lope de Vega and the Limits of Conformity*. Rochester, N.Y.: Tamesis, 2000. An examination of Lope de Vega's portrayal of the monarchy in his works. Bibliography and index.

Morrison, Robert R. *Lope de Vega and the Comedia de Santos*. New York: Peter Lang, 2000. This study examines the religious drama of Lope de Vega. Bibliography and index.

Ostlund, DeLys. *The Re-creation of History in the Fernando and Isabel Plays of Lope de Vega*. New York: Peter Lang, 1997. Oslund examines the historical aspects of the dramas of Lope de Vega. Bibliography and index.

Smith, Marlene K. *The Beautiful Woman in the Theater of Lope de Vega: Ideology and Mythology of Female Beauty in Seventeenth Century Spain*. New York: Peter Lang, 1998. A discussion of the feminine beauty as portrayed in the works of Lope de Vega. Bibliography and index.

Wright, Elizabeth R. *Pilgrimage to Patronage: Lope de Vega and the Court of Philip III, 1598-1621*. Lewisburg, Pa.: Bucknell University Press, 2001. This study focuses on the patronage system and the interactions between politics and the life and work of Lope de Vega. Bibliography and index.

Currie K. Thompson

Voltaire

François-Marie Arouet

Born: Paris, France; November 21, 1694
Died: Paris, France; May 30, 1778

Principal drama • *Œdipe*, pr. 1718, pb. 1719 (*Oedipus*, 1761); *Artémire*, pr. 1720; *Mariamne*, pr. 1724, pb. 1725 (English translation, 1761); *L'Indiscret*, pr., pb. 1725 (verse play); *Brutus*, pr. 1730, pb. 1731 (English translation, 1761); *Ériphyle*, pr. 1732, pb. 1779; *Zaïre*, pr. 1732, pb. 1733 (English translation, 1736); *La Mort de César*, pr. 1733, pb. 1735; *Adélaïde du Guesclin*, pr. 1734; *L'Échange*, pr. 1734, pb. 1761; *Alzire*, pr., pb. 1736 (English translation, 1763); *L'Enfant prodigue*, pr. 1736, pb. 1738 (verse; prose translation, *The Prodigal*, 1750?); *La Prude: Ou, La Grandeuse de Cassette*, wr. 1740, pr., pb. 1747 (verse; based on William Wycherley's play *The Plain-Dealer*); *Zulime*, pr. 1740, pb. 1761; *Mahomet*, pr., pb. 1742 (*Mahomet the Prophet*, 1744); *Mérope*, pr. 1743, pb. 1744 (English translation, 1744, 1749); *La Princesse de Navarre*, pr., pb. 1745 (verse play; music by Jean-Philippe Rameau); *Sémiramis*, pr. 1748, pb. 1749 (*Semiramis*, 1760); *Nanine*, pr., pb. 1749 (English translation, 1927); *Oreste*, pr., pb. 1750; *Rome sauvée*, pr., pb. 1752; *L'Orphelin de la Chine*, pr., pb. 1755 (*The Orphan of China*, 1756); *Socrate*, pb. 1759 (*Socrates*, 1760); *L'Écossaise*, pr., pb. 1760 (*The Highland Girl*, 1760); *Tancrède*, pr. 1760, pb. 1761; *Don Pèdre*, wr. 1761, pb. 1775; *Olympie*, pb. 1763, pr. 1764; *Le Triumvirat*, pr. 1764, pb. 1767; *Les Scythes*, pr., pb. 1767; *Les Guèbres: Ou, La Tolérance*, pb. 1769; *Sophonisbe*, pb. 1770, pr. 1774 (revision of Jean Mairet's play); *Les Pélopides: Ou, Atrée et Thyeste*, pb. 1772; *Les Lois de Minos*, pb. 1773; *Irène*, pr. 1778, pb. 1779; *Agathocle*, pr. 1779

Other literary forms • In addition to his plays, Voltaire wrote many poems, especially odes. Some of his most important longer poems are *Poème sur la religion naturelle* (1722); *La Henriade* (1728), an epic poem initially entitled *La Ligue* (*Henriade*, 1732); *Le Temple du goût* (1733; *The Temple of Taste*, 1734), on literary criticism; *Discours en vers sur l'homme* (1738-1752; *Discourses in Verse on Man*, 1764); *Poème sur le désastre de Lisbonne* (1756; *Poem on the Lisbon Earthquake*, 1764); and *La Pucelle d'Orléans* (1755, 1762; *The Maid of Orleans*, 1758, also as *La Pucelle*, 1785-1786).

Voltaire's main historical works are *Histoire de Charles XII* (1731; *The History of Charles XII*, 1732); *Le Siècle de Louis XIV* (1751; *The Age of Louis XIV*, 1752); and *Essai sur les mœurs* (1756, 1763; *The General History and State of Europe*, 1754, 1759).

Voltaire's current reputation is based on his *contes philosophiques* (philosophical tales), of which three of the principal ones are: *Zadig: Ou, La Destinée, Histoire orientale* (1748; originally as *Memnon: Histoire orientale*, 1747; *Zadig: Or, The Book of Fate*, 1749), *Candide: Ou, L'Optimisme* (1759; *Candide: Or, All for the Best*, 1759), and *La Princesse de Babylone* (1768; *The Princess of Babylon*, 1769).

Voltaire wrote numerous philosophical treatises, essays, polemics, and brochures, and he left behind a voluminous correspondence, compiled in *The Complete Works of Voltaire* (1968-1977; 135 volumes, in French).

Achievements • Voltaire dominated the eighteenth century theater by the number of his plays alone. He wrote fifty-two in all, of which twenty-seven are tragedies. He was the most popular dramatist of his time and the principal author for the Comédie-Française, which now only occasionally performs his plays. In his own time, Voltaire was regarded as one of the masters of French drama. More of his plays were performed than those of Pierre Corneille and Jean Racine together. Today, he is best known for his philosophical works, especially his tales, but during his lifetime he believed his immortality would rest on his dramatic accomplishments. Although he wrote most of his plays rapidly, he constantly reworked them and revised the failures, often bringing them to success, as with *Mariamne.*

Voltaire was the literary and philosophical bridge between the classical theater of the seventeenth century and the Romantic theater of the nineteenth century. It was he who kept the classical theater alive, both in subject matter (one-third of his tragedies are based on classical themes) and in form. He insisted on adherence to the Aristotelian unities of action, time, and place, and on verse, propriety, and verisimilitude. His style, though sometimes declamatory, is in accurate French *alexandrins*, elegant and frequently excellent poetry in the style of Corneille. Yet, as dedicated as he was to the values of French classicism in the drama, Voltaire was intrigued, if torn, by contemporary literary theories and foreign dramatic works, and at times he violated his own precepts in introducing into his plays—and into France—dramatic elements of the coming age.

Thus, while Voltaire kept French classical theater alive, he distinctly widened its frontiers. Voltaire's trip to England from 1726 to 1729 brought him into contact with the English theater, and especially with the plays of William Shakespeare. Critic Admad Gunny maintains that Voltaire also came to know and was influenced by the works of John Dryden, Alexander Pope, Jonathan Swift, Joseph Addison, John Milton, Laurence Sterne, Samuel Richardson, and Henry Fielding.

The influence of the earlier playwrights can be seen in many plays, among them *Brutus* and *La Mort de César*, based on Shakespeare's *Julius Caesar* (pr. c. 1599-1600); *Ériphyle, Semiramis, Oreste,* and *Tancrède,* all inspired by Shakespeare's *Hamlet, Prince of Denmark* (pr. c. 1600-1601); *Zaïre,* inspired by Shakespeare's *Othello, the Moor of Venice* (pr. 1604); and *Alzire,* inspired by Dryden's *The Indian Emperor: Or, The Conquest of Mexico by the Spaniards* (pr. 1665, pb. 1667). Although Voltaire was most influenced by Shakespeare, and his numerous literary essays on the English dramatist helped to make Shakespeare known on the Continent, Voltaire did not unreservedly accept Shakespearean drama, as is especially evident in his "Lettre à l'Académie Française" (1776). Yet his contributions in incorporating English dramatic theory into the French theater are the most significant of the eighteenth century and prepared the way for the Romantic drama of the nineteenth century as described in Victor Hugo's preface to *Cromwell* (1827), particularly in the emphasis on action rather than introspection.

Voltaire did not limit his subjects to classical sources, but widened the geographical boundaries of the tragedy. *Zaïre* is situated in Jerusalem, *Alzire* in Peru, *Zulime* in Africa, *Mahomet the Prophet* in Mecca, *The Orphan of China* in China, *Les Scythes* in Scythia, and *Les Guèbres* in Syria. There is, however, very little local color in these plays other than the settings and the names. Heralding Romanticism years before it would flourish, Voltaire used French national themes and names for his inspiration. *Zaïre* recalls the illustrious family of Lusignan; *Adélaïde du Guesclin* is based on fourteenth century Breton history; and *Tancrède,* in the style of historical romance, returns to the courtly love theme. The critic Thurston Wheeler Russel maintains that one of Voltaire's greatest literary innovations was his development of the heroic romance in the manner of

Dryden; Voltaire's plays in this genre, especially *Zaïre, Alzire, Tancrède,* and *Mérope,* almost operatic in nature, remain among his most popular.

Less successful in comedy than in tragedy, Voltaire, who greatly admired Molière, declared that comedy exists mainly to provoke laughter among the spectators. He did, however, allow tearful situations in his comedies, and his best comedies are sentimental in the vein of the *comédie larmoyante* ("weeping comedy"), as in, for example, *The Prodigal* and *The Highland Girl.* Voltaire intended comedy to be a faithful portrayal of manners and to rest on mistaken identity, historically two of the most important comic devices. His own plays illustrate these techniques and thus were rather successful in continuing the tradition of Molière and the classical comedy of Plautus and Terence. Critic Raymond Navès sees caricature as Voltaire's main accomplishment in comedy, and the use of prose in *The Highland Girl* as more effective than his ten-syllable verses in *The Prodigal* and *Nanine.*

Biography • François-Marie Arouet, known to his contemporaries and to posterity as Voltaire, was born on November 21, 1694, very likely in Paris, though there is some evidence for Châtenay. His father, a former notary, was a well-to-do bourgeois. Like Jean-Jacques Rousseau, Voltaire grew up without a mother, whom he lost when he was seven years old. From 1704 to 1711, he attended the aristocratic Collège Louis-le-Grand, where he received an excellent classical formation from the Jesuits. Despite his later anticlericalism, Voltaire maintained several attachments to his Jesuit teachers, among them Father Thoulié, who received him into the Académie Française in 1746. Voltaire also formed lasting bonds with his companions, especially Charles Augustin Feriol, comte d'Argental, his lifelong friend.

(Library of Congress)

Voltaire's father envisioned a career in law for his son, who felt no attraction to it, and preferred writing. He frequented the frivolous Society of the Temple, and in 1713 was exiled to Holland by his father, beginning a series of travels and romantic liaisons that were to characterize his life. At the same time, he began his literary career with an ode to commemorate the construction of Notre-Dame, soon to be followed by a play that was declared insulting to the Regent Philippe of Orléans, for which he was imprisoned in the Bastille in 1718. An expert in the art of flattery, he soon learned to court royal favor, and was well received until an argument with Gui Auguste de Rohan-Chabot, who had him beaten, necessitated exile in England. Thedore Besterman is of the opinion that this upsetting experience fueled Voltaire's lifelong passion for social justice.

Voltaire's three years in England, from 1726 to 1729, were important in his intellectual development. He became acquainted with new ideas on political economy and literary theory through association with Lord Henry St. John Bolingbroke, already his friend in France, Lord Charles Mordaunt Peterborough, Swift, Pope, John Gay, Edward Young, George Berkeley, and Samuel Clarke. He was later to popularize the new trend in thought in his *Lettres philosophiques* (1734; originally published as *Letters Concerning the English Nation*, 1733, also as *Philosophical Letters*; 1961). On his return he became acquainted with Mme Émilie du Châtelet, with whom he maintained an erratic liaison until her death in 1749. He lived most of the time at her château of Cirey, and there, under her influence, became interested in experimental science and Isaac Newton's physics. After her death, he spent two years, from 1750 to 1752, at the court of Frederick II of Prussia. Frederick had previously received Voltaire warmly, but gradually their relationship cooled, and it ceased in 1757.

From 1743 until his death, Voltaire's companion and mistress was his niece Mme Denis, with whom he settled at the estate of Les Délices, and at Ferney, near Geneva, from 1755 to 1778. The Calvinist pastors were not anxious to receive him among them, particularly since his anticlericalism was strongest at this time. He won his battles with them and with Rousseau on the theater, and in 1765 successfully rehabilitated the name of Jean Calas, who had been wrongly executed, and later the family Sirven and the Chevalier de la Barre (who was also killed), all victims of religious fanaticism. Voltaire created a model village at Ferney and became its provident patriarch. In 1778, he returned in triumph to Paris for the performance of his last tragedy, *Irène*. He died there on May 30, 1778, after having received the Sacraments of the Church. His nephew Father Mignot gave him secret Christian burial near Troyes. In 1791, the revolutionaries carried his remains in triumph to Paris, where they were placed in the Pantheon.

Analysis • Voltaire's theater is characterized both by innovation and by certain recurring themes. He draws primarily on the French classical theater, and uses techniques popularized by his contemporaries, such as Denis Diderot's bourgeois drama and heroic romance, and his rival Prosper Jolyot de Crébillon's recognition scenes. Voltaire's sources of inspiration include exotic settings such as China in *The Orphan of China*, America in *Alzire*, and French national history, as in *Adélaïde du Guesclin*. At the same time, he uses Greek sources in five plays: *Oedipus*, *Ériphyle*, *Mérope*, *Semiramis*, and *Oreste*. In these plays, the ancient theme of the avenging deity is uppermost, yet as early as *Oedipus* (1718), Voltaire displays his humanism in showing the hero as an innocent victim who protests his independence. Voltaire wrote four plays of Roman inspiration: *Brutus*, *La Mort de César*, *Rome sauvée*, and *Le Triumvirat*. Less successful than his Greek-inspired plays, they extol a patriotic and republican theme, to which Voltaire himself was not very committed.

In the classical tradition, Voltaire kept alive the three unities as well as *vraisemblance* (verisimilitude), and *bienséance* (propriety). Yet his innovative emphasis on action, the influence of Shakespeare, and his use of recognition scenes evidence his inexact observance of the classical rules of theater. Many plays fail in unity of action, as in, for example, his first play, *Oedipus*: The addition of yet one more character to the action, Jocasta's former lover Philoctetes, overdoes an already complex plot. The classical unity that Voltaire most frequently violates is that of place, as in *Mahomet the Prophet*, *Mérope*, and *Alzire*. In these plays, to give an appearance of exactness, Voltaire brings unlikely characters together in one location. Influenced by the English theater, at times Voltaire disregards the classical and contemporary French taboo against violence onstage, as in the murder scene in *Mahomet the Prophet*. (Such a case is an exception, however, since Voltaire generally preserves the French sense of delicacy with the classical device of a messenger who reports an act of violence.) Voltaire often fails in verisimilitude: The sudden change in Genghis Khan (in *The Orphan of China*) from a barbarous destroyer to a benevolent protector is unlikely; Semiramis's failure to recognize Assur as her husband's murderer is equally unbelievable; Mérope's blindness to her son's presence is improbable.

This lack of strict adherence to classical rules reflects Voltaire's changing dramatic theories. Although in many ways he resembles Racine, unlike that pillar of French classicism Voltaire subordinates psychological analysis to action, which in turn gives rise to an emphasis on staging and decoration—all highly untraditional at that time. Voltaire's later plays often resemble operatic performances. With *Tancrède*, Voltaire succeeded in eliminating spectators from the stage, where they had been accustomed to sit and witness characters discuss action that had taken place previously or offstage. The action in Voltaire's plays depends mainly on the *coup de théâtre* (an abrupt turn of events), surprise, and unexpected recognition scenes. Most frequently a child lost in early years is reunited with his or her parents. For example, in *Mahomet the Prophet*, Séide and Palmire, who plan on marrying, learn that they are brother and sister, the children of Mahomet's rival, Zopire. In *Mérope*, a suspected murderer is discovered to be Egisthe, Mérope's lost child, and Zaïre, about to renounce her religion for her lover, discovers that she is Lusignan's daughter. Even Voltaire's comedies use this device; the impoverished Miss Lindon in *The Highland Girl* is really Montross's daughter, who was taken from him at age five.

Although Voltaire made action primary in his plays, and used a variety of sources for his inspiration, he actually rewrote the same play again and again and shows a pattern in his themes. Some are hardly distinguishable: *Ériphyle* and *Semiramis*; *Zaïre*, *Alzire*, and *Mahomet the Prophet*; *Mérope* and *Mahomet the Prophet*. Because of Voltaire's belief in the theater as a moralizing device, he intended his plays to instruct spectators. In the theater, as elsewhere, Voltaire directed all his efforts against intolerance in religion and injustice in government. As early as *Oedipus*, Voltaire cited the danger in the power of priests. *Alzire* and *Zaïre* show the superiority of natural religion. In *Alzire*, the uninstructed Zamore is more compassionate than the inflexible Gusman, who compels the Indians to accept Christianity. *Mahomet the Prophet* is itself a fanatic apology for tolerance, falsifying history to present Muḥammad as a merciless murderer and adulterer. Although Voltaire dedicated his play to Pope Benedict XIV, its anticlerical intent was not lost on the critics, among them Voltaire's rival Crébillon, at that time a censor, who outlawed the play.

Voltaire's character analysis is for the most part rather superficial; his characters develop through action rather than through expression of their thoughts or through conversation. They resemble one another from play to play, usually revealing only one side, so that each character represents a human quality: Mérope and Idamé are maternal love; Alzire and Zaïre, romantic love; Zamti, patriotism; Mahomet and Polyphonte, tyranny. Yet owing to Voltaire's genius, his characters manage to be human and touching. They are usually victims of love, be it maternal or romantic, and are often on the verge of committing incest before the recognition scene. In many cases, Voltaire the humanist prevents his tragedy from becoming tragic (in the classical sense), for he spares the innocent victim, as in *The Orphan of China*. René Pomeau sees *Oedipus* as marking the end of traditional French tragedy, as the victim accuses the gods. In fact, it is for this humanizing dimension that Voltaire's plays are best appreciated, for he brought into a theater dominated by classical *reason* the Romantic trait of feeling, *sensibilité*, that was to characterize it in future years.

Oedipus • *Oedipus*, says Pomeau, is important because it is Voltaire's first tragedy, and among his best. In it, Voltaire announced the themes that he would spend his life proclaiming: justice and tolerance. Voltaire had begun the play before his imprisonment in the Bastille in 1718 and finished it there. It enjoyed a run of forty-five performances and featured two of the best-known actors of the time in the leading roles: Dufresne as Oedipus and Mlle Demarès as Jocasta. The play is obviously based on Sophocles' *Oidipous Tyrannos* (c. 429 B.C.E.; *Oedipus Tyrannus*, 1715), though at the actors' insistence Voltaire added the love scenes. The play was an enormous success, yet was attacked by critics as a plagiarism of Corneille, to which it does have strong resemblances. Voltaire responded to critics with several *Lettres philosophiques*, which form an excellent documentation of his literary views at the time.

Although Voltaire uses the story of Oedipus's search for the truth as narrated by Sophocles, like Corneille (whom he imitated), he complicates the plot with extraneous events. Such is the introduction of Philoctetes into the action of the story. Jocasta's former lover is accused of killing Laius but denies the charge. Although he still loves Jocasta, he is not jealous of Oedipus, who is noble and has saved the city. Oedipus in turn respects Philoctetes and even wishes to have him as his successor. Oedipus learns his identity from Phorbas, originally Laius's companion, and from Icarus, his former guardian. As in Sophocles' play, Oedipus blinds himself and Jocasta commits suicide.

Voltaire shows his anticlerical tendencies in act 2, scene 5, in which he points out the dangerous effects of priestly power. Voltaire also shows his humanism, differing from Sophocles in presenting an Oedipus who is not submissive to fate but assertive in protesting his innocence. Jocasta, too, defends Oedipus in act 4, scene 3; her suicide at the end is less convincing than her belief in justice. According to Pomeau, Voltaire's *Oedipus* is a new dimension in the theater, actually bringing to an end the traditional concept of tragedy.

Zaïre • *Zaïre* has always been one of the most popular of Voltaire's plays, with thirty-one performances in its first season alone and a long time in the repertory of the Comédie-Française. Voltaire's aim was that there should be "nothing so Turkish, nothing so Christian, so full of love, so tender, so furious," as *Zaïre*. He added the love element lacking in the unsuccessful *Ériphyle*; in fact, as Jean-Baptiste Rousseau commented, passion seems to triumph over grace. Set in Jerusalem, it shows the widening geographical frontiers of Voltaire's drama.

Zaïre is a captive of the sultan Orosmane, who loves her and wishes to marry her. She has abandoned her Christian faith for him and has forgotten Nerestan, who returns with her ransom. Orosmane, however, refuses to part with her or with the aged Lusignan. Lusignan, about to die, recognizes Nerestan and Zaïre as his lost children and as his last request wants to see Zaïre convert to Christianity. She accepts, though she does not wish to abandon Orosmane. He intercepts a letter that seems to indicate that Zaïre has betrayed him for Nerestan, and following a secret rendezvous, unknowingly stabs Zaïre. When he discovers his error, Orosmane frees Nerestan and then kills himself.

Zaïre's Deistic overtones were immediately perceived by the critics. Orosmane is as virtuous as Nerestan because Voltaire wished to show the equality of all beliefs. Zaïre herself states the relativity of religion: Had she been brought up along the Ganges, she would have been a "heathen"; in Paris, a Christian; she is a Muslim in Jerusalem. The play, however, is touching and very human; hence, Voltaire's daring ideas did not prevent its success.

Alzire • *Alzire* also treats the question of true religion, and has always been among the most popular of Voltaire's plays. In *Alzire*, for the first time in the French theater, the scene was set in America—in Peru—and according to critic Theodore Besterman it remains one of the most modern of Voltaire's plays because it deals with the problem of colonization and of "the relations between an occupying power and a subject people." Besterman believes that Voltaire does not solve this problem, but rather shows the triumph of force. This may be the de facto answer, but it is not necessarily the ideal proposed by Voltaire. The play is preceded by a lengthy preface, in which Voltaire declares his purpose: "to discover to what extent the true spirit of religion is superior to the natural virtues." For Voltaire, to harbor this true spirit is not to practice useless rituals, but rather "to consider all men as brothers, to do good and to forgive evil."

The brutal Spanish conqueror Gusman receives the governorship of Peru from his gentle father, Alvarez. Gusman is in love with Alzire, the Aztec king Montezuma's daughter, who refuses the man responsible for the death of her lover Zamore. Zamore, however, is not dead; in fact, he has saved Gusman's father, Alvarez, and returns to avenge the wrong done by Gusman. When Zamore arrives, Alzire has just been married to Gusman to appease the Spaniards. Alzire, though faithful to Gusman, pleads for mercy for Zamore, who in turn attacks Gusman. Both Alzire and Zamore are condemned, but are saved by Gusman's pardon of Zamore. Zamore, inspired by Gusman's gesture of forgiveness, accepts the Christian religion and will live to marry Alzire.

Although Voltaire extolled the virtue of forgiveness, he did not make a convincing case for Gusman's superiority. In fact, Zamore is equally virtuous, and Gusman's sudden change of heart is highly improbable. D'Argental, Voltaire's constant friend, found fault with the unconvincing ending, as do more modern critics, among them Pomeau and Besterman. Once again, however, Voltaire's play has charm because of the touching love story it recounts and the deeply human character of Alzire.

Mérope • The popular subject of *Mérope* is based on a nonextant tragedy of Euripides. Voltaire used the play by Francesco Scipione Maffei (*Mérope*, 1713), performed in Paris in 1717, as his main source. First planning a translation, Voltaire worked on the tragedy from 1736 to 1743, and dedicated it to Maffei. It was the best received of all Voltaire's plays, and broke all records in its proceeds. This was surprising, as the play has no love element other than maternal affection directly inspired by Racine's *Andromaque* (pr. 1667; *Andromache*, 1674). *Mérope* also repeats the theme of *Mahomet the Prophet* in Polyphonte, tyrant of Messène, who insists on blind obedience and fear in his followers. Besterman notes a Rousseauian element in Egisthe, "the virtuous man brought up far from cities and courts in an atmosphere of rustic simplicity."

Polyphonte, tyrant of Messène, wishes to marry Mérope, widow of the slain Cresphonte. She, however, detests Polyphonte and yearns only for the return of her lost son Egisthe. Egisthe has in fact returned, but his identity is unknown both to him and to Mérope, and he is accused of being the murderer of Mérope's lost son. Although Mérope wishes to punish Egisthe, the alleged murderer, at the same time she feels tenderness for him. The mystery of his identity is solved by Narbas, Egisthe's guardian; Polyphonte insists on punishing the young stranger, but on learning the truth, Polyphonte agrees to spare Egisthe on the condition that Mérope marry him and Egisthe swear homage to him. Egisthe kills the tyrant and becomes king in his place.

The critic Fernand Vial ascribes the popularity of this tragedy to its simplicity. Voltaire's contemporaries also hailed it as a model of true classical drama, although in fact it is not tragic, since the innocent triumph over the guilty. It is free from Voltaire's usual complications, however, though it does violate unity of place and has several improbable situations, such as the delays in recognition. Nevertheless, it is human and touching, and shows Voltaire's greatest merit as a dramatist: a sense of warmth and feeling, *sensibilité*.

Other major works

LONG FICTION: *Zadig: Ou, La Destinée, Histoire orientale*, 1748 (originally as *Memnon: Histoire orientale*, 1747; *Zadig: Or, The Book of Fate*, 1749); *Le Micromégas*, 1752 (*Micromegas*, 1753); *Histoire des voyages de Scarmentado*, 1756 (*The History of the Voyages of Scarmentado*, 1757; also as *History of Scarmentado's Travels*, 1961); *Candide: Ou, L'Optimisme*, 1759 (*Candide: Or, All for the Best*, 1759; also as *Candide: Or, The Optimist*, 1762; also as *Candide: Or, Optimism*, 1947); *L'Ingénu*, 1767 (*The Pupil of Nature*, 1771; also as *Ingenuous*, 1961); *L'Homme aux quarante écus*, 1768 (*The Man of Forty Crowns*, 1768); *La Princesse de Babylone*, 1768 (*The Princess of Babylon*, 1769).

SHORT FICTION: *Le Monde comme il va*, 1748 (revised as *Babouc: Ou, Le Monde comme il va*, 1749; *Babouc: Or, The World as It Goes*, 1754; also as *The World as It Is: Or, Babouc's Vision*, 1929); *Memnon: Ou, La Sagesse humaine*, 1749 (*Memnon: Or, Human Wisdom*, 1961); *La Lettre d'un Turc*, 1750; *Le Blanc et le noir*, 1764 (*The Two Genies*, 1895); *Jeannot et Colin*, 1764 (*Jeannot and Colin*, 1929); *L'Histoire de Jenni*, 1775; *Les Oreilles du Comte de Chesterfield*, 1775 (*The Ears of Lord Chesterfield and Parson Goodman*, 1826).

NONFICTION: *An Essay upon the Civil Wars of France . . . and Also upon the Epick Poetry of the European Nations from Homer Down to Milton*, 1727; *La Henriade*, 1728 (*Henriade*, 1732); *Histoire de Charles XII*, 1731 (*The History of Charles XII*, 1732); *Le Temple du goût*, 1733 (*The Temple of Taste*, 1734); *Letters Concerning the English Nation*, 1733; *Lettres philosophiques*, 1734 (originally published in English as *Letters Concerning the English Nation*, 1733; also as *Philosophical Letters*, 1961); *Discours de métaphysique*, 1736; *Éléments de la philosophie de Newton*, 1738 (*The Elements of Sir Isaac Newton's Philosophy*, 1738); *Discours en vers sur l'homme* 1738-1752 (*Discourses in Verse on Man*, 1764); *Vie de Molière*, 1739; *Le Siècle de Louis XIV*, 1751 (*The Age of Louis XIV*, 1752); *Essai sur les mœurs et l'esprit des nations*, 1756, 1763 (*The General History and State of Europe*, 1754, 1759); *Traité sur la tolérance*, 1763 (*A Treatise on Religious Toleration*, 1764); *Dictionnaire philosophique portatif*, 1764, enlarged 1769 (as *La Raison par alphabet*, also known as *Dictionnaire philosophique; A Philosophical Dictionary for the Pocket*, 1765; also as *Philosophical Dictionary*, 1945, enlarged 1962); *Commentaires sur le théâtre de Pierre Corneille*, 1764; *Avis au public sur les parracides imputés aux calas et aux Sirven*, 1775; *Correspondence*, 1953-1965 (102 volumes).

MISCELLANEOUS: *The Works of M. de Voltaire*, 1761-1765 (35 volumes), 1761-1781 (38 volumes); *Candide and Other Writings*, 1945; *The Portable Voltaire*, 1949; *Candide, Zadig, and Selected Stories*, 1961; *The Complete Works of Voltaire*, 1968-1977 (135 volumes; in French).

Bibliography

Besterman, Theodore. *Voltaire*. 3d ed. Chicago: University of Chicago Press, 1976. This biography by a Voltaire scholar provides coverage of the writer's life and works. Bibliography and index.

Bird, Stephen. *Reinventing Voltaire: The Politics of Commemoration in Nineteenth Century France.* Oxford, England: Voltaire Foundation, 2000. An examination of the critical response to Voltaire, particularly in the nineteenth century. Bibliography and indexes.

Carlson, Marvin A. *Voltaire and the Theatre of the Eighteenth Century.* Westport, Conn.: Greenwood Press, 1998. An examination of the French theater in the eighteenth century and Voltaire's role. Bibliography and index.

Gray, John. *Voltaire.* Great Philosophers 19. New York: Routledge, 1999. A biography of Voltaire that covers his life and works, while concentrating on his philosophy. Bibliography.

Knapp, Bettina Liebowitz. *Voltaire Revisited.* New York: Twayne, 2000. A basic biography of Voltaire that describes his life and works. Bibliography and index.

Mason, Haydn, ed. *Studies for the Tercentenary of Voltaire's Birth, 1694-1994.* Oxford, England: Voltaire Foundation, 1994. Contains essays on Voltaire's works and life, including one on the French theater in the 1690's. Bibliography.

Irma M. Kashuba

Wendy Wasserstein

Born: Brooklyn, New York; October 18, 1950

Principal drama • *Any Woman Can't,* pr. 1973; *Happy Birthday, Montpelier Pizz-zazz,* pr. 1974; *When Dinah Shore Ruled the Earth,* pr. 1975 (with Christopher Durang); *Uncommon Women and Others,* pr. 1975 (one act), pr. 1977 (two acts), pb. 1978; *Isn't It Romantic,* pr. 1981, revised pr. 1983, pb. 1984; *Tender Offer,* pr. 1983, pb. 2000 (one act); *The Man in a Case,* pr., pb. 1986 (one act; adaptation of Anton Chekhov's short story); *Miami,* pr. 1986 (musical); *The Heidi Chronicles,* pr., pb. 1988; *The Heidi Chronicles and Other Plays,* pb. 1990; *The Sisters Rosensweig,* pr. 1992, pb. 1993; *An American Daughter,* pr. 1997, pb. 1998; *Waiting for Philip Glass,* pr., pb. 1998 (inspired by William Shakespeare's Sonnet 94); *The Festival of Regrets,* pr. 1999 (libretto); *Old Money,* pr. 2000, pb. 2002; *Seven One-Act Plays,* pb. 2000

Other literary forms • Wendy Wasserstein, though best known for her plays, is the author of several teleplays, including *The Sorrows of Gin* (1979), an adaptation of John Cheever's short story, and *An American Daughter* (2000), an adaptation of her play. She also has written several unproduced film scripts. Her essays, which have appeared in numerous periodicals, including *Esquire* and *New York Woman,* have been published in two collections, *Bachelor Girls* (1990) and *Shiksa Goddess* (2001).

Achievements • Wendy Wasserstein has been hailed as the foremost theatrical chronicler of the lives of women of her generation. Her plays, steeped in her unique brand of humor, are moving, sometimes wrenching explorations of women's struggle for identity and fulfillment in a world of rapidly shifting social, sexual, and political mores. Most often against the backdrop of the burgeoning feminist movement, her characters navigate through obstacle courses of expectations—those of their parents, their lovers, their siblings, their friends, and, ultimately, themselves. They seek answers to fundamental questions: how to find meaning in life and how to strike a balance between the need to connect and the need to be true to oneself. Wasserstein's works, which deftly pair wit and pathos, satire and sensitivity, have garnered numerous honors, including the Pulitzer Prize, the Tony (Antoinette Perry) Award, the New York Drama Critics Circle Award, the Outer Critics Circle Award, and the Susan Smith Blackburn Prize.

Biography • Wendy Wasserstein was born on October 18, 1950, in Brooklyn, New York. She was the fourth and youngest child of Morris W. Wasserstein, a successful textile manufacturer, and Lola (Schleifer) Wasserstein, a housewife and nonprofessional dancer, both Jewish émigrés from central Europe. When she was thirteen, Wasserstein's family moved to Manhattan, where she attended the Calhoun School, an all-girl academy at which she discovered that she could get excused from gym class by writing the annual mother-daughter fashion show. Some years later, at Mount Holyoke, an elite Massachusetts women's college, a friend persuaded Wasserstein, a history major, to take a playwriting course at nearby Smith College. Encouraged by her instructor, she devoted much of her junior year, which she spent at Amherst College, performing in campus musicals before returning to complete her B.A. degree at Mount Holyoke in 1971.

Upon graduating, Wasserstein moved back to New York City, where she studied playwriting with Israel Horovitz and Joseph Heller at City College (where she later earned an M.A.) and held a variety of odd jobs to pay her rent. In 1973, her play *Any Woman Can't* was produced Off-Broadway at Playwrights Horizons, prompting her to accept admission to the Yale School of Drama and to turn down the Columbia Business School, which had simultaneously offered her admission.

It was at Yale University, where she earned her M.F.A. degree in 1976, that Wasserstein's first hit play, *Uncommon Women and Others*, was conceived as a one-act. Ultimately expanded, it was given a workshop production at the prestigious National Playwrights Conference at the O'Neill Theater Center in Connecticut, a well-known launching pad for many successful playwrights. Indeed, in 1977, the Phoenix Theater's production of *Uncommon Women and Others* opened Off-Broadway at the Marymount Manhattan Theater. Although some critics objected to the play's lack of traditional plot, most praised Wasserstein's gifts as a humorist and a social observer.

By 1980, Wasserstein, established as one of the United States' most promising young playwrights, was commissioned by the Phoenix Theater to write *Isn't It Romantic* for its 1980-1981 season. The play's mixed reviews prompted Wasserstein to rework it under the guidance of director Gerald Gutierrez and André Bishop, artistic director of Playwrights Horizons. There, with a stronger narrative line and more in-depth character development, it opened in 1983 to widespread praise.

In the meantime, Wasserstein had been at work on several new pieces—among them a one-act play, *Tender Offer*, which was produced at Ensemble Studio Theater, and, collaborating with Jack Feldman and Bruce Sussman, a musical, *Miami*, which was presented as a work-in-progress at Playwrights Horizons in 1986. In 1988, one of Wasserstein's most ambitious works, *The Heidi Chronicles*, which had been previously performed in workshop at the Seattle Repertory Theatre, had its New York premiere at Playwrights Horizons. It moved quickly to the larger Plymouth Theater on Broadway, where it opened to mostly positive critical response. The play earned for Wasserstein the Pulitzer Prize, the Tony Award, and virtually every New York theater award. Wasserstein's eagerly awaited *The Sisters Rosensweig* opened at the Mitzi E. Newhouse Theater at Lincoln Center in the fall of 1992. Receiving widespread critical acclaim, the piece augmented her already prominent presence on the American dramatic scene.

Wasserstein has branched out from her typical output to participate in several innovative theater events. In 1998 she was one of seven playwrights contributing one-act plays based on Shakespearean sonnets to the production of *Love's Fire*. In 1999, she was one of three playwrights creating librettos for *Central Park*, a New York City Opera production presented at Glimmerglass Opera and Lincoln Center. Her libretto, "The Festival of Regrets," was scored by Deborah Drattell, composer-in-residence for New York City Opera and Glimmerglass Opera.

At the age of forty-eight, Wasserstein became a single mother after treatment with fertility drugs. Her daughter, Lucy Jane, weighed only one pound, twelve ounces at birth. Wasserstein's essay about her struggle to conceive and her daughter's birth is one of the most moving pieces in *Shiksa Goddess*.

Analysis • Wendy Wasserstein's plays are, for the most part, extremely consistent in their emphasis on character, their lack of classical structure, and their use of humor to explore or accompany serious, often poignant themes. Throughout her career, Wasserstein's central concern has been the role of women—particularly white, upper-middle-class, educated women—in contemporary society. Though her plays are suffused with uproarious humor, her typical characters are individuals engaged in a struggle to carve out an identity and a place for themselves in a society that has left them feeling, at worst, stranded and desolate and, at best, disillusioned. This is not to say that Wasserstein's worldview is bleak. Rather, the note of slightly skewed optimism with which she characteristically ends her works, along with her prevailing wit, lends them an air of levity and exuberance that often transcends her sober themes.

These themes—loneliness, isolation, and a profound desire for meaning in life—are examined by Wasserstein chiefly through character. One of the playwright's great strengths is her ability to poke fun at her characters without subjecting them to ridicule or scorn. Her women and men, with all their faults and foibles, are warmly and affectionately rendered. They engage their audience's empathy as they make their way through the mazes of their lives, trying to connect and to be of consequence in the world.

Wasserstein is a unique and important voice in contemporary American theater. As a woman writing plays about women, she has been a groundbreaker, though never self-consciously so. Despite her often thin plot lines, she finds and captures the drama inherent in the day-to-day choices confronting the women of her generation. As a humorist, too, Wasserstein is unquestionably a virtuoso. Her ability to see the absurdity of even her own most deeply held convictions, and to hold them deeply nevertheless, is perhaps the most engaging and distinctive of her writing's many strengths.

Wasserstein is best known for her four full-length, professional plays, *Uncommon Women and Others, Isn't It Romantic, The Heidi Chronicles*, and *The Sisters Rosensweig*. The first three plays have in common their episodic structure and non-plot-driven narrative. In each of the three, scenes unfold to reveal aspects of character.

Uncommon Women and Others • *Uncommon Women and Others* begins with five former college friends assessing their lives as they reunite six years after graduation. The body of the play is a flashback to their earlier life together at a small women's college under the often conflicting influences of the school's traditional "feminine" rituals and etiquette and the iconoclasm of the blossoming women's movement. In each of the two time frames, events are largely contexts for discussions in which Wasserstein's women use one another as sounding boards, each one testing and weighing her hopes, fears, expectations, and achievements against those of her friends.

Isn't It Romantic • Similarly, in *Isn't It Romantic*, two former college friends, Janie Blumberg, a freelance writer, and Harriet Cornwall, a corporate M.B.A., move through their postcollege lives, weighing marriage and children against independence and the life choices of their mothers against their own. The play climaxes at the point where the two women diverge: Harriet, who has formerly decried marriage, accepts a suitor's proposal out of fear of being alone, and Janie chooses to remain unattached and to seek happiness within herself.

The Heidi Chronicles • *The Heidi Chronicles*, though more far-reaching in scope, is also a character-driven play. Here, Wasserstein narrows her focus to one woman, Heidi Holland, but through her reflects the changing social and political mores of more than two decades. From the mid-1960's to the late 1980's, Heidi, like Wasserstein's earlier characters, struggles to find her identity. Moving through settings ranging from women's consciousness-raising meetings and protests to power lunches in trendy restaurants and Yuppie baby showers, Wasserstein's Heidi functions as, in her words, a "highly-informed spectator" who never quite seems to be in step with the prescribed order of the day. In a pivotal scene, Heidi, now an art-history professor, delivers a luncheon lecture entitled "Women, Where Are We Going?" Her speech, which disintegrates into a seeming nervous breakdown, ends with Heidi confessing that she feels "stranded": "And I thought the whole point was that we wouldn't feel stranded," she concludes, "I thought the whole point was that we were in this together."

Isolation and loneliness and, contrastingly, friendship and family are themes that run throughout these three earlier plays. Heidi's wish, expressed in that luncheon speech, is for the kind of solidarity that exists among the women in *Uncommon Women and Others*, who, while constantly comparing their lives, are not competitive in the sense of putting one another down. On the contrary, they are fervent in their praise and support of one another, a family unto themselves. Janie and Harriet, in *Isn't It Romantic*, share a relationship that is much the same until something comes between them, Harriet's decision to marry a man she hardly knows because he makes her feel "like [she has] a family." Heidi, on the other hand, at the point when she makes her speech, has no close women friends. Presumably, they are all off having babies or careers. Her decision, at the play's end, to adopt a Panamanian baby girl, thereby creating a family of her own, is much akin to Janie Blumberg's decision finally to unpack her crates in her empty apartment at the end of *Isn't It Romantic* and make a home for herself.

This desire on the part of Wasserstein's characters for a family and a place to belong has at its root the desire for self-affirmation. It is evident in the refrain that echoes throughout *Uncommon Women and Others*, "When we're twenty-five [thirty, forty, forty-five], we're going to be incredible," as well as in Janie Blumberg's invocation, "I am," borrowed from her mother, Tasha. Though failures by the standards of some, Janie, Heidi, and the others can be seen as heroic in their resilience and in the tenacity with which they cling to their ideals—however divergent from the reality at hand.

Wasserstein's tendency to create characters who resist change can exasperate audiences, as her critics have noted. The women, in particular, who people her plays are often, like Janie with her unpacked crates of furniture, in a state of suspension, waiting for life to begin. In *Uncommon Women and Others*, there is a constant look toward the future for self-substantiation, as there is, to some extent, in Heidi's persistent state of unhappiness. Still, Heidi does ultimately make a choice—to adopt a baby, a step toward the process of growing up, another of Wasserstein's recurrent themes.

One of Wasserstein's greatest gifts is her ability to find and depict the ironies of life. This is evident in each of the three plays' bittersweet final images: the "uncommon women," their arms wrapped around one another, repeating their by now slightly sardonic refrain; Janie, tap-dancing alone in her empty apartment; and Heidi, singing to her new daughter "You Send Me," the song to which she had previously danced with her old flame, Scoop, at his wedding reception. These images are pure Wasserstein. In the face of disappointment, even the disillusionment, of life, her characters manifest a triumph of the spirit and a strength from within that ultimately prevails.

The Sisters Rosensweig • Wasserstein's *The Sisters Rosensweig* is a departure from her earlier plays in a number of ways. Most overt among these differences are the play's international setting (the action takes place in Queen Anne's Gate, London) and its concern with global issues and events. Also of note is the playwright's uncharacteristic use, here, of classical, nonepisodic structure, maintaining unity of time and place: in this case, several days' events in the sitting room of Sara Goode, the play's main character and the eldest of the three sisters for whom the play is named.

Sara shares many of the characteristics of Wasserstein's earlier protagonists—that is, her gender (female), ethnic group (Jewish), social class (upper-middle to upper class), and intelligence quotient (uncommonly high). She is, however, considerably older than her forerunners. *The Sisters Rosensweig* centers on the celebration of Sara's fifty-fourth birthday. This is significant in that Sara, a hugely successful international banker who has been married and divorced several times, does not share the struggle for self-identity carried out by such Wasserstein heroines as Heidi Holland and Janie Blumberg. With a lucrative, challenging career (noteworthily, in a male-dominated field) and a daughter she loves, Sara has achieved, to some degree, the "meaning" in her life that those earlier characters found lacking and sought.

As the play progresses, however, it is revealed that Sara, despite her self-confidence and seeming self-sufficiency, shares with Heidi, Janie, and the others a deep need to connect—to find, create, or reclaim a family. As she fends off and at last gives in to a persistent suitor, Merv Kant, a fake-fur dealer, and plays hostess to her two sisters (Pfeni Rosensweig, a sociopolitical journalist turned travel writer, and "Dr." Gorgeous Teitelbaum, who hosts a radio call-in show), Sara manages, at last, to peel back the layers of defense and reserve that have seen her through two divorces and the rigors of her profession and to rediscover the joys of sisterhood and the revitalizing power of romantic love.

It is not Sara alone who serves Wasserstein in her exploration of her characteristic themes of loneliness, isolation, and the search for true happiness. Pfeni, forty years old, the play's most seemingly autobiographical character, a writer who has been temporarily diverted from her true calling, has been likewise diverted from pursuing "what any normal woman wants" by remaining in a relationship with Geoffrey, a former homosexual. Jilted and distraught over the havoc that acquired immunedeficiency syndrome (AIDS) has played with the lives of his friends, Geoffrey has wooed and won Pfeni, only to leave her in the end to follow his own true nature. Pfeni's ceaseless "wandering" as well as her self-confessed need to write about the hardships of others to fill the emptiness in her own life is much akin to Heidi Holland's position as a "highly informed spectator," waiting for her own life to begin.

The Sisters Rosensweig harks back to Wasserstein's *Isn't It Romantic* in its concerns with the profound role that both mothers and Judaism play in shaping women's lives. Here, Sara rejects, and attempts to cast off, the influences of both. An atheist expatriate in London, she has reinvented her life, purging all memories of her Jewish New York upbringing and her deceased mother's expectations as firmly as she has embraced the habits and speech patterns of her adopted home. Sara's eventual acquiescence to Merv, a New York Jew, along with the rekindling of her emotional attachment to her sisters, represents, at the play's end, an acceptance and embracing of the past that she has worked so hard to put behind her.

Like all Wasserstein's works, *The Sisters Rosensweig* presents characters whose spirit triumphs over their daily heartaches and heartbreaks. While they long to escape the tangled webs of their lives ("If I could only get to Moscow!" Pfeni laments, in one of the play's several nods to Anton Chekhov's *Tri sestry*, pr., pb. 1901, rev. pb. 1904; *Three Sisters*, 1920), they manage to find within themselves and in one another sufficient strength not only to endure but also to prevail.

As in *Uncommon Women and Others*, *Isn't It Romantic*, and *The Heidi Chronicles*, there is a scene in *The Sisters Rosensweig* in which women join together to share a toast, affirming and celebrating their sisterhood and themselves. Be they biological sisters, sorority sisters, or sisters of the world, Wasserstein has made sisters her province. With *The Sis-*

ters Rosensweig, she adds three more portraits to her ever-growing gallery of uncommon women, painted, as always, with insight, wit, and compassion.

Other major works

NONFICTION: *Bachelor Girls*, 1990; *Shiksa Goddess: Or, How I Spent My Forties*, 2001.

SCREENPLAY: *The Object of My Affection*, 1998 (adaptation of Stephen McCauley's novel).

TELEPLAYS: *The Sorrows of Gin*, 1979 (from the story by John Cheever); *"Drive," She Said*, 1984; *The Heidi Chronicles*, 1995 (adaptation of her play); *An American Daughter*, 2000 (adaptation of her play).

CHILDREN'S LITERATURE: *Pamela's First Musical*, 1996.

Bibliography

Bennetts, Leslie. "An Uncommon Dramatist Prepares Her New Work." *The New York Times*, May 24, 1981, p. C1. Written as *Isn't It Romantic* was being previewed, this piece provides a look at Wasserstein's entry into writing and theater during her high school and college years. Wasserstein discusses feminism and women's difficulty in making choices in life. Contains photographs of Wasserstein and Steven Robman, the director of *Isn't It Romantic*.

Berman, Janice. "The Heidi Paradox." *Newsday*, December 22, 1988. This article, in which Wasserstein defines herself as a "feminist," discusses the male and female characters in *The Heidi Chronicles* and refers to Wasserstein's earlier plays. Contains photographs of the playwright, of Joan Allen in *The Heidi Chronicles*, and of Christine Rose and Barbara Barrie in *Isn't It Romantic*.

Nightingale, Benedict. "There Really Is a World Beyond 'Diaper Drama.'" *The New York Times*, January 1, 1984, p. C2. This two-page piece discusses *Isn't It Romantic* in the context of plays that focus on adult children struggling to sever ties with their parents. It compares Wasserstein's play with those of Tina Howe and Christopher Durang. Includes a photograph of the "mothers" in *Isn't It Romantic*.

Rose, Phyllis Jane. "Dear Heidi—An Open Letter to Dr. Holland." *American Theatre* 6 (October, 1989): 26. Written in letter form, this essay is a provocative, in-depth feminist critique of the images of women as presented in *The Heidi Chronicles*. Rose emphasizes Heidi's complicity in surrendering her independence to men, referring to Aeschylus's *Oresteia* (458 B.C.E.; English translation, 1777) as a means of furthering her point. Contains numerous photographs of scenes from *The Heidi Chronicles*.

Shapiro, Walter. "Chronicler of Frayed Feminism." *Time*, March 27, 1989, 90-92. Written shortly after *The Heidi Chronicles* moved to Broadway, this article provides insight into Wasserstein's impetus for writing the play. Shapiro offers a brief look at the feminist subtext throughout Wasserstein's work, as well as a more lengthy examination of her New York roots and family. Contains a full-page photograph of Wasserstein.

Wallace, Carol. "A Kvetch for Our Time," *Sunday News Magazine*, August 19, 1984, 10. Wallace focuses on *Isn't It Romantic* as a chronicle of the women of Wasserstein's generation. She also discusses Wasserstein's overachieving siblings, her New York youth, and her years at Mount Holyoke College. Includes a photograph of the playwright.

Anne Newgarden,
updated by Irene Struthers Rush

Oscar Wilde

Born: Dublin, Ireland; October 16, 1854
Died: Paris, France; November 30, 1900

Principal drama · *Vera: Or, The Nihilists*, pb. 1880, pr. 1883; *The Duchess of Padua*, pb. 1883, pr. 1891; *Lady Windermere's Fan*, pr. 1892, pb. 1893; *Salomé*, pb. 1893 (in French), pb. 1894 (in English), pr. 1896 (in French), pr. 1905 (in English); *A Woman of No Importance*, pr. 1893, pb. 1894; *An Ideal Husband*, pr. 1895, pb. 1899; *The Importance of Being Earnest: A Trivial Comedy for Serious People*, pr. 1895, pb. 1899; *A Florentine Tragedy*, pr. 1906, pb. 1908 (one act, completed by T. Sturge More); *La Sainte Courtisane*, pb. 1908

Other literary forms · Oscar Wilde's character and conversation were in themselves striking enough to gain for him the attention of the reading public, but in addition to playwriting, he practiced all the other literary forms. He began writing poetry at an early age, commemorating the death of his sister Isola with "Requiescat" in 1867 and winning the Newdigate Prize for Poetry at Oxford with *Ravenna* in 1878. Wilde's *Poems* appeared in 1881; *The Sphinx* in 1894; and *The Ballad of Reading Gaol*, his last literary work, in 1898. His efforts in fiction include "The Canterville Ghost" (1887), which was made into a movie in 1943; *The Happy Prince and Other Tales* (1888); *Lord Arthur Savile's Crime and Other Stories* (1891); *A House of Pomegranates* (1891); and his novel, *The Picture of Dorian Gray* (serialized in *Lippincott's Monthly Magazine* in 1890, published in book form in 1891). Oscar Wilde's best-known essays and literary criticism appear in *Intentions* (1891). *De Profundis*, the long letter the imprisoned Wilde wrote to Lord Alfred Douglas, was published in 1905; his collected letters, edited by Rupert Hart-Davies, appeared in 1962.

Achievements · To accuse Oscar Wilde of anything so active-sounding as "achievement" would be an impertinence that the strenuously indolent author would most likely deplore. Yet it must be admitted that Wilde's presence, poses, ideas, and epigrams made him a potent influence, if not on the English literary tradition, at least on the artistic community of his own day. More visibly than any British contemporary, Oscar Wilde personified the doctrines of turn-of-the-century aestheticism—that art existed for its own sake and that one should live so as to make from the raw materials of one's own existence an elegantly finished artifice. Wilde's aestheticism, caricatured by W. S. Gilbert and Sir Arthur Sullivan in their operetta *Patience: Or, Bunthorne's Bride* (1881) and in Robert Smythe Hichens's novel *The Green Carnation* (1894), mingled ideas from his two very different Oxford mentors, John Ruskin and Walter Pater, with the influence of the French Symbolists and, for a time, certain theories of the American painter James McNeill Whistler. However, Wilde's Irish wit and eloquence made the articulation of this intellectual pastiche something distinctively his own.

Wilde's literary works are polished achievements in established modes rather than experiments in thought or form. His poems and plays tend to look across the English Channel to the examples of the Symbolists and the masters of the *pièce bien faite*, though his *Salomé*, a biblical play written in French after the style of the then acclaimed dramatist Maurice Maeterlinck, was to engender a yet more significant work of art,

Richard Strauss's opera of the same title. If they are not intellectually or technically adventurous, however, Wilde's works are incomparable for their talk—talk that tends to be Wilde's own put into the mouths of his characters. The outrageous, elegant, paradoxical conversation volleyed by Wilde's languid verbal athletes have given English literature more quotable tags than have the speeches of any other dramatist save William Shakespeare.

Biography • Oscar Fingal O'Flahertie Wills Wilde was born on October 16, 1854, in Dublin, Ireland, to parents who were among the most colorful members of the Irish gentry. His father, Sir William Wilde, one of the foremost Victorian oculists and surgeons, numbered crowned heads of Europe among his patients. He was equally famed for his archaeological research and his amorous adventures. Oscar Wilde's mother was no less remarkable. Born Jane Francesca Elgee, she gained public notice for the patriotic pieces she published under the pseudonym Speranza. When one of Speranza's essays brought Sir Charles Gavan Duffy, leader of the Young Ireland party, to trial for high treason and sedition, the tall and dramatic authoress rose in court, proclaimed "I alone am the culprit," and on the spot became one of the heroines of Ireland.

This colorful background and his mother's doting attention must have fostered young Wilde's imagination. His mind received more discipline and direction when, through good fortune, he was brought into contact with a series of fine teachers. At Trinity College in Dublin, Wilde's Greek tutor, the Reverend John Pentland Mahaffy, inspired him with a love of Hellenic culture and, by his own witty example, honed and polished the younger man's conversational talents. Next, having won a demyship to Magdalen College, Oxford, in 1874, Wilde encountered Ruskin (then Slade Professor of Art), whose social conscience, love of medieval architecture, and belief in the necessary connection between art and life were to become part of Wilde's own creed. Even more important to Wilde's development was Pater, the skeptical latter-day Epicurean famed for his *Studies in the History of the Renaissance* (1873). In the light of Pater's intellectual advice to the youth of the day, most memorably distilled in his observation that "to burn always with this hard, gemlike flame, to maintain this ecstasy, is success in life," the Oxonian Wilde's famous ambition, "Oh, would that I could live up to my blue china!" seems a less frivolous objective.

In 1879, Wilde went to London, where, sharing rooms with the artist Frank Miles, he became one of the central figures of the aesthetic movement and made the acquaintance of many of the celebrities of the day, particularly the lovely Lily Langtry, whose career as a professional beauty had been launched by Miles's drawings. The tall, heavy, epigrammatic young Wilde was soon known in society for his eccentric dress and his paradoxical wit. Caricatured as Reginald Bunthorne in Gilbert and Sullivan's *Patience*, he became the epitome of aestheticism for the wider public as well. The shrewd producers of the comic opera, which was to go on an American tour, realized that the presence of Bunthorne's prototype would fan the flames of interest, so with their sponsorship, Wilde embarked on an extended tour of the United States that permitted him to see the notable places, to meet the notable people, and having done so, to conclude, "When good Americans die they go to Paris. When bad Americans die they stay in America."

On his return to England after a short stay in Paris, Wilde launched himself on what was to be his period of eminence. He made friends with the painter Whistler and became engaged to the pretty but conventional daughter of an Irish barrister, Constance Lloyd, whom he married in 1883. They had two sons, Cyril and Vyvyan. In need of

(Library of Congress)

funds to finance his luxurious mode of life, he cultivated his literary career, if not in earnest, then at least with more enterprise than he would have wished to acknowledge. He lectured, reviewed books, and for a time edited *The Woman's World.* His prose works appeared in rapid succession: short stories (*Lord Arthur Savile's Crime and Other Stories, The Happy Prince and Other Tales, A House of Pomegranates*), a novel (*The Picture of Dorian Gray*), and a collection of critical essays (*Intentions*).

With his fiction, Wilde solidly established his reputation in the world of letters, but his great period of financial success began only when he turned to writing for the popular theater. Although he found the enforced discipline of playwriting difficult and never regarded his social comedies as anything more than well-crafted potboilers, Wilde managed in a span of three years to write four plays that paid him exceedingly well and made him even more famous. *Lady Windermere's Fan* (premiering in February, 1892) was followed by *A Woman of No Importance* (April, 1893), *An Ideal Husband* (January, 1895), and *The Importance of Being Earnest* (February, 1895). After completing *Lady Windermere's Fan*, Wilde went to France, where he wrote *Salomé*, a poetic drama intended to make his artistic reputation on the Continent and at home. Wilde offered the title role in that play to Sarah Bernhardt, who accepted and began rehearsals for a London production that was never staged: The Lord Chamberlain banned it for violating the old law forbidding the theatrical representation of biblical characters.

Having reached its zenith, Wilde's star rapidly sank to oblivion in the spring of 1895. Since 1891, Wilde had been friends, and more than friends, with the handsome, talented, spoiled, unstable Lord Alfred Douglas, a younger son of the eighth marquess of Queensbury. The relationship was not discreet. Lord Alfred took pleasure in flaunting himself in the role of minion to the celebrated Wilde and in flouting the authority of his father. As his letters reveal, Wilde in his turn expressed his feelings for the elegant youth whose "slim gilt soul walks between passion and poetry" with his customary extravagance. Finally, in what was to be one of the most perverse and distasteful interludes in the history of English jurisprudence, Wilde was provoked to sue the ferocious marquess for criminal libel when that rash peer had culminated a campaign of harassment by leaving at Wilde's club a card bearing the words "to Oscar Wilde posing as a somdomite [sic]."

For his defense, Queensbury collected a small parade of blackmailers and male prostitutes to testify to the accuracy of his epithet. Unwisely persisting in his suit, Wilde failed, on Queensbury's acquittal, to seize his chance to flee the country. Having lost his battle with the marquess, Wilde in turn was arrested, tried, and ultimately convicted for practicing "the love that dares not tell its name." He was sentenced to two years at hard labor.

Wilde's twenty-four months of imprisonment were a continuous mortification of body, mind, and spirit. He had lost his honor, his position, his fortune, and his family. Although he was to write one more fine work, *The Ballad of Reading Gaol*, his life was behind him. Released from prison on May 19, 1897, he left England behind as well. Under the name Sebastian Melmoth, Wilde resided abroad, principally in France and Italy, until his death in Paris in 1900.

Analysis • Oscar Wilde completed seven plays during his life, and for the purpose of discussion, these works can be divided into two groups: comedies and serious works. The four social comedies Wilde wrote for the commercial theater of his day, *Lady Windermere's Fan, A Woman of No Importance, An Ideal Husband,* and *The Importance of Being Earnest,* brought him money and prestige but not artistic satisfaction. There were three plays intended as serious works of art: *Vera, The Duchess of Padua,* and *Salomé.* None of these three plays gained popular regard, critical acclaim, or theatrical success in Wilde's lifetime.

One can disregard the first two serious plays and lose little by the omission. *Vera,* published when Wilde was only twenty-five, is an apprentice piece that unsuccessfully mingles revolutionary Russian politics (particularly ill-timed, for Czar Alexander II had recently been assassinated, and the consort of his successor was sister to Alexandra, wife of the prince of Wales), improbable psychology, creaky melodrama, and what was already Wilde's dramatic forte: witty, ironic speech. *The Duchess of Padua* is a derivative verse drama in the intricate, full-blown style that worked so well in the hands of the Jacobeans and has failed so dismally for their many and often talented imitators. When read, the play has its fine moments, but even at its best, it is nothing more than a good piece of imitation. In *Salomé,* however, Wilde offered the world a serious drama of unquestionable distinction, a work that further enriched Western culture by providing a libretto for Richard Strauss's fine opera of the same title.

Salomé • The English-speaking public, to whom Wilde's four comedies are familiar enough, is less likely to have read or seen performed his *Salomé,* yet this biblical extrapolation, with its pervasive air of overripe sensuality, is of all of his plays the one most characteristic of its age and most important to the European cultural tradition. Wilde wrote his poetic drama in France, and in French, during the autumn of 1891. Wilde's command of the French language was not idiomatic but fluent in the schoolroom style.

This very limitation became an asset when he chose to cast his play in the stylized, ritualistic mold set by the Belgian playwright Maeterlinck, whose works relied heavily on repetition, parallelism, and chiming effect—verbal traits equally characteristic of a writer who thinks in English but translates into French. Like the language, the biblical source of the story is bent to Wilde's purposes. In the New Testament accounts of the death of John the Baptist (or Jokanaan, as he is called in the play), Salomé, the eighteen-year-old princess of Judea, is not held responsible for John's death; rather, blame for the prophet's death is laid on Salomé's mother, Herodias. Furthermore, as Wilde's literary executor, Robert Ross, and a number of other critics have observed, Wilde's Herod is a synthesis of a handful of biblical Herods and tetrarchs. Although Wilde's license with the language and sources of his play is sometimes deprecated, it should not be faulted. As a poetic dramatist, a verbal contriver of a symbolic ritual, his intention was not to transcribe but to transfigure.

The action of Wilde's *Salomé* takes place by moonlight on a great terrace above King Herod's banquet hall. The simple setting is deftly conceived to heighten dramatic effects. On this spare stage, all entrances—whether Salomé's, and later Herod's and Herodias's by the great staircase of Jokanaan's from the cistern where he has been imprisoned—are striking. In addition, the play's ruling motifs, moonlight and the recurrent contrasts of white, black, and—with increasing frequency as the play moves toward its grisly climax—red, emerge clearly.

As the play begins, a cosmopolitan group of soldiers and pages attendant on the Judean royal house occupy the terrace. Their conversation on the beauty of the Princess Salomé, the strangeness of the moon, and the rich tableau of the Tetrarch and his party feasting within sets a weird tone that is enhanced by the sound of Jokanaan's prophesies rising from his cistern prison. Salomé, like "a dove that has strayed . . . a narcissus trembling in the wind . . . a silver flower," glides onto the terrace. The prophet's strange voice and words stir the princess as deeply as her beauty troubles the young Syrian captain of the guard, a conquered prince now a slave in Herod's palace. At her command, the Syrian brings forth Jokanaan from his prison. The prophet's uncanny beauty—he seems as chaste and ascetic as she has just pronounced the moon to be—works a double charm of attraction and repulsion on Salomé. His body like a thin white statue, his black hair, his mouth "like a pomegranate cut with a knife of ivory" all kindle the princess's desire. His disgusted rejection of her love only fans the flames of lust. She must have him: "I will kiss thy mouth, Jokanaan," she chants, as the Syrian who adores her kills himself at her feet and the prophet who despises her descends once more to his cistern.

At this point, Herod and Herodias, attended by their court, enter. Their comments on the moon (to Herod, "She is like a mad woman, a mad woman who is looking everywhere for lovers"; to Herodias, "the moon is like the moon, that is all") introduce the significant differences in their equally evil natures. Herod is superstitious, cowardly, obliquely cruel, a tyrannical yet vacillating ruler; Herodias is brutal with the callous directness of an utterly debased woman. Salomé's strange beauty tempts Herod just as Jokanaan's tempts Salomé. Despite Herodias's disapproval and Salomé's reluctance, Herod presses the princess to dance. He offers her whatever reward she may request, even to the half of his kingdom. Having exacted this rash promise of the infatuated despot, Salomé performs her famous dance of seven veils and for her reward requires the head of Jokanaan on a silver charger.

As horrified by this demand as his ghoulish consort is delighted, the superstitious Herod offers Salomé a long and intricate catalog of alternative payments—the rich, rare, curious, and vulgar contents of an Oriental or *fin de siècle* treasure chest. With the sure instincts of the true collector, Salomé persists in her original demand. Unable to break his vow, the horrified king dispatches the Nubian executioner into the cistern. Presently, in a striking culmination of the play's color imagery, the Nubian's arm rises from the cistern. This ebony stem bears a strange flower: a silver shield surmounted by the prophet's bloody head. Delirious with ecstasy, Salomé addresses her passion to the disembodied lover-prophet she has asked for, silenced, and gained. "I have kissed thy mouth, Jokanaan," she concludes as a moonbeam falls on her. At Herod's cry, "Kill that woman!" the soldiers rush forward, crushing her beneath their shields.

Even so brief an account as that above demonstrates that the play has potential in sheer dramatic terms, as the great Sarah Bernhardt realized when, though much too old for the title role, she agreed to play the role of Salomé in a proposed London production that was not to be. *Salomé* is a richly fashioned tapestry. The play's prevailing mode, presentation of typically talkative Wildean characters articulating rather than acting on their emotions, gives way at three powerful moments—when Salomé dances, when the arm bearing Jokanaan's head rises from the cistern, and when the silver shields crush the dancer and her reward—to pure act, unsullied by words.

The play's psychological and symbolic suggestiveness are equally rich. One of Wilde's great contributions to the Salomé story was to provide psychological underpinnings for the sequence of events. To Wilde's invention are owed Salomé's spurned love for the prophet and the mutual hostility that counterbalances the sensual bond between Herod and Herodias. As an expression of love's ambivalence, *Salomé* is "the incarnate spirit of the aesthetic woman," a collector who (much in the spirit of Robert Browning's duke of Ferrara, it would seem) does not desire a living being but a "love object" handsomely mounted. Richard Ellmann finds something more personally symbolic in the tragedy. Jokanaan, says Ellmann, presents the spirit-affirming, body-negating moral earnestness of Wilde's "Ruskinism"; Salomé, who collects beauty, sensations, and strange experiences, who consummates her love for the prophet in "a relation at once totally sensual and totally 'mystical,'" stands for the rival claims of Pater. Herod, like his creator, vainly struggles to master these opposing impulses both within and outside himself.

Lady Windermere's Fan, A Woman of No Importance, and An Ideal Husband ·

Wilde's first three comedies, although each has its particular charms and defects, are sufficiently similar to one another, and sufficiently inferior to his fourth, *The Importance of Being Earnest*, to be discussed as a group rather than individually. Always lazy about writing (which was an arduous process for a verbal artist with his high standards) but perpetually in need of money to pay for the great and small luxuries that were his necessities of life, Wilde agreed in 1891 to write a play for George Alexander, the actor-manager of St. James's Theater. The result was *Lady Windermere's Fan*, a modern drawing-room comedy set in high society and frankly aimed to engage the interest of the London playgoing public. The financial results were gratifying enough to encourage Wilde to write three more plays in the same vein, though he never much respected the form or the products. Only in *The Importance of Being Earnest* was he to overcome the inherent weaknesses of the well-made society play, but each of the other three pieces is fine enough to win for him the title of best writer of British comedies between Richard Brinsley Sheridan and George Bernard Shaw.

Lady Windermere's Fan, A Woman of No Importance, and *An Ideal Husband* all center, as their titles suggest, on relationships between men and women, or more precisely between gentlemen and ladies. The plays were up-to-the-minute in providing fashionable furnishings and costumes to charm both segments of their intended audience. Late Victorian society people enjoyed seeing themselves reflected as creatures of such style and wit, while the middle classes delighted at being given a glimpse into the secret rites of the world of fashion. In fact, one might suspect that Wilde's stated concern for the Aristotelian unity of time in these plays springs less from belief in that classical standard than from the opportunity (or even necessity) that placing three acts of high life in a twenty-four-hour period provides for striking changes of costume and set.

In each of these elaborate "modern drawing-room comedies with pink lamp shades," as Wilde termed them, one finds recurrent character types: puritanical figures of virtue (wives in *Lady Windermere's Fan* and *An Ideal Husband*, an heiress soon to be a fiancé in *A Woman of No Importance*), mundanely fashionable hypocrites, and exceptional humanitarians of two types—the dandified lord (Darlington, Illingworth, and Goring) and the poised and prosperous "fallen woman," two of whom (Mrs. Erlynne in *Lady Windermere's Fan* and Mrs. Chevely in *An Ideal Husband*) go in for wit and the other of whom (Mrs. Arbuthnot of *A Woman of No Importance*), though equally unrepentant, specializes in good works. Clever, epigrammatic conversation is what these characters do best; guilty secrets and the situational intricacies they weave are the strings for Wilde's verbal pearls.

In *Lady Windermere's Fan*, the initial secret is that Mrs. Erlynne, the runaway mother of whose continued existence Lady Windermere is utterly ignorant, has returned to London to regain a place in society and is blackmailing Lord Windermere, who seeks to protect his wife from knowledge of the blot on her pedigree. Misinterpreting her husband's patronage of a mysterious lady with a hint of a past, Lady Windermere is led to the brink of unconsciously repeating her mother's error by eloping with another man, thereby prompting Mrs. Erlynne to the one maternal gesture of her life: The older and wiser woman sacrifices her own reputation (temporarily, it turns out) to save that of her daughter.

In *A Woman of No Importance*, Gerald Arbuthnot, a youth reared in rural seclusion and apparent respectability by his mother, happens to encounter the man who is his father: worldly Lord Illingworth, who when young and untitled had seduced Gerald's mother and, on learning of her pregnancy, refused to marry her. This complex situation allows Wilde to expose several human inconsistencies. Previously uninterested in the child he had begotten and also unwilling to marry the beautiful young mother, Lord Illingworth is now so full of paternal feeling that he offers to marry the middle-aged woman to retain the son. Gerald, who has just vowed to kill Lord Illingworth for attempting to kiss a prudish American girl, on hearing of Illingworth's past treachery to his mother wants her to let the offender "make an honest woman" of her. Mrs. Arbuthnot professes selfless devotion to her son but begs Gerald to forgo the brilliant prospects Illingworth can offer and remain with her in their provincial backwater.

In *An Ideal Husband*, the plot-initiating secret is a man's property rather than a woman's, and political intrigue rather than romantic. Sir Robert Chiltern, a high-principled politician with a rigidly idealistic young wife, encounters the adventuress Mrs. Chevely, who has evidence that Chiltern's career and fortune were founded on one unethical act—the selling of a political secret to a foreigner—and who attempts to use her knowledge to compel him to lend political support to a fraudulent scheme that will make her fortune. Acting against this resourceful woman is Chiltern's friend Lord Goring, an apparently effete but impressively capable man who can beat her at her own game. In brief, then, all three of these plays are formed of the highly theatrical matter that, in lesser hands, would form the stuff of melodrama.

Wilde's "pink lamp shade" comedies are difficult to stage because of the stylish luxury demanded of the actors, costumes, and sets, but the plays are not weaker for being so ornate: They accurately mirror a certain facet of late Victorian society. Similarly, the pervasive wit never becomes tiresome. The contrived reversals, artful coincidences, predictably surprising discoveries, and "strong curtains" may seem trite—but they work onstage. The defect that Wilde's first three comedies share is the problem of unreconciled opposites, implicit in *Salomé*. In *Lady Windermere's Fan*, *A Woman of No Importance*, and *An Ideal Husband*, part of Wilde is drawn to admire wit, style, vitality, and courage regardless of where they may be found, and part of him has a serious social or moral point to make. Even with this divided aim, Wilde wrote good comedies. When he solved the problem, he wrote a masterpiece: *The Importance of Being Earnest.*

The Importance of Being Earnest • What makes *The Importance of Being Earnest,* unlike the three Wilde comedies that preceded it, a masterpiece of the theater rather than merely an eminently stageable play? Perhaps a good clue to the answer can be found in the play's subtitle, *A Trivial Comedy for Serious People.* This typically Wildean paradox has been variously interpreted. Whatever the author may have intended by it, one thing the phrase suggests to readers is that *The Importance of Being Earnest* is worth the attention of "serious people" because it, unlike Wilde's other three comedies, succeeds in being utterly trivial and thereby attains pure comic excellence.

Eric Bentley has remarked of the play that "what begins as a prank ends as a criticism of life." Here at last Wilde offers witty wordplay and exuberant high spirits in an undiluted form. There are no melodramatic ambiguities or dark, complex emotions in *The Importance of Being Earnest,* where the chief events are flirtations that lead to engagements and prodigious consumption of tea and cucumber sandwiches. Whereas *Lady Windermere's Fan, A Woman of No Importance,* and *An Ideal Husband* take place in the stylized but recognizably real world of contemporary London society, this play unfolds in a world apart, one that, despite its containing a Mayfair flat and a Herefordshire manor, is as perfectly artificial yet completely valid as are Shakespeare's Forest of Arden in *As You Like It* (pr. c. 1599-1600) and Athens in *A Midsummer Night's Dream* (pr. c. 1595-1596).

The Importance of Being Earnest contains some of the stock theatrical devices Wilde relied on to galvanize his previous three comedies. There is mysterious parentage: Jack Worthing confesses to having been found in a handbag in Victoria Station. Characters run away from responsibility: Jack, in order to escape the country and get to town, has invented a wicked younger brother, Ernest, who lodges at the Albany; and Algernon Moncrieff, to escape from London to the country, has concocted an imaginary rural friend, the perennial invalid Bunbury. The comedy contains false identities: Both Jack and Algernon propose to and are accepted by their respective loves, the Honorable Gwendolyn Fairfax and Cecily Cardew, under the name "Ernest Worthing." There are misplaced possessions as significant as Lady Windermere's fan: Finding a cigarette case inscribed "From little Cecily, with her fondest love to her dear Uncle Jack," enables Algernon to discover his friend's double identity. The governess Miss Prism's unexpected, happy, eloquent reunion with the handbag she had mislaid twenty-eight years before brings the climactic revelation of the play: Through this recovery of the long-lost handbag, Jack, a comic Oedipus, discovers his true parentage. In all these cases, the dramatic machines of potential tragedy or melodrama are operated in the spirit of burlesque. There are no lapses or incongruities to drag down the lighthearted mood.

Similarly, the emotional developments, reversals, intrigues, and deceptions that were threatening in Wilde's other comedies are harmless in *The Importance of Being Earnest,* chiefly because the play is not about established relationships. It does not present married people with domestic differences; former lovers who should have married but failed to do so; present lovers already yoked to other people; parents, who through love, guilt, selfishness, or honor, influence the behavior of their children; or children who similarly manipulate their parents.

The play's four principal characters—Jack Worthing, Gwendolyn Fairfax, Algernon Moncrieff, and Cecily Cardew—are all young, single, and, with the exception of

Gwendolyn, parentless. The Reverend Dr. Chasuble and Miss Prism are, to use their own words, "ripe" but "celibate." Early in the play, Lane, Algernon's manservant, admits that, with regard to marriage, he has had "very little experience of it myself up to the present." Of all the characters, only the marvelous Lady Bracknell is mature, married, and encumbered with children. Even so, Lord Bracknell is completely under her control; that pitiful peer, who dines upstairs at her command, does and knows only what she prescribes. Her daughter Gwendolyn, on the other hand, is completely free from her domination; the poised young lady listens politely to her dogmatic mother and then acts precisely as she chooses. As a consequence, Lady Bracknell's personal essence and the behavior it determines are modified by neither spouse nor child.

With this array of singularly unfettered characters, *The Importance of Being Earnest* is not about domestic complications but about the act of committing oneself to domesticity. The social comedy of the play parallels the movement of a Jane Austen novel: Characters who exist as pure potential define and place themselves by choosing to marry and by selecting their particular mates. The choreography of this matrimonial ballet is exceptionally elegant, particularly in the commonly known three-act version. (The original four-act version, first staged by the New Vic in 1980, contains material that is not essential, though not uninteresting.) The dialogue is so uniformly delightful that it is impossible to single out a high point or two for quoting. For the first time, Wilde's comedy is a brilliant whole rather than a series of sparkling effects. Indeed, the play's final interchange between Lady Bracknell and her newfound nephew (soon-to-be son-in-law) Jack could be the dramatist talking to himself, for by taking comedy seriously enough to stay within its bounds, Wilde the dramatist finally achieved his goal of creating a play not merely well-made but perfect of its kind:

> LADY BRACKNELL: My nephew, you seem to be displaying signs of triviality.
> JACK: On the contrary, Aunt Augusta, I've now realized for the first time in my life the vital Importance of Being Earnest.

Other major works

LONG FICTION: *The Picture of Dorian Gray*, 1890 (serial), 1891 (expanded).

SHORT FICTION: "The Canterville Ghost," 1887; *The Happy Prince and Other Tales*, 1888; *Lord Arthur Savile's Crime and Other Stories*, 1891; *A House of Pomegranates*, 1891.

POETRY: *Ravenna*, 1878; *Poems*, 1881; *Poems in Prose*, 1894; *The Sphinx*, 1894; *The Ballad of Reading Gaol*, 1898.

NONFICTION: *Intentions*, 1891; *De Profundis*, 1905; *Letters*, 1962 (Rupert Hart-Davies, editor).

MISCELLANEOUS: *Works*, 1908; *Complete Works of Oscar Wilde*, 1948 (Vyvyan Holland, editor); *Plays, Prose Writings, and Poems*, 1960.

Bibliography

Belford, Barbara. *Oscar Wilde: A Certain Genius*. New York: Random House, 2000. An examination of Wilde's life with a somewhat revisionist view of Wilde's post-prison years.

Ellmann, Richard. *Oscar Wilde*. London: Hamish Hamilton, 1987. A richly detailed, sympathetic account of Wilde's life and art, with balanced views of his accomplishments and significance for modern culture. Ellmann presents a forceful analysis of the events that caused Wilde's trial, imprisonment, and eventual early death. Contains many illustrations, notes, a select bibliography, two appendices of books by Wilde's parents, and an index.

McCormack, Jerusha Hull. *The Man Who Was Dorian Gray.* New York: Palgrave, 2000. A scholarly scraping together of the life of Wilde's model.

McGhee, Richard D. "Elizabeth Barrett Browning and Oscar Wilde." In *Marriage, Duty, and Desire in Victorian Poetry and Drama.* Lawrence: Regents Press of Kansas, 1980. Comparing the art of Wilde and Browning, this study focuses on their contrasting emphases on duty and desire, with some similarity in their motives for attempting to reconcile the opposition between such values. Wilde's dramas are closely examined along with his lyric poems and critical essays. Notes and index.

Small, Ian. *Oscar Wilde: A Recent Research, A Supplement to "Oscar Wilde Revalued."* Greensboro, N.C.: ELT Press, 2000. A follow-up to Small's earlier work on Wilde that surveys new biographical and critical materials. Bibliography.

Peter W. Graham,
updated by Richard D. McGhee

Thornton Wilder

Born: Madison, Wisconsin; April 17, 1897
Died: Hamden, Connecticut; December 7, 1975

Principal drama • *The Trumpet Shall Sound*, pb. 1920, pr. 1927; *The Angel That Troubled the Waters and Other Plays*, pb. 1928 (includes 16 plays); *The Happy Journey to Trenton and Camden*, pr., pb. 1931 (one act); *The Long Christmas Dinner*, pr., pb. 1931 (one act; as libretto in German, 1961; translation and music by Paul Hindemith); *The Long Christmas Dinner and Other Plays in One Act*, pb. 1931 (includes *Queens of France, Pullman Car Hiawatha, Love and How to Cure It, Such Things Only Happen in Books,* and *The Happy Journey to Trenton and Camden*); *Lucrece*, pr. 1932, pb. 1933 (adaptation of André Obey's *Le Viol de Lucrèce*); *A Doll's House*, pr. 1937 (adaptation of Henrik Ibsen's play); *The Merchant of Yonkers*, pr. 1938, pb. 1939 (adaptation of Johann Nestroy's *Einen Jux will er sich machen*); *Our Town*, pr., pb. 1938; *The Skin of Our Teeth*, pr., pb. 1942; *The Matchmaker*, pr. 1954, pb. 1956 (revision of *The Merchant of Yonkers*); *A Life in the Sun*, pr. 1955, pb. 1960 (in German), pb. 1977 (in English; commonly known as *The Alcestiad*; act four pb. 1952, pr. 1957 as *The Drunken Sisters*); *Plays for Bleecker Street*, pr. 1962 (3 one-acts: *Someone from Assisi; Infancy*, pb. 1961; and *Childhood*, pb. 1960); *The Collected Short Plays of Thornton Wilder*, pb. 1997-1998 (2 volumes)

Other literary forms • Thornton Wilder came to national prominence in 1927 with what has remained his best-known novel, *The Bridge of San Luis Rey*, which won for him the first of his three Pulitzer Prizes. The year before, his first published fiction, *The Cabala* (1926), had appeared, and in 1930 came his third novel, *The Woman of Andros*. These works were followed in 1934 by *Heaven's My Destination*—his first fictional work about the American experience—and, at lengthy intervals, by three additional novels. *The Ides of March*, the story of Caesar told from fictional diaries, letters, and records, and quite probably Wilder's most significant novel, appeared in 1948; *The Eighth Day*, winner of the National Book Award, was published in 1967; and his last novel, the semiautobiographical *Theophilus North*, was published in 1973. In 1942, Wilder cowrote the screenplay for Alfred Hitchcock's motion picture *Shadow of a Doubt* (1943). Over the years, Wilder wrote a number of essays, including several that develop his theory of drama; some that introduce works by other writers as varied as Sophocles, Gertrude Stein, James Joyce, and Emily Dickinson; and a few scholarly articles on the Spanish playwright Lope de Vega Carpio. These works have been collected posthumously in *American Characteristics and Other Essays* (1979).

Achievements • Thornton Wilder was a true man of letters, equally accomplished and highly regarded at various points in his career as both a novelist and a dramatist. None of his works of fiction, however, seems likely to endure as a classic in the way that two of his plays, *Our Town* and *The Skin of Our Teeth*, most assuredly will. Wilder admittedly has always been, as the foreword to *The Angel That Troubled the Waters* insists, a decidedly and deliberately religious playwright, not in any parochial sense of espousing a specific body of theological doctrine but in the larger sense of consistently posing moral and metaphysical questions. As he makes clear in that preface, however, if the religious artist today is to reach a sizable and responsive audience, that artist generally must couch his or her views "in that dilute fashion that is a believer's concession to a contemporary standard of good manners." By birth, Wilder was a Christian; by education and training, he was a humanist. By his own reading and intellectual inquiry later in life, he became an existentialist. Several of the playlets in his first volume reveal the intersection of pagan and Christian myth, showing how the former is implicit in and fulfilled by the latter. Continually, Wilder emphasizes the "presentness" of the past and how the best that has been thought and said throughout the ages continues to be of value. Always he asserts the importance of reason even in ages of faith.

Wilder was one of the most learned and erudite of all American dramatists. Throughout his life, he was a teacher as well as a writer, and his plays teach effortlessly, engagingly, and entertainingly. Much of American drama centers on the family, and Wilder's plays are no exception. His family, though, is the Family of Man, the human community throughout history. Because of the allegorical and parabolic nature of his plays, Wilder's works might appear at first to be lacking in subtlety and complexity, yet, through the simple means he employs, they touch on the most vital of ideas. The timeless rituals in which his families participate are the universal ones of birth and growth, love and marriage, sickness and death. If Wilder perhaps reflects Henri Bergson and Marcel Proust in his own philosophy of time as duration and memory as a simultaneous coexistence of all past experiences, he is a child of Ralph Waldo Emer-

(Library of Congress)

son and Walt Whitman in his vague transcendentalism and almost religious belief in the value of democracy. Wilder insists that life has a purpose and a dignity, so it must be lived and cherished and nurtured. If this purpose and worth have become increasingly clouded, that simply makes artists all the more vital, for on them rests the task of revealing the divinity within human beings yet of showing them that they can become divine only by first being fully human.

He received numerous awards during his lifetime, beginning with the Pulitzer Prize in Fiction in 1928 for his novel *The Bridge of San Luis Rey*. He was awarded the Pulitzer Prize in Drama in 1938 for *Our Town* and in 1943 for *The Skin of Our Teeth*. He received the National Book Award for *The Eighth Day* in 1968. Among the many honors that came to Wilder late in life were the Gold Medal for Fiction of the American Academy of Arts and Letters, the United States Presidential Medal of Freedom, and the National Medal for Literature.

Biography • Thornton Niven Wilder was born on April 17, 1897, in Madison, Wisconsin, into a family with a strong New England Protestant background: Congregationalist on his father Amos's side, Presbyterian on his mother Isabella's. An older brother, Amos, became a professor of theology and commentator on religious poetry, and among Wilder's three younger sisters was Isabel, with whom he would later make his home and share the closest emotional attachment of his life. When their father was appointed consul general to Hong Kong and later to Shanghai in the first decade of the new century, the family lived with him for brief periods in each city, though the young Wilder was educated mostly in California. After he was graduated from Berkeley High School in 1915, Wilder went to Oberlin College in Ohio, later transferring to Yale, from which he received his bachelor of arts degree in 1920. While in college, he wrote numerous "three-minute plays," some of which would be included among the sixteen somewhat precious and pretentious closet dramas that reached print as *The Angel That Troubled the Waters and Other Plays*, as well as his first full-length effort, *The Trumpet Shall Sound*. Somewhat similar to Ben Jonson's *The Alchemist* (pr. 1610) in its incidents and thematic emphasis on justice, this early play was finally produced by the American Laboratory Theatre in New York in 1927.

While studying archaeology at the American Academy in Rome after college, Wilder began writing fiction. After returning to the United States, he taught French at the Lawrenceville School for Boys in New Jersey for much of the 1920's, staying there—with time out to attend Princeton for a master of arts degree and for a stint writing at the MacDowell Colony in New Hampshire—until after the critical acclaim of his second novel, *The Bridge of San Luis Rey*, which was awarded the Pulitzer Prize in Fiction in 1928. In 1930, Wilder began lecturing for part of each academic year in comparative literature at the University of Chicago, where he made the acquaintance of Gertrude Stein, whose theories of time and language exercised a powerful influence on all of Wilder's subsequent writing for the theater.

During the 1930's, Wilder published six additional one-act plays in his volume entitled *The Long Christmas Dinner and Other Plays in One Act*. In 1961, the title play became the libretto for an opera with music by Paul Hindemith. In addition, Wilder adapted both André Obey's *Le Viol de Lucrèce* (1931) and Henrik Ibsen's *Et dukkehjem* (pr., pb. 1879; *A Doll's House*, 1880) for Broadway before writing his most famous work, *Our Town*, which won for him the Pulitzer Prize in Drama in 1938. The same year saw the unsuccessful production, under the direction of Max Reinhardt, of *The Merchant of Yonkers*, later revised as *The Matchmaker* for performance at the Edinburgh Festival in Scotland in 1954 and in New York in 1955; in a still later transformation (1964), dressed up with a musical score by Jerry Herman, *The Matchmaker* became *Hello, Dolly!*, one of the greatest successes in the history of American musical comedy. In 1943 while serving in the United States Army Air Corps during World War II, Wilder won his second Pulitzer Prize for *The Skin of Our Teeth*, perhaps one of the most original and inventive of all American comedies.

At the beginning of the 1950's, Wilder was Charles Eliot Norton Professor of Poetry at Harvard, lecturing on the American characteristics in classic American literature. In 1955, his last full-length drama, *A Life in the Sun*, was performed at the Edinburgh Festival. In 1962, it, too, became the libretto for an acclaimed German opera, *Die Alkestiade*, with music by Louise Talma. At the time of his death on December 7, 1975, he left incomplete two cycles of plays on which he had been working for more than a decade, "The Seven Deadly Sins" and "The Seven Ages of Man," whose titles suggest the allegorical and mythic nature of Wilder's best work for the theater. Perhaps the cumulative effect of the complete cycles would have been greater than the sampling of their parts that reached Off-Broadway production in 1962 under the collective title *Plays for Bleecker Street*. The three one-act plays, *Someone from Assisi*, *Infancy*, and *Childhood*, were Wilder's last original works produced for New York audiences.

Analysis • Thornton Wilder's contributions in style and technique to American drama are akin to the innovations that Alfred Jarry in France, Luigi Pirandello in Italy, and Bertolt Brecht in Germany made to world drama in the twentieth century. Basically, Wilder was an antirealistic playwright, reacting against the tenets and presuppositions underlying the type of drama that held sway during the nineteenth century and continues to be a potent force even today. During a play that, as part of its attempt to create the absolute illusion of reality, employs a box set so that the audience sees the action through an imaginary fourth wall, there is a complete separation between actors and audience, stage space and auditorium. The audience, even though it implicitly knows it is in a theater watching a play, pretends for the duration that it is seeing reality on the stage; in short, the audience makes believe that it is not making believe. On the other hand, in theater that makes no attempt at achieving such an absolute illusion of reality, the audience readily accepts that what it is seeing is make-believe or pretense.

In his important essay "Some Thoughts on Playwriting" (1941), Wilder argues that the theater in its greatest ages—Periclean Athens and Elizabethan England, for example—has always depended heavily on conventions, what he calls "agreed-upon falsehoods" or "permitted lies." Such accepted conventions help to break down the artificial boundary between play and audience by inviting a fuller imaginative participation in the action; by increasing the audience's awareness of itself as audience; and by emphasizing the communal and ritualistic nature of the theatrical experience. In Wilder's view, the traditional box set, because it localizes the action to a particular place and restricts it to a definite time, renders the action less universal and hinders its ascent into the desirable realms of parable, allegory, and myth. In contrast, Wilder sought a theater in which the large, recurrent outlines of the human story could be told through particular examples less important in themselves than the universal truths they stand for and embody.

The Happy Journey to Trenton and Camden • Wilder's brand of minimalist theater can be illustrated by looking at *The Happy Journey to Trenton and Camden*, which the dramatist himself regarded as the best of his one-act plays. The action is simple: The

Kirby family (father, mother, son, and daughter) takes a brief automobile trip to visit a married daughter/sister, whose baby died shortly after birth. Because the literal journey is less important than the metaphoric one, it is appropriate that the bare brick walls of the backstage remain visible; that the automobile is merely suggested by four chairs and a platform, with Dad Kirby working an imaginary gearshift and steering wheel in pantomime; that the towns through which the family travels (including Lawrenceville, where Wilder once taught) are simply mentioned in the dialogue; and that a Stage Manager is available to serve as property man, to read the parts of all the minor characters, and to act the role of service station attendant. When the car must stop for an imaginary funeral procession to pass, it allows the family an opportunity to recall their son and brother Harold, who died in the war, and to remember that every human being must be ready for death.

As is typical in Wilder, the central female figure carries the weight of the play's meaning and expresses the dramatist's simple faith. Ma Kirby is the Eternal Mother, preserver of the family, who is close to God and to the nature that shadows forth the divine. She understands the process-oriented quality of existence: All things are born and they die; some, in fact, are born only to die. Further, she maintains her confidence in a providential order at work in the universe. Although human beings cannot know the ways of God, they must continue in faith that all things in life are for the best. What tempers Wilder's optimism and often prevents it from becoming sentimental is that he always keeps before his audience the dark side of human nature—human beings' myopic vision that limits them from being all that they might become—and the dark side of human existence—the fact of death, especially of dying without ever having really lived.

Our Town • When the Stage Manager steps out onto the stage at the beginning of *Our Town* and locates the mythical and microcosmic New England village of Grover's Corners, New Hampshire, firmly in time and space, he creates a place so palpably present to the American imagination that most people in the audience might expect to be able to find it on a map. This is, truly, anyone's and everyone's town, and the people who are born and grow up and live and marry and suffer and die there are clearly Everyman and Everywoman. Wilder's opening stage directions specify "No curtain. No scenery."

The absence of a curtain conveys the timeless quality of elemental experiences; the action has no specific beginning, because these daily events have been occurring since time immemorial and will continue to go on, despite an ever-changing cast on the world's stage. The almost complete lack of scenery, with only "two arched trellises" permitted as a concession to the unimaginative and literal-minded in the audience, indicates that the action is unlocalized and not tied to only one place at one time, but could, and does, happen everywhere. The pantomimed actions—perhaps influenced by the style of the Chinese theater, with which Wilder was well acquainted—achieve the same effect. The audience has no difficulty recognizing them, precisely because they are common actions (such as getting meals) that everyone performs.

The play's action is as basic, and yet as universal, as the setting: neither more nor less than the archetypal journey of man and woman through life to death and beyond. In this respect, the title play from *The Long Christmas Dinner and Other Plays in One Act* serves as a precursor to *Our Town*. In that short work, Wilder presented ninety years in the life of the Bayard family. Characters enter through a portal on one side of the stage, which symbolizes birth; partake of a Christmas dinner over the years that symbolizes the feast of life; and then exit through a portal, on the opposite side of the stage, that symbolizes death. One generation replaces another, even uttering many of the same lines of dialogue.

Act 1 of *Our Town*, called "Daily Life," focuses on the ordinary, day-to-day existence of two neighboring families: Editor Webb, his wife, older daughter, and younger son; and Doc Gibbs, his wife, older son, and younger daughter. In act 2, called "Love and Marriage," the playwright shows the courtship and wedding of George Gibbs and Emily Webb; the audience becomes an extension of the church congregation as the young couple enter and leave the ceremony via the theater aisles. Act 3, which is left untitled, is set in a cemetery with chairs for graves and an umbrella-protected group of mourners; it is the funeral of Emily, who died in childbirth and has been united in eternity with something like an Oversoul.

Although the action literally begins in May, 1901 (the hopeful springtime of a new century), *Our Town* is, unlike a play such as Eugene O'Neill's *Ah, Wilderness!* (pr. 1933), more than simply a nostalgic recollection of a bygone era of American democratic egalitarianism. Nor is the picture of life from the dawn of the twentieth century to the outbreak of World War I as sentimentally one-sided and limited in its awareness of evil and the darker forces of existence as has sometimes been charged. Along with Simon Stimson, the town drunk and eventual suicide, Wilder portrays petty gossip and backbiting, even among the church choir ladies; lack of communication between husband and wife and parent and child; the pain of separation and loss through death; and war (looking forward, since the action per se ends in 1913). The continuing importance of *Our Town*, however, should not be looked for on so basic a level as that of its story. Rather, it is a philosophical examination of time and the proper way of seeing, stressing the necessity for escaping from the narrow, myopic view of existence that human beings ordinarily take and embracing, with the poet's help, a God's-eye view of human history.

Wilder's attitude toward time as a continuum is made concrete in the way he conveys events that occurred before or will happen after the twelve-year scope of the action. Not only does the local expert, a college professor, Willard, provide a lengthy report about the geological formation of the region and the anthropological data of the area, but also the Stage Manager, in his casual shifting of verb tenses from present to future or future to past, points to a perspective that is both inside secular time and outside time, transcending it.

Wilder's laconic Stage Manager, with his understated and homespun New England manner, performs several functions: He is narrator, bridging shifts in time and place, setting the scene for the audience; he is actor of minor roles, including drugstore owner and preacher at George and Emily's wedding; he is property man, constructing the soda fountain from a few boards; he is chorus, philosophizing for the audience; and he is destroyer of the theatrical illusion, reminding the audience that they are in a theater watching a play. Distanced from the action that is filtered through his eyes, the audience begins to see with his sometimes ironic perspective. He possesses a Godlike omniscience, overseeing the progression of human history as God would. It is this kind of sight and insight that the audience, too, must develop.

In a seemingly inconsequential exchange of dialogue (perhaps influenced by a similar passage in James Joyce's *A Portrait of the Artist as a Young Man*, 1916), Wilder hints at the idea on which the entire work pivots. George Gibbs's sister Rebecca tells about a letter that a minister sent to a sick friend; included as the final words of the address on the envelope was the location, "the Mind of God." Wilder, who himself acted the role of the Stage Manager in the Broadway production, tells his audience that if it could only plumb the mind of God, where everything—from least to most, from smallest to largest, past, present, and to come—exists simultaneously as part of a purposive, providential order, then they would live life wholly and even be able to cope with death.

The tension and tragedy of the human condition, however, arise because, paradoxically, it is possible to gain the perspective necessary for seeing life steadily and seeing it whole only after death. Emily dies giving birth, a poignant image not only of mutability but also of the way in which life and death are inextricably bound in nature's cycle. Only after she dies and is given the opportunity to relive the most "unimportant day" in her life does she see that even the most ordinary and banal of life's experiences is full of wonder and learn to treasure more what she has lost. Sadly, only the "saints and poets" seem to recognize this wonder and beauty while they are still alive. The end of a human life, union with some larger spirit, is in its beginning hinted at even in the most common events of daily living—if only that person, like the poet, could see.

The Skin of Our Teeth • While *Our Town* displays some affinities with medieval morality plays, *The Skin of Our Teeth* is influenced by the medieval mystery cycles in its structure: In capsule form (and stylistically akin somewhat to a comic strip), it recounts human history from the beginning of time to the present and on into the future. The Antrobuses, Wilder's Family of Man in this play, begin each of the three acts on the upswing, feeling positive about themselves and the human race; see their fortunes descend to a nadir, through either a natural disaster or human culpability; yet finally finish each act—and the play as a whole—having narrowly muddled through "by the skin of their teeth." In each instance, temptation is overcome, sinful action somehow compensated for.

In act 1, with its echoes of the Garden of Eden story from Genesis, son Henry's killing of the neighbor boy (he earlier killed his brother, for which he received the mark of Cain) prompts Mr. Antrobus to despair, but daughter Gladys' ability to recite in school a poem by Henry Wadsworth Longfellow restores his faith. In act 2, with its underpinning of the Noah tale, the father's lack of faithfulness to Mrs. Antrobus sends shock waves through the family, as Gladys dons red stockings and Henry attacks a black person with a slingshot. Yet Mr. Antrobus, unlike the other conventioneers at Atlantic City who writhe in a snakelike dance, is among the remnant of faithful ones saved from the Deluge. Act 3 finds the family returning to normalcy after the war (any war), but the anarchic Henry threatens the stability of the family unit just as the forces of totalitarianism almost destroyed the world, until he is finally reconciled with his father, who puts his confidence in the best ideas from the past to sustain the human race. The overall structure, therefore, embodies Wilder's concept of cyclic time, with one result being that time can be handled anachronistically. The play, which began with a slide of the sun rising, ends with the equivalent lines from Genesis: "And the Lord said let there be light and there was light."

In its techniques, which extend the nonillusionistic style adopted in *Our Town*, *The Skin of Our Teeth* reflects the influence of Surrealism and even points forward to the multimedia effects of the 1960's and 1970's. The scenery, with its angles askew, the dozen lantern slides projected onto the set, the talking dinosaur and mammoth, the cardboard cutouts and flats, the lighting and noises—all contribute to a carnival atmosphere, anticipating the playful techniques of some Absurdist drama while also suggesting a dream happening without conscious control.

Mr. Fitzpatrick, Wilder's director/stage manager here, not only stops the play so that he can rehearse volunteers taking over the parts of sick actors, but also is mildly satirized for his literal-mindedness and prosaicism; even Ivy, the costumer, understands the meaning of the play better than he does. Significantly, the substitute actors are needed to play the hours of the night who cross the stage; that they recite passages from Benedict de Spinoza, Plato, Aristotle, and the Bible (as similar characters also had in *Pullman Car Hiawatha*) demonstrates that the enduring ideas of the past are not out of reach of the common man. The illusion of reality is further destroyed when Lily Sabina Fairweather, a compound of temptress, mistress, camp follower, and maid, steps out of character and, as the actress Miss Somerset, speaks directly to the audience, requesting that they send up their chairs for firewood during the Ice Age of act 1 and, at the end of the play, sending them home to do their part in completing the history of the human race on earth.

Within the framework of his comic allegory of humankind's journey, Wilder's characters assume an archetypal dimension; each member of the Antrobus family, whom Wilder calls "our selves," seems to stand for an aspect of the archetypal man or woman's personality. Mr. Antrobus—the former gardener (Adam), self-made man, inventor of the wheel, the lever, gunpowder, the singing telegram, the brewing of beer and of grass soup—represents the power of the intellect, which can be a force for both creation and destruction. Appreciating the importance of the wisdom of past ages, he will not tolerate the burning of William Shakespeare's works even to provide life-sustaining warmth. Mrs. Antrobus, inventor in her own right of the apron, the hem, the gore and the gusset, and frying in oil, is humankind's affective side; her watchword is the family and the promise of love between husband and wife that helps them endure and makes even suffering worthwhile. As one who insists that women are not the subservient creatures the media make them out to be, she stresses woman's role as transmitter of the Life Force.

Lily Sabina (Lilith), with her philosophy of enjoying the present moment, embodies the hedonistic pleasure principle. The Antrobuses' daughter Gladys, who appears after the war with a baby, symbolically conveys hope for the future. Their son Henry is a representation of the strong, unreconciled evil that is always with humankind; though he is the enemy during the war and in general refuses to accept responsibility, he is still taken along on the ark at the end of act 2.

In act 3, the actors playing Mr. Antrobus and Henry break out of their roles, moving from stereotypes to more rounded human beings as they reveal the tension between themselves as men rather than as characters. Something in the attitude of the actor playing Antrobus reminds the one portraying Henry of how authority figures have always blocked and hindered him, and so they clash personally. Through this tension, the actor playing Antrobus recognizes that there must indeed exist some lack within himself that triggered this negative response in the other, and so he promises to change. He ends confident that humanity, always on the edge of chaos and disaster, will ultimately endure and prevail, if only people accept the chance to do the hard work that Providence demands of them.

Wilder, like George Bernard Shaw, has often been criticized for his romantic optimism, which seems out of keeping with the darker facts of human history—*The Skin of Our Teeth* opened, after all, only a year after Pearl Harbor and found its greatest success in post World War II Germany. Whether Wilder's optimistic belief in humanity's "spiral progression through trial and error" is found congenial or not, *The Skin of Our Teeth* remains a richly imaginative work and the seminal text of deliberately self-conscious art in the American theater.

The Matchmaker • Wilder's *The Matchmaker*—a revision of his *The Merchant of Yon-kers*, an adaptation of Johann Nestroy's 1842 Viennese comedy *Einen Jux will er sich machen* (pr. 1842, pb. 1844; *The Matchmaker*, 1957; which, in turn, was based loosely on John Oxenford's 1835 English comedy *A Day Well Spent*)—belongs to that most vener-able of dramatic traditions, the genre of romantic comedy. As such, it is characterized by a repressive authority figure who tries to thwart young love; mistaken identities and confusion between the sexes, including boys disguised as girls; and a ritualized dance to foreshadow the multiple marriages that resolve the plot. Along with these appear el-ements of good-natured, boisterous farce, including inopportune entrances and exits; hiding behind a screen, in closets, and under tables; and exploding cans of tomatoes shooting up through a trapdoor in the floor. What marks all of this traditional, even ste-reotypical material with Wilder's own signature are the themes and the manner in which he breaks down the illusion of stage reality.

A further alteration from the norm in romantic comedy is that in this play, the older couple, rather than the young ones, are the hero and heroine. Horace Vandergelder, the sly, miserly merchant from Yonkers (he seems a direct descendant of Ben Jon-son's Volpone, the fox) forbids his sentimental young niece and ward Ermengarde to marry the penniless artist Ambrose Kemper. They ultimately circumvent his author-ity through the agency of two older women: Miss Flora Van Huysen, the spinster fairy godmother in the play, and Mrs. Dolly Gallager Levi, the inimitable match-maker herself. Miss Van Huysen refuses to permit her own loneliness to be extended to others through the destruction of young love, and so she acts as the presiding deity over the three marriages: Ermengarde's to Ambrose; Cornelius Hackl's to Irene Mol-loy, the Irish widow and milliner; and Barnaby Tucker's to Minnie, Mrs. Molloy's as-sistant.

Dolly, who all along has her eyes on Horace for herself, is the only character among a cast of types permitted enough depth to probe into herself and her motives. In the manner in which she arranges the relationships of others and herself, there is some-thing of the artist in Dolly Levi; her vocation is to make life interesting, to make peo-ple less selfish, to spread enjoyment, to see that the community renews and fructifies itself. She must, first of all, tutor Horace in adopting a proper attitude toward money; for her, money must "circulate like rain water" among the people and be "spread around like manure" if it is to encourage life and growth. She must also, however, tu-tor herself into giving up her widow's weeds, so to speak, and completely rejoining the human community. Ever since the death of her first husband, Ephraim, she has al-lowed herself to become like a dying leaf and now must cure her underactive heart through marriage to Horace. For both Dolly and Horace, lonely old age is only nar-rowly averted. This emphasis on full participation in life and life's processes, of seeing that to everything there is a season and of not rushing before one's time toward death and decay, is peculiarly Wilder's. Also distinctively Wilder's is the emphasis on the need for "adventure" and "wonder," which are two of the key words spoken by nearly every one of the play's characters and are direct echoes of the attitudes espoused in *Our Town*.

The settings for the four acts of *The Matchmaker* are the most elaborately realistic box sets prescribed for any Wilder play. Precisely because they do form such a realistic background, replete with "obtrusive bric-a-brac," they make the several instances of direct address to the audience by the major characters all the more startling. The disjunction between the realistic sets and the very nonrealistic goings-on calls the audi-ence's attention to the fact that it is watching a play and turns stage realism on its ear.

The Matchmaker becomes, indeed, a playful and affectionate parody of the way that stage realism stifles life. To be doubly sure that the audience does not miss this point, Miss Van Huysen even repeats several times some variation of the line "Everything's imagination," which is another way of saying that all is make-believe and pretense: exactly what Wilder strives to provide for his theater audiences.

A Life in the Sun • Wilder's *A Life in the Sun* is, both in form and content, linked closely to the Greek drama of the fifth century B.C.E. Its form, a play in three acts (each of which could almost stand alone as a self-contained episode) and a satyr play, replicates that of the Greek trilogies, which were followed with a comic parody of the tragic action. Here, the satyr play (entitled *The Drunken Sisters*, which tells how Apollo tricked the vain Fates into allowing Admetus to live) is added by Wilder to make the point that the tragic and comic experiences are incomplete in and of themselves; in life, the two kinds of perceptions must coexist.

The content of Wilder's powerful retelling of the Alcestis story for modern man is religious and mythological in nature, with his act 2 corresponding closely to the material found in Euripides' original. Unlike T. S. Eliot's *The Cocktail Party* (pr. 1949), which uses the same myth allusively as a vague underpinning for a contemporary parable, or Eugene O'Neill's *Mourning Becomes Electra* (pr. 1931), which takes the outlines and psychology of the Orestes and Electra stories and redresses them at a different time and place, Wilder creatively adjusts the myth to reflect contemporary philosophical currents, especially existentialism, as Jean-Paul Sartre had done in *Les Mouches* (pr., pb. 1943; *The Flies*, 1946).

Act 1 begins with a confrontation between Apollo, the force of light, and Death, the force of darkness, who introduce the issues that inform the entire play: the relationship between the divine and the human and the problem of discovering a meaning to life. Although Apollo admits that there exists much that human beings are incapable of understanding, he insists that what meaning does exist flows from him. Death, on the other hand—and later Tiresias, the wizened seer, will echo him—argues that it is the gods who cause human torment. By meddling in human affairs, the gods make people unhappy and distraught.

On her wedding day, Alcestis decides not to marry the King of Thessaly unless she receives a clear sign from the gods; she will forsake humans, finite and of this world, to love only God, infinite and other-worldly. Alcestis desires absolute certainty and the assurance that the gods have not abandoned humankind; without that, life is reduced to meaningless nonsense, and humankind is left in a condition similar to that of the absurdists, with life made all the more unbearable because human beings have been given hope of some meaning only to see that hope dashed. The God Apollo, by becoming human in the form of one of Admetus's herdsmen, must save Alcestis by forcing her to recognize that God is within each and every person, that the divine can be found within the human, the infinite within the finite. When Admetus enters wearing a blue cloak like Apollo's, the sight is an epiphany for Alcestis, who pledges to marry him and live totally for him, ready even to die for him.

Act 2, which occurs twelve years later, finds Admetus at the point of death and Alcestis finally favored with the long-sought-for message from Delphi, which indicates that the gods do demand the difficult. The message challenges her to do what she was prepared to do at the close of act 1: die in place of Admetus. The Watchman, the old nurse Aglaia, and the Herdsman all offer to sacrifice themselves so that Admetus might live, but Alcestis insists that the role fall to her. It is not that Alcestis has no hesitation, for she dreads to cease to be, to leave the sunlight, and she still craves the right to understand the ways of God to humankind that would make human beings more than animals. Finally, though, her love for Admetus dominates her love for life; she will die for him and, what is perhaps even harder, die from him, believing a divinity shapes her end. Yet, as Apollo intervenes in act 1, here Hercules, though in fear and trembling, descends into the Underworld to bring back from the dead the all-forgiving Alcestis, the "crown of women." The last image of the resurrected Alcestis led forth from Hell provides a further instance for the audience of the way in which classical and Christian myth and iconography fuse in Wilder: Apollo/Christ became man; Alcestis/Christ died and rose so that others might live.

If act 2 forms a meditation on death, act 3 is a metaphysical inquiry into the existence of human suffering, with Death taunting Apollo to explain why so many innocent in Thessaly have died in the pestilence: Do the gods make human beings suffer only so that people will remember rather than reject them? Admetus is now dead, and Alcestis is an old slave under King Agis. Epimenes, the only surviving son of the former queen, returns to what has become a wasteland, vowing butchery and revenge, only to have his hand stopped by his mother. Rejecting all of those who see God's influence only in the evil in the world and never in the good, Alcestis says that the gods' ways are not human ways; they do not love one minute and then turn against the loved one in the next. She counsels Agis, whose daughter Laodamia dies in the plague, that evil does have a purpose within the divine scheme and that suffering can make him open his eyes and learn wisdom. Her final visionary pronouncement recalls that of Emily in *Our Town*: Human beings should despair at the point of death only if they have not really lived, if they have failed to experience fully and treasure the here and now. The meaning of life is in the living of life. Alcestis herself becomes the sign that life does possess a meaning in and of itself, and, freed from the grave by the grace of Apollo, she experiences an apotheosis as her reward.

A Life in the Sun, as much a paean to woman and her role in the cosmic order as are *The Happy Journey to Trenton and Camden* and *The Skin of Our Teeth*, provides a dramatic summation of much of Wilder's philosophy: To become divine, human beings must first be fully human; the extraordinary is to be discovered in the ordinary; the power of myth is timeless, cutting across cultures and religions, synthesizing the past and the present, making the past ever new and vital. The Watchman's words in act 1 of *A Life in the Sun*, a play that is essentially an undiscovered country for all but ardent enthusiasts of Wilder, might be paraphrased as an epigraph for all Wilder's dramatic works: The essential facts of human life do not change, nor should humankind expect them to, from millennium to millennium, from year to year, from minute to minute. What must change is human beings' way of seeing.

Other major works

LONG FICTION: *The Cabala*, 1926; *The Bridge of San Luis Rey*, 1927; *The Woman of Andros*, 1930; *Heaven's My Destination*, 1934; *The Ides of March*, 1948; *The Eighth Day*, 1967; *Theophilus North*, 1973.

SCREENPLAYS: *Our Town*, 1940 (with Frank Craven and Harry Chantlee); *Shadow of a Doubt*, 1943 (with Sally Benson and Alma Revelle).

NONFICTION: *The Intent of the Artist*, 1941; *American Characteristics and Other Essays*, 1979; *The Journals of Thornton Wilder, 1939-1961*, 1985.

TRANSLATION: *The Victors*, 1948 (of Jean-Paul Sartre's play *Morts sans sépulture*).

Bibliography

Blank, Martin, ed. *Critical Essays on Thornton Wilder.* New York: G. K. Hall, 1996. A collection of essays on the works of Wilder. Bibliography and index.

Blank, Martin, Dalma Hunyadi Brunauer, and David Garrett Izzo, eds. *Thornton Wilder: New Essays.* West Cornwall, Conn.: Locust Hill Press, 1999. A collection of essays containing critical analysis of the literary works of Wilder. Bibliography and index.

Bryer, Jackson R., ed. *Conversations with Thornton Wilder.* Jackson: University Press of Mississippi, 1992. A collection of interviews with Wilder, presenting interesting perspectives on the man and his literary works. Index.

Burbank, Rex J. *Thornton Wilder.* 2d ed. Boston: Twayne, 1978. In this updated version of the 1962 edition, Burbank traces the history of critical controversy surrounding Wilder's work, offers insights into his methods of fictional and dramatic composition, and assesses his work's relative merits. Chronology, bibliography.

Castronovo, David. *Thornton Wilder.* New York: Ungar, 1986. This biography of Wilder focuses on critical analysis and interpretation of his literary works. Bibliography and index.

Harrison, Gilbert A. *The Enthusiast: A Life of Thornton Wilder.* New Haven, Conn.: Ticknor & Fields, 1983. A biography of Wilder that covers his life and works. Bibliography and index.

Lifton, Paul. *Vast Encyclopedia: The Theatre of Thornton Wilder.* Westport, Conn.: Greenwood Press, 1995. An examination of the contribution that Wilder made to American theater. Bibliography and index.

Walsh, Claudette. *Thornton Wilder: A Reference Guide, 1926-1990.* A Reference Guide to Literature. New York: G. K. Hall, 1993. An annotated bibliography of works on or by Wilder. Indexes.

Wilder, Amos Niven. *Thornton Wilder and His Public.* Philadelphia: Fortress Press, 1980. An interesting account of the relationship between Wilder and his critical and reading public, written by Wilder's older brother, a theologian. His aim is to offer a sophisticated discrimination, both aesthetic and sociological, of his brother's work in the light of contemporary American reality, particularly its symbolism, dynamics, creative modes, and registers of meaning. Bibliography and appendix.

Thomas P. Adler,
updated by Genevieve Slomski

Tennessee Williams

Born: Columbus, Mississippi; March 26, 1911
Died: New York, New York; February 25, 1983

Principal drama • *Fugitive Kind*, pr. 1937, pb. 2001; *Spring Storm*, wr. 1937, pr., pb. 1999; *Not About Nightingales*, wr. 1939, pr., pb. 1998; *Battle of Angels*, pr. 1940, pb. 1945; *This Property Is Condemned*, pb. 1941, pr. 1946 (one act); *I Rise in Flame, Cried the Phoenix*, wr. 1941, pb. 1951, pr. 1959 (one act); *The Lady of Larkspur Lotion*, pb. 1942 (one act); *The Glass Menagerie*, pr. 1944, pb. 1945; *Twenty-seven Wagons Full of Cotton*, pb. 1945, pr. 1955 (one act); *You Touched Me*, pr. 1945, pb. 1947 (with Donald Windham); *Summer and Smoke*, pr. 1947, pb. 1948; *A Streetcar Named Desire*, pr., pb. 1947; *American Blues*, pb. 1948 (collection); *Five Short Plays*, pb. 1948; *The Long Stay Cut Short: Or, The Unsatisfactory Supper*, pb. 1948 (one act); *The Rose Tattoo*, pr. 1950, pb. 1951; *Camino Real*, pr., pb. 1953; *Cat on a Hot Tin Roof*, pr., pb. 1955; *Orpheus Descending*, pr. 1957, pb. 1958 (revision of *Battle of Angels*); *Suddenly Last Summer*, pr., pb. 1958; *The Enemy: Time*, pb. 1959; *Sweet Bird of Youth*, pr., pb. 1959 (based on *The Enemy: Time*); *Period of Adjustment*, pr. 1959, pb. 19s60; *The Night of the Iguana*, pr., pb. 1961; *The Milk Train Doesn't Stop Here Anymore*, pr. 1963, revised pb. 1976; *The Eccentricities of a Nightingale*, pr., pb. 1964 (revision of *Summer and Smoke*); *Slapstick Tragedy: "The Mutilated" and "The Gnädiges Fräulein,"* pr. 1966, pb. 1970 (one acts); *The Two-Character Play*, pr. 1967, pb. 1969; *The Seven Descents of Myrtle*, pr., pb. 1968 (as *Kingdom of Earth*); *In the Bar of a Tokyo Hotel*, pr. 1969, pb. 1970; *Confessional*, pb. 1970; *Dragon Country*, pb. 1970 (collection); *The Theatre of Tennessee Williams*, pb. 1971-1981 (7 volumes); *Out Cry*, pr. 1971, pb. 1973 (revision of *The Two-Character Play*); *Small Craft Warnings*, pr., pb. 1972 (revision of *Confessional*); *Vieux Carré*, pr. 1977, pb. 1979; *A Lovely Sunday for Creve Coeur*, pr. 1979, pb. 1980; *Clothes for a Summer Hotel*, pr. 1980; *A House Not Meant to Stand*, pr. 1981; *Something Cloudy, Something Clear*, pr. 1981, pb. 1995

Other literary forms • Besides his plays, Tennessee Williams produced essays, letters, memoirs, music lyrics, original screenplays, poetry, short stories, and novels.

Achievements • By critical consensus, Tennessee Williams ranks second after Eugene O'Neill among American dramatists. He was greatly influenced by Anton Chekhov in his ability to universalize strongly realized local settings, in his portrayal of frail characters in a cold and alien world, in his frequently superb use of symbol and in his development of a natural structure that does not call attention to itself. Like Chekhov's best works, Williams's best plays appear to unfold as naturally as life itself. Williams has been accused at times of "purple" writing, sentimentality, and an overemphasis on violence and depravity. Although such criticism may occasionally be justified, Williams remains one of the most dramatically effective and profoundly perceptive playwrights of the modern theater.

Biography • Tennessee Williams was born Thomas Lanier Williams in 1911 in Columbus, Mississippi, the son of Cornelius Coffin Williams and Edwina Dakin Williams. He lived his early years in the home of his grandparents, for whom he felt great affection. His grandfather was a minister, and Williams's father was a traveling salesperson, apparently at home infrequently. In about 1919, his father accepted a nontraveling position at his firm's headquarters in St. Louis. The move from a more or less traditional southern environment to a very different metropolitan world was extremely painful both for Williams and for his older sister, neither of whom ever really recovered from it.

The Glass Menagerie is clearly a play about the Williams family and its life in St. Louis, though Williams's *Memoirs* (1975) and other known facts make it clear that the play is by no means a precise transcription of actuality. On the other hand, *The Glass Menagerie* is not the only Williams play that has biographical elements. His father, his mother, and his sister (who became mentally ill) are reflected in his characters in various plays. Williams's homosexuality, which he examines in some detail in his *Memoirs*, is also an important element in a number of his plays, including *A Streetcar Named Desire*, *Cat on a Hot Tin Roof*, and *Suddenly Last Summer*.

(Sam Shaw, courtesy of New Directions)

Williams attended the University of Missouri and Washington University and was graduated in 1938 from the University of Iowa. His adult life involved considerable wandering, with periods in such places as Key West, New Orleans, and New York. After various attempts at writing, some of which gained helpful recognition, Williams first won acclaim with *The Glass Menagerie*. Most of his plays from that point through *The Night of the Iguana* were successful, either on first production or later. He won Pulitzer Prizes for *A Streetcar Named Desire* and *Cat on a Hot Tin Roof*, and New York Drama Critics Circle Awards for those two and for *The Glass Menagerie* and *The Night of the Iguana*. The many plays that he wrote in the last twenty years of his life, however, achieved almost no success, either in the United States or abroad. Depending on one's point of view, either Williams's inspiration had run out, or he was writing a kind of play for which neither the public nor most critics were yet ready. Williams died in New York on February 25, 1983, having choked on a foreign object lodged in his throat.

Analysis • If the weight of critical opinion places Tennessee Williams below Eugene O'Neill as America's premiere dramatist, there should be no question that the former playwright is without peer in either the diversity of genres in which he wrote or his impact on the cultural consciousness of mid-twentieth century America. In the course of his long career, Williams wrote essays; letters; memoirs; music lyrics; original screenplays, including that for the controversial *Baby Doll*; poetry; short stories; and novels, one of which, the bittersweet *The Roman Spring of Mrs. Stone*, was made into a major motion picture.

It is as a playwright, however, that Williams's genius shines most brightly, particularly from the early 1940's to the early 1960's, a period comprising *The Glass Menagerie, Summer and Smoke, A Streetcar Named Desire, The Rose Tattoo, Cat on a Hot Tin Roof, Orpheus Descending, Suddenly Last Summer, Sweet Bird of Youth*, and *The Night of the Iguana*. These plays encompass an unrelenting exploration of the dark underbelly of human experience: frigidity and nymphomania, impotence and rape, pedophilia and fetishism, cannibalism and coprophagy, alcohol and drug addiction, castration and syphilis, violence and madness, and aging and death. These themes place Williams squarely in the gothic tradition and reflect his early interest in the bizarre and grotesque. As a child he was fed large doses of Edgar Allan Poe by his grandfather. Tormented by a sense of existential loneliness, Williams was able to sublimate his dark vision into plays that bring to life such iconic characters as Big Daddy, Stanley Kowalski, Blanche Dubois, and Amanda Wingfield in language that has been compared favorably with William Shakespeare's. Williams is second to none among American writers whose works have been successfully made into major films. His plays have been translated into more than a score of languages and continue to be performed in theaters throughout the world.

The Glass Menagerie • Williams's *The Glass Menagerie* was regarded when first produced as highly unusual; one of the play's four characters serves as commentator as well as participant; the play itself represents the memories of the commentator years later, and hence, as he says, is not a depiction of actuality; its employment of symbolism is unusual; and in the very effective ending, a scrim descends in front of mother and daughter, so that by stage convention one can see but not hear them, with the result that both, but especially the mother, become much more moving and even archetypal. The play is also almost unique historically, in that it first opened in Chicago, came close to flopping before Chicago newspaper theater critics verbally whipped people into going, and then played successfully for months in Chicago before finally moving to equal success in New York.

One device that Williams provided for the play was quickly abandoned: A series of legends and images flashed on a screen, indicating the central idea of scenes and parts of scenes. This device provides a triple insight into Williams: first, his skill at organizing scenes into meaningful wholes; second, his willingness to experiment, sometimes successfully, sometimes not; and third, his occasional tendency to spell out by external devices what a play itself makes clear.

The Glass Menagerie opens on a near-slum apartment, with Tom Wingfield setting the time (the Depression and Spanish-Civil-War 1930's); the play's method as memory, with its consequent use of music and symbol; and the names and relationships of the characters: Tom, his sister Laura, his mother Amanda, and an initially unnamed gentleman caller. A fifth character, Tom says, is his father, who, having deserted his family years before, appears only as a larger-than-life photograph over the mantel, which on occasion—according to Williams's stage directions, but rarely in actual production—lights up.

Tom works in a shoe warehouse, writes poetry, and feels imprisoned by the knowledge that his hateful job is essential to the family's financial survival. Apparently, his one escape is to go to the movies. His relationship with his mother is a combination of love, admiration, frustration, and acrimony, with regular flare-ups and reconciliations. His relationship with his sister is one of love and sympathy. Laura is physically crippled as well as withdrawn from the outside world. She is psychologically unable (as one learns in scene 2) to attend business college and lives in a world of her phonograph records and fragile glass animals.

Amanda, a more complex character than the others, is the heart of the play: a constantly chattering woman who lives in part for her memories, perhaps exaggerated, of an idealized antebellum southern girlhood and under the almost certain illusion that her son will amount to something and that her daughter will marry; yet she also lives very positively in the real world, aware of the family's poverty, keeping track of the bills, scratching for money by selling magazine subscriptions, taking advantage of her membership in the Daughters of the American Revolution. She is aware, too, that she must constantly remind her son of his responsibility to his family and that if her daughter is ever to marry, it must be through the machinations of mother and son. Yet, on the other hand, she is insufficiently aware of how her nagging and nostalgia drive her son to desperation and of how both son and daughter act on occasion to protect her illusions and memories.

Scene 1 provides a general picture of this background; scene 2 is a confrontation between mother and daughter. Amanda has discovered that, rather than attending business college, Laura has simply left and returned home at the proper hours, spending her time walking in the park, visiting the zoo, or going to the movies. Amanda must accept the fact that a job for Laura is out of the question, and she therefore starts planning for the other alternative, marriage.

The scene introduces a second symbol in a nickname that Laura says a boy gave her in high school: "Blue Roses." Roses are delicate and beautiful, like Laura and like her glass menagerie, but blue roses, like glass animals, have no real existence. Scene 3 shows Amanda trying unsuccessfully to sell magazine subscriptions on the telephone and ends in a shockingly violent quarrel between mother and son, concluding with Tom throwing his overcoat across the room in his rage and unintentionally destroying some of Laura's animals. One of Williams's most notable uses of lighting occurs in this scene. A pool of light envelops Laura as Tom and Amanda quarrel, so that one becomes aware without words that the devastating effect on Laura is the scene's major point. Scene 4 shows Laura talking Tom into an apology and reconciliation, and Amanda taking advantage of Tom's remorse to persuade him to invite a friend from the warehouse home to dinner, in the hope that the "gentleman caller" will be attracted to Laura.

Scene 5 is long, building up suspense for Amanda and for the audience. Tom announces to his mother that he has invited a warehouse friend, Jim O'Connor, to dinner the next evening. Amanda, pleased but shocked at the suddenness of this new development, makes elaborate plans and has high expectations, but Tom tries to make her face the reality of Laura's physical and psychological limitations. Scene 6 shows the arrival of the guest and his attempt to accept Amanda's pathetic and almost comical southern-belle behavior and elaborate "fussing," and Laura's almost pathological fright and consequent inability to come to the dinner table. Dialogue between Tom and Jim makes clear Jim's relative steadiness and definite if perhaps overly optimistic plans for a career. It also reveals Tom's near failure at his job, his frustration over his family's situation, and his ripening determination to leave home: He has joined the merchant seamen's union instead of paying the light bill. The scene ends with the onset of a sharp summer storm. Laura, terrified, is on the sofa trying desperately not to cry; the others are at the dinner table and Tom is saying grace: a combination remarkable for its irony and pathos.

At the beginning of scene 7, the lights go out because of Tom's failure to pay the light bill, so the whole scene is played in candlelight. It is the climactic scene, and in it, Williams faced a problem faced by many modern playwrights: What kind of outcome does one choose, and by what means, in a situation where if things go one way they might seem incredible, and if they go the other, they might seem overly obvious? It is perhaps not a wholly soluble situation, but Williams did remarkably well in handling it. By Amanda's inevitable machinations after dinner, Jim and Laura are left alone. Jim—who has turned out to be the "Blue Roses" boy from high school, the boy with whom Laura was close to being in love—is a sympathetic and understanding person who, even in the short time they are alone together, manages to get more spontaneous and revealing conversation out of Laura than her family ever has, and even persuades her to dance. Clearly, here is a person who could bring to reality Amanda's seemingly impossible dreams, a man who could lead Laura into the real world (as he symbolically brought her glass unicorn into it by unintentionally breaking off its horn), a man who would make a good husband.

For the play to end thus, however, would be out of accord with the facts of Williams's family life, with the tone of the whole play up to that point, and with modern audience's dislike of pat, happy endings in serious plays. Jim tells Laura that he is already engaged, a fact made more believable by Tom's unawareness of it. Laura's life is permanently in ruins. What might have happened will never happen. When Amanda learns the truth from Jim just before he leaves, the resulting quarrel with Tom confirms Tom in his plans to leave home permanently, abandoning his mother and sister to an apparently hopeless situation. Yet as he tells the audience—who are watching a soundless Amanda hovering over Laura to comfort her by candlelight—his flight has been unsuccessful. The memories haunt him; Laura haunts him. Speaking to her from a far-off world, he begs her to blow her candles out and thus obliterate the memory. She does, and the curtain falls.

A Streetcar Named Desire • Williams's next successful play, *A Streetcar Named Desire*, is generally regarded as his best. Initial reaction was mixed, but there would be little argument now that it is one of the most powerful plays in the modern theater. Like *The Glass Menagerie*, it concerns, primarily, a man and two women and a "gentleman caller." As in *The Glass Menagerie*, one of the women is very much aware of the contrast between the present and her southern-aristocratic past; one woman (Stella) is practical if not always adequately aware, while the other (Blanche) lives partly in a dream world and teeters on the brink of psychosis; the gentleman caller could perhaps save the latter were circumstances somewhat different; and the play's single set is a slum apartment.

Yet these similarities only point up the sharp differences between the two plays. *A Streetcar Named Desire* is not a memory play; it is sharply naturalistic, with some use of expressionistic devices to point up Blanche's emotional difficulties. Blanche is not, as is Laura, a bond between the other two family members; she is, rather, an intolerable intruder who very nearly breaks up her sister's marriage. A more complex creation than anyone in *The Glass Menagerie*, she is fascinating, cultured, pathetic, vulgar, admirable, despicable: a woman who, unlike Amanda, cannot function adequately outside the safe, aristocratic world of the past, but who, like Amanda, can fight almost ferociously for what she wants, even when it is almost surely unattainable. Her opponent, Stella's husband, Stanley Kowalski, is also a much sharper figure than Tom Wingfield.

One of the major critical problems of *A Streetcar Named Desire* has been whose side one should be on in the battle between Blanche and Stanley. The answer may be one that some critics have been unable to accept: neither and both. Blanche's defense of culture, of the intellectual and aesthetic aspects of life, may be pathetic coming from one who has become a near-alcoholic prostitute, but it is nevertheless genuine, important, and valid. Life has dealt her devastating blows, to which she has had to respond alone; her sister has offered no help. Yet she herself is partly responsible for the horrible world in which she finds herself, and her attempts to find a haven from it are both pitiable and (because she is inadequately aware of the needs of others) repellent.

Stanley, the sort of man who might, in later years, be called "macho," uncultured and uninterested in culture, capable (as Blanche also is in her own way) of violence, is nevertheless an intelligent man, a man who functions more capably than do any of his friends in the world in which he finds himself, a man who loves his wife and would be pathetically lost without her. Stanley would find any intrusion into his happy home intolerable, but he finds it doubly so when the intruder is a woman who stays on indefinitely, a woman with Blanche's affectations, her intolerance of any lifestyle other than that of her own childhood, her obvious dislike of her sister's marriage, and her corrupt sexual past, which makes her attempts to attract one of Stanley's best friends more than Stanley can tolerate.

It is ironic that the play should end on a "happily-ever-after" note for Stanley and Stella (though surely Blanche can never be wholly forgotten), but this is life, not a model of life. Indeed, the life that both find, apparently, wholly satisfying and sufficient is itself a sort of irony. Stella has had to give up everything that Blanche believes in, everything from her own past, in order to accept it and welcome it.

The setting of *A Streetcar Named Desire* is the street and outdoor stairs of the building in which the Kowalskis live, and the interior of their two-room apartment. As scene 1 opens, neighbors are out front talking. Stanley and Mitch come in, prepared to go bowling. Stanley is carrying a package of meat. Stella comes out. Stanley throws the meat to her, and even the neighbors are amused at the symbolism. Stanley and Mitch proceed to the bowling alley, and Stella follows. Then Blanche comes around the corner, with her suitcase, dressed all in white—another ironic symbol—in a fashion appropriate to an upper-class garden party. In a stage direction, Williams compares her to a moth, and throughout the play, she fears the alluring but destructive light. She fears people seeing how she really looks. She fears facing the truth or having other people learn it. As she later says, she fibs because fibs are more pleasant; symbolically, she covers the overhead light bulb in the apartment with a paper lantern. Paper, indeed, is a recurring symbol throughout the play. For example, two of the melodies one hears from a distance are "Paper Doll" and "Paper Moon."

Blanche has never before seen Stella's apartment or met her sister's husband. To mark her progress through New Orleans to get to the apartment, Williams took advantage of actual New Orleans names (or former names); Blanche has to transfer from a streetcar called Desire to one called Cemeteries in order to arrive in the slum, called Elysian Fields. While the first of the streetcars gives the title to the play, Williams wisely makes use of the names only once after the opening scene. Blanche's progress in the play is from a wide range of desires (for culture, security, sex, and money) to a sort of living death, and while the slum may be an Elysian Fields for Stanley and Stella, it is a Tartarus for her. Williams also, like many earlier dramatists, gave some of his characters meaningful, and in this case, ironic names. Blanche DuBois is by no means a White Woods (though the name is a reminder of Anton Chekhov's *Vishnyovy sad*, pr., pb. 1904; *The Cherry Orchard*, 1908, and hence of the sort of life she has lost), and Stella is no Star. Such devices can be overdone: The name of their lost plantation, Belle Reve, may be an example.

A neighbor who owns the building lets Blanche into the apartment, and another neighbor goes for Stella. Blanche is alone. Like Laura on the night of the dinner, she is skittish, but her reaction is different: She spots a bottle of whiskey and takes a slug. Stella rushes in and, as is common in plays that begin with an arrival, the audience learns a great deal about both sisters as they talk—learns about their past, about Blanche's hostile attitude toward her environment, about the grim string of family ill-nesses and deaths, about the loss of the plantation. The sisters love each other but are obviously at odds in many respects. Blanche has been a schoolteacher, but one may doubt the reason she gives, a sort of sick leave, for being in New Orleans in early May while school at home is still in session. Stanley comes in with Mitch and another friend. Williams's description of him here, as the gaudy, dominant seed bearer, is famous. With Stella in the bathroom and his friends gone, Stanley encounters Blanche alone. He is surprised, but he tries to play the friendly host. Presently, he asks Blanche if she had not once been married. Blanche says that the boy died, promptly adding that she feels sick. The scene ends.

A prominent feature of this first scene, one that continues throughout the play, is the use of sound effects. There are sound effects in *The Glass Menagerie*, too, such as the glass menagerie thematic music and the music from the nearby dance hall, but in *A Streetcar Named Desire*, the sound effects are much more elaborate. As the curtain rises, one hears the voices of people passing and the sound of the "Blue Piano" in the nearby bar, and the piano becomes louder at appropriate points. Twice a cat screeches, fright-ening Blanche badly. As the subject of her husband and his death comes up, one hears—softly here but louder when Blanche reaches a crisis—the music of a polka, clearly a sound inside Blanche's head and hence an expressionistic device. At the end of scene 2, in which Blanche and Stanley have had a conversation that is both hostile and covertly sexual, a tamale vendor is heard calling "Red-hot!" Similar effects, nota-bly of trains roaring past, occur throughout the play.

Scene 2 begins with a dialogue between Stanley and Stella. It is the next evening. Stella is taking Blanche out to dinner in order not to interfere with the poker night Stanley has planned. Stanley learns of the loss of the plantation and is angry, especially after he examines Blanche's trunk and finds it full of expensive clothes and furs. Stella has postponed telling Blanche that she is pregnant. Blanche enters and, seeing the situ-ation, sends Stella on an errand so that she can have it out with Stanley. Stanley must accept the fact that the plantation has been lost because it was heavily mortgaged, and the mortgage payments could not be made. Blanche grows playful with him, and Stan-ley implies that she is being deliberately provocative. Stanley comes across Blanche's love letters from her dead husband, and Blanche becomes almost hysterical. Stanley tells Blanche of the coming baby. The men begin to arrive for poker. Stella returns and leads Blanche away.

Scene 3, entitled "The Poker Night," opens on a garish and, Williams says, Van Gogh-like view of Stanley and his three friends playing poker. Stanley has had too much to drink and is becoming verbally violent. The women return from their evening out. Blanche encounters Mitch at the bathroom door—she wants to take another of her endless hot baths—and they are clearly attracted to each other. Stanley, hating the presence of women during a poker game, becomes physically violent, and (offstage) hits Stella. The other men, who are familiar with this behavior but feel great affection for Stanley, subdue him and leave. Blanche, horrified, has taken Stella to the upstairs apartment. Stanley realizes what has happened, sobs, and screams for Stella, who presently joins him on the outside stairs. They fall into a sexual embrace, and he carries her inside. Clearly, this series of events has occurred before; clearly, this is the usual outcome, and is one of the attractions that Stanley has for Stella. Blanche comes down the stairs, even more horrified, and Mitch returns and comforts her.

In scene 4, Blanche returns from upstairs the next morning and is shocked to learn that Stella accepts all that has happened and wants no change in her marital situation. With some justice, Blanche describes Stanley as an uncultured animal in a world in which culture is essential—a speech that Stanley overhears. He comes in, and to Blanche's horror, Stella embraces him. It is in this scene that Blanche, uselessly and desperately, first thinks of an old boyfriend, now rich, as a source of rescue from her plight, a futile idea that she develops and tries harder and harder to believe in as her plight worsens.

Scene 5 contains an example of Williams's occasionally excessive irony: Stanley asks Blanche her astrological sign, and it turns out that his is Capricorn and hers is Virgo. The major import of the scene is that Stanley confronts Blanche with stories he has heard about her life back home—and afterward Blanche admits to Stella that some of them are true. Blanche and Stella agree that marrying Mitch is the solution to Blanche's problem, and Blanche is left alone. A young newsboy comes to collect money, and Blanche comes very close to trying, consciously and cynically, to seduce him. Clearly, sex, like alcohol, has been both a cause of and a response to her situation. Mitch arrives for a date, holding a bunch of roses, and the scene ends. Scene 6 opens with the return of the two from their date. Its major import is Blanche's telling Mitch about her dead husband, whom she encountered one evening in an embrace with an older man. Later that evening, while they were dancing to the polka she now keeps hearing, Blanche, unable to stop herself, told him he disgusted her. A few minutes later, he went outside and shot himself. Telling the story is a catharsis for Blanche and deeply enlists Mitch's sympathy. They are in each other's arms, and he suggests the possibility of marriage.

In scene 7, several months later, with Blanche still there and with the marriage idea apparently no further advanced, Stanley tells Stella of his now detailed and verified knowledge of Blanche's sordid sexual past, including her having seduced a seventeen-year-old student. As a result of this last action, Blanche lost her job, and Stanley, as he explains to Stella, has told Mitch the whole story. Stella is horrified, both at the facts themselves and at their revelation to Mitch. It is Blanche's birthday, there is a birthday cake, and Mitch has been invited. Scene 8 shows the women's mounting distress as Mitch fails to show up for the party; Stanley gives Blanche a "birthday present," a bus ticket back home for the following Tuesday; he makes it clear that Blanche's presence all this time has been almost too much to endure. Stella develops labor pains and leaves with Stanley for the hospital. Scene 9, later that evening, shows Mitch coming in with very changed intentions, tearing the paper lantern off and turning on the light to see Blanche plainly for the first time, telling her she is not clean enough to take home to his mother, and trying to get her to bed. She reacts violently, and he runs out.

In scene 10, the climactic scene, Stanley comes back. Blanche has been drinking and is desperately upset. With Stanley, she tries to retreat into fanciful illusions—Mitch has returned and apologized, her rich boyfriend has invited her on a Caribbean tour. Stanley exposes her lies, and her desperation grows, as indicated by lurid, darting shadows and other expressionistic devices. Their confrontation reaches a climax, and after she tries to resist, he carries her off to bed. In scene 11, some weeks later, one learns that Blanche has told Stella that Stanley raped her, that Stella must believe that the rape is merely one of Blanche's psychotic illusions if her life with Stanley is to survive, and that Stella has made arrangements to place Blanche in a state institution. A doctor and nurse come to get her. Blanche is terrified. The nurse is cold and almost brutal, but the doctor gains Blanche's confidence by playing the role of a gentleman, and she leaves on his arm, clearly feeling that she has found what she has been seeking, a man to protect her. All this occurs while another poker game is in progress. The play ends with Stella in Stanley's arms, and with one of the other men announcing, "This game is seven-card stud."

The brutes have won, and Stella has permanently denied her heritage, yet one must remember that the "brutes" are not without redeeming qualities. Stanley has displayed intense loyalty to his friends, genuine love for his wife, and a variety of insecurities beneath his aggressive manner. The other men have displayed loyalty to Stanley, and Mitch has shown much sympathy and understanding. As Blanche has said early in the play, Stanley may be just what their bloodline needs, and that point is emphasized when, near the end of the final scene, the upstairs neighbor hands Stella her baby. Life must go on; perhaps the next generation will do better; but long before the play opens, life has destroyed a potentially fine and sensitive woman.

Cat on a Hot Tin Roof • Of Williams's four plays analyzed here, *Cat on a Hot Tin Roof,* his next big success, is the only one that falls into a special Williams category: plays that at some stage or stages have been heavily revised. Williams has said that, because of advice from Elia Kazan, the director of the first Broadway production, he made changes in the third act. The changes include the appearance of one of the main characters, Big Daddy, who had been in the second act only, and adjustments changing the bare possibility of an affirmative ending to a probability. Revisions of considerably greater scope than this were made by Williams in other plays, including plays that were completely rewritten long after their original productions (*Summer and Smoke* into *The Eccentricities of a Nightingale,* and *Battle of Angels* into *Orpheus Descending*).

Cat on a Hot Tin Roof is famous for its somewhat expressionistic set, the bedroom of Brick and Margaret (Maggie) Pollitt. The two major pieces of furniture, both with symbolic value, are a large double bed and a combination radio-phonograph-television-liquor cabinet. The walls are to disappear into air at the top, and the set is to be roofed by the sky, as though to suggest that the action of the play is representative of universal human experience. The powerful expressionistic psychology of the play recalls the theater of August Strindberg, but *Cat on a Hot Tin Roof* is deeply embedded in revealed reality, with one major exception: One does not know the truth, one cannot know the truth, behind the crucial relationship between Brick and his dead friend Skipper; the degree (if any) of Brick's responsibility for Skipper's decline and death; or of Maggie's responsibility.

The bedroom, outside of which is a gallery running the length of the house, is in the plantation mansion of Brick's father, Big Daddy, on his twenty-eight-thousand-acre estate in the Mississippi delta. The first act is largely a monologue by Maggie, talking to a mostly inattentive and uninterested Brick, and interrupted only by brief appearances of Brick's mother, Big Mama, and his sister-in-law Mae and two of her five, soon to be six, children. Maggie, like Amanda and Blanche before her, is a loquacious and desperate woman who may be fighting for the impossible; unlike her predecessors, she lives entirely in the present and without major illusions, and hence fights more realistically. She wants Brick to return to her bed: She is a cat on a hot tin roof, sexually desperate but interested only in her husband.

As the largely one-sided conversation continues, one learns the circumstances underlying Brick's loss of interest in her. Maggie tells Brick the news that his father is dying of cancer. Brick and Maggie have been living in the house for several months. Formerly an important athlete, a professional football player, and then a sports announcer, he has given up everything and lapsed into heavy drinking. He is on a crutch, having broken his ankle attempting, while drunk the previous night, to jump hurdles on the high school athletic field. Mae and her husband, Brick's older brother Gooper, a lawyer in Memphis, are visiting in hope, as Maggie correctly guesses, of Big Daddy's signing a will in Gooper's favor, because, while Brick is Big Daddy's favorite, he will want the estate to go to a son who has offspring. Maggie is from a society background in Nashville, though her immediate family had been poor because of her father's alcoholism. Big Daddy himself is a Mississippi redneck who has worked his way to great wealth. Brick and Maggie met as students at the University of Mississippi. Formerly, according to Maggie, an excellent lover, Brick has made Maggie agree that they will stay together only if she leaves him alone. Unable to bear the frustration, Maggie is ready to break the agreement and fight to get Brick back.

The roots of Brick and Maggie's conflict are fitfully revealed when Maggie begins to speak of Skipper, their dead friend, any mention of whom greatly upsets Brick. In Maggie's version of the story, from college on, Brick's greatest loyalty was to Skipper. She says that Brick's standards of love and friendship were so pure as to have been frustrating to both Skipper and Maggie; that on an out-of-town football weekend when Brick had been injured and could not go, Maggie and Skipper, out of their common frustration, went to bed together; that Skipper could not perform, and that Maggie therefore, but in no condemnatory sense, assumed that he was unconsciously homosexual, though she believes that Brick is not. Maggie told Skipper that he was actually in love with her husband, and she now believes that it was this revelation that prompted Skipper to turn to liquor and drugs, leading to his death. Maggie now tells Brick that she has been examined by a gynecologist, that she is capable of bearing children, and that it is the right time of the month to conceive. Brick asks how it is going to happen when he finds her repellent. She says that that is a problem to be solved.

Act 2 is famous for consisting almost entirely of a remarkably effective and revealing dialogue between Brick and Big Daddy. The act opens, however, with the whole family there, as well as their minister, the Reverend Mr. Tooker. The minister is there ostensibly because of Big Daddy's birthday, and there is to be cake and champagne. From the family's point of view, he is also there because after the birthday party (which is as big a failure as Blanche's), they are going to tell Big Mama the truth about Big Daddy's cancer, and they want his help in the crisis. From his own point of view, he is there to hint at a contribution, either now or in Big Daddy's will or both, for ornamentation for his church. He is totally useless in the crisis and is therefore, in spite of Williams's deep affection for his own minister grandfather, typical of Williams's ministers.

The birthday party will take place in Brick and Maggie's bedroom because Brick is on a crutch: an ingenious pretext for limiting the play's action to a single setting. Big Daddy is one of Williams's most complex characters, and the contradictions in his nature are never fully examined, any more than they are with Blanche, because, as Williams says in a stage direction in act 2, any truly drawn characters will retain some mystery. Big Daddy is a loud, vulgar, apparently insensitive man who was originally a workman on the estate, then owned by a pair of homosexual men. He is now in a position of power and worth many millions.

Desperately afraid to show any real feelings, he pretends to dislike his whole family, although in the case of Gooper and Mae and their children, the dislike is genuine and deep. One never learns his real attitude toward Maggie. Near the end of his talk with Brick, with great difficulty, Big Daddy expresses the love he has for him. His real attitude toward Big Mama remains uncertain. He has always teased her, made gross fun of her, and in his ostensibly frank conversation with Brick, he says that he has always disliked her, even in bed. He is clearly moved, however, when at the end of the family-scene part of the act, she, who is in her own way both as gross and as vulnerable as he, yells that she has always loved him. The conversation with Brick reveals his sensitivity in another direction: his distress over the intense poverty he has seen while traveling abroad and particularly an instance in Morocco when he saw a very small child being used as a procurer.

The motivation for the long father-and-son talk is that Big Daddy, hugely relieved at having been told, falsely, that he does not have cancer, wants to find out why Brick has given up working, given up Maggie (as everyone knows, because Gooper and Mae have listened in their bedroom next door), and turned to heavy drinking. Apparently, he has attempted frank talks with Brick in the past, with no success, even though each clearly loves and respects the other, and because of Brick's lack of interest and determined reticence, it would appear that that is how the conversation is going now. Having just gone through a severe life crisis himself, however, Big Daddy is determined to help his son. He gets the beginning of an answer out of Brick by taking away his crutch so he cannot get at his liquor. Brick's answer is that he is disgusted with the world's "mendacity." Finding that answer insufficient, Big Daddy finally brings himself to make the climactic statement that the problem began when Skipper died; he adds that Gooper and Mae think the Brick-Skipper relationship was not "normal." Brick, at last unable to maintain his detachment, is furious.

In a stage direction, Williams says that Skipper died to disavow the idea that there was any sexual feeling in the friendship, but whether Skipper did have such feelings is necessarily left uncertain. Brick himself, in his outrage, makes painfully clear that the very idea of homosexuality disgusts him. The relationship, he believes, was simply an unusually profound friendship, though he is finally forced to grant the likelihood that, from Skipper's point of view, though emphatically not his own, sexual love existed. (Whether Brick is himself bisexual is left uncertain, but it is clear that he could not face this idea if it were true.) He grants that liquor has been his refuge from a fact that Big Daddy (who has no prejudice against homosexuals) makes him face: that Brick's unwillingness to believe in the possibility of a homosexual reaction in Skipper, and to help Skipper recognize and accept it, is the major cause of Skipper's death. In a statement strongly reminiscent of some situations in the plays of O'Neill, Brick says that there are only two ways out: liquor and death. Liquor is his way, death was Skipper's. Then, in a state of strong emotional upheaval, Brick makes his father face the truth as his father has made him face it: He is dying of cancer. There is justice in Brick's remark that friends—and he and his father are friends—tell each other the truth, because the truth needs to be faced. As the act ends, Big Daddy is screaming at the liars who had kept the truth from him.

In the original version, as act 3 opens, the family and the Reverend Mr. Tooker enter. Big Daddy, one must assume, has gone to his bedroom to face his situation alone. The purpose of the gathering is to have the doctor, who presently comes in with Maggie, tell Big Mama the truth. Brick is in and out during the scene, but—in spite of appeals from Maggie and from Big Mama—he remains wholly aloof and is still drinking. If the shock of his conversation with Big Daddy is going to have an effect, it has not yet done so. After much hesitation, the doctor tells Big Mama the truth, to which she reacts with the expected horror. He tells her that Big Daddy's pain will soon become so severe as to require morphine injections, and he leaves a package.

Big Mama wants comfort only from Brick, not from Gooper. The Reverend Mr. Tooker leaves promptly, and the doctor soon follows. Gooper tries to get Big Mama to agree to a plan he has drawn up to take over the estate as trustee. Big Mama will have it run by nobody but Brick, whom she calls her only son. She remarks what a comfort it would be to Big Daddy if Brick and Maggie had a child. Maggie announces that she is pregnant. Whether this lie is planned or spontaneous, one has no way of knowing, but Brick does not deny it. Gooper and Mae, whose behavior throughout the scene has been despicable, are shocked and incredulous. Big Mama has run out to tell Big Daddy the happy news.

Gooper and Mae soon follow, but just before they go, a loud cry of agony fills the house: Big Daddy is feeling the pain the doctor has predicted. Maggie and Brick are left alone. Maggie thanks Brick for his silence. Brick feels the "click" that results from enough liquor and that gives him peace, and he goes out on the gallery, singing. Maggie has a sudden inspiration and takes all the liquor out of the room. When Brick comes in she tells him what she has done, says she is in control, and declares that she will not return the liquor until he has gone to bed with her. He grabs for his crutch, but she is quicker, and she throws the crutch off the gallery to the ground. Big Mama rushes in, almost hysterical, to get the package of morphine. Maggie reiterates that she is in charge and tells Brick she loves him. Brick, in the last speech of the play, says exactly what Big Daddy had said earlier when Big Mama said she loved him: "Wouldn't it be funny if that was true." Apparently, he has yielded. The curtain falls.

The ending is dramatically effective, but in a different way from Williams's earlier endings. *The Glass Menagerie*'s ending is final in one way, because it is all in the past, and *A Streetcar Named Desire*'s in another, because Blanche is escorted off, and Stanley and Stella are reconciled. In *Cat on a Hot Tin Roof*, one can only assume that Brick will "perform," that the result will be a pregnancy, and that the eventual effect of Maggie's use of force and of Big Daddy's shock tactics may be Brick's return to normality. Even in its original form, as here described, that is what the ending suggests, and Williams's instinct to leave an element of uncertainty seems correct.

The Night of the Iguana • *The Night of the Iguana* was Williams's next (and last) unmistakably successful play, after a series of plays of varying degrees of stage success but with more or less serious flaws. Unlike all of his earlier plays except *Camino Real*, *The Night of the Iguana* is set outside the United States and does not in any significant sense concern southerners. It also differs from almost all the plays after *The Glass Menagerie* in being free of serious violence. Besides *A Streetcar Named Desire*, with the suicide of Blanche's husband, Williams had used castration, murder by blowtorch, death by cannibalism, and other extreme acts of violence, prompting the accusation, at times with some justice, of sensationalism.

The Night of the Iguana takes place on the veranda of a third-rate, isolated hotel in Mexico, in a rain forest high above the Pacific. Like several other Williams plays, it grew out of what was originally a short story. Unlike any of the others, except possibly the expressionistic *Camino Real*, its ending is affirmative, suggesting hope not only for the three major characters but also for humanity in general. The central male character, a minister who has been locked out of his church because of fornication and what was regarded as an atheistic sermon, may be prepared in the end for a life of self-sacrifice—which may turn out to be richly fulfilling, because the woman to whom he may "sacrifice" himself is a woman who knows what genuine love means. The other woman, who is the central character, is Blanche's opposite: a New Englander instead of a quintessential southerner, she is in no sense handicapped by the past; she retains a sense of humor; she sees things clearly; and she accepts her situation. She is tied to an elderly relative in a wheelchair but she is not bitter about it; the relative is neither a frustration nor an embarrassment. Finally, she uses whatever weapons she must to keep her grandfather and herself able, if sometimes only barely, to survive. Without being an obviously fierce fighter like Amanda, Blanche, or Maggie, she has come to terms with her circumstances and has prevailed. She is the first and only Williams character to do so, a new conception in his gallery of characters.

At the opening of act 1, Lawrence Shannon, the former minister, arrives at the hotel with a busload of female teachers and students on a Mexican tour for which he is the guide. He is in one of his periodic emotional breakdowns and has chosen to bring his tour party to this hotel in violation of the itinerary in order to get emotional support from his friends, the couple who run the hotel. It turns out, however, that the husband has recently drowned. The wife, now the sole owner, the brassy Maxine Faulk, clearly wants Shannon as a lover and may well be genuinely in love with him. Throughout the tour, and indeed on some previous tours, Shannon has ignored the announced tour route and facilities, leading the group where he chooses. He has also, and not for the first time, allowed himself to be seduced by a seventeen-year-old girl. The women are in a state of rebellion. Their leader, another of Williams's homosexuals, though an unimportant one, knows of the sexual liaison and later in the play reports the whole story to the tour company for which Shannon works, with the result that in act 3, he is replaced on the spot with another guide. He has the key to the tour bus, however, and refuses to relinquish it, so the passengers (most of whom never come up to the hotel) are helpless.

Shannon's situation is in some ways similar to, although milder than, Blanche's: He was pushed out of the church as Blanche was dismissed as a teacher; he is seriously distraught, and confused in his sexual orientation, he is attracted to young girls, as Blanche was to boys. Presently, there is another arrival at the hotel, Hannah Jelkes and her ninety-seven-year-old grandfather, whom she calls Nonno. She has pushed him up the hill and through the forest in his wheelchair. They are without funds, and she is desperate for a place for them to stay. Maxine, for all her rough exterior, cannot turn them away in their plight, but she is upset over their literal pennilessness. She is also upset over Hannah's desire to earn money, as she has done all over the world, by passing through hotel dining rooms so that, on request, her grandfather may recite his poetry or she may make sketches of guests.

The only other guests at the hotel, because it is the offseason, are a group of Nazis, whose presence in the play may seem puzzling, as they have nothing to do with the plot. They are in and out at various points, a raucous group, delighted with radio news of German successes in bombing Britain. Totally without feeling, they are probably in the play for contrast; their lack of feeling contrasts with Hannah's genuine sympathy for anything human except unkindness, with Nonno's sensitive artistry as a recognized minor poet, with Maxine's apparent ability to love, and with the growing evidence, as the play develops, of Shannon's potential for overcoming his self-centered and almost uncontrollable desperation.

The major focus in both act 2 and act 3 is on the dialogues between Hannah and Shannon, which, in revelation of character and effect on character, resemble the dialogue between Big Daddy and Brick. Indeed, act 2 and act 3 are so intertwined as to make it difficult to separate them. One learns about Hannah's past, about her having suffered from emotional problems similar to Shannon's, from which she recovered by sheer determination. In a sense, she has sacrificed her life to caring for her grandfather; she feels only pride and love for him, and concern over his age, his periods of senile haziness, and his inability to finish his first poem in twenty years.

In a moment of symbolism, one sees that Hannah is capable of lighting a candle in the wind. Seeking for God, she has so far found him only in human faces. In sharp contrast, Shannon's view of the world is summed up in a memory of having seen starving persons searching through piles of excrement for bits of undigested food. Hannah's insight into Shannon's problem is deep, and she is adept in techniques, from sympathy to shock, to help bring him out of his somewhat self-indulgent despair. At one point in act 2, the Mexican boys who work for Maxine bring in an iguana and tie it to a post, planning to fatten it and eat it: a normal occurrence in their world. It escapes once and is recaptured. Maxine threatens to evict Hannah and Nonno but relents when Hannah makes her understand that she is not a rival for Shannon. Nonno provides embarrassing evidence of his intermittent senility. The act ends in the early evening with a heavy thunderstorm.

Early in act 3, later in the evening, Shannon's replacement arrives, and the bus key is taken from him by force. Shannon, growing more and more hysterical, tries to pull the gold cross from his neck and threatens to go down to the ocean and swim straight out to sea until he drowns. Maxine and her Mexican boys tie him in the hammock. Maxine tells Hannah that Shannon's behavior is essentially histrionic, and Hannah soon sees for herself that he is deriving a masochistic pleasure from the situation. She tells him, in a key speech, that he is enjoying an ersatz crucifixion, thus denying Shannon the role of Christ-figure that Williams had tried unsuccessfully to give his central male characters in certain earlier plays. Hannah as model and as psychiatrist begins to have an effect. He releases himself from the ropes, as she has told him all along he is able to do, and their conversation reveals enough about Hannah's past to make him admire her stamina, her hard-won stability, and her love of humanity, and to make him want, perhaps, to emulate her. He learns of the minimal, pathetic encounters she has had with male sexuality—in one instance, a man with a fetish for women's undergarments—and while they in no way disgusted her, since nothing does except cruelty, she is nevertheless a permanent virgin who is comfortable with her virginity.

Shannon suggests that they should travel together, platonically. She rightly refuses, and puts in his mind the idea that Maxine needs him, as Nonno needs her, and that he needs to be needed in order to achieve stability. Hannah persuades Shannon to free the iguana, which is, as he has been, "at the end of its rope." Nonno wheels himself out of his room, shouting that he has finished his poem. He reads it, and they find it moving. Maxine persuades Shannon to stay with her permanently, though Williams seems undecided as to whether one should regard Shannon's acquiescence as a sacrifice. In any case, however, it is evidence that he may no longer be sexually askew and that he may be capable of living a life that has some kind of meaning.

The change is quicker than the change that may occur in Brick in *Cat on a Hot Tin Roof*, though both plays take place in a few hours, and though Williams says in a stage direction in *Cat on a Hot Tin Roof* that even if events have occurred that will result in changing a person, the change will not occur quickly. Perhaps one may say that the difference is justified in that Big Daddy, for all his love and honesty, is no Hannah—there are very few Hannahs in the world. Hannah's own trials are not over: After Maxine and Shannon go off together, as Hannah prepares to take Nonno back to his room, he quietly dies. Hannah is left alone. No one needs her any more. The curtain falls.

The play is notable for its atmosphere, its memorable characters, its compassion, its hard-won optimism. The ending of *The Glass Menagerie* is devastating. The ending of *A Streetcar Named Desire* may represent the best solution for Blanche and happiness for Stanley and Stella, but there is nevertheless a sense in which all three are victims. In *Cat on a Hot Tin Roof*, it is possible that the future will bring happiness to Brick and Maggie, but it is far from certain; the future means a horrible death from cancer for Big Daddy, a life deprived of much of its meaning for Big Mama, and wholly meaningless and despicable lives for Gooper and Mae. The contrast with *The Night of the Iguana* is enormous. With his poem, Nonno has at last, like his granddaughter, "prevailed," and one must assume that he is ready for death, a death that, in contrast to Big Daddy's, is swift and peaceful. Maxine is no longer alone and has someone to love. Shannon seems on the road to psychological recovery and a useful and satisfying life. Hannah, to be sure, is left alone, as Tom and Blanche are alone in their worlds, but the contrast between her and those others is sharp and unmistakable. She has faced previous crises, survived, prevailed. Happy endings in modern drama are rarely successful at a serious level. In *The Night of the Iguana*, Williams wrote that rare modern dramatic work: a memorable, affirmative play in which the affirmation applies to all the major characters and in which the affirmation is believable.

Other major works

LONG FICTION: *The Roman Spring of Mrs. Stone*, 1950; *Moise and the World of Reason*, 1975.

SHORT FICTION: *One Arm and Other Stories*, 1948; *Hard Candy: A Book of Stories*, 1954; *The Knightly Quest: A Novella and Four Short Stories*, 1967; *Eight Mortal Ladies Possessed: A Book of Stories*, 1974; *Collected Stories*, 1985.

POETRY: *In the Winter of Cities*, 1956; *Androgyne, Mon Amour*, 1977; *The Collected Poems of Tennessee Williams*, 2002.

SCREENPLAYS: *The Glass Menagerie*, 1950 (with Peter Berneis); *A Streetcar Named Desire*, 1951 (with Oscar Saul); *The Rose Tattoo*, 1955 (with Hal Kanter); *Baby Doll*, 1956; *The Fugitive Kind*, 1960 (with Meade Roberts; based on *Orpheus Descending*); *Suddenly Last Summer*, 1960 (with Gore Vidal); *Stopped Rocking and Other Screenplays*, 1984.

NONFICTION: *Memoirs*, 1975; *Where I Live: Selected Essays*, 1978; *Five O'Clock Angel: Letters of Tennessee Williams to Maria St. Just, 1948-1982*, 1990; *The Selected Letters of Tennessee Williams*, 2000.

Bibliography

Bloom, Harold, ed. *Tennessee Williams*. Modern Critical Views series. New York: Chelsea House, 1987. This collection of critical essays carries an introduction by Bloom that places Williams in the dramatic canon of American drama and within the psychological company of Hart Crane and Arthur Rimbaud. Authors in this collection take traditional thematic and historical approaches, noting Williams's "grotesques," his morality, his irony, his work in the "middle years," and the mythical qualities in his situations and characters.

Kolin, Philip, ed. *Tennessee Williams: A Guide to Research and Performance*. Westport: Greenwood Press, 1998. A helpful collection of twenty-three essays devoted to individual plays except the last three, which are devoted to Williams's fiction, poetry, and films respectively. Contains three indices that allow the reader easily to locate specific information.

Leverich, Lyle. *Tom: The Unknown Tennessee Williams.* New York: Crown Publishers, 1995. This is a sympathetic and meticulous study of Williams's life and work concluding with the theatrical triumph of *The Glass Menagerie* in 1945. Divided into five parts, this massive work contains a detailed genealogy of Tennessee Williams; numerous photographs of Williams, his ancestors and friends; and a useful index. Although Leverich felt that writing a biography of someone as sensitive and prickly as Williams was akin to "performing an autopsy on a living person," he admirably fulfills Williams's request to "report, in truth, his cause aright" even as he presents divergent views of this complex man. Of particular interest are the opening pages on the writer's death by strangulation in New York's Hotel Elysee and his convoluted relations with his parents and sister, Rose.

Rader, Dotson. *Tennessee: Cry of the Heart.* Garden City, N.Y.: Doubleday, 1985. The title and opening, explaining the author's first encounter with a "flipped out" Williams, give a flavor to this chatty biography. Although it does not have the virtue of notes or a scholarly biography, it does have the appeal of a firsthand account, filled with gossip and inside information, to be taken for what it is worth.

Rondane, Matthew C., ed. *The Cambridge Companion to Tennessee Williams.* Cambridge, England: Cambridge University Press, 1997. A collection of fourteen essays using a variety of critical approaches with an introduction by the editor summarizing each. Particularly useful are Jaqueline O'Connor's survey of Williams scholarship, "Words on Williams: A Bibliographic Essay," and R. Barton Palmer's "Hollywood in Crisis: Tennessee Williams and the Evolution of the Adult Film." Contains a chronology from Williams's birth in 1911 to 1996, seven photographs of major actors in scenes from stage productions of the plays and a selected bibliography.

Spoto, Donald. *The Kindness of Strangers: The Life of Tennessee Williams.* Boston: Little, Brown, 1985. Spoto's literary biography begins with a description of Williams's parents, Cornelius and Edwina. Beginning with early separation, the Williams couple gave their children a stormy beginning in life. Spoto's lively chronicle details in ten chapters Williams's encounters with such diverse influences as the Group Theatre, Frieda and D. H. Lawrence, Senator Joseph R. McCarthy, Fidel Castro, Hollywood stars, and the homosexual and drug subcultures of Key West. Forty-two pages of notes, bibliography, and index.

Williams, Dakin, and Shepherd Mead. *Tennessee Williams: An Intimate Biography.* New York: Arbor House, 1983. One of the more bizarre duos in biographical writing, Williams (Tennessee's brother) and Mead (Tennessee's childhood friend) produce a credible biography in a highly readable, well-indexed work. Their account of the playwright also helps to capture his almost schizophrenic nature. A solid index and extensive research assist the serious scholar and general reader.

Windham, Donald. *As if . . .* Verona, Italy, 1985. This reminiscence of Williams's onetime friend portrays the writer as a man of bizarre contradictions and reveals in telling vignettes the downward spiral of his self-destructive lifestyle.

Jacob H. Adler,
updated by Rebecca Bell-Metereau
and Robert G. Blake

August Wilson

Born: Pittsburgh, Pennsylvania; April 27, 1945

Principal drama • *Ma Rainey's Black Bottom*, pr. 1984, pb. 1985; *Fences*, pr., pb. 1985; *Joe Turner's Come and Gone*, pr. 1986, pb. 1988; *The Piano Lesson*, pr. 1987, pb. 1990; *Two Trains Running*, pr. 1990, pb. 1992; *Three Plays*, pb. 1991; *Seven Guitars*, pr. 1995, pb. 1996; *Jitney*, pr. 2000, pb. 2001; *King Hedley II*, pr. 2001

Other literary forms • Although August Wilson is known primarily for his plays, some of his poetry was published in black literary journals, such as *Black World*, in 1969. He published a teleplay, *The Piano Lesson*, in 1995, and a nonfiction work, *The Ground on Which I Stand*, in 2000.

Achievements • Critics have hailed August Wilson as an authentic voice of African American culture. His plays explore the black experience historically and in the context of deeper metaphysical roots in African culture. Since 1984, his major plays have been successfully produced by regional theaters and on Broadway; in fact, he is the first African American playwright to have had two plays running on Broadway simultaneously.

Wilson has received an impressive array of fellowships, awards, and honorary degrees: the Jerome Fellowship in 1980, the Bush Foundation Fellowship in 1982, membership in the New Dramatists starting in 1983, and the Rockefeller Fellowship in 1984. He has also been an associate of Playwrights Center, Minneapolis, and received the McKnight Fellowship in 1985, the Guggenheim Fellowship in 1986, six New York Drama Critics Circle Awards from 1985 to 2001, the Whiting Foundation Award in 1986, the Pulitzer Prize in Drama in 1987 (for *Fences*) and 1990 (for *The Piano Lesson*), the Tony Award by the League of New York Theatres and Producers (for *Fences*), the American Theatre Critics Award in 1986, the Outer Circle Award in 1987, and the Drama Desk Award and John Gassner Award in 1987.

Wilson's goals are "to concretize the black cultural response to the world, to place that response in loud action, so as to create a dramatic literature as powerful and sustaining as black American music." While the form of his plays breaks no new ground, the substance and language produce powerful emotional responses. Rooted in the black experience, Wilson's plays touch universal chords.

Biography • August Wilson was born in Pittsburgh, Pennsylvania, on April 27, 1945, in the Hill District, a black neighborhood. He was one of six children born to Daisy Wilson from North Carolina, and a German baker, Frederick August Kittel, who eventually abandoned the family. Wilson left school at fifteen when a teacher refused to take his word that a twenty-page paper on Napoleon was his own work. He spent the next few weeks in the library, pretending to be at school. It was through reading, especially all the books he could find in the "Negro" subject section, that Wilson educated himself.

Later, he worked at odd jobs and spent time on street corners and at a cigar store called Pat's Place, listening to old men tell stories. Coming into adulthood during the Black Power movement of the 1960's, Wilson was influenced by it and participated in the Black Arts movement in Pittsburgh, writing and publishing poetry in black journals. With longtime friend Rob Penny, he founded the Black Horizons Theatre Company in Pittsburgh in 1968. He produced and directed plays, but his efforts at playwriting in those years failed, he later recalled, because he "didn't respect the way blacks talked" so he "always tried to alter it." He formed a connection with the Penumbra company in St. Paul and moved there in 1978. It was in this much smaller black community that he learned to regard the "voices I had been brought up with all my life" with greater respect.

Married in 1981 to Judy Oliver (he has a daughter, Sakina Ansari, from an earlier marriage), Wilson began to write scripts for the children's theater of a local science museum. This effort led him to submit his scripts to the National Playwrights Conference at the Eugene O'Neill Center in Waterford, Connecticut. His work caught the attention of conference director Lloyd Richards, who was also the dean of the Yale School of Drama and the artistic director of the Yale Repertory Company. Under Richards's direction, a staged reading of *Ma Rainey's Black Bottom* was performed in 1982 at the Eugene O'Neill Center, followed by a production at Yale and a Broadway success. The succeeding plays by Wilson followed the same pattern, with intervening production at regional theaters. Wilson eventually dissolved his relationship with Richards and turned to director Marion McClinton to stage *Jitney* and *King Hedley II.*

Divorced in 1990, Wilson moved to Seattle, Washington, where he continued to write his cycle of plays. He also participated as a dramaturge at the Eugene O'Neill Center when one of his own works was not being produced. After *Seven Guitars*, Wilson and his co-producer, Ben Mordecai, formed a joint venture called Sageworks, which gave Wilson artistic and financial control of his plays both as a writer and producer. Wilson refined his plays through a series of separate productions, writing and editing through each production's rehearsal process. Before reaching its New York run, *King Hedley II* received six regional productions. Wilson married Constanza Romero, and they had a daughter, Azula.

Analysis • Each of August Wilson's major plays dramatizes the African American experience in a different decade of the twentieth century, and the action of each play is driven by the arrival or presence of a character who has what Wilson calls the "warrior spirit," the quality that makes a man dissatisfied and determined to change or disrupt the status quo. Each of the plays is affected by Wilson's feeling for the blues, music that he calls the "flag bearer of self-definition" for African Americans. Characters sing the blues, music is called for in scene transitions, and

August Wilson in 1989 (AP/Wide World Photos)

the rhythms of the dialogue reflect the blues. His plays are written to be performed on a single setting with action that is chronological. While he writes within the genre of psychological realism, each play displays a different degree of adherence to structure and plotting. His characters, mostly men, are African Americans uncertain of their own places in the world.

One of Wilson's greatest strengths is with language: The authenticity and rhythms of the dialogue and the colorful vitality of metaphor and storytelling connect him to the oral tradition of the African American and African cultures. He discussed in an interview the indirect quality of black speech, with its circling of issues and answers that are not answers. Characters answer the question they think is intended, not necessarily the one that is expressed. This language, in fact, often becomes the unique poetry of his drama. The language is full of implied meanings and dependent on tonal quality for interpretation. Wilson also places increasing emphasis with each play on the superstitions and beliefs that affect his characters. These superstitions seem to come from a mixture of Christianity, ancient African religions, and street wisdom.

Ma Rainey's Black Bottom • In *Ma Rainey's Black Bottom*, Wilson uses a historical figure, "Mother of the Blues" singer Ma Rainey, and invents a story around her. The setting is a simultaneous representation of a 1927 recording studio and a band-rehearsal room. Overlooking the studio from the control booth are Ma's white producer and white agent, their presence and location a graphic symbol of white society's control over black music.

The dialogue seems to meander through silly and inconsequential matters. The underlying seriousness of these matters becomes apparent as the characters reveal their ways of coping with the white world. Ma Rainey plays the prima donna (note the pun in the play's title) while she acknowledges to her band that, like all black artists, she is exploited. Her music is her "way of understanding life." Wilson centers her in the play, a dynamic and colorful presence, but the character central to the action is Levee.

Levee has that warrior spirit. The tragic irony is that when he lashes out and kills, he kills the only educated band member in the play. His urge for self-sufficiency (to have his own band and make his own music) becomes self-destructive. By application, Wilson suggests that the misplaced rage of his race can result in self-destruction. The grimly serious resolution to this play does not describe the tone of lightness and humor in much that precedes it. It is Levee's appetite that drives the play, sometimes comically, and it is his frustrated hunger that causes an unnecessary death.

Fences • Wilson's second major work, *Fences*, won a Pulitzer Prize in Drama as well as Tony Awards for Wilson, the director, and two actors. It centers on the dynamic, volatile character Troy Maxson and takes place primarily in 1957. Troy is the warrior character whose spirit disrupts his own life as well as those of his sons and wife. Often inviting comparison with Arthur Miller's *Death of a Salesman* (pr., pb. 1949), the play dramatizes the life of a baseball player prevented from realizing his big-league dreams by the color barrier, overcome too late for him. *Fences* is about a man's battle with life and his emotional, sometimes irrational way of facing unfairness, pain, love, and hate. The fence that Troy built around his life, like that built around his home, could neither shut out the world's injustice nor protect his family or himself from his shortcomings. The final scene occurs after Troy's death in 1965, when others can express feelings about Troy that were not articulated before. This scene provides a quietly emotional contrast to the intensely alive Troy of the previous eight scenes. It is a necessary scene and yet points up the failure of father and son to express directly what they felt in their earlier confrontation.

Troy's brother, Gabriel, whose head injury from the war has made him believe himself to be God's angel Gabriel, provides a kind of mystical presence. Wilson uses his madness for a theatrically effective closing to the play. When Gabriel discovers that his horn will not blow to open the gates of heaven for Troy, he performs a weird "dance of atavistic signature and ritual" and howls a kind of song to open the gates. This marks the beginning of Wilson's increasing use of ritual, myth, and superstition in his plays.

Joe Turner's Come and Gone • In *Joe Turner's Come and Gone*, Wilson reaches farther back into the historical black experience. As in the old blues song of the same title, the brother of the governor of Tennessee, Joe Turner, found and enslaved groups of black men. Herald Loomis, the mysterious central character in this play, was so enslaved in 1901 and not released for seven years. The play dramatizes his search for his wife, which is actually a search for himself. His arrival at a Pittsburgh boardinghouse in 1911 disrupts and disturbs, creating the tension and significance of the drama.

Another boardinghouse resident, Bynum, establishes his identity as a "conjure man" or "rootworker" early in the play. Bynum's search for his "shiny man" becomes a thematic and structural tie for the play. At the end of the first act, during a joyous African call-and-response dance, Loomis has a sort of ecstatic fit, ending with his being unable to stand and walk. Some kind of dramatic resolution must relate Bynum's vision and Loomis's quest. It comes in the final scene when wife Martha returns and Loomis learns that his quest is still unrealized. Wilson describes Loomis's transformation in actions rather than words. His wife does not restore him, nor does her religion restore him. In desperation, he turns a knife on himself, rubs his hands and face in his own blood, looks down at his hands, and says, "I'm standing. My legs stood up! I'm standing now!" It is at this point that he has found his "song of self-sufficiency." Wilson's rather poetic stage directions articulate a redemption that Loomis cannot verbalize, risking audience misinterpretation.

Bynum's final line of the play recognizes Loomis as a shiny man, the shiny man who can tell him the meaning of life. The suggestion of a Christ figure is unmistakable, and yet Loomis's soul is not cleansed through religious belief. He has denied the Christ of the white man, despite Martha's pleading. His epiphany is in finding himself. Joe Turner has come but he has also gone. Herald Loomis finds his identity in his own African roots, not in the slave identity that the white Joe Turner had given him.

The Piano Lesson • With his fourth major play, Wilson crafts a more tightly structured plot. In fact, *The Piano Lesson* is stronger thematically and structurally than it is in character development. The characters serve to dramatize the conflict between the practical use of a family heritage to create a future, and a symbolic treasuring of that heritage to honor the past. The piano, which bears the blood of their slave ancestors, is the focus of the conflict between Boy Willie and his sister, Berniece. Its exotic carvings, made by their great grandfather, tell the story of their slave ancestors who were sold in exchange for the piano. Its presence in the northern home of Berniece and her Uncle Doaker represents the life of their father who died stealing it back from Sutter.

Berniece is embittered and troubled not only by the piano and her father's death but also by her mother's blood and tears that followed that death and by the loss of her own husband. In contrast, Boy Willie is upbeat and funny, an optimistic, ambitious, and boyish man who is sure he is right in wanting to sell the piano to buy Sutter's land.

He has the warrior spirit. Throughout the play, the presence of Sutter's ghost is seen or felt. Sutter's ghost seems to represent the control that the white man still exerts over this family in 1937. Boy Willie chooses to ignore the ghost, to accuse his sister of imagining it, but ultimately it is Boy Willie who must wrestle with the ghost.

Wilson has said that this play had five endings because Berniece and Boy Willie are both right. The conflict is indeed unresolved as Boy Willie leaves, telling Berniece that she had better keep playing that piano or he and Sutter could both come back. The lesson of the piano is twofold: Berniece has learned that she should use her heritage, rather than let it fester in bitterness, and Boy Willie has learned that he cannot ignore the significance of this piano, which symbolizes the pain and suffering of all of his ancestors. There is little in the play that deviates from the central conflict. The skill of Wilson's writing is seen in the interplay of characters bantering and arguing, in the indirect quality of questions that are not answered, and in the storytelling. While characters may serve primarily as symbols and plot devices, they are nevertheless vivid and credible.

Two Trains Running • The disruptive character in Wilson's fifth play is Sterling, but the theme of *Two Trains Running*, set in 1969, is found in the character Memphis, the owner of the restaurant in which the action occurs. Memphis came north in 1936, driven away by white violence. He has always meant to return and reclaim his land. In the course of the play, he learns that he has to go back and "pick up the ball" so as not to arrive in the end zone empty handed. He must catch one of those two trains running south every day. He must not surrender.

The major characters in the play represent varying degrees of tenacity. Wilson skillfully builds a plot around two threads: Memphis's determination to get the city to pay his price for his property, and Sterling's determination to find a place for himself and gain the love of Risa. Hambone is a crazy character, driven mad almost ten years ago when the butcher Lutz across the street refused to pay him a ham for doing a good job of painting his fence. Hollaway, a commentator character, observes that Hambone may be the smartest of them all in his refusal to give up—each day going to Lutz and asking for his ham. The unfortunate fact is, though, that his life has been reduced to this one action; all he can say is "I want my ham. He gonna give me my ham." Risa, a woman determined not to be dependent on a sexual attachment, has scarred her own attractive legs to make herself less desirable. In spite of herself, she is attracted to the vitality and optimism of Sterling, and Sterling is most tenacious of all. His warrior spirit has landed him in prison and may do so again, but his zeal and good humor are compelling.

The constant reminders and presence of death give resonance to the lives and efforts of these people. When the play opens, the Prophet Samuel has already died and the offstage mayhem surrounding the viewing of his body is evident. Characters talk about several other deaths, and no sooner is Prophet Samuel buried than Hambone is discovered dead (again offstage). The reactions to his death make up the ending of the play. Memphis and Sterling, trusting in the prophecies of the 322-year-old seer Aunt Ester, both triumph. Sterling runs across the street, steals a ham, and presents it to Mr. West, the undertaker, to put in Hambone's coffin. This final flourish of the play is an assertion of character identity and life. *Two Trains Running* may be Wilson's most accomplished work in blending character, plot, and theme.

Seven Guitars • *Two Trains Running* was followed in 1995 by *Seven Guitars*. Set in the 1940's, it tells the tragic story of blues guitarist Floyd Barton, whose funeral opens the play. The action flashes back to recreate the events of Floyd's last week of life. Floyd had arrived in Pittsburgh to try to get his guitar out of the pawn shop and to persuade his former lover, Vera, to return with him to Chicago. A record he made years earlier has suddenly gained popularity, and he has been offered the opportunity to record more songs at a studio in Chicago.

The play's central conflicts are Floyd's struggle to move forward in his musical career and his personal strife with Vera and his band mates. A subplot centers on Floyd's friend Hedley and his deteriorating physical and mental health as his friends attempt to place him in a tuberculosis sanitarium. The play contains some of Wilson's familiar character types, including the mentally aberrant Hedley; the troubled-by-the-law young black male protagonist, Floyd; the capable and independent woman, Louise; and the more needy, younger woman, Ruby. It also contains elements of music, dance, story telling, violence, and food.

Jitney • Wilson reworked an earlier, short play *Jitney.* Becker, a retired steel-mill worker, runs a jitney station, serving the unofficial taxi needs of the black community of Pittsburgh's Hill district during early autumn of 1977. The jitney drivers are a rich collection of troubled but hard-working men. The station offers the men a living and a sense of independence that is threatened by the city's plans to tear down the neighborhood in the name of urban renewal. Becker also faces a personal crisis. His son, Booster, is about to leave prison after serving twenty years for murdering his well-to-do white girlfriend. Father and son have not spoken for two decades. Becker is bitter that his son threw away a promising career, and Booster sees his father's lifetime of hard work and submissiveness to white landlords and bosses as demeaning. Father and son never reconcile, but they indirectly attempt to redeem themselves to each other. Becker decides to organize the jitney drivers and fight the urban renewal. Yet, just as Becker begins the move to resistance, he falls victim to his rigorous work ethic and dies unexpectedly. As the dispirited drivers praise his father, Booster begins to respect his father's accomplishments and prepares to carry on Becker's mission to save the jitney station.

King Hedley II • *King Hedley II* takes place in the back yard of a few ramshackle houses in the Hill District of Pittsburgh in 1985. Its protagonist, King Hedley II, is a petty thief and a former convict engaged in selling stolen refrigerators. Believing that he is being held back while everybody else is moving forward, Hedley dreams of a better life. His partner in crime is a shady character named Mister. Hedley's wife, Tonya, is pregnant with a child she does not want to raise in the rough life she knows. Hedley's mother, Ruby, is a former jazz singer who is reunited with an old lover, the con man Elmore. The next-door neighbor, Stool Pigeon, is a crazy old man who stacks old newspapers in his hovel. He is the play's mystic messenger who buries a dead cat in the backyard and brings to its grave various tokens that he believes will bring the animal back to one of its nine lives. The yard, barren except for weeds and garbage, is a major symbol. Hedley tires to raise plants in it, even fencing off a small patch with barbed wire. However, like Hedley's efforts to better himself, the attempt to grow something is doomed.

Other major works

NONFICTION: *The Ground on Which I Stand,* 2000.

TELEPLAY: *The Piano Lesson,* 1995 (adaptation of his play).

Bibliography

Bigsby, C. W. E. *Modern American Drama, 1945-1990.* Cambridge, England: Cambridge University Press, 1992. The author interviewed Wilson for pertinent biographical data and includes some in-depth analysis of the first four plays.

Bogumil, Mary L. *Understanding August Wilson.* Columbia: University of South Carolina Press, 1999. Bogumil provides readers with a comprehensive view of the thematic structure of Wilson's plays, the placement of his plays within the context of American drama, and the distinctively African American experiences and traditions that Wilson dramatizes.

Brustein, Robert. *Reimagining American Theatre.* New York: Hill and Wang, 1991. Brustein, critic and former artistic director of the Yale Repertory Theatre before Lloyd Richards, is one of the few negative voices criticizing Wilson's drama. He finds particular fault with the mechanisms and symbols of *The Piano Lesson* and hopes that Wilson will work to develop the poetic rather than historical aspects of his talent.

Elkins, Marilyn, ed. *August Wilson: A Casebook.* New York: Garland, 1994. The essays investigate such thematic, artistic, and ideological concerns as Wilson's use of the South and the black human body as metaphors; his collaboration with Lloyd Richards; the influences of the blues and other writers on his work; his creative method; and his treatment of African American family life.

Herrington, Joan. *I Ain't Sorry for Nothin' I Done: August Wilson's Process of Playwriting.* New York: Limelight Editions, 1998. Herrington traces the roots of Wilson's drama to visual artists such as Romare Bearden and to the jazz musicians who inspire and energize him as a dramatist. She goes on to analyze his process of playwriting—how he brings his experiences and his ideas to stage life—by comparing successive drafts of his first three major plays.

Hill, Holly. "Black Theatre into the Mainstream." In *Contemporary American Theatre,* edited by Bruce King. New York: St. Martin's Press, 1991. Hill's analysis of the plays sets them in the context of their period.

Nadel, Alan. *May All Your Fences Have Gates.* Iowa City: University of Iowa Press, 1994. Nadel deals individually with five major plays and also addresses issues crucial to Wilson's canon: the role of history, the relationship of African ritual to African American drama, gender relations in the African American community, music and cultural identity, the influence of Romare Beardern's collages, and the politics of drama.

Theater 9 (Summer/Fall, 1988). This special issue includes the script of *The Piano Lesson* with an earlier version of the ending, production photographs, and two informative essays. The articles "Wrestling Against History" and "The Songs of a Marked Man" explore Wilson's themes, especially the importance of myths and superstitions.

Wolfe, Peter. *August Wilson.* London: Macmillan, 1999. A comprehensive analysis of Wilson's theater. Wolfe sees the dramatist as exploding stereotypes of the ghetto poor, through his juxtapositions of the ordinary and the African American surreal, which evoke anger, affection, and sometimes hope.

Sally Osborne Norton,
updated by Rhona Justice-Malloy

Lanford Wilson

Born: Lebanon, Missouri; April 13, 1937

Principal drama • *So Long at the Fair*, pr. 1963 (one act); *Home Free!*, pr. 1964, pb. 1965 (one act); *The Madness of Lady Bright*, pr. 1964, pb. 1967 (one act); *No Trespassing*, pr. 1964 (one act); *Balm in Gilead*, pr., pb. 1965 (two acts); *Days Ahead: A Monologue*, pr. 1965, pb. 1967 (one scene); *Ludlow Fair*, pr., pb. 1965 (one act); *The Sand Castle*, pr. 1965, pb. 1970 (one act); *Sex Is Between Two People*, pr. 1965 (one scene); *This Is the Rill Speaking*, pr. 1965, pb. 1967 (one act); *The Rimers of Eldritch*, pr. 1966, pb. 1967 (two acts); *Wandering: A Turn*, pr. 1966, pb. 1967 (one scene); *Untitled Play*, pr. 1967 (one act; music by Al Carmines); *The Gingham Dog*, pr. 1968, pb. 1969; *The Great Nebula in Orion*, pr. 1970, pb. 1973 (one act); *Lemon Sky*, pr., pb. 1970; *Serenading Louie*, pr. 1970, pb. 1976 (two acts); *Sextet (Yes)*, pb. 1970, pr. 1971 (one scene); *Stoop: A Turn*, pb. 1970; *Ikke, Ikke, Nye, Nye, Nye*, pr. 1971, pb. 1973; *Summer and Smoke*, pr. 1971, pb. 1972 (libretto; adaptation of Tennessee Williams's play; music by Lee Hoiby); *The Family Continues*, pr. 1972, pb. 1973 (one act); *The Hot l Baltimore*, pr., pb. 1973; *Victory on Mrs. Dandywine's Island*, pb. 1973 (one act); *The Mound Builders*, pr. 1975, pb. 1976 (two acts); *Brontosaurus*, pr. 1977, pb. 1978 (one act); *Fifth of July*, pr., pb. 1978 (two acts); *Talley's Folly*, pr., pb. 1979 (one act); *A Tale Told*, pr. 1981 (pb. as *Talley and Son*, 1986; two acts); *Thymus Vulgaris*, pr., pb. 1982 (one act); *Angels Fall*, pr., pb. 1982 (two acts); *Balm in Gilead and Other Plays*, pb. 1985; *Say deKooning*, pr. 1985, pb. 1994; *Sa-Hurt?*, pr. 1986; *A Betrothal*, pr., pb. 1986 (one act); *Burn This*, pr., pb. 1987; *Dying Breed*, pr. 1987; *Hall of North American Forests*, pr. 1987, pb. 1988; *A Poster of the Cosmos*, pr. 1987, pb. 1990 (one act); *Abstinence: A Turn*, pb. 1989 (one scene); *The Moonshot Tape*, pr., pb. 1990; *Eukiah*, pr., pb. 1992; *Redwood Curtain*, pr. 1992, pb. 1993; *Twenty-one Short Plays*, pb. 1993; *Collected Works*, pb. 1996-1999 (3 volumes; Vol. 1, *Collected Plays, 1965-1970*; Vol. 2, *Collected Works, 1970-1983*; Vol. 3, *The Talley Trilogy*); *Lanford Wilson: The Early Plays, 1965-1970*, pb. 1996; *Day*, pr., pb. 1996 (one act); *A Sense of Place: Or, Virgil Is Still the Frogboy*, pr. 1997, pb. 1999; *Sympathetic Magic*, pr. 1997, pb. 2000; *Book of Days*, pr. 1998, pb. 2000; *Rain Dance*, pr. 2000

Other literary forms • Besides stage plays, Lanford Wilson has written works in a number of other dramatic forms: several teleplays, *The Migrants* (1973, with Tennessee Williams), *Sam Found Out: A Triple Play* (1988), and *Taxi!* (1978, not to be confused with the television series *Taxi*); two unproduced screenplays, "One Arm," written in 1969 and based on a Williams story, and "The Strike," based on the book *Last Exit to Brooklyn* (1988), by Hubert Selby, Jr.; and the libretto for Lee Hoiby's opera *Summer and Smoke* (1971), adapted from the Williams play.

Achievements • Lanford Wilson's plays have been produced throughout the United States and abroad; several have appeared on television, and *The Hot l Baltimore* was adapted as a television series. Wilson is the winner of numerous awards: a Vernon Rice Award (1967); Obies for *The Hot l Baltimore*, *The Mound Builders*, and *Sympathetic Magic*; a Pulitzer Prize and a New York Drama Critics Circle Award (as best-of-best) for *Talley's Folly*; the American Theater Critics Award for best play for *Book of Days*; the Brandeis

University Creative Arts Award, and fellowships from the Rockefeller and Guggenheim foundations. He was admitted to the Theatre Hall of Fame in 1995, and the Missouri Writers Hall of Fame in 1997.

Biography • Lanford Eugene ("Lance") Wilson was born April 13, 1937, in Lebanon, Missouri, the son of Ralph Eugene and Violetta Tate Wilson. When he was five years old, his parents separated (and later divorced), his father leaving for California, his mother taking Lanford to Springfield, Missouri, where she worked in a garment factory and he attended school. When he was thirteen, his mother married again—a dairy inspector from Ozark, Missouri—and they moved to a farm. Wilson attended Ozark High School, where he painted, acted, and was on the track team.

Although his childhood was relatively happy, Wilson never quite recovered from his parents' marital breakup. At eighteen, after a term at Southwest Missouri State College, he headed for California for a reunion with his father, by then a San Diego aircraft-factory worker with a new wife and two younger sons. The reunion, painfully mirrored in Wilson's autobiographical play *Lemon Sky*, was unsuccessful: Wilson and his father were thoroughly incompatible. After a year in his father's household, during which he worked at his father's factory and attended San Diego State College, Wilson left for Chicago. He lived for six years in Chicago, where he worked as an artist in an advertising agency, studied playwriting at the University of Chicago, and wrote his first plays (none produced).

In 1962, Wilson moved to New York, worked as an office clerk—in a furniture store, at the Americana Hotel, and in the subscription office of the New York Shakespeare Festival—and surveyed the theatrical scene. He was disgusted by Broadway but stunned by an Off-Off-Broadway performance of Eugène Ionesco's *The Lesson* at Caffé Cino, a coffeehouse theater in Greenwich Village. Soon Wilson began waiting tables and writing plays for Caffé Cino: His first play produced was *So Long at the Fair*, in 1963, and he achieved his first success in 1964 with *The Madness of Lady Bright* (which was given 250 performances Off-Off-Broadway). In 1966, Wilson had his first Off-Broadway success with *The Rimers of Eldritch*.

Wilson's rise had been swift, but then he began experiencing some setbacks. In 1967, he lost his home base at Caffé Cino when Joe Cino, the owner-manager, committed suicide; in 1968, *The Gingham Dog* failed on Broadway, followed in 1970 by *Lemon Sky*. After the failure of *The Gingham Dog*, Wilson stopped writing for a time. He got back into playwriting by first doing mundane jobs for the Circle Repertory Company, which he had recently cofounded with actress Tanya Berezin, actor Rob Thirkield, and director Marshall W. Mason. In 1973, that company produced *The Hot l Baltimore*, and Wilson's career was back on track. All of his major plays during the following decade were initially produced by them and directed by Mason.

Over his career, Wilson has collaborated with Mason on nearly forty productions, and he has continued to prefer working with regional theater companies, even after the Broadway success of *Talley's Folly*. In the late 1990's he accepted a commission to write a play for former Circle Repertory Company member Jeff Daniels, executive director of the Purple Rose Theatre in Chelsea, Michigan. That play, *Book of Days*, was called his best in twenty years and was followed in 2001 with *Rain Dance*, also produced at the Purple Rose.

Analysis • During his first period of playwriting (1963-1972), Lanford Wilson struggled to learn his trade—mainly in the convivial atmosphere of Off-Off-Broadway, where it did not matter if sometimes audiences did not show up. His plays from this period, mostly one-act dramas, are clearly apprentice work. They contain echoes of Tennessee Williams, Arthur Miller, and the Theater of the Absurd. Experiments include the use of overlapping and simultaneous speeches, free-floating time sequences, and characters who are figments of the main character's imagination. Perhaps the most effective of the plays from this decade are *Home Free!*, about a bizarre, incestuous relationship between brother and sister; *The Madness of Lady Bright*, about "a screaming preening queen" losing his beauty to middle age; and two impressionistic "montage" works that draw on Wilson's small-town Missouri background: *This Is the Rill Speaking* and *The Rimers of Eldritch*.

With the exception of *The Rimers of Eldritch*, a two-act play, Wilson had trouble sustaining longer plays during his apprentice decade; his longer works of this period tend to be uneven, diffuse, almost plotless. Their subject matter provides the main interest. *Balm in Gilead*, set in and around an all-night café on Upper Broadway, pictures the New York City subculture of pimps, prostitutes, pushers, and users. *The Gingham Dog*, financially unsuccessful but favorably reviewed when it opened on Broadway, portrays the rancorous breakup of an interracial marriage. *Lemon Sky* is autobiographical—about a young man's efforts to reunite with his father, who fled years before and is rearing a second family in Southern California.

As he gained experience, Wilson's work became more substantial in every sense: His mature plays are generally longer, more conventional, more realistic, and more successful than those of the decade of his apprenticeship. Wilson's breakthrough was with *The Hot l Baltimore*, an Off-Broadway success (with 1,166 performances) produced in 1973. *The Hot l Baltimore* shows the playwright in control of his material, displays his sense of humor, and illustrates the format on which Wilson has relied (in lieu of plot) with repeated success—an updating of the old parlor or weekend drama that brings together a group of disparate characters in an interesting setting (usually threatened, usually around a holiday) and allows them to interact. Other plays falling into this format are *The Mound Builders*, *Fifth of July*, *Angels Fall*, *Talley and Son* (a revised version of the 1981 *A Tale Told*), *Burn This*, and *Book of Days*. Even the Pulitzer Prize-winning *Talley's Folly*, a romantic tour de force with only two characters, repeats the format on a smaller scale. Wilson reveals one source of this recurring device in his 1984 translation of Anton Chekhov's *Tri sestry* (pr., pb. 1901; *Three Sisters*, 1920).

The public has been accurate in judging *The Hot l Baltimore*, *Talley's Folly*, and *Burn This* the best of Wilson's plays: They are the most tightly knit and evenly written, though some critics find them marred by sentimentality. *The Mound Builders*, his most ambitious work, is Wilson's favorite, but it shares, with *Fifth of July* and *Angels Fall*, a tendency toward rambling, uneven dialogue that is witty one moment and dull the next. *Angels Fall*, in particular, is burdened with intellectual baggage, something not found in Wilson's early work.

One simply does not look for highly structured, suspenseful plots from Wilson (the description "tightly knit," used above, is only relative), though his plays usually rise to a climax, even if it is sometimes forced or artificial. Rather, Wilson's work is significant for its characters and themes. His plays contain the greatest menagerie of characters in contemporary American drama—drag queens, freaks, prostitutes, academics, priests—for the most part likable because Wilson has a special sympathy for the losers and lost of society (a category that, in his work, includes almost everybody). Wilson does not really need intellectual baggage, because his characters carry his themes much more powerfully: In the world of Wilson's plays, only "angels fall" because his characters are already down—but never out. This sense of humanity is Wilson's most sterling quality.

Heartland dramas • Wilson represents the most recent stage of an American cultural phenomenon that could be aptly termed "the heartland drama." Wilson's predecessor and fellow Missourian Mark Twain celebrated American innocence; Wilson mourns its loss. The loss occurred precisely on August 6, 1945, when Harry S. Truman, the presidential Huck Finn, ordered that the atomic bomb be dropped on Hiroshima. The United States had been trying hard for a long time to lose its innocence, but once it was gone, the nation regretted its loss. Apparently, the famed innocence had been the source of American wholeness, of Fourth of July optimism, of childlike wonder.

Wilson centered his version of this American heartland drama on the family, where, according to Sigmund Freud, all the history of the world is played out. It is in the family, once the bastion of American innocence, that signs of the disintegration are most noticeable and its effects most far-reaching, and it is there that wholeness must be restored. Longing for the old innocence is expressed in Wilson's plays through titles that sound as if they are from nursery rhymes or children's games (some are). It is also expressed through the constant efforts to mend splintered families or to construct surrogate families. Yet the longing and the efforts are mostly in vain: The nursery-rhyme titles are mockeries, and the versions of home and family depicted are little better than cruel parodies.

Extreme examples can be found in *Home Free!*, in which a brother and sister, huddled in their apartment in an attempt to shut out the world, play husband-wife and father-mother; in *The Madness of Lady Bright*, in which the fading drag queen Lady Bright, lonely in his apartment, reminisces about former lovers (whose autographs are on the wall), talks with an imaginary "Boy" and "Girl," and waits in vain for a phone call; and in *The Hot l Baltimore*, in which the condemned urban hotel of the title is the home of prostitutes and poor retirees. Unfortunately, in modern America, these bizarre examples are only too real. For those seeking a substitute for the American family's lost wholeness, Wilson has some news: There is very little balm in Gilead, especially if one locates Gilead in such places as the New York City subculture of prostitutes and drug addicts.

Ultimately, in Wilson's work, the American heartland drama is not only played out in the family but also the family itself—real or surrogate—mirrors and becomes a metaphor for the whole society. Such is the case in *Fifth of July*, where the extended Talley family and its holiday guests mirror the post-Vietnam state of the nation. The older generation is blessedly dead or slightly dotty; the middle generation, now over thirty, is burnt out, subsisting on drugs and memories of Berkeley idealism and sexual entanglements; and the younger generation has a precocious vocabulary and sophistication that leaves little doubt that the era of old-fashioned Fourth of July innocence is finished. Similarly, the surrogate family group (including real families) gathered for an archaeological dig in *The Mound Builders* mirrors the larger tensions in American society, particularly the tensions between preservation and development. In both plays, the sense of America's loss—of its values, its history—is acute.

The Rimers of Eldritch • In dramatizing America's loss, Wilson occasionally takes on the tones of an Old Testament prophet. Nowhere is this more the case than in *The Rimers of Eldritch*, the best example of Wilson's early experimental work. Reminiscent of Thornton Wilder's *Our Town* (pr., pb. 1938) and Dylan Thomas's *Under Milk Wood: A Play for Voices* (pr. 1953, pb. 1954), though with a different emphasis, *The Rimers of Eldritch* treats a somewhat worn subject, now a television standard—the hypocrisy of a small town. Just one big down-home family, the town's citizens close ranks to heap their evil on a poor scapegoat and thereby preserve their appearance of innocence, but the town's evil remains, its corruption confirmed.

Appropriately, the printed play has the following epigraph from Jeremiah (the reference to balm in Gilead appears two verses later): "The harvest is past, the summer is ended, and we are not saved" (Jeremiah 8:20). *The Rimers of Eldritch* takes place during one spring, summer, and fall, but the play skips backward and forward in time, from one conversation to another, creating a montage effect rather than presenting a chronological sequence. Less confusing than it sounds, the montage dresses the worn subject in mystery and suspense, ironic juxtapositions, different versions of what happened (thereby mimicking small-town gossip), and a memory-like quality.

The town is named Eldritch and, true to the meaning of its name, Eldritch displays a weird collection of small-town characters, descendants of Sherwood Anderson's midwestern grotesques: farmers; a garage mechanic; a trucker; Cora Groves, owner of the Hilltop Café, who is carrying on with her young and transient lover; Patsy Johnson, prettiest girl at Centerville High, who gets pregnant by the transient lover and arranges a quick marriage to a hometown boy; Skelly Mannor, the town hermit, who goes about peeping into people's windows and who is suspected, according to an old rumor, of bestiality (boys follow him in the street shouting "Baaa!"); the town hero, a stock-car driver, now deceased, who was impotent and beat women; and a group of gossips who could substitute for the Eumenides. What characterizes the town, however, is not only its individual members but also its collective mentality. As Skelly says, the town's citizens see what they want to see and think what they want to think, all in the name of good Christian living.

The play's slight, makeshift plot dramatizes this observation. The plot revolves around an innocent fourteen-year-old crippled girl, who dreams of flying like Peter Pan and sowing autumn rime over the town. She compares the rime to sugar, but it turns out to be more like salt. Out of her sexual curiosity, she provokes her equally innocent boyfriend to try to rape her. Skelly happens on the scene and prevents the rape, but a nearby neighbor emerges with his gun and, naturally thinking that Skelly is the molester, kills him. The two "innocents" tell the Skelly-the-molester story to the judge and jury—a story the town is only too ready to believe. As the preacher (who doubles as judge) points out to the accompaniment of hymn singing, the town is to blame for not shooting the fellow sooner.

The Hot l Baltimore • Wilson's roots in the Bible Belt make him sound like the prophet Jeremiah in such plays as *Balm in Gilead* and *The Rimers of Eldritch*, but, in his *The Hot l Baltimore*, they also lead him to discover Mary Magdalene, whom he immediately forgave. An example of Wilson's mature work and his most popular play, *The Hot l Baltimore* is a warm and witty comedy—bittersweet, to be sure, but farcical at times. Apparently tired of turning his audiences into pillars of salt straining backward toward the lost past, Wilson set out deliberately to entertain in *The Hot l Baltimore*—and happily succeeded with a realistic, conventional play that even observes the classical unities.

The play is set during one twenty-four-hour period ("a recent Memorial Day") in the lobby of a seedy Baltimore hotel. Once an ornate showplace of the railroad era, the Hotel Baltimore is now scheduled for demolition. It is the home of the expected motley assortment of Wilson characters: hotel workers, retirees, transients, and—most notably—three warmhearted prostitutes. Like an extended family, from grandparents down to teenagers, they gather in the lobby to share each other's company and experiences. The prostitutes, in particular, share some ribald experiences concerning their clients. April observes, "If my clientele represents a cross section of American manhood, the country's in trouble," citing as one of the representative samples the fellow who scalds himself in the bathtub. Occasionally these scenes obtrude onstage, as at the hilarious end of act 1, when the outraged but otherwise unhurt Suzy, beaten and locked out of her room by a client, creates a commotion in the lobby by appearing wrapped in her towel and then nude.

Beneath the repartee and rough sexual humor, the audience is constantly reminded of the parallel between a troubled United States and the rundown hotel. The hotel's residents will be losing their home, the workers, within a month, their jobs, and other people with troubles appear: Mrs. Bellotti, whose crazy, thieving, alcoholic son Horse has been kicked out of the hotel and whose diabetic husband has had his leg amputated; Paul Granger III, a refugee from a reform school who is searching for his lost grandfather; and Jackie and Jamie, a sister and brother who bought salty desert land in Utah and now lack money to get their car on the road. All represent typical cases of the American blues, just as the hotel setting represents the transience of American values and society in general.

Presiding over this scene, ministering to the troubled in spirit, is the trinity of prostitutes, Suzy, April Green, and the Girl. These angels of mercy provide not only sex but also therapy, laughter, and sympathy. Significantly, they, among all the characters, show the most concern about family ties—about Mr. Bellotti disowning Horse, about Paul Granger III giving up the search for his namesake grandfather, about Jackie's abandonment of Jamie; they also have the strongest feelings about the scheduled demolition of the hotel and the dispersal of its workers and residents. "We been like a family, haven't we?" says Suzy. "My family." She is so broken up that she moves in with a rotten pimp, because she needs "someone; . . . I need love!" The prostitutes have lost their illusions along with their innocence, but they retain their sense of values, their humanity. As the Girl says, "I just think it's really chicken not to believe in anything!" For Wilson, still mourning the loss of American innocence, the prostitutes were an important discovery: One takes one's balm, however little there is, wherever one can get it.

Talley's Folly • This philosophy of balm, discovered in *The Hot l Baltimore*, prevails in *Talley's Folly*, Wilson's Pulitzer Prize-winning work. *Talley's Folly* introduces two mature misfits who have about given up on love but finally find solace in each other's arms. As this simple plot suggests, *Talley's Folly*, like *The Hot l Baltimore*, observes the unities, only more so: Matt's wooing of Sally takes place entirely in an old boathouse (an ornate Victorian structure called Talley's Folly), and the time required coincides with the playing time (ninety-seven minutes, no intermission).

Family is a particularly important consideration in *Talley's Folly*, one of an ongoing series of Wilson plays about the Talley family of Lebanon, Missouri (the other plays are *Fifth of July* and *Talley and Son*). As in so many Wilson plays, however, here again the families depicted experience friction or breakup. Thirty-one-year-old Sally Talley is the family outcast, first because tuberculosis left her sterile and thus unfit to seal the

Talley-Campbell family business partnership by marrying Harley Campbell, and second because her political views are anathema to the family, with its conservative small-town values (she sides with the union against the family's garment factory and is fired from teaching Sunday School). Forty-two-year-old Matt Friedman, a radical Jewish accountant, seems a likely mate for Sally, satisfying even her family's exacting requirements (though her brother Buddy runs Matt off with a shotgun). Matt does not even want children: Because the rest of his own family was wiped out in the Holocaust, he has resolved never to be responsible for bringing a child into this world.

Before the two can come together, they have to break down each other's solitary defenses. Matt has been melted down by Sally the summer before, with a few sessions in the boathouse, so now he takes the initiative. The play consists of their love sparring—Matt's persistence, Sally's attempts to chase him away, their anger, their jokes and repartee, their reminiscences, and finally their confessions—until Matt wins her hand. A fine vehicle for two good actors, *Talley's Folly* shows that, even in a bleak and hurtful world—no place to raise children—one can still find some balm in personal relationships.

Talley and Son • The third play in the Talley family cycle, *Talley and Son*, a revision of the 1981 *A Tale Told*, is set in Lebanon, Missouri, on July 4, 1944, precisely the same evening as in *Talley's Folly*. A darker play than *Talley's Folly*, this play is about the financial and other machinations of three generations of Talleys, who, together with the Campbells, have run two of the most profitable businesses in Lebanon: the clothing factory and the bank. Because of the liberal use of plot devices, this story of meanness and greed has often been compared with Lillian Hellman's *The Little Foxes* (pr., pb. 1939).

Angels Fall • Lest Wilson be accused of recommending retreat from the world, it should be added that in *Angels Fall*, he has used his family metaphor to extend the possibilities of reconciliation and hope. In *Angels Fall*, the surrogate family is a group of travelers taking shelter in a New Mexico mission church from a nearby nuclear accident. The play's title, perhaps implying that only angels stand tall enough to fall, suggests that Wilson has become reconciled to the loss of American innocence. Here the characters are all forgivably flawed and, in their mutual danger, in their mutual need, lean on one another and show a caring attitude. (Whether a nuclear accident is necessary to bring this about is unclear.) Even if the traditional American family is a dying institution, the play suggests, some of its values are still preserved in the bigger family of humankind—or perhaps in the family of God: What Wilson considers to be the fountainhead of these positive possibilities is implied in the setting (a church) and its presiding official, the genial Father Doherty.

Burn This • *Burn This*, which premiered in January, 1987, is shocking, outrageous, and larger than life. It presents Wilson's views on art, human sexuality, and love. Like Sally and Matt of *Talley's Folly*, the characters Anna and Pale conclude the play as a couple, but here the union may be a mistake. It is a poetic and cataclysmic work, in which art is seen as a sacrament, as an outward sign for inward, often chaotic but exhilarating truths. *Redwood Curtain*, a disturbing yet compassionate drama that depicts Vietnam veterans eking out primitive lives in the forests of Northern California, is perhaps equally powerful.

Book of Days • *Book of Days* was heralded as Wilson's "comeback" play, his most significant production in two decades, or perhaps in his entire career. The play is set in the small town of Dublin, Missouri, a spiritual sister city to Lebanon, the setting of the Talley family plays. When a Hollywood director named Boyd Middleton arrives in town to direct a community theater production of George Bernard Shaw's *St. Joan*, he sets off a chain reaction of events that upset the quiet lives of the other characters. The biblically named Ruth, cast in the role of Joan of Arc, stands up to evil in the form of big business after the mysterious murder of the owner of the local cheese factory.

Wilson has returned throughout his career to thinking about the Midwest where he was born. In the Talley family plays and *The Mound Builders*, he explored Midwest family dynamics, creating families that survived or unraveled after meeting outside forces. In *Book of Days*, Wilson moves beyond the family unit to ask serious questions about how towns, especially in the Midwest, can preserve their values against the threats of the Christian right and corporate greed.

Book of Days echoes elements found in Wilson's earlier work. Small towns such as Dublin, Missouri, marred by hidden corruption, have appeared in Wilson's plays since *The Rimers of Eldritch*. Ruth and Len, who manage to stay happily married because they are loyal to each other and because they have simple and honest dreams, are reminiscent of Sally and Matt of *Talley's Folly*. Doubts about the roles of art and artists in healing individuals and communities are raised in *Burn This*. What is intriguing in *Book of Days* is the combination of these elements, and the unusual political nature of the underlying conflict.

Other major works

TELEPLAYS: *One Arm*, 1970; *The Migrants*, 1973 (with Tennessee Williams); *Taxi!*, 1978; *Sam Found Out: A Triple Play*, 1988; *Lemon Sky*, 1988; *Burn This*, 1992; *Talley's Folly*, 1992.

TRANSLATION: *Three Sisters*, 1984 (of Anton Chekhov's play *Tri sestry*).

Bibliography

Barnett, Gene A. *Lanford Wilson*. Boston: Twayne, 1987. The most valuable general study of Wilson. This book carries chapters on all the major plays through *Talley and Son*. It also includes a family genealogy and a family chronology for the entire Talley clan.

Bryer, Jackson R. *Lanford Wilson: A Casebook*. New York: Garland, 1994. This collection includes ten critical articles, covering plays through *Burn This*. Also includes an introduction and chronology, and two interviews with Wilson.

Busby, Mark. *Lanford Wilson*. Boise, Idaho: Boise State University, 1987. Busby's brief monograph focuses on how Wilson's own family history has influenced his dramatic themes of longing for the past and conflict between generations. Literary influences, including Franz Kafka, and the influence of Wilson's early theater-going experiences, are also explored.

Dean, Anne M. *Discovery and Invention: The Urban Plays of Lanford Wilson*. Rutherford, Md.: Fairleigh Dickinson University Press, 1995. Written with the cooperation of Wilson, Marshall Mason, and other members of the Circle Repertory Company, this passionately affirming book examines Wilson's themes and the use of realistic yet poetic language, particularly in *Balm in Gilead*, *The Hot l Baltimore*, and *Burn This*.

Herman, William. "Down and Out in Lebanon and New York: Lanford Wilson." In *Understanding Contemporary American Drama*. Columbia: University of South Carolina Press, 1987. Herman's chapter includes explications of Wilson's major plays. He praises Wilson for the "delicate poetic language at the heart of his style" and for his "epic encompassment of American experience and mythologies."

Robertson, C. Warren. "Lanford Wilson." In *American Playwrights Since 1945*, edited by Philip C. Kolin. New York: Greenwood Press, 1989. An accessible reference to primary and secondary sources through 1987. Robertson provides a complete primary bibliography of Wilson's works and brief discussions entitled "Assessment of Wilson's Reputation" and "Production History." The article also includes an informative survey of secondary sources and a complete secondary bibliography.

Harold Branam,
updated by James W. Robinson, Jr.,
and Cynthia A. Bily

William Wycherley

Born: Clive(?), near Shrewsbury, Shropshire, England; May 28, 1641(?)
Died: London, England; December 31, 1715

Principal drama • *Love in a Wood: Or, St. James's Park*, pr. 1671, pb. 1672; *The Gentleman Dancing-Master*, pr. 1672, pb. 1673 (adaptation of Pedro Calderón de la Barca's play *El maestro de danzar*); *The Country Wife*, pr., pb. 1675; *The Plain-Dealer*, pr. 1676, pb. 1677; *Complete Plays*, pb. 1967

Other literary forms • Although William Wycherley's reputation among modern readers rests entirely on his work as a playwright, he wrote poetry as well, most of it in his later years. Twenty-eight years after his last play, he published *Miscellany Poems: As Satyrs, Epistles, Love-Verses, Songs, Sonnets, Etc.* (1704), a collection of unremarkable pieces on a variety of subjects. The volume has lighter verses, songs of wine and women, but to the reader of the plays, there is matter of perhaps greater interest. Certain poems suggest that the dark vision of the later dramas continued to grow in Wycherley until he despaired of any hope for humanity.

Achievements • William Wycherley's dramatic canon consists of only four plays, and his stature in English letters depends almost entirely on a single work, *The Country Wife*. In his own day, *The Plain-Dealer* was his most popular comedy, but more recent criticism has called attention to certain problems with that play that have diminished its reputation. Interestingly, the play's flaws are a result of Wycherley's excessiveness in the very quality that makes his dramatic achievement unique. More than his contemporaries, Wycherley deals bluntly (some critics have said crudely) with the tendency of social conventions to corrupt natural human instincts. More specifically, he posits the need of men and women to come together in relationships of love and mutual respect, and he exposes the ills that result when that need is perverted by marriage for purely material reasons. As the real meaning for marriage, the strongest bond between two individuals, becomes infected and weakened by social concerns, so the more casual relationships between men and women suffer corruption as well. Finally, Wycherley's vision is a world of grotesques, moral cripples, through which a very few good people grope their way in search of honorable relationships.

Biography • It is not certain exactly where and when William Wycherley was born. The year may have been 1640 or 1641 and the place Clive in Shropshire or Basing House in Hampshire. His father, Daniel Wycherley, was serving as teller to the Exchequer at the time of William's birth; later, he served as chief steward to the marquis of Winchester and came under suspicion of embezzlement. In 1655, young Wycherley was sent for education to France, where he became a favorite of Madame de Montausier, who was instrumental in his conversion to Roman Catholicism, although he returned to the Anglican Church in 1660. Wycherley stayed in France for four years, then returned to England and entered Queen's College at Oxford. He took no degree from Oxford and soon entered the Inner Temple. Law, however, was never a genuine interest for him. Court life held far greater appeal, and the ingratiating young man became a favorite of the duchess of Cleveland, King Charles II's mistress. It was to her that he dedicated his first play, *Love in a Wood*, which opened in 1671 at the Theatre Royal in Drury Lane. He wrote only three more plays, and his entire career as a playwright spanned only a relatively few years.

In 1678, as a result of ill health, Wycherley was sent to Montpellier for a rest at the expense of Charles II. When Wycherley returned, the king offered him the position of tutor to his son, the young duke of Richmond. The salary of fifteen hundred pounds a year, in addition to a pension when his services were no longer needed, was unusually generous. Unfortunately, Wycherley lost this fine opportunity and royal favor through a rash marriage. One day in 1679, he happened to meet a young woman in a London bookstore looking for a copy of *The Plain-Dealer*. Wycherley introduced himself to the young woman, who proved to be Countess Laetitia Isabella, daughter of the earl of Radnor and widow of the earl of Drogheda. Shortly after that meeting, they married in secret, but Charles and the duchess of Cleveland soon found out and, furious, banished him from the court.

Wycherley's new wife was ill-tempered and jealous, and her wealth was less than her debts. Their marriage was short-lived and ended with Isabella's death in 1681. Wycherley fell ever deeper into debt and in 1685 was confined to Fleet Prison, but the new king, James II, who believed that Manly, the protagonist of *The Plain-Dealer*, was a representation of himself, arranged for Wycherley's release and partial payment of his debts. The grateful author became a Roman Catholic once more.

Wycherley's later years were rather uneventful. In 1704, he published his *Miscellany Poems* and began a correspondence with Alexander Pope, who was then only sixteen. In 1715, he married young Elizabeth Jackson, the intent apparently being to deny any inheritance to a despised nephew. "Manly" Wycherley, as he was known after his most popular character, died only eleven days after his wedding. He was buried in St. Paul's, Covent Garden.

Analysis • When read in the sequence of their production on the stage, William Wycherley's four plays make an interesting study of a dramatist gaining mastery of his art. The early plays display a number of structural flaws and basic problems with dramatizing a story. Through what could only be deliberate experimentation, the several elements of drama are shaped, weighed, and positioned in a variety of ways until a near-perfect formula is achieved in *The Country Wife*.

Love in a Wood • The highest plot line of *Love in a Wood*, Wycherley's first play, concerns the adventures and trials of Valentine and Christina, idealized lovers who would seem more at home in a romance than a Restoration comedy of manners. Valentine, who had fled England for France after wounding a man in a duel, has secretly returned and is staying with his friend, Vincent. Ranger, another friend of Vincent, met Christina by chance while investigating the activities of his own mistress, Lydia. Through no fault of her own, Christina has now become the object of Ranger's desire, and this he has hastened to tell Vincent. Valentine concludes that Christina has been untrue, and five acts of the expected misunderstandings and confusions are needed to convince him that his jealousy is unfounded and to unite the pair in matrimony. A second level of the play concerns the adventures of Vincent and Ranger that do not directly involve Valentine. The fop, Dapperwit, also moves on this level, and together these three gallants generate the witty dialogue and bawdy action expected by a Restoration audience. The lowest level is occupied by an array of rogues and whores. Central are the efforts of the procuress, Mrs. Joyner, to match a mistress, a husband, and a particular suitor with the old usurer (Alderman Gripe), his sister, and his daughter, respectively.

Love in a Wood is much more complex than this simplified summary suggests. Minor characters and story lines clutter the action to such an extent that all but the most attentive viewers must, like the characters, find themselves lost in a wood. The play is obviously the work of a new playwright, one who is still learning the craft. Wycherley knew well all the things that might go into a drama. He knew Ben Jonson and the humors, and he understood his age's fondness for wit and was himself at least witty enough to satisfy that appetite. He was aware that ideal, romantic love could always find an audience, and he understood the importance of effective dialogue and could write it forcefully and naturally, if not elegantly. Unity, too, he was certain, was one of the several ingredients that a playwright should add to the pot.

Conscious attention to all of these elements can be seen in this first play, but also apparent is Wycherley's failure to understand that a cook need not empty his entire pantry to prepare one dish. *Love in a Wood* simply tries to do too much. There are too many characters, too many plots. Unity, which should be the natural effect of careful plotting and characterization, is lost in the stew. The rather artificial attempts to build in a kind of unity are obvious. For example, the play begins on the level of the low plot, with Mrs. Joyner being berated by Gripe's sister, Lady Flippant, for not finding her a rich husband. More low characters are added before the action shifts to the level of the wits, as Ranger and Vincent prepare to seek new love in St. James's Park. Ranger encounters Christina, and the audience is introduced to the high plot. In only two acts, Wycherley, in sequence from low to high, introduces his principals and plots, but there the neat if obvious organization ends as the action shifts among characters and levels quickly and too often without clear purpose.

Another and again only partially successful unifying device is the use of certain key characters as links between the three major plot levels. Both Vincent and Ranger serve to tie the world of Valentine and Christina to that of the wits; Ranger is actually the catalyst for the action involving the ideal lovers. Dapperwit exists in a limbo between the wits and the low characters. He does keep company with Vincent and Ranger but is clearly more fop than wit, and unlike them, his existence affects but little the world of Valentine and Christina. Dapperwit is much more at home with Mrs. Joyner and Lady Flippant, and on this level he does help to move the action. Thus, the low is directly linked to the middle and the middle to the high. There is still, however, a quite obvious gap between the high and the low; no single character links the extremes.

Construction and theme cannot be separated, and Wycherley's failure to achieve effective unity of design is reflected in his ambiguous message. Happy marriage based on ideal love appears possible. Valentine and Christina exist in the real world of Restoration London, and their love survives nicely in that world, but there, too, live Gripe, Flippant, and Dapperwit, and their message must leave the audience quite confused as to what ideal love is really all about.

The Gentleman Dancing-Master • Wycherley's second play, *The Gentleman Dancing-Master*, adapted from Pedro Calderón de la Barca's *El maestro de danzar* (wr. 1651), suggests that he was aware of the problems with *Love in a Wood*, but that he was unsure as to how to resolve them, for *The Gentleman Dancing-Master* is the pendulum at its opposite extreme. While *Love in a Wood* has three major plot levels and a host of minor intrigues and adventures, *The Gentleman Dancing-Master* has only one story to tell, and this it does with a cast of major characters only half the size of that of the first play. Hippolita, the fourteen-year-old daughter of Mr. Formal, is unhappily engaged to Mr. Paris, her cousin and an absurd Gallophile. Mr. Formal, almost as absurd in his devotion to Spanish manners and fashion, would do all in his power to preserve his daughter's virtue, and with the help of his widowed sister, Mrs. Caution, keeps her under careful watch. Hippolita, however, is smarter than the lot of them, and, with the unwitting help of Paris, she manages to conduct an affair with a young gallant, Mr. Gerrard, who at her suggestion poses as a dance instructor. The lovers plan an elopement, but Hippolita's doubts about Gerrard's motive—love or her money—and assorted other diversions postpone the nuptials until the end.

In his first play, Wycherley had aimed at too many targets. *The Gentleman Dancing-Master* aims at only one, a broad, comedic effect assisted by a large dose of farce. Wycherley himself was less than proud of this work as an indicator of his real literary skill, and critics have generally agreed that it has little to admire. First, there is the problem of the genre itself. Farce, while very popular with Restoration audiences, was held in low esteem by scholars. Truth to life was the principal criterion by which a play should be judged; so said most of the great English critics, including John Dryden, the leading dramatist, poet, and critic of the age. Believability is the least concern of a farce, for everything that contributes to a believable effect—fine characterization, realistic dialogue, tight plot development—must yield to the hilarity of the episode. Moreover, as farces go, *The Gentleman Dancing-Master* has been judged by many modern critics as especially uninventive.

To be sure, Wycherley's second play would never be studied as an example of Restoration comedy at its finest. Still, it is not without merit, and a brisk stage rendition reveals strengths that are lost in a reading. For example, the single plot line tends to hold together the broadly comic episodes, achieving a sense of unity that is most often lacking in farce. The play is about Hippolita's efforts to find a suitable husband, and a Hippolita well acted can keep that design always before the audience. Hippolita, certainly one of Wycherley's more interesting characters, is responsible for adding a rather larger dash of satire than is commonly found in farce, not so large a dash as to make the flavor noticeably bitter—after all, she does get her man—but still enough that the reader of Wycherley's later, darker comedies can look back to *The Gentleman Dancing-Master* and notice a hint of what was to come.

In this glimpse of Restoration society, a fourteen-year-old girl only recently returned home from boarding school is complete master of the revels. She rejects her father's choice of a husband, engineers her own courtship, and marries the man she wants, all under her father's roof and her aunt's close guard, and neither is aware of what has happened until the closing lines of the play. It is she who invents the dancing-master fiction and transforms a shallow young man, who is more interested in a dowry than a good marriage, into acceptable husband material. She displays the naïveté and frankness of a child and the insight and cleverness of a mature adult and can move between these extremes in a matter of a few lines. Yet all of this talent and effort is needed to obtain what ideally should be taken for granted: an assurance that the words of the wedding vow will be sincere, that her marriage will be based on mutual love, honesty, and respect. In Wycherley's world, however, such assurances are difficult to find. Even a child must be devious to accomplish what is right, when her own father and intended husband are themselves prime examples of misrepresentation.

Mr. Paris, who would be known as Monsieur de Paris, and Mr. Formal, who prefers to be called Don Diego, are as contemptible as they are absurd. Wycherley created the roles for James Nokes and Edward Angel, two of the most famous comic actors of the day. Indeed, Paris's part is the largest in the play, for it was doubtless Nokes as a French fool that the audience came to see. Both Formal and Paris have rejected what they are, Englishmen, to ape foreign manners: It is small wonder that they are so unaware of Hippolita's machinations. They have their own lies to live and would rather argue with each other as to whose lie is better than to see the reality of what is happening. That a fourteen-year-old girl with a sense of purpose can manipulate the adult world says little for that world. That the best husband available is a man so easily directed, a man who must be tested for sincerity before deemed acceptable, adds little reason for optimism, and finally that that fourteen-year-old is herself unsure of the true nature of her young man and is after all only adept at fooling fools must bring small reassurance. *The Gentleman Dancing-Master* is a comedy, a farce, but already the darker shadows have begun to fall.

The Country Wife • With his third effort, Wycherley brilliantly overcame the problems of his first two plays. *The Country Wife* is generally acknowledged as one of the finest comedies of the Restoration, and it is still frequently acted, not so much as a historical curiosity but because it is good theater. The plot is somewhat more complex than that of *The Gentleman Dancing-Master*, but it is tightly unified by linking characters who have real business in the variety of situations; there is none of the baffling confusion of *Love in a Wood*. The main action is moved by Horner—who, as his name suggests, delights in making cuckolds of the London husbands. To that end, he has caused the false rumor of his own impotence to be spread about the town; as expected, husbands who would never let their wives near Horner have foolishly relaxed their guard. Lady Fidget, Mrs. Dainty Fidget, and Mrs. Squeamish are among his willing conquests.

The adventures of Margery Pinchwife, the title character, form a second but closely related plot. Jack Pinchwife married his country wife because he was hopeful that such a woman would be ignorant of the fashions of the city and the promiscuity of the gallants and ladies. This decision, however, was not motivated by a sense of higher morality; indeed, Pinchwife may well be the most immoral character in the play, for, as his name suggests, his every action is directed by his intense fear of being made a cuckold and by a jealousy that can move him to viciousness. Despite her husband, Margery has learned of the way of the world and is anxious to sample it. She realizes that there are better relationships than that which she enjoys with Pinchwife and so cultivates an affair with Horner. The third plot does not relate quite so directly to the main plot, but the characters and action provide some obvious contrasts that serve to clarify and further comment on the play's theme. Alithea, Pinchwife's sister, is engaged to Sparkish. She is an intelligent woman of genuine honor; he is the usual ridiculous fop that so delighted Restoration audiences. Fully aware that her fiancé is a fool, she is resolved to go through with their arranged marriage, though in fact she loves Harcourt, a friend of Horner, and he loves her. At the last, Sparkish's misunderstanding of Alithea's part in the typically confusing episodes and intrigues that follow results in a broken engagement and a clear way to her union with Harcourt.

While Alithea's role is a relatively minor and unimpressive one on the stage, she does make a significant contribution to an understanding of Wycherley's message. Alithea stubbornly insists on behaving honorably in a world where there is no honor. She is obliged by custom and contract to go through with the marriage arranged by

Pinchwife and respects that obligation, though the union must result in a life of misery and wasted talent for her and in material gain for men who neither need nor deserve it. In Alithea, the audience sees real virtue turned against itself by corrupt marital customs that not only make cuckolds of fools, which may not be so bad, but also make honorable people victims of their own honor, which is intolerable. Still, at the end, it is only Alithea who appears to have a chance for real happiness. Mrs. Pinchwife's unhappy fate is to return to her husband, while the husbands return to their fool's paradise, as Horner convincingly reaffirms the lie about his impotency.

Before concluding that Wycherley's message is to proclaim the inevitable rewards that come to virtue, one should remember that he had little choice but to inject some measure of happiness at the ending (the play is a comedy), and that Alithea's deliverance from Sparkish has nothing to do with the power of virtue. She is freed from the contract by Sparkish's stupidity and the chance outcome of the intrigues of the other characters. In the world of *The Country Wife*, honor is as impotent as Horner pretends to be, and if anything is temporarily set right, it is only because of luck.

The corruptive power of marriage without love is seen from a different perspective in the title character, Margery Pinchwife. Alithea shows the system's effect on honor; Margery shows its effect on innocence. She enters the world of fashion a complete ingenue, and so Pinchwife would keep her, but all that is said to her and all that she sees writes on the blank slate of her character. Her jealous husband foolishly describes the pleasures of city life, pleasures to be avoided, and thus awakens her interest in them; he takes her to a play dressed as a man, so that she will not draw the attention of other men, which gives her the inspiration to assume a disguise when she visits Horner.

Marlowe it would not be altogether accurate to say that Margery is corrupted, for at the end of the play, her naïve belief that she can exchange Pinchwife for Horner as her husband and live a happily married life ever after shows a character who has really learned nothing of how the system works. She does, indeed, do things that conventional morality would deem wicked, but she is merely aping what she has seen: These are the proper city responses, written on the slate by the characters around her, and against the background of her innocence, their conduct is brought into sharp relief. Hers is rightly the title role, for through her the audience clearly sees the nature of the other characters and the world they have created. There is no happy ending for Margery. Luck does not smile on her; she has not learned the true cunning of Horner that would allow her to make the best of the situation, and she is not one of the fools who can delude themselves with happy lies. She strikes a note at the end that is not quite comedy.

Mr. Harry Horner has been attacked by three hundred years of critics as one of the most immoral creations of the Restoration stage. In fact, there is no question of moral or immoral conduct in the high society in which he moves. The clearly moral alternative simply does not exist, and heroes are recognizable only by their superior wit and not at all by their deeds. Thus, though Horner does invent an obscene lie to help him bed other men's wives, his contempt for his victims manages to make him something more than simply another rake. He has honor of a sort, but certainly not Alithea's passive honor, not the honor of the martyr. Horner's honor allows him to use the weapons of the system against itself, and to him is the victory, for, with his lie still intact, he leaves the field strewn with cuckolds. That lie, however, is more than a tool for undoing fools; it is Wycherley's comment on the society. As the action moves the audience among various couples, it becomes increasingly clear that marriage has nothing to do with love or basic nature. It has become a thing arranged on paper and bought with money. Horner's impotence is a fiction. Ironically, the real sterility exists in the marriages of his victims.

The Plain-Dealer • Wycherley's final and longest play, *The Plain-Dealer*, confirms what was apparent in *The Country Wife*: The author had learned well the lessons of plot construction and structural unity. It poses other problems of characterization, however, that make it less a masterpiece than his third effort. The story is simple. There are only two plots, and all the principal characters occupy the same social level and have occasion to interact, thus creating a sense of unity.

Captain Manly, the title character, is described by the author as honest, surly, and good-humored. He believes firmly in plain dealing, and the shortage of others who share that belief has led him to misanthropy. After losing his ship in the Dutch wars, Manly has returned to London to seek another vessel. He soon discovers that his mistress, Olivia, thought to be a plain dealer like him, has married another man and appropriated the money Manly had left in her care. Torn between contempt and affection, Manly sends his young aide, Fidelia, to arrange a meeting with Olivia. Instead, Olivia develops a passion for Fidelia, who in fact is a wealthy young heiress disguised as a boy to be near Manly, whom she loves. Manly next discovers that Olivia's secret husband is Vernish, the only man he really trusted. At Olivia's home, Manly fights Vernish, takes back the money, and discovers that Fidelia, who lost her wig in the commotion, is really a young woman. He immediately decides that Fidelia is a more proper object for his affection, and together the couple plan their future in the West Indies.

In the second plot, Lieutenant Freeman, a young friend of Manly, attempts to marry the cantankerous old Widow Blackacre for her fortune. The widow, whose only delight is in controlling her own business and suing people, wants no part of such an arrangement. When Freeman persuades the widow's stupid son to accept him as his guardian with full power over his inheritance, Widow Blackacre retaliates by claiming that her son is a bastard and not a legal heir. Freeman, however, discovers this to be a lie, and in order to avoid a charge of perjury, the widow is forced to grant him a handsome annuity.

Captain Manly is perhaps the most puzzling character in Restoration drama, and the difficulty of the audience in interpreting him obscures the theme of the play. Like that other famous voyager, Lemuel Gulliver, Manly suffers from misanthropy, and the distorted judgment to which it leads him makes it difficult to judge how representative a spokesperson for the author he is intended to be. Certainly he has qualities to be admired. In relation to the collection of liars and frauds that surrounds him, his utter contempt is justified and his bluntness is refreshing. Still, he recognizes neither hypocrisy nor plain dealing when he sees them, and at times he is as willing to overlook or condone deliberate deception as he is at other times anxious to condemn it. Moreover, he is, like Horner, quite willing to practice a little deception of his own if it suits his purpose.

If Manly were not wrong and self-contradictory most of the time, there would be no play, for his mistakes move the plot. His greatest mistake is his choice of Olivia. She mouths the same philosophy of plain dealing as Manly but marries and steals in secret. Fidelia is the cause of another mistake; the plain dealer wanders through five acts unaware that his aide, the person with whom he plots revenge against Olivia, is a woman, and when her gender is discovered, he transfers his affection with embarrassing rapidity. Throughout those five acts, he has remained blind to the fact that Fidelia displays a faithfulness and devotion rare in a human being, and when he decides at last to love her, he is equally unconcerned that her disguise, while for a good purpose, was hardly consistent with plain dealing.

There is also the problem of Freeman. The lieutenant is really Manly's best friend, for Vernish turns out to be a villain. In fact, Freeman is the only character who deals plainly with Manly. He quite frankly tells his captain that truth is a handicap in the social world and honestly confesses his motives in the wooing of Widow Blackacre. Manly cannot tolerate the company of most dissemblers and hypocrites, but Freeman is an exception; apparently, honest hypocrites are acceptable.

Despite Manly's several mistakes and inconsistencies, he is still clearly the hero of the play, and Wycherley certainly intended the general audience response to be positive. After all, Manly does have the love of a good woman, who seems willing to suffer almost any humiliation for his sake, and he does have the sincere friendship of Freeman, something of a rogue, to be sure, but a likable rogue. The problems with Manly's philosophy of plain dealing are more apparent in a careful reading than they are in a lively performance, and his confusing behavior is in part a result of his being made to interact with Freeman and Fidelia, who have characterization problems of their own. Fidelia in almost any other play would present no difficulty. She is an idealized female who would be quite at home in a romance, but she seems strangely out of place in a world that requires a misanthrope for a hero. Moreover, her male disguise, which jars with Manly's love of plain dealing, is a conventional comedic device that would present no problem on another stage. Freeman, too, is a conventional figure, but confidant to Manly is not a proper job for a lovable rogue, and while Freeman would make an ideal friend for Horner, his role in *The Plain-Dealer* confuses the message.

Wycherley's final play, then, cannot be judged his best. It may well be, however, his darkest comment on society. Manly is certainly the closest thing to direct spokesperson that Wycherley ever created, and in *The Plain-Dealer* that spokesperson was finally allowed to comment openly on the world of knaves and fools and hypocrites and whores that had been presented with increasing pessimism in the three earlier plays. The problems with Manly may well be the inevitable culmination of Wycherley's vision: Society corrupts honor and innocence and infects with confusion even the best efforts of the best people. There is no firm ground on which a plain dealer can stand.

Other major work

POETRY: *Miscellany Poems: As Satyrs, Epistles, Love-Verses, Songs, Sonnets, Etc.*, 1704.

Bibliography

Markley, Robert. *Two Edg'd Weapons: Style and Dialogue in the Comedies of Etherege, Wycherley, and Congreve.* New York: Oxford University Press, 1988. This study is concerned with the comic style and language of Sir George Etherege, Wycherley, and William Congreve as the rewriting or adaptation of systems of theatrical signification in predecessors, as the reflection of particular cultural codes of speech and behavior that would be accessible to their audience, and as a comment on the culture of which they and their audience were a part. Bibliography.

Marshall, W. Gerald. *A Great Stage of Fools: Theatricality and Madness in the Plays of William Wycherley.* New York: AMS Press, 1993. Marshall examines the concept of mental illness as it appears in the works of Wycherley. Bibliography and index.

Thompson, James. *Language in Wycherley's Plays: Seventeenth Century Language Theory and Drama*. Tuscaloosa: University of Alabama Press, 1984. Thompson discusses how Wycherley used language in his dramas and relates his usage to the broader context. Bibliography and index.

Vance, John A. *William Wycherley and the Comedy of Fear*. Newark, N.J.: University of Delaware Press, 2000. An analysis of Wycherley and his works with the focus on his treatment of fear. Bibliography and index.

Young, Douglas M. *The Feminist Voices in Restoration Comedy: The Virtuous Women in the Play-Worlds of Etherege, Wycherley, and Congreve*. Lanham, Md.: University Press of America, 1997. A study of feminism and women in the works of Wycherley, George Etherege, and William Congreve. Bibliography and index.

William J. Heim,
updated by Genevieve Slomski

William Butler Yeats

Born: Sandymount, near Dublin, Ireland; June 13, 1865
Died: Cap Martin, France; January 28, 1939

Principal drama • *The Countess Cathleen,* pb. 1892, pr. 1899; *The Land of Heart's Desire,* pr., pb. 1894; *Cathleen ni Houlihan,* pr., pb. 1902; *The Pot of Broth,* pr. 1902, pb. 1903 (with Lady Augusta Gregory); *The Hour-Glass,* pr. 1903, revised pr. 1912, pb. 1913; *The King's Threshold,* pr., pb. 1903 (with Lady Gregory); *On Baile's Strand,* pr. 1904, pb. 1905; *Deirdre,* pr. 1906, pb. 1907 (with Lady Gregory); *The Shadowy Waters,* pr. 1906, pb. 1907; *The Unicorn from the Stars,* pr. 1907, pb. 1908 (with Lady Gregory); *The Golden Helmet,* pr., pb. 1908; *The Green Helmet,* pr., pb. 1910; *At the Hawk's Well,* pr. 1916, pb. 1917; *The Player Queen,* pr. 1919, pb. 1922; *The Only Jealousy of Emer,* pb. 1919, pr. 1922; *The Dreaming of the Bones,* pb. 1919, pr. 1931; *Calvary,* pb. 1921; *Four Plays for Dancers,* pb. 1921 (includes *Calvary, At the Hawk's Well, The Dreaming of the Bones, The Only Jealousy of Emer*); *The Cat and the Moon,* pb. 1924, pr. 1931; *The Resurrection,* pb. 1927, pr. 1934; *The Words upon the Window-Pane,* pr. 1930, pb. 1934; *The Collected Plays of W. B. Yeats,* pb. 1934, 1952; *The King of the Great Clock Tower,* pr., pb. 1934; *A Full Moon in March,* pr. 1934, pb. 1935; *The Herne's Egg,* pb. 1938; *Purgatory,* pr. 1938, pb. 1939; *The Death of Cuchulain,* pb. 1939, pr. 1949; *Variorum Edition of the Plays of W. B. Yeats,* pb. 1966 (Russell K. Alspach, editor)

Other literary forms • Throughout a literary career spanning a half century, William Butler Yeats distinguished himself principally by means of the production of some dozen volumes of lyric poems. His early work is most clearly indebted to the English Romantics, but his commitment to the cause of the Irish Literary Revival, of which he was the leader, and to the management of its showcase, the Abbey Theatre, gave him an increasingly public voice. The poetry of his last twenty years contains his most complex, modernist, and profound work and is often considered the highest achievement in that genre during the twentieth century.

Yeats was also the author of a considerable body of essays, reviews, and introductions during a career of literary journalism and theatrical management: *Essays and Introductions* (1961), *Explorations* (1962), and *Uncollected Prose by W. B. Yeats* (two volumes; 1970, 1976). He collected and edited writings and promoted the work of such collaborators as Lady Augusta Gregory and John Millington Synge. Yeats's early excursions into short fiction are collected in *Mythologies* (1959). Autobiographical fragments are found in *Autobiographies* (1926, 1955) and *Memoirs* (1972). *A Vision* (1925, 1937) sets forth a symbolic ordering of history and human character in a manner chiefly useful in explicating his poetry, while *The Senate Speeches of W. B. Yeats* (1960) gathers some of his public statements from the 1920's. The Yeats correspondence is partially collected in *The Letters of W. B. Yeats* (1954) and in *Ah, Sweet Dancer: W. B. Yeats, Margot Ruddock—A Correspondence* (1970).

Achievements • William Butler Yeats's reputation as one of the masters of modern literature rests mainly on his achievements in poetry, and his dramatic work has long been regarded less favorably as "poetry in the theater." This aspect of his work has, however, been reassessed, and he has come to be regarded as one of the boldest and most original dramatists of the twentieth century. As one of the founders, first playwrights, and lifetime directors of the Abbey Theatre, Yeats was the central figure of the Irish Literary Renaissance. The example of efforts to develop a modern and national literature that drew on Celtic mythology, folklore, and the oral tradition of Ireland provided incentives for the latent talents of such dramatists as Lady Augusta Gregory, John Millington Synge, Padraic Colum, and Sean O'Casey.

(© The Nobel Foundation)

Although Yeats experimented with several dramatic styles, including peasant realism, farce, and naturalism, his genius found its true métier in a highly sophisticated drama that combined poetry, dance, mask, and symbolic action to represent a world of ideals and pure passion. These plays, borrowed from the tradition of the Japanese Nō for their form and from Celtic heroic tales for their subjects, expressed Yeats's views of the primacy of imaginative or spiritual realities of which historical change and the differentiation of human character are emanations. Yeats was therefore at odds with modern realism and with its interest in individual character and social relations: An attitude of detachment and impersonality shaped his works into intensely ritualized expressions, having affinities both with religious drama and absurdism.

Yeats lived through revolutions in politics and sensibility. Most important, through a lifelong remaking of dramatic and lyric form and style, Yeats achieved a continuous renovation of his own spirit. Thus, he became one of those primarily responsible for the restoration to Ireland of its cultural heritage, at the same time forging an idiom that the modern world at large considers its own.

Biography • The eldest of the four children of John Butler Yeats, the painter, and his wife, Susan Pollexfen, William Butler Yeats was born in Sandymount, near Dublin. When he was nine years old, the family moved to London, where he attended the Godolphin School in Hammersmith, taking his holidays with his maternal grandparents in County Sligo in the rural west of Ireland. The Yeats family returned to Dublin in 1880, and the young Yeats thereafter completed his education at the high school and the Metropolitan Art School. During this time, from 1883 to 1886, he came under the influence of George Russell (Æ) and a circle of Dublin mystics, as well as John O'Leary, the aged Fenian leader.

These various influences turned the introverted boy from art to literature; from religious confusion (his mother was a Protestant, his father an agnostic) to Theosophy, the occult, and Rosicrucianism; and from the Oriental themes of his earliest literary efforts to Irish subjects. Yeats moved back to London in 1888. In 1890, he helped organize the Rhymers Club, where he made friends with many of the leading poets of the time, including Arthur Symons, William Morris, and Lionel Johnson, with whom he founded the Irish Literary Society in 1891.

In 1888, Yeats had met Maud Gonne, an actress and activist in behalf of Irish nationalism. A lifelong, unrequited obsession with her (she rejected marriage proposals in 1891 and again in 1916) accounts for the periodic intensification of his enthusiasm for nationalist politics, the subject of much of his poetry and two of his early plays, *The Countess Cathleen* and *Cathleen ni Houlihan.*

Yeats returned to Dublin in 1896, and in 1899, he collaborated with Edward Martyn and Lady Gregory in founding the Irish Literary Theatre, which in 1904 became the Abbey Theatre. The affairs of this theater—playwriting (peasant and Celtic themes), daily management, the promotion of playwrights with Irish subjects (Synge was the most notable)—were his preoccupations until about 1910.

After Ezra Pound introduced him to the Japanese Nō drama, Yeats wrote his *Four Plays for Dancers*: formal, symbolic, ritual plays based on Celtic, Irish, and Christian themes. He married Georgina Hyde-Lees in 1917 and, discovering her capacities as a medium, revived his interest in Spiritualism. With her assistance, he produced the systematized *A Vision*, which illuminates much of his mature drama and poetry. The couple lived in Dublin and at Thoor Ballylee, a restored Norman tower in County Galway, and had two children. During the last twenty-five years of his life, Yeats produced his most mature work in poetry, prose, and drama. He was appointed a member of the senate of the Irish Free State from 1922 to 1928, lectured widely in Europe and the United States, and received widespread recognition, including honorary doctorates and the Nobel Prize in Literature in 1923. In 1932, along with George Bernard Shaw and Æ, he founded the Irish Academy of Letters, and in 1936, he edited the controversial *Oxford Book of Modern Verse.* Failing health forced him to abandon Thoor Ballylee, and in the 1930's, he spent progressively more of each year in Italy and France. In 1939, shortly after completing his last play, *The Death of Cuchulain,* he died in the French Riviera and was temporarily buried there. His remains were returned to Drumcliff, County Sligo, his grandfather's parish, in 1948.

Analysis • William Butler Yeats's reputation justly rests on his achievements in poetry, yet a considerable portion of that work is written for two or more voices and, therefore, is dramatic. Indeed, his first literary compositions were long dramatic poems, and throughout his life, he continued to publish his plays and poems side by side. Yeats believed that the language of poetry best represented imaginative reality, the life of the soul, or the introspective or subjective consciousness, as opposed to the spirit of science, the modern, extroverted age, the objective consciousness that draws its identity from external circumstances and that finds its appropriate expression in dramatic realism. Therefore, throughout a career as a dramatist consisting of four distinct phases, Yeats's sympathies remained mystical, Symbolist, and removed from the mainstream of popular drama. Nevertheless, he is one of the genuinely original dramatists of the twentieth century, with influences on verse drama and the work of Samuel Beckett.

The Countess Cathleen • When Yeats joined talents and ambitions with Lady Gregory and Edward Martyn to form the Irish Literary Theatre in 1899, his first contributions to the venture were *The Countess Cathleen* and *Cathleen ni Houlihan.* The former is a rather static verse drama in which a heroic native aristocrat sells her soul to merchant-demons in order to save the starving peasants. The play aroused controversy over its doctrinal content in Roman Catholic Ireland, and its author's doughty defense of independence in artistic and patriotic self-expression established a pattern that was often to repeat itself.

Cathleen ni Houlihan • Yeats's most dramatically successful early work, however, is *Cathleen ni Houlihan,* one of several peasant plays that Yeats wrote. The play depicts in realistic terms the diversion of a young man's intentions from his impending marriage to a phase of the 1798 rebellion in Ireland. An anonymous old woman becomes a young queen because of the heroic commitment of Michael Gillane. Here is *The Land of Heart's Desire* rewritten in nationalist terms: The thrifty realism of the peasants gradually yields to the incantatory power of the old woman's lament, and the political allegory is triumphantly announced in the famous curtain line.

With Maud Gonne in the title role reciting the credo of nationalist Ireland, Yeats was accused of producing unworthy propaganda. He protested that it came to him in a dream, but like the subject matter of all of his early work, its origins are demonstrably in the native folklore that Yeats had been collecting and studying since his conversion to the cause of Ireland's cultural distinctiveness. The theme of this particular play is, indeed, traceable through popular ballad to the Gaelic *aisling* (vision) convention and to the theme of the lady and the king found in medieval Irish literature. Its power on an Irish stage is therefore attributable to more than its last line. Yeats was to wonder, with some justification, how much this play contributed to the Easter Rebellion of 1916.

The Cuchulain plays • Before the heroism of that week burst on his and the nation's consciousness, Yeats was cultivating in himself and on the stage of the Abbey Theatre a renewed appreciation of the literature of ancient Ireland and its exaltation of heroic individualism, eloquence, aristocracy, and paganism. In the figure of Cuchulain, the hero of the Ulster Cycle, Yeats found the embodiment of these virtues, and he wrote a series of five plays dramatizing episodes from the hero's lone defense of Ulster, beginning with *On Baile's Strand.* Among Cuchulain's challengers is a young man in whom Cuchulain notes a resemblance to his abandoned wife, Aoife. Caught between his natural affinity for this image and his oath to King Conchubar to defend the province against intruders, Cuchulain is driven to combat. Too late, he discovers that the dead boy is his own son, and in his anguish, he rushes, sword in hand, into the waves until he drowns.

This play marks a significant advance in technique on Yeats's early dramatic efforts in its tight control and complexity of theme. The theme of conflicting loyalties operates at several levels simultaneously, so that Cuchulain's roles as loyal soldier, independent hero, father, and son all conspire to bring on his tragic self-destruction. The framing device of the Fool and the Blind Man functions as an ironic lowlife commentary on the serious central action, while at the same time casting up counterpart images of Conchubar and Cuchulain as creatures guided by similarly fitful lights.

Yeats went on to write four other Cuchulain plays, *The Golden Helmet, At the Hawk's Well, The Only Jealousy of Emer,* and *The Death of Cuchulain,* as well as several others drawn from Celtic sources made available by translators such as Lady Gregory. His dissatisfaction with modern realism, however, with its focus on the drama of individual character, distanced him from the kind of work that made the Abbey Theatre popular. When Ezra Pound introduced Yeats in 1913 to the Nō theater of Japan, Yeats recognized the tradition which would enable him to shape his own ideas into a successful poetic drama.

The Dreaming of the Bones • The Japanese Nō drama dates from the late Middle Ages, has strong Zen elements, and is highly stylized. It is a symbolic drama, developing the resources of mask, gesture, chanted dialogue, slow rhythmic dance, ornamental costume, chorus, and flute and drum to create an atmosphere of passionate reverie contained beneath an elegant repose. Yeats was attracted by the tone of gravity, detachment, mystery, grace, and nobility in these plays. His Spiritualist sympathies predisposed him to appreciate plays that featured figures in the process of "dreaming back" moments of extreme passion in their lives as they sought release from human desires and entrance into final peace. In his *Four Plays for Dancers*, especially *The Dreaming of the Bones* as well as in several later plays, these influences are evident.

The Dreaming of the Bones is designed in two scenes joined by a choral interlude, according to the structure of a fantasy-style Nō such as *Nishikigi*. The Subordinate Player (here the Young Man) encounters the Main Players (here the Stranger and Young Girl) in a historical spot (the Abbey of Corcomroe) at a historical moment (1916). The Main Players tell the story of the place and ask for prayers and forgiveness of the Young Man, finally revealing themselves as the ghosts of Diarmuid MacMorrough and Dervorgilla (the twelfth century couple whose marriage was instrumental in the Norman invasion of Ireland). Because the Young Man is a modern Irish patriot for whom that liaison was the original sexual-political transgression, he refuses, and the couple is left to continue their purgatorial "dreaming back" of their tragic sin. The various themes of the play—dream, war, resurrection, cyclic change—coalesce in the emblems of the birds in the Musicians' final chorus. Subsequent experiments with the Nō form demonstrate Yeats's greater facility in adapting it to the expression of his own views of the afterlife and his mythologization of the Irish past—especially in *The Only Jealousy of Emer*, *The Words upon the Window-pane*, and *Purgatory*.

The Words upon the Window-Pane • *The Words upon the Window-Pane* is a daringly successful combination of naturalism, Spiritualism, the "dreaming back" from the Nō and Yeats's latter-day identification with eighteenth century Anglo-Ireland. In this dramatization of a Dublin séance, the tortured spirit of Jonathan Swift is invoked, though remaining unrecognized by any except the literary scholar John Corbet. Swift, the representative of intellectuality, classical ideals, and the natural aristocracy of Ireland, "dreams back" his rejection of the opportunity for fatherhood offered by Vanessa, thereby sharing Yeats's rejection of the "filthy modern tide" that would likely be their issue. In his management of middle-class character and dialogue, Yeats shows his capacities in the naturalistic style, but the dramatic coup here comes in the final scene, when these conventions are broken and the audience is left alone with an order of reality beyond the reach of skeptic or scholar.

Purgatory • In *Purgatory*, one of his last plays, Yeats achieved his most concentrated work for stage. The setting and action are symbolic, the language a brilliant fusion of colloquial and poetic idiom. The Old Man, the product of a marriage between a big house and a stable, lost his aristocratic mother at his birth and later murdered his drunken father. Now, accompanied by his son, the Old Man visits the scene of his parents' unfortunate wedding—unfortunate because it betrayed class and because it produced him, a parricide. In an attempt to break the chain of evil, the Old Man stabs his son, but to no avail: The spirits of his parents are trapped in a perpetual repetition of their crime, unless God intervenes. Here, Yeats has devised a complex dramatic symbol for the demise of aristocratic Anglo-Ireland, the approach of global conflict, and the relationship between the living conscience and the stages of spiritual purgation to be encountered after death. The play is thus a summary exposition of Yeats's social and philosophical views in the later years of his life, drawing on the disciplines of language and construction that he had refined over a lifetime of experimentation.

Other major works

SHORT FICTION: *John Sherman and Dhoya,* 1891, 1969; *The Celtic Twilight,* 1893; *The Secret Rose,* 1897; *The Tables of Law; The Adoration of the Magi,* 1897; *Stories of Red Hanrahan,* 1904; *Mythologies,* 1959.

POETRY: *Mosada: A Dramatic Poem,* 1886; *Crossways,* 1889; *The Wanderings of Oisin and Other Poems,* 1889; *The Countess Kathleen and Various Legends and Lyrics,* 1892; *The Rose,* 1893; *The Wind Among the Reeds,* 1899; *In the Seven Woods,* 1903; *The Poetical Works of William B. Yeats,* 1906, 1907 (2 volumes); *The Green Helmet and Other Poems,* 1910; *Responsibilities,* 1914; *Responsibilities and Other Poems,* 1916; *The Wild Swans at Coole,* 1917, 1919; *Michael Robartes and the Dancer,* 1920; *The Tower,* 1928; *Words for Music Perhaps and Other Poems,* 1932; *The Winding Stair and Other Poems,* 1933; *The Collected Poems of W. B. Yeats,* 1933, 1950; *The King of the Great Clock Tower,* 1934; *A Full Moon in March,* 1935; *Last Poems and Plays,* 1940; *The Poems of W. B. Yeats,* 1949 (2 volumes); *The Collected Poems of W. B. Yeats,* 1956; *Variorum Edition of the Poems of W. B. Yeats,* 1957 (P. Allt and R. K. Alspach, editors); *The Poems,* 1983; *The Poems: A New Edition,* 1984.

NONFICTION: *Ideas of Good and Evil,* 1903; *The Cutting of an Agate,* 1912; *Per Amica Silentia Lunae,* 1918; *Essays,* 1924; *A Vision,* 1925, 1937; *Autobiographies,* 1926, 1955; *A Packet for Ezra Pound,* 1929; *Essays, 1931-1936,* 1937; *The Autobiography of William Butler Yeats,* 1938; *On the Boiler,* 1939; *If I Were Four and Twenty,* 1940; *The Letters of W. B. Yeats,* 1954; *The Senate Speeches of W. B. Yeats,* 1960 (Donald R. Pearce, editor); *Essays and Introductions,* 1961; *Explorations,* 1962; *Ah, Sweet Dancer: W. B. Yeats, Margot Ruddock—A Correspondence,* 1970 (Roger McHugh, editor); *Uncollected Prose by W. B. Yeats,* 1970, 1976 (2 volumes); *Memoirs,* 1972; *The Collected Letters of William Butler Yeats: Volume I, 1865-1895,* 1986.

MISCELLANEOUS: *The Collected Works in Verse and Prose of William Butler Yeats,* 1908.

Bibliography

Bornstein, George. *Material Modernism: The Politics of the Page.* New York: Cambridge University Press, 2001. A study of Modernism in Ireland, England, and the United States, focusing on Yeats and James Joyce. Bibliography and index.

Brown, Terence. *The Life of W. B. Yeats: A Critical Biography.* Malden, Mass.: Blackwell, 1999. A biography that examines the intellectual life of Yeats as well as his works. Bibliography and index.

Chaudhry, Yug Mohit. *Yeats, the Irish Literary Revival and the Politics of Print.* Cork, Ireland: Cork University Press, 2001. A study of Yeats's political and social views as well as a critique of his writings. Bibliography and index.

Holdridge, Jefferson. *Those Mingled Seas: The Poetry of W. B. Yeats, The Beautiful and the Sublime.* Dublin: University College Dublin Press, 2000. A study of Yeats's poetry that suspends it between the philosophies of both Kant and Burke, focusing on the source of the power of Yeats's mysticism.

Larrissy, Edward. *W. B. Yeats.* Plymouth, England: Northcote House in association with the British Council, 1998. A basic biography of Yeats that examines both his life and works. Bibliography and index.

Maddox, Brenda. *Yeats's Ghosts: The Secret Life of W. B. Yeats.* New York: HarperCollins, 1999. Maddox examines Yeats's connection to spiritualism and the occult. Bibliography and index.

Richman, David. *Passionate Action: Yeats's Mastery of Drama.* Newark, N.J.: University of Delaware Press, 2000. Richman examines the dramatic works of Yeats and discusses Irish literature. Bibliography and index.

Cóilín D. Owens,
updated by Peter C. Holloran

Paul Zindel

Born: Staten Island, New York; May 15, 1936
Died: New York, New York; March 27, 2003

Principal drama • *Dimensions of Peacocks*, pr. 1959; *Euthanasia and the Endless Hearts*, pr. 1960; *A Dream of Swallows*, pr. 1964; *The Effect of Gamma Rays on Man-in-the-Moon Marigolds*, pr. 1965, pb. 1971; *And Miss Reardon Drinks a Little*, pr. 1967, pb. 1972; *The Secret Affairs of Mildred Wild*, pr. 1972, pb. 1973; *The Ladies Should Be in Bed*, pb. 1973; *Ladies at the Alamo*, pr. 1975, pb. 1977; *A Destiny with Half Moon Street*, pr. 1983; *Amulets Against the Dragon Forces*, pr., pb. 1989; *Every Seventeen Minutes the Crowd Goes Crazy!*, pr. 1995, pb. 1996

Other literary forms • Paul Zindel once considered himself primarily a playwright, and in 1990 said, "basically, I'm a dramatist"; he enjoyed great success as a writer of novels for teenagers, however, and it is in this capacity that he is best known. His first such work, *The Pigman* (1968), sold in the millions, and sequels such as *The Pigman's Legacy* (1980) followed. A 1989 book, *A Begonia for Miss Applebaum*, was critically well received, and the autobiographical *The Pigman and Me* was published in 1992. Zindel's teen characters confront the pangs and thrills of young adult reality as they reach for friendship, for romantic love, for mature perspectives on sexuality, and for success or at least survival in school or work. In 1984, Zindel published his first novel for adults, *When a Darkness Falls*. During the 1990's Zindel began writing series chapter novels including comedy, mystery, and horror for pre-teen audiences.

Zindel wrote screenplays for *Up the Sandbox* (1972), *Mame* (1974), *Runaway Train* (1983), and *Maria's Lovers* (1984), and a teleplay, *Let Me Hear You Whisper* (1966). He also wrote for periodicals.

Achievements • Paul Zindel's *The Effect of Gamma Rays on Man-in-the-Moon Marigolds* gained acceptance not only in the form of broadcasts on National Educational Television in New York but also through stage performances at the Alley Theatre in Houston, Texas. Zindel secured a Ford Foundation grant as a playwright-in-residence at the Alley in 1967. In 1970, the play opened in New York, Off-Broadway; then it moved to the New Theatre on Broadway. It closed on May 14, 1972, after 819 performances. *The Effect of Gamma Rays on Man-in-the-Moon Marigolds* received an Obie Award for the best Off-Broadway play in 1970. Also in 1970, Zindel won the New York Drama Critics Circle Award for Best American Play and the Vernon Rice Drama Desk Award as the most promising playwright of the season. In 1971, he received an honorary doctorate from his alma mater, Wagner College, and a Pulitzer Prize in Drama.

The success of *The Effect of Gamma Rays on Man-in-the-Moon Marigolds* was followed in 1971 by a Broadway production of *And Miss Reardon Drinks a Little*, a play previously staged in Los Angeles in 1967. The Broadway production, starring Julie Harris, ran for 108 performances, and the play made the list of the ten best plays for the 1971 season. Zindel next brought a comedy to Broadway, *The Secret Affairs of Mildred Wild*, which lasted for only twenty-three performances.

Joining the Actors Studio in 1973, Zindel extensively revised earlier material to produce *Ladies at the Alamo*, which he himself directed at Actors Studio for a two-week run in 1975. He directed the same play in a brief Broadway run in 1977, as well as a New York revival of *The Effect of Gamma Rays on Man-in-the-Moon Marigolds* in 1978. The Coconut Grove Playhouse in Coconut Grove, Florida, premiered Zindel's *A Destiny with Half Moon Street* in its 1982-1983 repertory.

Zindel's plays have moved from little and regional theaters to Broadway and back. Critics say that his later plays have not fulfilled the expectations raised by his initial success. Still, Zindel's plays continue to be performed in high school, college, touring company, and regional repertory productions.

In 1998 Zindel was honored, along with forty-three other notable dramatists such as Edward Albee, by a walk-of-fame bronze star on the Playwrights' Sidewalk outside the Lortel Theater in Greenwich Village. In 2002, the year before his death, Zindel received the Margaret A. Edwards Award for his lifetime writing contribution to literature for young adults, an honor presented by the Young Adult Library Services Association.

Biography • Paul Zindel was born on May 15, 1936, in Staten Island, New York, to Paul and Betty (née Frank) Zindel. His father, a police officer, abandoned his wife and two small children, Paul and a sister. Betty Zindel, a practical nurse, launched into numerous ventures, ranging from real estate to dog breeding, and sometimes took in terminally ill patients for board and care. The family moved almost annually.

This transient lifestyle and his mother's unwillingness, if not inability, to form meaningful relationships acquainted young Zindel with various forms of loss. Pets allowed at one home might be forbidden by the next landlord. Dogs raised for sale would eventually be sold. Board-and-care patients would sometimes die. The frequent moves, too, kept the boy, more often than not, in the role of newcomer in a neighborhood. It grew simpler to enjoy the worlds of imagination and, when possible, the manageable environments of aquaria and terraria.

In school, Zindel occasionally acted in plays and skits, some of which he wrote himself. At fifteen, he contracted tuberculosis and spent about eighteen months in a sanatorium, the sole youth in an otherwise adult community. He learned some parlor games and studied piano during his stay; more important, he became an interested observer of adult behavior. Returned to health and to high school, Zindel wrote a play for a contest sponsored by the American Cancer Society; it centered on a young pianist who recovers from a serious illness to play at Carnegie Hall. The play won for Zindel a Parker pen.

Zindel majored in chemistry at Wagner College in New York City. While completing his bachelor of science degree, he took a creative writing course with Edward Albee and wrote a play, *Dimensions of Peacocks*, during his senior year. Zindel was graduated in 1958, and after working briefly as a technical writer for a Manhattan chemical firm, he decided that he wanted to teach.

Completing a master of science degree at Wagner in 1959, Zindel began teaching chemistry and physics at Tottenville High School on Staten Island. His *Dimensions of Peacocks* received a minor staging; more significant, he attended his first professional theater production, Lillian Hellman's *Toys in the Attic* (pr., pb. 1960), and left with his appetite for theater whetted.

For the next several years, Zindel continued to teach and to write. A second play, *Euthanasia and the Endless Hearts*, had a brief coffeehouse production in 1960, and a third, *A Dream of Swallows*, managed a single performance Off-Broadway in 1964.

The Effect of Gamma Rays on Man-in-the-Moon Marigolds fared better. In 1965, it opened at the Alley Theatre in Houston, Texas. New York's National Educational Television ran four showings of its abridged teleplay format. Recognition grew, with the Ford Foundation underwriting Zindel as playwright-in-residence at the Alley in 1967. By 1969, Zindel felt sufficiently established in theater to resign from teaching. Playing in New York, *The Effect of Gamma Rays on Man-in-the-Moon Marigolds* accrued its various awards that prefaced the Pulitzer. From the New York plaudits, Zindel went to writing screenplays in California. Paul Newman produced and directed a movie version of *The Effect of Gamma Rays on Man-in-the-Moon Marigolds* in 1972, and Zindel wrote screenplays for *Up the Sandbox* and *Mame*.

When *The Effects of Gamma Rays on Man-in-the-Moon Marigolds* was on the rise, a publisher suggested that Zindel should write fiction for the teen market. His first teen novel, *The Pigman*, was both a critical and a popular success, as were several subsequent teen novels. Some critics have complained that while the argot of the young constantly changes, the teen dialogue in Zindel's later novels was indistinguishable from that found in his novels of the late 1960's and early 1970's. In other ways, too, Zindel was accused of merely repeating a successful formula.

In 1973, following the year in California, Zindel made two major decisions. He married Bonnie Hildebrand, a screenwriter with whom he later had two children, Elizabeth and David, and he joined the Actors Studio in New York to learn the language of acting and directing as well as playwriting. At the same time, he resumed work on a manuscript that National Educational Television had turned down in 1970 as too explicit. In its earlier version, the play had centered on the exchanges and revelations of a group of women playing bridge and watching an exhibitionist in a building across the street. Zindel shifted the setting to a theater in Texas, and the conflict to a battle for control of the theater. To make the five characters more authentic, Zindel conducted in-depth interviews with five actresses from the Actors Studio. The result was *Ladies at the Alamo*.

Beginning in the mid-1970's, Zindel became more active as a novelist than as a dramatist, but he continued to be involved in the theater, producing new work as well as adaptations. He occasionally traveled to regional productions of his plays as part of publicity campaigns (as he did for the 1990 Cleveland Playhouse revival of *The Effect of Gamma Rays on Man-in-the-Moon Marigolds*), and to be active as a moderator for the Actors Studio West, in the Los Angeles Playwrights Unit. According to interviews, the process of filmmaking was destructive for him. His young adult novels are sometimes turned into plays; for example, *Confessions of a Teenage Baboon* (1977) began as a novel but became *Amulets Against the Dragon Forces*, produced at the Circle Repertory Theatre in 1989. Zindel's 1995 play *Every Seventeen Minutes the Crowd Goes Crazy!* was written on commission for the American Conservatory Theater's Young Conservatory in San Francisco. Zindel intended that the play would address what he believed was the most critical issue of the decade, the failure of parents to fulfill traditional roles. At the time, his own children had recently left home for college. Zindel wrote for a big cast, believing that young actors needed and deserved as much time onstage as possible.

Analysis • Paul Zindel's plays closely follow his own life experience; certain features of his early years recur in his drama. His mother was bitter, transient, reclusive, and presumably uncertain of her place in life. Zindel's major plays commonly depict women struggling for identity and fulfillment, often damaged, if not destroyed, by betrayals or deaths of loved ones. These women in turn fail to provide the adequate care so desperately needed by the young people for whom they are left responsible. Another theme of Zindel's plays is the notion that modern society has replaced traditional religion with a secular faith of scientism accompanied by unbridled self-indulgence.

Zindel's marvelous storytelling ability has captivated millions, and several of his works have been translated. His plays, certainly not as well accepted by critics or the public, still appeal. Zindel describes the drama form as one in which the players must shout the message of the work. In this vein, his characters and events exhibit unsettling qualities: the old people border on grotesque, shambling versions of death; events are capped by illogical and unpredictable outcomes; and character motivations result in bizarre behaviors. However, Zindel's repugnant misfits lay claim to the compassion, empathy, and integrity of the audience. As Zindel explains in commenting on his more recent prose works, humor and horror have much in common, and these qualities are readily apparent in a majority of his dramatic works.

The Effect of Gamma Rays on Man-in-the-Moon Marigolds • *The Effect of Gamma Rays on Man-in-the-Moon Marigolds* opens to observers the lives of Beatrice Hunsdorfer and her two teenage daughters, Ruth and Tillie. Beatrice, overtly modeled after Zindel's mother, is a cynical, verbally abusive paranoid schizophrenic. Her untidy home was once her father's vegetable store. Her husband left her long ago and later died of a heart attack. For income, Beatrice boards an aged woman who needs a walker to creep slowly from bed to table to bathroom and back to bed.

Ruth, the elder daughter, is the more physically attractive yet is emotionally unstable and subject to convulsions in times of stress. Tillie, the younger, is bright and eager to learn. Beatrice, more concerned about her girls' looks and marriageability than about their intellectual growth, badgers both daughters but is most severe with Tillie.

Act 1 opens with Tillie, in darkness, marveling that the atoms in her hand may trace back to a cosmic tongue of fire predating the birth of the sun and the solar system. As lights rise on the home scene, Beatrice fields a telephone call from Mr. Goodman, Tillie's science teacher. He is concerned about Tillie's absences. Beatrice responds with several defenses. She thanks Mr. Goodman for giving Tillie a pet rabbit and compliments him on his looks. Claiming that Tillie does not always want to go to school, Beatrice says that she does not want to put too much pressure on Tillie, lest she turn convulsive, as Ruth has done. The phone call ended, Beatrice derides Tillie and Mr. Goodman, then orders Tillie to stay home. The girl is anxious to see a cloud-chamber experiment in science class. Beatrice threatens to kill the rabbit if Tillie goes. In contrast, Beatrice encourages Ruth to go to school, lets her rummage through mother's purse for lipstick, and gives her a cigarette on request. Ruth scratches Beatrice's back and gives negative reports on Tillie's activities at school. She also reveals that she has seen the school file on the family. It records the parents' divorce, the absent father's death, and Ruth's nervous breakdown.

The scene fades to darkness, and again Tillie speaks. She describes the fountain of atoms visible in the cloud chamber, a phenomenon that could go on for eternity. Rising lights reveal Tillie preparing to plant irradiated seeds. Beatrice, scanning realty advertisements, mixes conjecture on the potential of various properties with questions about Tillie's science project. Nanny, the aged boarder, begins the slow trek to the ta-

ble as Tillie tries to explain the concept of atomic half-life to Beatrice. Beatrice dispar-
ages Nanny, her daughters, and herself through derisive double meanings for the term
"half-life."

Beatrice phones Mr. Goodman, expressing concern that Tillie's seeds were irradiated, turning aside his explanations. After several other demonstrations of instability
and cruelty, Beatrice shows another aspect of her character. During a thunderstorm at
night, Ruth suffers another seizure. Beatrice orders Tillie back to bed in typically harsh
fashion but cradles Ruth with genuine compassion and tells how her father, Ruth's
grandfather, used to sell fruit and vegetables from a horse-drawn wagon. Beatrice's
mother had died quite early, and her father fell seriously ill while Beatrice was still
rather young. Anxious for her future, he urged her to marry for security's sake. She still
sees her father's face in her nightmares.

The following scene shows Beatrice again lashing out at Tillie and Nanny until Ruth
dashes in. She reports excitedly that Tillie is a finalist in the science fair. The principal
calls to ask Beatrice to attend the final judging and awards. Beatrice is rude and eva-
sive. Her first thought is that people will ridicule her. Only after Tillie runs off in tears
does Beatrice realize how her paranoiac response has hurt Tillie.

Act 2 opens with the Hunsdorfers about to leave for the final science fair presentations. Working as an attendance aide for Mr. Goodman, Ruth has overheard gossip
about Beatrice, who used to be called "Betty the Loon." Ruth blackmails Tillie into giving her the rabbit by threatening to tell Beatrice the school gossip. Tillie concedes—
she deeply wants her mother to share this one significant event in her life, even at the
cost of her pet—but when Beatrice orders Ruth to stay home with Nanny, Ruth ex-
plodes with the epithet "Betty the Loon," and Beatrice crumbles emotionally. Ruth
goes to school in Beatrice's place. In a scene change through a lighting shift, another
science fair finalist, Janice Vickery, superficially explains the past, present, and future
of her cat skeleton. Back at the Hunsdorfer home, Beatrice makes two phone calls.
One is a bitter call to the high school. The other is to Nanny's daughter: Beatrice wants
Nanny out of the house the next day. Finally, Beatrice heads upstairs with a bottle of
chloroform.

In another shift by spotlight, Tillie cites the past, present, and future of her project.
Lightly irradiated seeds produced normal plants. Moderately irradiated seeds produced various mutations. The heavily bombarded seeds either died or produced
dwarfs. Knowing the range of effects, she believes some mutations will be good. She
declares her faith in the strange, beautiful energy of the atom.

Beatrice is drunk when the girls get home. She has begun to refit the living room for
a tea shop. Ruth brings the dead rabbit downstairs and goes into convulsions. The play
closes with Tillie declaring her curiosity about the universe, her sense of place in the
order of things, and her fascination with the atom.

The Effect of Gamma Rays on Man-in-the-Moon Marigolds presents a family, broken as
Zindel's was, in financial straits, deriving income from a board-and-care patient, as
Zindel's family had. Beatrice's unfinished real-estate and beauty classes mirror the varied attempts Zindel's mother made at supporting the family. The significance of
Beatrice's preparation, in the last scene, for a tea shop is open to question. The move
hints at growth in her character, yet she has killed the rabbit, the symbol of warmth
and tenderness for the daughters. Tillie's success at least has stirred Beatrice to a new
beginning.

Ruth has shifted from contempt for Tillie to pride in Tillie's achievement. That
pride, however, seems rooted more in Ruth's concern for social status than in genuine

understanding of either Tillie or the experiment. Tillie herself has not changed significantly in the play. At the outset, she speaks of her fascination with science. At the end, her success confirms her self-esteem and potential for growth in spite of the abuse from home.

Thus, the play relies on revelation of character more than on development of character in response to conflict. In a decade accustomed to "slice-of-life" literature and ambiguous if not bleak conclusions to many stories and plays, *The Effect of Gamma Rays on Man-in-the-Moon Marigolds* presents a positive faith in the future through science, and hope for one character in overcoming the emotional damage common in modern life.

And Miss Reardon Drinks a Little • *And Miss Reardon Drinks a Little* offers a different constellation of women but still mirrors several aspects of Zindel's personal experience. The three Reardon sisters, Ceil, Catherine, and Anna, embody many of the ills of teachers long settled in the education system, ills well-known to Zindel and anyone else with some teaching experience.

Of the three sisters, Ceil has been the assertive one. She has taken the courses necessary to carry her from classroom to administrative work with the board of education. She took the chance of marrying Edward Adams, although Catherine dated him first. Ceil, too, arranged for their dead mother's estate to be settled seven months before the night of the play's action, and now Ceil is the one bringing papers for Anna's commitment for psychiatric care.

Act 1 begins with Mrs. Pentrano, the wife of the building superintendent, entering the Reardon sisters' apartment. She asks if the new lock has satisfied Anna and expresses concern for Anna's condition. A delivery boy brings groceries, including chopped meat, which Catherine arranges in a candy box. Untipped, the delivery boy exits with flippant sarcasm. Mrs. Pentrano has been pressing Catherine for a cosmetics and toiletries order despite Catherine's objections. Ceil arrives and dismisses Mrs. Pentrano with little more than a greeting.

Catherine berates Ceil for making scant contact since their mother's death. She also complains that her fellow faculty members believe that Catherine's position as assistant principal is a consequence of Ceil's being on the board of education. Ceil cuts through the criticism with questions about Anna; she also expresses her concern for Catherine, who, people say, has taken to drinking. During their exchanges, Catherine eats raw meat from the candy box. Since her breakdown, Anna has turned vegetarian and wants no meat or animal byproducts in the apartment. Slaughter of animals is too reminiscent of human death.

Catherine explains to Ceil the development of Anna's condition. During a trip to Europe after their mother's death, Anna suffered a cat bite. She grew convinced that she had rabies. She demanded shots for the disease and thereafter was on tranquilizers so that she could return to teaching in September. Suffering harassment by students, however, Anna eventually broke down, committing some unspecified form of sexual indiscretion with a male student.

Anna enters. Groggy with medication, she had forgotten that Ceil was due for dinner. Catherine goes about preparing fruits and vegetables for their meal. Anna worries about the presence of Mother's old pistol in the apartment. Ceil assures her that Mother kept only blanks in the gun. Anna searches desk and bookcase until she locates the pistol in an album. Anna rambles about her condition, criticizes Ceil for taking Edward away from Catherine, then fires the pistol. Catherine tries to humor

Anna, retrieves the pistol, and puts it back in the album, saying that Ceil can take it away later.

The second act opens with the sisters, still at dinner, interrupted by Fleur Stein. Fleur, an acting guidance teacher at the school where Catherine and Anna work, brings an official faculty get-well gift. Her husband, Bob, is getting the package from the car. Fleur says she debated whether the gift should be religious. Anna responds with a long story of losing religion because she saw a puppy hit by a truck. When Bob presents the gift, Anna loses control. They have brought her leather gloves. She throws them across the room. Ceil explains Anna's aversion to animal products, and Catherine belatedly introduces Ceil to the Steins. Fleur is counselor for the boy involved in Anna's case, and she pressures Ceil for help in securing her guidance teacher's licensure. In return, she will persuade the boy's parents not to sue for damages. Fleur downplays judgment on the incident, attributing a loss of traditional religious attitudes to modern acceptance of science. Bob Stein, given certain provocations, bluntly attributes Anna's breakdown to lack of male companionship. He offers to get Anna a date for the evening and drapes Fleur's fox fur stole over Anna's shoulders. She screams and kicks the stole away, deploring the cruelty of the fur trade. Bob reacts in anger, insulting all three sisters in turn. Catherine suggests that Anna show Bob their mother's album.

As the third act opens, Anna fires the pistol at Bob's face. Bob grabs the gun, telling Anna that she has real problems. Anna, in response to an earlier comment by Fleur, asks Bob why he never uses his own bathroom at home. He retorts that he hates the soaps and rough paper that Fleur steals from the school. Fleur attempts to smooth over Bob's irate exit, assuring Ceil that she will do her best to help. With the Steins gone, Ceil wants to discuss business with Catherine alone, but Anna insists on staying. She reminisces about an eccentric principal they once knew. Ceil brings out the commitment papers and tells Catherine to get Anna packed for travel the next day.

Catherine rebels at the order. Anna asks Ceil how Edward makes love to her. Furious, Ceil shoves meat from the candy box in Anna's face. She screams and runs off to wash. Ceil keeps Catherine from following Anna. Catherine finally admits that she hates the dominance in both their late mother and Ceil. In return, Ceil rebukes Catherine for leaving her choices in life to others. Ceil throws the commitment papers down and leaves. Catherine now must take responsibility for either keeping Anna home or committing her for psychiatric care.

Examining the lives of professional educators, Zindel presents a family with the occupational stability and social standing he himself experienced in his first career. The Misses Reardon, like Tillie and Ruth Hunsdorfer, have suffered from an unhealthy family situation: an absent father and a domineering mother. Ceil, assertive in her own right, made choices that carried her out of Mother Reardon's sphere of control and eventually to the top echelon of her profession. Her progress is a logical extension of the strength of character Tillie Hunsdorfer maintains despite Beatrice's dominance. Catherine and Anna, in contrast, show the effects of remaining under Mother's control to the end. Catherine shrinks from asserting herself: She cannot briskly dismiss Mrs. Pentrano as Ceil can; rather than cope with awkward comments by the Steins, she runs the blender; instead of confronting Anna with her own preference of diet, she sneaks meat into the house and eats it raw. Both Catherine's craving for raw meat and Anna's indiscretion represent inordinate reactions to unfulfilled needs.

In addition to the parallels in family dynamics, there is another link between *And Miss Reardon Drinks a Little* and its predecessor. Tillie Hunsdorfer's youthful faith in science has evolved, in Fleur Stein, into the laconic conclusion that science has supplanted religious faith in modern life. Anna, in contrast, cannot rationalize pain and suffering; she traces the loss of her religion to the death of a pup. Ceil makes no claims regarding religion. She does live by the premise, however, that a person must accept responsibility for choices in life and must seize opportunities for change and growth. At the close of the play, she leaves Catherine with the choice of compensating for Anna's incapacity at home or committing her for psychiatric care. Catherine seems, at last, ready to accept the responsibility.

Amulets Against the Dragon Forces • *Amulets Against the Dragon Forces*, a revision of *A Destiny with Half Moon Street*, is exceptional for Zindel in that the protagonist and antagonist are both male; however, these characters also struggle with the issues of disappointment, inadequacy, and betrayal. A cycle of abuse is revealed as an old woman who had long ago attacked her son for his budding sexuality is brought home from the hospital to die. The son, Floyd, is the antagonist of the play. He is now a nearly deranged adult and has a history of alcoholism and child abuse, one featuring the habitual use of young male prostitutes, a series of whom he has brought to the family home where he exchanges shelter for sexual favors. A divorced, itinerant practical nurse has been engaged to care for the dying mother, and she brings her own son, the protagonist Chris, into the household.

Being the youngest and most innocent character, Chris retains some characteristics of childhood, including a hobby of creating balsa wood replicas of local landmarks populated by models he has carved. These "amulets" are mere charms and seem unlikely to stave off the "dragon forces" of the play's title. Chris uses the figures to represent characters in made-up stories. He hopes to become a writer—an ambition suggested to him by a mentally unstable teacher. For the near future, Chris plans to escape life with his kleptomaniac mother by going to Florida to live with his father, but the father refuses. Chris's mother does finally succeed in buying a home for herself and her son, barely completing the transaction before the old woman she is caring for dies. The play ends as Floyd suggests to Chris that the passage of time may someday allow the boy to accept his own disquieting sexual urges. Zindel has indicated that this is the last play he plans to write set in Staten Island and using events and factors influential in his own upbringing.

Every Seventeen Minutes the Crowd Goes Crazy! • *Every Seventeen Minutes the Crowd Goes Crazy!* portrays a family of teenage children recently abandoned by their parents, who communicate with the youngsters infrequently and then only via a fax machine. Written on commission for the American Conservatory Theater's Young Conservatory, the play addresses the breakdown of family life as caused by the societal ills of commercialism and hedonism. The parents prefer the thrill of the track, where the horse races finish "every seventeen minutes," and so have fled their failing careers and dependent offspring—children they find to be unbearable users. They express regret over leaving the youngest child, Ulie, who is only twelve years old, but predict his inability to escape a future of self-centeredness. The older children plan various means of economic survival, including charging admission to regular keg parties, but they are meanwhile cleaning out any remaining cash advances available on their parents' credit cards. The overall effect is ironic and painful as the young protagonists bravely hide or perhaps even abandon their feelings of disappointment and longing for a return to a more normal life. A one-act play, the work begins and ends with the "Oprah-

Speak Gap Chorus" chanting a jumble of slogans, ads, and *National Enquirer*-type headlines.

Other major works

LONG FICTION: *When a Darkness Falls*, 1984.

SCREENPLAYS: *Up the Sandbox*, 1972; *Mame*, 1974; *Runaway Train*, 1983; *Maria's Lovers*, 1984.

TELEPLAYS: *Let Me Hear You Whisper*, 1966; *Alice in Wonderland*, 1985 (adaptation of the story by Lewis Carroll); *A Connecticut Yankee in King Arthur's Court*, 1989 (adaptation of the novel by Mark Twain).

CHILDREN'S LITERATURE: *The Pigman*, 1968; *My Darling, My Hamburger*, 1969; *I Never Loved Your Mind*, 1970; *I Love My Mother*, 1975; *Pardon Me, You're Stepping on My Eyeball!*, 1976; *Confessions of a Teenage Baboon*, 1977; *The Undertaker's Gone Bananas*, 1978; *A Star for the Latecomer*, 1980 (with Bonnie Zindel); *The Pigman's Legacy*, 1980; *The Girl Who Wanted a Boy*, 1981; *To Take a Dare*, 1982 (with Crescent Dragonwagon); *Harry and Hortense at Hormone High*, 1984; *The Amazing and Death-Defying Diary of Eugene Dingman*, 1987; *A Begonia for Miss Applebaum*, 1989; *The Pigman and Me*, 1992 (autobiography); *Attack of the Killer Fishsticks*, 1993; *David and Della*, 1993; *Fifth Grade Safari*, 1993; *Fright Party*, 1993; *Loch*, 1994; *The One Hundred Percent Laugh Riot*, 1994; *The Doom Stone*, 1995; *Raptor*, 1998; *Reef of Death*, 1998; *Rats*, 1999; *The Gadget*, 2001; *Night of the Bat*, 2001.

Bibliography

Barnes, Clive. "Troubled Times for a Teen." Review of *Amulets Against the Dragon Forces*, by Paul Zindel. *New York Post*, April 7, 1989. Barnes finds a "commonplace honesty" beneath the play's pretentiousness in this review of the Circle Repertory Company's production. Barnes finds "the same quality of compassion" as in *The Effect of Gamma Rays on Man-in-the-Moon Marigolds*. Barnes states that the play has "the air of a work written to enable its author to get something off his chest."

DiGaetani, John L. *A Search for a Postmodern Theater: Interviews with Contemporary Playwrights*. New York: Greenwood Press, 1991. In one chapter, DiGaetani interviews Zindel about the influences of psychoanalysis on his work and the reasons for his gradual transition to young adult novels. Zindel's destructive relation with Hollywood is also discussed with considerable candor. Asked which playwrights Zindel admires, he replied, "I'm happy to say none."

Evett, Marianne. "'Moon-Marigolds' Author in Nostalgic Return Here." *Cleveland Plain Dealer*, November 4, 1990. This preview of Cleveland Playhouse's revival of *The Effect of Gamma Rays on Man-in-the-Moon Marigolds*, with Marlo Thomas in the role of Beatrice, includes a telephone interview with Zindel, who remembers the first productions and his "bubbly publicity agent (Bonnie Hildebrand). I ended up marrying her." He reports here that he "escaped East [from Hollywood] to keep my sanity intact."

Fischer, David Marc. "Paul Zindel: The Shouting Play, the Whispering Novel." *Writing* 24 (February/March, 2002): 20. Presents an interview with Zindel covering a discussion of his career as teacher and writer with emphasis on distinguishing between the style of language and writing appropriate for drama as opposed to the novel.

Forman, Jack Jacob. *Presenting Paul Zindel*. Boston: Twayne, 1988. A basic biography that includes criticism and interpretation focused primarily on Zindel's fiction. Useful indexes and bibliography.

Lesesne, Teri. "Humor, Bathos and Fear: An Interview with Paul Zindel." *Teacher Librarian* 27 (December, 1999): 60. Zindel discusses his thematic emphasis on teenage misfits in young-adult novels and drama, citing a scene from *The Effect of Gamma Rays on Man-in-the-Moon Marigolds* as an example of his best work.

Slaight, Craig, ed. *New Plays from ACT's Young Conservatory.* Vol. 2. Lume, N.H.: Smith and Kraus, 1996. Contains the text of *Every Seventeen Minutes the Crowd Goes Crazy!* with commentary by Slaight, Zindel, and student actors from the play.

Zindel, Paul. "Beyond Man-in-the-Moon Marigolds." Interview by Helen Dudar. *The New York Times*, April 2, 1989, p. B5. A long interview on the occasion of Zindel's later work, *Amulets Against the Dragon Forces*, twelve years after his last New York opening. He recaps his career, mostly in teen novels, and his sense of destructiveness in the maw of Hollywood. Good biographic profile, with a photograph.

Ralph S. Carlson,
updated by Thomas J. Taylor
and Margaret A. Dodson

Dramatic Terms and Movements

Absurdism. See *Theater of the Absurd.*

Academic drama. See *School plays.*

Act: One of the major divisions of a play or opera. The practice of dividing a play into acts probably began in Rome but is derived from Greek drama, which separated the episodes of a play by choral interludes. In classical theory (notably in France in the seventeenth century), a play is divided into five acts; since the eighteenth and nineteenth centuries, however, the typical number of acts has varied from four to one, while some plays have entirely eliminated structure by acts and use only scene division. (See also *Scene.*)

Action. See *Plot.*

African American drama: Drama written by or focusing on African Americans that emerged formally in the twentieth century but has precedents in the mid-nineteenth century. Playwrights in this vein include August Wilson, James Baldwin, Ed Bullins, Lorraine Hansberry, Adrienne Kennedy, and Suzan-Lori Parks.

Afterpiece: Short farce meant to follow a serious play, a practice adopted in France by 1650, which became a standard part of English drama during the Restoration.

Agitprop: Word combining "agitation" and "propaganda" to describe drama performed as social protest rather than for its dramatic or literary merit. A German labor group called the Prolet-Bühne first used this term in New York City in 1930. Agitprop drama was performed throughout the 1930's by the American labor movement and continues to be performed in Europe and in the United States.

Agon: Greek, meaning "contest." A segment of Greek drama in which two participants become involved in verbal conflict. The two participants may be a character and the chorus; two characters, each backed by part of the chorus; or two parts of the chorus.

Alazon: Impostor or braggart of Greek comedy. The type survives in Roman comedy, as with the *Miles gloriosus* (*The Braggart Warrior*, 1767) of Plautus. (See also *Miles gloriosus.*)

Alexandrine: In French, a verse of twelve syllables generally containing four accents (in English, the iambic hexameter is sometimes referred to as an "Alexandrine"). Established as the standard form for French tragedy in the mid-sixteenth century, the Neoclassical dramatists of the seventeenth century (Pierre Corneille and Jean Racine, for example) used the Alexandrine to create the serious, elevated tone that was theoretically considered proper for the tragic mode.

Alienation: German dramatist Bertolt Brecht developed the theory of alienation in his epic theater. Brecht sought to create an audience that was intellectually alert rather than emotionally involved in a play by using alienating techniques such as minimizing the illusion of reality onstage and interrupting the action with songs and visual aids. Brecht hoped an intellectually alert audience would relate the dramatic action to problems in the real world and seek solutions to those problems. (See also *Epic theater.*)

Allegory: By representing abstract ideas or concepts through the symbolic use of character, plot, and situation, allegories are intended to instruct the audience in moral or political values. Allegory is an important component of classical drama and medieval morality plays.

Anabasis: Greek, meaning "a going up." The rising of an action to its climax. (See also *Rising action.*)

Anagnorisis: Recognition or discovery. Aristotle uses this term in the *De poetica* (c. 334-323 B.C.E.; *Poetics*, 1705) to refer to the moment of recognition in which a character moves from a state of ignorance to one of knowledge. In Sophocles' *Oidipous Tyrannos* (c. 429 B.C.E.; *Oedipus Tyrannus*, 1715; also know as *Oedipus Rex*), which Aristotle considered the ideal example of tragedy, an anagnorisis occurs when Oedipus discovers that he himself is the slayer of his father, as predicted by the seer. This recognition is accompanied by a "peripeteia" (or reversal) in which the whole action of the play is reversed.

Antagonist: Major character in opposition to the protagonist or hero.

Antimasque: Grotesque interlude within a masque which contrasts violently to the beauty and harmony of the preceding episodes. Ben Jonson created the antimasque, which typically includes grotesque dances of clowns and monsters. (See also *Masque.*)

Antistrophe: In classical Greek drama, the antistrophe is a stanza-like unit of song and dance responding to the strophe and mirroring its structure. (See also *Strophe.*)

Apollonian and Dionysian: Friedrich Nietzsche proposed in *Die Geburt der Tragödie aus dem Geiste der Musik* (1872; *The Birth of Tragedy out of the Spirit of Music,* 1909) that Greek tragedy was composed of two opposing elements, which it held in tension and finally unified. One element, the Dionysian, represented the savage, frenzied, passionate nature of humanity. The Apollonian stood for reason, moderation, and order. Nietzsche believed that the choral songs provided the Dionysian element and the dialogue the Apollonian element. Characters were often torn between these opposing forces within their personalities, which personified larger philosophical and moral issues.

Apron stage: The apron is that part of the stage that extends beyond the proscenium arch. A stage that consists entirely or primarily of an apron and on which the action is not "framed" by a proscenium may be called an "apron stage."

Asian American drama: Form of drama that emerged from the identity politics and student radicalism of the 1960's and 1970's. "Asian American" was coined in the 1960's as a replacement for "Oriental," a term that many considered a demeaning colonialist description that exoticized all individuals to whom it was attached. Thematic orientation focuses on varied topics such as the struggle against racism, ethnic profiling, economic discrimination, shared cultural heritage and ethnic identity, and invisibility. Playwrights include Frank Chin, Philip Kan Gotanda, Jessica Hagedorn, Velina Hasu Houston, David Henry Hwang, Genny Lim, and Elizabeth Wong.

Aside: Short passage generally spoken by one character in an undertone, or directed to the audience, so as not to be heard by the other characters on stage.

Auto sacramental: Renaissance development of the medieval open-air Corpus Christi pageant in Spain. A dramatic, allegorical depiction of a sinful soul wavering and transgressing until the intervention of Divine Grace restores order.

Avant-garde: Term describing plays intended to expand the conventions of the theater through the experimental treatment of form and/or content.

Ballad opera: Type of burlesque opera popular in eighteenth century England and modeled upon (as well as parodying) contemporary Italian operatic conventions. The story is conveyed in both spoken dialogue and songs (the latter mirroring the arias of the more serious form) set to old folk songs or ballads. The most successful work in this genre was John Gay's *The Beggar's Opera* (pr. 1728).

Beijing Opera: Complex theatrical style of drama known in Chinese as *Jingju* (Wade-Giles, *ching-hsi*), commonly called Beijing Opera. It was begun by Anhui actors sometime in the 1830's, when two modes of music, *erhuang diao* and *xipidiao*, were brought together. By the 1870's it had become the predominant form of Chinese drama and remains the major force in modern-day Chinese theater. The form is characterized by lavish costumes, percussive music, acrobatic dance, and colloquial lyrics.

Black comedy: General term of modern origin that refers to a form of "sick humor" that is intended to produce laughter out of the morbid and the taboo. The term is sometimes inappropriately confused with "dark comedy."

Blank verse: Unrhymed iambic pentameter, blank verse that first appeared in drama in Thomas Norton and Thomas Sackville's *Gorboduc*, performed in 1561, and that later became the standard form of Elizabethan drama.

Boulevard drama: Body of plays produced in the mid- and late nineteenth century in Paris by writers such as Ludovic Halévy and Eugène Labiche. The term properly refers to comedies of some sophistication, designed as commercial products.

Bourgeois drama: Term generally used to describe the modern realistic drama which deals with the situations and social problems of the middle class.

Bunraku: Japanese puppet theater. It emerged in the twelfth century but did not become firmly established until the turn of the seventeenth century, when narrations chanted to musical accompaniment were added to puppet performances.

Burlesque: Work which, by imitating attitudes, styles, institutions, and people, aims to amuse. Burlesque is distinguished from a closely related form, satire, in that its aim is ridicule simply for the sake of amusement rather than for political or social change. An example of burlesque drama is Gilbert and Sullivan's comic opera *Patience: Or Bunthorne's Bride* (pr. 1881), which is a parody of the aesthetic movement in late nineteenth century England.

Burletta: Short comic play with music that was popular in eighteenth and nineteenth century English theater.

Buskin: Half boot covering the foot and calf, worn by actors in Greek tragedy, also known as a cothurnus. The purpose of the buskin was to designate the stature of the characters; while comic actors wore low, flat foot coverings, tragic figures wore platform buskins. "To put on buskins" became a term for performing or writing tragedy. (See also *Sock*.)

Capa y espada: Spanish for "cape and sword," a term referring to the Spanish theater of the sixteenth and seventeenth centuries dealing with love and intrigue among the aristocracy. The greatest practitioners were Lope de Vega and Pedro Calderón de la Barca. The term *comedia de ingenio* is also used.

Cape and sword play. See *Capa y espada*.

Caroline: Of or referring to the reign of King Charles I of England, lasting from 1625 to 1649. Political strife and the violent opposition to the theater by the Puritans informed Caroline drama with a rather decadent morality and generally a quality inferior to the plays of the preceding Jacobean and Elizabethan periods, although

Caroline drama did produce the noted tragedian John Ford and his counterpart in Caroline comedy, James Shirley. Caroline drama was effectively halted in 1642, when the Puritans closed all public theaters for the next eighteen years.

Catastrophe: The conclusion of a play or narrative, especially tragedy, the catastrophe is more often called the "denouement," meaning the unknotting or resolution of the situation. (See also *Freytag's pyramid.*)

Catharsis: Term from Aristotle's *Poetics* referring to the purgation of the emotions of pity and fear in the spectator aroused by the actions of the tragic hero. The meaning and the operation of this concept have been a source of great, and unresolved, critical debate.

Cavalier drama: Type of play performed at court in the 1630's during the reign of Charles I of England until the ascendancy of Oliver Cromwell in 1642 and the closing of the theaters. The plays featured elaborate plots, political conflicts, lustful villains, beautiful and virtuous ladies, and their brave, honorable lovers. Dialogue was typically florid and artificial. The most notable dramatists in this genre were Thomas Killigrew and John Suckling.

Centre 42: Early 1960's British movement designed to bring theater to people outside London and to factory districts and areas where little or no theater was performed.

Character: Personage appearing in any literary or dramatic work.

Chorus: Originally a group of singers and dancers in religious festivals, the chorus evolved into the dramatic element that reflected the opinions of the masses or commented on the action in Greek drama. In its most developed form, the chorus consisted of fifteen members: seven reciting the strophe, seven reciting the antistrophe, and the leader interacting with the actors. The development of the role of the chorus is generally seen as one of diminishing importance: In Aeschylus, the chorus often takes part in the action; in Sophocles, it serves as a commentator; and in Euripides, its function is sometimes purely lyric. The Romans adapted the Greek chorus to their own stage, and the Elizabethans occasionally imitated the Roman chorus (reducing it to a single actor), but it never became an integral part of the structure. The chorus has been used during all periods, including the modern (for example, in T. S. Eliot's 1935 *Murder in the Cathedral*), but has survived most prominently in the opera and other forms of musical theater. (See also *Parodos.*)

Chronicle play: Dramatization of historical material (or material believed to be historical), the chronicle play became popular at the end of the sixteenth century. Drawing heavily on the chronicle histories of Raphael Holinshed and Edward Hall, dramatists originally strung together loose scenes from history, but the form later developed greater unity in works such as Christopher Marlowe's *Edward II* (pr. c. 1592) and the *Henry IV* (pr. late sixteenth century) plays of William Shakespeare. Also termed "history plays," the chronicle plays developed into subtle studies of character and became more important as examinations of human strengths and frailties than as accounts of historical facts.

Classical drama: Classical drama originally referred to the literature and theater of ancient Greece and Rome, but later the term also included theater composed in imitation of the Greco-Roman tradition, which was often called "neoclassical." In more common usage, the term refers to art which possesses at least some of the following characteristics: balance, proportion, control, unity, and simplicity.

Climax: Moment in a drama at which the action reaches its highest intensity and is resolved. The major climax of a play may be preceded by several climaxes of lesser and varying intensity.

Closet drama: Play meant to be read rather than performed. Two examples of closet drama are Alfred de Musset's *Fantasio* (pb. 1834, pr. 1866; English translation, 1853) and George Gordon, Lord Byron's *Manfred* (pb. 1817, pr. 1834). Also, a play which, although meant for performance, has survived only as literature.

Comedia: Principal form of nonreligious drama during the Spanish Golden Age (*Siglio de Oro*) of the sixteenth century that mixed tragic and comic elements in a complex, suspenseful plot, used a variety of verse forms, and favored realistic language and action. The *comedias* of the early sixteenth century were written in five acts, but by the 1580's the number of acts had been reduced to three by playwrights such as Lope de Vega.

Comedia erudita: "Learned comedy." In the Renaissance, scholarly imitations of classical comedies (particularly Roman) were created by such writers as Pietro Aretino, Ludovico Ariosto, and Niccolò Machiavelli (the latter's *La mandragola*, pr. 1520; *The Mandrake*, 1911; is frequently cited as an example of the genre).

Comédie ballet: Theatrical form mixing elements of comedy, farce, and musical-balletic spectacle popular in seventeenth century France. Molière's *Le Bourgeois Gentilhomme* (pr. 1670; *The Would-Be Gentleman*, 1675) and *Le Malade imaginaire* (pr. 1673; *The Imaginary Invalid*, 1732; also known as *The Hypochondriac*) are the two best examples of the form.

Comédie larmoyante: French term meaning "tearful, or weeping, comedy." This sentimental comedy was popular in eighteenth century France. A development from the earlier style of comedy, *comédie larmoyante* aimed to produce not critical laughter (as in the earlier style exemplified by Molière) but pleasurable tears. The chief practitioners were Philippe Destouches and Pierre-Claude Nivelle de La Chaussée. (See also *Sentimental comedy.*)

Comedy: Generally, a lighter form of drama (as contrasted with tragedy) that aims chiefly to amuse and ends happily. Wit and humor are used to entertain. The comic effect typically arises from the recognition of some incongruity of speech, action, or character development. The comic range extends from coarse, physical humor (called low comedy) to a more subtle, intellectual humor (called high comedy). When comedy tends toward the judgmental or critical, it is referred to as satiric; when it is mixed with sympathy or pathos, it moves in the direction of tragedy. There are many specific comic forms and manifestations. (See also *Burlesque, Burletta, Comedia erudita, Comédie larmoyante, Comedy of humours, Comedy of manners, Commedia dell' arte, Dark comedy, Farce, High comedy, Interlude, Low comedy, New Comedy, Old Comedy, Romantic comedy, Satire, Sentimental comedy, Slapstick, and Tragicomedy.*)

Comedy, drawing room. See *Drawing room comedy.*

Comedy, laughing. See *Laughing comedy.*

Comedy, sentimental. See *Sentimental comedy.*

Comedy of humors: Type of drama developed in the late sixteenth and early seventeenth centuries by Ben Jonson and George Chapman that dealt with characters whose behavior is controlled by some single characteristic, or "humor." In medieval and Renaissance medicine, the humors were the four bodily fluids (blood, phlegm, yellow bile, and black bile), any excess of which created a distortion or imbalance of personality (by extension, the term came to mean "mood" or "disposition"). Jonson used this theory of character in several of his works, such as *Every Man in His Humour* (pr. 1598) and *Every Man out of His Humour* (pr. 1599).

Comedy of manners: Sometimes known as "genteel comedy" (in reference to its lack of coarseness), a form of comedy that arose during the eighteenth century, dealing with the intrigues (particularly the amorous intrigues) of sophisticated, witty members of the upper classes. The effect and appeal of these plays are primarily intellectual, depending upon quick-witted dialogue and cleverness and facility of language. The Restoration period was particularly fond of this form, as can be seen in the plays of such dramatists as William Congreve, Sir George Etherege, and William Wycherlcy.

Comic relief: Humorous incident or scene in an otherwise serious or tragic drama intended to release the audience's tensions through laughter without detracting from the serious material.

Commedia dell'arte: Dramatic comedy performed by troupes of professional actors, which became popular in the mid-sixteenth century in Italy. These troupes were rather small, consisting of perhaps a dozen actors who performed stock roles in mask and improvised upon skeletal scenarios (often derived from the traditional material of ancient Roman comedy). The tradition of the *commedia*, or masked comedy, was influential into the seventeenth century and still, in fact, exerts some influence. Some of the more famous stock roles are Pulchinella, Harlequin, Arlecchino, Pantalone, II Dottore, and II Capitano.

Commedia palliata: Roman comedy produced in Greek costume and refined by Plautus during the second century B.C.E.

Corpus Christi plays: These religious plays depicting biblical events were performed on Corpus Christi Day in England during the fourteenth, fifteenth, and sixteenth centuries. The plays originated in the liturgy of the Church, but they came to be staged outdoors on large wagons that moved through towns (such as York and Chester) in a procession, so that each play was performed before several different audiences. (See also *Liturgical drama, Miracle play, Trope.*)

Cothurnus. See *Buskin.*

Counterplot: Secondary action coincident with the major action of a play. The counterplot is generally a reflection on or variation of the main action and as such is strongly integrated into the whole of the play. A counterplot may also be referred to as a subplot, but this more general term may refer to a secondary action which is largely unrelated to the main action. (See also *Subplot.*)

Coup de théâtre: An unusual, striking, unexpected turn of events in the action of a play.

Cup-and-saucer drama: Type of play that furthers the illusion of reality onstage through the realistic portrayal of domestic situations among the upper classes and through the use of realistic sets and authentic properties. The English playwright Thomas William Robertson (1829-1871) was the chief practitioner of this type of drama.

Curtain raiser: An entertainment, sometimes a one-act play, performed at the beginning of a program. In the late nineteenth and early twentieth centuries, a curtain raiser often served to entertain an audience during the arrival of latecomers, thus avoiding disturbances when the main presentation began.

Cycle play. See *Miracle play.*

Dada drama: Short-lived but important experiment in the capacity of the stage to present something other than familiar reality was Dada, an early twentieth century movement which began as a cabaret experiment in Switzerland. The guiding spirit of Dada was the Romanian poet Tristan Tzara, who asserted that the first order of business for the new artist was to raze all existing structures, including logic itself, in order for a new world to be built on cleared ground. Consequently, the Dadas looked at reason and logic and proceeded to do the direct opposite. Tzara's *Le Coeur gaz* (wr. 1921, pb. 1946; *The Gas Heart,* 1964), Guillaume Apollinaire's *Les Mamelles de Tiresias* (pr. 1917; *The Breasts of Tiresias,* 1961), and Jean Cocteau's ballet scenario, *Les Mariés de la tour Eiffel* (1921; *The Wedding on the Eiffel Tower,* 1937), are examples of Dada drama.

Dark comedy: Term coined by J. L. Styan in *The Dark Comedy* (1962), referring to the modern concept of the play between tragedy and farce (which evolved from the work of a wide range of predecessors, such as Euripides, medieval mystery plays, Shakespeare, and Molière). The concept reflects the existential belief in a disjunctive world where there is no possibility for conventional notions of heroism and tragedy. Such a concept imposed upon drama tends to produce a catharsis from moment to moment (not a climactic one). The term is broad enough to encompass most of the innovative works of the contemporary repertoire.

Deaf theater: Form of theater that is unique because it is typically defined by its physical method of performance rather than by its literature, play script, or intended audience. Plays performed in American Sign Language (ASL), regardless of their source, content, or intended audience are said to delineate deaf theater. Spoken language scripts are translated into ASL, a process reverse from that found in other niche-based drama. Deaf theater is usually performed simultaneously in two languages, manual ASL and spoken English. The development and proliferation of deaf theater reflects first the joining of spoken and manual languages and then the struggle to separate them. Deaf theater began to embody the ASL literature of the deaf culture in the early twenty-first century.

Denouement: Originally French, this word literally means "unknotting" or "untying" and is another term for the catastrophe or resolution of a dramatic action, the solution or clarification of a plot.

Deus ex machina: Latin, meaning "god out of a machine." In the Greek theater, the use of a god lowered by means of a mechanism called the *mechane* (usually a crane with rope and pulleys) onto the stage to untangle the plot or save the hero. In *Poetics,* Aristotle condemned the use of the *deus ex machina,* arguing that ideally the resolution of a dramatic action should grow out of the action itself. The term has come to signify any artificial device for the simple or easy resolution of any dramatic difficulties.

Deuteragonist: Second actor in Greek drama, the addition of whom was an innovation of Aeschylus. The term is often synonymous with antagonist. In subsequent usage, the term has indicated a major character of secondary importance or position, such as Claudius in William Shakespeare's *Hamlet, Prince of Denmark* (pr. c. 1600-1601)

Dialogue: Speech exchanged between characters or even, in a looser sense, the thoughts of a single character.

Dionysia: An annual drama festival and play contest that began in the sixth century B.C.E. in honor of the god, Dionysus, and is said to mark the beginnings of Greek drama. The Dionysia was celebrated in March and was eventually followed by a second festival in Dionysus's honor, the Lenaea ("wine press"), held in the winter.

Dionysian. See *Apollonian and Dionysian.*

Dithyramb: Originally a choral hymn sung and danced during the ancient Greek rites of Dionysus, the tone of which was passionate and excited. In *Poetics,* Aristotle postulates that the tragic form developed from the dithyramb.

Documentary drama: Also popularly referred to as "docudrama," this term refers to the dramatization of actual events in a journalistic style that explores the ethics and responsibility of issues of public concern. Documentary drama developed in West Germany in the 1960's and is represented by works such as German dramatist Rolf Hochhuth's *Der Stellvertreter: Ein Christliches Trauerspiel* (pr. 1963; *The Representation,* 1963; also known as *The Deputy,* 1964) and American dramatist Eric Bentley's *Are You Now, or Have You Ever Been: The Investigation of Show-Business by the Un-American Activities Committee, 1947-1958* (pr. 1972).

Domestic tragedy: Serious and usually realistic play, with lower-class or middle-class characters and milieu, typically dealing with personal or domestic concerns. The term has been used to refer to works from the Elizabethan age to the present. Examples of domestic tragedy include George Lillo's *The London Merchant: Or, The History of George Barnwell* (pr. 1731), Thomas Heywood's *A Woman Killed with Kindness* (pr. 1603), several of the plays of Henrik Ibsen, and Arthur Miller's *Death of a Salesman* (pr. 1949).

Drama: Generally speaking, any work designed to be represented on a stage by actors (Aristotle defined drama as "the imitation of action"). More specifically, the term has come to signify a play of a serious nature and intent which may end either happily (comedy) or unhappily (tragedy).

Dramatic irony: Irony is a means of expressing a meaning or significance contrary to the stated or ostensible one. Dramatic irony often lies more in the action or structure of a play than in the words of a character. Oedipus' search for the murderer of Laius (whom he later discovers to be himself) is an example of extended dramatic irony. Dramatic irony may also occur when the spoken lines of a character are perceived by the audience to have a double meaning.

Dramatis personae: Characters in a play. Often, a printed listing defining the characters and specifying their relationships.

Dramaturgy: Composition of plays. The term is occasionally used to refer to the performance or acting of plays.

Drame: French term employed chiefly by Louis-Sébastien Mercier (1740-1814) to denote plays that mixed realistic and comic elements with a serious, often tragic, plot. Such plays featured middle-class characters and situations and a preponderance of sentimentality.

Drame héroique. See *Heroic drama.*

Drawing room comedy: Nineteenth century form, related to the comedy of manners form, that elevated the comedy's moral tone by banishing much of the witty sexual innuendo that had long characterized the genre. The setting is usually the drawing room, in which the social games being played are exposed for the audience's amusement as well as for its admiration, the latter being reserved for characters who can best play the game. Dion Boucicault's *London Assurance* (pr. 1841) illustrates the type.

Dumb show: Dramatic performance communicated entirely through gestures, not words. The play-within-a-play in *Hamlet, Prince of Denmark* is a famous example of the dumb show. The term "pantomime" is occasionally used to signify the same type of performance. (See also *Play-within-a-play.*)

Elizabethan: Of or referring to the reign of Queen Elizabeth I of England, lasting from 1558 to 1603, a period of important developments and achievements in the arts in England, particularly in poetry and drama. The era included such literary figures as Edmund Spenser, Christopher Marlowe, William Shakespeare, Ben Jonson, and John Donne. Sometimes referred to as the English Renaissance.

Entr'acte: Brief performance, often musical, intended to entertain an audience between the acts or scenes of a drama.

Environmental theater: Production style developed by the experimental theater groups of the 1960's, emphasizing a flexible approach to the total theater space and aimed at eliminating the traditional separation between audience and stage. Environmental theater is often performed in "found" spaces such as streets, warehouses, and fields.

Epic theater: Style of drama in which the action is presented in loosely related episodes, often interspersed with song, that are designed to distance the audience from the drama. Epic theater was developed by the German director Ervin Piscator in the late 1920's but came to be associated chiefly with the work of Bertolt Brecht. (See also *Alienation.*)

Epilogue: Closing section of a play, or a speech by an actor or chorus at the end of a play, which makes some reflection upon the preceding action or simply, as in Puck's speech at the end of *A Midsummer Night's Dream* (pr. c. 1595-1596), requests the approval and applause of the spectators. The term is sometimes used to refer to the actor who recites such a closing speech.

Episode: In Greek tragedy, the segment between two choral odes. In the larger sense, an episode is a portion of a plot or dramatic action having its own coherence and integrity.

Exodos: Final scene in a classical Greek drama.

Expressionism: Movement dominant in the decade that followed World War I, particularly referring to German painting. External reality, including the appearance of objects, is consciously distorted in order to represent reality as it is felt or "viewed emotionally." Among examples of expressionist drama (which often used distorted scenery, props, music, and unrealistic lighting effects) are Frank Wedekind's *Die Büchse der Pandora* (pr. 1904; *Pandora's Box*, 1918), Eugene O'Neill's *The Hairy Ape* (pr. 1922), and the operas of Alban Berg (*Wozzeck*, pr. 1925; English translation, 1952; and *Lulu*, pr. 1937, English translation, 1977). A play may contain expressionistic devices without being specifically expressionistic (for example, Tennessee Williams's *The Glass Menagerie*, pr. 1944, or his *A Streetcar Named Desire*, pr. 1947).

Extravaganza: James Robinson Planché (1796-1880) developed this form in England. An elaborate musical presentation, the extravaganza was usually based on a fairy tale.

Falling action: Part of a play following the climax. (See also *Freytag's pyramid.*)

Farce: From the Latin *farcire*, meaning "to stuff." Originally an insertion into established Church liturgy in the Middle Ages, "farce" later became the term for specifically comic scenes inserted into early liturgical drama. The term has come to refer to any play that evokes laughter by such low-comedy devices as physical humor, rough wit, and ridiculous and improbable situations and characters. A play may contain farcical elements without being, properly speaking, a farce.

Feminist theater: Theater that works to highlight women's social and political struggles, while in the process exposing patriarchal structures in society and the politics of prevailing gender roles. Feminist playwrights include Alice Childress, Tina Howe, Caryl Churchill, Megan Terry, Wendy Wasserstein, and Marsha Norman.

Flashback: Scene in a play (or in film or literature) depicting events that occurred at an earlier time.

Foil: Any character who sets off or contrasts with another by means of different behavior, philosophy, or purpose.

Folk drama: Generally, plays on folk themes performed at popular or religious festivals by amateurs. Sometimes the term is used to indicate plays written by sophisticated, practiced dramatists on folk themes or in "folk settings" and performed by professional actors. John Millington Synge's *The Playboy of the Western World* (pr. 1907) may be considered, in some sense, a folk drama by this latter definition.

Fourth wall: Theatrical convention intended to heighten the illusion of reality onstage and employed extensively in the late nineteenth century. An invisible fourth wall is imagined to exist between the audience and a stage, enclosed on three sides by the stage set and framed on the fourth by the proscenium arch. The audience, in effect, looks in on the action "through" the fourth wall.

Freytag's pyramid: In 1863, the German critic Gustave Freytag described the theoretical structure of a typical five-act play in *Die Technik des Dramas*. He categorized the dramatic action into the following segments: introduction, rising action, climax, falling action, and catastrophe—all of which can be diagramed in a pyramidal form with the climax at the apex.

Fusion theater: Form of experimental theater which combines elements of non-Western traditions of acting, dramatic and storytelling conventions, music, and performance styles with its Western counterparts. New York's Café La Mama and Berkeley's Zellerbach Playhouse are popular playhouses that promote fusion theater. (See also *Experimental theater.*)

Gay and lesbian drama: Dramatic works written by or focusing on gay issues and lifestyles. Early twentieth century playwrights that subtly treated the subject of homosexuality included Noël Coward, Lillian Hellman, Edna St. Vincent Millay, and, in the 1950's, Robert Anderson. Mart Crowley's *The Boys in the Band*, produced in 1968, paved the way for gay drama in the decades that followed. Among the most honest presentations of homosexuality since 1968 have been John Hopkins's *Find Your Way Home* (pr. 1970), Marvin Hamlisch and Edward Kleban's *A Chorus Line* (pr. 1975), Harvey Fierstein's *La Cage aux Folles* (pr. 1983), and Tony Kushner's pair of plays, *Angels in America: A Gay Fantasia on National Themes*, Part One: Millenium Approaches (1991) and Part Two: Perestroika (1992). The AIDS crisis, homophobia, and political representation have become modern thematic orientations of gay and lesbian drama.

Grand Guignol: Type of theatrical presentation in which horror is the desired effect. This is typically achieved by skillfully naturalistic depictions of situations causing physical pain, such as amputations, eye gougings, and burnings. The effect is invariably grisly and is sometimes meant to produce an uncomfortable sort of laughter.

Hamartia: Greek word for "error," specifically an error in judgment. Aristotle, in *Poetics*, states that a true tragic hero should be a character "preeminently virtuous and just, whose misfortune, however, is brought upon him not by vice and depravity but by some error." This error of judgment may proceed either from ignorance or from moral fault and is sometimes referred to as a "tragic flaw."

Harangue: Speech, usually of some length, often addressed to a crowd to influence the attitudes and actions of the addressees. Antony's ironic speech to the citizens of Rome over Caesar's body in William Shakespeare's *Julius Caesar* (pr. c. 1599-1600) is a well-known example.

Harlequinade: Play or pantomime in the *commedia dell'arte* tradition featuring Harlequin, the stock buffoon who has a shaved head and parti-colored tights, and carries a wooden sword.

Hero/Heroine: Most important character in a drama. Popularly, the term has come to refer to a character who possesses extraordinary prowess or virtue, but as a technical dramatic term it simply indicates the central participant in a dramatic action. (See also *Protagonist.*)

Heroic drama: Type of play usually written in heroic couplets and of elevated diction and seriousness of action (although there might be a happy ending). Heroic drama was popular for a short period, predominantly during the Restoration in England, and its practitioners were John Dryden, Bronson Howard, and Thomas Otway, among others. In France, the *drame héroïque* was likewise popular during the seventeenth century (here the verse form was the Alexandrine). The *drame héroïque* reached a level of accomplishment and art far surpassing its English counterpart. The great French practitioners were Pierre Corneille and Jean Racine.

High comedy: Term broadly used to refer to comedy whose impulse is often satiric and whose appeal is primarily intellectual. Intellect, wit, style, and sophistication are the trademarks of this type of comedy. Plays such as William Congreve's *The Way of the World* (pr. 1700), Molière's *Le Misanthrope* (pr. 1666; *The Misanthrope*, 1709), and Oscar Wilde's *The Importance of Being Earnest: A Trivial Comedy for Serious People* (pr. 1895) are all examples of high comedy.

History play. See *Chronicle play.*

Hubris: Greek term for "insolence" or "pride," the characteristic or emotion in tragic heroes of ancient Greek drama that causes the reversal of their fortune, leading them to transgress moral codes or ignore warnings. An example of hubris in Sophocles' *Antigonē* (441 B.C.E.; *Antigone*, 1729) is Creon's overweening pride, which, despite Tiresias' admonitions, brings about the deaths of Antigone as well as those of Creon's wife and son.

Humors, comedy of. See *Comedy of humors.*

Hypokritēs: An expositor performing recitations in early Greek tragedy that advance the action by brief dialogues with the chorus.

Imitation: From the Greek mimesis, used by Aristotle in his *Poetics* to describe tragedy as "an imitation of an action" of a good man. Aristotle perceived artistic imitation not as an exact replica of life but as an artistic representation that transcends reality to convey universal truths, which produces pleasure in the observer. This term has remained central to Western literary and dramatic criticism, although it has been subject to various interpretations through the centuries.

Improvisational theater: Performance in which action and dialogue are created spontaneously by the actors, and which is often based upon a rough scenario rather than a written, rehearsed script. The *commedia dell'arte* of the Italian Renaissance featured improvisation, and many contemporary theater groups use improvisation both as a performance and as a training technique.

Interlude: Short play, often a farce, popular in fifteenth and sixteenth century England. The English interlude has Continental counterparts in such works as the anonymous French farce *Pierre Patelin* and the comedies of the German mastersinger Hans Sachs. Henry Medwall and John Heywood were practitioners of the interlude in England.

Intrigue: Incidents that make up the plot or action of a play. The term is most frequently applied to plots that are elaborate and in which the schemes of various characters are involved. A play such as William Congreve's *The Way of the World* is sometimes referred to as a "comedy of intrigue."

Irony. See *Dramatic irony.*

Jacobean: Of or pertaining to the reign of James I of England, who ruled from 1603 to 1625, the period following the death of Elizabeth I, which saw tremendous literary activity in poetry and drama. Many writers who achieved fame during the Elizabethan age were still composing (notably William Shakespeare, Ben Jonson, and John Donne). Other dramatists, such as John Webster and Cyril Tourneur, achieved success almost entirely during the reign of James I. The theater of this period is particularly noted for its interest in the violent and the fantastical.

Kabuki: Form of theater in Japan which was, traditionally, established by a former priestess of the early seventeenth century, Okuni. Okuni organized a troupe of actors that included both men and women. Kabuki enjoyed immediate popular success, and the number of companies (with both male and female performers) increased rapidly. As early as 1629, the presence of female performers caused a scandal and was banned. Female impersonators kept the tradition alive and remain very popular. Kabuki actors wear no masks (unlike the performers of the aristocratic Nō theater). The Kabuki drama is typically melodramatic and violent, with complex plotting.

Latino drama: Drama that emerged in the 1950's and 1960's, written by or focusing on the numerous groups that belong to Latino culture in the United States: Mexican Americans or Chicanos (American-born Mexicans), Puerto Ricans or Nuyoricans (New York Puerto Ricans), and Cuban Americans, whose modern theater has acquired several names, including Cuban American and Cuban exile theater. Identity issues, immigration, socioeconomic status, and a postmodern political consciousness of "the other" as both outsider and insider typically grounds the thematic orientation of Latino drama.

Laughing comedy: Term coined in 1772 by English playwright Oliver Goldsmith to describe a comedy, such as his *She Stoops to Conquer* (pr. 1773) or Richard Brinsley Sheridan's *The Rivals* (pr. 1775), that exposes human follies and vices for the amusement and edification of the audience, as opposed to the sentimental comedy, which dominated eighteenth century drama and which was intended to move audiences to pleasurable tears with sentimental stories about the middle class. The respective merits of these two types of comedy were hotly debated throughout the 1770's.

Lazzo: Improvised comic dialogue or action in the *commedia dell'arte*. Lazzi (plural) were among the prime resources of the *commedia* actors, consisting of verbal asides on current politics, literary topics, manifestations of terror, pratfalls, and similar actions.

Leitmotif: From the German, meaning "leading motif." Any repetition—of a word, phrase, situation, or idea—which occurs within a single work or group of related works and which serves to unify the work or works. The term has special meaning in musical drama (a signal melody or phrase of music), and the technique was used by the nineteenth century composer and theoretician Richard Wagner not only to unify his operas (most notably the four-opera cycle *Der Ring des Nibelungen*, pr. 1876; *The Nibelung's Ring,* 1877; also known as *The Ring of the Nibelung,* 1910) but also to add dramatic and psychological resonance and depth to the action.

Libretto: Italian for "little book." The text or script of an opera, operetta, or other form of musical theater.

Liturgical drama: Plays performed as part of the liturgy of the Church during the Middle Ages. The origin of these plays was in the tropes or interpolations into the Latin text of the liturgy, which was chanted by the clergy. These interpolations were expanded and eventually developed into independent performances in the vernacular. The performances eventually moved out of the church proper and were performed by members of the laity. While the plays ceased to be liturgical, they continued to deal with religious themes, particularly drawn from the Old and New Testaments. (See also *Corpus Christi plays, Miracle play, Trope.*)

Low comedy: Term broadly used to refer to the coarse elements in a play designed to arouse laughter. Such elements include physical comedy (slapstick, practical jokes) and off-color humor. Low comedy elements are to be found not only in such comic forms as farce but also in plays of high artistic repute, such as William Shakespeare's *A Midsummer Night's Dream* and *The Merry Wives of Windsor* (pr. 1597).

Manners, comedy of. See *Comedy of manners.*

Masque: Courtly entertainment popular during the first half of the seventeenth century in England. Derived from Italian court entertainments, it spanned from the latter part of the reign of Elizabeth I through that of James I and into that of Charles I. It was a particularly sumptuous form of spectacle including music (song and dance) and lavish costumes and scenery (the great Baroque architect Inigo Jones and the great Baroque composer Henry Purcell were frequently involved in the nonliterary aspects of these productions). Masques often dealt with mythological or pastoral subjects, and the dramatic action often took second place to pure spectacle. Ben Jonson was the greatest writer of masques during this period, and even the young John Milton composed a masque, *Comas* (pr. 1634), whose interest was, atypically, more literary than spectacle-oriented. (See also *Antimasque.*)

Melodrama: Originally a drama with occasional songs, or with music of any kind (*melos* is Greek for "song"). It was also one of the original Italian terms for opera. By the early nineteenth century, the term acquired a new meaning: a play in which characters are clearly either virtuous or evil and are pitted against one another in suspenseful, often sensational situations. Late eighteenth century French playwright Guilbert de Pixérécourt was a well known melodramatist, best remembered for his *Sélico: Ou, Les Nègres généreux* (pr. 1793). This type of play became so common that the term took on a pejorative meaning which it still retains today: any dramatic work characterized by stereotyped characters and sensational, sometimes improbable situations.

Method, the: An approach to acting developed by the Russian director Konstantin Stanislavsky. Commonly referred to as "the Method," this approach emphasizes a realistic acting style based on each actor's self-knowledge and on the entire cast's careful analysis of the script. An understanding of the motivation behind the character's speech and actions is essential to a believable performance, according to the rules of the Method, which was popularized in the United States by the noted acting instructor Lee Strasberg.

Miles gloriosus: Braggart soldier character type found in many plays from antiquity to the modern age, particularly in Elizabethan and Jacobean drama. The term derives from Plautus's play of the same title. Nicholas Udall's *Ralph Roister Doister* (pr. c. 1552) and William Shakespeare's *Sir John Falstaff* are quintessential examples of the type in sixteenth century English drama. (See also *Alazon.*)

Mime: Dramatic action portrayed by means of gesture and movement without speech. An actor who performs such actions is also called a "mime."

Mimesis. See *Imitation.*

Miracle play: In English drama, this term refers to medieval religious plays dramatizing the lives of the saints and divine miracles. The term "mystery play" (derived from the French term *mystère*) is used to designate plays derived from the Scriptures as opposed to those dealing with saints' lives. These plays were originally associated with the celebration of saints' feast days and with religious processions (particularly the Corpus Christi festival) and were performed in Latin as part of the liturgical services. Later, these plays were expanded, performed in the vernacular, and moved into the streets. Trade guilds were often responsible for the performance of a particular play, so that in time a series of performances by various guilds would create a cycle of plays. Some examples of subjects derived from Scripture include Christ's Passion, the Fall of Man, and the story of Noah. This form of dramatic entertainment reached its height in the fifteenth and sixteenth centuries. (See also *Corpus Christi plays, Liturgical drama, Trope.*)

Mise-en-scène: Staging of a drama, including scenery, costumes, movable furniture (properties), and, by extension, the positions (blocking) and gestures of the actors.

Modernism: An international movement in the arts that began in the early years of the twentieth century. Although the term is used to describe artists of widely varying persuasions, modernism in general was characterized by its international idiom, by its interest in cultures distant in space or time, by its emphasis on formal experimentation, and by its sense of dislocation and radical change. Seeking to revolutionize dramatic structure, playwrights often presented fantasies, hallucinations, nightmares, and other subjective experiences. In addition, they developed new lighting and staging techniques—particularly the turntable stage—that portrayed myriad moods rather than a single mood, and they excluded irrelevancy. Influenced by German expressionism, Symbolism, and Sigmund Freud, many of these playwrights were antinaturalistic. (See also *Symbolism, Expressionism, Naturalism.*)

Monodrama: Theatrical presentation featuring only one character. Jean Cocteau's *La Voix humaine* (pr. 1930; *The Human Voice*, 1951) is an example of this form.

Monologue: An extended speech by one character in a drama. If the character is alone onstage, unheard by other characters, the monologue is more specifically referred to as a soliloquy. (See also *Soliloquy.*)

Morality play: Dramatic form of the late Middle Ages and the Renaissance containing allegorical figures (most often virtues and vices) that are typically involved in the struggle over a person's soul. The anonymously written *Everyman* is one of the most famous medieval examples of this form.

Motoriae: Loosely structured play, refined by the Greek writer Epicharmus of Cos during the fifth century B.C.E., the violent action of which combines mythological plots with realistic stories.

Mummery: This term refers broadly to a theatrical presentation in which actors or dancers are masked or in disguise. The term is occasionally used to refer to acting in general.

Musical comedy: Theatrical form mingling song, dance, and spoken dialogue which was developed in the United States in the twentieth century and is derived from vaudeville and operetta. In its earliest stages, the music often had little to do with the libretto (the text or script), but a closer integration of these elements has occurred since the early 1940's. (See also *Musical theater, Opera.*)

Musical theater: Dramatic production in which music, lyrics, and sometimes dance are fundamental elements. Opera, operetta, and musical comedy are all forms of musical theater. Proponents of this genre include Claudio Monteverdi, George Frederick

Handel, Wolfgang Amadeus Mozart, Gioacchino Rossini, Vincenzo Bellini, Giuseppe Verdi, Richard Wagner, Richard Strauss, and Giacomo Puccini. (See also *Musical comedy, Opera.*)

Mystery play. See *Miracle play.*

Native American drama: Dramatic works by Native Americans and/or about their experience in North America. The search for identity in the United States and the hope of rectifying the cultural image of the Native American commonly held in American society are often thematic poles of such works. Works often integrate religious themes, rituals, and dances that began to perish at the end of the nineteenth century with the increasing removal of Indian peoples to reservations. Representative playwrights include Hanay Geiogamah, William S. Yellow Robe, Jr., Roxy Gordon, and Leanne Howe.

Naturalism: Naturalism was a type of realism, aimed at overturning theatrical convention, created in the late nineteenth century by a school of French and American writers including Émile Zola and Theodore Dreiser, who elevated the style nearly to a philosophical movement. As a genre, it professed to be unsentimental and, consequently, antibourgeois. Naturalistic drama sought to mirror life, even at its seamiest, in all its cruelty and degradation. Henry Becque and Gerhart Hauptmann were two naturalistic playwrights. (See also *Realism.*)

Neoclassicism: Aesthetic movement that influenced seventeenth century French and English drama and was characterized by an admiration for and an emulation of classical Greek and Roman culture. French neoclassical drama is best represented by the tragedies of Pierre Corneille and Jean Racine, who followed the strict rules of unity and verisimilitude advocated by the Académie Française. In England, neoclassical dramatists such as John Dryden wrote heroic tragedies, which were highly artificial dramas featuring exotic settings, improbable and spectacular action, and high-flown language, usually written in heroic couplets. (See also *Renaissance drama.*)

New Comedy: Greek comedy of the third and fourth centuries B.C.E. that coincided with the decline of Greek political power and with the decline of the satiric comic theater of Aristophanes. The New Comedy featured stereotyped plots and characters: courtesans, young lovers, foolish miserly old men, and scheming servants. After many amorous intrigues, the plays typically ended in a happy marriage. Menander was the chief proponent of the form, and the Romans Terence and Plautus were much influenced by it, finding in it an abundant source for material.

Nō: Form of theater developed in fourteenth century Japan from ritual dance associated with Shinto worship. The plays were designed for aristocratic audiences and were highly restrained and stylized. The plays are typically mysterious and gloomy in plot and atmosphere. Performers (who are always male) wear masks and employ a distinctly unrealistic form of acting. The text is sung or chanted to musical accompaniment in low- and high-pitched voices. The influence of this Eastern form can be seen in the West in certain twentieth century works such as William Butler Yeats's *At the Hawk's Well* (pr. 1916) and *The Only Jealousy of Emer* (pr. 1922).

Obligatory scene: Scene that a playwright has led an audience to expect (usually an emotional confrontation between characters) and without which the audience would be disappointed (also called a *scene a faire*).

Old Comedy: Greek comedy of the fifth century B.C.E. that originated in the fertility festivals in honor of Dionysus. Of the plays in this form, only those of Aristophanes survive. His work is notable for its biting personal and political satire as well as its lyric beauty. The chorus takes an important role in the action, notably delivering the parabasis, an extended speech usually expressing the views of the playwright. With the decline of Greek political power in the fourth century B.C.E., this form was replaced by New Comedy. The plays in this form relied heavily on stock characters and situations.

One-act play: Although there have been short, unified dramatic works that might properly be termed one-act dramas earlier on, this term has typically been employed for such works written since the late nineteenth century. The one-act play is usually quite limited in number of characters and scene changes, and the action often revolves around a single incident or event.

Opera: Form of dramatic entertainment consisting of a play set to music. Opera is the most important and most sophisticated form that combines music with theatrical representation. It is a complex combination of various art forms—music (both vocal and instrumental), drama, poetry, acting, stage design, dance, and so on. Like other art forms, it has its own conventions; these are sometimes derived more from a musical perspective than from a purely theatrical perspective or tradition. The origin of opera in the late sixteenth and early seventeenth centuries in Italy resulted from the attempts of certain Humanist literary figures and musicians to recreate classical Greek drama, with its combination of speech, music, and dance. From its inception through the present, opera has undergone a diverse history of its own (which sometimes mirrors the history of purely spoken drama). Practitioners of the form include Claudio Monteverdi, George Frederick Handel, Wolfgang Amadeus Mozart, Gioacchino Rossini, Vincenzo Bellini, Giuseppe Verdi, Richard Wagner, Richard Strauss, Giacomo Puccini, and Alban Berg. (See also *Musical comedy, Musical theater.*)

Pageant: Originally the platform or movable stage upon which medieval miracle and mystery plays were performed, the term has come to refer to any large-scale outdoor procession or performance.

Pantomime: Dramatic action communicated entirely by gesture and movement but not speech. Also, a type of theatrical entertainment developed in England in the eighteenth century. The story was usually acted out in both song and dance, and the scenery and stage effects could be quite lavish and spectacular. The form still survives in England in special Christmas entertainments designed for children.

Parabasis: Seven-part choral number occurring toward the middle of a Greek comedy that makes a direct appeal to the audience, requesting a prize or offering advice on current events.

Parodos: In classical Greek tragedy, the first scene in which the chorus appears and the first ode that the chorus sings are called *parodos.* The name derives from the entryway used by the chorus for entrances and exits. (See also *Chorus.*)

Passion play: Play that depicts the life, or incidents from the life, of a god. These plays had their origin in the pagan rites of ancient Egypt and the Near East. In Christian Europe, many medieval plays presented episodes from the life of Christ and are also referred to as Passion plays. The form still survives in various pageants in Europe and the Americas (particularly notable is the famous Oberammergau Passion play of Germany, performed every ten years).

Pastoral drama: Form of tragicomedy that was popular in the sixteenth and seventeenth centuries, originally a dramatic imitation of the bucolic idylls of Horace and Vergil. Pastoral drama represented a neoclassical vision of the rustic, Arcadian life and typically mingled such elements as unrequited love, intrigues of jealousy, and threats of death to the protagonists. These tragic elements are often happily resolved by the revelation of true relationships between characters or the triumph of love. The masterpiece of the genre (and one of the most influential theatrical works of the sixteenth century) is Battista Guarini's *Il pastor fido* (pr. 1596; *The Faithful Shepherd*, 1602). Another famous example is Torquato Tasso's sixteenth century play *Aminta* (pr. 1573).

Pathos: Quality in a dramatic character that evokes pity or sorrow from the audience.

Peripeteia: Sudden reversal of situation in a dramatic action. Aristotle gives as an example the arrival of the messenger in *Oedipus Tyrannus*, who believes he will relieve Oedipus's anxiety and accomplishes the reverse effect.

Pièce bien faite. See *Well-made play.*

Pièce de thèse. See *Problem play.*

Play-within-a-play: Play or dramatic fragment, performed as a scene or scenes within a larger drama, typically performed or viewed by the characters of the larger drama, such as the farcical "whodunit" in Tom Stoppard's *The Real Inspector Hound* (pr. 1968). In Elizabethan drama, the play-within-a-play was often performed as a dumb show, as in the players' scene in *Hamlet, Prince of Denmark*. (See also *Dumb show.*)

Plot: Sequence of the occurrence of events in a dramatic action. A plot may be unified around a single action, but it may also consist of a series of disconnected incidents—it is then referred to as "episodic."

Political theater: Broad term that typically refers to any production of a play that carries either an overt or covert sociopolitical message, provokes serious contemplation of social issues, or invokes an understanding of and sympathy for political causes. Often a dynamic tool for public instruction, propaganda, and entertainment, political theater instigates, examines, and sometimes suggests solutions for the problems inherent in human society. The two most common types of political theater include plays used to make a statement in order to change public sentiment concerning a social issue and those used directly to instigate social change as an agent of propaganda. Arthur Miller's *The Crucible* (pr. 1953), Amiri Baraka's *Slave Ship: A Historical Pageant* (pr. 1967), and Caryl Churchill's *Cloud Nine* (pr. 1979) are examples of political theater.

Postcolonial theater: Theatrical works primarily driven by, focused on, or concerned with the political, social, or cultural effects or aftermath of colonial dominance after a nation's independence. Postcolonial literature and theater often focuses on the "subaltern" (that is, those who are in a subordinate power position who fight, or have fought, the process and results of colonialism) finding their voice. Themes revolving around the intersections of nationalism, identity, and race, as well as protest and cultural revival, are often present in postcolonial dramatic works. Examples includes David Henry Hwang's *M. Butterfly* (pr. 1988), which studies the issues of Western colonialism, and Athol Fugard's *MASTER HAROLD . . . and the Boys* (pr. 1982) or *My Children! My Africa!* (pr. 1990), which examine the colonial legacy in South Africa.

Postmodernism: Term loosely applied to the various artistic movements that followed the era of so-called high modernism, represented by such giants as James Joyce and Pablo Picasso. The term typically refers to a work that calls attention to itself as an artifice rather than a mirror held up to external reality. In drama, the mixing of several available forms and styles, often in fanciful, experimental ways, is now labeled postmodernism, a special form of which is performance art. Typified by artists such as Laurie Anderson, a performance art piece might include an artist working alone and presenting a statement through multimedia, music, singing, storytelling, and stand-up comedy. Examples of postmodern plays include Dario Fo's *Morte accidentale di un anarchico* (pr. 1970; *Accidental Death of an Anarchist,* 1979), Caryl Churchill's *Top Girls* (pr. 1982), and Edward Albee's *Three Tall Women* (pr. 1991).

Presentationalism: An approach to playwriting and stage production that presents drama as an artificial, theatrical event rather than as a realistic representation of life. For example, classical Greek drama, with its masks, chorus, and circular stage, and Elizabethan drama, with its stark stage sets and blank verse, are presentational. (See also *Representationalism.*)

Problem play: Drama in which a social problem is illustrated and, usually, a solution is suggested. This form is also referred to as a thesis play (from the French *pièce de thèse*) and originated in the mid-nineteenth century in France. *Le Fils naturel* (pr. 1858; *The Natural Son,* 1879), by Alexandre Dumas, *fils,* is an early example. A number of Henrik Ibsen's plays can be categorized broadly as problem plays.

Prologue: Opening section of a play that often provides introductory information concerning the central action of the play. Also, a speech by an actor or chorus at the beginning of a play of an expository nature. The term is sometimes used to refer to the actor who recites such an introductory speech.

Properties: Usually abbreviated as "props." Properties are the movable objects (other than scenery or costumes) that appear on stage during a dramatic performance.

Proscenium: Part of a stage in front of the curtain. Also, the wall that separates the stage from the auditorium of a theater and provides the arch that frames the stage.

Protagonist: Originally, in the Greek drama, the first actor, who played the leading role. In a more general sense, the term has come to signify the most important character, usually a hero, in a drama or story. It is not unusual for there to be more than one protagonist in a play. (See also *Hero/Heroine.*)

Protasis: Section of a classical drama in which the characters are introduced and the dramatic situation is explained. The term "protatic character" has come to signify a character used only to assist in the exposition of a play and appearing nowhere else in the action.

Proverbe dramatique: Play—typically of one act—illustrating an aphorism that forms the play's title. This form began in France in the eighteenth century and was developed by Carmontelle, but its most famous practitioner was the nineteenth century poet and dramatist Alfred de Musset.

Psychological realism: Sigmund Freud's analysis of the complex psychological motivations behind human behavior led dramatists in the late nineteenth century to try to reproduce this psychological complexity in their characters rather than relying on character types. One of the earliest proponents of this psychological realism was August Strindberg (1849-1912), who argued that since human actions are caused by complex motivations in real life, they should be similarly portrayed on the stage.

Radio drama: Drama written for and performed over radio and popular in the United States between 1920 and 1940. Orson Welles was a well-known practitioner of radio drama.

Raisonneur: Character in a play, typically somewhat detached from the action, who acts as a spokesman for the author. This character observes the other characters involved more directly in the action and comments upon the action, expressing the author's views.

Realism: Broadly, any mode of art that attempts to present a replica of real life (as opposed to a fantastic or an ideal vision of life) and engage the audience in a reaction to the work as though it were real life. Particularly, realism was a reaction, beginning in the late nineteenth and early twentieth centuries, to fantastic, superhuman, melodramatic, idealistic, and otherwise Romantic forms of art and theater. Because realism sought to put forth the actual over the ideal, it necessarily replaced the exotic with the ordinary, the superhuman with the human, poetic and elevated language with familiar dialogue, the overblown and spectacular with the understated and domestic, and exaggerated or grandiose actions with those that are more plausible and often verbal or cerebral. Realist theater—characterized by a well-devised dramatic plot, with its emphasis on psychological truth and human pathos—tended to be sentimental and moralistic and to preach social reform. Realist playwrights rejected the idea of the well-made play with its mechanical artifices and slick plotting, as well as exaggerated theatricalism. Henrik Ibsen is considered the leader of this revolution in drama, and chief pioneers of dramatic realism in the twentieth century included Eugene O'Neill, Tennessee Williams, Arthur Miller, and Edward Albee. (See also *Romanticism, Russian realism, Well-made play.*)

Recognition. See *Anagnorisis.*

Renaissance drama: European drama produced from the early sixteenth to the late seventeenth centuries and often characterized by a concern for the classical ideals of composition and structure that are set forth in Aristotle's *Poetics* and are demonstrated in the works of classical dramatists such as Seneca, whose five-act plays were considered to epitomize the classical structure. Renaissance drama was also characterized by a humanitarian interest in secular subjects such as history, politics, and social issues, and this interest constituted a quite marked departure from the exclusively religious/allegorical concerns of medieval drama, evidenced in the miracle and morality plays. Renaissance drama first appeared in Italy during the early and mid-sixteenth century with playwrights such as Niccoló Machiavelli, Ludovico Ariosto, and Giangiorgio Trissino.

Repertory: Theater troupe or company that presents several different plays in alternation during the course of a season.

Representationalism: An approach to playwriting and staging that seeks to create the illusion of reality onstage through realistic characters and situations and/or through the use of realistic stage sets, properties, and acting styles. The Naturalistic drama advocated by the French novelist Émile Zola (1840-1902) and practiced by French director André Antoine (1858-1943) at the turn of the twentieth century is an example of representationalism. The opposite approach to drama is presentationalism, which presents drama as a stylized, theatrical event. (See also *Presentationalism.*)

Restoration: Period in English history beginning with the restoration of Charles II to the throne, bringing an end to the Puritan interregnum, which had abolished the monarchy in 1649 and closed the theaters. The Restoration period has no precise end but is commonly held to have ended about 1700. As a result of the reopening of the London theaters, there was a surge of theatrical activity, and the period was known for the wealth of new drama produced by such dramatists as William Congreve, Sir George Etherege, William Wycherley, George Farquhar, and Oliver Goldsmith.

Revenge tragedy: Type of drama, particularly associated with the Elizabethan and Jacobean periods, in which revenge is the central motive. Thomas Kyd's *The Spanish Tragedy* (pr. c. 1585-1589) is said to have established the genre in English drama. Some other examples are Christopher Marlowe's *The Jew of Malta* (pr. c. 1589) and

John Marston's *Antonio's Revenge* (pr. 1599). William Shakespeare's *Hamlet, Prince of Denmark* is, in an enlarged and very sophisticated sense, an example of this type of drama.

Reversal. See *Peripeteia.*

Revue: Theatrical production, typically consisting of sketches, song, and dance, which often comments satirically upon personalities and events of the day. Generally there is no plot involved, although some semblance of a unifying action or theme may unite the individual sketches and musical numbers.

Rising action: Part of a play preceding the climax. (See also *Anabasis, Freytag's pyramid.*)

Romantic comedy: Play in which love is the central motive of the dramatic action. The term often refers to plays of the Elizabethan period, such as William Shakespeare's *As You Like It* (pr. c. 1599) and *A Midsummer Night's Dream,* but it has also been applied to any modern work that contains similar features.

Romanticism: Broad term that at times fails to capture the complexity and multiplicity of European Romanticism, which was manifested in different ways and different periods in European regions during the late eighteenth and nineteenth centuries. Generally, the genre exalted individualism over collectivism, revolution over conservatism, innovation over tradition, imagination over reason, and spontaneity over restraint. Romanticism regarded art as self-expression; it strove to heal the cleavage between object and subject and expressed a longing for the infinite in all things. It stressed the innate goodness of human beings and the evils of the institutions that would stultify human creativity. Other values associated with various schools of Romanticism include primitivism, an interest in folklore, a reverence for nature, and a fascination with the demoniac and the macabre.

Russian realism: Beginning in the mid-nineteenth century, a movement whose leaders included Ivan Turgenev, Aleksandr Ostrovsky, Leo Tolstoy, and later, Maxim Gorky. Anton Chekhov's plays *Chuyka* (pr. 1896; *The Seagull,* 1909), *Dyadya Vanya* (pr. 1899; *Uncle Vanya,* 1914), *Tri sestry* (pr. 1901; *The Three Sisters,* 1920), and *Vishnyovy sad* (pr. 1904; *The Cherry Orchard,* 1908) are the best examples.

Satire: Dramatic satire employs the comedic devices of wit, irony, and exaggeration to expose and condemn human folly, vice, and stupidity. Although subject to political and societal repression throughout the centuries, dramatic satire appears in the classical Greek comedies of Aristophanes, in the personification of vices in the medieval morality plays, in the Renaissance plays of William Shakespeare and Ben Jonson, in the social satires of Oscar Wilde and George Bernard Shaw in the late nineteenth and early twentieth centuries, and in the twentieth century dramas of such dissimilar playwrights as Sean O'Casey and Harold Pinter.

Satyr play: In Greek drama, a performance composed of choric dances performed exclusively by actors dressed as satyrs. Not necessarily comic, the story was often derived from epics or legends and was associated with Dionysus.

Scenario: An outline of the dramatic action (plot) of a theatrical work, specifying the characters and the order of acts and scenes.

Scene: Division of action within an act (some plays are divided only into scenes instead of acts). Sometimes scene division indicates a change of setting or locale; sometimes it simply indicates the entrances and exits of characters; this latter case was, for example, the typical practice of the French neoclassical dramatists such as Pierre Corneille and Jean Racine. (See also *Act.*)

Scène à faire. See *Obligatory scene.*

School plays: Plays performed at secondary schools in sixteenth century England. These plays showed the influence of the classical comedy of Terence and Plautus and were composed both in Latin and in English. The earliest known example of the form in English, of about 1566, is Nicholas Udall's *Ralph Roister Doister.*

Sentimental comedy: With the rise of the middle class in the eighteenth century, a "new" audience patronized the theater, demanding drama which related to their social class and milieu and which upheld the traditionally accepted moral code that had brought them into increased position and power. The sentimental comedy was a type of play generally centered on the distresses of the middle class and intended to evoke the sympathies of the audience. Good and bad characters were often presented in a very schematic way without psychological complexity. Pleasurable tears, not laughter, were the mark of the successful sentimental drama. In England, the Restoration playwright George Farquhar anticipated some of the features of the sentimental comedy, but the true practitioners of the unadulterated form were playwrights such as Sir Richard Steele, Hugh Kelly, and Richard Cumberland. The corresponding development in French eighteenth century drama was the *comédie larmoyante* (tearful comedy), of which Philippe Destouches and Pierre-Claude Nivelle de La Chaussée are the chief proponents. (See also *Comédie larmoyante.*)

Set speech: Long, uninterrupted speech made by a single character to set forth a number of points. This device is prevalent in verse drama.

Setting: Time and place in which the action of a play happens. The term also applies to the physical elements of a theatrical production, such as scenery and properties.

Slapstick: Low comedy in which physical action (such as a kick in the rear, tripping, and knocking over people or objects) evokes laughter.

Social realism: Philosophical movement, begun in the early twentieth century, that raised political consciousness of the working classes and often criticized governments and regimes. By focusing on topics of social justice, the attitudes and problems of several social classes, and émigré identity, the form became popular with many "ethnic" dramatists by the 1960's and 1970's, including Latino, Native American, and Asian American playwrights.

Sock: Flat foot covering worn by actors in Greek comedy. In contrast, tragic actors wore high platform boots (buskins), which endowed them with increased stature, both physically and metaphorically. The sock was literally more down-to-earth. (See also *Buskin.*)

Soliloquy: Properly, an extended speech delivered by a character alone on stage, unheard by other characters. Soliloquy is a form of monologue, and it typically reveals the intimate thoughts and emotions of the speaker. (See also *Monologue.*)

Sottie: Form of medieval French farce that presented political, religious, or social satire.

Stasimon: Term for the odes sung by the chorus in classical Greek tragedy after the chorus had taken its place on the stage.

Stichomythia: In dramatic dialogue, a term referring to single lines, spoken alternately by two characters, which are characterized by repetitive patterns and antithesis. The Elizabethans, modeling after classical drama, used this type of dialogue with some frequency.

Stock character/situation: Frequently recurring dramatic type or dramatic incident or situation.

Strophe: In the choral odes of Greek drama, the strophe is a structural unit of lyric song and dance, similar to the stanza. The chorus sang and danced a strophe, followed by an antistrophe, which corresponded in form to the strophe. (See also *Antistrophe.*)

Sturm und Drang: Dramatic and literary movement in Germany during the late eighteenth century that took its name from Friedrich Maximilian Klinger's play of that title, published in 1777. Translated in English as "Storm and Stress," the movement was a reaction against classicism and a forerunner of Romanticism, characterized by extravagantly emotional language and sensational subject matter.

Subplot: Secondary action coincident with the main action of a play. A subplot may be a reflection (by means of contrast or similarity) upon the main action, but it may also be largely unrelated. (See also *Counterplot.*)

Surrealist drama: The term *drame surréaliste* (literally, "superrealistic drama") was originally coined in 1918 by Guillaume Apollinaire to describe his play *The Breasts of Tiresias* and was later modified and expanded by André Breton to describe a form of drama that focuses upon subconscious reality. The composition of such drama was often achieved by the practice of "automatic writing" and the study of dreams. The goal of Surrealist work is to restore the neglected subconscious to its rightful place alongside conscious perception.

Symbolism: Term commonly signifying a literary movement that originated in France in the latter part of the nineteenth century. Symbols have always been used in literature and drama, but as a conscious movement and practice, Symbolism achieved its most highly developed and defined form in the poetry of Stéphane Mallarmé and Arthur Rimbaud and in the plays of Maurice Maeterlinck. Drama was conceived as taking place in the mind and soul and was not felt to be truly expressed by outward action. The Symbolists, therefore, avoided the more traditional apparatus of dramatic construction: There are no strong, detailed characterizations; no true locus of crisis or conflict; no message or catharsis is intended. Action exists almost exclusively on a symbolic level and is conveyed through symbolic language, settings, lighting, sound effects, and so on. The influence of Symbolism was widespread and appears in the work of dramatists such as Leonid Andreyev, William Butler Yeats, Sean O'Casey, Anton Chekhov, and Eugene O'Neill.

Tableau: Silent, stationary grouping of performers in a theatrical performance. Also, an elaborate stage presentation featuring lavish settings and costumes as well as music and dance.

Theater of Cruelty: Term coined by French playwright and theorist Antonin Artaud to signify a vision in which theater becomes an arena for shock therapy. The characters undergo such intense physical and psychic extremities that the audience cannot ignore the cathartic effect in which its preconceptions, fears, and hostilities are brought to the surface and, ideally, purged. Startling noises, violent gestures, incantatory words or phrases, and unnerving lighting, music, and scenic effects all contribute to an atmosphere conducive to this curative goal.

Theater of the Absurd: General name given to a group of plays that share a basic belief that life is illogical, irrational, formless, and contradictory, and that human beings are without meaning or purpose. This philosophical perspective led to the abandonment of traditional theatrical forms and coherent dialogue. Practitioners have included writers as diverse as Eugene Ionesco, Samuel Beckett, Jean Genet, Harold Pinter, Edward Albee, and Arthur Kopit.

Theater of the Unspoken: (Théâtre de L'Inexprimé): A form of theater developed in France after World War I that emphasized the nonverbal elements of drama. It was created in response to the perception that earlier French theater was too verbose, containing too much dialogue. Practitioners include Jean-Jacques Bernard.

Théâtre Libre: French for "free theater." A private theater club founded by André Antoine in Paris in 1887 for the production of new Naturalistic plays. The innovations in settings, dramaturgy, direction, and acting had a great influence on the modern theater, helping liberate the stage from its early and mid-nineteenth century artificiality.

Thesis play. See *Problem play.*

Thespian: Another term for an actor; also, of or relating to the theater. The word derives from Thespis, by tradition the first actor of the Greek theater.

Three unities. See *Unities.*

Tirade: Technical term used in French drama (and particularly associated with the seventeenth century neoclassical theater) for a long set piece or uninterrupted speech delivered by a single character to other characters on stage. A tirade is not necessarily of an angry or violent nature, as signified by the English cognate. The English term "harangue" is sometimes used as the technical equivalent.

Tragedy: In its broadest sense, a form of drama that is serious in action and intent. More specifically, Aristotle defined tragedy as an imitation of an action that is serious, complete in itself, and of a certain magnitude. He also specified that this action rouses pity and fear in the audience and purges these emotions. These rather broad criteria originally had specific meanings, which have undergone tremendous evolution from their inception through the present age—a single example is the notion of the tragic hero. Where in the ancient Greek theater the tragic heroes were typically personages of high rank and position (a king, queen, or nobleman), in the modern concept (particularly since the rise of the middle class in the eighteenth century) he or she would be a member of the middle or lower class. There has been much debate on the issue of whether "true tragedy" is even possible in the modern theater, and playwrights such as Eugene O'Neill and Arthur Miller have tried to incorporate the criteria of Aristotelian concepts in evoking tragic feeling or effects.

Tragedy, heroic. See *Heroic drama*

Tragedy, revenge. See *Revenge tragedy.*

Tragic flaw. See *Hamartia.*

Tragicomedy: Play in which the dramatic action, which ostensibly is leading to a tragic outcome, is reversed and concluded happily. This somewhat loose form mingled elements theoretically associated with tragedy (such as noble characters and an action ending in death) and those theoretically associated with comedy (such as lower-class or trivial characters and an action ending happily in celebration). The term is often associated with the early seventeenth century plays of Francis Beaumont and John Fletcher. Wolfgang Amadeus Mozart's opera *Don Giovanni* (pr. 1787) is a famous example of this form in musical theater.

Trope: Brief dialogue, often accompanied by music, used in early medieval religious services to dramatize certain portions of the liturgy. As tropes became more elaborate, they were separated from the religious service and evolved into liturgical drama, which later evolved into the medieval mystery and morality plays. (See also *Corpus Christi plays, Liturgical drama, Miracle play.*)

Unities: Set of rules for proper dramatic construction formulated by Italian and French Renaissance dramatic critics (particularly Ludovico Castelvetro), purported to be derived from the *Poetics* of Aristotle. The "three unities" were concerned with the standards governing the action, time, and setting of a drama: A play should have no scenes or subplots irrelevant to the central action, should not cover a period of more than twenty-four hours, and should not occur in more than one place or locale. In reality, Aristotle insists only upon unity of action in tragedy, and simply observes that most extant examples of Greek tragedy covered a period of less than a full day (there is absolutely no indication of the concept of unity of place). This formulation held particular sway over dramaturgy in France in the seventeenth century and persisted there virtually unchallenged until the introduction of the Romantic drama in the early nineteenth century.

Vaudeville: Variety show popular in the United States and Europe from the 1890's to the 1930's, vaudeville featured songs, comic playlets, animal acts, and sketches. These theatrical entertainments were a refined version of the nineteenth century form of burlesque.

Verse drama: Written in a poetic form and intended primarily as theater rather than as literature, verse drama was the prevailing form for Western drama throughout most of its history, comprising all the drama of classical Greece and continuing to dominate the stage through the Renaissance, when it was best exemplified by the blank verse of Elizabethan drama. In the seventeenth century, however, prose comedies became popular, and in the nineteenth and twentieth centuries verse drama became the exception rather than the rule.

Weeping comedy. See *Comédie larmoyante.*

Well-made play: From the French term *pièce bien faite,* a type of play constructed according to a "formula" which originated in nineteenth century France. The most prolific practitioner of the form was Eugene Scribe (1791-1861). Scribe took dramatic devices, which had been part of comedy and tragedy since the classical theater, and wove them into a formula that he repeated with little or no variation as the underlying frame for the plot construction of his enormous theatrical canon. The plot of a *pièce bien faite* often revolves around a secret known only to some of the characters, which is revealed at the climax and leads to catastrophe for the villain and vindication or triumph for the hero. Misunderstanding, suspense, and coincidence are some of the devices used in the unraveling of the plot. The well-made play provided a form for the developing social drama of such playwrights as Emile Augier and Alexandre Dumas, *fils,* and influenced later playwrights such as Henrik Ibsen and George Bernard Shaw.

Zanni: Stock buffoon character from the *commedia dell'arte* representing the madcap comic servant. Harlequin is the best known of this type.

Theodore Baroody, revised by the editors

Time Line

Date and place of birth

Date and place of birth	Playwright
525-524 B.C.E.; Eleusis, Greece	Aeschylus
c. 496 B.C.E.; Colonus, Greece	Sophocles
c. 485 B.C.E.; Phlya, Greece	Euripides
c. 450 B.C.E.; Athens, Greece	Aristophanes
c. 254 B.C.E.; Sarsina, Umbria	Plautus
c. 190 B.C.E.; Carthage	Terence
November 25, 1562; Madrid, Spain	Lope de Vega Carpio
February 6, 1564; Canterbury, England	Christopher Marlowe
April 23?, 1564; Stratford-upon-Avon, England	William Shakespeare
June 11, 1573; London, England	Ben Jonson
April 18, 1580 (baptized); London, England	Thomas Middleton
January 17, 1600; Madrid, Spain	Pedro Calderón de la Barca
June 6, 1606; Rouen, France	Pierre Corneille
January 15, 1622 (baptized); Paris, France	Molière
August 19, 1631; Aldwinckle, England	John Dryden
December, 1639; La Ferté-Milon, France	Jean Racine
May 28, 1641(?); near Shrewsbury, Shropshire, England	William Wycherley
1653; Fukui, Echizen Province, Japan	Chikamatsu Monzaemon
January 24, 1670; Bardsey, Yorkshire, England	William Congreve
1677 or 1678; Londonderry, Ireland	George Farquhar
November 21, 1694; Paris, France	Voltaire
November 10, 1728 or 1730; Pallas, Ireland	Oliver Goldsmith
January 24, 1732; Paris, France	Pierre-Augustin Caron de Beaumarchais
August 28, 1749; Frankfurt am Main (now in Germany)	Johann Wolfgang von Goethe
October 30, 1751; Dublin, Ireland	Richard Brinsley Sheridan
November 10, 1759; Marbach, Württemberg	Friedrich Schiller
January 22, 1788; London, England	George Gordon, Lord Byron
March 20, 1828; Skien, Norway	Henrik Ibsen
November 18, 1836; London, England	W. S. Gilbert
January 22, 1849; Stockholm, Sweden	August Strindberg
March 15, 1852; Roxborough, Ireland	Lady Augusta Gregory
October 16, 1854; Dublin, Ireland	Oscar Wilde
May 24, 1855; London, England	Arthur Wing Pinero
July 26, 1856; Dublin, Ireland	George Bernard Shaw
January 29, 1860; Taganrog, Russia	Anton Chekhov
June 13, 1865; Sandymount, near Dublin, Ireland	William Butler Yeats
June 28, 1867; Girgenti, Sicily	Luigi Pirandello

Date and place of birth · Playwright

Date and place of birth	Playwright
April 1, 1868; Marseilles, France	Edmond Rostand
April 16, 1871; Rathfarnham, Ireland	John Millington Synge
July 1, 1876; Davenport, Iowa	Susan Glaspell
March 30, 1880; Dublin, Ireland	Sean O'Casey
September 26, 1888; St. Louis, Missouri	T. S. Eliot
October 16, 1888; New York, New York	Eugene O'Neill
July 5, 1889; Maisons-Laffitte, France	Jean Cocteau
January 9, 1890; Malé Svatoňovice, Bohemia	Karel Čapek
May 23, 1891; Växjö, Sweden	Pär Lagerkvist
September 13, 1894; Bradford, England	J. B. Priestley
April 17, 1897; Madison, Wisconsin	Thornton Wilder
February 10, 1898; Augsburg, Germany	Bertolt Brecht
June 5, 1898; Fuentevaqueros, Spain	Federico Garcia Lorca
October 9, 1898; Alexandria, Egypt	Tawfiq al-Hakim
December 16, 1899; Teddington, England	Noël Coward
June 20, 1905; New Orleans, Louisiana	Lillian Hellman
June 21, 1905; Paris, France	Jean-Paul Sartre
April 13, 1906; Foxrock, Ireland	Samuel Beckett
July 18, 1906; Philadelphia, Pennsylvania	Clifford Odets
November 26, 1909; Slatina, Romania	Eugène Ionesco
June 23, 1910; Cérisole, near Bordeeaux, France	Jean Anouilh
December 19, 1910; Paris, France	Jean Genet
March 26, 1911; Columbus, Mississippi	Tennessee Williams
May 15, 1911; Zurich, Switzerland	Max Frisch
June 10, 1911; London, England	Terence Rattigan
May 3, 1913; Independence, Kansas	William Inge
October 17, 1915; New York, New York	Arthur Miller
March 14, 1916; Wharton, Texas	Horton Foote
February 19, 1917; Columbus, Georgia	Carson McCullers
January 5, 1921; Konolfingen, Switzerland	Friedrich Dürrenmatt
February 9, 1923; Dublin, Ireland	Brendan Behan
March 7, 1924; Tokyo, Japan	Kōbō Abe
January 14, 1925; Tokyo, Japan	Yukio Mishima
May 15, 1926; Liverpool, England	Peter Shaffer
July 4, 1927; Bronx, New York	Neil Simon
March 12, 1928; Virginia	Edward Albee
January 9, 1929; Killyclogher, near Omagh, Northern Ireland	Brian Friel
December 12, 1929; London, England	John Osborne
March 22, 1930; New York, New York	Stephen Sondheim
May 19, 1930; Chicago, Illinois	Lorraine Hansberry
October 10, 1930; London, England	Harold Pinter
June 11, 1932; Middelburg, South Africa	Athol Fugard
July 27, 1932; Deep Creek, Alberta, Canada	George Ryga
January 1, 1933; Leicester, England	Joe Orton
July 13, 1934; Ijebu Isara, near Abeokuta, Nigeria	Wole Soyinka
October 7, 1934; Newark, New Jersey	Amiri Baraka

Date and place of birth	Playwright
May 15, 1936; Staten Island, New York	Paul Zindel
October 5, 1936; Prague, Czechoslovakia	Václav Havel
October 21, 1936; Hayling Island, England	Simon Gray
April 13, 1937; Lebanon, Missouri	Lanford Wilson
July 3, 1937; Zlin, Czechoslovakia	Tom Stoppard
November 21, 1937; New York, New York	Tina Howe
September 3, 1938; London, England	Caryl Churchill
April 12, 1939; Hampstead, London, England	Sir Alan Ayckbourn
February 25, 1940; Berkeley, California	Frank Chin
June 26, 1940; Delano, California	Luis Miguel Valdez
June 25, 1942; Montreal, Canada	Michel Tremblay
December 6, 1942; Griffen, Austria	Peter Handke
November 5, 1943; Fort Sheridan, Illinois	Sam Shepard
April 27, 1945; Pittsburgh, Pennsylvania	August Wilson
November 30, 1947; Chicago, Illinois	David Mamet
October 18, 1948; Trenton, New Jersey	Ntozake Shange
January 2, 1949; Montclair, New Jersey	Christopher Durang
October 18, 1950; Brooklyn, New York	Wendy Wasserstein
May 8, 1952; Jackson, Mississippi	Beth Henley
April 24, 1953; Woburn, Massachusetts	Eric Bogosian
July 16, 1956; New York, New York	Tony Kushner
August 11, 1957; Los Angeles, California	David Henry Hwang
May 10, 1963; Fort Knox, Kentucky	Suzan-Lori Parks

NOTABLE
PLAYWRIGHTS

Geographical Index

Categorized Index

Subject Index